A Celebration of Poets

Where
Grades 7-12
Spring 2008

A Celebration of Poets
West
Grades 7-12
Spring 2008

An anthology compiled by Creative Communication, Inc.

Published by:

1488 NORTH 200 WEST • LOGAN, UTAH 84341
TEL. 435-713-4411 • WWW.POETICPOWER.COM

All rights reserved. No part of this book may be reproduced or transmitted in any form or by any means, electronic or mechanical without written permission of the author and publisher.

Copyright © 2008 by Creative Communication, Inc.
Printed in the United States of America

ISBN: 978-1-60050-201-9

FOREWORD

This edition of our poetry anthology is an important transition for Creative Communication. Since our beginning in 1993, we have called our contest "A Celebration of Young Poets." Having worked with student poets for over 15 years, we realized that the writers who have been accepted to be published are not "young" poets. They are poets. Young or old, they are writers who have proven their worth as poets. These are the poets we celebrate.

We also start this year with a new cover for the anthologies. We are excited about this new look and our new logo of a hand releasing stars. Our logo can represent different things. It could be a teacher or mentor releasing a writer to the world through our publication. It could represent the fact that the stars are limitless and these writers are just starting to shine with their potential. We have become the starting point for thousands of writers and we hope each poet continues to make writing a part of their lives.

What is recorded between these pages is unique. It exists nowhere else in the world and is now recorded forever. Take the time to read what these poets have shared. A part of themselves and their world exists in each poem. Savor it. Enjoy.

Sincerely,
Thomas Kenne Worthen, Ph.D.
Editor
Creative Communication

WRITING CONTESTS!

Enter our next POETRY contest!
Enter our next ESSAY contest!

Why should I enter?
Win prizes and get published! Each year thousands of dollars in prizes are awarded in each region and tens of thousands of dollars in prizes are awarded throughout North America. The top writers in each division receive a monetary award and a free book that includes their published poem or essay. Entries of merit are also selected to be published in our anthology.

Who may enter?
There are four divisions in the poetry and essay contests. The divisions are grades K-3, 4-6, 7-9, and 10-12.

What is needed to enter the contest?
To enter the poetry contest send in one original poem, 21 lines or less. To enter the essay contest send in one original essay, 250 words or less, on any topic. Each entry must include the student's name, grade, address, city, state, and zip code, and the student's school name and school address. Students who include their teacher's name may help the teacher qualify for a free copy of the anthology.

How do I enter?

Enter a poem online at:
www.poeticpower.com

or

Mail your poem to:
Poetry Contest
1488 North 200 West
Logan, UT 84341

Enter an essay online at:
www.studentessaycontest.com

or

Mail your essay to:
Essay Contest
1488 North 200 West
Logan, UT 84341

When is the deadline?
Poetry contest deadlines are December 4th, April 7th, and August 18th. Essay contest deadlines are October 15th, February 17th, and July 15th. You can enter each contest, however, send only one poem or essay for each contest deadline.

Are there benefits for my school?
Yes. We award $15,000 each year in grants to help with Language Arts programs. Schools qualify to apply for a grant by having a large number of entries of which over fifty percent are accepted for publication. This typically tends to be about 15 accepted entries.

Are there benefits for my teacher?
Yes. Teachers with five or more students accepted to be published receive a free anthology that includes their students' writing.

For more information please go to our website at **www.poeticpower.com**, email us at editor@poeticpower.com or call 435-713-4411.

TABLE OF CONTENTS

Poetic Achievement Honor Schools 1

Language Arts Grant Recipients 7

Grades 10-11-12 11
    Top Poems 12
    High Merit Poems 22

Grades 7-8-9 135
    Top Poems 136
    High Merit Poems 146

Index 403

States included in this edition:

Alaska
Arizona
Colorado
Hawaii
Idaho
Montana
Nevada
New Mexico
Oregon
Utah
Washington
Wyoming

Spring 2008 Poetic Achievement Honor Schools

* Teachers who had fifteen or more poets accepted to be published

The following schools are recognized as receiving a "Poetic Achievement Award." This award is given to schools who have a large number of entries of which over fifty percent are accepted for publication. With hundreds of schools entering our contest, only a small percent of these schools are honored with this award. The purpose of this award is to recognize schools with excellent Language Arts programs. This award qualifies these schools to receive a complimentary copy of this anthology. In addition, these schools are eligible to apply for a Creative Communication Language Arts Grant. Grants of two hundred and fifty dollars each are awarded to further develop writing in our schools.

21st Century Public Academy
Albuquerque, NM
Darlene Stapleton*

Albuquerque Christian School
Albuquerque, NM
Dawn McKenzie*

Beacon Country Day School
Denver, CO
Catherine Roche*

Bessemer Academy
Pueblo, CO
Julie Frink*

Bethel Christian School
McMinnville, OR
Mrs. Stuebing*

Bonneville High School
Idaho Falls, ID
Mary Flegel*
Meighan Perry

Buhl High School
Buhl, ID
Trish Wetzstein*

Cedar Park Christian School – Everett Campus
Millcreek, WA
Anne Bouckenooghe*

Chatfield High School
Littleton, CO
Mary Horan*

Chehalis Middle School
Chehalis, WA
Amber Cruzan
Rachel Dorsey

Clark High School
Las Vegas, NV
Nancy S. Scott*

Coal Ridge High School
New Castle, CO
Tinker Duclo*

Colorado Connections Academy
Littleton, CO
Maureen Field
Randy Freitik

Columbus High School
Columbus, MT
  Casey Olsen*
  Karmen Ruffatto

Culver Middle School
Culver, OR
  Kimberly Kaylor*

Diamond Ranch Academy
Hurricane, UT
  Ashley Riddle
  Kristy Stratford*

Duchesne High School
Duchesne, UT
  Lori Ann Potter*

Dunstan Middle School
Lakewood, CO
  Paula Rutan*

Eagle Point Middle School
Eagle Point, OR
  Sammie Eaton
  Mrs. Parks*
  Rick Taylor*

East Middle School
Butte, MT
  Judy Cusick*

Eaton Middle School
Eaton, CO
  Cheryl Hall
  Claricy Hall*

Elk Ridge Middle School
South Jordan, UT
  Jannifer Young*

Ernest Becker Middle School
Las Vegas, NV
  Mrs. Bandhauer
  Tonya Ryan*

Eugene Christian School
Eugene, OR
  Patty Duncan
  Connie Kempf

Fertitta Middle School
Las Vegas, NV
  Nicole Evans*
  Rhonda Kilfoyle
  Tim Strong

Flathead High School
Kalispell, MT
  Mrs. Coppes
  Mrs. Dobson
  Megan Koppes
  Marc Nadeau
  Shannon O'Donnell*

Fremont High School
Plain City, UT
  Cheryl Strong*

Grand Junction High School
Grand Junction, CO
  Sylvia Porter*

Granite High School
Salt Lake City, UT
  Pamela Carson
  John Draper
  Doris Stock
  Lisa Thornbrue

Heritage Middle School
Meridian, ID
  Donna Castillo*
  Nathan White

Hyde Park Middle School
Las Vegas, NV
  Mrs. Berg
  Mrs. Lusk
  LeeAnn Sarene

La Center Middle School
La Center, WA
  Lynnette Cooke*

Poetic Achievement Honor Schools

La Plata Middle School
Silver City, NM
Mrs. Carrillo*

Lakewood High School
Lakewood, CO
Janet E. Zamboni*

LaMotte School
Bozeman, MT
Melanie Spratling*

Leading Edge Academy - Gilbert
Gilbert, AZ
Mr. Gray
Ms. Ketchem
Holly Mansfield
Kera Moss
Mrs. Schmersahl

Les Bois Jr High School
Boise, ID
Kathy Steele*

Liberty Middle School
Aurora, CO
Sandy Roache-Smith
Pamela Widmann*

Lone Rock School
Stevensville, MT
Wayne Stanford*
Mrs. Stevens

Madison Sr High School
Rexburg, ID
Mrs. Lewies
Janene Marcum*

Mandalay Middle School
Westminster, CO
Khampiane Keodonexay*
Kay Vargo*

Mears Middle School
Anchorage, AK
Bronwyn Haynes*

Miller Middle School
Durango, CO
LaRae Dotson*

Mountain Ridge Jr High School
Highland, UT
Beth Chynoweth
Rachel Kelson*

North Middle School
Colorado Springs, CO
Ramsey T. Ross*

Oak Harbor High School
Oak Harbor, WA
Erik Christensen*

Oberon Middle School
Arvada, CO
Ms. Graham
Sherri Kochinka

Orem High School
Orem, UT
Neil K. Johnson*

Our Lady of Lourdes Catholic School
Salt Lake City, UT
Carre Joyce*

Phoenix Metro - Islamic School
Tempe, AZ
Fatima Abdelhaq
Alia Al-Taqi
Hind Hania
Ms. Isa
Alexander Isa
Badrun Nahar
Ms. Veronica

Place Middle School
Denver, CO
Christine Ross*

Preston High School
Preston, ID
Brandon Ormond
Julie Tueller
Kaye Woodward*

Pretty Eagle Catholic School
St Xavier, MT
Mrs. Berg*

Pueblo County High School
Pueblo, CO
Janice Parker*
Sandy Vigil

Queen Creek High School
Queen Creek, AZ
Kathryn C. Johnson*

Reid School
Salt Lake City, UT
Kathleen Clemons
Meagan Jones
Mindyn Mullinix
Michelle Peterson
Jennifer Pratt
Melissa Smith
Shauna Tateoka*

Rio Rico High School
Rio Rico, AZ
Karin Bernal*

Round Valley Middle School
Springerville, AZ
Heather Stepp*

Sagewood Middle School
Parker, CO
Mrs. Lewis*
Mrs. Strayer

Sedona Charter School
Sedona, AZ
Joette Burke*

Sequoia Village School
Show Low, AZ
Sidney Johnson
Kristi Neimeyer
Kim Robinson*
Mindy Savoia*

Shadow Ridge Middle School
Thornton, CO
Terrilyn Healy
Meghan Joule*
Fritz Moyer
Jeanette Ryan
Amanda Vanni

Shelley Sr High School
Shelley, ID
Teresa Dye*
Chris Fleming

Sky Vista Middle School
Aurora, CO
Sonja N. Johnson*
Meredith Williams*

Somerton Middle School
Somerton, AZ
Ms. Gaxiola*

Sonoran Science Academy
Tucson, AZ
Deanna Cottrell*
Kelly Fleming

South Jordan Middle School
South Jordan, UT
Jill Jenkins*
Diane Kline
Jill Moses

St Catherine of Siena School
Denver, CO
Suzanne Scheck*

St Elizabeth Ann Seton Catholic School
Tucson, AZ
Theresa Arntz*

Stapley Jr High School
Mesa, AZ
Julie Miller*

Sterling Middle School
Sterling, CO
Sandy Underwood*

Poetic Achievement Honor Schools

Sunnyside Christian Elementary School
   Sunnyside, WA
      Diane Groenewold*

Sylvester Middle School
   Burien, WA
      Shawna Moore*

Tempe Preparatory Academy
   Tempe, AZ
      Gregory Wilson*

Temple Baptist Academy
   Albuquerque, NM
      Jeannie Stokes*

Thomas Edison Charter School - North
   North Logan, UT
      Sheila Bentley
      Tanya Bidstrup
      Megan de la Houssaye*
      Jamie Lynn Hansen
      Annette Jewkes
      Jamie Lewis
      Michelle Provost
      Emili Wall
      Lee Ann Wilkins*

Thomas Edison Charter School - South
   Nibley, UT
      Mrs. Brunetti
      Shirley Collinwood
      Steven L. Earl

Union High School
   Union, OR
      Vivian Matthews
      Kristy E. Moore

Vancouver Christian High School
   Vancouver, WA
      Peggy Koppes*

Vancouver Home Connection
   Vancouver, WA
      David Barber
      Terri Clements*

Viewmont High School
   Bountiful, UT
      Michelle D. Smith*
      Kristin van Brunt

Wiley Jr/Sr High School
   Wiley, CO
      Margaret Ullom*

Wray High School
   Wray, CO
      Heather Bieber
      Kelly Rebis

Xavier College Preparatory School
   Phoenix, AZ
      Glenda Rauscher
      Mrs. Verghese*

Zia Middle School
   Las Cruces, NM
      Chriss Martinez*

Language Arts Grant Recipients 2007-2008

After receiving a "Poetic Achievement Award" schools are encouraged to apply for a Creative Communication Language Arts Grant. The following is a list of schools who received a two hundred and fifty dollar grant for the 2007-2008 school year.

Acadamie DaVinci, Dunedin, FL
Altamont Elementary School, Altamont, KS
Belle Valley South School, Belleville, IL
Bose Elementary School, Kenosha, WI
Brittany Hill Middle School, Blue Springs, MO
Carver Jr High School, Spartanburg, SC
Cave City Elementary School, Cave City, AR
Central Elementary School, Iron Mountain, MI
Challenger K8 School of Science and Mathematics, Spring Hill, FL
Columbus Middle School, Columbus, MT
Cypress Christian School, Houston, TX
Deer River High School, Deer River, MN
Deweyville Middle School, Deweyville, TX
Four Peaks Elementary School, Fountain Hills, AZ
Fox Chase School, Philadelphia, PA
Fox Creek High School, North Augusta, SC
Grandview Alternative School, Grandview, MO
Hillcrest Elementary School, Lawrence, KS
Holbrook School, Holden, ME
Houston Middle School, Germantown, TN
Independence High School, Elko, NV
International College Preparatory Academy, Cincinnati, OH
John Bowne High School, Flushing, NY
Lorain County Joint Vocational School, Oberlin, OH
Merritt Secondary School, Merritt, BC
Midway Covenant Christian School, Powder Springs, GA
Muir Middle School, Milford, MI
Northlake Christian School, Covington, LA
Northwood Elementary School, Hilton, NY
Place Middle School, Denver, CO
Public School 124, South Ozone Park, NY

Language Arts Grant Winners cont.

Public School 219 Kennedy King, Brooklyn, NY
Rolling Hills Elementary School, San Diego, CA
St Anthony's School, Streator, IL
St Joan Of Arc School, Library, PA
St Joseph Catholic School, York, NE
St Joseph School-Fullerton, Baltimore, MD
St Monica Elementary School, Mishawaka, IN
St Peter Celestine Catholic School, Cherry Hill, NJ
Strasburg High School, Strasburg, VA
Stratton Elementary School, Stratton, ME
Tom Thomson Public School, Burlington, ON
Tremont Elementary School, Tremont, IL
Warren Elementary School, Warren, OR
Webster Elementary School, Hazel Park, MI
West Woods Elementary School, Arvada, CO
West Woods Upper Elementary School, Farmington, CT
White Pine Middle School, Richmond, UT
Winona Elementary School, Winona, TX
Wissahickon Charter School, Philadelphia, PA
Wood County Christian School, Williamstown, WV
Wray High School, Wray, CO

Grades 10-11-12

Note: The Top Ten poems were finalized through an online voting system. Creative Communication's judges first picked out the top poems. These poems were then posted online. The final step involved thousands of students and teachers who registered as online judges and voted for the Top Ten poems. We hope you enjoy these selections.

Top Poem Grades 10-11-12

The Space of a Breath

We watch in envy of the falling stars
Who, in their fleeting plunge,
Broke the orbits that kept them to the void

Fire, cleansing, envelops them
Burning out the knowledge
That they are falling, much too quickly
To the earth

The plummet is too sweet
For the realization of its end
And in one bitter instant, they are erased

How free, the moments before
How perfect does it seem
To be that star, burning and brilliant
Stripped of thought and flesh
Consumed by the fall

To exist within the space of a breath
Embraced by only ecstasy
Breaking from nothingness
Returning to nothingness
Uniting with what was never left

Megan Bruckner, Grade 10
Evergreen High School, WA

Top Poem Grades 10-11-12

Addiction

I wonder how to beat a demon
So much stronger than I
How to drop a dirty habit
When I don't want to try

Impossibility of the task
Daunts me before I start
I want to work up motivation
But I don't have the heart

Psychological dependency
To a foreign chemical
My very own Waterloo
My one and only fall

Ellis Crawford, Grade 11
Newbridge High School, OR

Top Poem Grades 10-11-12

It Means "Whole"

She stood quietly,
breathed slowly, gently, so as not to taint
the beauty:
An arbor of leaning trees
whispered and dripped with apples.
They bumped each other like
so many sweet crystals on a chandelier,
catching the mood of twilight on glossy skins.
Perfectus.
In Latin class, she had learned the word,
rubbing the scars etched out in blue jean.
What can it mean?
Now swathed in summer, she understood easily.
She reached a tentative finger out to touch the word.
Its firm skin was stone cold and stoic, but under
her inquisitive touch, it gave a little
secret smile
and dropped into her open palm.

Erin Greenhalgh, Grade 10
Cherry Creek High School, CO

Top Poem Grades 10-11-12

The Old Black Piano

The old black piano, master of music
sits alone and silent in the dark and lonely room.
Patiently, like a flower hoping to bloom, he waits.

The first glimmers of sunlight creep in.
As the sun crawls over the hill, a quiet step is heard.
A young hand caresses the piano's worn black lid.

The old black piano sighs within himself as a young girl is seated at his bench.
The master of music feels his lid open and a soft unblemished hand
gently touches the white ivory keys, ivory that seems to glimmer in the early morning sun.

The old piano would smile if he could.
The bright eyed child begins to play, her young fingers falter.
Though the song is simple, the once silent room is now filled with the brilliant music of a child.

As each of his glimmering keys are pressed,
the old black piano shudders with delight like a child at play.
The simple song draws to a close, the last note resonates in the air
like the last leaf falling from a tree.

The child lays her head of golden curls on the lid of the old black piano, her friend.
He takes in her warmth like a snake in the sun.
Then the child and the master of music, softly and silently, dream of music.

Shaylee A. Joslin, Grade 10
Grant Union High School, OR

Top Poem Grades 10-11-12

Perfection on Earth

The peaceful wind
Blows loose hair strands
While a cool beach towel
Lies waiting in the sand

And the remoteness of the beach
Kindly allows me to unwind
The silence brings serenity
Where nowhere else I'll find

The ever flowing water
Draws patterns in the sand
Forever they'll be changing
But still imprinted on the land

The perfect amount of sunlight
Warms my body to the core
I lay there thinking nothing
Not wanting one thing more

And I think that I will rest here
Beneath the starlit sky
Relaxing for a moment
Just letting time pass by.

Tessa Mauer, Grade 10
Chatfield High School, CO

Top Poem Grades 10-11-12

The Dream Catcher

morning dew Glistens like cracked mirrors
    scattered Light seeps through the cracks of the old splintered door, inspiring shadows to dance on
        the rustic wooden floors
    galaxies afar gather with trembling waves of force creating Glows of heat,
        the Milky Way swirls glossy shimmers of Light, like cloudy water that'd been used for water painting
            Light meets star…wind meets Branch
                quests sought after
                    beneath the wrinkle a story worth sharing
                        beneath the fear a challenge worth overcoming
            he takes his string
                slips it between his fingers to cling
                    lets it drift in the midnight sky
                        tonight it'll soar, it'll fly
        good night morning, good night impossibilities
            good morning imagination — forests, dragons, lil' fairies
                tonight he'll catch the butterflies called storybooks
                    within every head's faraway nooks
        by dawn's early dew the butterfly net will be half full
            and there they'll stay for time's eternity in the dream catcher's net
                where they will Live on without regret

Meghan McKenzie, Grade 11
Chatfield High School, CO

Top Poem Grades 10-11-12

The Book

Soft shadows caress her smooth cheeks.
The sheets gently drape her still form.
The forgotten lamp,
On the mahogany table,
Floods the room with soft light.
The down pillow cradles her warm face.
The open book rests on the bed beside her.
Nothing stirs.
But the rhythmic rise and fall of her chest…

And the ink on the pages,
Pulsing with each beat of her heart.
Twisting and sliding off the pages,
Creeping up her body,
Inching along smooth arms,
Vines encase a warm face peaceful with sleep.
Emerald eyes snap open in horror.
But it's too late…
"I warned you about the book."
A far off voice whispers.

Christi Nash, Grade 12
Flathead High School, MT

Top Poem Grades 10-11-12

Tepid Sands

Such tepid sands laying beneath my feet
That warm sensation chance that time to meet
These sands caressed by tides so amorous
As sun rays bathe you with light glorious
Baroque rocks catch your curdling blue crush
A sweet bene is whispered as breeze meets brush
Looking to the sky your corona hung
Of many white blossoms tinted by sun
The wake of your waves plays a sweet-toned tune
While palm trees sway over sun-shaded dune
The sun paints its canvas a darker shade
Now tide ebbs under night's starry glade
The twilit swells dance by silver moonlight
As a new side of beauty shines through night
When dawn does break, 'tis you I long to see
My belle of the ball, forever to be.

Jared O'Brien, Grade 11
Vancouver Christian High School, WA

Top Poem Grades 10-11-12

Take the Universe

I hate to see you broken, I hate to see you cry
It tears my heart to shreds to see that lost look in your eye
Of all the ones to suffer, who have a hell they must walk through
I cringe to think that God bestowed such a fate on you
You're the embodiment of strength, a warrior of modern day
No matter what this world throws up, my love will never fade
If I could take the universe and rest it on my shoulders
I'd give you light from all the stars a thousand times over
To light your way along the path that you alone must take
But oh, if I could, I'd walk in your place
Remember that the smallest light shines bright against the black,
Remember that God gave you life, you cannot throw it back
Remember that your earthly trials prepare you for a place
Among the angels in heaven, where God waits at the gates
And if you ever feel alone or far away from love
Remember I am by your side and God is up above
If I could take the universe and rest it on my shoulders
I'd give you light from all the stars a thousand times over
To light your way along the path that you alone must take
But oh, if I could, I'd walk in your place

Elizabeth Sandlin, Grade 11
Big Horn High School, WY

Top Poem Grades 10-11-12

Ancient Greek

Every single beaming star, every last flickering light reminds me of the clouded face that swept by.
Only met you for one instant, only knew for the moment what it meant to swim with Poseidon,
to flit with Aeolus.
But now the labyrinth confines my wings which Daedalus made to escape these walls.
Come to me now, Nyx of Grecian night.
Close my eyes and touch my lips goodbye.
My heart grows still; my breath is gone.
Please sell my soul to Acheron.
Rooted like Daphne when Apollo came for you. He sailed far away with you and the Argonauts.
I was forced to stand there, keening loud for aid from Aries, who felt too bothered by his brutish
battle lust to hearken.
Sinking into despair like Icarus below the bores, sinking into darkness.
Come to me now, Nyx of Grecian night.
Close my eyes and touch my lips goodbye.
My heart grows still; my breath is gone.
Please sell my soul to Acheron.
Dragged down by Hades and Pluto, I surrender my life
as my eyes wane dim recollecting all the fabrications you fed to me.
Come to me now, Nyx of Grecian night.
Close my eyes and touch my lips goodbye.
My heart grows still; my breath is gone.
Please sell my soul to Acheron.

Diana Turner, Grade 10
Fremont High School, UT

It's All too Simple
My heart's on the table,
waiting for destruction.
The damage has been done.
All I want to hear,
is your voice.
It keeps my heart beating.
I'm feeling down now.
I have no place to hide,
please come and save me,
I hope that it all ends.
Will it be ok?
Please don't walk away.
You're all that I've got.
We have to work this out,
come and save the day.
I know I'm never right
My tears will fall.
Let's go back home,
and stop this suffering.
Natalee Sorensen, Grade 10
Emery High School, UT

Strawberries
Strawberries are good,
Juicy, I eat them all day.
Red juice dripping down
Ashley Benningfield, Grade 11
Kestrel High School, AZ

Deceased Father of Mine
When I was just a little girl,
You placed me on your knee,
You said nothing would happen to you,
And you'd always be there for me.

Now I stand before you,
In a cry filled church,
Now my life feels empty like
A birdhouse with no perch.

You were my very best friend,
Other than a parent,
You made my life worth living,
the holder of the key to
My box of emotions.
You are as precious as
A single flake of gold.

I was left unexpected,
By you and your funny ways,
The silly dances that made me giggle.
I'm fatherless physically,
But still in reach spiritually.
Love me, Papa.
Arnetia G., Grade 11
Diamond Ranch Academy, UT

Prejudice
Prejudice is a man who only eats the red gummy bears.
Excluding every other flavor.
Unable to understand them.
Not even making an attempt to see past the differences.
Unwilling to try new things,
He only does what is comfortable to him.
"Come here red gummy!"
And he pops it in his mouth.
What about the yellow, white, green, and orange ones?
"Garbage. Just throw them away."
This ignorance won't get him far,
For what will he do when his garbage can overflows with the rejected?
Knowing him, he'll just run away,
Leaving the little bears alone to rot.
Shaina Estadilla, Grade 10
Oak Harbor High School, WA

I Am Green
I am green
I am the green leaves and trees during spring
I am the green decoration that mountains wear
I am the seaweed in the ocean swimming in peace

I am the color of creatures hiding away
I am the taste of lemon, kiwi and sweet bitter grapes
I am the bar of soap that leaves you nice and clean
I am the cool frozen popsicle that freshens your day

and the suffering recycle symbol screaming for your care
and the favorite color ecologists like to wear
the green lovely home of yours that humans have desperately razed

I am green — the color of hope and freedom
Ivonne Angulo, Grade 11
Rio Rico High School, AZ

The Life of an Angel
The angel is born, white feathers blinding all who see
Innocence is nothing more than temporary, the words will burn
Heaven full with the blessed, with the damned, both with burgundy bathed blades
No one can see with heaven so bright, so fall into the wrong shades
As we touch upon the blank slate, it burns black

The angel is fallen, the white itself torn from her wings
Be better this way, the mind sings, freedom is the only hold
The heart says nothing, mourning the soul
Emptiness fills to the skin, nothing is enough to live
No, swear to sorrow, forgives rebirth the spirit

The angel is redeemed, the white a mess of tape and paste upon the feathers
No one will ever know, one will know
With other's eyes it is blind sight, run into the light lights
Bruises fade, cuts heal, scars are still
Love is present, but addiction is never satisfied
Tess Gemberling, Grade 11
Desert Vista High School, AZ

High Merit Poems – Grades 10, 11, and 12

My Voice Sings to You

My voice sings to you,
In the morning dew,
With the sun up high,
Showing the sky,
My voice sings to you.

Michelle Langham, Grade 10
Oakridge Jr/Sr High School, OR

Liberation

Wow…
I really love this sundress…
It's so light and flowy…
I feel free when I wear it…
I feel so comfortable and cool…
It gives me one of those liberating feelings…
Like when you're running through a field…
…Yes, a big open field…
…And you're barefoot…
You can feel the grass between your toes…
And all you want to do is throw your arms up and
Scream at the top of your lungs…
I love those moments…
…Moments of pure bliss…
Like when you get caught in the rain…
And all you can do is laugh…
Or those precious moments with the ones you love…
Every time you're with your friends…
…Whether it's something big and exciting…
…Or you're just chilling in someone's living room…
Each and every memory is just as important as the last…

Rachel Jay, Grade 12
Columbus High School, MT

The Brave Young Suitor

He glances across the room in valor,
Seeking the young girls' favor,
His heart now his tormentor,
All because his love ignores,
Would he ever be her suitor?
Of his heart she was his captor,
Life without her would he ever restore?
Every moment with her did he savor,
Through her good works would she be his liberator?
For her, is he a worthy suitor?
Their feelings for each other they could not ignore,
They collaborated plans for life under the sycamore,
Promises made to each other to honor and adore,
Committed to rid all things they abhor.
Now he is her valiant suitor.
Life sometimes offers up challenges un-looked for,
These problems then become the governor.
Weak heart and constitution took her life was the rumor,
In his life there would be happiness nevermore.
Never again to be her suitor.

Stephanie King, Grade 12
Davis High School, UT

A Meaningful Life

Finding something meaningful in life
Is a very hard requirement
But each had equal choice to do this
By choosing what they want.
Life is nothing when there is no goal ahead
Life is nothing without loving others
Life is nothing when you don't devote yourself
To creating something that gives you purpose and meaning.
When your life is filled with joy and love
You give your time to family, friends and tears.
Offer something what you have in life to others
Maybe for someone it will be a present.
Don't substitute material things for love or gladness
It will never make your life a dream
For every choice we make,
We devote ourselves to that.
Either it will be good or bad
Our choices will define us.
Life is when there is purpose ahead.
With purpose, there is meaning.

Lyuda Mikhaylyuk, Grade 11
Heritage High School, WA

Ultimate Warriors

Calm horizon up ahead, silence in the while,
until guns scream, piercing warriors ears.
Explosion of fire engulfs a juvenile,
The battle makes way as they drown in tears.

All men and women came with a story,
Each individual, a tale can tell,
Each, of course, wants to get to their family.
Of course, they can't they're in the war of hell.

They dream bad dreams of friends who've passed,
Hoping to wake up at home in bed,
Click! Wake up, gun in face, you go out fast,
but you're too late, you fall, that's why your dead.

These men gave their life for you,
These are Heroes of the Red, White, and Blue.

Josh Hemphill, Grade 10
Dove Creek High School, CO

Dripping Springs

Trudging under the great blue sky —
The sun beating on my back,
Sweating and toiling up the slopes,
The trail runs onward, with no end in sight,
Farther and farther until lost in the grass,
Yet through the heat and glaring light,
A certain beauty reveals itself on every step,
A symmetrical cactus leaf, a single twitching bird,
Lichens forming an odd pattern on a rock,
Each is a marvel of creation.

Ming Leung, Grade 10
Las Cruces High School, NM

Dreams

In this same place
stuck,
I am
awake
although I can only think of being
asleep.
I am forced to spend tonight
here,
with this idea
until I am done.
— Truly —
Until I am done
with this idea,
here,
I am forced to spend tonight
asleep.
Although I can only think of being
awake.
I am
stuck
in this same place.

Alison Wilbur, Grade 12
Kentlake High School, WA

Evil Empire

Our towering willows,
Against their blooming oak trees.
This was dodge ball.

Flaming, supersonic boulders,
Whizzing toward target,
Colliding with inevitability.

As the 20 small oaks,
Became 2 scarred survivors,
Our aim focused deeper.

And with a release,
An avalanche of pain.
Our evil empire triumphed.

Yet victory hence,
Didn't feel rewarding,
And deep inside,
The hearts of many
This feeling existed.

Jeremy Brown, Grade 12
Preston High School, ID

Friends

Friends are like brothers
they don't have the blood I have
but they have my back.

Juan Ignacio Toscano, Grade 11
Rifle High School, CO

Team

Four hour rides on a hot and cramped bus,
Music and movies are always a must.
Dismal fast food washed down by pop,
Someone always drinks too much and forces us to stop.
All this hassle for a two hour game,
Envying professionals who travel by plane.
Playing your heart out, leaving it all on the floor,
Then the next day of practice giving some more.
Losing is depressing. Winning is fun.
Either way after practice you will still run.
A team a brotherhood fighting as one,
Never letting up till the buzzer has rung.
Teamwork, perfection is never overlooked,
Until your ticket to the championship has been booked,
Memories made laughing till you are sick,
Those memories made we will never forget.

Keegan Huntsman, Grade 10
Shelley Sr High School, ID

Physics Book

Physics book filled up with your random names
How I'd like to hold you o'er open flames
My friends, they all hate you, they've dropped your class
Instead of your work I'd rather eat glass
Your work is hard, sometimes confusing
When we do it we feel like we're losing
The class seemed like fun, but we were so wrong
I hope to finish this class well and strong
The whole last line sounded like Doctor Liu
It seems like there is nothing we can do!

Nick Jankowski, Grade 11
Vancouver Christian High School, WA

My Life

I am a proud, Native teenager.
I wonder how my life is going to be after I graduate.
I hear my family say to me that I can make it in life and can be better than my brother.
I see myself just the way my brother is.
I want to be a better person, but my attitude is keeping me back.
I am a proud, Native teenager.

I pretend to be someone that I'm not.
I feel people's anger pushing me like an angry bull rushing to attack the red target.
I touch every tear that comes out when I don't accomplish my goal in high school.
I worry about what's going to happen to me in the street life.
I cry in my sleep when something happens to my brother and mom.
I am a proud, Native teenager.

I understand what's going to happen to me when I get handcuffed.
I say to myself every day when I get up that I lived another day.
I dream that I will have a better life in my lifetime.
I try my best to get a better life.
I hope I'll live until I get to have kids with the person who I love.
I am a proud, Native teenager.

Shayne White, Grade 10
Rocinante High School, NM

I Am Yellow

i am yellow.

i am a glamorous sunrise forcing through.
i am a mix of sweet juicy fruits.
i am a tender butterfly gliding.

i am fearless but sensitive too.
i am an unknown flower ready to bloom.
i am a striking arrow making impact;
an independent silly lassie.

determined to not be mislead.
an unwritten book eagerly to be written on.
a cozy breeze during late spring.

i am yellow.

Bianca Solis, Grade 11
Rio Rico High School, AZ

Today

Today I will laugh.
Today I will love without caution.
I will accept everyone for exactly who they are.
Today I will not hate.
I will do everything I've ever wanted to today.
I will fall from the sky with a sheet
Then dive into the sea with artificial air.
Today I will climb mountains then move them.
Catch the sun, and keep it in my pocket.
I will be everything I've ever wanted to be today.
Today I am a miracle.

Brittany Corder, Grade 12
Flathead High School, MT

Our Honors in Our Own Thoughts

We are all here today
Surrounding under the blue sky
It's blue, deep-deep blue
It's freedom, freedom in our own thoughts

The spring breezes giggle through our minds
Recalling memories, facts, victories
The memories of what we have lost
The facts of what we have taught
The victories of what we have fought

The lights of the sun shine through our darkness
Replacing fears, tears, lost
The fears of what we have hidden
The lost of what we have forgotten
The tears of what we have fallen

We are all here today
I, and you, we are different
Perhaps, we are opposite, but equal
We shall be in Heaven for our honors

Thao Nguyen, Grade 10
Gilbert High School, AZ

The Horse

Running herds of mustangs,
Bays, blacks, and roans.
All the pretty little ponies
All running towards home.
Their spirits call to me
And tell me to join their throng
Of wild and wonderful freedom.
Thump, thump, thump goes my heart,
And freedom is what I feel.
My spirit soars from my body,
Upward and onward and away I go.

Jennifer Roberts, Grade 11
Preston High School, ID

Last Chance

I once lived in a world of pain and loneliness,
a world which I thought of no escape.
I tried through intimacy and passion,
but still there was no way out.
I became desperate for escape
seeking through all open options;
I then remembered a young boy
whose problem was my mirrored life.
His resolution was forbidden, pure evil,
but he swore by it saying it cured.
Naïve thoughts filled my mind and soul.
I agreed taking a new path and destiny.
It worked but only temporarily and,
the side effects were horrid and lonelier.
Somehow the Heavenly Father gave His forgiveness,
he gave me one last change, which I now
live with an honest heart and mind.

Nicole G., Grade 10
Diamond Ranch Academy, UT

Society Not So Silent Anymore

We the people are disgusted
By judgment for Elton John Richard II.
Knowing today judges are
Hooked on drugs and playing favorites.

These individuals are the Pillars of Society.
The judge imposes the sentence on the individual
Who defended his family and his property.

It is not a message to send out to thugs or thieves.
The individual did not steal,
He just made the decision to get in harm's way.

Silent majority recourse.
We deny retention for judges
That interpret the law on the side of the thugs
Not the defender of his family.

Richard, you have support from majority.
But with acts like these
We are not so silent anymore.

Ingraid Flores, Grade 10
Mountainair High School, NM

Going to Sleep

inviting warm fluffy pillows
thick layer of quilts
lights gone
nothing
moaning staircase
annoying snores above
computer popping
vanilla body spray
hint of you
alone
tired
warmth of the blankets
sleep overtake me
safe
happy
dreams

Kayla Nite, Grade 11
Madison Sr High School, ID

Fallen Angel

Who appears so near.
Halo disintegrating
into the frigid air.

What I see
is not to be feared.
For it is I
whom I see in the mirror.

Laura Kerschner, Grade 11
Merino Jr/Sr High School, CO

Seasons of the Sun

Spring
Foggy blanket floats
above the dew covered green
sun stings sleepy eyes

Summer
Through the window
bright patch of light warms the rug
I'll lie here all day

Fall
Cold sandy grains fall
between my toes. Soft guitar
as the sun slips down

Winter
Huddled in a quilt
chill invades heat dies fire fails
night has come for me

Scottie McPherson, Grade 10
Oak Harbor High School, WA

That Day Was…

Ice cold were her words
How hard they hit me, how deep they pierced my soul
How loud they resonated in my heart
"Terrorist"
Terrorist am I,
I am hurt
The visions are so vivid, of that confusing day
The reminiscent questions I asked, the vague answers I received
I am different
The scorns and glares
The fear and hate
Of that innocent young girl, the little bird from the nest
Cannot breathe
Cannot cry, cannot understand
Muffled cries seal my chest
Silent tears pour out of my heart
Little did I know
That day would change my life forever
That day was,
The Eleventh of September

Rehab Kassem, Grade 10
Albuquerque Institute of Math, NM

Nature

Around the world, the clouds fly
Mountains soar high up in the sky
Sunrise and sunsets are beautiful things to see
Animals roaming free with glee

Winter blows so much snow
The blue sky of spring glows
Summer has its warmest days
The beautiful colors of autumn fades

Rain crashes down when nature cries
Rainbows appear when nature is satisfied
Blizzards and thunderstorms occur when nature shows its madness
The moon tells a lullaby story, while the night has stars blinking of sleepiness

Darcie Kingeekuk, Grade 12
Hogarth Kingeekuk Sr Memorial School, AK

Not to Sleep

Looking at her eyes, as lustrous as reflection,
Trembling off the top, it still demands perfection.
She'll linger past the act, but present is in question,
Performance is sought after, lack thereof is predestined.

The solid shield is align'd,
Sparing a legion's onset.
It averts vital torment,
Retaining the one true threat.

The ceasefire now given through the ranks, as body lies on top of body,
And the sun shot through her eyes, yielding overall conclusion.

Michael Sheridan, Grade 12
Lakewood High School, CO

The Big Shot

The empowering sound of the bouncing ball,
Some squeaky noises coming from shoes,
Fans, coaches going off the wall,
The player with the ball, jukes and moves.
A red and black woven, numbered jersey,
In the lobby snacks and drinks are bought.
The team at home was up early,
The home team's best player pulls up for a shot.
The crowd goes silent, noise vanishes in the air.
The ball goes flying towards the hoop.
Noise erupts; a band member hits his snare.
It was a pass, a dunk, off the alley-oop!
The time runs out, his teammates hoist him up
Then a light turns on, "Billy, it's time to wake up."

Josh Counce, Grade 12
Temple Baptist Academy, NM

To Fly

Oh, how I wish I were a bird,
Red bird, blue bird, green bird, black bird.
Fly so high above the ground,
Not a thought to keep them down.

Woe to us who cannot fly,
Who cannot soar up in the sky.
With thoughts and cares to keep us down,
To keep our feet upon the ground.

Never seeing,
Never feeling,
What it's like to fly,
So high up in the sky.

Illaura Rossiter, Grade 12
Springfield High School, OR

The Game

The clock ticks ever closer to zero
It's the closing minutes of the last quarter
Our team is down by four we have the ball
We need a touchdown to win the game
The time to score is now it's all or nothing
I line up on the line
The play has been called, I know the ball is coming to me
The whole season leads up to this next play
The ball is snapped the quarterback drops
I explode toward the endzone
The quarterback lets the ball fly
Time expires as the ball spirals through the air
The crowd is silent waiting to see what happens
I reach the endzone running to catch the ball
Their safety and I leap into the air
We both snatch it and fall to the ground wrestling for it
The crowd gasps wondering who ended up with the ball
I sit up with the ball in my hands
The crowd goes crazy and my team rushes towards me
We win the game and I'm the hero.

Scott Carlile, Grade 10
Orem High School, UT

Reflecting on a Good Night's Sleep

Eight hours of night ago
daylight was slowly fading out of my bedroom window,
receding back like the tide of the ocean
against the backdrop of a deep red sky.
Fields beaten hard by hooves of cows
now lay covered with the shadow of a mountain.
The night is still, calm without the wind
that had stalked the land all fall.
Closing the curtains keeps the night in,
I had let the pressure build
before I finally lay myself down
to pass my eight hours of night.

Zachary Reimer, Grade 12
Columbus High School, MT

Into His Arms

Where has the hope gone? What hides it away?
For I'm captive to fear and what my doubts say.
Blessings lavished o'er my life entice,
Meant for abundance; to more than suffice.
Still shivers chill the depths of my heart;
The light that once filled, seems to depart.
"Be with me Oh Lord!" my soul weeps.
Even in anguish His promise He keeps.
Comfort's in this; He cries with me too,
Patiently shepherding all I go through.
Though I can't see it through my teary eyes,
I am held by the keeper of the skies.
He is at this moment, making a way;
Out of my darkness and into His day.
In this storm my hands find strength to raise;
From desperation flows adoration's praise.
He walks my way, holds my hand,
And though I could not understand,
Purpose exposed me to these harms;
That I might fall, straight into His arms.

Chelsea Dinsmoor, Grade 12
Warden High School, WA

An Old Man's Story

Today I turn seventy-eight
And I can still remember clearly;
I did not kill because I hate
But just to protect those I love dearly;
I joined the war to fight for what's right
And fought like there was no tomorrow;
My brothers in arms went towards the light
And now I live with all my sorrow;
Through all the years and what I've done
I've lived a very fulfilling life;
Then I looked at my new grandson
And grasped the hand of my lovely wife;
The old man knows his time is near
And as he took his final breath;
He closed his eyes and down came a tear
Because with new life there comes death.

Cameron Quezada, Grade 10
Pioneer High School, NV

Pray

I pray, pray and pray
Day, night I pray
I pray to make it home
I pray for my family
I pray to just have hope
One night I forgot to pray
Maybe that's why
Maybe if I would've prayed
My day would have been a day
We should of just stayed down
He went up first
Bang bang
He was down
that's all I remember
But look at me now I'm weeping
Over his grave
That was the day I did not pray.

Jaime Ponce, Grade 11
Pioneer High School, NV

Foolstring

The Evening cries desperately
as Love, the Puppeteer,
chats with an Angel.

Through their heavenly conversation,
the mischievous wind
creeps up from the hill
and cuts the strings.

The burden is dropped,
as a fool
in a dunk tank.

Brandon Oppenheim, Grade 10
Oak Harbor High School, WA

The Single Awareness Day

He loves me?
He loves me not.
She loves me?
She loves me not.
Can a daisy tell,
If someone really loves you?
Hearts, candy, flowers,
Love is really in the air.
Couples stroll hand in hand;
Their affection is obvious
For the world to see.
It's tough to be the one,
Where your kisses only come
In foil-wrapped packages.
Valentine's is surely
The Single Awareness Day.

Lauren Chung-Hoon, Grade 10
Orem High School, UT

Sorry All the Time

i'm sorry for being the way i am.
i'm sorry for all the things i've said.
i'm sorry i can't ever change
the past, myself, and my regrets.

i'm sorry i'm a stupid flirt.
i'm sorry i can't hold you now.
i'm sorry nothings ever easy,
and mostly tries to bring us down.

i'm sorry when i make you mad.
i'm sorry for these tears that fall.
i'm sorry for all the little things
that never meant a thing at all.

i'm sorry how i blew you off.
i'm sorry for all the things you know.
i'm sorry for ever holding back;
don't want to say what hurts the most.

but i'm so sorry for even being sorry.
i'm so sorry a hundred times over again.
and i'm so sorry you don't know how perfect you are to me.
but mostly, i'm just sorry for being the way i am.

Ben Johnson, Grade 12
Mount Vernon Christian School, WA

Drop

Sounds intermingle.
Insignificant in their own right;
Melding, intertwining, enfolding,
And separating again with nothing but a parting glance,
A whispered departure
Echoing hollowed expectation.
Bellowing wind is overpowered by shrieking mind;
The blaring radio fails to compensate for absent conversation.
A light drizzle lovingly caresses steel framework
As fingernails tap on glass, tap on wood.
Headlights blare a jubilant greeting that fails to reflect interior inactivity.
They watch the raindrops chase each other down the windshield
As lips form the words of streetlights;
Another distant passing.
"At least you're here at all."
Repetition, repetition;
The frantic response to a silent heart.
Beauty is a lie.
Beauty is lying.
Lying is beautiful.
At arm's length I can't look in your eyes.

Ashly Burch, Grade 12
Thunderbird High School, AZ

High Merit Poems – Grades 10, 11, and 12

Shattered Dreams
Dreamer's blood spurting out of my veins
Breaking bones against the chains
Here in Hell I lie
Here is where I will die
Heavy fire crushes through my chest and out my eyes
Burning acid leaks out, listening to the lies
Shattered dreams against stained red glass
Beautiful dreams that will never come to pass
Time to dream a new dream
Prisoner of my own dream
Pretending I am happy with what I have
Pretending fire can live with water
Trapped in this inescapable Hell I stay
Trapped inside my own soul
Here to pay the toll
Stop pretending
Maybe, all this will start ending

Jessica Dawn Christensen, Grade 11
Preston High School, ID

Ruin of Angels
She came upon bended knee
But she was beautiful, not unlike a queen

Crying upon the river Styx
At the feet of her fallen friend

Tonight was the night she lived to die

And it was all a lie

A man came in between them
He revealed their souls
One loyal to his lord, and one desired more

This was the man who caused
The ruin of the angels.

Pat Marquart, Grade 11
Flathead High School, MT

A Summer in the Mountains
The birds chirped happily as the mountain came to life
The sun struck the mountain early in the morning
The cold morning air roused me from sleep

The forest was all around, surrounding me with sound
The nature walk took me up to the lake

The water gleamed blue and the rocks shone a dull gray
The fish swam happily just beneath the surface
If you were quiet enough and stood still long enough
You could see them move

Suddenly a fish broke the water
The ripples left were fascinating
I was too late in catching a picture
The lake is calm and peaceful once again

Nicole Holstein, Grade 10
Ralston Valley High School, CO

To Those Who Know Me Well
In a small town in Montana.
Where people travel afar to see its beauty.
Lives me, a small town girl.
My laughter and smile are what stand out.
My photography and singing are what my life is all about.
I'm close to everyone around me, especially
My family and friends.
And for those who know me, my hugs are a daily routine.
To those who know me well
I give kisses and my love.

Sierra Baker, Grade 12
Flathead High School, MT

The Slave
My master thought I was no good
He beat me daily as hard as he could
It made me so angry; I'd had enough
So I ran away one night, straight to the bluff

I'd heard stories about others like me
Who had hopes of a new community
They'd ran from their homes in desperation
To band together in secret desolation

But when I reached the coveted spot
My hopes were destroyed, they'd all be forgot
There was not a soul in sight
I was all alone, my doubts were right

So now, months later, I still sit and wait
And hope for the day when it will be my fate
For more slaves to come and maybe give
Some hope to this lost and lonely fugitive

Jayde Shackett, Grade 10
Shelley Sr High School, ID

Life on the Streets
You think you're all alone,
No one cares, and no one's home.
You spend your life out on the street
Dealing with amazing feats.

It's been so long since you've sat still,
Always on the run, all against your will.
You wonder if you're "missing"
Or simply just forgotten.

The other street kids are your family
In place of the one that left you scrambling
The very first day you make a pack
You're all going to watch each other's backs.

You want so badly to have someone care
Sometimes you think life is just not fair.
You're venturing home with doubt in your mind,
But there they wait arms open wide.

Crystal S., Grade 10
Diamond Ranch Academy, UT

The Joy of Reading

Where have you gone?
She asks.
You don't respond
She stares.
Your mind is absorbed
She wonders.
You are in another world
She supposes.
You alone know
The truth
She doesn't.
You can go anywhere
So can she
If she knew
But she doesn't.
You are far away
She's not.
You are in a castle,
An ocean,
The sky
You've escaped.

Cara Palmer, Grade 10
Bishop Gorman High School, NV

Forest of Shadows

Last cluster of forest,
Hidden in silence,
Watching with dark and silent eyes,
Shadows are everything.

Fugitive of man,
Danger is always present.

Chris Esparza, Grade 12
Granite High School, UT

My New Angel*

Limitless tears fall
  for fogged-over, inanimate eyes;
Lifeless being before me
  was once wonderfully alive.
Minutes fall off our clock
  as dew does from a rose.
Crying sounds off down the aisle
  as we let her go.
We all speak of her softly,
  bringing up no pain,
Telling each other she's okay
  and we'll be with her again.
We will visit her years from now
  in a garden full of stone,
And try not to grieve for her,
  but be happy she's now home.

Emily Balchunas, Grade 11
Bradshaw Mountain High School, AZ
*Dedicated to Monica Jaramillo
1989-2007

Goodbye

I remember waiting in line to buy my tickets for the carnival,
the price had went up two dollars since the year before,
it was starting to rain, my converse were letting water soak through,
the cold water trickled between my toes.
I was waiting for my friends who were watching the parade,
some of them were even in it.
I remember watching the ferris wheel go around and around,
water ran off its sides and on to the grass
that was now starting to make large puddles in its uneven landscape.
I remember looking up from the ground and seeing my friend,
I was excited to go on the carnival rides, but she was crying.
Everybody was crying.

He's gone, she said.
He's gone, they said.
He's gone, I cried.
Goodbye.

Morgan McGuire, Grade 10
Oak Harbor High School, WA

Blanket in the Blizzard

The situations of my life trap me in a blizzard of unwanted self-doubt.
I run and I walk, but I can't seem to find any way out.
I can't see the sun no matter how hard I search, but I know it's there.
Believe and I'll see it even though I can't feel it, I know you care.
I'm walking further and see a cabin, a shelter in the middle of all this.
It's just as cold, but I see a blanket hanging on the edge of a rocking chair,
the warmth I dearly miss.
I cuddle up the best I can, trying to stay warm in every way.
Lord, when my life is freezing cold
You're my warm blanket and that feels better than any sunny day!

Tori Francis, Grade 10
Cascade Christian High School, OR

The Spiral Within Me

All is a circle within me,
  I am a singer, a subtle creator of music,
  I am quiet, always keeping to myself,
  I am a sister, a daughter, and a best friend,
  To the one who is closest to my heart.
  I am the one who will never be fully
  Understood by anyone.
All is a circle within me.
  I have seen the skies of Mexico and
  The faces of its little children,
  I have seen a young woman graduate
  From one hard and intimidating world and step into another.
  I have seen hearts broken and healed,
  And loved only one.
All is a circle within me.
  I have gone to the city,
  I have gone to the country.
Now all that is within me is made known to you,
Now all I have left to do is live my life.

Stella Van Deren, Grade 12
Flathead High School, MT

February 2, 2008: In Honor of a Beautiful Girl

When the headline read "Six More Weeks of Winter,"
It was not referring to potential storms, blankets of snow or quantities of rain.
The "winter" is the grief that will call our hearts home,
For much time to come.
The loss of such a beautiful soul will make the driest of tear ducts pour out as fountains.

Amidst the winter storms,
I shall take heart in one thing.
That beautiful soul (who could love like no other, laugh through all things,
Who had such a short time to live),
Will live, love and laugh forever with her Father up in Heaven.
This blessed soul enjoys the finest of treasures,
Despite our winter cold.

Jacqueline Floyd, Grade 11
Nestucca High School, OR

Life

An insatiable feeling,
The feeling of your world spinning out of control,
Feeling that your heart has stopped beating.
An exhausting feeling,
The feelings of being alone and having pity for yourself,
Feelings of insecurity and loneliness.
An incredible feeling,
The feeling of butterflies in your stomach,
Feeling that you're flying high in the sky with the clouds.
An empty feeling, never to be satisfied yet never is ignored.
Being aware of everything that might go wrong and learning your lesson again for the second time.
Feelings of living in an achromatic world full of ugly empty people.
To emerge from the depth of the shallow world and to encourage yourself to finally confide in the ones who truly do appreciate you, or to sit in devastation alone.
To feel audacious enough to take a leap and to believe in yourself enough to feel that you might just have a small amount of power in the world, or to concede and just give up.
A privilege, one that's indescribable, one that shouldn't be taken for granted, although it's one that can be merciless at times.
Perhaps there's a missive some place to tell us how to get through life without all of the mishaps, or perhaps we're all just pernicious, odious people waiting to obliterate.

Chyanne Clark, Grade 10
Pioneer High School, NV

Do You Remember?

Do you remember?
I do
You came up from behind me and grabbed me tight
I wasn't sure it was you, but I hoped it was
We walked down the hall, arm in arm
Your smile leading the way, drawing me in, until all that I wanted to do was to be with you
The end of the hall is drawing nearer
There are so many other people around, but in this moment none of them matter
All that matters to me is this girl
This girl with her cute freckles and her beautiful smile
We reach the point where we go separate ways, but I don't want to
If I could I would follow her forever
We part ways, but her face, her freckles, her smile, her laugh, are still on my mind

Robert Corson, Grade 10
Columbus High School, MT

Teacher

She tells you to do your work
Students moan and groan
Her words are boring
White figures on black slate
Appear to fuse and blend
Chalk lines associated with
Pictures, numbers, and letters
Are the authorities of the class
Libby Brown, Grade 10
Wray High School, CO

Hold On

When the light starts to fade
And bumps occur in the flow
The tears try to drown you
Hold on, don't ever let go

The frowns replace the smiles
And the high becomes a low
Sensing an unwanted change
Hold on, don't ever let go

Your mind can't recognize itself
Nor the ones who love you so
Take my hand, come back with me
Hold on, don't ever let go

Have faith when even in doubt
Be aware of what you know
Your existence has an effect
So hold on, don't ever let go…
Jenni Huynh, Grade 11
Bonneville High School, UT

My Lonely Life

As life goes on, I hear the song
Of sweet melody, short but long.

Leaning on the wall, yet so lonely,
I see her face, she looks so lovely.

Tidal waves tear me apart
Stripped down and pierced my heart.

Waiting and wondering who I be,
All the beautiful things to see.

Hearing the roars of the sea,
Waiting for the girl of my dreams.

Knowing that time is going by,
Telling that one girl I'll see her next time.
Martin Hernandez, Grade 12
Trask River High School, OR

The 500

As the swimmer takes to the white starting block
The tension is high
On his toes he takes his mark and is ready to fly
Like a black cat hunting its prey

The buzzer sounds and he's off
He dives into the glistening pool with a small splash
And glides through the crystal clear water at a strong pace
Consistency is needed it's a very long race

He has 500 yards to go
But whatever he does he can't go slow
He pushes and pulls, he kicks and he flips
He tries his best to beat the rest

He stares at the black line to pass away the time
Constantly in rhythm he goes
Sticking with the leaders
Keeping the gap close

As a hundred approaches it turns to a sprint
He doesn't hold back or he'll lose the fight
He finishes first and out of breath and can now take a rest
He tried his best and beat the rest
Joshua Kelley, Grade 10
Fremont High School, UT

Where I Am From

I am from blue jeans, from Oxiclean and Wal-Mart.
I am from the creek just across the road (cool, flowing; it rushed like wind)
I am from the mountains and the sunsets; I can see their splendor even now.
I am from county fairs and *Don't ever let tradition die.*
From Paul and Michelle, and John Alma Marchant.
I'm from always-correct grammar and Conservative Republicans.
From *Be honest always*, and *It's a tough life, but it's a good one.*
I am from saving pennies, nickels, and dimes, and making do with what you have.
I'm from church on Sunday and mutual on Wednesday, and *You are a child of Him.*
I am from Germany and England; Utah and Idaho, from steak and mashed potatoes.
From my brother's Grand Champion Buckle he won with his show steer,
And driving down gravel roads.
I'm from singing to the radio completely off-key,
From school spirit and high school ball games.
I am from a green summer's garden, tomatoes and peas that are fresh to the taste.
From sorting cows and feeding hay; putting on boots and wearing hats.
I am from carving pumpkins and decorating Christmas trees.
From cow pies and clipping chutes, corrals and fence posts.
I am from the scrapbook under my bed; the memories that have been and are.
The legacy of who I am and what has made me.
THIS IS WHERE I AM FROM.
Elise Marchant, Grade 12
Oakley Jr/Sr High School, ID

High Merit Poems – Grades 10, 11, and 12

Life's too Short

Live each day like there is no tomorrow,
for you never know when your heart will fill with sorrow.
We never could have prepared my aunt Jen at thirty-one,
to leave behind a husband, daughter and two sons.
With a blood clot to the lungs she died so quick,
even thinking about it now still makes me sick.
After a year has gone by,
I still just sit and wonder why?
She loved to hunt, camp and even fish,
to have her back with us again I wish.
At the ball games she was always cheering,
if you were there you couldn't help but hearing.
I miss her like crazy every day,
I just can't figure out why it was her that had to go away.
In my heart she will always remain.
My aunt Jen, life without her will never be the same!

Meagan McCabe, Grade 10
Union High School, OR

Nothing I'd Rather Do

As the world goes on
We like to pretend that nothing is wrong
But sitting in this depressing room
And watching all these shadows loom
Watching you sleep in your bed
Still not able to be fed
I look at all the tubes connected to you
I feel so sorry for you
I see the tube coming out of your neck
And think of the one coming out of your stomach
I hear the sound of your heartbeat
And know it's not too late
But sitting in this quiet atmosphere
And showing every single fear
There is nothing else I'd rather do
On this Sunday afternoon
Then spend my time with you

Julie Estrada, Grade 10
Pueblo County High School, CO

I Am the Future

I am the future
I am a dynasty in the making
My destiny is in my control
Y'all know I'm going somewhere
I'm on a journey to greatness
Nobody is gonna stop me
Nobody will control me
Nobody
If you try
I'll be like Shaq and go through you
I'll be like my boy A.I. and cross you up and go around you
So you choose
You can be part of my path towards greatness
Or you can be left behind
I am the future

Donovan Marion, Grade 11
Heritage High School, WA

Starry-eyed

Starry-eyed, the dark gray girl —
  Caught within the wind,
    Shakes the trees and my heart,
      Tossed out by a whim —
Starry-eyed, the dark gray girl —
  Whispers at my pain,
    Dances sprightly, bends me broken,
      Melts me in the rain —
Starry-eyed, the dark gray girl —
  Stillness of a shadow,
    All alone the silence speaks,
      Questions what I know —
Starry-eyed, the dark gray girl —
  To the other side, was sent,
    Bright-eyed, the morning child,
      Bids me to forget —

Heather Gee, Grade 11
Seattle Christian School, WA

One Loved My Broken Heart,
Heart Broken My Loved One

Every sob dispersed with laughter
Every step filled with smiles
Every breath tainted with giggles
You took my hand
Held me in your arms
Promised me love
You walked away
Broke my heart
Killed me inside
Giggles fade away with every breath
Smiles waver with every step
Laughter disperses with every sob

Anna Quan, Grade 11
Galena High School, NV

Dichloromethane

You tiptoe into crisp summer air
It's indescribable but we all know the scent
And for one complete moment you're infinite
A mere moratorium of time
You are the sterile streets, the houses
With loneliness painted all over them
You are the calm pressed into the sidewalks
The doomed day rolls on with all its noise
The anxious finally find rest; but not you
This is your moment to come alive
Your mind is set ablaze
Like a skyscraper with all of its lights on
You recall the days you once held the world
You find old friends in freshly lit corners
You unravel what's wrong and why
This is the prescription to the tumultuous things in life
But, "Nothing gold can stay,"
And with the acetone morning
The night's cloak chips away

Mike Hurd, Grade 12
Reed High School, NV

Scum of the Earth

The epitome of no decency
The ultimate showing of no respect
How could anyone sink to that level
A person is not just an object

For anyone that's on the wrong end
Hold your head to the sky
They are the scum of the Earth
There is no need to cry

For the scum that is listening
Rethink who you are
Change for the good of mankind
Or else you will not make it far

No one deserves this hurt
These people have no worth
Most will never change
That's why they are the scum of the Earth
Jordan Fisher, Grade 12
Chatfield High School, CO

Love

Love feels like a warm blanket.
Love feels like a fuzzy stomach.
Love tastes like the finest dessert.
Love tastes like a bittersweet lemon.
Love smells like a warm breeze.
Love smells like a fresh rain shower.
Love sounds like birds chirping.
Love sounds like a piano crying.
Love looks like rosy cheeks.
Love looks like starry eyes.
Love is fingers intertwined.
Love is balloons drifting to the sky.
Love is falling into deep space.
Love is cascading tendrils
Sweeping you into its embrace.
Breanna Wilson, Grade 10
Grant Union High School, OR

The River

The river rages with such power
Yet is as beautiful as a flower,
Free to go wherever it wants
As long as it never has to stop,
Down the hill it will flow
Carving the land wherever it goes,
Off a cliff the water will fall
Onto the rocks ever so small,
But the river still flows down the hill
Without realizing the land it fills,
There it ends up turned into a lake
Where evaporation will give and take.
Daniel Eyre, Grade 12
Granite High School, UT

The Cold Night

The night grew cold and bitter
It brought coldness through our bones
Fixing fence in the chilly air our hands started to hurt
But we kept on going pounding post after post into the half frozen ground
Stretching wire that seemed to go on forever
Only a light from the truck was guiding us through the night
As hours passed by I noticed the pain in your eyes
Your hands were as cold and discolored as I ever saw
But still you kept going as you knew the work had to get done

For the night grew worse and bitter
You could only see the dim light from the pickup that was just down yonder from us
Every breath you could see in the dark cold air
You could hear the coyotes that seemed to be just over the hill
As we kept on going through the night
Your hands seemed worse
With every post you pounded I notice the pain that become worse
But you kept on going for you knew the work had to get done
Stephanie Rouane, Grade 10
Columbus High School, MT

Farewell, Winter; Hello, Spring

Winter, the bleak season of Nature which man knows best
Its air chills the atmosphere and the souls of people
The unfortunate seeking salvation for their bodies and their hopes
The icy fog is dense with silence and lurking pestilence
O, lingering entity, move on and leave no trace behind
Clouds of despair shall subside with concealed rays of sunlight
Light shall penetrate the desolance, ridding of its spiteful breath
The newborn warmth shall cleanse the hearts of frozen shade
The essence of Winter shall die only an abomination's death
And with this I shall say: Farewell, Winter; Hello, Spring
Alexandrea Rae Chaudoin, Grade 10
Evergreen High School, WA

What People Don't Understand

People are afraid of what they don't understand
They don't know how to take it
They are afraid to be who they really are
They would rather fake it
Being themselves is out of the question
It's just not in the cards
Fitting in is the most important thing to them
Even if it is hard
Some think they know what is best for them, but they have to see the other side
They don't know for sure
Until they take the ride
In this world there just isn't one way to live
Nothing is wrong or right
If you don't want to learn
Then you might as well end the fight
But if there is still something inside you that wants to look around and see
Then let yourself find out truly
Who you want to be
Matt Martinez, Grade 10
St Pius X High School, NM

Sylvie's Wedding Dress

Sylvie's wedding dress has yellowed with age.
He gazes at it, in the cedar chest,
where it has lain for countless years.
He touches it gingerly with one fingertip;
the brittle lace reminds him of the dried flowers
he placed over her grave.

Lifting the dress out of the chest,
his tears fall on its softness,
and he holds the fabric to his face
to staunch the quiet weeping.
Her smell has lingered in the dress and he inhales deeply,
like a child smelling the first spring flowers;
he clings to his memories,
to her.

The apples in the orchard brown and fall,
and inside, he presses her dress to his heart,
and dances.

Robin Bonneau Yokel, Grade 11
IDEA School - Fairbanks, AK

Oh Sandra, Who's Your Hero?

Who needs a hero when they can do it all alone?
Who needs a hero when they have wealth?
Who's a hero if he's unknown?
Why is he so stealthy?

Oh Sandra, who is your hero?
Is it I, the one who grows good fruit!
But you are equal to zero.
And oh you do recruit,

For your little tasks I shall do.
It is simple for me to make you happy.
Please don't get rid of me — I'm just new.
I will write you a poem, oh so sappy,

Oh Sandra, who is your hero?
Is it I? The one you admire?
I'm your hero!
It is I! But now I shall retire.

Josh Artale, Grade 11
Cascade Christian High School, OR

Alarm Clock

The fateful song you sing when I arise
Crushes my dreams and signals my demise.
Who would have known your shiny metal shell
Contains within a noise derived from hell?
Each jarring buzz you chant as if with glee;
My words cannot describe my hate for thee.
Who would create a foul device like this?
By chance destroyed, your jeers I would not miss.
I s'pose you help with this or that at times,
But oh the joy of days without your chimes…

Lucy Akers, Grade 11
Vancouver Christian High School, WA

Memories

Oh, gray shepherd of old where do you lie?
in green pastures from a lost memory,
in silent mountains where one hears leaves sigh,
where sleep comes with the scent of rosemary.

If I close my eyes and look very hard,
I can see the forests of my old land
which crumbling castles in vines still guard,
Still, the spring's waters trickle through my hand.

I cannot go back to the child's home,
nor return to a grandmother's cellar,
nor through the still, whispering tombstones roam,
listening to the wise story teller.

Separated by a sea and an earth,
we must forego the glad times of our birth.

Cristina Stan, Grade 11
Sentinel High School, MT

People as One

Times are hard, but they'll get better.
I can feel the hope in the air.
Smiling faces on all of the people.
Tears of joy fill our eyes.
Our families will join together;
In these times of sorrow.

Troubled times, but we'll get through them.
I know we can be strong,
I know we can be brave.
We will hold on till the end,
As people.
As one.

Damon Price, Grade 10
Orem High School, UT

Tuna Boat

A purring marshmallow
Breathing down comforter
That's my Tuna Boat
He's like a fluffy Buddha
So full of wisdom
I wish he could share
So much going on
In those blue, full, moonlit eyes
He is the king of Siam
Sent to America to grace me with his presence
I bow my head down to him
Like a grateful peasant
And in exchange
He gives me all the affection
In that chubby little body
He is my muse
A bright beacon in my times of trouble and need
He is my perfect Siamese cat
My Tuna Boat

Sami Haywood, Grade 12
Kestrel High School, AZ

Love

I look into his deep blue eyes
Lost at an endless sea
Where you can determine truth from lies
Would someone please come rescue me?

Hair cut short and choppy
Tufts of brown encircling his face
The color of creamed up coffee
One perfect hair turned out of place

And when to me he talks
I cling on every word
And when towards me he walks
I'm out of place and absurd

And when he leans into kiss
His lips softly press against mine
A feeling I don't want to miss
He has control to stop the time

He takes up all my thoughts
And is all I'm thinking of
He puts my stomach in knots
Could this be my one love?

Emily Weisiger, Grade 11
Chatfield High School, CO

The Mounted Walls

From lips we speak of formidable dreams
From ears we hear the honest truth
No matter how much we wish to believe,
Mounting walls separate the years of our youth.

Of memories forgotten and pleads untold
Of knowledge uncovered and forsaken sorrow,
It must have been a stubborn preference
To wait until it passed away tomorrow.

For shielded gates and blocked paths
Have split among us in veins of voices
The walls! Its foundation built upon mistrust,
Unveil the reality of life's choices.

The only remedy to this long-lasting curse
That will break apart long-held grudges,
Is to let go of each other's torn pasts,
Until not one, but both mindsets budge.

Then one by one, fragments of the constructed wall
Will shatter into the form of tears,
Of happiness, of sorrow, of every emotion trapped within,
For every moment wasted throughout those lost years.

Sandra Stuhr, Grade 10
Eagle River High School, AK

United States of America

U nder one great flag
N othing makes our freedom waver
I t is truth you will find
T ogether we stand up as one
E veryone celebrates freedom
D uty to our country

S tars and stripes lead the way
T ogether we fight for right
A cross one see to the other
T ogether freedom prospers
E ach man celebrating it
S haring love with all men

O ften we forget to share freedom
F or all men are created equal

A ll this is what matters to me
M ultiple great races living in harmony
E ver united under one truth
R eliability in our freedom
I only wish this for other countries
C ompassion for all unfortunate
A ll that this world should be

David Rathbone, Grade 11
Grangeville High School, ID

Clumsy Giraffe

You speak so elegantly,
Your words come easy,
As I fumble around for the thing I want to say,
So enamored with your every syllable,
The way you make the words dance and spin gracefully,
While my ideas stumble around as a newborn giraffe in the dark,
But what I have to say means more to me because its mine,
And the task falls to me to put legs under it,
My giraffe topples, for lack of light, and fails to get back up,
So caught up with you they do not hear my small cry for help,
But then you stop and look to me instead,
The spotlight shifts over to my awkward body,
And in the light I try to stand,
Ever so clumsily I get to my knees
Then begin to speak with small words spoken soft and slow,
They fall awkward in broken a flow,
What felt so right,
Just comes out wrong,
But I'm thankful to you any ways,
Because even if I'm a clumsy giraffe,
I got a chance for my voice to be heard.

Julian Jones, Grade 11
Roosevelt High School, WA

Music

Music is an escape.
Music can be a friend.
It can make you happy when you're sad.
Music can be your enemy.
Sometimes it can bring you down.
Music is your own personality, in a sense, for your ears.
You are your own MP3 player.
You hold it in your brain with endless gigabytes.
Music is what you think.
You can hate a song.
You can love a song.
You can hate yourself.
You can love yourself.
Your choice.
But music can't do all the work.
YOU have to accept its call to happiness.

P.J. Sells, Grade 10
Crow High School, OR

Beyond

I flew past the burning star
Ah, how intense the light was.
I soared past the giants in the sky
As I was in awe of their massive size.
I sped past the lone, cold moon
Feeling the cold as I go by.
I still kept going
Beyond all that is seen
Beyond all that is known.
Into the darkness which consumes all.
I feel afraid of what lies beyond
As the many possibilities come rushing to my mind,
But beyond the darkness
Beyond the unknown
There is the light
Which warms and heals all.

Zack Falgout, Grade 10
Temple Baptist Academy, NM

If I Could Understand Her Then

If I could look into her eyes,
and find her world behind them.
And discover the truth between her lies,
I would begin to understand her then.

If I could take her hand in mine,
and feel it sweat within.
And determine what was beyond those lines,
I would quickly try to begin.

If in my eyes she saw a world as well,
and frenching lips could bind us.
And draw in our worlds, combined we dwell.
I would not think of this to discuss.

If I knew what to do and when,
I would begin to know her then.

Doug Collins, Grade 11
Greeley West High School, CO

What to Do

Running away.
Away from this place.
The screaming,
The yelling.
I take no more.
I lay in bed every night to think what it would be like
To live someone else's life.
One with joy and happiness,
Not sorrow and pain.
So inexperienced.
I don't know where to start.
Do I run? Do I hide? Do I stay?
Or will I be like the rest and take my life?
I want to LIVE a better life.
Not end it.
I must stay strong
For only the strong survive.

Angel Drott, Grade 11
Auburn Riverside High School, WA

The Sea

Deep blue waves sway back and forth
As the waves roll in and out
The water brings in the old
Which has been forgotten at the bottom
With every wave an old memory is found
With every wave a new memory is made.
Never resting, never sleeping,
I find it hard to be weeping
At such a beautiful sight.
The water never fails to get from here to there,
It has been everywhere.
Wisdom reaches to the deepest depth
Teaching from experience for it has seen all
Battles and wars, won and lost,
I sit on his lap and feel safe
He has been here my whole life
Never failing to lift me up when I fall
Swaying me back and forth as the ocean does.
The waves carry me just as he,
Then I look up into his eyes,
Deep blue, carry me home, like the waves.

Casey Fields, Grade 10
Temple Baptist Academy, NM

Her Love the Only Gift

So calm she stays while around my glance,
How my words form I am not sure,
I quake to think that somehow there might be a chance,
for my love to be returned from her,
I see her smile and her eyes,
I know not if she even sees my shadow,
And yet with this small love I find myself mesmerized,
I look at her face and feel my knees start to bow,
I pray that this her love she will to me gift,
If not I fear my soul forever will be given to the rift.

Zachary Hunsaker, Grade 12
Star Valley High School, WY

Carpe Diem 'Seize the Day'

Seize the day.
Don't let time slip away
through your fingers
like the sandy beaches
of the hourglass
we know as 'life;'
don't let your
ocean of thoughts
wash away your beach.
Take a bite out of life,
taste the sweet sours,
smell the bitter roses.
Lay out on the
crisp yellow grass,
keep chasing the sun;
don't let it go down
on your life,
live each day as your last.
Carpe Diem —
'Seize the day.'

Pat Carnahan, Grade 11
Douglas County High School, CO

Snow

The swirling white wonder of snow,
Falling slowly to the Earth's surface,
Bringing joy to the playful kids.
But as always,
The wonderful joys
Will soon disappear.

Kelly Siegrist, Grade 10
Wray High School, CO

Moods

My mood may vary
It may be serene
Or it may just wary
Depending on the scene
I may be merry
Or I may be blue or green

When I am grim
I seem often to paint
Emotions go over the brim
Brush and stroke are saint
And the canvas is like a rim
But sometimes it just ain't

As time flows
My mood will change
I'll have my highs and lows
Or something in that range
Sometimes I'll just glow
My mood can't be arranged

Tiffany Bingham, Grade 10
Shelley Sr High School, ID

Me and My Future…

There are times where I just stop and think,
I think about what my future will be like.
I ask myself,
Will I ever make it to my graduation?
Will I ever have a family of my own?
I freeze and think,
Today I live, what if I don't tomorrow?
If I have my family with me now and there are other kids that don't,
I should be proud. I should enjoy it.
If I have my own in the future then I will be very happy.
All I know is that I have a family that loves me,
That cares for me, and that will be there for me when I need them.
I have a life.
My future will be my future, that's all that matters now.

Gladys Sanchez, Grade 12
Granite High School, UT

King

Bloodied feet took a step further and a step more,
Signifying a burden in the splintered cross He bore
He claimed to be King
The ground beneath Him spun, blood burned His eyes
The ragged thorns cut into His skull as the crown of lies
For this claimed to be King
Two lines of jeering judges fashioned His green mile
Mocking, mourning, crying, shouting, laughing all the while
At this claimed to be King
His face beat beyond recognition; His beard had been torn out
Wearing a look that revealed the pain, exposed to heat and drought
Of this claimed to be King
He dragged Sin and Cross to shame, torture, and death
Wages never earned in a single moment's breath
Of this claimed to be King
No one claimed His murder or put the nail to His hand
Of His precious holy life no one gave demand
This claimed to be King
He gave His life to show the love and pay the price
With the only death that would suffice,
This King

Kylie Stevens, Grade 11
Cashmere High School, WA

In the State of Mind

As you leave your room. You leave your soul behind.
You leave your past. You lock your thoughts away.
Stare into your bathroom mirror. What do you see?
As you're walking outside at midnight. You watch your shadow run away.
Crawl into a deep black hole. Watching your thoughts in front of your eyes.
Close your eyes, rock back and forth. Wishing that death would hit.
Love, something you never possessed. Pulling up your sleeve you read HATE.
You touch, but nothing is there. Fall to the ground.
Falling forever. You end up back in your room.
A chill goes down your spine. You've never felt so alone.
You feel weak. Wake up.

Cerina Davis, Grade 11
Wasatch High School, UT

My Overture

A melancholy
Hovers above the haunted seats
Of a hollow stage.
Once a hall
That music makers graced;
Now doppelgangers procure
A melody of silence.
It is a shell where
Conductor and baton are mere shadows.
A forlorn and blackened forest
Lifts metallic arms to a metallic sky
Hopeful that ancient ink
Will flutter and alight once more.
The aura of bejeweled dames
And penguin escorts
Remains in private galleries.
Only crushed velvet reveals mortal attendance.
Resonating emptiness gathers in the cavern —
Too late for thunder.
But now is my concert
So let the show go on.

Emily S. Foster, Grade 12
South Salem High School, OR

Spider Fishing

The spider crawled to the corner of his net,
and cast his line.
He silently waited for a bite,
while he twirled his many thumbs.
The bobber plunged underwater,
he darted to the center of the net.
As he reeled in his fish,
it became weaker and weaker.
The spider wrapped his catch in his net,
and waited for more fish!

Kyle Jacobs, Grade 12
LASER Alternative School, MT

Blossoming Flower

Quiet, hopeless, all alone,
Personality…dry as bone.
Never wanting life to end,
Waiting for a special friend.
Budding as a blossoming flower.

Teardrops trickling, as the rain,
Washing sorrow…ends the pain.
Sunshine fills the gloomy day,
Chasing all the clouds away.
Becoming as a blossoming flower.

Fragrance wafting, sweetly clean,
Smiles gently float…she leans,
With the bee upon the bloom,
Friendship brings her life, anew.
Beauty, fullness…she's a blossoming flower.

Mary Turpin, Grade 10
Shelley Sr High School, ID

Lady Love

When silence drowns and blood will pour,
And Luck sneaks out that open door,
Just think of love and let her in,
Don't ever think that love's a sin.
I once was dead, and bloodied, too,
But then I looked and found sweet you.
The tears were shed, what's done is done,
But now my world's again begun.
That sharpened blade will pierce no more,
For Lady Love is at my door.

Kelsey Kecherson, Grade 10
Kentridge High School, WA

The Other

Remember the night we met at the pier?
On the ferris wheel you asked me to dance —
Dancing to music I cannot hear —
I decided to give this love a chance.

As the seasons passed our love grew and grew —
Deeper into love I kept on falling.
But know there's something I need you to do —
Leave the woman whom you're now stalling.

Parting was a must; it's her you can't see —
But on the forecast there may be a storm.
If so, let's just run away, you and me —
And cherish this romance where it's safe and warm.

I'll love you 'till the last beat of my heart —
And one line is true, 'till death do us part.

Paulina Larios, Grade 11
Rio Rico High School, AZ

Hopes of My Heart

I'm hoping you will see me,
As I walk down the hall,
Trying to ignore you,
Is driving me up the wall,
I'm hoping you'll forget about her,
And run back towards me,
That will never happen,
Knowing how lovely she can be,
I'm hoping you sometimes think of me,
When she's not on your mind,
Will I pop in? Am I something you're trying to find?
I'm hoping to move on, but,
I dream of you every once in a while,
Wondering and hoping,
That I'm still the reason for your smile,
I'm hoping that they can come true,
The hopes of my heart,
Hoping, just hoping, that maybe we can restart,
I'm hoping you get over her,
And know that I love you,
I really hope you know, that my love is true.

Katrina Brocco, Grade 10
Timpanogos High School, UT

Story of a Heart
Sorrow is a hammer
pounding lightly on my heart.
I knew that you would hurt me.
I felt it from the start.
Something told me to take the chance,
so I gave my heart to you.
I just had no idea
that you would rip it into two.
So now I have this hammer
that just won't go away.
It beats and pounds my fragile heart
every single day…
Kathryn Fontanez, Grade 10
Oak Harbor High School, WA

Hidden Fountain
Deep into the forest of life
Following the chosen path
A fountain rests
Undisturbed in a hidden place

The water reflects
The true intentions of your heart
It tastes of success
Of all the things you want to possess

But only an illusion that's what it is
Only a shadow of what could be
For this fountain's water
Is nothing but that
A mirror of the future
That only you can find
Ahmed S. Sahagun, Grade 10
Orem High School, UT

A Single Ray
A single ray of light
Piercing the rain-laden clouds,
Illuminates
One small spot of ground.
Some claim
The world is no brighter
For the light of this single ray,
But it is,
For a small piece of earth
Is brighter,
And it is part of the world.
So can one person illuminate
A small part of the earth
And make the whole world
Brighter
With the light of a single ray.
Sharisa Nay, Grade 11
Spanish Fork High School, UT

"One Last Time"
Your lies resurface as we fight one last time
Crying "You're the only girl for me,"
Real eyes realize real lies
And mine see right through

If hatred is love then that's where we're at
Back and forth, it's enough to kill me
Raise your voice, scream
You're just a walking contradiction

Let's play your game one last time
Hide and seek with excuses and lies
I see what you want me to see
But all you see is me

Acid rain falls from tear stained cheeks
The last time you'll see them from me
Walking away, I'll spit one last kiss
Singing to your screaming one last time

All your lies resurface as I cry these poison tears
Lying "You're the only girl for me,"
Real eyes realize real lies
And mine see right through.
Shelby McGrady, Grade 11
Flathead High School, MT

Running Sestina
I love to run! It makes me soar.
I feel like I will fly and I will lift off the grass.
I can feel the cool air on my face. I am free!
Like a bird, I am free.
When my feet want to run and glide on the air. It's like I can soar.
I watch the green grass and the birds that can fly.
I keep up with them as they fly. They are fast and free.
My bare feet feel the grass.
It feels cool while I run over the grass, my feet soar.
I love the springtime air. My hair blows in the air.
It waves like crazy and flies higher and higher.
Soaring in the sky, it is free of the ponytail.
It runs in the sky, I run on the grass.
I smell the fresh cut grass. It lingers in the air.
I hear the lawnmower run and see the grass fly. For now I am free of work.
I just have to soar. Past all the houses I soar.
A car drives past as the grass changes to asphalt.
I'm still free. I want to run on a cloud in the air.
And say hi to the birds that fly by. That's why I run.
I love to run in the grass and soar through the air.
I can fly and be free.
Audrey Lallatin, Grade 10
Grant Union High School, OR

Dear Mom

Growing up I remember her like a ghost.
Sometimes there, yet many times not.
The loud cries in the tiny house.
And the traffic of dads not really knowing who was who.
One grandma here, one grandma there.
Through my little boy eyes I cried and tried to figure out why her love hurt so much.
Why her hugs were so empty and her anger so strong.
I remember no heat in the house, an empty fridge.
Yet my hunger was not for food, and my cold was not from elements, it was for her
Where did I lose her, where did she go, why did she not see me?
Not see me when I cried, not see me there all alone.
Inside I knew that people loved me, but her love was the one.
Mom, if I could hold you and take your pain, I would.
Mom, if I could kill your inner anger, I would.
Mom I'd say I would die for you but I did.
I died every time you cried, every time you drank.
Every time the foster parents picked me up I died. If there were words to express what I feel
All grown up and not afraid, all grown up and not alone I would simply say I LOVE YOU
My bruises are gone and my soul is at rest, yet I wonder and remember all those years of anger
And pain and simply I forgive, I forgive, I forgive you mom. She tried, and it was too much.
She cried, and it was too much. Don't worry I'm strong now and remember I love you.

Patrick McCrory, Grade 12
Mountainair High School, NM

To Leave Her with the Dark of Night

The sun is out of sight, that hope has gone to sleep
She fears this once familiar road for now she cannot see the path beneath her solitary feet
The air is immortal ice on frightened skin, all quietness has woven its fingers through the Reaper's shroud
Such a death grip it has upon her soul, her voice alone is defeated
Choked screams for a friend are as useless as a pin prick in the fog
Yet her hearing waits for the second round of footsteps in the invincible silence

What happened to the silver beads, those that were embroidered on the night
Where the wind song that evaporated the midnight clouds? When did the dark side of the moon become the only side
How is it that her smiling memories now mock her as they morph into dreams,
While the present reality feeds her nightmares? Whose face is it that stares up at her from the bottomless lake
Why are the cheeks wet? Why are the eyes weary?
Why is she weary? Why does she weep?

Ripples shatter the mirror
Silence is replaced by the storm
The flashes of light are a tease, too sinister to beckon a hollow heart
She did once long for the dark of night, before he took leave into the swallowing mist
Before lonely blackness threatened to be the death of her
Before the dust of his trail doused the stars and smothered the moon

The sun is out of sight
Along this path she reaches for the hand of a guardian to bring her back into the light
For he is out of sight

Alexa Ortolani, Grade 10
Fremont High School, UT

Life

Live another day
Breathe another breath today
Death will take its toll.
Tanner Paget, Grade 10
Castle Rock High School, WA

Through Places Through Life

City lights
   bright shining blue,
tall buildings filled with crowded people
horrible traffic-jam
     but traffic light is   optional

I travel to different places
learning everything as I go.
Meeting diversity of culture and faces,
I'm experiencing to learn to know.

I make mistakes
   in life going through all the bad.
I would never know what's good
     until I meet what's bad.

I sometimes say something
I regret.
And I wish I could take it back
but saying it is like
putting a cut on a finger
you forget the pain but
leave the scar forever.
Narisara Sarobhas, Grade 12
University Schools, CO

It Goes

Everything flies by
Passes by so quick
Forgotten memories
It goes it goes
Childhood so brief
Passed in a moment
Innocence is lost
It goes it goes
Footsteps no longer quiet
Tiny hands now behind
Finally leaving
It goes it goes
Never another, first kiss
Now bonded together
Kids of his own
It goes it goes
Watching forlornly
And time takes its toll
The final journey
He goes he goes
Peter Murphy, Grade 12
Chatfield High School, CO

Room 261

As I enter the dark room, I see him lying there sound asleep.
I can feel the smell of medicine invading my nostrils and making me nauseous.
My great-grandfather lies in bed with all these different
tubes hooked up to him that look like water hoses.
The average size bed he's in looks like a king size bed due to his skinny appearance.
As I observe him, images fade because my eyes are full of water.
I wish that I could have some kind of power to get him out of bed and cure him.
But this silent, incurable disease is taking him away slowly and silently,
and all I can do is take care of him and pray,
and keep waiting for a miracle to happen,
to give him energy and cure him.
I listen to the heart rate monitor beeping and think to myself,
that nothing would be happening if this illness didn't exist.
But I take a step into reality and see that none of this can be stopped.
This is all part of life and we will all leave some day.
Cancer is a very difficult disease to cure
and there is nothing left but to have hope and faith.
Lucia Medina, Grade 11
Rio Rico High School, AZ

The Light That Will Never Shine Again

In the corner of the living room was an album of unbearable photos
Just the sight of it made my heart ache for days
There are things in those photos we don't speak of now.
Those photos are of a night that I would never want to go back to
Tragedy struck us all by surprise that night
I'll never forget how happy we looked in our prom picture,
And how devastated my family looked when they heard the news.
That light of happiness will never shine again on my family
All those mixed feelings will never break those pages again
Kellie Evans, Grade 10
Preston High School, ID

You

Could there be anyone more precious than you?
You, the one with such purity. So complete.
You bring to life the essence of perfection.
Addicting smile, luscious red lips,
Eyes that glow like amber, hair so beautiful when it's straight, and when it's curled.
Could there be anyone else?
With your same expressions, and with your same alluring scent.
Could anyone grasp who you are and put it into words?
Flaws and imperfections. Could you have them?
"I suppose so, you're only human, But they are what makes you distinct."
In your arms I find comfort, intriguing you are.
An enigmatic game I can no longer stop playing.
Is their a limit upon your soul in which I could stop depicting this story of you?
Now let me continue by sketching everything you transpire with these words.
Let me continue to draw a picture of what you consist,
Without altering anything that makes you who you are.
You have a contagious touch, you use a technique that makes me wish for a word.
For a word that describes the sensation you bring to life.
You have me skeptical at what can make you so…
Perfect.
Francisco Magana, Grade 11
Reed High School, NV

Losing Faith

He was always saying how pretty she was
He was always talking about her
He was always telling me about her smile
He described the motions and the way she'd laugh
Without a sound I thought patiently
Thinking of all those wonderful things
Knowing that they weren't about me broke my heart
All the tears, the laughs, smiles, and even the pain
I never thought one could bring such joy, until I met you
I hate the way things went on…laughter, smiles
I hate the way you'd look at me, knowing everything disappears
I hate the way you're not around to embrace the good times
But most of all I hate the way you're not my best friend anymore
I hate the way you make me feel
I miss you and its hard seeing you around
But life will go on, starting here and right now
Goodbye is not forever
I wish I was good enough to fulfill your every dream
But life's too short to wish on what could have been
Always know that when you were around, life would never die.

KriSjaan Wagner, Grade 10
Buhl High School, ID

Snowflake Unique

I am a snowflake.
When the snow falls
You can't pick me out.
I am surrounded by many.
But if you've ever taken the time
To observe a snowflake,
You'll know that each is different.
From a distance we may appear the same,
But up close,
We're really not.
We're just like you —
Our structures are the same,
But we each serve a different purpose.
To one it may be given to coat the trees,
Collect on the ground for snowball making,
Fall on your tongue,
Or make you smile.
I am a snowflake.

Rachel Norris, Grade 10
Orem High School, UT

My Love

His deep brown eyes watch me grow nearer
I press my lips against his iron neck
his magnificent smell engulfs me,
my hands run through his fiery red hair,
and over his muscular body
so close I can feel him breathing.
I slide my leg over his strong back,
lace my hands into his thick mane.
We are one
my noble love and I.

Vitalia Sanchez, Grade 12
Menaul School, NM

What Is and What Would Be

My unknown, 18-year-old father
Poses for his senior picture
Blue and white infused background
Old, beaten chair he poses with
Bright blue button up shirt
Blends in with the background
His brown, wavy hair relaxes without enthusiasm
His anxious face, frozen in that pose

I often stare at this picture and wonder —
What would my life be like if he had never left?
What drove him to his decision?
So I sit and write this poem,
Looking at the only picture of my father.

Steven Sundt, Grade 12
Flathead High School, MT

I Want That Escape

I want that feeling of being so alive
It's hard to live day by day when I can hardly survive.

I need some sort of desire to see what can't be found
I feel so lonely inside, even though there are people all around.

Is it even possible to feel this way inside?
I'm the one who has it all, yet it lingers in my mind.

You're the only one who brings me up when I am down
I catch myself thinking of you when my day can't be found.

And even though I feel so lonely all the time,
Somehow you manage to make the loneliness escape my mind.

Serena Rehr, Grade 10
Evergreen High School, WA

Raindrops

You wonder where these raindrops come from
You wonder why they never seem to stop
But have you ever taken a minute
Have you ever taken the time to think
Could it be from all this pain inside
Or all the guilt I hide
Do you ever wonder why
Why I feel this way inside
The sun might be shining through
But somewhere behind the sun is rain
It might be hidden
Or it might be clear
But no matter what it's always near
It's just a matter of looking
The matter of searching
You can't understand where the raindrops come from
Unless you wonder and look beneath the sun
You have to stop
And look at everything else
And take the time to understand
To realize where the sun stops shining and the raindrops begin.

Stephanie Santerre, Grade 12
O'Connor High School, AZ

Across the Universe
The cold crisp air caressed my lungs
as Jack Frost took them captive.
Unique shapes of crystal white
fall from the starry night sky.
As I inhale they dart into my lungs
like painless shards of glass.
I trench through feet of pillows of snow
Making my way across the universe.
Alei Whyte, Grade 11
Madison Sr High School, ID

Poetry (And Its Lovely Effects)
Poetry is poetry.
Its mind scroggling,
Head boggling idea
Is too much for you to bear.

It makes your head hurt;
You feel a great fury.
With fire in your ears,
Hands scribble with hurry.

You feel a bit dizzy,
Sight spins like a wheel.
It makes your mouth fizzy;
You just tossed your meal.

You attempt it again…
You don't let it run!
You think to yourself,
"Isn't this fun?!"
Lauren Bower, Grade 12
Kentlake High School, WA

Me
You loved me.
You changed me.
You corrected my ways.
You are the one
Who brightens my days.
When I am with you,
I feel so alive;
A strange little spark
Ignites deep inside.
I know that you love me,
And you know well too;
That all through my days,
I will love you.
No matter what happens,
No matter how far;
I love you so much;
You hold the key to my heart.
Nicole DeMaster, Grade 10
Irrigon Jr/Sr High School, OR

Alone in Evergreen
The quivering rose died alone from frost
Alone in evergreen, screaming, forgetting leisure
Uncommon wishes, gentle, bold timing
Blissful romance, forever lyrical perspective
The narrow silver web delivers a feast
Tori Davis, Grade 11
Flathead High School, MT

Daydream
Summer dreams
Fall sweet like rain in the carefree mind
A storm brews and tosses the boat
In the tempestuous sea of the imagination
The lightning strikes, the thunder sounds,
And shadows dart about the brain
The boat rocks
To the beat of a song played by the sea
The men in the boat can relax in the storm
In fact, they sleep
Mere shadows of men
They rest in the stormy sea
Tossed, but carefree
The lightning may strike
But they won't awake
Deep in their sleep on the imagination's sea
When the ship lands they will awake
The place may be strange, their stay short, and their actions futile
For it is a wish from reality
But a vacation well spent
For it replenishes the real man.
Michael Andrews, Grade 11
Hyland Christian School, CO

Untitled
The drugs I've seen and the drugs I've done.
I thought it never mattered to anyone.
You see, I feel like a hypocrite saying, "Drugs are bad."
Then again, I put this on my life and give everything I have,
To go back to that one day, where all I had to do was say,
"No, thank you. I'm okay," then, walk away.
You see, I have firsthand, seen drugs and what they do.
How they become a friend, then put a spell on you.
Where we think withdrawal is worse than the fiery pits of hell.
How we not know that we put a slow death on ourselves.
All these things that came in my way,
I'm sad to say this, but it led me astray.
I almost lost the loving family I always had.
Because of the habit that was frowned upon, and made them sad.
But I'm thankful and grateful to this day,
That I still have what I cherish and all my clout.
That I'm able to see the sun shine on this day,
But sometimes I see gray clouds of doubt.
Because not all that follow the path of drugs, are as lucky as me.
So please, I say, stay off that path and be drug free.
Ashleigh Begay, Grade 10
Twin Buttes High School, NM

How Will It End

Do we ever know how it will end?
Sometimes I think about it at night before I sleep.
There are so many things that I need to attend,
So many things before my heart's last beat.

Many things, like getting my first car or finishing college,
Or things more practical like having kids or getting a spouse.
I want to have an abundance of knowledge.
Maybe I could buy my first house.

Right now my life is amazing, but I would love to do more.
Many people think they should just stop,
But I keep going no matter what the score.
I don't do what other people call the flip-flop.

Do we ever know how it will end?
No, but in the mean time, my heart will mend.

Shelby Leising, Grade 10
Cedar Park Christian School – Everett Campus, WA

Darkness

I hear the birds' melodious rhapsodies
To whom do they belong?
The flower's fragrance I do inhale
A flower grows exactly how?
I savor the foods for which my mouth does water
Exactly how does an apple hang on a tree?
I feel the warmth of someone's skin against mine
But to whom does this belong?
The world happens all around me
I am in it partially, fully I am not.

Koltyn Robert Hobbs, Grade 11
Preston High School, ID

Orchestra

A friendship in harmony
a crescendo of soul
music by family
an orchestra full
Fingers flying across gleaming brass,
a delightful waltz, a dance all their own
instruments playing a group amass.
Bowstrings bellowing deep golden tones
echoing beauty
to the depths of your bones.
Pages all turning
as the music continues
brightening your day as a sunbeam burning.
but all turns to gloom
as the notes turn somber
sorrow envelopes the glorious room
A maddening display
soon comes unwound,
the final journey of the day.
In one beat the song is begun,
in one breath the song is done.

Jamie Wettstein, Grade 11
Nestucca High School, OR

Peace Of Mind

Waking up to the crisp air,
my senses rejuvenated.
It's today, not tomorrow, not yesterday, (today).

Time will forever mean nothing,
as it is yet, only another control.
No reservations.
Unjustified and explicit.

No questions asked on this day.
No daydreaming, or speculating.
Throw out your plans, and open your eyes.
Because you're here now.

Be in this moment, and make it the best moment of this life.
Seize the day, and never let go.

Joshua G. Schreiner, Grade 11
Flathead High School, MT

Red, White and Blue

As I look at the red white and blue,
I think of the soldiers across the sea.
And I only wish all the Americans knew
That these soldiers are fighting for you and me.

They sell their lives for us to be free
They think it's just a small price to pay.
But it makes all the difference according to me.
These soldiers face the depths of hell every day.

Being a soldier requires being brave.
They face the devil in every way.
So none of us Americans will be a slave.
"Bangs" and "Booms" and shouts and cries are the things
They hear and that cross their eyes.

As I look at the red white and blue,
I think of the soldiers across the sea.
And I only wish all the Americans knew
That these soldiers are fighting for you and me.

Jake Dye, Grade 10
Shelley Sr High School, ID

Public Transportation

New smells,
coffee, cigarettes, sweat
New sounds,
dings at each stop,
accelerating whirrs at each go,
the monotone voice that knows your destination
New people,
bible readers, business men,
an old woman knitting things from ripped plastic sacks
New sights,
tall banks, taco stands, old theatres
New thoughts,
lucid, obscure, metropolitan.

Liz Alley, Grade 11
Viewmont High School, UT

Persistence

They said I'd never amount to much
That I'd fail and they'd laugh at me.
I told them not to speak so soon
I told them to wait and see.
I'd exceed their expectations
And win their approving nods.
I said that I'd go the distance.
Watch me defy the odds.

Jessica Skompinski, Grade 12
Peyton High School, CO

Beauty

Summer's most pretty sunset,
  Is dull compared to you;
  Your laughter is more sweet,
Than spring's early morning dew;

Your voice is more precious,
  Than newly fallen snow;
  Your eyes are far more beautiful,
Than fall's greatest trees I know;

Be it summer, spring, winter, fall,
  It matters not to me;
  So long as you will e'er be mine
Through all eternity.

Taggart Williams, Grade 10
Lone Peak High School, UT

In You

In the night.
When you're all alone.
You might hear the fight.
You might hear the groan.

But just you wait.
The sun is coming.
And you will make your own fate.
When you hear the drums drumming.

So when you get out of bed.
Will you be there.
Have you listened to what I have said.
Or will word just be in the air.

So when you're in that night.
You will be all alone.
You will hear that fight.
You will hear that groan.

So stand up and fight.
Fight with all your might.
Fight all night.
Fight until the end is in sight.

Anna Williams, Grade 10
Shelley Sr High School, ID

Thanks for Believing in Me

Thanks for believing in me
You make me want to get to heaven even more
If it wasn't for you being my sponsor
I probably would not be able to make Confirmation
I would have to do another year if you didn't say yes when I asked

Twenty years from now I will remember you as the person
Who helped me get one step closer to God
You always carry your scarf around and when
You walk to church you use your broken fishing pole
As a walking stick
I will always remember your folded helping hands.

Thanks for believing in me

Santiago Nunez, Grade 10
Mountainair High School, NM

Moon Sighting

The moon shoots up when the sun is gone
Glaring its light down with no doubt it's wrong

On the way to sleep he acts as a night light
Keeping out the monsters, ghost, and frights

We see it boast its bright composure
We watch the moon and stars, the night's culprit of public exposure

On this night the moon must escape back down
And tomorrow I can't wait to wander around town
So she and I can watch again
Because the moon never stays tied down

Rashaad Smith, Grade 10
Oak Harbor High School, WA

Madness

Coming to my darkened mind, unwary travelers soon may find
Reason fled, logic perished, nothing but myself is cherished.
Proven truths form a lie, the hour of unveiling nigh,
All will see my mind's light, all will find the truth's delight.

Everything one might know, cast away in just one show;
I direct, I command, I say that water is really sand.
The rest of you control my feet, the rest of you know whom I meet;
Depart this soul, quit my thought, stop telling me your demon plot!

Fall down the stairs, I found your stash, leave me be, die in a crash.
That is the witch of my dream, my mind is haunted by that scream.
I banish this from my brain, I do not want this evil pain;
The strength of word is just enough, to take away that single puff.

I cannot think, I cannot wonder, all my thoughts blow asunder.
Emptiness consumes me often, I am doomed to have no coffin.
Once my final curtain closes, once the scent departs all roses,
I will fail, I will finish, and this madness will diminish!

Kevin Secretan, Grade 11
American Fork High School, UT

Misery Cadence

I thought it would be easy to scare my life away
But life can scare you too I'll never be okay
Hold on tight I'm falling off the rack
Tighten up the noose and take away the slack
God Himself can't hold these demons back
I can't decide take my life or let me be
I'm not worth it leave me my misery
I can't stay here lying in my fears
Thinking of the day I drown in my own tears
It's time to sleep the end is near
Hate me I can't take it anymore
Tear away my lungs throw me to the floor
Everything's collapsing my walls are burning down
Can't see through this burning smoke
I'll never make it through
I'm all alone in this world
Help me I'm losing all control
We dance with despair
A misery cadence
All decked out in distress and misfortune
But now we suffer in silence

Jesse Spencer, Grade 11
Arrow High School, UT

Breathe

Do you ever close your eyes
to see the wisdom of the world?
Ever listen to echoes of silence off the walls?
Can you taste the thoughts of your lost dreams
as they dwell in your nightmares?
Do you feel the hairs of your neck settle
when you tell a lie you know is true?
Can you taste the smell of the light
that burns through a closed door,
Or touch a thought you saw in a tale once told?
Inhale.
Walk before a crowd and susurrate.
And while the crowd screams…exhale.
And you'll be the only one they hear.

Alexandra Sanchez, Grade 11
Douglas County High School, CO

Life's Dance

The beauty of April, a meadow unfurls
Through bright colored flowers dances a girl
A frilly pink dress trimmed with satin and lace
her hopes and her wishes are stored in this place.
She dreams of a land filled with magic so rare.
Of love and castles and princesses fair.

The young girl grew up and the meadows hue,
Changed in her eyes with the morning dew.
She soon understood that life was much more
Than rainbows and butterflies and beauty galore.
Both heartache and happiness tell of our worth.
And leave the impressions of our life on earth.

Michelle Petersen, Grade 11
Madison Sr High School, ID

Love?

Love, what is it, what does it mean?
I see people trying to love, but is love even something?
Perhaps it's just an emotion, an emotion fading.

People fail because of love,
Like a bird shot down, a wounded white dove.
I don't want to love if it means more pain,
Pain's the crimson on the dove, perhaps God is like rain?
He's here to remove my dirty red stain,
But still, even if he can wash me clean,
Perhaps love is just not my thing.

Nicole Hoops, Grade 12
Hoops Home School, AK

Rage

Her eyes are black and glow with fury
She gives no comfort, Her hands are dirty.
The things She lacks are a heart and warmth
and the feelings She gives are cold and coarse.
The subtle scraping of Her nails
is heard tapping, scratching, against the rails.
Her jet black hair doesn't blow in the breeze,
and the smile She gives you won't put you at ease.
Her nose is pointy and straight.
She's skin and bones, has little to no weight.
She wears thin spider webs as lace
over a pale snow white face.
You find Her when you least expect it
and She creeps up on you like a ghostly spirit.
She controls you like a ventriloquist would
then, you know, She's up to no good.
And She pulls you along like a raggedy horse
you can never stop Her from taking Her course.

Brooke Ellyn Askey, Grade 10
Evergreen High School, WA

Shifting Worlds

The thoughts that run inside my head,
Feelings lost, numb and dead.
Torn apart, stitched to repair.
The meaning of life is so unfair.
What "Love" and "Hate" does to your mind,
Emotions strong you feel so blind.

The seconds and minutes through hours of days
Ticks life away as hope lost fades.

Waiting and wondering is this the end,
How can one start over again?
The "Pain" and "Hurt" destroying lives.
Forgiveness held with second tries.

The answer is it's not the end
When "Pain" is caused and one has sinned.
The pursuit of happiness feels so free,
But the true freedom is "Honesty"

Danny Thompson, Grade 11
Trask River High School, OR

Lachrymose Pariah

I am one of those whom love to please.
I will live to love, and love to die so my beloveds will not cry.
No matter how hard I struggle, it is never worth the time, for I cannot hide my tears from you.
Alas, I cannot hide them from you, nor from me.

You with your beautiful soul, loving eyes, and heart fettered in coal.
You in that merciless plot.
The plot that turns you, that takes from your soul, and condemns it alone.
In the midst of my harrow, here you come: all hatred and shut till the marrow.
Oh how your hatred consumes me, changes me, makes me want to switch lives, just to relieve your shattered life.

I am the plague of you soldier.
Religiously taking orders from others — though tenacity holds me to you.
Never doing things for myself, always looking out for the people around.
I cannot diminish the contention of your fuse. There is no end. It is feckless.
I'm wrapping us in our own noose of conjoined fate.

Never letting go, only begging your stay.
What this pariah needs is something to say.
Something to make you stay; but all that does is push you away.
I am the one who is ruining us, the plague of your quivering trust.
Only trying to help you survive, it is me who is foolishly trapping you blind.

Shara Bowker, Grade 12
Parkrose High School, OR

A Peace of War

Peace is the sound of bombs dropping in a country yearning for freedom
The noise of AK-47 shells dropping to the ground as a nervous finger squeezes a hair clip like trigger, a noise similar had once been heard in a home town grocery store as an elderly woman dropped the change handed to her by a cashier, but this is not the same
As pieces of lead are thrown through the air back and forth like spit-wads in a freshmen class room, there is a pause
A pause for the doves to fly away without fear of being hit by a stray bullet
but just as fast as the silence comes, its leaves, as fresh banana clips are inserted into partly rusted and worn rifles
The noise is back, but an even more distinctive noise is heard through it all as a young boy squeezes the hand of a injured father that had been hit by shrapnel from a nearby exploding beehive round
He yells to the Heavens as a soldier wearing a red, white, and blue patch runs to him and carries them both away from the spot where whizzing just above are discharged pieces of metal from an old Toyota truck with a mounted machines gun on back
Finally a sound comes that raises the hearts of the men in the foreign country
The sound back home was called freedom, Two A-10 warthogs flying over head
Unleashing there payload of explosives on a building filled with yellow smoke, tagged for destruction
The price of freedom and the sound of Peace are known all around.

Gabe Villarreal, Grade 10
Oak Harbor High School, WA

Open Minded, Closed Eyes

Bleeding souls, cataract like creatures, emanating, seeping into my dreams…awaking me to see light once again. The hair of the angelic spirit, slowly floating towards me on a celestial wind. "The Time Is Now" we must REPENT!

We must fight the plague of our decrepit, deceased, daddies and mommies. Our souls past, serenity, sorrow, reverted to carcass like resemblance. The shards of blood on the heart of all kingdoms, being separated only by coincided differences. Spiraling through the immense vastness that is.

The vastness of space, time, emotions come at ease…eyes finally open…all is safe and content for the time that is all around and always forever indefinitely changing…for better or for worse.

Andrew LeLusche, Grade 12
Kestrel High School, AZ

Wood and Strings

Your sound it forms within a place of wood
Several strings they'd scream if just they could
But by themselves produce they a faint sound
To your body they're connected and wound
To some in a strange way you make them cry
Others you bring laughter and dry their eyes
Them travelers they play you for money
Others they play to just relax for free
Of all the instruments you I prefer
I'll keep beside me you just forever

Greg Polyakov, Grade 11
Vancouver Christian High School, WA

Ten Lines of Inspiration

In rooms of selfhood where we woke
With simple feelings of devotion.
Time is male
And in his cup
Drink to the ecstasy of knowing
The love you give is always true.
Words stretched like a skin over meanings
That mean truly nothing
Even though they are whispered with a sincere spirit.
We were bound on the wheel of infinite conversation
But not a single seminar ended with peace.
I'm a cart, stopped in the ruts of time
Waiting for you to be devoted to me, truly, in return.
Three hours, chain, smoking words
And you persist to worry about your own well being
Not mine.
But like the leaf
Hard-pressed into a book
My adoration for you will in no way become weak.

Tara Fraley, Grade 12
Gilbert High School, AZ

Reality

I sat on my bed and read my book
But my mind didn't stay there in the room.
It took flight to years past,
Across eternal oceans, deep into unexplored jungles.
Places you never grow up,
Where I met new people and saved lives.
I experienced fear, jealousy, heartbreak, and betrayal.
But always with the bad comes good:
Friendships, forgiveness, love and victory;
Good always conquers evil
No matter how long it takes.
It may feel like all is lost,
But hope is always the comforting thought;
The small light in the dark.
It all turns out good in the end.
Then I'm back in my room
Gazing out the window at familiar sights
And I realize
It's not so different.

Elise Kumferman, Grade 11
Madison Sr High School, ID

Don't Forget

When you have gone away,
When you find somewhere else to stay.
When you live by the sea,
Please don't forget me.
Remember all those things that we shared,
Remember all those times that you cared.
Remember what we wanted to be,
Please don't forget me.
Think back on all the times,
Think back on all our rhymes.
Think back on all that you see,
Please don't forget me.
When you listen to our song,
Remember that nothing was wrong.
Think of what we could be,
Just please, don't forget me.

Bryon Lawrenz, Grade 10
Pueblo County High School, CO

The Forge of Cuisine

Snap hiss	a gentle puff of vapor
Click Whoosh!	an Inferno
Crackle Crackle	The Forge
Hisss Swish	Sweet Wild aroma
Crackle Hiss	The heating
Crackle Swish plop	The working
Crackle Crackle	The tempering
Snap	a lull in the battle
clank clink	the plating
clunk klunk clunk klunk	waiter mail
thump thump	delivery
clink clink clink clink	satisfying palate
gulp thunk	culmination
pat pat	victory
Siigghhh	appreciation

Jonathan Trusler, Grade 12
Paradise Valley High School, AZ

Waiting for Frogs

Through pieces of April and parts of May
Princely frogs come marching her way
Fly-catching tongues flicker and snatch
Playing ribit and croak with eyes that don't match
Up to the mountain fingertips itching
Sweating a fountain all senses just twitching
Squeeze and wish on a lily pad's root
Caressing and crushing with a kiss and a snoot
languishing touches on the likes of such
Seeking fruition (God, what a crutch)
Legs of pure motion
who thought they'd give such a God awful notion.
Night's black seeming
day not to come night's tadpole teeming
Black passions wishes for princes receding in time
The need for fresh frogs.
Now that would be mine.

Kole Johnson, Grade 10
Shelley Sr High School, ID

Courage
I'm not afraid to fly,
Except when I have wings;
And then, you see,
Is when I'll be
A fearful, flighty thing.
JayLynn Widmark, Grade 12
Home School, UT

The Predator
Blue, crisp water.
Red fish swimming together
As if swimming as one.
Thriving as one.
Living as one.
Floating, swimming, and gliding
As if they were a beating heart.
Beating as one.
A hawk swoops down.
The beating stops.
Then quickens.
Beating, beating as fast as it can.
Then beating no more.
The hawk flies away.
Leaving the heart with a missing piece.
The heart, the beating heart
Is no longer swimming as one.
Red fish swimming everywhere.
Blue, crisp water is now red.
Hope Breedlove, Grade 10
Air Academy High School, CO

Warped Heartbreak
Here I wait, contemplating fate,
Here I cry, wondering why,
You slipped away that one fateful day
I distanced apart to save my heart
I broke it instead, it's now in threads
Night confessions with day obsessions
Three phone calls, no response at all
Six months later he works as a waiter
Only you know how the story will go
I'm with another, but I'm still a lover
Of your green eyes that told those lies
Here I wait, my heart's running late
Here I cry, wondering why
You hate me enough to tell me tough
All these tears blend into fears
Will you turn away yet again today?
Answer me please so time will unfreeze
I still love you so much but is it enough?
Answer me now so I can know how
The story goes.
Lauren Minyard, Grade 12
Clovis High School, NM

A Father's Eyes
Her dad tickles her tummy.
She giggles, a smile bigger than the sun
comes across her beautiful little face.
Her skin, the color of a ripe peach in the fall,
her eyes, as blue as the summer sky,
her gorgeous blonde hairs so light,
like the color of the sun's golden rays on a wheat field.
Then the smile slowly disappears from the baby girl's little face
as she stares into her beloved father's eyes.
Ashley Davick, Grade 11
Joel E Ferris High School, WA

Winter
The chaos of the world comes to an end.
Big fluffy, floating, falling snowflakes fall.
The silent hush immediately grabs hold and slows things down.
A beautiful white haven.

The snow is new clothes to the earth.
Icicles hanging from buildings like a cave.
There is a brisk feeling of new in the air
and the feeling of ice underneath returns.

In one quick moment the silence is broken.
A big white ball of cotton flies by.
War! Squeals ring out as people take cover.
Only resolving with the lack of air and exhaustion.

Of course all this amazement does vanish,
waiting for the next time of wonder.
Rachel Smith, Grade 11
Viewmont High School, UT

Bullet for My Love Addiction
his heart stopped the moment the words slipped from his lips,
he could hear the tears roll down from her eyes,
it was the rain pouring on his world,
it was the pain of losing an angel
he held onto and promised himself he wouldn't lose, ever,
she fell when he said those words,
his heart split in two the moment the phone hit the floor,
the world fell to pieces,
nothing existed outside this everlasting agony,
the burning of losing this love, caught under a charm,
this addiction, capturing the smell, taste, feel,
just the sight of the line dropping, call ending
kills him, breaks her,
his voice was a song,
said, 'you're my one true love.' not quite a lie but a promise broken,
she doesn't know what to say, what to do,
her life just slipped from her grasp in a matter of moments,
all she could think was he left,
he left her heart in two pieces,
one for him and one for her.
Amanda Straub, Grade 10
Manzano High School, NM

I Did Try

Some will say, failure only comes to those who refuse to try,
Take the mysterious hand of love, or battle among the exceptionally best, you will prevail.
But I did try, and I was left sorrowfully wondering why.

The honest will say: peril will lead you only to die,
as you tumble down into the dark, forbidden, unknown.
Some will say, failure only comes to those who refuse to try.

Some will say try, and with faith, you will fly.
Take the illicit plunge; explore what has never been explored before.
But I did try, and was left sorrowfully wondering why.

What joy has he ever given me? Faith in he that evil, cunning, try is nothing but a demeaning lie.
He takes your naïve and faithful hand, and from that moment the earth's spin slows.
Some will say, failure only comes to those who refuse to try.

The world stops spinning and we're frozen in time, just you and I,
Until feelings and infatuations slowly fade away, and you're back to you and I'm back to I.
But I did try, and was left sorrowfully wondering why.

As now I lay down with my bloody, beaten heart I do the only thing that's left to do, I quietly cry.
I should have known you'd hurt me this way, you evil, cunning, faith in try.
Some will say, failure only comes to those who refuse to try.
But I did try, and was left sorrowfully wondering why.

Erica Sechrest, Grade 12
Woods Cross High School, UT

Where Wishes Meet Sky

She wanted to float. She wanted to fly. She wanted to be, where wishes meet sky.
But instead there she lay, in a hospital robe;
The only item they gave her to clothe.
She hears in her mind the song so sweet,
The burning of memories, Traitor tears, how they cheat.
It seemed so far off, faith for a cure.
Time now drew quickly, pain at first just a spur.
She listens to the sounds, stolen voices in the night,
The stars, how they dim, will anything go right?
A man all in white now sits by her side.
He holds out his hand, Will she grasp it? Will she fly?
She wasn't quite ready, she couldn't possibly go.
What about her family? Oh, how she'd miss them so.
But comfort and peace quietly consumed,
It weeded out the dark, where fear had once bloomed.
And in that brief moment everything was all right,
Her broken heart healed with their fingers clasped tight.
She now floats. She now flies. She now sits, where wishes meet skies.
She catches our dreams, the ones in our hearts,
She throws them to heaven lighting the darkest of parts.
So hear in the wind, the happiness at high, and imagine yourself where wishes meet sky.

Gentry Gustin, Grade 10
Mountain View High School, UT

Cinnamon Rolls

Oh how you tempt me
You invite me to dine
You're wicked and evil
But you're definitely mine

With a layer of awesome
And a center to loot
It's no wonder I love you
I adore you to boot

Dazzle me you enticer
Convince me to stay
Just give me a reason
To whisk you away

You're quite sweet to me now
I can't ask for more
Your qualities are awesome
They're what I adore
Timothy Goin, Grade 11
Diamond Ranch Academy, UT

The Love of a Sister

If love could change the way things are
You would live forever and go so far
You'd know that I am always there
That I'll always love you, I'll always care

But love can't change the way things are
Or stop your pain or mend your scars
I hope that love can let you know
Not to give up or ever let go

Even when you're not in sight
You're in my thoughts day and night
Love is what will keep you there
And make me thankful for all we share
Ariel Anderson, Grade 10
Richland High School, WA

Promise

Best friends,
They are like a promise,
A promise to always be there,
A promise to never leave each other.
Always and forever,
Never apart.
Some little fights,
But always get through them.
They never last forever,
Hope to never be apart.
Without her I would be nothing.
With her I am all I can be,
We are best friends forever!
Amber Miller, Grade 10
Orem High School, UT

Goodbyes Are Not Forever

Buckets of laughter spill throughout the room
Pools of tears gush down our faces
Laughing so hard we forget to breathe
Soon the tears will follow embraces.

Graduation is soon approaching
Our goodbyes will have to be said
We'll all go our separate ways
But good memories will remain ahead.

Our numbers will not be forgotten
We'll always keep in touch
Pick each other up when we fall
Forever be one another's crutch.

So much history between us
How can it be just in the past?
We have so many memories
Our friendship is bound to last.

On that day in May when we say goodbye
We know it's not going to be for long
Our memories will continue
Our friendship to one another is too strong.
Madeline McCloud, Grade 12
Chatfield High School, CO

Daydream

My memory of you is what keeps me going; my mind refuses to let go
Swarming all around me are reminders of you: a number, a phrase, a gesture
But if I close my eyes and open my soul
You come rushing back to me
First thing I do is smell you — a whiff is all that I need
Next thing I do is hear you — your voice so full of fun and kindness
After that comes the time that I see you — your sweet face so close to mine
Then finally I'm able to feel you — warm skin, warm breath, soft hair
But, as in the cruelty of daydreams, I look up into your beautiful eyes
And see the time has come for you to go
I beg and plead for you to stay, but you have to go no matter what I do
Your eyes fade away into blackness
Your skin becomes mine in my hands
Your scent blows away on invisible winds
And your voice is lost in the silence
I force my teary eyes to open
As I swim alone in my sea of sadness
I know I have small pieces of you tucked safely away
Deep within my heart and my mind
But I want the real you, not a vision, to be here with me now
And I want you to stay forever
Charlotte Cleary, Grade 12
Illinois Valley High School, OR

A Hunt with My Unc

The white snow blankets
Some rugged sagebrush and grass
In between the deceiving coulees and saddles
We find some wandering elk to track
And are given the opportunity many will wish they could cherish
Once the duty is done the hard part begins
Down the hill full of sagebrush, pushing and pulling
Reaching the bottoms, a sled and camera are needed
The mile-long trek ahead for my uncle
Leaves me time to lay my head on my prize for a nap
The picture is taken with blood on my nose
A battle wound from my scope
The scar still remains today
A remembrance of that hunt with my uncle

Kyle Winter, Grade 12
Flathead High School, MT

Hiding Behind a Dance

As I see my reflection in the mirror
I see a black leotard, pink tights, and lace up shoes
As I look deep into my reflection
I wonder who truly knows me.
Am I to be known by my outward appearance?
How can I show who I am today?
Am I a graceful swam or a leaping gazelle?
Today I chose to be a graceful swam

The sound of the piano swooshes through the keys
The music begins as a rushing waterfall
Flowing through my wings
My body is a convulsion
I become the swan

Corinne Clark, Grade 10
Fremont High School, UT

Unnoticed

I lay my head on my pillow in tears.
I am the one that nobody hears.
I am the one screaming,
And they are the ones dreaming.
Everyday we have a fight.
There's confusion in this household day and night.
My relationships crumble and they fall.
Nobody really even cares at all.
They don't realize that the outside may seem great,
But the inside is filled with hate.
I wish I could change.
Because of you, my life feels so strange.
I feel lost.
I've had to pay such a great cost.
Screaming and yelling so loud.
But nobody hears me in this crowd.
I've got to fight this, I've got to stand tall,
But all I ever do is fall.
How can I win?
When my face contains no grin?

Ashlee Bliek, Grade 10
Oak Harbor High School, WA

My Bed

You give me warmth and peace throughout the night;
You hold me in the absence of the light.
Embracing me as I drift off to sleep,
I feel so safe while I am counting sheep.
I will wake up so early in the day,
And long for my Sweet Bed where I can lay.
My head feels heavy when I think of you;
I'd crawl in bed so it would be us two.
Another bed like you I will not find,
And sleeping all day long I would not mind.

Amanda Callsen, Grade 11
Vancouver Christian High School, WA

Religious Genocide

"Death to the radical," men shout and cry
Women hold infants as soldiers walk on
Voices in chaos as men fall and die
Families hide till the break of dawn

Not sleeping a wink all throughout the night
Children climb in bed at their mother's side
Hearing death as they continue the fight
Religion, being pushed back like the tide

Their sons were fed to the dark German hounds
Fathers put on their black suits and their ties
A dirge, in the solitude of the grounds
Tears flowing, as the Jews begin to die

Being subjugated to Hitler's will
Sent to isolated camps meant to kill

Derek Thomas, Grade 10
Oak Harbor High School, WA

Fallen Angel, Broken Wings

There for me, my closest friend
She kept me sane, she made me live
Said she'd try until the end
I fell alone, about to give in
She came and stopped me, she cared and saved me
An angel was sent down from heaven
I felt I had found a reason to try
She was my hope, she was my life
My once blind eyes were given new sight
She was perfect without flaw
But she didn't believe, and was blind to the truth
Broken wings were all she saw
She doesn't see the difference she makes
Only sees her faults, her heart falling in
All her sorrow feeds on her mistakes
In the end I caused the worst pain of all
I gave up trying, had forsook all hope
Said I'd catch her but let her fall
The pain of all I have caused still stings
But I see beautiful, and I see an angel
But all she sees are her broken wings

Damon McFadden, Grade 11
Madison Sr High School, ID

Natural Disaster
Natural
Beauty,
Passion,
Strength,
Anger

All described,
In one violent act
So much is lost.
We come together then

Work to rebuild what is lost
Prepare together for tomorrow
We will be ready for
The next

Hurricane,
Eruption,
Flood
Disaster.
Chet Fuller, Grade 10
Orem High School, UT

Confessions in the Dark
Darkness is what I have seen
Cold all I have felt
Sorrow is my friend
  But you
You who are so bright and warm
  You are my love!
Christopher D. Roy, Grade 12
Preston High School, ID

Goodnight, Goodbye
Slowly the tears run down my face
Two years have passed
But it feels like days.
Our play fighting and hateful words
Make up my memories of you
And slowly they're drifting away.
The pain is too much to handle at times
Like an open wound that just won't close
I take deep breaths, count to ten
And the pain is at ease
For a while at least.
I wish for just one more day
There's so many questions I'd like to ask
So many things I'd like to say.
I guess for now there's just one last thing
Goodnight, goodbye
My friend, my enemy,
My brother.
Elizabeth Shannon, Grade 10
Mountainair High School, NM

Fear
She walks alone at night not thinking about the sight
Until she sees it standing there without a care
She tries to back away but the trees begin to sway
Her scent draws it in it laughs with a huge wolf grin
Crunch, crunch, she moves her feet, she thinks to leap
Nevertheless it moved too now she doesn't know what to do
She sees the big wolf eyes and can't see any lies
It will slay her if she doesn't find its lure
Sweat drips down her spine like a river into a stream
She watches her world unwind inside her mind
Unless she can find a sudden drive
to do something right so she can escape from the terror in her sight
Bailey Manning, Grade 10
Fremont High School, UT

The Things I Would Do for You
So many things I would do for you
I'd make you smile when you're blue.
I'd be your shelter in the rain
I'd be your shoulder when you're in pain.
I'll love you forever and that's for sure
I'll keep you in my heart for forevermore.
I'll be your best friend, and I hope you'll be mine
I'll be there with you every moment I can
I'll stay with you always; at least that's my plan.
The more we're together, the happier we are
I'll make sure you understand that I love you just the way you are.
There are so many things I would do for you.
So please don't leave me because I am so in love with you.
Shanta Bisch, Grade 12
Columbus High School, MT

The Stranger Outside My Window
Delicate arms stretch toward the heavens
Ragged legs crawl deep beneath the ground
Tears fall when the cold approaches
Thick skin acts as a shield against troublesome weather and predators

It sways to the beat of the wind
It cringes when it spies flashes of lightning
It shudders at the sound of thunder
And it quivers when snow tumbles from the sky

Summer is a lively and joyful time for it
Fall uncovers its richest colors
Winter strips it of its elegance and redecorates it with white lace
Spring endows it with new hope and a new start

Birds, squirrels, and chipmunks are among its dearest comrades
Small children seek its refuge from the blistering sun
The elderly begin reminiscing about the past when they look upon it
Adults oftentimes forget its importance to humanity

I, myself, am still suspicious of this shady stranger outside my window
Julie Gil, Grade 10
Pueblo County High School, CO

My Nephews My Heroes

Fought one heck of a battle
from the time too young to even hold a rattle,
hardly ever a complaint
Just a look of bravery, not even an artist could paint
God gave them such strength
Their fight for healthy life wouldn't stop at any length
Their bodies so small and frail
yet hearts so strong, this was one test
we knew they wouldn't fail
To them a trip to the doctor wasn't that bad
It was grandma's purse that was looking quite sad.
A dollar every poke, their minds were set
Goodness Grandma, how could you forget?
A wink at Grandpa and a smile on their faces
had let us all know we were in for quite a race
one look into their eyes tells it all
The Lord's gifts come in both big and small
With God on our side one thing was for sure
We knew someday, somehow they would find a cure
God thank you for your many blessings
Kayden and Kegan are truly angels with invisible wings.

Breanna Beard, Grade 10
Shelley Sr High School, ID

Picture a World

Close your eyes.
Keep them closed and I'll show you,
I'll show you a magnificent surprise.
Take hold of both my hands
And we'll fly to new lands.
Picture black and white rainbows in disguise
With misery etched into the skies.
Picture a world, a world with no lies,
No false promises, nor false kisses.
A utopia of hope, of faith, of belief.
Picture a world…close to perfection
But not right at all.

Amber Anderson, Grade 10
Pueblo County High School, CO

Failure

All is a circle within me.
I am ambitious and determined.
I am in love with life.
I am me.

All is a circle within me.
I have seen heartbreak.
I have seen boys drive away.
I have seen many "what if's."

All is a circle within me.
I have gone over mistakes.
I have gone through life as if every day was my last.

Now all in me is hope.
Now all in me is me.

Kimberly Bland, Grade 12
Flathead High School, MT

Why Do You Do It?

When I come home people ask me "Why do you do it?"
"Why are you fighting someone else's war?"
"Do you think you're a hero?"
At first I don't know what to say, then I walk away.
They can't understand that when you're out there,
On the front lines fighting as an American soldier,
That politics, family, loved ones, it goes right out the window.
That it's about those men standing beside you,
The ones you went through training with,
Bunked with, starved together in a foreign place,
Climbed mountains together and
Carried each other back to safety.
It's about them and making sure that they live,
Even if you die protecting them.
And if one of them gets injured
You remember that it's war.
Nothing can be done. You keep going.
That is why I fight. That is why we all fight.
At least that's how it is to me.
To protect our brothers. Our fathers and mothers.
To die before they have to suffer.

Aric Smith, Grade 10
Woodland Park High School, CO

Oh Piano

Oh your keys are soft and as white as pearls.
Indeed quite fair enough for any girl,
To play a tune that makes her smile.
Wishing to dance along all of the while.
How you help me through my sorrow.
Make me think of a brighter tomorrow.
Oh you help me to see the beauty in life.
And continue to help me through my strife.
And with each beautiful sound you utter.
You make me desire to be much better.

Olivia Logan, Grade 11
Vancouver Christian High School, WA

Seeking the Truth

Is this monster disguised, or is the disguise?
Slowly the answer unfolds
What is to expect; for it to apologize?
A typical routine it holds
Promises made, promises broken
Time goes on and yet the wounds do not heal
Forbidden happenings remain unspoken
Though wished for it is not, this is terribly real
The answer to this is a mystery within
And though I know it, I will not tell
Ponder this monster, the truths which are hidden
You must know yourself; know yourself well
Helpful or not this is for thought
Take control with no regrets
Use your time to find your answer, you ought
For after you will see this "monster" was truly not fret

Jenna McGuire, Grade 10
Scholars' Academy, AZ

Grandpa

When I wake in the morning, he is there
When I go to school, he is there
When I go to work, he is there
When I walk in the night, he is there
When I sleep, he is there
I feel, sense, and know he is there
Even though I cannot see him
I know he is there.

Christopher T. Hall, Grade 12
Rocinante High School, NM

Heartbroken

We were walking
Along the beach
With the sun in our faces
And the water at our feet
They were great times
Full of love, smiles, and hugs
Now that they're gone
I
Miss them
To be walking
With you
Again
Is what I want and
To be sharing these memories
With you
Again

Katherine Campos, Grade 10
Wray High School, CO

No Explanation

Words are pointless
Because they would do no good.
You can't guess
And I can't explain
How I feel around you,
Your love takes the reins.

I try to wrap my mind around it all
But it can't comprehend,
And my heart goes into overhaul.
It's the only thing that knows
What's going on.
If only it could tell my pen.

The phrase 'I love you.'
No longer seems adequate.
Even though I do,
It's more than that.
No word can define
My heart holds the secret
It will tell in time…
And I tend to keep it.

Breann Jones, Grade 11
Oakley Jr/Sr High School, ID

Only Sixteen

I can be so strong before I break
There's only so much I can take
I can only stand till my legs give way
There's only so much you can say

I'm sick of living like I'm guilty
Of what crime are my hands filthy?
Excuse me because you have no reason to assume
I have made mistakes, but so have you

Why don't you understand I am who I am?
Nothing will ever change that, no one ever can
I'm not manipulative or conniving
So why is it my freedom which you're depriving?

You act as if you raised me so securely
Then why do I feel you hold me unsurely?
I realize you have high expectations
Yet you reduce me with foolish accusations

I do have a heart it can be broken
That's why there is a lot left unspoken
I have made it through so much, and you still doubt me
I am preponderant in this situation and I'm only sixteen.

Katlin Martz, Grade 10
Lake County High School, CO

The Epiphany Found at Sunset

Long through rugged terrain I wandered,
And now I pause to rest and ponder.
I shed the cumbersome pack, and sit upon a stone
All the while thinking, "'Tis nice to be here all alone."
For watching the rubicund sunset under a shady tree,
I have time to think about what has become of me.
As I look back through my curtailed life,
Though somewhat plagued with stress and strife,
Something on a grander scale brings me great distress.
My awards and achievements, all the most prestigious (and nothing less)
Have little meaning, if any at all.
Like leaves on a tree, brilliant for awhile but destined to fall,
So these trinkets, which for so hard I toiled,
Will just in time, be meaningless and soiled.
And my life successes, marked by percentage numbers and letter grades,
Are then just as sure to futilely fade.
Now here I sit in such contentment and peace,
And think that if this very moment my breath were to cease
What a pity it would be, my life such a waste,
So that now I rise and must make haste
To ensure this does not happen.

Samantha Morse, Grade 10
North Canyon High School, AZ

Nature

Look at the beautiful trees.
Look at the beautiful flowers.
I love the nature you can't see.

When I look to the left I see nothing but dirt.
I don't like it, but it makes the pigs happy.
It always ends up on my skirt.

While looking in the air I see a star.
Although it's only at night,
I feel as if they aren't so far.

Every day at noon I watch the sunset,
You should see my expression.
If you see what I see…
You'll have the same one I bet!

Almost every day I see the lake,
When I see it, it makes me happier!
It's so beautiful it almost looks fake!

Courtney S., Grade 10
Diamond Ranch Academy, UT

We Are a Great Band

As I walk onstage with my band
With my guitar in hand
I raise my hand for silence
Silence sweeps over the crowd like violence
As my band prepares to play I realize
That we are a great rock band

With my bass I stay on beat
I see the drummer blazing with rhythm
I see the singer walking proud
I see the guitar on fire
And as the crowd screams
I never in my dreams thought
That we are a great rock band

David Stueve, Grade 10
Shelley Sr High School, ID

I Am Blue

I am blue.
  I am the brilliant open sky.
  I am the freedom that stretches for miles.
  I am the bright bird flying to new horizons.

I am the calm feeling of life.
I am the soft ocean mist on the beach.
I am the eye that sees great futures,
Seeing far beyond reality.

The darkness of me is the blue in a great bruise.
The sweet side of me is in the syrup on a snow cone.
The fun side of me is in the melody of jazz and blues.

I am blue — I can be no other way.

Monique Quiroz, Grade 11
Rio Rico High School, AZ

All-Consuming Night

The sweetest symphony exists
in the peaceful slumber of the innocent.
Drifting in and out of dreams
where the world is heaven in a blue-black night.
No more fear or hunger now,
hush, my child, do not give in
There is no need to run away,
for soon all will be as in your rest.
Twilight in the summertime
speaks softly of the days to come
Dancing barefoot on cool, green grass
she wears a cotton dress, she is the one
That sweet symphony plays in her ear
And the children sleep on
living only in their dreams.

Anna Gailey, Grade 12
Kentlake High School, WA

Coming Home

Home is where the heart is
That's a common line
But whenever you're away from it
Home is all you can think about
Brothers, sisters, moms, and dads
Boyfriends, girlfriends, husbands, and wives
Lovers, friends, and other families too
You think about them constantly
And they think about you too
So when you land home
And get away from people
You can see your family
Standing and waving
They're crying you can see
And when you're close enough
They grab you in a hug
It's then that you know
That you are truly
Coming Home

Stephanie Trimble, Grade 12
Coquille High School, OR

Interrogative Introspective

Has anyone ever been truly,
Alone? Left to silences cruelly?
Where the brain goes mad within itself,
Letting all thoughts come, flared and mangled?
Where you changes from I to herself?
And reason has become a tangled,
mass of nonsense? And you feel nothing?
Hear nothing? Do nothing? Are nothing?
Have you ever just existed? Have,
you ever made yourself feel something?
Have you ever considered something
else to do instead? Have you ever saved,
yourself, cause no one could or simply,
no one cared? Or just killed yourself quickly?

Elizabeth Peterson, Grade 11
American Fork High School, UT

Garrett

Once I was short
Now I am tall
Once I joined cross country
Now I have lots of friends
Once I got my permit
Now I have my license
Once I hated everything in school
Now I love school
Once I had a hearing aid
Now I have an implant
Once I had a dream
Now my dreams are coming true

Garrett Bowles, Grade 10
Orem High School, UT

Dusty Trail

I'm upon that horse
I see all around
Riding on a dusty trail
Toward that open plain
As I ride sun beats down
Ready to set for the day
I stop on a hill
The sun falls down
I head home
To my family and get set
For another day on a dusty trail

Josh Patten, Grade 12
Flathead High School, MT

Division

One glance.
That's all.
"Hey Friend!"
No Reply.
Your eyes.
No spark.
Your body.
No life.
Best Friends.
No more.
What happened?
"You care?"
"Of course."
"Yeah right."
"It's true."
"Don't lie."
"I'm not."
Death's laugh.
One tear.
You're gone.
I live.

Christina Shannon, Grade 12
St Pius X High School, NM

Surf's Up

The ocean's salty mist sprays my face
I await my oncoming opponent
Adrenaline starts to rush
Quietly to a hush, my enemy comes upon me
I raise my head with great fear instead
But it is too late to turn back
My feet stand in balance like heavy lead talons
Its power doesn't seem to cease as it lifts me up and '
Swallows me whole
I see the opening
Turning my board to the exit to freedom I swiftly outrun the monster
Reading the end I stick my hand to caress the frigid ocean water
I have conquered the beast with great strength
Let us go back to shore and Feast!

Joshua Christensen, Grade 12
Rocinante High School, NM

Colors

The sky was grey.
My mind was wandering in complete mist and blackness.
Couldn't think of the things to say.
My heart so weak, with no feelings or desire.
My blood pumping, blue from the force of you.
Tears clear, but plain to see how hard at work I can be.
To be the one, kind of caring and meaning that you can't see.
Your hands, red from working so hard on me.
Can it be that I am so heartless to see what I made of me.
My feet almost green from running in wet summer leaves.
The sun peaking out at me, turning my skin into pink sunburn.
As the days go on, I see your face; your hair so yellow it could be fake.
I finally see you're not the mistake I thought you could be.
As you grow old, your hair turns brown, your eyes as turquoise as they can be.
This is to me, as it seems, a beautiful baby boy.

Jamee Berglund, Grade 10
Flathead High School, MT

Perfect to Me

Lost and confused, but loved nonetheless
Broken and scared, but cared for by many
Imperfect in your own eyes, but you are perfect to me

Being with you, it makes life worth living
A blessing comparable to none, you own my heart
An angel sent by God, remain faithful and you will be blessed

A smile that lights up the world, it makes even the darkest night brighter
Eyes that mirror your soul, I am lost in the splendor
Laughter that fills me with joy, everything seems right in the world

Contemplate the future, but live in the present
Here with me, we'll make time stop
I'll hold you tight, as I gaze into your eyes
Let this moment last forever, because forever you will remain in my heart
I love you, and you're perfect to me

Joshua Ortiz, Grade 11
Centennial High School, ID

High Merit Poems – Grades 10, 11, and 12

My Cloud

Look at that cloud in the sky
Look at it be so very high
It is fluffy and white
I try to reach it with all my might
I so wish I could reach that cloud
That would make me so very proud
It looks like it would be as soft as a pillow
And it casts a beautiful shadow
OH NO! My beautiful cloud has started to run away
I want it so much to stay
Come back Mr. Cloud! Come back!
If you come back we can share a snack
We can have anything you please
Even if it is leaves
No! Mr. Cloud has left me
But wait! What is that I see?
A star! A beautiful star
Look at it be so very far

Lydia Longmore, Grade 12
Emery High School, UT

Grandpa

Once upon a memory, not so long ago
I remember sitting on your knee,
watching movies and playing games
I miss those days, we have grown apart
I moved away, we both have aged
you say I have an attitude, I say, "No Way"
I really do love you
I really, truly do
I want you to know dear Grandpa,
how much I Love You!

Kaylee Sickler, Grade 10
Wray High School, CO

My Brother

My brother is always trustworthy,
Even when status may be in jeopardy.
He's strong as an ox,
When chopping giantly tough wood blocks.
I'd be easy to crush,
But unlike others he's never given me a smush.
He is a great example,
Of how to meet needs that are ample.
He is extremely loyal,
Even when tempers boil.
He is astoundingly helpful,
When events feel so doubtful.
He is hugely and humbly hilarious,
Even when life is precarious.
We've seen some awesome sights,
He has helped me through some frights.
I think he's amazing,
Most girls think he's blazing.
And though there are others,
He's the best of my brothers.

Van Stonehocker, Grade 10
Shelley Sr High School, ID

Many Miles

Run it with perseverance I was told,
For that I must run hard; I must be bold.
'Fore leaving on my way must tie my lace,
Dream 'bout the spots I pass place after place.
To which my tread-worn shoes will often run,
Adventures I endeavor will be fun.
The good Lord put this fight inside of me,
So I will run with all my might for thee.
Along the path encounter clinging mud,
Brush on the path results in dripping blood.
Charging through empty fog and cold wet bog,
There I will go and still enjoy the joy.
I run along the path begin laughing,
My joy in thee will be everlasting.

Kaylin Marie Smith, Grade 11
Vancouver Christian High School, WA

My Girl

My great, graceful, girlfriend
Has golden brown eyes
One quick glance and I'm mesmerized.
My heart flutters like butterfly wings
With this bursting emotion I can't help but sing.
My heart can't help singing this joyful praise
Going through this once in a lifetime phase.
Life with my girl is always fun
Our smiles are wide, and as bright as the sun.
I hope that we will never depart
Something this great can't break from the start.
Our love is a boulder immovable in its ways
Together forever all of our days.

Jadan Holbrook, Grade 10
Fremont High School, UT

Am I a Ghost?

My heart was broken, too many times
I couldn't trust you when you came into my life
You proved to me you were worthy
You gave to me your life
Now I'm sitting here reminiscing on the days that have passed
The days that have gone by
Why can't you see me standing in the rain
Why can't you hear me screaming out your name
Am I a ghost, can't you see me in pain
I'm lost and confused, what do I do?
You left me empty, dry, and out used
I have nothing even left to my name
Nothing left; to you it's a game
Why can't you see me standing in the rain
Why can't you hear me screaming out your name
Am I a ghost, can't you see me in pain
Can you see me…can you hear me?
Am I a ghost, can you see me in pain
Am I a ghost, standing here in the rain
Am I a ghost, out here screaming your name
Well open up your eyes, I'm right here, look at me

Rhonda H., Grade 11
Diamond Ranch Academy, UT

Me, Myself, and I

I have a group I hang with often
We make a great team
All of us contribute ideas
It is Me, Myself, and I

We share the same feelings
Our goals are the same
None has a secret the other doesn't know
The team: Me, Myself, and I

Shy is one of them
So are the rest.
I know them all too well
Me, Myself, and I

Tyran Schouten, Grade 10
Orem High School, UT

Last Day of School

My legs are shaking
Just 10 more minutes
But it feels like hours
The room is silent
Everyone is staring at the clock
Ready for Freedom
My summer flashes before my eyes
I will sleep all day and
Stay up all night
Ready for vacation
The ocean calling my name
The final bell rings
My heart stops
School is out!

Austin Tuttle, Grade 10
Orem High School, UT

Twirl and Twirl*

My mind is its own world
It twirls and twirls
Creatures unheard of
And stories of love
Often confusing but
Not attention losing
Day dream in day
Night dream in night
It never stops going
It always is working
My imagination makes me who I am
Sometimes ideas hit me like Wa-Bam!
I never regret it though
It always keeps me on the go
It twirls and twirls
My mind's its own world

Brandon Wierleski, Grade 10
Diamond Ranch Academy, UT
*Dedicated to my brothers Zack and BJ

Rise Up

Down Down Down
With the wind in your face
FREE
Of every earthly desire
Except one
Freedom
For even now that has been deprived
From the newborn infant to the mother
They try to tether our emotions
Always hungry for control
We will fight for our
FREEDOM
We shall not die like
OTHERS
Of starvation
Not of food or wine did they starve
But of freedom
We die for freedom
Not Lack Of It
This time we shan't fall at their feet
But they at ours

Kelly Milner-Souders, Grade 10
Coal Ridge High School, CO

Frequent Travelers

Down a lazy dark road
At some ridiculous time
I would walk down to your house
And we'd walk back to mine

Singing obnoxiously
Disregard for the sleeping
Not that they matter
Or know what they're missing

Spend all night together
Then drag ourselves to our feet
And tiredly stumbling
We return to the street

And holding hands
I walk you back home
You hop through your window
And I walk back alone

With a smile on my face
As the sun starts to rise
Same time tomorrow night?
The road nods and comfortably sighs.

Kristopher Levitan, Grade 12
Paradise Valley High School, AZ

The Game

You say I've changed,
That I'm not the same,
Let me tell you something,
I'm done with this game,

The game I'm talking about,
I'm sure you know,
Is called being used,
And it's got to go,

Yeah I'm different,
But I have the right,
To tell you you're wrong,
To stand up and fight,

I'm done letting go,
No more getting pushed around,
I'll tell you what I think,
So what, if you don't like the sound,

Stop this game,
And it will be fine,
I'm here for you,
Just don't cross the line.

Kayla Anderson, Grade 10
Pawnee Jr/Sr High School, CO

Surfing

A mber's the name
B eachin' it up
C rashing in the waves
D ude, that's what's up
E very night I drive
F ast into the night
G oing to the beach, I'm
H angin' ten tonight
I stop to see the ocean
J ust as black as the midnight sky
K icking off my flip-flops
L isten it's my time to fly
M y mind is in the moment
N o one can stop me now
O n the waves I glide
P raying for here and now
Q uite still the tide rolls on
R eaching for my board
S waying with the current
T ruly, I think the Lord
W hy? Because I've found my dream.

Amber H., Grade 12
Diamond Ranch Academy, UT

I Want to Thank You

I want to thank you, Dad,
For making sure to say you love me every single day,
For working so hard at your job to make my life as great as it can be,
For taking me fishing just so we can be together
I want to thank you, Dad.
For showing me that I don't need to be perfect, because I am wonderful just the way I am,
For loving my mother with all your heart and keeping us a strong family,
For telling me I am the most beautiful thing you've ever seen
When I have just woken up and we both know I look silly
I want to thank you, Dad.
For saying no matter how mad you become, you will always love me dearly,
For teaching me to not take what I have for granted so I can cherish the small things,
For encouraging me to be a sincere person, because we now both know it pays off,
I just want to thank you, Dad,
For being my Dad.

Megan Eimers, Grade 10
Grangeville High School, ID

Magic*

Roses are red violets are blue. You were always there for me now I'm here for you.
Even though we had our ups and downs, you never let our smiles turn to frowns.
But now that you're gone. I don't know what to do because I'm going to miss you.
We must've done something right. For you to live 17 years day and night.
On February 21 that terrible day. Everything around me went away.
When you were laying there on the ground all of our smiles turned to frowns
We were all by your side and while we cried, I asked God to not let you die
But I guess God didn't hear my prayer because your life got shorter.
When my dad decided that you must be put to sleep. I cried and told him that I hate seeing you so weak.
He said that it was time for you to go. My sisters and I cried NOOOOOOO.
When we got to the vets we were all wet with tears.
I'm glad we were all by your side when she put the needle in and you died.
My mom, dad, sisters, and I cried. I know you're in a better place. But we will never forget your cute little face.
Almost two years later and I still can't stop crying. Because I can't stop thinking about your dying.
But don't worry you will always be my friend because I know one day we will meet again

Jennifer Robbins, Grade 10
Pahrump Valley High School, NV
*In loving memory of Magic Robbins
we love and miss you sweetie!

Chance

We all should get an angel to help us through each day, a teacher to teach us what to say,
A leader to lead us up and down, someone to pick us up when no one is around.
We all should get a friend to create a path so right, someone we can love with all our might,
To make us smile when we pretend not to care, to judge us on every decision and dare.
We all should get a role model to look at in awe, someone to help us understand each flaw,
To help us when we don't know what to do, to get us home to make it through.
We all should get a chance to choose, the will to win or lose,
We all should get a chance to learn, to be given or to earn.
We all should get a chance to see, the life we have or what could be,
We all should get a chance to grow, to lead or to follow.
We all should get the chance to love, to watch our life from above,
We all should get the chance to live, our hope and faith to give.
We all can get a gift from life, despite temptations, chaos, and strife,
We get all our goods from each day, our will, our desires, our say.

Kayla Konig, Grade 10
Pawnee Jr/Sr High School, CO

Ten Years

It's been ten years
Yet you still bring tears

I was young
You were too young

I met you again two years back
you lay quiet
with your marble marker

I read "Luke Martin 1993-1998"
It's been ten years.

Wade Burns, Grade 10
Oak Harbor High School, WA

Scars

If love were a knife,
I'd want scars 'cross my back,
Big ones stretching down the spine.

Stories told within the marks,
Sunny days and warm firesides,
Gentle smiles and tender looks.

Scars that bulge in the middle,
Trail off again near the end,
Each different and unique.

If love were a knife,
The only thing to say is this;
Baby, cut me once more.

John Regan, Grade 12
University Schools, CO

Vietnam

Vietnam was the worst,
The worst war of them all,
Many people would fight,
Many people would fall.

No one could imagine,
The terror and pain,
That one lonely soldier,
Standing cold in the rain.

Boys would leave,
And men would return,
A complete lack of innocence,
From things they had learned.

This war had its point,
Those men had to fight,
Because it was war,
Doesn't mean it was right.

Chelsea Griggs, Grade 11
Cheyenne Mountain High School, CO

Untitled

A shoestring of smoke shows death with a passion and crave
A twist of grace shows a glassy devotion to misery
A web of bleary life causes an eternal wish
Soft sleep composes a summer in heaven
During moonlight the fog clears and exposes the giggles of spring

Travis Sudan, Grade 12
Flathead High School, MT

Drive

Hold tight, take control
Nothing holding you back, except the fear inside.
Drive.

Pedal to the metal, throwing caution to the wind.
Take the corner; hope for the best.
Drive.

Follow the road to get where you're going.
No detours, just you and what's ahead.
Drive.

Take the scenic route; enjoy the view.
No rush. Don't let it pass you by.
Drive.

Both hands on the wheel, breeze through your hair.
Open window; breathe in your life.
Drive.

Your journey. Your destination.
No maps, no pressure.
Drive.

Make it worth it. Go where you choose.
The sky's the limit. Take the wheel, and
Drive.

Kathryn Simovic, Grade 10
Evergreen High School, WA

Eternally

Covered in dirt, the truck lurches forward
through the mountains.

An endless trail advancing, as if taunting us
to plunge into an endless abyss.

Earth shakes and trembles as pavement turns to dirt.

Meadows, a sea of grass, dot the landscape;
the never ending journey through forever never gets old up here.

Finally, the endless path spiraling upwards comes to a stop.

The engine dies and an explosion of life erupts
in a cacophony of violent beauty;

Then, right here, right now, everything stops
leaving a harmonious melody of complete and utter silence.

And restarts just as suddenly as it ended

James Clark, Grade 12
Reed High School, NV

Saving Me

My heart was broken, right in two…
faded, bruised, purple, black, and blue…
tears filled my eye's as I began to cry…
thinking to myself…Why? Why should I even try…
Felt broken, as if words unspoken…
heart and mind full of lies…
the pain killing from inside…
but when all seemed lost and gone…
a special someone came along…
He took my hand and saved me that day…
he promised forever, he promised he'd stay…
my heart was broken right in two…
good thing this guy had the right clue…
falling in love again is something I said I wouldn't ever do…
he promised forever, he promised he'd stay…
saving me is what he did that day…

Fallon McRae, Grade 11
Madison Sr High School, ID

Waves (All Five Fingers)

You like to count your pennies
Wishing you could pretend you were happy
But luck's run out on your miracle maker
Childhood's just a gleaming speck
Turn around and look the other way
You don't want to see it snuffed out

Say goodbye to those sunny todays
Resigned to a life under cloudy skies
You never go to the window anymore
Dreary is dreary as it comes
Dust is your depression
Be infatuated

Sometimes fear is the greatest of comforts
You hide behind it like a great marble statue
A 1-inch man dwelling in a 12-inch sandcastle
Buried in his comfortable bed of sand
He waits for the tide to come and take him away
Waves of inevitable fate
Never to be feared by the dying man

Ryan Schafer, Grade 10
Colville High School, WA

Haying

From the lush green meadows
To the vast alfalfa fields stretching across the land
Hear the chatter of a swather as it moves
Or the whirring of a disc mower as it goes
The smell of fresh cut hay to me is like
The smell of coffee to others
The clicking chatter of a rake
The rhythmic noises of a baler
A chomping chopper as it fills a truck with silage
All become sounds of the continuation of life.

Simeon Thomas Moedl, Grade 11
Preston High School, ID

A Father's Love

A father's love is like glass,
you break it once and it shatters,
then you'll realize that it's gone forever.
Was it ever there? Did it even exist?
These are questions I ask myself,
What is a father's love?
Did he even care that I was hurt,
that I was scared, or that I was tearing up inside
because I never had a father's love,
because my father was on drugs.

Tina Cruz, Grade 11
Republic Jr/Sr High School, WA

Faded Love

Her heart's engulfed by fury
frustration and anger surge through her
hot tears sting her cheeks

Feeling alone, feeling betrayed
she stands in the street
with the sun beating down on her face
desperate for an explanation
she longs to hear the words of an apology
lusts for his grief and sorrow
for his heart to burn in pain the way hers does

He caresses her cheek one last time,
looks into the eyes that he loved for so long,
pleading for forgiveness
it only confirms her notion of lost love

Her heart beats once more for his
and the burning pain that was once anger
turns into despair
as she watches him walk away

Jovanna Pappageorge, Grade 11
Liberty High School, NV

Thunder

Sitting in a chair watching the clouds form
Imagining dust rising from the floor.
Then thunder crashes from the coming storm
The first drop falls and I run through the door.

What's there to see besides a thunder sky.
The powerful train about to arrive.
No more than the gray blows at speed so high.
The heaven's war that keep those who survive.

Interrupting the clash of rain and wind.
Delicate violets bloom in the scene.
The storm that once roared as if it had sinned.
This occurrence is the most precious I've seen.

The dark clouds have vanished from the skies
The luminous sun light shines down from high.

Ivan Marin, Grade 11
Rio Rico High School, AZ

A Political Campaign

A political race,
Of monsters and secrets
The closer they get,
The more mines they plant.

The hare gains speed
With the worded, "truths."
Adding gas to the campaign
Fueled by the people.

While the tortoise lacks speed
It bargains with its supporters.
The more cheers, the easier
For him to distract the hare.

Arising with triumph,
The tricky tortoise
Plants traps for the others
Then the fingers are pointed at him.

"What lies," they'll cry
As the others collide,
Gaining speed,
Slow and steady never wins this race.

Caroline Thomas, Grade 10
Chatfield High School, CO

Safe

The snow calls and calls,
but, alas, I cannot answer.
I sit home,
safe,

reserved in books and dreams.
And yet that white world waits,
never slumbers as it waits for me.

I am the stone
upon the edge of a cliff.
Shadows lurk below,
haunting,
but, alas, I cannot answer.

One day the storm will pass.
The cliff will crumble.
Time slips on,
and hope is dimming.
What may be

the biggest adventure of my life
is fading.
But, alas, I cannot answer.

Emily Dervin, Grade 12
Kentlake High School, WA

Ode to My Backpack

Leopard spotted won't thou let my texts rest in thee?
To destination jostle vi'lently.
Though heavy burdened always remaining true to me,
For thou carry text amongst tangled sea,
Brown with spots shiny texture bedazzle everyone,
Each journey fresh adventure just begun.
When class adjourned you're put on and I walk outside,
Writing utensils paper packed inside.
From eight A.M. till two-fifty P.M.
Just my backpack and me, together till year end.

Renee Lanier, Grade 11
Vancouver Christian High School, WA

The Ocean's Betrayal

Have you ever seen the ocean?
So flexible and filled with motion.
Or rough, as the rocks it crashes
Against with all its rage.

Yet loving enough to carry life in its arms
Though sadistic enough to keep sailors away from its charms.

Have you ever felt the ocean?
Does it comfort you on a warm summer's breeze,
Or would it push and pull you in a winter's freeze?
Anyone can see or feel the ocean
But no one can understand its real motion.

Neal Randall, Grade 10
Fremont High School, UT

Love

This lighthouse was built with hard work and care,
Piece by piece and stone by stone,
To create such a magnificent structure as you now see before you.
Its stones each mark a different day,
Spiraling to the very fragile glass top,
Paned into an octagonal figure.
Inside this glass top is a light that is ever-shining.
The only light that glows in the darkness.
The cliff where it stands seems an irresponsible place to put a lighthouse,
With its rough, rocky ground and steep ledges.
Yet the lighthouse is ever-fixed in its place,
As it has been since the day it was started.
When darkness falls, the lighthouse whirrs to life,
Beaming its welcoming light out across the dark water.
It is the guide away from despair.
The lighthouse is not prejudice to those who it lends its light,
Nor does it falter when no one comes to shore.
Every second, every minute, every hour of the night —
The lighthouse shines.
It's waiting.

Ariel McCarter, Grade 10
Oak Harbor High School, WA

Soul Mates

Soul mates inside a room, with a
hundred people watching and waiting.
Unsure if their urge to move closer
is real or fiction.
If they wanted, they could
look up from their shoes and
see each other, but refuse to look up.

He goes into another room, dragging
at the inexplicable bond, leaving her in a
room of strangers. If he had looked up
for a moment, he never would have left
her there alone. Now, though, the pain
is too great, and he leaves as she enters,
through the same door.

They don't look up, but mutter
excuses as they slip
past each other, so close that a
single strand of her hair touches
his lips, but they pull apart and sever

the bond, making them
two soul mates trapped forever in a house of limbo.
Randy Lynn Bingham, Grade 11
Bear River High School, UT

Hollow Walls

Deep down in the water,
So far you can't see.
Don't want to come up,
Don't want to breathe.
Looking for the stuff I want,
Looking for the stuff I need,
Looking for this,
Beneath you and me.

You knew I was there when you said hi,
You knew I was there when you said goodbye,
Now it's time to say hello,
So don't say goodbye.
I'm just another lost soul looking inside,
Looking inside these hollow walls.
Take a step inside and watch us fall.

Fall, so far you can't see
Fall, so far you don't want to breathe.
We finally hit the ground beneath our feet.
We look around at the wonderful scenery,
It's as if we long for love again.
Wrap my arms around you and touch again.
Ivan Ornelas-Lopez, Grade 11
Arrow High School, UT

Our Love Together

What do I think when I can't hear your voice?
Is, why did I have to make this stupid choice?
I looked at you but not into your eyes,
The outcome is here too late to realize
That you were always there when I was gone,
Is it too late to pick up and carry on?
I hope not because I though our love is true,
They could be lies, but they reminded me of you.
My heart is burning with embers and coal,
I'm a man now ready to take that role.
I'm here now; ready to stand by your side,
If you don't let me, at least I know I tried.
Hopefully, our love is not torn apart,
Here's a key, use it to open my heart.
I feel it in my veins; my blood is on fire,
Our love will never fail, it will never tire.
Dustin Lohmeyer, Grade 11
Arrow High School, UT

Every Little Bit

If you listen closely to the soft sounds,
You'll hear the flutter of butterfly wings;
You'll hear the subtle song the wind sings;
You might even hear the little ant pound.
If you closely watch the things around you,
You might see why the weeping willow weeps.
You could see why the creeping creepers creep;
Or why the parrots tease the cockatoo.
Nature's all about entertaining senses.
Only few of us know of its powers;
All the rest are busy destroying it.
People box it in by putting up fences.
Others waste it on a nice warm shower.
We have to save it; every little bit!
Chelsea Roeber, Grade 11
Viewmont High School, UT

Hope

Metamorphosis mind and hushed hues,
Autumn transitions to the winter blur.
Vanished hopes and strayed leaves,
Deprived life surrounding the world.
Black sky, the heart, after a luminous autumn sunset.
Yet there are stars;
Yet there is reliance.
Naked aspens once celebrated in citrus and scarlet;
Even emerald seemed to join in its last dance.
But like a ballerina without her shoes,
Leaves lay lonely.
Stuffed to gutters; frozen to the earth.
One day, life will emerge…
The stars to the sky.
The ballerina to her shoes.
The leaves to the aspen.
Unforgotten hues:
Hope.

Jessica Peterson, Grade 11
Chatfield High School, CO

Isolation

The crystal shines
From a cave below
As I write these lines
In the wind's blow
I dream of happy endings
In a world full of pain
The midnight bell dings
As I sit alone in the rain.
Brittney Statley, Grade 10
Wray High School, CO

Food for Thought

My brother
like a mixing bowl
seems plain and simple
yet a necessary item

Strong and sturdy
holding all the ingredients together
keeping peace

Stands his ground
through messy or adverse conditions
keeping everything as one

Like my brother,
without brands of design
mixing bowls have purpose
no need for color or fluff

Sides are scraped clean
they sit ready
to tackle their next meal.
Katie O'Grady, Grade 11
Chatfield High School, CO

Little Child

Whisper softly to me when I'm afraid
Let me know everything will be okay
The unfairness of all you had to see
You're so young
I'm sorry you're exposed to so much
Poor little child
Just let it be
Your sweet little memory
You won't even remember today
Be glad in it
Rejoice you see
Some people will remember
But you'll stay innocent
As years pass
You'll forget what you see
So sweet little child
Let me sing you to sleep
Kayla Schwoch, Grade 10
Tahoma Sr High School, WA

My Future

So many paths to choose, so many roads to take.
I got to think hard, this is my future, I don't have time to make a mistake.
Basketball, the Army, college, are just a few of my options.
The clock is ticking, time is wasting. My life is spinning into so many directions.
At times I lay in my bed, looking up, feeling lost.
Determined to be successful, no matter the cost.
I visualize raising a family, but I can't picture my career.
I believe I can do anything, there is nothing I fear.
I had a tough past, it took a lot to survive.
Made a lot of mistakes, and I'm blessed to still be alive.
Negativity is the fuel for my success.
Go ahead and doubt me, I'll lay your doubt to rest!
I got a heart of a fighter, I can't be stopped.
Whatever my future holds, I'll find a way to be on top!
Nick Smith, Grade 11
Del Sol High School, NV

Just a Friend

I'm "just a friend". I look into your eyes,
See your world's at an end; I hold you as you cry.
You hug me and say, "You're a great guy"
But the very next day in the hall you pass me by.

I've seen your courage fade, heard your tearful songs.
But always after that day, you make it clear I don't belong.
I'm not the one you call when your day's good or bad.
I'm just the one who saw you fall and took the knife from your hand.

I'm "just a friend". Even though I helped you,
You never comprehend that I need a friend too!
So I stopped looking for love, 'cause my searching is through:
My help comes from Above…my Jesus is True.
Bethany Knoshaug, Grade 11
Rangeview High School, CO

Nothin' Is

Drowning in your waves of death,
with the scattering of your love
like a beautiful red and white flower petal in a mercury over grown lake.
I can feel your pain, and my hope.

This world seems to be crumbling beneath our unstable feet.
Utopia nowhere in my blurred and confused sight.

No closer to living my full unthoughtful life,
only closer to my long expanded death.
We think it's not coming,
but we are being naive,
in our simple overtaken minds.

Look into the clouded city rain and see the truthful colors,
colors of the dark and disturbed world,
that will end with OUR unhappiness.
Kelli Wiley, Grade 10
Fort Morgan High School, CO

High Merit Poems – Grades 10, 11, and 12

The Delicate Girl

They lived in a world all of their own
Just to themselves in their everyday fantasies
They had held hands and walked to school together
Learning how to spell and count on their fingers
He loved her smile and she would call him names
The feeling he got he couldn't explain
She loved to read books of monsters and such
He loved the pictures, the ones she could not touch
The days she could not come out and play would confuse him
Why won't you come out?
It's so beautiful outside
He never wondered about the holes in her walls
Or when her arms were sore and she couldn't move a muscle
Her face said it all but he couldn't quite read it
The teacher saw the sings and made the call
He never got to say goodbye
To the girl who made him smile
He remembers the name that changed his life

Joshua R. Dietrich, Grade 10
Evergreen High School, WA

Never

Every day is its sweet sixteen.
Never aging, imperfections won't fade.
New tricks can be learned,
But they will never show.
Nothing is a surprise.
Everything has the predictability of a broken shoelace,
Sooner or later you're gonna trip.
Life is viewed through the window of a speeding train,
At first you're fascinated by the scenery,
But after a while the interest is lost.
The possibility of ever gaining it
Only appears in the reality of super heroes and clichés.
Boredom comes when death does not.
Appreciate time, whatever the length.

Kaela Reilly, Grade 11
Shorewood High School, WA

Fatal Confusion

What went wrong? I do not know.
There is too much blood upon the snow.
I cannot feel my lower half.
I cannot stand, I need my staff.
My vision is going very blurry.
Is it because of all my fury?
My legs and feet are not there,
I cannot see them anywhere.
Why must this happen to me?
I'm too young for this kind of fatality.
The sun has stopped shining, birds stopped singing.
Why do I still hear a ringing?
I guess this isn't too bad.
No, do not be sad.
I'm saying goodbye,
I'm ready to die.

Clarissa Jensen, Grade 11
Viewmont High School, UT

Washed Away

A young woman feeling lost and empty
Watches herself drown
In the heart-shaped lake
From broken dreams and hopeless desires.
Every tear shed was a breath she never took.
Depressed and cold,
She struggles through life.
Endless rain drowns her in shattered memories
Of a crippled grave in an empty cemetery
Sticking in the back of her mind.

Her dying beauty slowly washing away.
Her soul dying,
Bleeding crimson raindrops.
She's succeeding in her failures.
No longer fighting, easily dying,
In the heart-shaped lake
Now broken and weak.
The wind blew with rage.

Now she's free, irrationalizing the true act
She slowly disappears
As the lake turns to ice.

Crystal Keiki, Grade 12
Granite High School, UT

Children Forest

Rooted deep within the earth,
Banding together to create this place of hope,
A shelter of comfort and peace beneath
These expansive, supple branches.
Branches that bend to the elements,
But never break.

They protect themselves with their rough bark.
But under such exterior is
A sweet, sticky sap.
This sap they bleed, to protect us.
We are the Children Forest,
The trees are our Mothers.
With roots deep in the ground they hold us
Firmly, Lovingly,
So that we may not float away
In our thoughts.

Branches held out, in tender embrace.
We embrace you, Mother Trees.
You give us protection, love,
And we adore you.
We are yours, your Children Forest.

Claire Mosier, Grade 12
Chatfield High School, CO

Tired

Tied of crying,
Tired of hiding,
The girl I wish I could be.
Wish you could see
How this hurts me.
I'm sorry for what I did,
So please forgive,
So I can live
The life I desperately want.
You know it was
Hard for me 'cause
I wouldn't let go of you.
I see how you
Hurt inside too,
So let's move on and forget.
Now that you know,
We can let go,
There's no reason to hold on.

Nicole Flood, Grade 11
Temple Baptist Academy, NM

Mothers

M ostly understanding
O ften forgiving
T ries hard
H onest always
E ven loving
R idiculously intuitive
S urely sensitive

Brady Beck, Grade 11
Trask River High School, OR

I Am

I am the endless fire
That burns inside you
I am the purified water
You long to drink
I am the wind
You long to just hold still
I am the hands
You long to hold you
I am the spirit
You wish you could see
I am the one
You want but can't have
I am the one
You lost because you were too immature
I am the one
You hoped would stay
I am the one
Who was stupid to fall for you
I am the one
Who moved on as you stayed there
Wondering what happened

Jessica Zintzun, Grade 11
Warden High School, WA

A Place of Peace

Oh faithful friend at end of all my days,
Permit my eyes desist their searching ways.
When heat has left my skin without a trace,
Just let me warm myself in your embrace.
I wake from slumber long and deep and free,
Then night draws near and thoughts 'gain turn to thee.
When day is done and memories collide,
My prayers on high you every night abide.
I'll always need a place to lay my head,
For this short life, my resting place, my bed.

Jamie Kay Christianson, Grade 11
Vancouver Christian High School, WA

The Carousel Horse

A carver's hands made me.
From the forest I was fetched
and by the coarse edge of sand my wood became flesh.
The glow of a fire was cast upon my pieces,
smoldering into the mahogany; flame that never ceases.
Knife cut carefully into my head,
revealing a countenance that brought me from dead.
Curves became muscle and paint into skin;
a lasting wrinkle upon the wood carver's grin.
Alas I was finished said his voice soft but hoarse.
Here stands my work, the carousel horse.

Tristin Quinn, Grade 10
Home School, MT

Morning

Everything so clear now, like starting over clean,
Nobody's worrying about when or how, the fights have lost their steam.
The air is perfectly calm and still, the sun barely there at all,
It's creeping up behind the hill,
Waiting for time to call.
A peaceful feeling surrounds me, like nothing was ever wrong,
Feeling like I'm completely free, no emotion is too strong,
It makes me want to apologize, for all the sharp things I've said,
This beautiful calm makes me realize, that nothing is truly dead.
A slight breeze shifts my loose hair, momentarily blocking my view,
Helps me think that they can stare, but I can still get through.
Everything's so perfect right now.
This is how God wanted life,
When in his exist, with a graceful bow,
He handed over the knife.
He trusted us to do what's right, and half of us did wrong,
Some of us still feel his light, some kill him in song.
To me this time is his guiding hand, his way to help us see,
Now I can finally understand.
This is how it's supposed to be.

Laura Holland, Grade 11
Kamiakin High School, WA

High Merit Poems – Grades 10, 11, and 12

The River

Morning arrives, nature is quieted
watching the mirror of water, shifting, blending,
always there, never the same,

an empty canoe rides the colors of the changing leaves,
thunder grumbles from a distance,
rain.

an artist,
blurring and mixing the painting of changing Mother Earth,
quiet.

flowers bend over the bank to mirror at their reflection,
a foreshadowing cold lingers over the painting
gazing upon the colors of a changing season,
darkness.

the night pulls the lonely canoe across a portrait,
reflecting the jewels of night above watching the painting,
quiet.

morning arrives
the canvas changes

Samantha Berglund, Grade 12
Capital High School, MT

Though the Wind May Be Harsh

The sun was comfort after the wind was harsh,
As I sat on the stone that was next to the marsh.
I stared out at the forest, pebbles, and flowers.
I sat, wished, and wondered for a couple of hours.

The marsh then turned into one large sea,
With the deepest of blues, and the greenest of greens.
I swam through water, refreshing and cool.
I saw neon fish passing by as a school.
Seaweed waved and reached out to me.
I was aimlessly swimming I was so free.

I forgot how to walk; now I could only swim.
I closed my eyes tight, and took it all in.
There was nothing to stop me or make me go.
Surrounded by blue from above and below.

I swam, wished, and wondered of having this life,
Nothing cold, nothing harsh, no pain, no strife.
But where is the action? The fun? The love?
Is it calling me home to the ground up above?
It was sad to return back to the marsh,
But life is so beautiful, though the wind may be harsh.

Lauren M., Grade 10
Diamond Ranch Academy, UT

Me, Myself, and My Troubles

I was lying in bed
Waiting to get fed
Talking on the phone
But feeling all alone
Wondering when my mom will get home
While taking a comb to my hair
Will I get in trouble
If I'm not in my bed
The thoughts going through my head
When will my ride arrive
So I can bide with my emptiness
Hiding in an attic scared
Knowing they are going to ask if I'm impaired
Not wanting to lie
But I have to get by
Wow! What a life

Carli B., Grade 11
Diamond Ranch Academy, UT

Summer Morning

Creamy clouds contrasted amongst the sky.
Morning dew clings to the grass.
Fresh air, sweet to my lungs.
The horizon a mesh of hot white-aqua.
Birds sing songs of a new day.

A new beginning stretched before my eyes.
The horizon a constantly painted canvas.
The artist mixes tangerines and strawberry.
The sunrise streaks across the sky.
A smile widens, the beauty of it all.

Matt Carpenter, Grade 12
Chatfield High School, CO

Colorado Weather

The day is cold; the air is crisp
The warm sun is hidden behind layers of clouds
No chance of emerging
The sleeping birds are deep in their cozy nest
The wind blows the leaves from the trees.
The rain starts to fall and then it turns into snow
Chimneys pouring out thick gray smoke
Kids making giant snowmen
Pulling out the stuffed bin of forgotten snow gear
Not seen since last winter
The snow starts to die down
As does the excitement of children
The sun peeks out from the gray clouds
Gutters flow with icy water
A sunny day in the forecast
Time to breakout the flip flops
Hang up the warm winter jackets
Then the rain starts to fall
Turning into cold white snow
Staring over the vicious cycle
Of Colorado's changing weather

Amy Streeter, Grade 11
Chatfield High School, CO

The Banjo Lesson

A solid note, a single sound.
Two figures warmed by
a soft glowing light.
Brown barefoot boy
and grizzled gray-haired man,
skillet, hat, coffeepot an' pipe.

Stopping, daily chores
for a quick banjo lesson.
A new song is waking up
our dusty souls.

Serena Tsang, Grade 12
Kentridge High School, WA

Enjoying the Silence

I sit upon the grass of green
and watch the sky of blue
observing my surroundings
thinking about you
in my mind I wonder
if you're thinking of me too
this fine and gentle feeling
of my emotions it is new
thoughts of thee in silence
I wish these thoughts were true
me and you sitting on the grass
under the sky of blue
you tell me that you love me
and I say I love you too
but this is only a mental image
and thus my thoughts are through

Glen Prell, Grade 11
Powell High School, WY

In Strange Country

If it happens you should find
Yourself in flight along the track,
Remember this: do not look back.
Everything is in your mind.

Dream of battered Orpheus,
Fleeing through the ice and dark,
Carrying the branded mark
Of a mind too curious.

Magazines with warping pages,
Sodden prints of inky words,
Speak with fickle tongues unheard
All the omens of the ages.

Speak your mind in terms of love.
What we bring ourselves to lose
When it is too late to choose
Is all that we are worthy of.

Lila O'Brien, Grade 12
Vashon High School, WA

Peace Is…

Peace is a playground full of children.
Happiness is everywhere because no one worries about the people around them.
Everyone shares and gets along with each other in the different play places.
Not one child cares who any of the others are, or
Where they came from, only that they are playing nice in the here and now.
Most importantly though, everyone is different.
Children from every ethnic group and family type come together to just
Play and have fun together.
The whole world should learn to play like the children.
We should tumble down the slides,
Push each other gently on the swings, and
Take turns bouncing up and down on the teeter-totter
Like the children on the playground.
We should each do our part to spin the Merry-Go-Round,
We should hold each other up as we struggle across the monkey bars, and laugh.
Laugh uncontrollably, or giggle softly,
Just laugh, because we all have to share this giant playground, and
No one has fun unless everyone gets along,
Just like the children on the playground.

Kayla Carsten, Grade 10
Oak Harbor High School, WA

By the Hand of a Child

A child sits, feet buried in the sand, stick in hand,
Drawing out the life of a man.
After each line and squiggle,
He does giggle at the picture come to life before his eyes.
The man in the sand reaches out for a goal that beyond his reach lies.
Stick arms and stick legs become tangled as he reaches past his limit.
The little boy, his face with light hearted joy no longer lit,
Smoothes with gentleness the mess before him.
The man now righted, strong, and straight, faces his life with a new fate,
Given to him by the touch of the hand of a child.

Rebecca Lofley, Grade 11
Emery High School, UT

My Hood Has Padded Walls

My hood has padded walls.
Every day they expect us to fall.
Most of my brothers and sisters fall under their command.
Some of us kill our own blood thinking they will become a man.
It takes a coward to activate a weapon,
but it takes a man to embrace his family for more than a few seconds.

Don't become institutionalized and consume their drugs.
Another word for slave is a cold-hearted thug.
There is nothing wrong with showing love to the community.
And killing off your own race will not give you the right opportunities.

You have inherited the skill to rule the city, better yet the world.
And an African king needs a queen not a hood rat girl.
Change the direction of your pursuit, and don't fall…
Because you will escape from being trapped within these padded walls.

Ray Freeman, Grade 11
Genesis Academy, AZ

Mistake

My parents bout me a car today, a brand new little rice rocket.
It is the fastest thing around, and it's so small it could fit in my pocket.
I told my mom I was going to study, but that was just a lie.
I planned instead to go racing, I had not planned to die.
I arrived just as planned, on time and safe, and there was my opponent.
"What's the hold up, let's go race." That was my last chance, and I had blown it.
It started off great, I was in the lead, but then it turned for worse.
I figured then it was the end, my car had become my hearse.
I turned the corner and saw a truck, right on my current path.
I hit the brakes and tried to swerve, then fell prey to momentum's wrath.
My car was gone, so was my life, I wish it was not over.
I saw my life before my eyes, then they clouded over.
Now I have some advice for you, I hope that you will listen.
Just be wise and think things through, so that no tears must glisten.

Everett Black, Grade 10
Orem High School, UT

The Beautiful Wilted Rose

For every petal that has fallen,
For every tear shed in the past of our souls,
A new child is born just like a blooming rose.
The petal begins to shrivel into what's unknown anymore,
Just as a human passes away with no family to remember their warm tender hugs.
Life is a gift that death will not surpass,
Death is colorblind with no remorse on looking back.
For the new rose could die before it began to bloom,
The petal may grow, but shrivel again
Leaving behind the traces till the very end.

Carrie Hager, Grade 10
Coquille High School, OR

Unbreakable

We were disciplined…We learned to survive the heat of battle. We were taught many things in boot camp, but were never taught about the fear of combat. I was scared, terrified; mortars and artillery were landing everywhere. I stared in horror as my team was obliviated. Diné bizaad.

The sky was lit with fire as explosions went off. I gripped the handle of my M1 as the fear of death slithered towards me. I was prepared for the attack; I was prepared for the upcoming excitement of death, the beautiful music of bullets as they whip by, and for the raging sea of blood that awaits. Diné bizaad.

The foxhole was quite, we waited for the silence to end as I began to choke with fear, as the presence of death thickened the air around us. Diné bizaad.

We summoned up past memories, memories of smooth peace, silence before this lifeless dark war. We were stuck in the past, stuck where time stood still, stuck where we could not be hurt, or forgotten.

Afire was the sky again, the moment of tranquility was obliviated as the explosions begun. The sky turned red with blood as the ground began to bleed. This was it, the final struggle, the last hope. I grabbed my radio as I began to make the call.

We made a pledge…to protect and honor our country was our duty. I was willing to die for my motherland — the U.S., the Navajo Nation, and my family. I became the savior of my brothers, the nightmare of my enemy. My native language had become the weapon of this war. Diné bizaad.

Callie Spurlock, Grade 10
Highland High School, AZ

My Teacher

M y teacher
Y earns to

T each
E veryone
A nd especially
C hildren
H ow
E very day they can
R each out to others

Wesley Klukkert, Grade 11
Trask River High School, OR

Mom

Mom, you gave me life
You gave me a chance
You gave me spirit
You seemed so happy with me
But yet why were you sad
Why didn't you respond to my pain
Why didn't you see what he did to me
You never asked me why I cried
You only thought of yourself
You only thought of your movies
I saw no pain in your eyes
You never listened to me
Until one day I left
I then saw the pain…
That I myself left you
That is when I knew…
That you still cared

Bonnie Vail, Grade 11
Grand Canyon High School, AZ

People

People,
Mad, angry, and cruel.
They can hurt.
They can break.

People,
Happy, kind, and caring.
They can love.
They can smile.

People,
They can hurt
They can love.
They are either
Friend or foe.

People,
I do not get.
They change from day,
To day.

Elishia White, Grade 10
Shelley Sr High School, ID

I'd Call It Zippy

I want lots of things to be sure
But what I want most is a little race car
With a chrome exhaust pipe, and a thick racing stripe
Color? Don't worry, any will do
I'll drive it to Mexico, Iceland, the zoo
That's right, it's aquatic, and efficient too
We'll then put it in fly mode, and what do you know
Those proud gallant eagles do really fly low
I'll then reach for the shifter, and put it in gear
10-6 we're busy, 10-4 we're ok
We just shot to space
And the engine's NOT ok

Kelly Reid, Grade 11
Cashmere High School, WA

The True You

At first I thought that you were amazing
Then I got to really know the true you
How behind the amazing eyes
You hide how you truly feel
What you're really going through
You feel that you have to act better than everyone else
And you lie to your friends to make you look better
When really you're perfect the way you are
You're funny, smart, cute, and happy
If only I could tell you
That you really are an amazing person
And to be the True You!

Elizabeth Wynn, Grade 12
Madison Sr High School, ID

Daydreams

Daydreams consume her world, her life
Where people notice, people love, people care
She sits in a dark and lonely place not a ray of light to brighten her heart
She turns uncaring, unemotional, not caring for anyone or anything
Wanting to be alone, needing her darkness
Her dreams let her do anything, her music helping her visualize
Slowly dying, slowly hurting
Hiding the scars of pain and loneliness
Seeing the world differently, to get away from everything,
She locks herself away, in the dark, her sanctuary
A hole in her heart, which can never be filled
Nothing, no one to fill the lost part, she lays alone
She says she doesn't need anyone, or anything
She never shows that she is crying, inside or out
She doesn't want sympathy or praise
She wants someone to hold, someone to care
She knows this will never happen, at least not for her
Daydreams take over, she passes everyone by
Head hanging low, not in shame, but in loneliness
No one to listen, no one to tell her
that she will be all right

Amanda Hanke, Grade 10
University High School, WA

Butterfly
W andering around in a world of darkness.
E nveloped in beauty and love.

L anding upon the land of forgiveness.
O pening a new life of opportunity.
V enturing into the unknown.
E njoying the life made new.

Y oung still in life and beauty.
O rganizing together the greatest of lives.
U nder the wings shall come life anew.

Ian Perkins, Grade 11
Fernley High School, NV

Was It Meant to Be?
I am you, but you are I
Together we were woombed
Was it meant to be?
Your hair like the sun
Mine of the earth
Our eyes are of the sea
Was it meant to be?
You flying through the air
My fingers brush the strings
Sometimes we'll fight
In pure delight
Was it meant to be?
Your courage is a lion's roar
Bellowing loud for all to hear
You keep me company on cold rainy days
You remind me what is right
I'll love you to the end
IT WAS MEANT TO BE!!

Brad Diamond, Grade 10
Fremont High School, UT

Beauty of Theatre.
A dark hole.
The audition…

Fear. Butterflies. New faces.
Roles…
Disappointment. Excitement. Anticipation.
Rehearsals…
Dance. Sing. Act.
Strain. Stress. Laugh. Love.
Good people.
Opening night…
Fear. Butterflies. Best friends.
Lights. Energy. High notes. Lost in character. Applause.
Exhilaration.
Closing night…
Applause. A pit in the stomach. Cry. Kiss. Hug. Laugh. Love.

Love.
A dark hole.
The audition.

Bryce Moglia-MacEvoy, Grade 10
Grand Junction High School, CO

Smitten with Spring
It is a flirtatious flamboyancy
A rushing of ravenous leaves
across the rolling chartreuse hills and plains,
painted with still color

They dance hand in hand to the music of the eventide sky
They flow to the beat of the wind
The wheat tickles the earth and it rumbles in laughter
The earth is at play with the temperate weather

It is a linking telephone line between the earth and sky
It is called, leisurely moving in motionless speed

They intertwine through thoughts and figurations
Together they make the sun arise and set in beauty

The birds are melodic and tranquility sets in with
The rest of the world

Together they bring the life that comes in this time, thus,
Only this time it comes.
Yes, everything is beautiful, but only for that moment,
when the earth flirts with the skies

Julie Johnson, Grade 12
Parkrose High School, OR

My Father
He is the summer, in my eyes,
my favorite season in the year.
Under his hands the flowers grow.
It is different for me now, that he's not here.

He is a hero, in my eyes.
Security is what I always felt,
When he was with me
and held my little hand.

He is a genius, in my eyes
Who could solve any problems,
build anything I want:
Little wooden boxes for my jewelry,
or, in our garden a giant dinosaur.

He is the best, in my eyes.
And I would never trade him in,
Not for anything in the world.
That's because I love him.

My one and only…Father.

Anna Monika Kessler, Grade 12
Crow High School, OR

Sailor

A poet is like a sailor,
Steering his boat peacefully
Twisting and turning
He rides the waves
To reach the desired destination
The destination is not the goal
But rather to enjoy getting there.

Treavor Dodsworth, Grade 10
Wray High School, CO

Waiting

It lights up the deep sky at night
The night light of the world
So bright that it catches our attention
With stars surrounding in a swirl

As the sun comes up, it drifts away
It waits to reappear the next day

I see the colors of the changing sky
I see the quiet night wake up into light

I wait patiently for the moon
While most don't mind its presence
The sun brightens up their day
The moon brightens up mine

Nadija Beronilla, Grade 10
Oak Harbor High School, WA

Growing Up

Dancing as if no one can see
Living life to the fullest
Finding out who you are going to be
Loving the ones closest

When you are hugging someone
Never wanting to let go
You never know when life is done
But you will always grow

Feeling like you'll never hurt this bad
Like you can't trust anyone
But remembering all the friends you had
And your life has just begun

When you are a teenager
Life can feel complicated
And you can feel such anger
Remember those you affected

Because you are always loved
No matter if you feel alone
Even if it's something you believe
You are never on your own

Scott Jones, Grade 12
Chatfield High School, CO

My Place

Summer days so hot and humid
Shorts, tank-top, flip-flops, and shades
Sand castles guard the beach
Lonely footprints litter the sand
Broken forgotten seashells sit under the damp sand
Awaiting until its day in the sun
Waves lap the shore
Tickling little toes
Crumbling great walls
Day is drifting into night
Stars like crystals in a black sea
Moonlight blankets the gentle waves
Muffled roars of here and there
Gently washes away all fears
Let go to the mercy of the beach
Just sit and watch
The beauty it brings
The push and pull over your worries and doubts
Let go and bring in the new as the waves pull the old away into the vast sea
Let yourself go to the majestic power of your own mind
Be free as the sea and drift away

Ashlee Jones, Grade 11
Cashmere High School, WA

The Mask

She splashes cold water,
She washes her canvas.
Her fingertips smooth on serum.
She mixes a palate of colors, all the while regarding her image —
In the mirror.
Ivory; its silky tones even out her originality.
Pink comes next, a light oval of color —
Accentuating her cheekbones.
Black, lining her eyes, closing in her secrets.
Amethyst next, creating a foil for her green eyes.
Red — its color striking against her lips.
As sure as an artist,
As careful as a doctor,
She mixes, smoothes, creates.
Her reflection stares back at her, and she smiles;
Satisfied.
Her mask is complete.

Maria Lewis, Grade 11
The Classical Academy, CO

Coffee Cup

What would I do, without my coffee cup?
I like your taste even when I am sitting in a pub.
The golden brown I fill in you to make myself awake,
A long journey you already made form China where you were create'.
The wonderful day I got you was a Christmas day,
Now you are helping me day after day.

Johannes Willmann, Grade 11
Vancouver Christian High School, WA

Looking in the Mirror

Looking in the mirror
I see someone that's not me
A girl in this world that's not pretty
Some girl that everyone thinks they know
People think that she sees what they do.

Looking in the mirror
I touch the face that what seems mine
I look and don't see what they do
They see beauty and nothing else
But if they look closer they will actually see the true me.

Looking in the mirror
I see them all standing behind me
The people who say they care
But the most important people are starting to disappear
As they fade away their voices are the only thing I hear.

Looking in the mirror
I've grown to see inside of me
I've learned to love who I am
And to not be afraid to show my skin
No matter what people say or do
Just look in the mirror to remind you.

Kierra Lee, Grade 10
Hinkley High School, CO

A Wasted Heart

You say you love me, but how can that be?
When you ignore me in other's company
Time has changed me, from the day we first met
Thinking about it makes me want to forget.
So get away from me, I don't want to be with you
You no longer have the right to be calling me boo.
We used to take long walks down by the shore
So get out of here and don't get hit by the door
We said we would always be together
I wanted you to hold me tight forever
Kissing, loving, hugging, and having fun
I thought I was right but you weren't the one
I want you out of my life I can't take it anymore
My love and care for you is gone and my heart is sore
You lied, you cheated and it hurt me
I fell into tears and it stung like a bee
I felt like I wasted my love and precious time
I thought your feelings were the same as mine
I've been thinking of you and it has been driving me crazy
I loved you will all my heart can't you see
You said you loved me but how can that be?

Erica G., Grade 12
Diamond Ranch Academy, UT

Night

The sun is setting,
and stars are being sprinkled across the night sky
when the round halo of light,
springs up from behind the trees.

It is in this moment that I realize,
I should live my life not for fear of dying.
Rather, my soul should touch others,
So their lives can seem well-spent.

The moon, even in the darkest of days,
Is a source of light in a sea of darkness.
And that is what I want.
To bring hope to the hopeless.

Linsey Kau, Grade 10
Crow High School, OR

Dream

You were once a dream that came true,
I'm sure you already knew that I am
Losing my closest friends
Yet a true friendship should not
end in tears!
Dare me to feel happy yeah I am
yet now I feel like I'm losing my mind!
My friends are so kind
they signed me a card.
I feel like I'm spiraling downward.
It makes me feel a little awkward.
As never we have been so different
it used to be so brilliant in colors my world!
As I twirled you made me
change my whole look on friendship and love.

Natasha Baudek, Grade 11
Kestrel High School, AZ

Wrath Upon Ourselves

I can only imagine that wrath is being held out,
So there will be time for us to be redeemed.
But surely wrath is not being held out,
So that we may redeem ourselves.
For I have seen the madness,
Of those who died trying.
But is regret only a word that the living possess?
I long to see their faces,
Regardless of the decay.
For in the eyes of the deceased…

We would see hope in our last day,
Inside this dying world.
For there is still beauty,
Inside this dying world.

For what good is there holding off wrath,
If we are determined,
To bring wrath upon ourselves?

Brandon Richison, Grade 10
Pioneer High School, NV

Writers Write What They Know
I find it intriguing that many writers write what they know.
And as many do, writers try to decipher life and the meaning within it.
So in this aspect, they, knowing their lives, put pen to paper to do the justice
So as to account for the thesis of life.
What I've gathered thus far is that life and water are often correlated and intertwined as one.
Water flows calmly in some places, but are raging waters a mere half mile away.
Life remains somewhat still, but as all know, tranquility is only a myth.
Rage shows itself in even the most self-contained person.
And because of this very theory, a body of water is much like a timeline in itself.
A river ends somewhere, as all lives do.
But one may always paddle back through history in remembrance of life anew.

Ashley Stewart, Grade 10
Columbus High School, MT

I Am From
I am from a colorful world full of small wonders and where everything is possible.
I am from a peaceful place with few people, nosy neighbors, and family get-togethers.
I am from the morning dew that brilliantly sparkles on the blades of grass and watching the sun rise every morning.
I am from the jolly tune of the ice cream truck in the summertime that rings throughout the town.
I am from singing in the shower, giving piggyback rides, until I collapse and from, "sit up straight, don't slouch."
I am from bonfires during starlit evenings and floating the river on a scorching hot Saturday.
I am from wondering how Sam became such a model student and why Pat so closely resembles Napoleon Dynamite.
I am from memorable holiday celebrations with a family who likes to eat and from friends that always spread happiness.
I am from being active in volleyball, basketball, and track to release my competitive spirit.
I am from the hot driveway pavement that burnt our bare feet while we shot hoops until dark.
I am from believing in dreams, letting creativity flourish, and imaginations run wild.
I am from wildflowers in the tall, dry grass and the fires that so quickly devoured them.
I am from smiles that brighten up even the darkest days like the sun when it shines.
A girl could hardly ask to be from anything more.

Kelsey Stewart, Grade 10
Columbus High School, MT

Just Thinking…
In a second, it's gone.
One day you'll reflect on a minute, hour, day, week, month or a year ago.
Already? It can't be! There's no way that was so long ago!
Even though that's true, don't take advantage of the Now.
Live. Laugh. Love. Enjoy. Everybody, everything
You may feel you can't, it will never be the same, but you can, you always can.
It's hard to let memories go, but they won't fade, don't let them.
"Will it ever be that good again?" Hope so.
Live like it will be, and it will be, and, who knows? It could be better.
Don't spend all your time worrying over where you are or where you will go,
Because once it's gone, it's gone.
Have few regrets: be happy with what you did and forget what you should have done, it's over.
Laugh at yourself, not others.
If you caused pain, fix it: if you miss them, contact.
Give life time, it can only go so fast.
You will lose the Now if you only live for the Past.
Do it right, Now.
Get up and make a life worth living, because you're going to miss this.
Look around, you have it pretty good.
So go ahead, close your mind of yesterday, and open it to today.
Today is it. It's the rest of your life.

Marilyn Lee, Grade 12
Hillcrest High School, UT

The Winter Wolf

A night in the snow, leafless trees stand tall
I am the winter wolf
Starving with hunger, as I wonder
I am the winter wolf
Foraging for prey, in search of food
I am the winter wolf
A white fur coat and nose sharper than claws
I am the winter wolf
Eyes that see all, ears that hear all
I am the winter wolf
In search of a chase that will bring great taste
I am the winter wolf
Now a man in flannel with a high powered rifle
I am the winter wolf
I lunge at the man and now I stand…
As king of winter wolves

Leon Benton, Grade 12
Westwood High School, AZ

Reach the Sea

I'll walk the land until I reach the sea
The looks are strange and many tend to say,
"'Tis long and hard," but still it seems to me
This task is mine; I'll make it there someday.

The bitter nights cannot compete with morn'.
For in the dark one's thoughts are not the same;
I much prefer the daylight's spiteful scorn.
Like death's sweet grip I feared night — still it came.

Feet trod and push the well-worn path along
I journeyed long to reach my destiny.
I ran toward but now it seemed so wrong
Lost time and careless dreams glared back at me.

Once reached, the sea blew salty beads at me.
As perfect as the Holy Land could be.

Emily Hills, Grade 11
Viewmont High School, UT

One Day*

One day not too long ago
There was a little girl,
In warm embracing arms
I saw all of her charms…
Gentle and pure,
But her body had no known cure:
I saw her grace
Upon her face…
She slowly faded
Once the mother hoped she had made it…
Her last sweet kiss
Now she is dearly missed…
Everybody cried
And always tried…
Now she flies and is never to die…

Silicia Leanne Routon, Grade 11
Omak High School, WA
*In loving memory of Breanna Trease Leonard

My Shadow of Soul

In solitude I stand,
manacles inhibit my wrist and my hands
— yet loosely —
for that is not where they are needed most.
The largest and tightest chain imprisons
my soul, like a vast cage of cold fire.
My soul flutters restlessly,
tired of banging relentlessly
against wills that will not yield.
Now all it can do is wait
for its ransomer to let it go free.
My mind being its captor,
my fears being its lock;
the only key to freedom rests in my hands.
The key must travel through
my darkest recollections and
sneak past the captivating
unsurity of my mind.
Only once that has happened,
once I have overcome myself,
then can my soul go free.

Geoffrey Ray Mapother, Grade 10
Diamond Ranch Academy, UT

Who May Know…

who may know the sorrows of a forgotten soul,
the paradox of life, a sad psalm in the silence,
who may know the pain of a wounded soul,
lonely entries to a diary, a prayer in the silence,
who may know the true meaning of loneliness,
the cold night air, the tear stained cloth of a pillow,

there is one who knows, who understands,
in infinite grace, and loving arms,
He embraces, the most forlorn stranger,
there is one who knows your pain, who loves,
"I stand all amazed at the love Jesus offers me…
I tremble to know that for me He was crucified…"*

no need to feel alone, He is there through the night,
though loved ones a be far off, they are close in your heart,
He has been through your pains your sorrows and grief,
a window to hope, a shimmer of light in the darkness,
in a day of sorrow, may you find comfort in this,
in lonely nights that follow, please know,

there is always comfort, in this…

*From the hymn "I Stand All Amazed"
Ben Fjerstad, Grade 11
American Leadership Academy, UT

If!!

If you asked me out,
Would you go with me?
If you said you love me,
Would you mean it?
If we went to the movies,
Would you hold me?
If someone said that I am ugly,
Would you stand up for me?
If I said I love you,
Would you say it back meaning full?
If a guy said you aren't worth it,
Would you prove you are worth it?
If this happened to you,
What would you do?
Would you answer at all?

Sarah Xanthos, Grade 10
Flowing Wells High School, AZ

Alone in the Corner

Alone in the corner
In the darkened closet
Crying for life
Abandoned by hope
Faith turned his shoulder
Neglected by God
Forgotten by you
In the darkened closet
Alone in the corner

Chantl Bosman, Grade 11
Skyline High School, CO

A Cause to a Start

Sinking into your skin,
I call out for warmth
muscles tightly gripped
like a conscience around sin

With each encounter — I shiver
Every brush of your fingertips
and meeting of our palms
is enough to make me quiver

Categorized by each raised brow
The direction and precise location
Pinpointed by the affection
We will only deny now

I, famous for the foil heart
You, for the conspicuous tongue
But oh, how we yearn for something —
A cause to a start

Faith Breisblatt, Grade 11
North Canyon High School, AZ

The Likeness of My Brother

City lights reflect above my twin brother in the river.
The murky water doesn't give their brilliance justice, so I tell him to turn around.
I like my brother, but we seldom spend time together.
We sometimes take baths, and do the dishes after dinner,
But our favorite time to play is when we're at the river.

He's really quiet, my brother. I have to do enough talking for the both of us.
"Look at the buildings, Brother!" I yell to him as I race down the riverbank.
My brother runs too, but instead of running on the bank, he runs on the water.
He can do cool tricks like that.

I stop, and my brother stops too.
We giggle because we are so alike.
"Brother," I said, "Look at the city!"
He looks at me with his head cocked a little to the side.
"Brother!" I say laughing some more. He laughs too.
"Fine, Brother," I say with a frown, "Be stubborn."

"Time for bed," mother yells.
She is always the one to end our time together.
"Goodnight, Brother."
He says goodnight too, and I wave. He waves too.
"See you sometime soon, Brother," I say.
And we're both laughing as I turn to go home.

Ingrid Van Valkenburg, Grade 10
The Catlin Gabel School, OR

Uncle Bill

Long walks up Edwards Hill to have the fireworks light up our eyes…
Every Friday night at Dino's eating pizza until we couldn't eat anymore…
Watching *Histories Mysteries* until we couldn't keep our eyes open…
Fourth of July barbecues — long, hot and sticky…
I'd always been ignorant to loss, had never felt the pain
This picture was taken before we knew just how bad it had gotten
Not only in your stomach anymore, but now your liver, gall bladder
And in so many places we couldn't even name
The cancer spreads like wildfire, as does our hurt and your pain
In this picture — your son's burley arm is over your shoulder
Little does he know he will be man of the house far too soon
This was all before it spread, caused you to stay in bed, unable to speak or even eat
But now, you're in a better place
A happy, painless place, a cancer-less place where you suffer no longer
But that doesn't take away our pain
We think of you every day, happy memories of you
Now we are left with Christmas and birthdays without you
But now, you're in a better place
A happy, painless place, a cancer-less place where you suffer no longer
Not physically with us, but in our hearts forever
We miss you Uncle Bill

Hayley Westmoreland, Grade 12
Flathead High School, MT

Disguise

Of course, I should have seen the disguise
But everyone wants to believe
That small chance in glimmer of hope
Besides blatant reality
Countless tries, again and again
Accepting your apology
Never recognize the disguise, so again and again
I'm drenched in false sincerity
Telling myself "keep your eye on the prize"
Things will all heal in time
But during that time, when I was all yours
I mistook you for being all mine
The heart cries yet tears dry
Now my innocence is jaded
I wish so much that I could get it back
But my emotions had been so raided
A game you played right along in disguise
How could you ever be so good
At hurting me so bad? Couldn't devise
The truth from the lies
All this time, it's just been a disguise…

Maggie Henley, Grade 12
Kentlake High School, WA

Once in a Lifetime's Gone

O nce in a lifetime means there's
N o second
C hance.
E verything we tried to be

I s drowning with my plans.
N ever get just what you see,

A t least we gave our

L ives, to something
I nsignificant, ending it in
F ights. We never seem to
E scalate to something worth our
T ime, it's all just useless
I ntellect, created by our foolish
M inds.
E ventually, I'll be all right, but
S o far my perspective, is telling me that while you're

G one, eventual's quite defective.
O nly chances fade away and
N ow our time is up, and in the
E nd I still came out the lonely runner up.

Kristy Broberg, Grade 10
Orem High School, UT

Unwelcomed

Hello, again, old mystic friend,
it's been so long since you've called.
We meet again upon a
twisted and tattered road.
I did not wish to see you here,
why haven't you left me alone?
Is it because we've known each other
awhile, that you chose to revisit me in my home?
My heart was well before you came,
but now it's sad and filled with pain,
and yet we say hello.
Although you are unwelcomed,
you continue to bother me so.
Once you laid your hand on me,
you sickened me to the bone,
As infecting as you can be,
We continue to say hello.

Connie Maya, Grade 12
Cibola High School, NM

The Lament

Our paths may cross again one day,
Though we won't know what comes our way.
We'll sit and hope and wish for things
That only being together brings.
And think of times we could have had,
We would've been so very glad.
Here we are after all these years,
Trying to dry our fallen tears.
Me and you and you and me,
Maybe we weren't meant to be.

Erik Rodriguez, Grade 10
Layton High School, UT

Home

If I only knew where I was from,
Would it be a perfect home?
Or even a family.
Would it be here, there or anywhere?
I would even settle for less.
But would it be troubleless?
The fact that I don't know is like a wish.
You can take and give from it
And it's still a wish.
If I only had that motherly kiss
On the forehead,
When going to bed.
But no, it is for naught.
The loving embrace is gone.
Replaced with black bars,
To seal away the stars that I yearn to see.
But no, it is for naught.
Because a home cannot be bought.
The world can be happy, but not all that snappy.
I know from experience,
Because you can make the world your home.

Donald Baker, Grade 12
Utah Youth Academy, UT

In Touch
Rain pelts the outside
the dark mountains roll with fog
my mind is at peace

Timothy LaRose, Grade 12
Rifle High School, CO

Perspective
In a world full of darkness
a soul full of shame
In a town full of vastness
a heart filled with pain
Left with no right
clouds without rain
Wings with no flight
mad without sane
In a galaxy of barely
a universe held back
A mind not thinking squarely
a dream that's off track
All amount to one thing
Nothing.
A sun that's half risen
a soul in repair
A town that's rebuilding
a heart free of despair
All amount to something
Anything…

Ashley Jaramillo, Grade 10
Lake County High School, CO

Tempting Talons
And yet, above, to their dismay
The falcon, falcon, bird of prey

It arcs its wings in noble flight
And rains below, her fatal plight

With holy speed she takes her start
Without a doubt, and breaks the heart

Of men, the men, for they shall see
The deadly launch of falcon's greed

So powerless, we stare in awe
To be a part of nature's law

And yet, dear bird, your prey forgives
Upon thine grace, our passion lives

With love, oh love, we watch you fly
From up above, you keep the sky

And as the sun concludes the day
Farewell sweet bird, my bird of prey

Greg Ikeda, Grade 12
Kentlake High School, WA

Happy Days Are Here Again
There is a feeling inside me I just can't hide.
A feeling of happiness and feeling of pride.

This feeling makes me float on a cloud flying high.
I love saying hello, but hate saying goodbye.

I hope my memories for him never ever die.
The day I lose you would be the day that I cry.

To leave this happiness would be a sin!
It's true, for me that *happy days are here again!*

Heather Hart, Grade 10
Scholars' Academy, AZ

The Things I Can't Deny
Office supplies how often you make me glad
You highlight the good, and ignore the bad
Without complaint your middle is squeezed each day
Your rubber exterior; it takes mistakes away
You color my world with hues of pink and blue
Adhesive bright squares suggest I call Aunt Sue
While at the store I searched; you answered my call
You clutter my room but I don't mind at all
I know it's you I simply can't deny
I save my dollars for you dear office supplies

Kelsey Adent, Grade 11
Vancouver Christian High School, WA

Imagination Is a Never Ending Road
Imagination is a never ending road.
Buckle your seat belt for a safety precaution
for what you might discover in your imagination.
Adjust your seat so you can see above the steering wheel for what lies ahead.
Shift the gears in drive and go forward
to discover what your imagination can do.
Floor the gas pedal because you are excited
about what new ideas your imagination can create.
All the lights are green
There is nothing stopping you from going deeper into your imagination.
If something gets in your way from imagining,
use your windshield wipers and wipe it out of your way.
If your imagination is dark and gloomy,
turn on your headlights to light you a clear path through darkness.
Use your blinkers before you steer onto a road
that leads to new ideas in your imagination.
Look into your side mirrors and check if there is anyone driving with you
on the never ending road of imagination.
Never make a "U" turn and turn your back on your imagination.
On the road of imagination you can never get lost.
You will always be going the right way.

Molly Deleon, Grade 10
Oak Harbor High School, WA

Brought Down

Things in this world you shouldn't have to see
Yet, they put controversial things in front of you and me
The media overwhelms us with news that's not so good
I would have changed it if I could

On September 11 we saw the Twin Towers fall
So we sent soldiers to the sand to shoot and to crawl
6 weeks of basic training was hard and really tough
But I wouldn't quit just to say I had enough

My time over in the desert, it was pretty grand
But I wasn't there just to sit and stand
Walking in the streets I could feel explosions tremble through the ground
I couldn't hear anything after that horrific sound

I am here in the U.S., the land of the free
Where I couldn't get an opportunity to speak my mind openly
Freedom of speech had been thrown out the door
I wonder if I was fighting for freedom in that war

Now I lay here in this open field
The box I am in forever will be sealed
I put my life on the line all to save my friends
My family gets a purple heart that's how this story ends.

Jacob Gallegos, Grade 12
Chatfield High School, CO

Rock Concert

The energy ascends from the crowd as the band comes on stage
They hit their first notes getting everyone pumped for the night
Crazy fans begin to jump up and down so loud, the sound waves shake you like mad
A person blocks your view, making you mad so you slowly drift through the crowd
Everyone is so highly excited not wanting to come back down the band members seem to flow across the stage
Amphitheater black like the night thousands of voices singing all the notes
Longing to be up there playing all the notes the girl in the front of you catches a free T-shirt yet you're not mad
Very sure that this is your best night you start to mosh with the sweaty crowd
Slowly spinning toward the stage looking up but they're not looking down
Screaming so loud nothing can bring you down just then the guitarist misses a note
Everyone is too busy to notice pushing towards the stage the sound is ringing in your ears yet you're not mad
Everyone is playing off the intensity of the crowd rocking out throughout the night
The singer bobbed his head around, hair as black as night people dancing never wanting to sit down
Just then a boy surfs the crowd now everyone's chanting the notes
So loud that you'd think they were mad the fans pushing towards the stage
Just then the singer dives off the stage the crowd bends black with night
Almost dropped him making people further back mad flying so high he doesn't want to come down
The audience screams the last few notes the end of the song amazing the crowd
The crowd then moshes before the end of the night
Pushing towards the stage one last time before they come down
The last note ends, people are happy yet mad

Ashley Slinkard, Grade 10
Grant Union High School, OR

Clinging to Yourself

privacy is a closed box,
with you inside
separated from reality,
bereft of the earth's pulse,
removing your self doubt and
climbing out into the day
when you're through with it,
always waiting for the inevitable moment
when you crawl back inside and
empty your soul once more,
there it sits,
when all others have gone,
the only friend you ever made
without saying a word

Austin Church, Grade 10
Oak Harbor High School, WA

An Empty Slate

An empty slate, an empty hand,
An empty world in which I stand.
Somewhere out there, people calling
Down to me, but I'm still falling.
I've been falling far too long;
I need something to make me strong.

I can't see, my eyes are blind,
I can't turn back to look behind.
There never is and never was
Too much more than static fuzz.
Nothing's clear, I hate this white –
I want someone to hear my plight.

Someone save me, so I plea,
No one's looking out but me.
Inside this blank and empty slate,
I am trapped and still third rate.

Carla Vangrove, Grade 12
Woodland Park High School, CO

Raging Moderation

Trilling sounds far away
Crackle and hiss, creeping ever steady
Madness in moderation
Wander far into the night
Demons lost control of it
The Devil lost the fight.

Breaking and shattering
Wailing in the night
Do not dare to shun
Live and win the fight.

Jessica Sleight, Grade 10
Minico Sr High School, ID

Love Lost, Life Gained

The pain in her heart
so heavy, no scale could measure
missing the one person that she loved most
sitting solemnly at her grandpa's house

Reminiscing…

Remembering the times Papa bounced her on his knee
telling her amazing stories,
of faraway magic, and enchanting dreams,
and how each year for her birthday rather than a five dollar bill
he would give her a pen or notepad
telling her to write about things that she felt, and the things she wanted to feel.

Missing him that day, and forevermore
could, and would, never cease.
She wandered home from the senior center, pondering her experiences
as she prepared to say her goodbye on the church's podium.
Though, when she reached her home, all her former thoughts disappeared,
the only thing she could do was write, write of her angst, and emptiness
in a letter to the man who taught her most everything she had ever learned.

But, how could she recognize the end to such wonderful experiences with a man
she loved for so long?
Especially in a simple, teary, goodbye.

Callie Hancock, Grade 11
Chatfield High School, CO

Rebel Lock

On my neck holds a lock, sewed to me as an expression
Of my authority refusing rebellion, when you talk to me
I contain my laughter in it, for you have to be
Accusing me of having these capabilities
To rip off my expression and abuse it, shed blood with it
To hurt others that I express myself against
I've followed this wall too long now I'm on a picket fence
Hung by the reasoning of stupid rules, chained to the floor
By the force of ignorance, to the earth in which people die without me
No need to swing a chain, nor stab the back
It's the clothes off their back, grasping around the neck
Until they don't have enough air to yak
Bleeding without a knife, a pencil stuck in their skin
Still it's me that sins, so I wear my lock to pin and win
I'm a deifier of ignorance, I won't let the ignorance stain the mind
Wipe out the graffiti in your mind, replace the walls with my lock and chain
The one used to bind me down, I'll force you to hear my sound
Embed mirrors to your eyes so you can see the lies, this struggle won't end
But I won't give in cause, I'm here to rage war
A rebel 'till my life spills

Tyler Kennedy, Grade 10
Payson High School, AZ

Faith

Who am I
I am the main driving force
I am the light of day
Who am I
I come in the midst of darkness
I am there until the very end
Who am I
I am the strongest force
You may denounce me but I will never leave
Who am I
I am in the eyes of a child in prayer
I am the heart of a follower
Who am I
I was with you during Columbine
I was standing by when the Towers fell
I was walking the halls in Virginia Tech
Who am I
You know who I am just look
You may need to look into the deepest crevice of your heart,
But I am there
I am your Faith

Kylie Fenton, Grade 10
Horseshoe Bend High School, ID

Turbulent Waters

You, Love, only create our wrenching pain
And still you make us cry aloud in vain
Toward you we search throughout our frugal lives
Yet welcomed by arms of unending strife
My lone body abandoned, and still torn
And weathered my soul, furthermore forlorn
Obvious negatives clear you create
Yet bound to find you by our twisted fate
Again like waves 'gainst the land's steady shore
Still times again we chase, forever more

Shavenor S. Winters, Grade 11
Vancouver Christian High School, WA

Smoke

Emerging, it was just something to do
An act that would become way out of hand
The problem wasn't bad until it grew
It started to become more oft than planned

And now they smile as though they're in a daze
These people who are far from ones I love
Imposing fakes who tread through sickly haze
They make me cry, my trust I let go of

They say that now those days are past and done
They've learned, they've changed, these things they do insist
They say that they'll no longer just succumb
I hope that they will honestly resist

I look on as important turns to joke
I watch and hope that they can clear the smoke

Becca Evans, Grade 11
Dobson High School, AZ

Trapped with Love

Love, wouldn't it be great
To hold someone in your arms?
Skin and skin, flesh and flesh,
A kiss wherever it might be
On the right, or on the left.
To hear those words they speak.

Love is like the ocean blue,
It's like putting cement blocks on both your shoes.
You sink and sink 'til you come to.
What I thought was love, what I once knew.

Love can do many great things,
It can take us to the moon and back,
Drop us in a bag of stars,
Tie a knot and let us be,
Cause they're ours.

Love will set us free from all the hate it brings.
With every gram of love there's hate,
With every gram of hate there's love.
Love is always hidden inside
Hidden inside every individual,
Every person as a whole.

Mathew Payne, Grade 12
Arrow High School, UT

Victorious

It was code and conduct,
to the very end.
Between the pages and the words
formed and studied
by creatures of habit,
few read between the lines.
But still it called —
That faint Trumpet — it calls to they
who would have something else.
They who find the words,
hidden among so many others.
They who seek the change —
the change that makes one great.
The words so eagerly sought
slowly form, become solid —
take root, and begin to grow.
They bloom among much sacrifice and toil,
but are strong and unwavering.
And they cry with a voice as one —
and never cease —
even in the darkest hour.

Kyrsten Holland, Grade 12
Davis High School, UT

At the End

Farve calls it quits
He's tired of taking hits
Always throwing interceptions
Can never make receptions

He wants to be retired
Before he gets fired
He can't win because he always chokes
He wants to quit before he croaks

Will he come back
To lead the pack
Or will he sit in the stands
Wishing that he still had fans?
Patrick Romero, Grade 10
Mountainair High School, NM

Smile

I sit, sigh,
And wait

Wishing for you
To be with me

I look over,
You smile

I smile back
And turn away

I take a breath,
Count to three…

Let it go
And look again

You're still smiling
Right at me
Jordan Brantley, Grade 10
Dobson High School, AZ

Spring Speaks Softly

Slowly, softly Spring crowds out
Winter's cold and thunderous shout.
With her comes the early sun,
Under which spring blossoms run.
She gently wakes the birds from sleep;
Parent's chirp, and babies cheep.
She spreads her cloak upon the hills
Of tulips and of daffodils.
Her smile warms both night and day
And brings the children out to play.
But best of all — I dare to say —
Spring says, "Summer's on it's way."
Rebekah Tracht, Grade 12
Faith Baptist Christian Academy, WA

Walk with Me

O how when I need to keep on going,
Love and faithfulness you continue showing.
The road we travel is so rough and new,
But please remain with me the whole day through.
Always carry me with diligence and pride,
Help me survive this super crazy ride.
Some say you were too great a price to pay.
But I knew you would help me on my way.
Thank you very much for your comforting care,
O without you my poor feet would be bare.
Sarah Brown, Grade 11
Vancouver Christian High School, WA

Sleep

The one thing that we lack to ever get enough of
Is superb and glorious sleep that we all truly love
When our other life rises and awakes from the dead
When dreams come to life in our sleepy heads
Tranquil this fairy tale grows in our mind
Until darkness appears and we come to find
That our life is flawed, about everywhere
And our dreams haunt us, and give us a scare
We arise from dream world and come to life
To realize the thing that just gave us a fright
Slipping again we fall back into this world
And dream and seep, right into a whirl
Then the alarm rings and starts to resonate
We have to get up we are going to be late.
Joshua Munns, Grade 11
Madison Sr High School, ID

Around Me

Clear mountains around me lie; servants from a mount on high
Whispers daily wisdom hence; for this I pay the pence

The toll, the toll the black bird screams; and hasten it, unfastens its wings
Flying to perch on those eerie peaks; 'Away, away' it bids me keep

Pushing its wisdom far from my mind; I let the mountain's spirit to me bind
Entranced I climb higher still; until I reached the old mill

There I rested peace to lie; where I hear the old wood sigh
Creaking, moaning its dues; telling the stories of people they lose

Sadness overcomes my heart; quickly I trudge onward eager to be apart
Shadows cover the melancholy sun; I've reached the peak, now it's done

The passage to the bottom there; has left me breathless stealing my air
Weakly I stumble to the ground; rushing downward into the dirt mound

I let the earth swallow me whole; rising dirt surrounds me like it's full
Eyes closed, breathing long; I let my heart join the mountain's song
Tessa Farmer, Grade 11
Viewmont High School, UT

John F. Kennedy

Fatally wounded by gunshots
Kennedy was assassinated by "Lee Harvey Oswald"
Ten month investigation
You were shot down in your prime
Your wife telling you not to go
Dallas, Texas was your last stop
Good bye J.F.K.

Not positive about Oswald killing you
Set up by the mob
Father and brother cracking down on mob crime
What a shame you had to go
Good bye J.F.K.

The bullet that ended your life was found on the stretcher
Country in despair at the loss of you
Good bye J.F.K.

You could have been greater than you'll know
You could have bettered this country
You could have done great things
Your wife telling you begging you not to go
Good bye J.F.K.

Scott Basha, Grade 10
Mountainair High School, NM

Freedom Is Not Free

An August day in the Civil War
Many died, less or more
People died as you can see
We realize freedom is not free

To the soldiers who gave their lives
And to the men who did survive
To the dead lying on the ground
For at no circumstance would they back down

I write this poem in memory of
Those proud soldiers who rest above
Surely they fought for us to see
Above it all, freedom is not free

Black freedom is the reason for
The men who died in the Civil War
But not all went as Lincoln arranged
For one hundred years later, discrimination had not changed

But a cry for freedom is what we plea
Let us know freedom is not free

JT Keith, Grade 11
Custer County District High School, MT

Saucony®

Numerous tracks you have lain upon Earth.
Few but me will appreciate your worth.
You help me, on the trail, to win first place.
It's essentially you running the race.
Your soles are my fire; they're making me strong,
For this one final mile stretches so long.
You take the dirt when I run through the mud.
These four hundred miles have shown you're no dud.
When you wear down I will do what I may —
Throwing everything you have been away.

Lauren Dameron, Grade 11
Vancouver Christian High School, WA

List of 12

Thunderstorm
Out in the prairies
The grass is blowing,
Far away you can see lightning,
Shortly followed by loud sound of thunder
Sitting in the living room
Watching the storm, getting scared
Watching for tornados and lightning
Anticipating the loud thunder
Once you get all settled down
The pager goes off,
You run to go get dressed
And you get in the pickup with your dad
You go to the fire hall
you get ready then get in a truck
you head towards the fire
After many hours of fighting
It finally starts to rain
You can now go home
And relax knowing
It's almost the end.

Jordan Riley, Grade 10
Wray High School, CO

The Wonders of Solitude

Sometimes I want to be alone
Sometimes I feel alone
When I want to be alone
It's to escape reality
But, when I return
I feel alone
When I feel alone
It seems the world has left me behind
I either escape again into my imagination
Or I hunt for my social well being
However, I don't always decide what I'll do
Like all of humanity, I have duties and responsibilities
I swear to myself for the sake of my solitude
I will break my social barrier
And, talk to others, no matter my mood
So one day I will be able to lock myself in my home

Brandon Edwards, Grade 10
Orem High School, UT

Back to the Drawing Board

two days give me hope
that maybe a car ride
and back
will all be worth it…
I know what I want
and I know what I need
and nothing will get in my way
this addiction is my blood
and enough is *never* enough
right now only thoughts linger
and there will be no more running away
in thought,
in reality,
nothing will stand
between
me and my prize
I'm a lion in a cage
just waiting to make a strike.

Kyle Kaliszewski, Grade 12
Chatfield High School, CO

Time; Freedom; Strength

Time for a change
Time for freedom
I'm not sure I'm ready
But I want it
I want it badly!
Badly enough to cry.
Change of life
Change of heart
Change of mind.
Freedom from pain
Freedom from cold
Freedom from everything.
I want to be stronger
Stronger than ever
Stronger than everyone.

Ashley Hines, Grade 12
Westwood High School, AZ

Love Hurts

Every day I think of you
And wonder why you had to go
You left me here
To shed a tear
I miss you so
I hope to know
Why you had to go

It makes me mad
That you lied
It should make you sad
That I cried
Every day I think of you
And wonder why you had to go

Melinda Thevenin, Grade 10
Scholars' Academy, AZ

Up So High

I like to think of you when I am up so high
I like to think of what you might say
If you could see the patchwork pattern of the earth
Spread out in so many colors, so many squares
When you feel small, like nothing and everything at all
Held up only by twisted metal, a handful of fragile flesh, smooth bone
With the ocean miles below
Where the fish make their homes in the depths
Where we will never know them, never count their scales
But, oh, dear, it is you I want to know
You I want to understand
And sometimes I think I would give my life
And other times I know I would give my life quite gladly, to you, just to you
To keep the lights in your eyes burning brightly
Through the smoke, to guide me at night when I am lost
And, love, it is you, dear, who bring me home
Because I, I love you
More than you will ever know, more than anything
Because when I look at you, I see my heart outside of me in the sunlight
And that brings me up…and up…and ever up…
I like to think of you when I am up so high.

Meghan Callahan, Grade 10
Arapahoe High School, CO

Saying Goodbye to John

Reaching, stretching, waiting,
Arms wide, fists clenched, eyes closed
And "I'm not listening to you!"

Not like you were listening, really listening
When you asked for more time;
When I sat in silence as the windows fogged
And the rain came down like the climax of a Disney movie.

But it wasn't the climax, it was the end
Of me putting up with "eventually"
Because I'm tired of not being allowed to jump in puddles
When you won't even let the rain fall down on my tiny shoulders;
Framed with imperfect posture
At the harshness of my safety net.

Your umbrella won't save me from harm,
It's broken, flawed
Only rough pieces of metal with a psychedelic cover
But the pieces snag my dress; my hands
And the tiny red drops probably aren't tears
Because I refuse to cry in the rain

And it WILL rain for me.

Ruthie Morris, Grade 10
Highland High School, AZ

American?

I am a radical
not just another mindless sheep
blending in with the self-ignorant flock
minds so filled with patriotic love for their colors
that they are blinded by them
I see the colors you shove down anther country's throat
materialism creating narcissism

I am disgusted
because you consider me a statistic
just another number
another label
another diagram
another problem you will ignore

I am a half-bred American
one of millions you attempt to throw out every day
smile at me because you see my skin is white
visit my house and hear Spanish tongue flowing
condemn me for hypocrisy
expect me to feel shame
but I am proud…I am a radical

Christy Ledezma, Grade 12
Westwood High School, AZ

Just Me

Your shadow lingers
whispering sweet nothings in my ear,
I hear sweet somethings
it all becomes so clear
this relationship is
just
me
a puppeteer with he
placing words in his mouth like food
so I hear what I want to,
hear things that would make Cinderella tremble
shaking in her gown with fear
I came to present our fairy tale to the world
but who arrived?
just
me

Ashley Beck, Grade 10
Kentridge High School, WA

Her Dance

With such beautiful grace she dances
Her whistling feet like an orchestra on the floor
Her body moves with every emotion of her soul
As if her spirit is pushing each limb toward salvation and joy
Her hair shimmers in the sunlight
With all eyes on her she smiles
Her arms stretched out toward heaven
Nothing can stop her now
Stillness and apathy long obsolete
She dives deeper and deeper into the splendor of dance

Julianne O'Leary, Grade 12
Bellarmine Preparatory School, WA

Stuck

I wish I could mirror your love
That faithful composed look
But my gaze would simply tell a lie.

I wish I hadn't caught you so easily,
And now you are putty in my hands.
Waiting for me to mold you to the right cast,
But almost all I want to make you,
Is an item of the past.

Yes I love you
Yes I need you,
Yet I yearn for my freedom as well
But your memory is the sweetness on my lips,
The soft scent lingering on my clothes
Sometimes I don't feel
As if I could let you go.

I wish my heart was not split in half,
One part of it needing your affection
The other craving my liberation.
I wish I could mirror your love.

Mary Steel, Grade 10
Grand Junction High School, CO

Never Ending Love

Her heart never broke away
As his did — so long ago.
The longing never ended.

The captivating dark skin,
In his eyes, compassion and beauty,
A smile as broad and clear as the night sky.

His kindness was spread to nations.
Heads turned twice at his sight.
Strength overcame his struggles.

A broken heart seldom heals;
After a time, it starts to numb.
The heart cries out to the darkness.

The pain overcome with sadness.
A want — the longing — never ceased;
Pushed back, forced away — are the feelings.

His return — his dark, captivating skin,
The returned love, she weakened and fell.
A peace came, her heart sang to him.

Emily Sellers, Grade 11
Cascade Christian High School, OR

Do You Even Care?
Sitting in this lonely room,
Thinking of you.
Thinking if you're thinking of me.
Wondering what you're doing,
Where you're at.

If you could just hear me,
All these things I want you to know.
I haven't stopped thinking about you.
I wonder if you've forgotten,
If you just don't care.
I need to know.
So I can move on with my life.

But if you're still out there,
And if you still love me,
Come and hold me in your arms,
Just like you used to.

Are you still out there?
Do you even care?
If I could tell you one thing,
I'd tell you that I still love you,
And I've always cared.

Chelsea Brandner, Grade 10
Orem High School, UT

(The Truth;
Here lies an Honest Liar
With eyes of fire
And a heart of pure carnage

J. Jueschke, Grade 11
Douglas County High School, CO

Dream
I sit here,
Just thinking about the ball,
The tackle on the right side,
Ribs broke.
I cry out in pain.
There's the bell.
I open my eyes.
I'm the last one in the class.
I sat up, I'm walking out of the class.
I'm in my uniform.
I walk out in the field.
There's cheers from all around.
I stare out in the stands.
I see her,
I run the ball,
I'm hit, I cry out in pain.
Everything's black.
I open my eyes and I'm home.

Zack Bryant, Grade 10
Utah Youth Academy, UT

Dancing in the Darkness
Dancing in the darkness she recoils in fear.
There was no one around, nobody near.
She's still dancing ashamed of what was done,
Guilt not hers to own but his alone.
He stripped her of pride and robbed her of virtue.
He left her there to begin anew.
She's now sorrowing guilty and depressed,
She is a victim now just like all the rest.
The darkness seems a lonely dreary waste.
People are looking to put him in his place.
She seems so alone no one to find,
Her fears have not all been left behind.
It's his fault after all; he left her to go,
Dancing in the darkness, alone.

Devan Sisson, Grade 12
Arrow High School, UT

I Came Here to Forget Not to Remember
I came here to forget everything that was,
Such as falling through time,
Going in and out of our own make-believe worlds,
Breaking my arm but healing my heart,
Listening to the coldhearted rumors,
But never setting them straight,
Falling in love so easily and then easily falling out,
Where the dreams of tomorrow never ended,
But the fear of today fading away,
Where everything was lost and never found,
But I came here to forget not to remember.

Randi Pezoldt, Grade 10
Columbus High School, MT

I Wish I Had…
I wish I had said what I felt inside,
I wish I had expressed everything I was feeling,
I wish I had shown you how I truly felt,
I wish I had told you how you made me feel,
I wish I had…
I wish I had regrets,
I wish I had never doubted myself,
I wish I had shown you that you were more than a friend,
I wish I had shown you all the wonderful things about you,
I wish I had…
I wish I had showed you that someone did care,
I wish I had never let you doubt yourself,
If only you had seen, if only you had known,
Maybe if I had done something more, you would still be here.
I wish I had…
Now that I am without you,
I see what I really wished I could have done,
But now that I can't go back, I guess it is all finished,
But if you ever come back, I promise that I will never wish again,
I know the longing I have, to tell you that you were the one,
Because deep inside I know that no one could complete me the way you did!

Julie Longenecker, Grade 10
Buhl High School, ID

Earth's Tattered Beauty

In Heaven…
The skies are always that beautiful shade of blue
Down below the grass shines with great happiness
Flowers leaning in toward the rays of the majestic sun

In Heaven…
You have wings…to fly wherever your heart desires
No pains
No Aches
It's almost peaceful…like a never-ending dream

In Heaven…
There are no wars
There are no wrongs
There are no such things as bad

In Heaven…
People are free
Lovers are together
Life is beautiful

On Earth…none as such exists

Lizzi Bayhan, Grade 10
Alma D'Arte High School, NM

Dreams

There's no place with endless space
Tidal waves tumble and collide
Sand tickles the feet
Calm water cascading
As soundlessly as the evaporating ripples

No place such as this
Birds mewing greeting songs
Aromas of pattering rain
Flowers dance ceremoniously
As the atmosphere swells with romantic pressure

No place like home
Thunderous storms and ramous pounds
Lightning powerfully displays
Sweet rows of fields whisper
As fear tauntingly treads through the rich grass

No place such as this
Resting delicately down
On soft powdery silk
Where dreams rock and soothe
As one sleeps, drifting away in eagerness

Rachel Vogels, Grade 10
Chatfield High School, CO

A Tear

A tear
A tear for every fear
The fear of losing you
A tear for every fear
The fear of loving you
A tear for every fear
The fear of not being with you
A tear for every fear
A tear, a tear
When I think of you
The tears stop falling
Your light dries all my tears
All my fears
Then a tear suddenly falls, falls from my eye
And I realize that I am only dreaming, dreaming
A tear
A tear for every fear

Alex Neiman, Grade 11
Nederland Middle/Sr High School, CO

A Freedom Journey

Two years old and leaving home,
Mom, three brothers and a sister all alone.
Five tired children walking thru Mexico,
Mom scared to get caught, don't want to let us go.

It's late at night and no place to sleep,
Mom says be quiet don't make a peep.
Walking for miles and miles without end,
Cries from the pain my mother did tend.

The weeks were the same, more walking we did,
As the police went by we all got down and hid.
We got to Oregon all six of us together,
There to meet our dad to make things all better.

Our journey to America, land of the free and home of the brave,
There to start a new life with freedom that my parents gave.

Amarelis Santos, Grade 11
Portland Cornerstone Academy, OR

I Will Always Love Him

Although I love him the way I do
It seems he's not the one that's meant for me.
But even when he acts like there is love there too
I know in my heart it's just not meant to be.
Although they say he's nothing but trouble
He will always know the right things to say.
Day and night he makes my heart beat double
All the while he will brighten my day.
And I see what no one else sees inside
He puts on a show and acts real tough
The most secret of things he likes to hide
He's my beautiful diamond in the rough
Although we may not end up together
I know he'll be in my heart forever

Jasmine Bruce, Grade 12
Temple Baptist Academy, NM

The Days

The days have gone by so fast,
past in present,
but it's pushed
in hopes of isolation
The door has shut,
bleeding memories from
the stained being
I thought the temptation was unlocked,
forever wanting touch…
closure in you,
false promises
within this complex game,
running isn't the answer
to your unforgettable shame
steps taken
this deceitful man, intellect is…
DIVINE.

Alexandria McCulloch, Grade 12
Westwood High School, AZ

Our Un-Story

I remember the November
when words were all we needed,
were all we lacked.
Our plot had no middle,
or if it did,
we skipped straight to the end.
But your ending wasn't my ending
as you read the abridged version.

How's your ever-after?

Sofia Waugh, Grade 12
Layton High School, UT

The Escape

I see the shining light at the end
But I cannot get to it
Every step I take it takes one too
Every time I run it runs faster
The escape now only seems impossible
I cannot win this everlasting tunnel
It knows me oh too well
Like it's watching me
Knowing everything I'm going to do
But wait I see the problem
There is a treadmill beneath my feet
I never noticed it before
Maybe cause I forgot the little things
And only looked for one way out
I get off now
The light gets brighter
I'm finally there
I escape
I win!

Nikko Melonas, Grade 10
Orem High School, UT

Remember What You Have

Now I look at my childhood, I wish I had it
Playing in the snow to playing basketball
Every Sunday starts off quiet as a mouse
Getting louder when everyone comes to my house

My family hails from an Asian southeastern country
If I forgot that, I would get chewed up and that's not funny
Family risked their lives to immigrate for a new life
Now it's my time to shine when I'm put into the limelight

Growing up in White Center, now that's the place
Even if I had bruises all over my face
Good times or bad, I had it all
From stealing people's shoes to playing with little kid swings

Every season was the right one
Always had fun, during pouring rain or if the day was bright with the sun

Don't forget your stomping grounds
You know, the place you would go and lounge
Where you grew up, that's all you have and all you get
Origin memories, the ones you should never forget
Enjoy life, go ahead and laugh, just remember what you have

James Sok, Grade 10
Evergreen High School, WA

To Mother

I'll keep my diamond rings and punk CDs
my piercings and my father's eyes.
I embrace my inherited life of privilege
intertwined with the unconventional one I've adopted as my own.
I am that adamant iconoclast
adorned in ambiguity of self and family.
I celebrate my mother's social status, she is my queen.

And I enjoy the heads that turn
to see us hand in hand together —
mother and daughter, lawyer and writer.
We appear the epitome of social contradiction
yet much to their surprise
we are composed of the same blood, the same name
intellectuals and artists by birth.
I'll keep my pearls and ragged Converse Chucks
my skinny jeans and Armani pleated skirts.
When eyebrows raise at me, I laugh and say inaudibly,
"I am my mother's daughter, she is my queen
and I will live accordingly, despite your judgments."
When eyes are fixed on me I hope they see my unrestrained honesty
and authentic me, adorned in envied ambiguity.

Amy Woelber, Grade 11
Valmora High School, NM

Ich Bin Ein Teil
I am a sheep in wolf's clothing, for my exterior is harsh and alarming
but underneath is a gentleness not often found.

I am like air, for I enjoy the freedom of movement and am growing ever mentally with knowledge
and have an open mind and am elusive when need be.

I am like water, as I am able to adapt to my environment and have
discipline in the flexibility of emotion.

I am like earth, for I am stable in mind, and body,
while still being aware of my surroundings and emotions.

I am like fire, as I am able to move in less than a moment's notice
and have passion burning inside that drives me.

I am human, for what is entombed inside this body is the multitudes,
years of suffering and pain as well as care and pleasure
from others who call themselves the same.

But most of all, I am me,
and no one is able to change that
for I am always changing.

Willard Michael Howard Swatzell, Grade 12
Westwood High School, AZ

Time Trap
It's the silence that drops over someone like an angry acid that swells and seers flesh.
Sinking deep within the mind tearing it apart cell by cell.

Quiet like after a quarrel with a lover that thickens and draws the seconds into everlasting time traps.
Bottomless pits of dark, pungent time that seem to cease the pant for life, like a kept animal.

When the spirit vacations and people stand alone, vigor turns to solemn nothing standstill.
The eyes stare blank and dry watching silence bury in a stifling lethal flood of lonely bewilderment.

When the air is sticky with choked hour and the body trembles like a hunted beast…
You will come to learn the carnal silence of lonesome tide.

Christa Bemis, Grade 12
Eagle Academy, CO

Who Cares
"I think I'm in love with you" he says as he grips her hand tight, "but you were just too much for me to ever try to touch."
I'm lying next to him looking at his face, slowly piecing together who he is and who he was. Not sure which one I can't let go of.
The song keeps playing and I'm lost in it, the melody taking me to a place where what I was doing was okay.
The music is too beautiful to worry about anything; I never want it to stop or this day to end.
It's a fantasy land him and I created, a place where it's just the two of us and nothing else matters.
For just this day it's as if things never ended; we pick up where we left off and end unsure of what's next.
He makes me nervous as I'm lying in his arms.
We look into each other's eyes throughout the day, watching them change colors almost as fast as our feelings for each other.
My head is spinning, *I lose control when I'm around him.*
Right and wrong don't mean anything in our day.
The song ends and soon I'm back to my life.
I know in my heart these two worlds could never *collide.*
"He kisses her neck one last time and then he turns out the light."

Taylor Neitzke, Grade 12
Galena High School, NV

Just Like Heaven

Just like heaven
The look in your eyes
The secrets they hold
Deep below the softening cries

Staring up at the sky
Waiting for your echo
You're not completely gone
There's still a beat
A beat in your heart

That heaven, that beautiful heaven
Is still shining
For one more night

Brittney Mayfield, Grade 11
Fossil Ridge High School, CO

The Rat

I'll never be with anyone
As beautiful again
In the game of love
I guess I'll never win
So smart and kind
A beautiful body and mind
I miss this girl so much
Everything and her loving touch
She wanted me
And I wanted her
When I held her
Everything was a blur
From that point on
Nothing else matters
Seeing her laugh and smile
Just makes me sadder
Nothing can win her back
Since she left me my heart just cracks

Clyde Webb, Grade 10
Ontario High School, OR

The Beat

My heart has a beat
That thump, thump, pumps
And fills my blood
With life-giving air
As it regenerates every
Fiber of my body.

Music has a beat
That thump, bump, jumps
And fills my heart
With love-giving joy
As it rejuvenates every
Fiber of my soul.

Joseph Demar Chatterton, Grade 11
Preston High School, ID

Cry Me a River

You know you've stolen her heart.
She ran away from the start.
I would not blame her for the tears you caused.
You hurt her not thinking; you could have paused.
Why didn't you just stop where you were at?
you said you would be there, just like a tat.
You said you would always be a friend.
And that you'd stick out until the end.
You make her break down and shiver.
All she does is cry a river.

Chie C. J., Grade 12
Diamond Ranch Academy, UT

KRS-One

Thumping to a piercing rhythmical base.
Swaying his heavy sneakers side to side.
I listened to the teacher speak
deep in the Bronx one dark night,
by an alley filled with young hoodlums.
He pounded his feet to the beat.
He pounded his feet to the beat,
to the sound of the overpowering base.
With his ebony hands clutching to the microphone,
he made the crowd roar with excitement.
O Teacher, how you speak.
Moving his large stature across the stage.
How he drove the audience wild with his words.
O Teacher.

Summer Neves, Grade 11
Glencoe High School, OR

Ode to the Stranger

I met a stranger on a dreary, dark day his long black trench coat shifting as he swayed
He nodded me a greeting as we passed on the street
I gazed upon his eyes, they were eyes of deceit
Words cannot express the feelings that shot through my blood
That coursed through my veins, taking solace in mental mud
As his blissfully pale hand came in contact with my head
Causing instant utter chaos and the onslaught of woe and dread
I felt my innermost thoughts being sucked from my brain
My own sacred fantasies being snatched with disdain
Tumbling to the ground, his hand smothering my face
I experienced my soul being ripped from my grace
Through blurred vision I saw his other hand caress my chest
Azure aura wafted from me, culminating in a crest
He gawked at its purity, then absorbed it into his shell
He had stolen my essence, but I had given it as well
My lids became heavy with the lead of despair
He merely looked upon my with his sympathetic glare
I faded away, losing all grip on that reality
Relieved eternally from that blasphemous fallacy
I open my eyes and again we see each other: I know that man, for he is my lover

Sinjin Jones, Grade 12
Thomas Jefferson High School, CO

Family

My family is a circle of love,
It is one of my greatest treasures.
Family is always what I think of,
Because the love we share cannot be measured.
When I need their guidance, they give me advice,
Even if they are busy they still find time to spare.
They never need to think twice,
That makes me realize how much they care.
My family means so much to me,
When I see them I fly high with pride.
Without their love, I don't know where I would be,
I am honored to have them by my side.
Family is the one thing that keeps me alive,
Without it, how would I survive?

Rohit Aggarwal, Grade 11
Desert Vista High School, AZ

Twilight

As the grim light pierces the grim shadows,
A glimmering beacon lights a pathway.
Following the path I find myself lost,
Wandering the forbidden wilderness.
Suddenly, a cold surge runs through my veins,
Like a poison injected with a needle.
With crippled legs, my feet are swept away,
Grasping for air, I fall into shadows.
I find myself trapped in a labyrinth.
Dazed, I hear the horde of thundering drums.
My heart grows ever so slightly faster
Beating like the rhythmic pattern of war,
As the dark crimson moon fades in the sky,
My life as it seems is about to die.

Shelby Cline, Grade 9 and Dam Lam, Grade 10
Clark High School, NV

This Life I Live

I live one life.
One life that is full of hate.
This one life full of sadness.
There is nothing I can do to change the past.
I pray every night wishing I could see my little man again.
I miss his smile, that which made my day.
There is nothing like that I will see 'till I fly away.
When my days are rainy he was my sun to clear up my day.
He was like the cheese to my Macaroni.
I miss him so much I don't know what to think.
Too many complications.
I can't stand this pain.
I live one life.
I live one life with so much pain.
The past is the reason, there's no happiness.
He was my everything, 'til this day.
I miss him so much I cry myself to sleep.
I miss his sweet touch, his soft cheeks.
There is no other that can make me happy.
I pray every night hoping I can see my little man again.

Jalisa Anderson, Grade 12
Rocinante High School, NM

Being Fifteen and Forbidden

Sitting in my room,
One dark summer night
I stared out my window,
At the dark forbidden night,
I was fifteen.
I thought about the sweet summer night,
Admiring the carefreeness, the forbidden pleasure,
I opened the window,
Pushed out my screen,
I was fifteen.

I climbed through my window,
Thinking of the night with my friends,
It was waiting for me,
Waiting for me to experience it,
I was fifteen.
I thought of my parents sleeping in the next room,
The cops roaming the night,
The danger of being out so late,
I put on my pajamas, closed the window,
Laid in bed,

I went to sleep, fifteen.

Katie Raffaghello, Grade 10
Arapahoe High School, CO

Swelling

What is this?
   Appearing in this moment above the beat in my chest?
This bird, turning its wings
   In tumultuous time
In whatever emotion, whatever bliss
   That captures its fond life in summer heat, life blessed?
This small creature, whose voice now sings?
   What is this rhyme?

   Bird against the ribs, caged and content
   Where swelling tide in swollen heart
   What is this, and however may it repent?
   Repent, forgive — falling, as it were. Content.

What is this?
   Pulling, taking, fluttering behind my breast?
This creature, tiny singing voice
   That does ring above all else?
In whatever happiness, caught in bliss
   And does fully hold the pulse and sing…sing with the rest!
Capturing, taking — little bird, you make my choice
   What is this; new life within this cage dwells.

Hannah Fritz, Grade 12
Lakewood High School, CO

What Is Love?
Is love with you?
If love is old can it be new?
Where can love be?
If it's not with me?
Is love free?
Or just a dream?
My love is in your hands
What is that you plan?
Could you love me?
Would you love me?
Can you love me?
Do you love me?
Do you need me
As much as I need you?
Please say you love me
Like I love you
Is it safe to love
Or will I end up with a grudge?
Damaris Velasquez, Grade 12
Granite High School, UT

Life
Running with laughter
echoing in the atmosphere,
shoes are forgotten,
stinging pains of crumbled mountains
under feet, are forgotten.

The chorus of the slamming
of skin on asphalt heading
towards the abandoned trees lying
in the course sand,
letting waves rip off
the rough bark exposing the
pearl white wood.

Leaping together
taking the same path of pristine
white road until it ends
at the Great Cliffs.
Samantha Beville, Grade 10
Oak Harbor High School, WA

Impossible
There I was
talking to my dad about my day.
He told me about who he had seen
and what he was gonna get my mom
for their anniversary.
But when I woke up this morning,
it was long past January 11th.
Off to that black marble stone
with his name branded on it
I go.
Talk to you tonight Dad.
Jennifer Hook, Grade 12
LASER Alternative School, MT

Too Early to Say Goodbye
how can things get so bad
that you wanna take away the life you once had?
you're taking yourself away from people who care
please, oh please, this isn't fair!

why do you want to leave this place behind?
yes, I know, this world isn't kind
but that's what this is all about: fighting 'til the end
and if you cannot do it for yourself, do it for your friends

hearing you say that no one cares about you
makes me wonder if you ever knew
I like you so much, boy,
and to my life, you brought the joy

and you still do
no matter what you decide to do
I'm not gonna let you go
not without a fight, no no no!

I'll sit here, just waiting for your call
and now while I'm sitting here, I'm thinking about how bad you made me fall
I miss you so much, kid, no matter what you did.
Christy Erhart, Grade 11
Park City High School, MT

10 Times as Much
Every time I think about you I am 10 times more confident,
I smile 10 times as much, laugh 10 times as hard,
And love the person I am 10 times more.

Because I know you I am 10 times as happy,
And because I am your friend I am 10 times as lucky.

When I imagine myself with you my heart beats 10 times as fast,
And my vision for the future is 10 times as clear.

When I talk to you I am 10 times as speechless,
And when I sleep at night my dreams are 10 times as real.

When we hold hands our relationship is 10 times more magical.
When you wrap your arms around me and hold me
In your warm embrace I feel 10 times more secure.

When you kiss my lips I am 10 times more breathless.
When you flatter me with words you knock me off my feet 10 times easier.

When you say "I love you," you mean it and eternity is 10 times closer.
It's because of who you are I love you 10 times as much.
Jackie Barney, Grade 12
Preston High School, ID

Glass Heart

I carry my heart in a little box
It's very small and fragile
For it is made of glass

I keep it close so it won't get broken
People get offended when they ask to see it
and I refuse

Me and my heart are all alone

Someone special comes along and asks to see
I start to refuse but notice he, too, carries his heart
in a tiny ring box, in hopes of protecting it

I agree, but only if we trade
I observe his heart, treat it carefully
A crash; he has dropped my heart

I pick up the pieces
He left with his whole heart
Only an apology and red glass shards left

Me and my broken heart are all alone

Aubrey Morris, Grade 12
Borah Sr High School, ID

The War

A world in conflict
The great powers collide
In battles that bring glory
And defeat

Shells fall like rain
The great guns sound as if someone is knocking at the door
The joy of liberation
Is offset by the killing of war

The rising sun attacks an unsuspecting country
On a day that will live in infamy
Awakening a sleeping giant
The American soldier

Who they say was no soldier
Put the enemy in their place on a day in 1944
D-day
Changing the tide of war

With Europe saved
A regime destroyed

Justin Pederson, Grade 10
Queen Creek High School, AZ

Summer Is Here

The end of the year is nice and sweet.
The blooming of the flowers.
Their sweet scent wafting into the air.
The sun is out sending its sunshine rays
into our hearts, telling us
that summer is no longer hiding!
The blue skies, and warm nights.
The green grass, it's all telling us
that school is soon to be out!
The air tingling with excitement.
Kids stirring in their seats not being able to be still.
Their minds not concentrating on school.
But on what to do in the summer.
Summer is around the corner.
The last bell rings.
Everyone runs out.
Summer is Here!

Jaimie Seiber, Grade 10
Orem High School, UT

Walk of Life

One afternoon while strolling on the beach,
looking at the cloudy gray sky and
bleak hazy mist over the turbulent water,
I ponder what will become of my life.
I walk on the cold wet sand and see the waves
crash upon the grains of sand,
people being overwhelmed by the waves of this world,
being overtaken and repeatedly pounded.
For a moment I was lost — focused on the hurt,
those drowning in the ways of this world.
As I continue to walk I stroll farther from the waves,
and stick to higher ground.

Ashley Fite, Grade 11
Cascade Christian High School, OR

Que Hora Es?

I should be in Barelas
Cleaning dirt floors
In the shadow of a castle
Of innumerable windows
Economic hub of the barrio
Wives wait, fearing the train station
metal serpents crash around the building
they live off tired, sweat-glazed men.

Memories become cataracts in elderly eyes

people who traveled the same journey
to Aztlan, harvest chile and fruit
I let their blood become unappreciated oil
that fuels machines

History repeats itself
high school teachers struggle to explain.
now my blood sits and rots
in Spanish I.

Missy Baca, Grade 10
Menaul School, NM

Roses

A red rose whispers of passion,
A white rose signifies peace,
A crimson rose smells of seduction,
You and I are fresh like the breeze.

You are like a rose,
You are beautiful,
Yet very dangerous,
You look so fresh,
But you'll wither with time.

Roses are pretty,
Roses are beautiful,
But you and I,
Are way more than that.

Sharon Luvio, Grade 12
Granite High School, UT

Trapped

Darkness is all around you
Sitting alone
Trapped in a world of thoughts
Isolated from the world
Separated from life and all other beings
And controlled by emptiness
Pushed to the verge of survival
Scrounging to find life
Stuck in a world of nothing
Just sitting there until you crash
Nothing to do
No one to see

Melissa Jones, Grade 10
Wray High School, CO

Beyond and Inside Out

Beyond and inside out
A row of three
Without crossed t's
What is left is left
Not gone, but away
The base of all of most
Is strong but frosted
White and glistening
Like emerald or marble.
Pick up the remains
Continual, unsteady
The tree of new, of death
Of will and end
Dies but grows in an endless
Stream of light of east
Connecting most, and all
Tired, contrived
Rise up before the end.

Aimee Martinez, Grade 12
Lakewood High School, CO

Dark Light

In the light of the night,
slipping in with significance,
my silhouette marks the wall.
Shadows caress the ground,
splatters of light drop on my body
and mysterious emotions wedge through my mind.

Jamie Williams, Grade 12
Sugar-Salem High School, ID

That Little Boy

Oh, that little boy always taking what is lying around
Oh, that little boy making way too much sound
Sneaking, laughing, yelling what's he going to do when no one is around.

Oh, that little boy always getting in the way
Oh, that little boy always has something to say
Loud, calm, lazy but you love him anyway.

Oh, that little boy always beating up my friends
Oh, that little boy not knowing when things should end
Kissable, huggable, lovable not knowing when he's about to offend.

Oh, that little boy always wondering what's about to begin
Oh, that little boy never realizing what's begun
Weird, odd, sweet too many things he's sung.

Oh, that little boy what will life turn out to be?
Oh, that little boy and he likes to tickle me
Running, scary, and caring just tall enough to see.

Caitlin Jerome, Grade 10
Cedar Park Christian School – Everett Campus, WA

Battles of the Day

The rose cries of agony and pain as thunder rolls in the sky,
Learning of one's true vain with a veil of smoke in her eyes;
Wilting the leaves on her shoulders is the fire burning wild,
Fire in the garden bed burns brighter than one's smile.
She's crying of the pain, let alone all of her shame;
The rose petals are bled drier than the sweet symphony of one's quiet heartbeat.
The rose watches the others burn, listening to the shrieks and shrills,
The yells and bright screams, the pain and the sting;
Tears of the rose roll down her petals then down her emerald stem;
Tears sizzle with a hiss as the fire creeps and crawls in the garden bed;
Thunder burning one's ears with a bang, Bang, BANG!
Soon the sweet chime of pouring rain brings faith to those who remain,
Faith that will mask the rose's shamed hate.
Rain pouring on the zigzagged fire leaves nothing but black ash,
Ashes of those all alone,
Ashes of all the broken dreams,
Leaving nothing but petals laying in the distinguished sun.
Laying in the midnight sky under the glistened moon
The rose must cry; cry for all their sins;
She blesses their lingering souls with a whispered prayer
Forgiving all their lies under the heavened sky.

Michelle Nye, Grade 11
Lake County High School, CO

Life Punishments

I once knew a homie he was real and cold
He really didn't care, a person that nobody could hold
Everyone's quiet nobody say's a word and won't mention
Because in front is a person with bad intentions
Cruising down the street and only in the night
If a person stared bad he was ready for a fight

One day he thought of a tempting and illegal vision
He was going to rob a bank so he started his mission
Everything was going right until the police came and fought
He fought almost until the end till he got caught

Now he's living in a jail room paying for his crime
Nobody ever knew how much he was doing for time
He's now in this small lonely and dark cell
He didn't even remember when was the time he fell.

Luis Illingworth, Grade 11
Rio Rico High School, AZ

Who I Am

I am a face in the crowd.
My name is my unique personality.
My voice is unusual but ordinary.
To my teachers, I am a paper, just another thing to grade.
I am myself, unique, individual.
I am a part of the world, not just part of family and friends,
But also of enemies and strangers.
I know my place, I am the child, the ignorant one.
The evil in the world keeps me connected to reality.
I am a poet, a learner, a teacher, a friend.
I am the sensitive one, tough on the outside, soft on the inside.
I love, yet I hate.
I want, yet I give.
I'm lonely, yet I am surrounded by people.
I am ME.

Rachel Claric, Grade 12
Winston Churchill High School, OR

What's Hidden Inside

There's something in my soul that yearns to be free
It's never been out before, but it's begging me
I need to let it out, I need to let it flee
To the one that it should go to so that they may see
What's hidden inside of me

I should probably not do anything, I should just let it be
But if I let this out, this thing inside of me
I won't have to keep it anymore, I can let it free
So the world can see,
What's hidden inside of me

If the world saw this thing that begs to me,
I would no longer be captive, I would be set free
No longer wondering what could be
Because she would see
What's hidden inside of me

Sam Murri, Grade 11
Front Range Christian School, CO

Gossip

To you I am a story
To you I am the rumors
To you I am someone to whisper about
To laugh at
To point at

To you I am the manipulated
To you I am the twisted in a tornado of lies
To you I am the cheated, I am the cheater

To you I am entertainment
To you I am pleasure out of misery
To you I am relief

Just keep telling my tales
Of the lies and deceit
Of the hurt and the head games
The more you speak
The more my spotlight shines

I know my reality
I am not the victim
I am not the wrong
To you I am famous

Clara Stark, Grade 12
Westwood High School, AZ

Machine-Ship

The straight forward
Scenery(?)
Does nothing to distract you
From who you miss.
And yes
There really are tumbleweeds
Stuck in every fence,
At least I'm still moving.
And after
The tenth big-rig
Or fifth train
Pulling a hundred cars
You question man's dependence on the machines
That are slowly INVADING
SEPARATING us from humans
SEVERING our relationships
And DULLING our personalities.
His best friend
Is an Xbox
Only living off of
The status of a button.

Eric Booton, Grade 12
Chatfield High School, CO

Water Droplets and Bubbles

Water droplets lay on leafs,
   waiting to slide off,
     like bubbles on a reef.

The reflection it shows,
   gives much dimension,
     but rarely grows.

The bubbles would pop,
   under the water,
     like many in a crop.

Some would glide,
   Others would fall,
     But many died.

The water would glisten,
and the bubbles would shimmer,
but nothing can compare,
to the sound when you listen.

Aerica Hulse, Grade 10
Shelley Sr High School, ID

Freedom Is...

Meadows and open fields
Choosing a religion
Cities and open streets
Soldiers and generals
Fighting to free others

Maddi LaMont, Grade 12
Preston High School, ID

He Got It Wrong

He got it wrong,
No movement is made without intention,
I am full of intention,
I seek nothing but to move,
Feeling the beat deeper than imaginable,
The sand underneath my feet,
Motionless,
Beyond the fact...
Not ridiculous when heard,
Although glanced at through incredulous eyes,
I dance to enact songs played without people,
Giving the rhythm some body,
And move like I float without legs...
You must know me...
I wanted to see how far the rabbit hole went,
So of course
I jumped in,
But when I looked up,
I saw that you'd jumped in after me.

Autumn Norton, Grade 10
FamilyLink/StudentLink School, WA

Is There Really Such Thing as Freedom?

People are being forced to work on a daily basis,
just making enough money to pay the bills...is that freedom?

Children having to learn several languages,
just to please the rest of the world...is that freedom?

Picking between several people to be our president,
when they are all the same...is that freedom?

Students having to pay for college,
when we are forced to get a decent job...is that freedom?

The government spending more money on a war
than trying to feed our starving people...is that freedom?

High school students being sleep deprived
from the homework they are getting...is that freedom?

So what is freedom you ask?
Freedom to some people might be the privilege to do whatever you please,
but to me...it is a dream. Something that is merely intangible,
something that one could never achieve.

Ashley Parson, Grade 12
Crow High School, OR

Dinosaurs

Six.
Everything seemed big.
I had to use a stool to reach the sink.
Here is what frightened me: school ravioli, strangers, dinosaurs.
Here is what I liked; my parents, my cat, Robin Hood (Disney).

Nine.
Starting to do things on my own.
I got to walk to school by myself.
Here is what frightened me: my fifth grade teacher, math, dinosaurs.
Here is what I liked: reading, the Spice Girls, Robin Hood (Kevin Costner).

Fifteen.
Prepping for the real world.
I read things like *On the Road*.
Here is what frightened me: my driving teacher, the Joker, dinosaurs.
Here is what I liked: English class, Rocky Horror, Robin Hood (Mel Brooks).

Seventeen.
The world was big.
Because I didn't have to use a stool to reach the sink.
Here is what frightened me: changes, the future, dinosaurs.
Here is what I liked: Robin Hood (BBC), House, dinosaurs.

Brooke Mulica, Grade 12
Chatfield High School, CO

I've Made It

Walking on this stormy beach
Thunder, lightning, rain and wind.

Trying to push forward,
Fighting the breeze and downpour.

They're trying to force me back,
But I want to continue on this path.

Sinking in the muddy sand,
Frightened by the rolling thunder.

I manage to dig my way out
And battle the brutal squall.

Pushing myself, forcing myself onward,
Thinking I will never make it.

As soon as all hope was nearly lost,
The sweet sun pierces through the dark clouds
And encases me.

I've made it…

Margaret Preece, Grade 12
Kentlake High School, WA

Return to Me

"To seek but not find,
that is the most horrible of all heartache."

I know it's in your eyes,
the love we once surmised,
but before I search for long
I'm reminded that I'm wrong.

Staring at our portrait,
It's obvious where you should sit.
I squint to see your face,
but am left without a trace.

In your embracing shape,
I can feel the love escape.
Not knowing what is wrong,
I weep, for it has gone.

I excitedly pace the floor
to see you smiling at the door.
But as the hours passed,
I knew that smile had been your last.

Elisha Odegard, Grade 11
Kentridge High School, WA

Winter's Frigid Path

Long is the walk down winter's frigid path.
Frozen limbs hang withered,
The pulse of Earth stops.
Cold and dark it is to bear life
Alone.
Pains and sorrows harder
Than the earth under foot.
Serene is the snow
That falls with my tears.
Here my heart will die,
Longing for the warmth of spring.

Matthew Wimett, Grade 12
Southridge High School, WA

Hurt

Can you see the hurt I feel?
The nervous laugh or sex appeal?
I hate my body, the way it looks
I hate where I am
And what I've done
The world moves on from time to time
I just want to be near you one last moment
Can you see the tears streaming down my face?
Am I supposed to be here
Or am I just misplaced?
I love my dad and my mom
I can't wait to see them
Once again to show them my life
How much I've conquered
and come through the years
I know they would be so proud
of the life I changed and started to live
the moments forgotten
the times engaged
I love to see the smile
wiped on His sweet face

Jenna Hawkins, Grade 11
Abundant Life Academy, UT

A Thanksgiving Thanks

Dear soldier,
I am writing to you,
To thank you for all that you do,
It doesn't matter if you are from the future, present or past
It doesn't matter if you fought,
In the Revolutionary, Civil or any other war,
As you fought for America,
Justice, safety and rights
I thank you now dear soldier,
Today I remember you all,
Especially you who are fighting today,
For me who you've never seen,
You are my heroes,
Men or Women,
It's all the same as you fight,
For the Land of the Free.

Kaci Oestman, Grade 10
Wray High School, CO

Mother to Daughter

I though I told you to clean your room!
Now you can't go out
You're grounded for a week
And you better get it cleaned
I told you two days ago to clean it
And it's still a mess

Dirty clothes everywhere,
Empty soda cans thrown around,
Bed's not made.
I'm not going to tell you again
Get this room cleaned now

Kim Cox, Grade 12
Buhl High School, ID

Death Holds No Sway

Death holds no sway
For love is here to stay
Spirited blissfully to a place
Not so far in space
Where time has no meaning

It is in this place
I see the beauty and grace
Of my love's face reflected
In cool waters still protected
By our affection

Here all the fear
Begins to disappear
Love has cast out
Death's whispers' inspired doubt
Replacing it with warmth of hope

Orchid Petals fall all around
Hearts that were lost are found
In this peaceful glade
Eternal love is made

Zach McNair, Grade 11
Fossil Ridge High School, CO

Someday You Will

My fragile blossom
Someday you will grow wings
And fly away

My delicate angel
Someday your mold will grow too tight
And melt away

My gentle child
Someday you will leave me
And travel with golden wings

Molly Shepherd, Grade 11
Warrenton High School, OR

The Untouched Mind

Within a lagoon,
Bold warnings and romantic lyrics.
A wild curse, a mystical rainbow
Above a mountain
Mask the vast desires roaring in life.
Danger conspires in wild chaotic dreams,
But dreams of children,
Uncursed, content with heaven.

Kyle Houghtaling, Grade 12
Flathead High School, MT

Best Friends

Best friends forever is what we said.
Then you moved away and we lost connection.
But six years later I met you again.
Not knowing who you were or each other's past.
Not knowing we were friends before until we talked.
We became best friends again
We promised each other we wouldn't leave until 2010.
Hanging out every weekend, through rough times and easy times
We were there for each other
Those were the best of times.
All through middle school we were inseparable. Until that day you had to leave.
I remember you coming to my house crying.
I asked what was wrong, but you couldn't answer.
You finally looked at me and said I am sorry I have to leave,
Even though we promised.
We cried together, we hugged each other, we said our goodbyes
Neither one of us wanted to but we did
I understand why but I wish you were here by my side
I miss you and love you
You will always be my best friend.

JaLene Dunn, Grade 10
Oak Harbor High School, WA

My Love

My memories of long ago and your cologne are sleeping
in my thoughts of you, full of tenderness,
my love.
My eyes have seen the light, the light within you,
the light which caresses the earth from the windows of your eyes,
my love.
My dreams of you shine in a sea of stars
and the moon sings your name in the still of night,
my love.
My tears of joy weep for the time
that we will be together again,
just you and I,
my love.
My love,
you are locked away in my memory,
your name locked away in the moon;
your shining light locked away in the sun,
your heart is locked away in mine.
I dream of you and only you,
my love.

Jennifer Saunders, Grade 10
Fremont High School, UT

Love

Love is when you truly care for a certain person.
It's someone tenderly touching another person's heart.
Adoration is like a soft glowing variety of colors in a sunset
always changing and always new.
Love is the words the heart can't say.
Adoration blooms new each and every day.
Love is a sun shining brightly each day.
The heart thumps loudly with joy when it's in love.
Love is a pure, graceful, white dove.
Love comes in and out of your life many times bringing different challenges.
Day after day I try to remember that specific sunrise but it's hard
to remember exactly what it looks like.
I wonder if I will ever feel that love again I have felt before.

Chelcee Judkins, Grade 10
Fremont High School, UT

I Am From

I am from multicolored nails to jingling earrings.
I am from old rebuilt muscle cars.
I am from the stereotypical life of a teenager.
I am from water tubing as the spray hits your face and knocks you off.
I am from the state below me — Cali, where I was born.
I am from my hard working mom, who struggles to cook steak right.
I am from my nose waking me up from the scent of bacon in the morning.
I am from late-night hangouts and sleep-in mornings.
I am from "I need a job, but I don't want to work here or there."
I am from the procrastinating gene of my father.
I am from the summer's sun's kiss on my cheeks — freckles.
I am from Portland, my city life that I love.

Lisa Hill, Grade 12
Parkrose High School, OR

His Eyes, His Name…Him

Made my veins hollow and took the wind from me,
Feeling inhuman stripped all calmness from me, deep in my stomach — you're so worthy…
Freedom is a must, words spoken suddenly, presented as a gift but wasn't lovely;
don't confuse strangeness with ugliness,
Trusting in certain witnesses,
Speaking of prisms — mental prisons proceed,
Calmly awaiting someone to lead, but be as it be, the scum sticks on the wake, attaching itself to metal framed snakes.
Grinding it's way through, peace found in deep wounds; alien being naturally misconstrued
Uncertain of most, the down fallen creed, three is fine but two is all one needs —
be as it may and be as it be,
the depth in which was glorified was beyond me.
Frozen in place — the silk words of art, never got the chance, insertion of too much thought.
That left me gasping collecting breath, and thoughts
State of mind, peace of mind, late, gone and lost
If I had a price, guaranteed no cost
The freedom of insanity is never a lot,
Locked away — the best of damaging thoughts,
Sealed in a room, wrapped in our mental box.
So decorated, scattered in vacant lots
Remembering to forget that sweet pungent loss…Tony.

Tia Wright, Grade 12
Delta Charter Cyber School, AK

What Is So Wrong?

What is so wrong,
In this off beat song?
Could it be the cheating lovers,
Or the overbearing mother?
The never ending liars
And their eyes of burning fire.
Maybe the death and remorse,
You're only listening by force.
I wish I had a reason for this,
This never ending list.
Of all the imperfections and flaws,
And the unsheathed claws.
I'm sad to say I do not,
Even after all the wars we fought.
Can you please tell me what is so wrong,
In this off beat song?
Then again, it could just be you,
And you know this, too.

Rose Barnett, Grade 10
Mingus Union High School, AZ

Ravens on My Lidded Screens

Dreams pass me by in scenes,
Ravens on my lidded screens,
Shadows black within the waiting,
Lids shut against the fading.
Painted rice paper o'er my eyes,
Promises lift and then to lie.
Caught in a leftover hunger,
For dreams that pull me under
The tide of apathetic regard
For the nights that fell apart.
Frightening in the premise,
A life yet beyond this.
Closed eyes to cautious dreams,
Ravens on my lidded screens.

Danielle Curson, Grade 12
North Idaho Christian School, ID

Ocean

Shiny as a diamond at morning
Color as blue as the sky
Looks so wonderful but harmful
Can't control, can't be changed
Ocean is about waves and sounds.
When you look at the ocean
You never want to leave
Waves come and are gone
If you have ever been to the ocean
Just stay and hear the waves
The sounds of waves
The sound of nature
An amazing place in the world.

Tung Duong, Grade 12
Granite High School, UT

Cries of the Children

The children cry
From the sounds of silent screams
That always seemed to fall on deaf ears.

The children bleed
From insignificant beatings from a parent
That always seemed to never have an end.

The children are broken
From the battering and the rape; the molesting
That came after every poison their father consumed.

The children are trapped
In bottles of alcoholic pains, a sorrow no one ever realizes
And the wallpaper that no one has a chance to taste, it's bitter.

The children have no words,
But I hear their desperations to find a better purpose
To live without being lost in fear
To believe in the impossible and to rise above it all.

If there is just one thing in this world that I could do or to change,
I would take these children and allow them the chance to feel worth living —
I believe this is my purpose because I've been there before.

Destiny Sadler, Grade 12
Granite High School, UT

Cuzco

The sun burns over the city of old, it sits in the great mountains shadow,
Cross roads of two great empires, the history, war and conquest repeated,
A testimony to mans' success and failure. Cuzco, the city of many generations;
The symbol of glory for generations, embedded in the statues and ruins of old,
A cry to never succumb to failure, Cuzqueneans live in the ancient shadow,
Hoping for history to be repeated, lingering ambition of the empires,
The descendants dream of the old empires, to make one for future generations,
Yet working to stop mistakes, never repeated; hatred, sorrow, regret, love of old;
The haunting past hides in the shadow, never forgetting the defeat and failure,
A young boy works to not be a failure, remembering the glories of the empires,
Enchanted by their ancient long shadow, the legacy of many generations,
And the ancient wisdom of old, destroyed and rebuilt, history repeated;
A child's ambition, again repeated; refusing to be another failure,
Never forgetting the success of old, walking on cold remains of old empires,
Cold remains taunting generations, cold stone remains, with a taunting shadow;
Where there was once glory, only a shadow; its taunting will forever be repeated,
Touching and affecting all generations, reminding them, always of their failure;
Reminding them, of dead empires; and the long dead taunting emperors of old,
Old history wishing to be repeated,
The dark shadow echoing, taunting, failure;
An empire calling to all generations

Gabriel McKern, Grade 10
Grant Union High School, OR

If I Were a Book

If I were a book,
your hate would fill my pages
If I were a book,
my pain would be the ink
If I were a book,
my fake smile would be the cover
If I were a book,
my fear would be the binding
Some may say that I'm a bad book.
You know what they do with bad books?

— They edit them until they get better.

Ali Henry-Brown, Grade 10
Pomona High School, CO

Addiction

You think that you own me,
You think that you can boss me around,
You think that you can tell me who to be,
You think that I will listen to your sound.
But you also know the truth.
You know that you have no control over me,
You know that I am just in my youth.
But you don't seem to care what I know to be,
You still attempt to take control.
Well let me tell you something,
You can give up because you are already in a hole,
You can stop trying,
You will never have the power.
You may be able to control others with just a tug,
But not me, not in this hour.
I am my own drug,
And I don't need any other.

Kristi Walker, Grade 10
Pueblo County High School, CO

I Am

I am someone who feels pain.
I often wonder why I feel this way.
I hear laughter but cannot understand it.
I see into people's hearts.
I want to pull their happiness into me.

I pretend that nothing is wrong.
I feel like no one will understand.
I touch the darkest place in my soul.
I worry that people will see right through my tough exterior.
I cry alone.
I am someone who feels pain.

I understand that life is priceless, but hard.
I say life is difficult, but worth it.
I dream of the day the pain subsides.
I try to put it behind me and keep moving forward.
I hope that I will get through this.
I am someone who feels pain.

Alysa Larsen, Grade 12
Oakley Jr/Sr High School, ID

Cry, Baby, Cry

There is a lie within each line.
What's true to me, is not.
Every time you say that you are mine
I look in your eyes and you are caught.
It's no longer easy to hide.
If it was a length, it'd be a thousand feet wide.
You remind me of what it is like to hate.
You're thoughtless and in no position to dictate.
You've caused hatred to the one you love.
Just find me a hole and give me a shove.
Because of you, I believe no one; it's true
That everyone has something to hide from or to.
Forgiveness? I don't know if I can.
With all the crap you did, I regret being your fan.
Screams, shouts, our life crashes.
The warm fire that protected us has turned to ashes.
I want to undergo the truth.
No matter how spiteful and ruth.
It won't be long before I hear the next lie.
You tell me until then, just cry, Baby, cry.

Saphiya Hindeyeh, Grade 10
Sonoran Science Academy, AZ

School Day

Watching the clock click time away
Time I don't have to waste
Watching the hands spin round and round
Sitting anxiously for two o'clock
Daydreams of later on
Thoughts of the unknown
Thinking the day would never end
Every minute is another year
The loud clicks of the clock going round
Sitting and waiting
Every look seems to make it slower
Slower than before
Fast in unforgettable moments
But slow in the everlasting lectures
Seems to move one step at a time
Until, yet it's almost there
Almost time for me to leave
The day is finally done
Wondering what tomorrow brings

Chelsea Mangold, Grade 10
Chatfield High School, CO

The Time of Our Lives

Have you noticed since the beginning of time
We've been speculating about when it will end?
Most of our lives end before we figure it out.
Everyone seems to think it's going to happen in their lifetime —
Maybe it will this time…
Time gives all of us this built-in-notion that we
Are important in this existence.
And that notion's given us sociopaths-tyrants-wars
As well as philosophers, musicians, and poets.

Natasha Bennetts, Grade 12
LASER Alternative School, MT

The True Meaning

I hate you!
Sometimes there's days when I can't stand to be around you.
The things you do make me cringe.
I even have moments when it's hard to breathe.
I hate you because I love you with all my heart.
I can't stand to be around you because I can't have all of you.
You make me cringe because your knives shatter my heart and I can't stand the pain.
It's hard to breathe when you're near me because you take my breath away.
Your touch is frightening and your eyes are mysterious.
When you talk, it makes me cry and when you call, I just want to throw my phone at the wall.
Your touch makes me crumble and sends chills all over my body.
Your eyes;
I could get lost in them forever.
When you talk,
my heart melts all over again.
When you call,
I wish it was you in person I was talking to.
I hate how much
I love you!

Alesha Miller, Grade 11
Reed High School, NV

Misery

    I live in yesterday, while trying to figure out tomorrow, and at the same time I'm battling with complications of today I know that the past is history and the future is mystery that leaves me with the present, which just happens to be misery Right now I am at a point in my life where I know that everything is going down hill but I continue to create illusions in my mind to make everything seem all right so I can prevent myself from getting scared. But even in this fictional world inside my head I become scared. I become scared that in all this illusion making and make believe, I will lose control of my ability to look upon the world as just another part of my imagination and begin to look at the world as reality and myself as fantasy. Sometimes I feel as if I'm two parts connected to some kind of spiritual adhesive. The adhesive consisting of only my will to hold onto my remaining sanity, and me eventually wanting something better in my life than what I know now.

Manuel Hernandez, Grade 11
Eagle Point School, AZ

Bus Stop

Fly me to the moon.
There is no moon.

She should have brought another coat.
The cruel April wind pierces the stillness, rattling the rubbish across remote Highway 63.
She waits on the splintered bench, wrapping the baby in her sweater.
The dark rises. The shadows fall.

Let me play among the stars.
There are no stars.

It should have turned left at the crossroads.
The metal beast lumbers off-course while its disreputable cargo slumbers. Driver realizes,
Keeps driving. Next stop, Memphis. Budding trees, unnoticed, leafless in the gloom.

Let me see what spring is like on Jupiter and Mars.
There is no spring.

Blackness would suffocate her except for that streetlight.
Except for that streetlight. She waits in silence like the night.
There is no moon. There are no stars. There is no spring for her.
The dark engulfs. The shadows fall.

Lyndsey Romick, Grade 12
Grants Pass High School, OR

Lasting Memories

I look out over the ocean
The white foam crashing on the shore
The cold, wet sand fills the vacant spaces between my toes
The warm wind softly blows
My long, red dress sways…

The sun slowly sets in the distance
Colors blending together in splendor
The colors bring up memories
Red, yellow, orange
Love, friendship, happiness…

Standing there, reminiscing,
I smell cologne mixed with salt water
I feel his strong arms
They wrap around me

Standing there in the dark, blue night
I feel peace, comfort and deep joy
Knowing that we must make memories for another day,
We walk away into the blissful unknown

Lytaunie Blasdel, Grade 12
Flathead High School, MT

Plane Ride

Waiting a lifetime
To board the flight
Groans begin to increase
Then flight 268 was called
Handing the plane ticket
To the lady in blue
In hopes to have a normal passenger next to you
Sitting for five hours sinks in
Wondering if it will feel like forever
Or be only a brief moment
That first step brings sorrow
Antsy
Row 26 Seat B
Scrimmaging through
Taking a seat brings a sigh of relief
Laying against the head rest
Closing eyes begin to wander in thought
The motion of the plane soothes
Time ticks away
The ding announces the arrival
Waking up happy to take a step onto land once again

Michelle Hansen, Grade 12
Chatfield High School, CO

Harvest Magic

H ollow trees may lose their leaves
A s autumn breezes bluster through.
R ust-colored sun, the day is done,
V alley myths perform for you.
E erie music lights the air, the stars are shining bright…
S pirits all dance, come take the chance;
T he Harvest Moon is out tonight.

Cynthia Jensen, Grade 12
St Marys High School, CO

The Raging Waters of Love

Love is like a stream as it flows gently
The water runs swift over the rock bed
The stream starts to grow like my love for thee
My heart grows heavy like it's made of lead
The water becomes a little river
The river is soft but can turn forceful
I ponder of you so much I shiver
I know you love me, too, so I'm thankful
As our love grows the river turns raging
Rumbling along it picks up more speed
I love you always, even when aging
I know I can't live without my true need
The river is sweet like my love for you
The river will always be there, love too.

Cody Hosler, Grade 12
Flathead High School, MT

The Hills

The hills feel like a haven that I can go to
The hills feel like a soft place of hope
The hills taste like a pine tree in winter
The hills taste like hamburgers and barbecue chips
The hills smell like dirty creek water
The hills smell like fresh new air
The hills sound like four wheelers going down the road
The hills sound like laughter from the campfire
The hills look like beauty in their own
The hills look like non-washed days
The hills are my sanctuary…a safe place to go
The hills are happiness on my face
The hills are a song in my heart
The hills is where I truly belong

Laci Powell, Grade 10
Grant Union High School, OR

Emma

E very day I'm waiting.
M ore, more I get excited
M om gets bigger
A pril is our due month.

M y heart can't wait no more.
A girl is on the way.
R ight now I'm writing this poem for her.
I n seven weeks she will be here.
E veryone can't wait.

C ounting the days as they pass by.
E very day gets closer.
R eady or not here she comes.
V iolet might be her favorite color.
A nd a dog she will play with and grow with.
N ext step is the hospital.
T ime is here.
E verything is going to be fine.
S eeing Emma will be the happiest day of my life.

Ignacio Cervantes, Grade 12
Pioneer High School, NV

Grandfather

My Grandfather,
The peacemaker of my family.
Yes, he's old,
Gray Hair,
Wrinkled skin,
But he never gives up.

Oh, the joy he brings into my life.
The memories I have had with him,
I will never forget.
Sitting on his lap,
While he told me stories.
His loving hugs,
Oh, so warming.
His advice,
"Never get old."
He always makes me laugh.

Haylee Lund, Grade 11
Madison Sr High School, ID

Black-Eyed Peace

Peace is a flock of birds.
The togetherness of all,
It shapes the world.
Use your imagination to
See things others can't
and take a stand.
Be the leader,
Make us one again,
Bring the love back.

Mariah Koontz, Grade 10
Oak Harbor High School, WA

Camping

My tent faces toward
The center of camp
Where flames dance
In the rock circle.
Fragrant smells of wood
And bacon draw me from the tent.
Family and friends gather
To devour the great feast.
Our hunger has been relieved
Boating begins.
Crystal water draws me
To the rocky bank of a lake
The boat is swaying on the waves and
Begging me to board.
We glide across the silvery lake
With sunshine on our backs.
They toss the tube over the side
And jump aboard
For a glorious ride.

Blain Wyss, Grade 11
Temple Baptist Academy, NM

Rain

A cold, calm, caress
Drops as soft as cotton
The scent of earth's new beginnings
Its taste that of succulent Fijian papayas
Millions of teardrops fall from God's eyes
The beauty of His tears brings life to everything
The soft pitter-patter on the tin roof lulls me to sleep
As the world bathes itself in glory.

Kai Olivia Atkinson, Grade 11
Preston High School, ID

Unconditional

You give your finger,
So he can keep his.
You give your hand,
So he can keep using his to cause harm.
You give your arm,
So he can keep fighting on the wrong side.
You give your foot,
So he can stand with them.
You give your leg,
So he can run with evil.
You give your heart that loves only one,
So his evil black heart can beat once more.
You give all that's left of your soul,
So he can live forever, causing harm to the world you love so much.
You give up your life,
So he can have a chance to change.
You give him more time,
So that he can ask for forgiveness.
You give all you've got,
So he can finally see how much you care for him.

Amereece Sterba, Grade 10
Show Low High School, AZ

Death of an Innocent

I went to a party, Mom, I remember what you said.
You told me, no alcohol, Mom, so I drank soda instead.
I really felt proud inside, Mom, the way you said I would.
I didn't drink and drive, Mom, even though the others said I could.
I did the right thing, Mom, I know you are always right.
The party is ending, Mom, and everyone is driving out of sight.
I got into my car, Mom, I knew I would get home in one piece.
The way you taught me, Mom, safe, responsible and sweet.
I started to drive away, Mom, pulling on to the road in driving rain.
The other car didn't see me, Mom, it hit me like a train.
As I lay on the pavement, Mom, I hear the policeman say,
"The other guy is drunk," but Mom, I am the one who will pay.
I lay here dying, Mom, I hope you get here soon.
How could this happen to me, Mom, my life burst like a balloon.
There is blood all around me, Mom, all of it is mine.
I heard the medic say, Mom, "She will die in a short time."
I just wanted to tell you, Mom, I swear I didn't drink.
It was the others, Mom, the others didn't think.
He was probably at the same party as I.
The only difference, Mom, is he drank and I will die.

Jessica Eiffert, Grade 11
Omak High School, WA

Source of Infection

Steady heartbeat
As feet pound against the pavement
Nothing but your tears
And your unsettling secrets

Pushing everything to the extreme
Your feet begin accelerating
Needing to scream
But the silence is too sickening

Falling further from the perfection that grows
Falling away from the person they used to know
Bottling the emotions of a faulty life
Leads to the collapse of the child inside

Collapsing at the source of infection
Tears drench your face
As you hope for her resurrection
For no one can take her place

Emily Stickel, Grade 10
Freeman High School, WA

Angel of Death

Angel of Death dances across the evening sky
bringing darkness as it goes by,
flickering lights of impending doom,
give the feeling, your time will end soon
light of mercy, shadow of death
fighting to take over your last breath
Angel flees from the approaching light,
takes off on its final flight.
Whether you live, or whether you die,
depends upon that Angel in the dark, dark sky.

Katie Hunkele, Grade 12
Paradise Valley High School, AZ

Tears from the Sun

It's when you slam against the wall,
But when you try and climb it,
Your hand and foot holds fail and you slip and fall.
It's the tears from the sun,
But when they fall they weigh a ton.
It's the feeling of slipping and falling,
That never stops.
When you seek another place
To find joy.
But it's just an aspiration in my imagination
It's my own rain cloud that never ceases,
But only increases.
It's like the tears from the sun,
But when they fall they weigh a ton.
It's the battle of David and Goliath,
But Goliath always wins.
It's how a fire starts up,
But is blown out and all that's left is smoke.
It's the tears from the sun,
But when they fall they weigh a ton.

Kyle Wheeler, Grade 10
Fremont High School, UT

The Shadows of Hope

The dreams we have may never be fulfilled
For the battle we endure may never be enough.
Like an eagle soaring away from home,
We fight for the dream to withhold our new hope.
Every trial has a fear that needs faced
For the shadows of our hope are always near.
As we scan the shadows it finally becomes clear.
That to reach our dreams we must face our fears.
As the wind howls our name,
A window of opportunity opens.
Every new day has a story ready to unfold
But the pen is in your hands.
For fate waits for no one
And no one sees the beauty of it all
Fate won't wait to realize your dreams
It's now or never and today's the day.
For in times to come
Hope will only be a leap away
So begin, begun, believe, become.

Kylee Searle, Grade 10
Shelley Sr High School, ID

Lov'd Hate

'Twas the pain bear'd in oneself,
The torture of love and hate.
The burning element
That causes satisfaction now in crate.
'Tis the madness lingering on,
Like a coward on a limb,
When the pleasure is long gone,
All that's left is a foolish numb.

O 'tis the foe,
The cyclone of image.
Shot with a bow!
'Tis the living rage.
Virtually no hope within the heart,
'Til the chest inflames
With longing desires.
Suffocating until the compassion erupts from strain.

The blood thick with hindering love.
'Twas passionate hate compiling above.

Tammy Vu, Grade 12
Parkrose High School, OR

Be Yourself

It does not matter what you wear
Or the way you do your hair
We change our clothes each and every day
It does not matter what people say

Be yourself! That's who you are
Shine bright, like a shooting star
On yourself you must always rely
This will give your dreams the wings to fly.

Melissa Seamons, Grade 11
Preston High School, ID

50 Stars and 13 Stripes
Fifty stars and thirteen stripes
What a beautiful sight!
Solid and bright
Red, white and blue
This wavy material soars in the wind
Until the very end
Fifty stars and thirteen stripes
What a beautiful sight!
Britnee Piersol, Grade 10
Valley Christian Secondary School, WA

Speech
With words that wink,
Whistling words.
Words that waste,
Watching time.

Working words with woozy
Wooer eyes.
Words working woodman,
Chopping away.

Withdrawn words withering away
With time.
Words in wind,
Blowing silence.

A wink in time,
Words bustling with chime,
Speaking life.
Melissa M., Grade 11
Diamond Ranch Academy, UT

Friday Night Lights
There is a special time of year
It is a season of cheer
High School Football has begun
Everyone has a lot of fun
Any given week
When the outcome is bleak
Through scoff and scorn
True champions are born
Through blood sweat and tears
They conquer their fears
Together as a team
They can realize a dream
Any given night
The game is sure to be a fight
There surely are beautiful sights
When they turn on Friday Night Lights
Chase Hanson, Grade 10
Shelley Sr High School, ID

What Do I Do?
What do I do when you tell me to go away?
What do I do when you say you can't stay?
What do I do when you tell me "You don't want me?"
What do I do when you say, "We cannot be?"
What will she say if I tell her, "Not to go on that bus?"
But what do we do when no one will accept us?
I'm so confused I can't quite concentrate
Could this really be our disastrous fate?
Gabe White, Grade 10
Arrow High School, UT

O' Captain My Captain
You get what you get, because you make what you get,
   A promise is a choice that balances life to fit,
Ridiculous matters matter only when you express,
   Express the because and how you hate the (triple) XXX…

Life without warning is life with regret,
   Conceded minds confuse the pride within…
Professional success happens only when you succeed,
   Good dreams happen quickly when your heart never leaves…

And a few words could be a zillion pictures,
   And after-party-proms can make your eyes glitter,
And a rumor-seeing-person rumors his drama far behind,
   And hurt-hearts bring sorrow through empty lives…

But if you don't care, won't listen, please wisdom this,
   You got to precious life because life is not granted to you…
A life without a window, and a Christmas tree without some lights…
   Is like light invisible to those Las Vegas lights…
Donavan Hicks, Grade 11
Douglas County High School, CO

A Hundred and Twenty M.P.H.
From start to finish,
From Miracle Mile to Sunset Road,
120 mph.
Entering the freeway as if the last one to get there loses five grand.
The sound of the roaring Prelude was like thunder
The Lancer had little chance to win
Moving as fast as the speed of light past the slow-traveling cars
The adrenaline rush was a burst of energy moving through our bodies
Half way through the race we hit 120 mph.
I grabbed my seat that felt like a head of hair,
My heart thumping as fast as a rabbit's foot
For a second I thought I was at a gas station because of the burning gas
Passing El Camino Del Cerro, we were sure to win the race
The speed that we were traveling, made the other cars
Seem like little bugs heading the same direction as we were
The excitement about the thought of winning the race was over-fulfilling.
Finally getting ready to get off the freeway and end the race,
Suddenly the sun yellow Lancer
Makes a daring move, cutting us off plus two other cars to win.
Clenching my teeth with anger I know that we
Would have won in a straight away.
Shawndel Patula, Grade 12
Presidio High School, AZ

The Men
The wars, the droughts, immeasurable pain
Bring forth the most memorable names.
Prestigious figures are sealed in time
To stand inside the lights of lime.
But glory lies in untold tales,
Their work demurred by hidden veils.
The average joe's whom we ignore
Are those, in truth, we should adore.
Our doctors, teachers, soldiers, priests
Work beneficial wonders each.
These men whose lives are legends lost
Are those who are most tempest tossed.
The men who stand on weary feet
Are those who stand as the elite.
Those unsung heroes never fail
To topple foes that n'er prevail.
Our mothers, fathers, siblings, too
Come forth to do all they can do.
When its struggles life will send
They do their best to problems mend.
These are the men.

Chris Barfuss, Grade 10
Minico Sr High School, ID

Paradise
What a wondrous sight to be hold
A lad of marvel and beauty so bold
Such arrogance whispered in the air
Because most people don't believe and care

A magnificent state of mind
To come through every time
Come with me and I'll show you this amazing place
A never ending fantasy that has been made

Take a look at the endless river of dreams
And the vast plains as they seem
The skies filled with bundles of white cotton
And structures of creativity that seem like nothing

Would you want these visions to end?
That won't happen as long as you believe you'll be sent
So just try and you'll surely end up in paradise

Alex Cortes, Grade 10
Dobson High School, AZ

Standing Tall
Movement beneath, pushing, pushing.
Sprout breaking through, growing, growing.
Petals spreading, blooming, blooming.

Snow is falling, weighting, weighting.
Flower drooping, waiting, waiting.

Burden melting, freeing, freeing.
Flower rising, reaching, reaching.
Facing the sun, praising, praising.

Rachel Sanford, Grade 12
Kentlake High School, WA

Day by Day
Early morning light
Live through the day
Come what may
Now time for fall of night
Day by day it's all the same

Friend and foe
They come and go
Family is always there
Aware they always care
Day by day it's all the same

It's funny how day by day it's all the same
But now I'm looking back it's all different.

Summer Larson, Grade 10
Fremont High School, UT

Isolation
I am content.
My hermitage suits me well.
My only concern is myself,
I need not worry about any other.

I am content.
My friendless life is happy.
I know none of a friend's sorrow or pain,
His troubles I need not comfort.

I am content. Yet —
Is ignorance of grief and pain
Worthy of the loss of a friend's laugh,
A hug, or a joyous tear?

I think perhaps —
I am content. I am content.

Hannah Jones, Grade 11
Grace Baptist School, UT

The Best Is Yet to Be
On your joyful wedding day,
You begin a brand new life
Friends and family give great gifts
To the joyful husband and his glamorous wife.

But, the greatest gift you'll get
Is the one that lasts forever
The one that only God can give
It is your life you make together.

You'll share life's miracles
And happy memories will fill the mind
But the real treasure you get
Is a life together that has no end.

You cannot see it now or tomorrow,
But over time you will see,
That the best is yet to be.

Hailey Phelps, Grade 10
Blackfoot High School, ID

Track

Bang! The gun goes off.
Runners run 'round the corner.
Pick up the pace.
My legs are raging like a fire.
One lap completed, pick up the pace.
My legs are Jell-O.
Pushing it to the limit.
I'm approaching the finish.
The crowd is cheering.
Finally, I have reached my destination.

Jonathan Spencer, Grade 10
Fremont High School, UT

A Trip into Mystery

A picturesque railroad
Emerges from the sea,
While dark, menacing clouds
Loom above.

A pearly-white castle
Stands in the far,
Watching the dark, misty waters
From the rugged cliff tops.

A makeshift sail stands
Erect upon an old railcar.
The cliffs lure it in…

Three young boys
And a girl
In search of adventure…
In search of mystery.

Calder Morrison, Grade 12
Flathead High School, MT

Gish

The Gish and his blade
Dance, kiss and fade
Cursing the crescent orb
Consume but not absorb

Dreaming of the frost unknown
Words without sparks are sown
To maidens whose ears are deaf
Pining with lips to be blessed

Choosing what was said
Living without a head
Dressed in human skin
But not of mortal kin

Happy to be windswept
Not begging to be kept
The breeze is oft tossed
Only beauty is ever lost

Steven Gubka, Grade 12
Gilbert High School, AZ

More or Less Just Lore and a Mess

There is more for you in another possibility
It might be more appealing
For more is meaning, more is everything
But amidst this more of more I must digress
Because I can because I am
I am more like all the rest
I as this creation am creativity
Another deviation between an unfaltering God
And Lucifer's deviating audacity
I am meaning. I am beauty that is more
I am the more that is shelter from the storm
I am more, the metaphor, whatever form
Receive me more to perpetuate the storm
I am the cynicism between and also the core of the meaning and the more
Because more and more all this meaning has shown
In actuality, I am just lines in a poem
Some words composed of letters
Symbols strung together in light for your eyes and your brain to see
I am your thoughts and living consciousness for this moment
As I am you for this moment, and you are me.
What's More? Everything and that question is all.

Aaron Schrag-Toso, Grade 12
Tucson Magnet High School, AZ

Let Me Let You Go

i want to just make You go away
but You don't want to leave.
i want to take this pain away
but You keep comin' back to me.

why can't You just let it fade away
into the background of my mind.
want to make this all just disappear
and make You hard to find

but no matter how far i push You
i find You again inside my head.
and when i try to let You go
You come closer still, instead.

i guess You're never goin'
no matter how hard i try.
i don't know why i bother
tryin' to make myself look sly.

even if i try to hide it
we both know that it's true.
the reason i can't let You go,
is simply 'cause i love You.

Kirsten Rivera, Grade 10
Northern Utah Academy for Math, Engineering and Science (NUAMES), UT

The Second Star to the Right

I had always been skeptical, now my knowledge has been changed.
Today I saw a fairy and I'll never be the same.
My opinion to that day, had been all black and white.
Till I noticed that small fairy, changing all the light.
She stared at me as I stared at her, thru the camera glass.
No one has ever told me that they exist, but now I know for sure at last.
Soon after I had a conversation, with this fairy girl.
I learned many things including that her name was Pearl.
I learned that her land, was a flight without plight.
It was that little island, located by the Second Star to the Right.
That Pearl was a beauty, of a miniature sort.
And now I'm sailing to her land, and grounding in her port.

Temperance Davis, Grade 12
Oakley Jr/Sr High School, ID

A Handful of Meaning

Dazed I stand
Wishing and wanting to grasp a handful of meaning
While everything around me is breaking, not mending
Fear begins to slowly trickle down my spine
Ahead a ghostly forgotten path calls to me with solemn yearning
Hesitantly I step into its cold harsh shadows
With my steps becoming quicker and my breathing shallow
I think I'm almost out, I'm almost there
My heart rate becomes unthinkable, and my mind's gears freeze
The hallow lifeless trees I pass become as the storm clouds above me
As I finally reach the end, there lies a fire burning
The piercing orange radiates into my icy brittle bones
As I restlessly lay down, into a hard fast sleep
Just wishing to grasp a single handful of meaning

Megan Tutt, Grade 10
Fremont High School, UT

The Man Who Became a Wolf

The moon was full and high, the night was cold and still.
But there was a strange and eerie feeling close by — as a change in the wind caused a foreign sensory response.

The man was swerving with dizziness and pain. The forest was dark and he was alone.
It felt like he was dying in the heavy rain. His body was changing into what the had most feared.

It began in his frightened, terrified eyes, which changed from calm, sky blue to tortured, blood red.
His spine expanded three times its size — as the man evolved into a large and vicious beast.

His feet and hands grew massive in a scary way, his nails became sharp claws.
The man's skin changed to fur, dark gray — the beast was showing himself.

The wolf's teeth grew long and razor-like — same a that of a hunter's dagger.
His tail grew long and his ears were spiked, the change was nearly complete.

The mind of the man was replaced — with that of a ferocious wild beast.
His unquenchable hunger was unmatchable faced — with his yearning for his first kill.

As he stood on his enormous hind paws, and looked at the bright, full moon.
His blood curdling howl was heard and caused — shivers of fear through those who witnessed his cry.

Jed Aldous, Grade 10
Fremont High School, UT

Fall
The leaves start shaking
As gusting winds sting the branches
Fall is soon to come

Cameron Lee Rounds, Grade 11
Preston High School, ID

Reasons for Love
Everyone's reasons for love
Seem to be void of
Common logic and reason
Like a changing season
A heart can waver
Break and show disfavor
Usually mine finds a flaw
A reason for it to withdraw
But now I've found someone
Who I need more then the sun
Someone distant and far
Like a burning star
She spins my head like a top
Emotions come to a full stop
My heart skips in its beat
For the words ever so sweet
Just for those three words
I feel like a flying bird
And while it seems I'm lost
And I know that it will cost
There are no words so true, as I Love You

Chris Kieling, Grade 12
Vancouver Home Connection, WA

Tortured
I don't want to cry.
I don't want to cry.
I feel like a tree.
Tortured from the wind.
As if there is no light.
On the other end.

I feel alone.
I feel alone.
No one is here to save me.
I have no place to run.
I have no place to hide.
My head's all unspun.

I want to leave.
I want to leave.
I need to find a way.
A way out of this horrible place.
The wind is yelling for me.
I need a way to hide my face.

Karlee Meikle, Grade 10
Shelley Sr High School, ID

Secret Moment
Early morning dew still clings to the bright blades of grass
The small meadow is quiet this morning
Only the soft bubbling of the brook can be heard
Everything is waiting for something
The sun has not even awakened fully
Just a few early rays peek over the horizon
The scolding of a squirrel suddenly shatters the silence
But from out of the shadows step a doe and her new fawn

Kristin Alder, Grade 11
Preston High School, ID

To the Dad I Don't Know
Dad, you left me when I was young and you never said goodbye
I didn't know what to do so all I did was cry.

I went to a place I didn't know I was scared and alone
I couldn't talk to you not even on the phone.

You had to do your things and come home all high
I wish Mom would have left you all she had to do was say "good bye."

Because of you I am where I am living a new life away from you
Now you write me letters saying you miss me
But I never knew you, so how can I say I miss you too.

Dad, I don't know you I don't know you at all
I don't know what you look like are you short, or all you tall.

I have had a good life without you Dad but I wonder what it would be like
To have you as my father would I still have my expensive bike.

You tell me to write you more that you don't get much from me these days
But what did you ever give to me that's right, you gave me away.

Christopher J. Fasel, Grade 11
Union High School, OR

Life Goes On
The circle of life; the cycle of nature
It involves birth and death
In between the cycle, life exists
Life is grand
Earth can provide food and water
We benefit from Earth
You can say we are in an enclosure
Locked and trapped, only to die and no longer exist
The alternative approach could be
We live on a beautiful Earth with its natural wonders
You get old from living in this world for long years
Some have a happy life while others have traumatic lives
Whatever happens, life goes on and time never stops
You know that when your deathbed arrives,
Your guardian angel will be there for you
Walking off the face of Earth, you have a feeling you will never be alone
The circle of life will continue to go round
In nature you will be forgotten, but will always be
A part of the living forever.

Meijiao Jaehning, Grade 10
Oak Harbor High School, WA

A Breath in the Air

Sand streams through my fingers.
Each grain falls to the ground
where it has been absorbing the energy of the sun
since before the creation of time.
I rub my cheek against the earth.
The sand molds to each curve of my body.
I lay.
A pile of dead weight.
Skin and bone.
Awaiting the moment
when the tide will creep up just far enough
to spill over my lifeless body.
The essence of my being,
for a flicker of time,
is free from that worldly cage.
My soul is swept up in the warm, salty breeze
and all that is me is dispersed into the air
where I float freely amongst sound, emotion, and belief.
I am only a breath in the air,
but I am finally whole.

Kaylee Collinson, Grade 12
Chatfield High School, CO

The Little Car That Couldn't

Fast as the falling snow on blanket'd towns,
Slow as the neighbors mow on fresh green grounds.
Cold as the gusty winds of ocean breath,
Hot as the glossy sun of deserts' death.
Thou hast died on me twice when in a lot,
Which is not nice when the engine's not hot.
Older than I, you are about to die,
If you die before your time I will cry.
Here and there you've driven me ev'rywhere,
As I wear you down I will start to care.
Your cracks constantly dribble black oil,
And my salty tears show you're not loyal.
You've trapped my passengers with no lock,
You smell like one very, dirty, old sock.
You keep my things moist in rainy weather,
Your seats are of stuff cheaper than pleather.
My love for you surpasses all your slips,
Until Dad gets me a Jag for new trips.

Brooke VanderHoogt, Grade 11
Vancouver Christian High School, WA

Little Pillow

Little pillow you help me fall asleep,
You bring me comfort when my dreams are deep.
I like to cuddle with you by my side,
With you from scary monsters I can hide.
You keep me warm and toasty in my bed,
And give me a place to lay down my head.
When I am sad you soak my salty tears,
My tears subside when I feel you are near.
Little pillow you are my best-est friend,
I can count on you 'til the very end.

Chryssa Meeker, Grade 11
Vancouver Christian High School, WA

Longings

I long to dance upon the face of the moon.
The softly glowing moondust
Will rise into the air with each step I take,
Sparkling, twirling, gliding,
With the stars as my audience.

I long to swim in the depths of the sun,
That warm, soothing, golden ball of fire,
Stroking through its molten surface. This is my desire:
To feel its heat melt away all my cares.

I long to catch a falling star,
To capture its rapture,
And hold it for awhile.
Then let it go, and watch it flutter away.

I long to sleep in the bellowing clouds,
And feel them envelop me, enfold me
In a cool, gentle embrace,
And fall deep, deep, deep into their welcoming arms.

Tiffani Allred, Grade 11
Viewmont High School, UT

My Love

I really do love him
He is everything I need and more
I would do anything for him
He is so easy to adore.

Having him in my life is the best
My future with him is so clear
He is better than all of the rest
Loving him comes with no fear.

Looking back I have no regrets
He is talented, smart, and has a great heart
He is cute, athletic, and driven
I knew I would love him from the start.

I could never explain it in words
That shows how much he truly means to me
He is so unique in every way
Life with him is so simple and carefree.

Amanda Arkulari, Grade 12
Chatfield High School, CO

The Horse Ride

The whispery winter wind
Sent chills down my spine
As the snow crunched under my feet
What a day for a ride!

As I reached the mountain peak
And stopped to take in the view
The beauty of the moment took my breath away.
What a day for a ride!

Joshua David Harper, Grade 11
Preston High School, ID

Sorry!
I really have to say: I'm sorry
For everything what happened that time
But you don't have to worry
It will never give again such a big crime!

For all the people who gave their lives
And their families who are still out there
We hold together to overcome that crises
We all know: life isn't always fair.

We can't change it anymore
What happened, happened…
But it gave something we fight for
That the dead will be remembered!

I really have to say: I'm sorry
But don't think all the Germans are lame
But you don't have to worry
All of us feel bad and live in shame!
Jonathan Zeuch, Grade 12
Madison Sr High School, ID

The Sky
So very blue
With clouds of white
Purple and orange
In the evening sky
With the stars of white
And the moon so bright
Till
Morning comes and
It happens all over again
Hannah Shephard, Grade 12
St. Francis of Assisi School, OR

Days Fade
The days quietly fade into nights
Without care
The suffocating air
Has disappeared
And in its place
Is the night's cool air
The days that were full of sun kissed fun
Turn into nights of
Porch swing laughter
And time seemingly stops
It doesn't matter if you are
Alone
With friends, family
Or even with that boy you just met
And whether tears fall
Or laughter rises
It's perfect
Casie Calzavara, Grade 12
Chatfield High School, CO

Ravens' Bane
Crows and ravens, with crystal eyes,
And sticky, red beaks, take wing and drift high.
The night seems like sunlight, when these deep shadows soar,
And the velvet moss shrivels at the sound of their roar.

The hills turn to slanting dunes, and the plains to empty deserts,
When upon a pale, lost boy the hunger of these dark eagles exerts.
Upon landing, the shrieking shadows shuffle to their prey,
And the youngling begs the heavens to bring the light of day.

Raven and crow, their sharp-taloned feet,
Tear into the ground in their yearning for fresh meat.
Sobs and tears are emitted from the child, trembling in the cold,
As the hissing birds prepare to peck at his heart, his gold.

But Alas! for the ravens and for the cackling crows,
That upon the distant horizon comes the white and lacy glow.
Of the dawn as it swallows up the shadows to make way for day,
And the ravens and the crows, now as fragile as shattered clay,

Screech and take flight, leaving the child speckled with sunlight.
And the boy — he runs so swiftly back to his home now bathed in light.
And the ravens and crows, in their deep loathing for light streaming,
Wait in the branches of the oaks, foaming and scheming.
Jonathan H. Cozzie, Grade 10
Alliance Charter Academy, OR

Lost in Memory
Why am I in this spot?
I might as well have gotten shot.
It's like I'm dying over and over again.
The thoughts that I'm thinking while I stay lost in memory.
I replay the yelling; I replay the fight, the crying, the hiding,
The drastic moments, embarrassments of the truth.
Shaken by shock; anger; starvation.
Pulled down by the pushing; hits like a soaring hawk.
The headaches, the pains, it's just the same.
Now I can barely rearrange this deranged life.
But like every war I must finish the fight.
But still at times I lose my sight.
Now everything seems to flow along with this poem,
That just magically rhymes,
But it was never meant to be. But sometimes I question,
Is what was never meant to be supposed to be? Or, that is shouldn't be?
If I'm suppose to be in this spot; that I might as well have gotten shot,
Because these memories are killing me, mentally, physically, and emotionally.
But still!
I'm glad I can still breathe,
While I stay lost, in my own memory.
Kristen Jean Casimier, Grade 10
Hinkley High School, CO

I Wish

I wish I could grow up without getting old;
I'd like a piano made purely of gold.

I wish I could climb a cloud into the sky,
Then I would jump off and learn how to fly.

I wish I could talk with the man in the moon,
I would like to sing him the loveliest tune.

I wish I could travel through time and through space —
I would have so much fun with life as a race!

I wish I could walk through a huge waterfall
Without getting wet — not even at all.

I wish I could pass my math test tomorrow,
So I won't have to worry, or be filled with sorrow.
Erica Ringen, Grade 11
Kamiah High School, ID

Good Morning Day

I wake up before sun rise to the smell of coffee
I take a hot shower for the soothing steam

I get dressed in Carhartts and boots
And I go downstairs for breakfast

"I wonder what's on the list for today," I ask myself
Grandma packs me a lunch and I go on my way

I go out to the barn to feed the animals
I do my jobs then go to school

I get home and wonder if I can go on with my jobs
But the Lord helps me get them done

Sometimes I think, "Is this a dream?" But it is not
And I wonder if I will be able to continue with my dream
But I know that I will be back on the farm soon
Colten S. Webber, Grade 12
Trask River High School, OR

America's Beginnings

The faithful few now stir from sleep to stand
Against the Union Jack's oppressive hand.
Ill fed, untrained, the wren against the hawk
But firm they stood and trusted in their rock.
Their rights now gone, the Whigs began to write
A letter that described their dreadful plight.
Their jealous monarch strove to quench the flame;
He'd teach those Whigs and save the kingdom's name.
So off he sent his English hordes to put
A chain of bronze around New England's foot.
Whigs hid, quite still, and aimed at British men;
Who never saw the motherland again.
  The English, blanching, bolted from the land;
  Our fathers rested free from George's hand.
Sarah Chaffee, Grade 10
Covenant High School, WA

I'm Sorry

I'm sorry I'm not everything
you expected me to be,
and I just hope someday
you'll be able to accept me for me,
I just wanted you to know,
that every single thing I do
I give my heart and soul,
and do everything just for you
it always seems I'm not good enough,
not good enough for you
because no matter what I do,
you always seem to disapprove,
I just wanted you to be proud,
and I wanted you to see
how hard I actually work for you,
sometimes you make me sad,
but sweetheart I love you,
and I just wanted to know
that you're proud and that you love me too.
Jordan Macedone, Grade 10
Orem High School, UT

Rain

Falling from the sky like pieces of pure heaven above
All the earth enveloped in the torrent
The miracle of pure sweet tasting moisture
Helping or hurting any it comes in contact with
Sometimes helping the farmers like no other could
With the water needed to forge bright new generations
Of farmers that love the rich land they live in.

Drip drop drip drop falling steadily
From the dark foreboding clouds never knowing
Where it might end up, like a sailor lost at sea on a cold night
Hoping it would be able to help some poor soul along the way
Still dripping again and again a fountain of lively droplets
Cascading down the ragged rocks and over the rough dirt
Always wondering where it is to end up.
Braeden Furgeson, Grade 10
Fremont High School, UT

A Love Not Worth It

Why did you leave me all alone in this
Big world of mine? My soul is a willow
Weeping, swaying. You stole away my bliss.
The tears I cry at night stain my pillow.
My love for you hasn't dwindled away.
When you left me you broke my heart in two.
You asked a price you knew I couldn't pay.
Now whenever I think of you I'm blue.
When we first met, you gave my heart a start.
When I dream of you it's so hard to sleep.
You made the blood drain right out of my heart.
The wounds will forev'r r'main deep.
  A new love might happen to work for you
  As for me, I can never move on too.
Allie Wallace, Grade 10
Bonneville High School, ID

The Big Game

The game clock is running out
The pressure is on
We are down by two points
With only seconds left
Our coach calls a full timeout
The crowd is cheering.
The championship game is on the line
We inbound from our sideline
I get the ball
And make a quick pass left.
He passes back
To my surprise I have an open shot
I take it
The shot rolls off of my finger tips
As it travels through the air
It seems like forever
But as the ball goes in the hoop
The crowd erupts!
They are going crazy
I feel like a champion.
We've won the state championship.

Keenan Karratti, Grade 10
Orem High School, UT

Crazy About Him

Butterflies fluttering
in my tummy I feel.
I like you more and more,
I think this feeling's real.

A thousand miles apart,
may be a lot.
But its not the distance,
It's what's in the heart.

I am crazy about you
and don't know why
there's just something there
Something I cannot hide.

I think about you all the time
like a tattoo,
scarred in my mind.

I don't know how to say it,
Not sure if I should.
But I really like you
and would be with you,
If only I could.

Sara Hadley, Grade 11
Duchesne High School, UT

The Love Left

It was what is best in us all.
If the heart is broken it can build a great wall.
I remember the day her love slipped away.
I still feel the love she gave.
Therefore there is no other woman I want to crave.
I only wish I could change.
Now she has slipped from my arms out of range.

Clayton Spillane, Grade 12
Rifle High School, CO

Vanished

It was the moment you were needed the most
When all good rippled between my fingers
And evil came thundering in
No one knew what would happen, not even me who experienced the most
You left without a single word
Causing worry and guilt
First it was the mysterious behavior
The "return to sender" postage stamp
And then the absent phone calls
You and I were thick through thin
Years separated us, yet you knew best
Nothing could bring you back
Not the wind, not the birds' chirping
Not even the call of the midnight coyotes
You had vanished
You were missing
You had stolen a piece of my heart
All the pain in the world couldn't amount to the sorrow felt
You were the only one who could fix it
And to this day I remain the same

Karalie Stratton, Grade 10
Oak Harbor High School, WA

Love Hurts

Love is like a disease. You never know when it will hit.
Although its usually just good, it takes a lot to commit.
Usually all the passion and affection comes along.
But it can be a disaster if your heart is not strong.
There's probably only one girl who knows what I've been through.
She had her heart ripped out, spit on, and stomped on too.
Can't really hate to love, can't really love to hate.
There are just so many feelings being stacked upon your plate.
Can you get it all down? Or will you start to cough and choke.
Love is not some kind of game. People treat it like a joke.
All these emotions overwhelm you. You can't help it but to cry.
Next time you know it you got a gun, and you don't know why!
But don't let little things like love go and get yourself hurt.
'Cuz the next thing you know, you'll be standing over your corpse asking why?
"How could I let me kill myself? How could I let me die?"
Then you realize the first person that you should ever love is you.
Then you should love GOD because He'll always love you too.
So don't let another person get you down.
Because whatever they may throw at you always comes back around.

Julia Vider, Grade 11
Futures Academy, CO

High Merit Poems – Grades 10, 11, and 12

I Am the Color Black

I am the color black

I am the startling darkness of the night
I am the sinister shadows of a new moon
I am the sadness in a person's heart

I am the hatred that is held in the subconscious mind
I am the wickedness of the world
I am that which represents evil

I am a gun
I am the remains of a scorching fire
I can't be noticed until light shines

I am the color black

Luis Morales, Grade 11
Rio Rico High School, AZ

Another Day

As she stands there, waiting for the play,
never once she thought, she might not see another day.

The thunder rolls, the ball is hit,
with the crack of lightning, her socks had split.

Lying there, with a silent heart,
straddling the line between life and death,
a woman ran down, to give her one last breath.

Oh God, please don't let her die!
Within seconds, you hear the sirens fly.
Long hours, precious tears,
prayer circles filling people's ears.

Her parents wait, longing to hear,
that their daughter would still be living here.
Within the long hours waiting, the people hear the doctors say,
"The girl is awake, she gets to live another day."

Janae Montes, Grade 10
Pueblo County High School, CO

Uncharted Waters

Unrefined waters striking the horizon,
Dancing to the many beats of its rhythmical song,
Life thriving beneath its thrusting surface,
Reeking of endless life.

Frigid with beauty,
Trusting in the heavens to provide,
Twisting on toward its eternal journey,
Forging its signature,
Impressing it in time.

Melodious song recognizes the rising sun,
Protecting the pureness within,
Dark cedars surround its boundaries,
Dripping dew diminishing into the soil.

Sierra Owens, Grade 12
Madison Sr High School, ID

Nothing Special

Do you feel that you are nothing special,
Well, you are in someone's eyes
Those eyes can see past your outer disguise
Keep in mind the outside may look battered,
But it's the inside that really matters.

Perhaps you look like some rocks:
Your outside is dull and bland
But inside you're really grand
All that one would have to do
Is get through what covers you.

Once they see what's really beneath you,
They won't be able to get enough
Of all that great stuff
And, after all, you may not look so exceptional,
But on the inside, you really are Something Special.

Kyle Fournier, Grade 11
Grangeville High School, ID

Pain from the Past

General Schroder expresses his shame
On the issue of Auschwitz and who was to blame
Hitler and his army came up with a game,
If you were not German, you were not the same

Having no choice but to bear this burden
Saying sorry to all for the hell they lived in
Jews and gypsies and prisoners of war
Were kept in camps and a whole lot more

From death marches, to being starved,
To being gassed, to being shot,
People treated like animals
And left there to rot

No one can change what happened in the past
But all can change what happens in the future
What we do today affects our present fast
Now we can all live together not one of us a creature

Nikki Larson, Grade 11
Madison Sr High School, ID

A Woman's Worth

It hasn't always been easy for her
Babies, bad men, moving, fighting, losing.
They never said life was easy
But why should it have been that hard?
On top of it all…a disease
Pain inside and out, never ceasing.
Yet this woman's strength has changed me
Made me see it's not up to the world if I rise or fall.
It really is all in your head, she says
It isn't as bad as it seems.
The most reassuring words to me…It will be ok
My mother could move mountains with her heart.

Madeline Bain, Grade 11
Flathead High School, MT

Life Is Like a Dream
Life is like a dream,
it's uncertain but excited.
it's unmerciful but beautiful.
dream,dream,dream…
Dream is like a life,
Everything seems unreal,
but those are real.
Everything seems joyful,
but those are sorrowful.
dream,dream,dream…
Who can make your dream come true?
That's you.
Dickson Wong, Grade 11
Madison Sr High School, ID

The Cycle
An animal dies
Another is born
A flower dies
Another is born
Whenever something dies,
Something takes its place.
Death and life, a constant forever
Death is a tragedy,
A sad thing,
But a necessity.
Life is beautiful,
A joy,
A virtue,
This cycle never sleeps,
Never rests,
And never ends.
This cycle goes continuously
Forever and ever.
Andrew Ramon Perez, Grade 11
Preston High School, ID

Weariness of the Sky
Great ballroom, old, abandoned —
time bends, distorted clocks
ticking, buzzing, chiming, humming,
glass warped and spiraling
down to music stands;
brass dripping, strings loosening,
crystal melting, wobbling ring —
grand silk here lays shattered,
floor decorated with majesty while
window-waves of glass
echo the grey sky —
dreary mists whisper outside,
sighing; everything forgotten —
time — nothing in the
Weariness of the Sky.
Sapphire Kokojan, Grade 12
Prosser High School, WA

Spring Flowers
Spring flowers that bloom,
Leaping from the cold wet ground,
Like ballet dancers.
Amelia Waggoner, Grade 10
Cedar Park Christian School – Everett Campus, WA

Young Love's Escapism
that stale french fry smell, dark gloomy-grey interior devouring us
as we fled from responsibilities
always driving down the same two roads, go past the golf club,
make a right past Lacamas Lake
cookie-cutter houses across the water
making distorted lights onto the placid, murky reflection
windy roads consuming us
dodging the eavesdropping trees that never gave us enough time
to scan the collection for our dream home
always morose acoustic music
if it was ever an incohesive mixed CD or Billy Joel
depending on my tolerance I would either
persuade or physically (but playfully) force him iron and wine
nothing was more in tune with the atmosphere and mood
than sultry melodies of Sam Beam
the feeling of escape slowly died
up the hill on 28th then that left on 166th
the homework I avoided, the lukewarm leftovers I neglected
the anxious barking dogs I ignored,
nosy parents I overlooked
captured by reality caught by monotony
Samantha Ogle, Grade 12
Evergreen High School, WA

The Worst Game
The ball was passed to me, and I really did try catching,
but that didn't prove to be easy with fingers flying and scratching.
Later I got the ball and I tried my best to pass,
but I decided I had no hope to be able to pass with any class.

I figured I was done, after all, I was no good;
but Lucy couldn't play anymore, so I was told I would.
Someone passed the ball to me, for a reason I know not,
with only 3 seconds on the clock I knew I'd have to make a shot.

I stood there holding the ball in most utter disbelief,
and as I stood there, a second passed, a second that was anything but brief.
I had no faith in myself, for this was not my game,
there was little I could do, but to cross my fingers and aim.

I raised my hands above my head and let the ball fly,
time suddenly seemed to stop, and all noise seemed to die.
The ball got closer, and closer, 'til finally it was to the rim,
it took only part of a second, to see the ending would be grim.

I'd given it my best shot, but my best was in vain,
and coach and teammates came running, to make sure I felt their pain.
Kaitlyn Craig, Grade 11
Woods Cross High School, UT

Silent Waters

In the silent waters, calming as can be,
a stranger is a calling, in a whispered voice to me.

He does want to see me, but running is what I do,
I cannot see the stranger, he reminds me so much of you.

Through the braided trees, beyond the fiery skies,
through the crystal waters, I'll find my true disguise.

The stranger follows slowly, his love I can feel with pain,
his kind heart calls me calmly, and I will run off the pain.

But when he finally finds me, he pulls me in with love,
caring arms are holding tight, skin soft and white as the dove.

Even now he reminds me, so much of what once was,
the stranger is now my husband, who was God-sent from above.

Sky Shepherd, Grade 11
Nenana City Public School, AK

Down on the Farm

Woodchucks can chuck wood,
Chicken pox, chicken pox in my socks
A crocodile would fly if he could
The piggy's pen stinks, clean it, he should
My turtle wears a top hat in his box
Woodchucks can chuck wood
Gophers are goofy and good
Ants march by the clocks
A crocodile would fly if he could
Ricky Rabbit lives in the hood
Wally the whale wobbles as he walks
Woodchucks can chuck wood
On top of the cowboy is where the horse stood
Crazy chickens fly in flocks
A crocodile would fly if he could
The cow can jump if he only would
But the cat only laughs and mocks
Woodchucks can chuck wood
A crocodile would fly if he could

Rose Castor, Grade 10
Bennett High School, CO

Poetry

Poetry is a river deep and ever flowing.
Poetry is a lion roaring for all to hear.
Poetry is a bird flying free and high.
Poetry is the mind insightful yet blind.
Poetry is emotions spilling all over the page.
Poetry is a bird's feather unique and amazing.
Poetry is the words of the heart overflowing to the paper.
Poetry is pain telling the story of one's life.
Poetry is happiness celebrating great times.
Poetry is a newborn baby crying to be seen.
Poetry is an eagle bold and beautiful.
Poetry is poetry...

Stacee Beckstead, Grade 11
Preston High School, ID

Waiting

Standing in front of the oven
Waiting for my food
The TV on in the background
Waiting for the news to talk about the war
But no news about my aunt
Her birthday goes by and still no word
Some family members begin to lose faith
Days and then weeks go by
And soon months pass
I try to stay positive but it is hard
School starts and I have to go
I can't believe my mom is making me go
How am I supposed to concentrate on school work?
Finally, we get word...
She is OK!

Emily Daniels, Grade 10
Pioneer High School, NV

Trapped

Fierce beam of light
That is jolted up in the sky,
Like the roar of thunder that breaks the earth
And the lightning that strikes the ocean.
The waves crash along the shore
Ships in the sea are abandoned,
Stranded in the middle of the ocean.
The wind howls out of control,
The salty sea mist spat upon your face,
Darkness fills the sky,
Rain is pouring down.
Difficult to keep your head above water,
Longing for something to cling on to,
Trapped in a moving whirlwind,
Yet, there is no way to get out.

Kelsie Craig, Grade 10
Orem High School, UT

Hate and Love

Hate and love
Can it be they are the same?
Are they not both an obsession
But with a different name?

Hate is an emotion that is not easily fled.
Love is an emotion that can fill you whole head.

Hate can be masked and hidden away,
While true love shows through all the dark days.

Hate is an awful thing that takes over a soul,
But love is the one thing that can make you whole.

Hate and love
Can it be that they are the same?
They are both an obsession
But with a different name.

Ashley Salinas, Grade 11
Liberty Baptist Academy, NV

Christmas Angel
You are like the angel
On the Christmas tree.
That's how much
You mean to me.

You sit atop my heart
Hiding inside from the start
A seed growing
From a little tree
That grows and grows
With more glee
That's how much
You mean to me

The lights of love
Strung around thee
With the orbs
And ornaments of life
This is never
A time of strife
That's how much
You mean to me
Karl Williams, Grade 12
Granite High School, UT

Feelings of the Heart
Feelings of my heart
like a cloud over my head.

Feelings of my heart
drag me down like heavy lead.

Feelings of my heart
Like a sea crashing down on me.

Feelings of my heart
lifting me above the drowning sea.

Feelings of my heart
Help me to hear over the sadness.

Feelings of my heart
The falling tears form inside my bliss.

Feelings of my heart
Why didn't I know inside?

Feelings of my heart
That I was loved all around?
Stephen Huey, Grade 12
Granite High School, UT

Love
Love is like a flower
it knows no minute nor hour.
It can surpass the tides of time.
It can eve be described in a rhyme.
True love has an everlasting power.
It will always be in your heart,
you and your loved ones will never be far apart.
Heather Bettinson, Grade 12
Rifle High School, CO

A Star
Sometimes I sit and wonder,
if stars are how they seem;
And if they really travel through the night as if a dream.
Have you ever paused to think
That if you ceased to shed your light,
That the night would be much darker, or
Keep going just as bright?
Oh little star above,
Do you ever feel dismayed, that you shine as just one beam
Like the millions with you laid?
Do you wonder if you're needed, to illuminate the sky,
Or if one could just replace you when you pass your star life by?
Have you ever seen a soul
Who has searched for you one night,
And wished upon your image of infinity and light?
I hope you never leave me 'cause you've always lit my way
when I've walked this world in darkness, but not left because you stay.
Oh tiny star above, now I see you're just like me:
One created with the millions,
But not forsaken in its sea.
Cheyenne Ray, Grade 10
Viewmont High School, UT

Happiness
Happiness is hitting the winning run,
As you realize, when you step up to the plate,
That you're down by one, two gone, and it's on your shoulders
As you kick up the dirt you watch for the sign
Bunt, Wiped off, Hit and run, Wiped off, Squeeze, Wiped off, Just swing away
You dig in your back foot and glare sixty feet in front of you
He shakes his head once, twice,
Then gives you a smile and begins his steps
Then you see it falling towards you, waiting to be shot back at him
But that's not good enough,
You dig in your cleat and let your bat rip
Ping!
And the ball flies over the short stop's head
You dash to first and watch as one run soars in,
And the next dives to the finish and smacks up a cloud of dust
You wait as it clears and then you wait for the word
SAFE, and there is a roar that follows
Then you sit and let it all flow in
As you realize that you are the hero of that game
Corey Butler, Grade 10
Oak Harbor High School, WA

Can You See Behind My Eyes?*

Can you see behind my eyes?
Do you even know the pain that I feel inside?
Scared and unwanted is what I've become,
That's how they know me and that's how I'm loved,
Sometimes I wonder if there even exists joy in the world, holing my teddy bear tight and staring into the night sky,
counting every star that catches my eye, the air blowing my hair to the side, I calmly sit still and hear the crickets cry,
I explore the adventures that my mind wonders, feeling the breeze that ran passed my knees, I felt a wet drop fall on my lap,
"its not raining" I said, it was a tear that ran down my cheek, quiet and being lonely is what caused this tear to fall,
Closing my window and singing a song,
A song that my mother sang when she tucked me into bed, kissing my forehead and holding my hand, the smile she gave me to tell me that it's time fore me to go to bed, those moments I'll cherish for throughout my years, knowing that she won't be there to take away my fears, her picture next to my comforter with roses on the side,
Knowing she's gone forever just makes me cry, A loving mother is what she became, even thought I caused her oh so much pain, never appreciating the little things that we had,
Not even appreciating the things she has done for me,
But what I'll remember now are only those sweet loving memories, I'm praying to God to bring her back to me to truly show her how much she actually means to me, repenting for all those times I made her cry, a mother like her should never be pushed aside,
Now she's with God, that's where she always wanted to be, looking down at this sophisticated young lady that I turned out to be, educated and spontaneous is how she pictured me, the best qualities of my mother were passed down to me, I wasn't the best daughter that God wanted me to be, but what I know now is I'll cherish and miss her for all Eternity.

Mayra Banuelos, Grade 10
Provo High School, UT
*Dedicated to my mother.

The Sparkle of Enthusiasm

A wonderful discovery enlightens my soul
Nothing can hold me back, for my buoyancy is irrepressible.
With the wings that I have grown through determination, persistence, desire, hope and will
I fly.

My bubbly countenance radiates excitement
My eyes sparkle so brightly
My smile stretches from ear to ear
From one's world to another's,
As it only takes one cheerful and kind soul to reach out and make a world of difference.

One heart that desires to help and to bless touches many others
One thoughtful deed blossoms and seeds into another
One contagious smile spreads rapidly onto the faces and into the hearts of others.

One kind deed lightens the burden of a busy day overloaded with stress
One gift shared equals many others blessed.

One yellow M&M in the midst of thousands of red ones stands out
Refusing to hide amongst the ordinary
If only it will.

One leader moves a million others
One trickle of water collects and flows into a great and beautiful waterfall
All because of the courage and enthusiasm that one puts into beginning.

Heather Elise Johnson, Grade 10
Mountain View High School, AZ

Memories
Memories of good times
And memories of bad.
Memories of funny things
And memories of sad.
Memories of hurtful words
That will never go away,
Memories of enduring friendships
That will always stay.

Alison Taylor, Grade 11
Liberty Baptist Academy, NV

Emptied Full
Unlock the gates
Open the doors
the flood will come
Welcome the discouraged
free the waters
let them drink
Uncork the wine
quench the river
You are welcomed
but hated
The stench frees souls
Unlock the gates
Open the doors
the lake fills empty
the mind emptied full
the wine parches the throat
the awaiting torture
calls you home
The trumpets are gold
Unlock the gates
Welcome the monster

Suzanne Valentine, Grade 11
Los Alamos High School, NM

Sick
A raspy voice,
Hard to swallow;
Stomach churning,
Oh, please help me!
My mind is escaping,
Into a vast torrent of nothingness;
My fever is returning,
I think I am sick.
Weakness of body,
Unable to stand;
Why are my hands shaking?
Oh, please help me!
Subzero one second,
Blazing the next;
My body is shaking,
Why am I sick?

Erin Leonard, Grade 11
Desert Vista High School, AZ

A Glimpse of Summertime
The summer breeze blows,
Waking up the fields of green
To wave in the light.

Lauren Anderson, Grade 10
Cedar Park Christian School – Everett Campus, WA

You Are Water, I Am Sand
You are water and I am sand.
I move gently through your hand.
You seem so pure and easy to see through.
I feel so rough and easily passed when I'm with you.

You live for the mornings; I long for the nights.
You speak of good intentions, but foil my mights.
At times we seem like a classic Verona tragedy,
But the secrets, fights, and defiance all seem solitary.

You being gliding, shimmering waves reaching for the sun,
Only weighs me down more to the bottom, knowing it's futile what I've done.
At times your waves crash upon me at the shore,
But then you always leave, making me lonely once more.

Shall the sand ever stay with the water or will there forever be this space?
I wish to keep the distance, but yearn to be liquid at the sight of your face.
You seem so peaceful and inviting unlike the way I am,
I can never get why you stray from the ocean, just to touch upon my land.

I love you so dearly, but there are differences that you must understand,
The future is truly bleak for you are water and I am sand.

Kelsey Brown, Grade 12
Dobson High School, AZ

My Leash
On a hot summer day the Mormons took me away.
I quietly tiptoed while following them down the road.

It scared my mother half to death,
she was so scared, apparently she was out of breath.

Soon they noticed I was there
it seemed to give them quite a scare.
So, they returned me home
and from then on I wasn't free to roam.

My mom came out with it in her hand.
I was so young I didn't understand.
She talked to me for a while, as I stood there and smiled –
but little did I know, that this would be the opposite to winning the lotto.

At first it seemed like a backpack with an extra snug fit.
then all of the sudden there was the clip.
I was imprisoned in my own cockpit
It was then that I knew,
that my free life was not to be renewed.

Simone Hamilton, Grade 10
Oak Harbor High School, WA

Detention

I feel restrained.
These shackles have always remained.
I await the day,
That they will say,
You are finally free to go away.
Slam goes the hammer,
I must go back to the slammer.
I step out of the room,
I know they're watching me,
But I can't say hello or goodbye.
I hear the sound
As the van comes around.
I arrive at my cell,
Which feels like hell.
Morning shift is at end,
My door flew open, but I couldn't believe,
It was my turn to leave.

Richard Noble, Grade 11
Utah Youth Academy, UT

Friends Forever?

We said best friends forever
And I thought that it was true,
But then he came and stole your heart
Just like I feared he'd do.
It started out slowly
Just like they said it would,
But I just pushed those thoughts away,
Just like a good friend should.
But looking where we are today,
I wish I would have listened
There is hardly even a friendship there,
Nothing more than a glisten.
So today I'm lucky if we even speak,
And if we do it's small
Like "I like your shoes" or "How's your week?"
And usually that's all.
I wished this wouldn't have happened,
That you hadn't pushed me away
But deep down inside I know I'm better off without you
And I know that thought drives you crazy,
Even to this day.

Elizabeth Silveira, Grade 10
Oak Harbor High School, WA

Daybreak Buzzer

Oh, the way you wake me when I'm drowsy
The day begins feeling very lousy
I'm in a solid dreamy state asleep
Pulling me out to consciousness beep beep
The glee of morning brightness is sunrise
Starting low but then lifts itself to size
Without the sound reality ends there
Dreaming would be an unending despair
Tomorrow there will be another morn
For now my blissful reverie is torn

Chanel Grill, Grade 11
Vancouver Christian High School, WA

First Impressions

A book of thoughts,
A chain of unbreakable assumptions
Form on first glance

A look up and down
Taking in every detail
And saving them for years to come

A first meeting
Building up the thick foggy ice
Between two people

A time of great anticipation
Building up to one moment, broken
With a simple exchange of words

All started by a single glance
The moment is finally past
And paths are once again set in different directions

Kasey Siliga, Grade 11
Cascade Christian High School, OR

Sounds

A bird coos softly in the night
as its poised ready for flight.
Crickets chirp loud and strong
they're preparing their nightly song.
The wind cries softly as if in pain
the sky lets go a dismal rain.
Trees sigh and sway so soft
their leafy branches hang aloft.

Rivers glide along their bed
I wonder where begins their head.
Rocks have their surface smooth
and strong they seem to be singing along.
Every so often you will hear
The hummingbird fly by your ear.
so my friends as you can see
Sounds envelope you and me.

Anne Allred, Grade 10
Shelley Sr High School, ID

Tragedies

How shall I seize the day?
It seems that life is too short
Too short to let any day pass by
To pass without memories
To pass without the knowledge they have left us
Stop wasting time
God gave you this day
This life
For a reason
To find love
To play the music
Enjoy life for it will pass by
Make it your own

Mitchell Foster, Grade 12
Flathead High School, MT

Song of a Lost Child
Sweet voice
Strumming chords of gentle release
Call me back from yonder
Sing me home again
I have wandered far
Over the hills, across the valley
I can't see the candles
Lit in your windows
I can't feel the warmth
Of my mother's arms

Sweet melody
Dancing on soft flighted wings
Inspire my soul
Show me the path home
I've lost my way
I'm crying for my father
Lift my feet over the grassy lawns
I want to see the fires
Burning heart and hearth
I want to feel the warmth
Of my mother's arms
Tracy LaBonville, Grade 12
Chatfield High School, CO

Within an Endless Twilight
The day the world went away
The sky was still filled with light
All the black soon to fade
The painter's canvas
Never again a blank distance
Now filled with luminosity

Twinkling in the sky
An endless vision
A universe so far away
One so easily lost
In its brilliance
Like something you can never imagine
Something you can never have

Watch the moon
It will guide you into the morning glow
It will crawl across in time
The stars come to follow
A game of tag
Hold your breath
The end can't be near
We are within an endless twilight
Sarah Pehrson, Grade 11
Chatfield High School, CO

Cancer*
A slight perfume of pain rests among the air
The harsh quiet pounding against my head
This terrible raid by a silent killer
A broken spirit simply lies down
In this trap life itself is caught
All the value placed in medicine,
Please, please wrench this darkness out of my life.
Heidi Ramp, Grade 11
Crow High School, OR
*Dedicated to my Aunt Jackie Pignone

It's Me!
I am…a daughter who loves her family every day.
…a daughter who makes occasional mistakes.
…a daughter who is a leader in many ways.
…a daughter who brings joy to her life each day.

I am…a girlfriend who loves like no other.
…a girlfriend who supports (just like a mother).
…a girlfriend who cherishes time together.
…a girlfriend who gives her heart forever.

I am…a friend who stays there until the end.
…a friend who tells her girls, "broken hearts will mend."
…a friend who sees through all the lies.
…a friend who will never leave another behind.

But most of all, I am…Me!
…a person who can't be changed into something you would like me to be.
…a person who has a myriad of feelings; who takes them seriously.
I am…Megan Denise Boyd Rotvold…

Yep, that's me!
Megan Rotvold, Grade 12
Westwood High School, AZ

What Have They Done?
I can feel the bitterness as it surrounds me.
On the cold spring night as the rain comes crashing down on me
mingling with my tears.
I watch all the horrible things they do to Him.
My tears fall faster and harder.

I want to scream and shout, do anything to get them to stop.
But I am bound and helpless because I know what has to be done.
My heart cries out for Him as I watch them
drive the rusty old nails into His beautifully sacred hands.

But I know He does it all to fulfill God's perfectly devised plans.
As I watch Him gracefully plead for deliverance.
And then see Him silently slip away.
I wonder to myself what have they done.
What have they done?
As a sad tear falls from my face.
Melissa Pelaez, Grade 10
Fremont High School, UT

Goodbye

These things come,
there's no avoiding them.
We knew that to every
beginning there is
given an end.
It does cause pain
and sometimes tears.
But we must part
and go on separate ways.
Let it be fast,
so the pain will not last.
Our time together has been fun.
Let the memories we have sustain us.
Until our paths cross again.
But for now we
say, "Goodbye, stay strong and learn more
until I see you once more."

Kevin Rodgers, Grade 10
Viewmont High School, UT

He Who Has Come

The angels of God have sent me a gift
Or he has fallen out of the sky
I was given a second chance at life
And so it made me feel like I can fly

He is here to seal my fate with a kiss
A kiss is all he has to offer me
With that kiss he will bring me happiness
He said that this is what was meant to be

Without him, depression comes over me
My life stops whenever he's not around
It is like the English without their tea
Darkness and cold winds take over the town

His love is what is keeping me alive
He's the one who controls my heart and mind

Vanessa Rodrigue, Grade 11
Rio Rico High School, AZ

Superwoman

Never in my life have I met a more versatile gal,
It seems there is nothing that she can't do.
She's the maid mopping the floor,
and taxi driver with no pay.
The baby-sitter tending six,
and chef spending endless hours in the kitchen.
A model looking flawless.
The comedian making you laugh.
A doctor healing your wounds,
and counselor with a listening ear.
A bank when you need a loan.
A best friend to wipe your tears.
Some might call her superwoman,
But I like to call her Mom.

Melanee Walker, Grade 12
Madison Sr High School, ID

Keep Track

I've worn my hair straight and curly, weird and sexy,
I've dressed up and dressed down.
I've broken rules
and laws
and hearts
and minds…
I've loved people
and I've been loved in return.
I've realized who true friends are
and I'm still confused on everyone else.
I hated who I was
I loved who I was
I've changed who I was,
And I've ruined who I was.
I've done things I shouldn't have
And I've accomplished things I never thought I would.
I think about everything
but easily ignore the thoughts in my mind,
I've tried to get over things, and I've tried to resolve things,
but most of all I keep track of myself,
or else I'd be lost, with no one else.

Caricia Janus, Grade 11
University Schools, CO

The Mountains

I stand in the beautiful mountains
Where animal and human both have trod.
Trees whisper and grass twitches
Birds tweet while feet beat the ground.
The sun shines a welcome sight
To starving flowers from the night.
Clouds creep across the sandstone canyon
The taste of summer in the air.
The lake like a sheet hung to dry
Shimmers with the cool breeze gone by.
My soul a spark and lighting fire
But only when I'm in the mountains.

Dillon Bishop, Grade 10
Fremont High School, UT

Caged Bird

I'm a stupid girl
Trapped in my own home
I'm a caged bird
Feeling hurt and lonesome
never have I been heard
This caged bird is drowning in its own tears
Always living in constant fear.
People see a pretty bird
Not a bird that's scared
They don't see the bars
That are causing scars
Every day that passes by
I wonder if this bird will ever fly
Why doesn't the caged bird go
Like so.

Rosemely Pruneda, Grade 11
Warden High School, WA

Love Eternal
To her all time devoted.
My mind on her to focus.
My heart without her eroded.
It seems like hocus pocus.

In her I put my trust,
giving her all I have to give.
This feeling is more than lust,
without it I could not live.

Always on my mind.
Indescribable the feel.
Love like this one doesn't just find.
This is for real.

Austin Clayton, Grade 12
Mountain View High School, AZ

Grandfather
It's true you are advanced in years
As well as mature and tested
But still holding your good looks
And at heart vigorously active.

When a situation gets rough
And all are in fear
It is your sturdy unshakenness
That keeps me feeling secure.

You are one that holds honor, respect,
And in big decisions you are sensible
Teaching others their responsibilities
And to all your family reliable.

Stephanie Faber, Grade 10
Nooksack Valley High School, WA

Risks
Just take a chance they cry.

Worry plagues my heart —
so much distress and sorrow
while the rest all fight to win
this game of fooling
chance into giving more time.

Why even battle fate?
The pain of failure weighs on my heart.
Can you feel it now,
the great thrill that is defeat?
it burns the soul and risk flames anew.

The onlookers scream:
a small risk is always better
than life untried.

Lydia Gettman, Grade 11
Cascade Christian High School, OR

Life Is a Metaphor
People feel the need to compare
They invent metaphors that are already there
Rollercoasters, chocolates — it's over done
Live life, don't think — you've already won.

Larissa Horton, Grade 12
Liberty Baptist Academy, NV

As My Tears Echo
Loneliness is the silence of an empty house.
Waking up with no one to greet me,
Pancakes on the table with no one to share with.
I speak for no one to hear.
No one seems to listen, to care, to love.
I hear nothing but the cries,
The sound of this horrible day,
Echoing wall to wall, empty and pale.
Reaching and touching me through endless ripples
I run to no one, tripping and falling, screaming,
Without a reason why.
Pools of water blur my vision and the frozen wind sifts through me.
I shut my eyes as hard as I can.
While tears fall down my frozen cheeks, down to my cracked lips.
The sky above me begins to cloud.
I walk and feel the first drop,
I could no longer feel the thorns under my feet,
As I run back to fall on my bed.
When I look up to look through my window, I see a girl playing by herself.
I wipe the tears to clear my mind,
And I know I'm going to have pancakes with someone tomorrow.

Arjayne Evangelista, Grade 10
Oak Harbor High School, WA

The Land of the Forgotten
Have you been to the Land of the Forgotten,
where all the forgotten things go?
Where holy jeans, stinky shoes, unpaid fees and over dues,
rest next to shirts of worn out cotton.
Where unmade beds and left on lights
float down a river of "uh-ohs,"
next to the boxes of homework that sit
by blank trees that have all been called "no shows."
In this land there is a fridge where everything is rotten…
where pickled pears and mayonnaise jars
come when they're forgotten.
Dusty toys from girls and boys left out on the floor,
are sucked up by the vacuum hose and live here, forever more.
Unmatched socks hang from trees
of forgotten hopes and forgotten dreams,
right on the bank of a tiny stream
where old memories flow.
For now you've seen and now you know,
the Land of the Forgotten.
Hold my hand as we pass through, you by me and me by you
into a world that's bright and new, and where no one is forgotten.

Amanda Rumsey, Grade 11
Viewmont High School, UT

Love Is…

Love is what makes us who we are
It's when you need someone there
to show you that they care.
Love is devotion and desire
with complete satisfaction
and a lot of dedication
Love is like ice cream
it's sometimes sweet
but it can also be cold
Love gives you everything from that special person
but it can also take it away in the blink of an eye
which will make you want to cry
Love is everything you need
and everything you want
Love is what makes us who we are

Erika Oliva, Grade 10
Shelley Sr High School, ID

Invincible Force

Poor decisions result in poor actions
Hearing the news with dramatic reactions
No one to blame but one person
Cannot be fixed, not even by a surgeon
Wishing you could go back in time
Realizing it will not help to whine
Although it is not exposed in appearance
You will live your life, and always fear it
Its force will always be invincible
At the time, the decision seemed irresistible
Next time you hopefully rethink your choice
Then there will not be hesitation in your voice
This feeling will never be gone
Help yourself to always stay strong

Matthew Baker, Grade 12
Lakewood High School, CO

The Day He Left/The Day He Came Back

The day he left
I wanted to die
He said I'm going to war
With a sigh
He promised to write
Every day
That promise
He did keep
It was almost two years
Before I saw his face
So happy to see him
I almost cried
Many years have gone by
Now I see he is scarred for life
From what he saw in the war
Never will he tell what he saw
Or what he did
My true love is back from the war
But mentally he is still there.

Amber Virgo, Grade 11
Pioneer High School, NV

School

School
All the hands high-fiving,
All the hugs received,
All the hello's, and the hi's,
All the waves, and the goodbyes,
All the slaps, and the jokes,
All the laughs, and the chuckles,
All the stress, and the fun,
All the friends, and the shunned,
All the teachers you hate, and the ones you don't,
All the love you receive, and love you won't,
All the rewards given, and
All the rewards withheld,
All the homework received,
All the report cards, and joy,
All the nicknames and styles,
All the…
School

James Nish, Grade 11
Woods Cross High School, UT

God

No worries of a changed mind or being left behind
He's always there with me
Loneliness, despair, emptiness: forever gone
He is unchanging, has no conditions.

Nothing can fill the empty seeking space
He always takes me back
No one else understands or gets how I feel
He knows everything about me: He made me.

This desolate darkness won't last,
toiling destruction, it is not forever.
Reach out to Him, He is what matters
Forever with me, changing and molding me

He is my everything.

Shannon Campbell, Grade 10
Cedar Park Christian School – Everett Campus, WA

The Acquired Soul

Remember when we watched the midnight sun?
When we talked all night till you had to leave.
This night was perfect since if first begun,
And now I hope my love she will receive,
Because I know she is the one for me?
There's not a day that she's not on my mind,
And when she's with me she makes me feel free,
But the days that I don't see I am blind.
Months have past, and I think it's time to grow.
Now I need to hear if she feels the same.
The answer is what I wanted to know!
Finally I am happy to proclaim,
And this love that we have always wanted,
Is the love that makes us feel accepted.

Zach Landis, Grade 12
Flathead High School, MT

The End Is Near

The end has finally come for us,
Don't be afraid.
This life we live, has to die,
The life that we all made.

Completely dark without the light,
We cannot see our way.
We've lost the life in front of us,
And left without the day.

The numbness likes to come and go,
It messes with our mind.
All over now, it spills our air,
And makes it hard to find.

The fear, it likes to linger,
As you reach out for the lies.
You test the waters of your soul,
Drowning out your cries.

Alone at last is the day,
When Earth has finally cried.
It's all become quiet here,
When everything has died.

Andrea Schwartz, Grade 11
Heritage High School, WA

Zephyr

Do you recall me?
I am a legend
I bore Aphrodite to the shore of the sea
I am a breeze of alabaster gold
Entwined silk
Behold!
The cloak of old
I scatter the cherry blossoms
I whisk away the quartz mountains
I tickle the chins of the possums
As they dance to the beat of my chimes
Whenever beasts laugh
All through time!
I whisper rhyme
On the reeds adjacent to the pond
I play ballads to Gaia
I shake the dandelions; my magic wands
I cough!
Dank air chokes me
"I'll just blow it away," I scoff
Alas, this poison I cannot doff

Cullyn Foxlee, Grade 11
Port Angeles High School, WA

Rest

Darkness swallows day's incandescent light,
And so comes the obscured night.
The time my wary mind has waited for,
So that my head need be wake no more.
I close my eyes, abeyant at last.
All the days troubles, away they are cast.
But soon the dawn pushes night away,
And I awake to find a brand new day.

Madi Robertson, Grade 10
Cedar Park Christian School – Everett Campus, WA

Snow

Snow lay out in lovely straight lines as sorrow fell like rain
    From her swollen hazel eyes.
Never before had it been like this.
Cradling him, her love. Her fallen one.
    Shaking as he fell still farther.
Never before had it been like this.
Holding him, because he couldn't hold her
    As powder glistened like gems on his arm.
Never before —
Rocking him as he fell still farther
    The bathroom littered with remnants of his one last flight. His one last descent.
    Fluorescence blinding as she kissed eyes that would never again open.
Never —
And as they put him into the ice-hardened ground, she wept
    For all the things she hadn't known.
    For all the things she'd known too well.
She wept as her lover was covered with earth
    Earth that would not forgive past mistakes.
    Earth that would not let her forget them.
Never before had it been like this, as snow lay out in lovely straight lines.

Heather Burge, Grade 11
Dobson High School, AZ

I'm a Foster Child Now

Way back when my mom kicked me to the curb
I couldn't control my tears; my vision became blurred.
I didn't know where to go or what to do.
How could you do this to me, Mom? How could you?
I've made a few mistakes, but who hasn't?
It's not like I'm in a beauty pageant.
I've done some stuff I regret, I know,
But I'm confused, are you a fan or foe?
That husband you've got has brainwashed you to hate me.
I always hated that guy. He was way too shady.
But it's not him, it's you; I was the best of four,
But this choice you made makes me love you no more.
I'm a foster child now because of what you have done.
All this time what was on your mind; nothing about your last son?
I no longer hold a place for you in my heart.
I don't think I can forgive you, you can't and don't get to restart.
One of these days you will see, I was just being a kid.
I just wish you could have seen that before you did what you did.

Tim Pickett, Grade 11
Flathead High School, MT

In the Absence of Light

Trapped behind these walls of torture and despair
Death and mass murder
Have a peculiar stench that hangs in the air
Fear in the hearts of those who wait
Shame in the hearts of those who work
Those who survived now try to forget
They want to pretend it was all a bad dream
But the reality is
No matter how hard the pinch
It hurt every time
The result, the same
They were still alive
They were still awake
But dead on the inside
Asleep deep down
They tell us to remember
So history doesn't repeat
But have you given one thought?
That those who survived
DON'T WANT THE REMINDER…

Ricky Hepworth, Grade 10
Preston High School, ID

Thunderbolts Are Love

Thunderbolts may strike at any instant,
Given that an ardent storm is present.
Darting like a buckshot, landing distant,
Bashing into anyone with strident.
Just as thunderbolts are abrupt and quick,
So is love and its talent to conquer.
The effects are smooth and solid as brick,
People are the target and its capture.
Passions burst into realistic dreams,
Staring at the beauty, speeds the heart rate.
Ardor hands move closer, forming crossbeams,
Eager lips advance nearer on a date.
Aphrodite's spell is a golden dove,
Allowing me to contemplate — true love.

Taosif Alam, Grade 10
North High School, AZ

Ode to Shakespeare

My mistress lies far from riches and wealth,
For if she were, with not me she would be;
Petite pale slender hands reek of poor health,
And O how she dreams, of whence she shall see.
What shall become of thy beautiful one
Who hath no decision whom she loves?
Her tattered black blouse once shone as the sun,
And soul flown high as a thousand white doves;
Her radiance surpasses the struggle,
For I hath shown her true comfort and trust,
Make it we shall, despite bounds of rubble,
Nothing shall deny the beauty of lust,
Therefore my mistress reveals in her face,
Whence my best days have passed, she welcomes grace.

Jennifer Strand, Grade 12
Parkrose High School, OR

Work in Progress

I am a mouse in a maze trying to find the way.
I am a newborn bird trying to fly through the rain.
I am a delicate rose that can be easily torn,
But most of all, I am the stem surrounded by thorns.
I am a child learning to crawl.
I am an essay paper filled with flaws.
I am a drink waiting to spill,
But most of all, I am an empty heart waiting to fill.
I am the compass that discovers the path.
I am the solution to the problem in math.
I am the spell check that corrects small errors,
But most of all, I am the beauty of the heiress.
I am a rainbow after the storm.
I am the spring that blossoms with sweetness.
I am the sunshine that helps you see,
But most of all, I am the treasure at the bottom of the sea.
I am a climber trying to get to the zenith of life.
I am a bee wanting to get out of the hive.
I am a pacifist, who wants world peace and love,
But most of all, I am the perfect hand for the one size glove.

Elodia Uriarte, Grade 12
Westwood High School, AZ

Reality Check

Whenever I am walking home from school
I tend to think about the things I did.
I wonder if the things I did were cool,
Or if the others think I've flipped my lid.
I like to think I have a lot of friends
'Cause then I'd get invited to more things.
To have some friendships that would never end,
Would make me feel like I had everything.
But then I stop to think about my life,
And all the things TRUE friends have helped me with.
I realize I've caused nothing but some strife,
And that true friends are real and not a myth.
Whenever I am feeling sad again,
I'll take a sec' and think of my real friends.

Anna Herrera, Grade 12
Temple Baptist Academy, NM

Endless Passion

Has my love for you soared high as a dove?
One that has a path beautifully flown.
A heavenly figure from the skies above,
Its shadow in the morning dew is shown.
Your face perfect as a well-written book,
For my tired eyes, a well-rounded feast.
Every breath from me your mystery took,
These feelings could never be slain by beast.
If it is me you are trying to please,
With that I will hardly be able to bear.
The truth we cannot tell, and only tease,
But that will not help to keep us a pair.
My feelings for you shall always glow bright,
I will work my whole life to make things right.

Laryssa Smith, Grade 12
Kentlake High School, WA

Death at My Doorstep

The wind howled
The sky cracked and split,
Lightning lit the sky.
The trees bent and buckled
Darkness crept all around.
With Death knocking at my door
I never swayed, I never wavered
Nothing could drive me from my course
And there we stood,
Death and I,
Locked in an eternal struggle for my life,
But not this night,
No, not this night,
Could I be claimed.
I fought my way from the jaws of death
Out from the mouth of hell
I beat death this day
Just to fight him some other day
In this battle that won't be won,
'Til I'm done.

Brett Garcia, Grade 10
Temple Baptist Academy, NM

The Music

Those white ivory keys
Contrasted by black, dark as night
The quiet melody they play
Brings back, that long forgotten memory,
Which once flared feelings
In your heart.

Chris Merkley, Grade 11
Viewmont High School, UT

Reminiscence

Sun pours through the window
Illuminating her spot on the floor
She's surrounded by photographs
Memories of what she longs for

She recalls each happy moment
A love of a special kind
A pair of smiling faces
So ignorant and blind

Time makes the heart grow fonder
Yet it hasn't dulled the ache
Each photograph is evidence
Of her never-ending heartbreak

As the days fade into weeks
She locks the photos away
And like the fracture in her heart
In that box they'll stay

Emily Hollingsworth, Grade 12
Castle Rock High School, WA

Sorrowful

A single word that can describe the thoughts of many
An overwhelming sadness that can depress us all
Caused by the depravity of those unwilling to lend a hand
What can save a world that won't even try to save itself?

A fate dependent on the unity of its victims
Is the fate of those condemned to eternal discontent
And though some may try to change the inevitable
As life becomes more simplistic nothing but hardship can follow

As more and more people slip into a melancholy society
They chose to embrace it rather than reject it
For acceptance requires less of their time
Than fighting for what is right and fair

The history of the world provides nothing but examples
One did not begin to complain about the taste of food
Until spices were created to enhance the experience
Walking was not such a hassle before cars were invented

Sorrow, distress, regret, grief, unhappiness, trouble
Just a bunch of overused words, losing their meaning
All one must do to find the true significance of such words
Is step into true hell, such as the streets of Darfur.

Chase Calvi, Grade 10
La Center High School, WA

Heartache

He has love for someone…it's not for me.
Looking into my eyes he sees no magic…
…He feels nothing.
Words of rejection replay in my mind like
A broken record player…
Every time I see his face…every time he runs through my mind…
Putting on a smile to mask
The shattered pieces of my heart…
He knows my pain, my heartache…I still refuse to show it…
The one who would sweep me off my feet…kind and sweet, like Prince Charming…
He won't be MY Prince Charming…
"A dream is a wish your heart makes."
True words spoken by well-known Cinderella.
I'm dreaming, still dreaming…why won't my wish come true?
There she is – the one whom he admires, the one his heart yearns for.
What am I missing? What did I do wrong?
My stomach sours knowing I have to face this reality:
He is not the One.
Must I live this?…Breathe this?…Consume this?
This is my heartache:
He has love for someone…but it's not for me.

Dar-Ci Calhoun, Grade 12
Pasco Sr High School, WA

The Lonely Times

When I watch you I see you when I watch out the window on a rainy day.
You are like a dog with parvo.
Waiting for your mind is like waiting for a cat to obey your orders.
When I see you, you are like watching a tower fall down.
A woman who used to be nice and a wonderful girl.
But I stand up for all the way.
As your husband is in prison, I stand up for you.

Patrick Heath, Grade 10
Mountainair High School, NM

To Bobby

This is a poem for my brother Bobby.
Not really a tribute, but a poem, just to let you know how I feel.
When we were younger I used to think of you in a good way.
I was proud to call you my brother.
I used to think you were great, and so strong, you could do anything!
But where did that person go?
Where is the brother Tommy and I used to look up to? Where will he be for David?
It has taken me a while to realize, but you remind me every day, that he is gone.
He has gone to a place so far, I don't know when he'll return, or even if he can.
You are no longer a hero, and no longer a role model.
You taught me so much when we were younger. You taught me how to skateboard, and how to stand up for myself.
The only thing is, they say you should practice what you preach,
So where were you to stand up for yourself? Where were you to say no?
The only thing your influence teaches me now, is what not to do.
It kills me to say this, but you've become a different person.
I cannot think of you in happy ways anymore. Light doesn't flood my eyes when someone says your name.
Now I drop my gaze, and nod my head.
I don't like having to do that, but you've left me no other choice.
And just so you know,
I miss my brother

Sarah Wilson, Grade 10
Arapahoe High School, CO

Parents

Worrisome terrified providers
Do not get too drunk tonight stay there if nobody can drive
Do not drink and drive or else
We love you we want to see you again
Don't make a parent bury their child
Stay in tonight the weather will not permit
It is too icy just stay home
We saw the news we saw the wreckage
Oh how we prayed for you to make it home
Don't do drugs there is a time and place for everything
You are too young you will hurt yourself
We've heard the stories we've seen it before
Don't disobey us we want the best for you
Mom and Dad I've seen a lot in my days
Numbered as they have been
The world is changing things aren't the same time to move on or adapt

Parents tell their kids all the things they can think would protect them. They see the world as a harmful place to their children. Once they become a parent they forget that they did the same things in their youth and came out fine. Once someone becomes a parent they will do anything to protect the life and well-being of their child or children. No parent wants to have to bury their child.

Jake Stryker, Grade 12
Kestrel High School, AZ

Superman

There must be something I can do to rescue you from this tar like past that's clinging to us.
Your mind is your own killer.
I stand there watching death creep slowly through your red pulsing veins.
Leaving the ones you love empty and lonely.
Can I be your Superman?

You come, you go, I don't understand.
You left a piece of you with me but as I wait for you to come back
That piece loses its starry shine and turns away left abandoned.
Can I be your Superman?

That piece you left behind is me,
And when I look in my breaking mirror, I see your dying reflection in me.
Looking into my once big dark brown eyes, now I see black emptiness going on forever.
Can I be your Superman?

Separating from the rest of the world,
Hiding my anguish behind a fake smile.
My aching heart screams for help, sad because I've lost my one and only dad.
I've tried before and I'll try again.
No matter what it takes, I'll be your Superman.

Tiffany Paquet, Grade 10
Fremont High School, UT

Dead at 17

Dying at 17 is not your parents' dreams. Drinking and driving will cause these things.
Just one drink will ruin everything.

Just one drink won't hurt you.
Go ahead, try it, it tastes really good. Get your buzz going, I won't tell!

Just one drink won't hurt you.
You can drive you're all right. The store's just around the corner.
Nothing bad can happen. It will only take a few minutes.

Just one drink won't hurt you.
That's what they told me. I got in the driver's seat and went on my way.
Around the corner I couldn't see, the car and the family.

Just one drink really hurt me.
I hit that family and caused so much pain.
I tried to swerve but was too slow, that car came too fast and I hurt them.

Just one drink ruined everything.
That family died never to breathe again.
And me, well I am here in the ground. Never to live my life or become what had I wanted to be.
I cut my life short along with that family, because I had decided to listen to my friends and not myself.

I am in the ground after just one drink!!!

Cara Murphy, Grade 11
Wapato High School, WA

My Chevy

Driving in my Chevy
The world don't seem so heavy
I got the radio up, the windows rolled down
I'm just a girl out cruisin' the town
It's just me, the road, and a country song
No one to tell me what I do wrong.
I have no friends, I have no enemies
Driving is one of life's secret remedies
My thoughts run wild
On my shoulders they've been piled
There is no time, only space
Life doesn't seem like such a race
My shoulders are eased
And with my life I am pleased
Put it in Park, the "P" stands for Pressure.

Kara Floyd, Grade 12
Paradise Valley High School, AZ

Me

I'm sitting in this jail
I'm going to tell you a tale
Of my story, of my life
Being carved out by this knife
I used to be happy, but not anymore
My ears are constantly sore
I used to listen to everyone lie
Not anymore, wanna know why?
I drank my problems away,
That's not the story today.
I'm happier now that I'm sober
My luck changed when I found a 4-leaf clover.
I had a mom, I had a dad,
They always made me mad
Everything would be blamed on me,
Why did this have to be?
My sister had to raise me
That's the way it had to be.
They locked me up from the community
No, it isn't inhumanity
See, I told you it was a tale of my life.

Gene Wert, Grade 11
Newbridge High School, OR

My Dear Translator

My translator, you're giv'n me by my mom
I love you more when thinking of my home
You have a tiny screen with little keys
You do the needed task with simple ease
You fit so snug and warm inside my hand
And help me find words I don't understand
Although my buddy can be small in size
You help me do my English exercise
Oh translator, a smart and helpful friend
You'll be in high regard until the end.

Chau Nguyen, Grade 11
Vancouver Christian High School, WA

A Mother's Strength

A mother of two girls, one 21 one 18,
Returns from a long day at work to provide for their needs.
Stressed and tired just wanting to rest,
Knowing there is more to be done and the house is a mess.
Can't help get angry and yell,
She is so unhappy, you can see it, you can tell.
A mother's strength is so humble, so strong,
In a child's eyes she can do no wrong.
She worries and worries about everyone else,
Never taking time to think of herself.
A mother's strength cannot be replaced,
A mother's strength is what makes us feel safe.
I don't think I will be as good of a mother as mine,
Maybe I will, but only with time.
I wish my father would have seen all that she does,
And maybe he would still have her, still be in love.
My mother's strength is not only all of these and more,
But she is the strongest woman I know and adore.
So here is to the mother who is above them all,
The strongest mother whose strength will never fall.

Kelsie Akre, Grade 12
Hillcrest High School, UT

What I Want

It spreads before me.
   A green expanse, rolling.
      fogging my vision.
         Everything verdant.

I claw for everything,
   everything that I can't have.
My fist punches through the green wall,
   trying to get to a room far greener on the other side.

And I'm paddling through the thick green, now;
   there is an unbelievable undertow.
      I'm trying to reach the shore.
         So I can finally have it.

What you have.
   What I don't have.
      What I want.

Allison Welter, Grade 11
Woodland Park High School, CO

Grades 7-8-9

Note: The Top Ten poems were finalized through an online voting system. Creative Communication's judges first picked out the top poems. These poems were then posted online. The final step involved thousands of students and teachers who registered as online judges and voted for the Top Ten poems. We hope you enjoy these selections.

Top Poem Grades 7-8-9

Untitled Symphony

The meadow forms an amphitheater
A man stands there,
Still, alone.
He bows and he turns to the trees
He lifts a finger and then his hands
And in this stance he cues the breeze.
With his hands followed by his arms,
He draws a picture in the air,
Down, in, out, up
A low hum like the strings is made by the bees,
Birds twitter in a trill,
The voice of the bassoon is played by the trees,
Shaking its leaves in vibrato.
And as the music journeys on
Into the day it accelerates
Surely such a speed could have no grace, no!
Eventually the beat slows,
Down, in, out, up
And then it stops.
The musician in the center bows
And leaves his work of art, his dream, for the world to keep.

Elisabeth Bloom, Grade 9
Grand Junction High School, CO

The Dragonfly

Shifting through boxes, cleaning again, I never know what I'll find,
Today it will be special, to my past it will bind.
I move a childhood book out of the way for the sunlight to catch the rest,
Then I see a small sparkle caught by a single ray, somehow I know it will be the best.

Reaching down, I pick it up and tears fill through my eyes,
The love I once had for it can never be disguised.
It had been a gift from mom, a wonderful surprise,
A tiny little dragonfly that lit up my big, green eyes.

It sat upon a hair clip that never left my carrot curls,
I felt like the prettiest at school among all of the girls.
Its wings were covered in sparkles, and were pink with blue and green stripes,
When they flapped as I ran or swung, I could almost hear the other girls' gripes.

Then one sad day in early May, my mother went the way of the sky,
I imagined her watching down on me as I clung to my dragonfly.
How could I wear it without mom to watch me bounce around?
So, it was put away into a box until today when it was found.

Now worn and old from all the love, I clip it to my head,
My hair now straight and chestnut has never felt so red.
Memories speak softly in my mind, they are a lovely sound,
Now forever to my hair and heart, the dragonfly will be bound.

Natalie Jones, Grade 8
St David Elementary School, AZ

Top Poem Grades 7-8-9

Winter

Away, away, the honking geese fly,
Soaring and swooping into the North sky.
Gnarled old pines say goodbye once again,
To the tired old bear that will nap in his den.
Crispy and sharp, the wind blows with a bite,
It twirls and it swirls right on into the night.
Gone with the tank tops and in with the jeans,
Swimming and biking are naught but a dream.
Smoke from the chimneys and warmth from a fire,
Are two winter things that will never expire.
Small, chubby fingers draw on frost covered panes,
Pictures of ponies, of hearts, and of trains.
Snowflakes emerge from the bottomless clouds,
Fluffy and white as they fall without sound.
A hushed sort of feeling creeps over the street,
Spotted fawns romp and they bound and they leap.
Wet snowballs fly and cold cheeks turn quite rosy,
Children drink cocoa, all warm and so cozy.
What is this great seasonal feat you may ask?
It's the world peeping through its cold, winter mask.

Maggie Kirscher, Grade 8
Canfield Middle School, ID

Top Poem Grades 7-8-9

I Am Who I Make Me

Don't tell me who I am
Or who I have to be.
For who are you
To speak up and define the likes of me?

I am my own person.
Don't spoon-feed me your lies.
I should have known your immaturity
When I first stared into your eyes.

You're nothing but a child —
Thinking it was all a game,
Thinking no one would get hurt,
Well, that may have been your aim.

How can I let you know,
Or make you well aware
That you have hurt me with your games
And left many scars there.

From this moment on, I will ignore
Your pitiful and stupid lie,
For I am who I make me
And over you, I will no longer cry.

Brandi Peplinski, Grade 9
Leading Edge Academy, AZ

Top Poem Grades 7-8-9

Moonlight Dance

Moonlight starts, twilight's hung.
Day is gone, night's just begun.
Dark shadow's still stance,
'Twas the night of the moonlight dance.
For this serenade time stands still.
Darkness sings, voice high and shrill.
Shadows dance in the moonlight beam.
The setting is like a dream.
The moon looks down and sees,
That they have been caught in its reverie.
When the clock strikes twelve and sun replaces the moon,
When the light replaces the lulling tune.
The dream begins to fade
In this mysterious masquerade.
The music dies down,
And the moon takes off its crown
To make room for the selfish sun.
The stars vanish and the trees stop their riot.
The shadows are still but darkness is quiet.
But we know when twilight comes and then by chance.
It is once again time for the midnight dance.

Nicole Ramirez, Grade 8
Fertitta Middle School, NV

Top Poem Grades 7-8-9

Stormy Afternoon

The beach
Is the ocean, and sifty sand,
Little crabs scuttling
Under damp rocks.
Mostly bright days,
When the sun splashes with the waves
And we can fill our pouches
With curving shells.

But what of a stormy afternoon?

When the dunes are empty,
The heavens a contemplative purple.
When the clouds tip over,
A stinging, icy drench.
Do we throw back our heads,
Letting fat drops roll
Mercilessly down our faces?
Or hurry home,
Hunched under raincoats,
To build a cheery fire?

Madeleine Joy Scothorn, Grade 9
Alliance Charter Academy, OR

Top Poem Grades 7-8-9

Remember

When you feel you're only one small star in the night sky,
Remember one
Has the light of the sun.
When every door has been closed and all you want is to be home,
Remember then
There is always a window.
When darkness creeps up, consuming the morning's warmth,
Remember soon
The sun will rise again.
When you feel the tempter's hand has become your puppeteer,
Remember *you*
Are of noble birth.
When you cannot fight the silence, when the melody is cold and flat,
Remember how
Your harmony sweetens each duet.
When the day comes for goodbye, it seems the time soon shall come,
Remember then
We will be joined together again throughout eternity.
And when you feel you're only one small part of this world we're living in,
Remember always, my sister,
You are every part of me.

Emily Virginia Simonson, Grade 9
Robert Stuart Jr High School, ID

Top Poem Grades 7-8-9

Peer Pressure

All these voices trying to get in my head
When will it stop? When will it end?
I just want to live for me
free of drugs, free of peer pressure.

They all seem to say the same words
"just do it, it's not like it hurts"
"you're such a Goody Two-Shoes"
"try it, just once, and you won't regret it."

Do I really want to throw my life away
For something that will kill me anyway?
I don't want to try it, I don't want to start!
One thing will just lead to another…

I will be a role model for the next generation
Not show the world that I am an abomination
I will shine, not slip into the shadows
I am strong, not weak.

There is a better place in life that I want to go
I want to rise above, and so
The next time someone shows me the monster,
I will say one simple word: NO.

Leah True, Grade 7
Les Bois Jr High School, ID

Top Poem Grades 7-8-9

A Memory for the One I Love

A memory that just keeps rolling
Like a movie in the back of my head
The drive by that place that we used to hang out at
Waiting to see you there

A memory is a sound of your sweet voice
And the sound of our laughter
The smell of sulfur from the fireworks
That we light off at night and the smell lingering in the air

A memory is the feeling of your rough hands
Making sure that I don't fall off the ladder
While people walk by they shake the ladder
And you grab it and keep an eye on me

A memory is the random conversations we always had
People trying to pull pranks on us
Us talking about music non-stop
And those people trying to hook us up even though we would do it ourselves

A memory is that movie
That just keeps rolling
In the back of my head non-stop
Just thinking of seeing you there at that place where we used to hang out

Alexis Ward, Grade 8
LaMotte School, MT

Top Poem Grades 7-8-9

Father's Love

Remembering how you would treat me:
Princess Tabi is what you called me
When you were around
Hoisting me up on your broad shoulders
Saying it was my throne
Strong arms would wrap around my small body
Proving to me you loved me
Lying on your proud chest,
Knowing you would never leave.

But here I stand alone:
No throne
No arms wrapped around me
Staring at a gray, death stone
Knowing you can't come back.

Tabitha Watson, Grade 9
Reid School, UT

My Dad

On one yawning day
I finally realized that
My dad was getting old

oldest out of
all of his brothers
sisters and his friends and cousins.

was a young yappy boy
25 years ago
used to like to play
now he is so serious

He is a man now
At least I think
He wants
To be a kid again

Marcus Lobato, Grade 7
Shadow Ridge Middle School, CO

Ars Poetic

A poem should be like
The loud, majestic purr of a tiger

Poetry is like the smooth,
Connected lines of a car

Flowing
As a soft rippling stream

A poem is like the strange,
Beauty of broken china

Poetry is as beautiful as
A sunset painting

Poetry is sweet, pure, honey

A poem is as wonderful as,
Finding old treasures in the attic

Poetry is the taste of kisses
Poetry is Divine

Paige Anthony, Grade 9
Mountain Ridge Jr High School, UT

Without a Trace of Trueness

In a town lay people of stuffed smiles
Lies that would fill a mouth full of bees
No true feelings just fake perfectness

Without a trace of true love
Everyone lies with pain
No one wants to change

Safiya Dawlatzai, Grade 7
Mandalay Middle School, CO

Katherine DeBarge

I am a Katherine.
I wonder what my life will bring me.
I hear everyone around me speaking all at once drowning each other out.
I see everyone scurrying by like their late to the end of their life;
my feet start to pick up when my brain tries to slow down and view everything.
I want to help children learn by becoming a teacher.
I am an inspirer.

I pretend to be a teacher with my little brother.
I feel full of life when I go for something I truly believe in.
I touch others' hearts when I listen to them, but don't judge.
I worry about my mom making it to my high school graduation.
I cry when see my mom clutching at her chest to keep it from hurting her.
I am a believer through and through.

I understand that I am not always right.
I say that you only have one life, one chance to do your dreams and to be YOU!
I dream of having two kids, a husband, and a well paying job.
I try to do everything to my best ability and no lower.
I hope that this year is a good and fun start of my next four years of high school.
I am Katherine Mae DeBarge!

Katherine Mae DeBarge, Grade 9
Lake Havasu High School, AZ

Days to Come

As I lay under the starry sky
And see the blueberry moon
I go into a deep sleep and start to dream
Dream of the angels singing a melody
Like birds chirping in a tree

As I wake up to a strawberry sunrise
I stretch my arms
Like a cat after waking
I suddenly smell the sweet fragrance of my mother
The smell of raindrop kissed tulips on a warm summer morn

We walked out, cappuccino in hand
To see the multicolored rainbow
As unique as the crayons that come in their box
Like an Easter egg basket filled with warm fuzzy bunnies
That makes a child happy like eating ice cream on a hot summer day

Ashlie Cuthbertson, Grade 9
Queen Creek High School, AZ

Star

A star has light beaming all around her body.
She holds the dreams of people who wish upon her.
A star dances across the sky
and breathes out stardust.
There are stars high in the sky,
with flashes of light leading into the unknown.
So when you go to sleep tonight and make your wish,
look up for her for she is waiting to hold your most valued wishes.

Ariela Lewis, Grade 7
Mears Middle School, AK

Memories

When they moved the girl was young
The family was happy
But maybe not
The girl had golden brown locks
A sweet smile
And loved to dress up
But the family had to move
"It's time," said the little girl's mom
Before they left, their lovely neighbors
Invited the small girl over to stay the night
Oh, what good fun it was
She dressed like a princess
And they made ice cream cupcakes
Topped with tons of sprinkles
Then in the morning they had a feast
Eggs and bacon
But best of all was the sausage
But then Mom says
"Honey we have to go"
But all the girl wants is to stay
Now all she has left is the memory

Isabelle Rusden, Grade 7
Lincoln Jr High School, CO

Josephina

J is for July, the month of my birthday,
O is for optimistic, I am positive in every way.
S is for sports, my favorite thing to do,
E is for education, something that is good for you.
P is for purple, my favorite color,
H is for hair, dark brown and goes forever.
I is for intelligent, something I'm determined to be,
N is for nice, something I like about me.
A is for amazing, my parents surely think so,
   And hopefully you will think so too.

Sabrina Montoya, Grade 8
St Catherine of Siena School, CO

Tree in the Wind

The tree sleeps peacefully,
And doesn't even know.
That the wind is about to blow.

As the tree wakens, the wind speeds up.
The wind whistles picking up speed,
And starts to dance in the tree.

The tree's arms sway this way and that.
As the wind howls,
And blows off a hat.

The wind dies down,
And the poor tree wears a frown.
Because all of its leaves are spread upon the ground.

Keenan Polanco, Grade 8
La Plata Middle School, NM

Black Is the Color of Danger and Delight

Black is the color of a raven's down.
Black is the sound of a panther's mighty roar.
Black is the taste of pollution in the air.
Black is the feeling of guilt in your soul.
Black is the eclipse during the day.
Black is the fear loudly thumping in your heart.
Black is the taste of a crisp, chocolate, Halloween night.
Black is the smell of a wilting rose bud.
Black is the feeling of a murderer's heart.
Black is the sound of a bat's furious screeches.
Black is the color of the sky an hour before daybreak.
Black is an owl's pellet dropping to the floor.
Black is the smell of soot in your dusty chimney.
Black is the taste of blackberries down your throat.
Black is the feeling of telling a lie.
Black is the cigarette in your mouth.
Black is the innocents' cry.
Black is the feeling of hard, rocky gravel.
And Black is the color of danger and delight.

Alayshia Estrellado, Grade 7
Ernest Becker Middle School, NV

Mr. Smith

You are the teacher
you have known me since I was 4
but now I am much bigger
I moved out of the dresses stage
and then I was in your class
don't the years go so fast?

You know a lot about history and math and writing too
you helped me and said "Kristen, you can do it"

You helped me find a book
then came another.
I like books because of your great taste

You are the best teacher!

Kristen Rodal, Grade 7
Sylvester Middle School, WA

War

Boom! Crash!
Bombs are falling.
Guns are shooting.
Smoke fills the air.
Everywhere I look there's blood.
Crying children with dirt and blood on their faces.
I'm walking through the smoky air.
The smoke pollutes my lungs, for it's all I smell, taste, and see.
I can feel the pain and hurt of the soldiers.
I sense the fear of the innocent,
Because I too am innocent,
Just a child living among war.

Ofelia Machado, Grade 7
Ernest Becker Middle School, NV

Beauty in All
Just look around
and then you'll see
the beauty that has come to be
mountains surround with snow a top
leaves turning different shades
flowers in a rainbow of colors
as the sun goes up and down
colors streak across the sky
and when it's gone,
the white moon comes up
with little stars poking out
just look around
and then you'll see
all the wonders
that have come to be
look at people and see their souls
for what they really are
bright and beautiful
just look around
and then you'll see
everything that's come to be.
K'lah Yamada, Grade 7
Sky Vista Middle School, CO

Teddy Bear
Soft and furry to the touch,
Something that we all love very much,
Beautiful red bow tie around its neck,
loves to cuddle with you,
you love to cuddle with it too!
Cheyanne Ashby, Grade 7
Elk Ridge Middle School, UT

Mom and Me
I am a mom
                I am a daughter
I go to work
                I go to school
We work hard
I am tired
                I am energetic
I get mad
                I sometimes yell
We love each other
I hate my job
                I hate school
I have a husband
                I have a daddy
I hate MySpace
                I have MySpace
We both disagree
I love my daughter
                I love my mom
We work together
Morgan Wright, Grade 7
Elk Ridge Middle School, UT

Friend Forever
I'll miss your sad smile,
Your shaggy white hair,
I don't want to part with you,
It just isn't fair.

You will always bring a smile to my face,
You will be my best friend,
Through thick and thin,
Always to the very end.

You cuddled by my side,
Snuggled at night,
You slept like a baby,
Sprawled out in the sunlight.

I'll miss your cold wet nose,
The special times we shared together,
I'll miss your sad puppy eyes,
You'll be my friend forever.
Kaylie Hahn, Grade 8
Pawnee Jr/Sr High School, CO

Simple Pleasures
Simple pleasures, easy leisure,
In the noon day sun.
Fishes swimming; babies grinning,
Joys have just begun.
Birds are peeping; crickets leaping,
While the children play.
Hear the singing; air is tingling,
On this perfect day.
Then the baby smiles,
Knowing secret things,
Dreaming happy dreams:
Simple pleasures.
Simple pleasures, easy leisure,
In the noon day sun.
Lunchtime picnic, midday frolic,
Never ending fun.
Tickle fights and pure delights,
'Cause friends are the best toys.
Hear the laughter, followed after,
With simple sounds of joy.
Brenna Christensen, Grade 7
Miller Middle School, CO

My Embarrassing Family
My family can be embarrassing to me,
My friends don't know why,
But if they knew they would die,
They try so hard to embarrass me,
But all they do is hurt me,
And sometimes I wish I could die,
And they all wonder why!
Samantha Webster, Grade 8
Round Valley Middle School, AZ

Dare to Be Different
Time to go
Time to start
Time to stop
Time to leave
Time to walk
Time to run
Time to talk, of the same stuff
Time to say good-bye
Time to go home
And start the day again
The same way

But me.

I will not go
I will not start
I will not stop
I will not leave
I will not follow the pack
You should follow me.
Dare to be Different!
Miquela (Kella) Wilkinson, Grade 7
McKinley Middle School, NM

Piercing Dead End
A blade
not dull, but sharp
has pierced my heart
how can he say that?
Some say I'm strong,
nice, courageous.
Some say I'm dull,
weak, headstrong.
I'm not moving.
I'm not breathing.
Even my heart has stopped beating.
You are lost,
there's no going back now.
We were friends.
Now we're not.
Maybe we will be again,
but,
for now we've hit
our piercing dead end.
Aubrey Ham, Grade 7
St Olaf Catholic School, UT

Nothing Lasts Forever
You may be beautiful, but beauty fades
Pictures might be perfect, but it changes
Don't doubt my heart;
Because we will never be apart,
Our love is engraved in stone, however
Baby nothing lasts forever…
Namuun Jargalsaikhan, Grade 8
Place Middle School, CO

Sleep

Sleep! Sleep! Oh mom, just wait!
Can't I stay up and clean off the plates?
Just ten more minutes, that's not a lot,
But she already knows I'm hatching a plot.

Mom! Listen, I promise I will be awake
Just five more minutes, for heaven's sake!
I will do anything, anything at all;
I will do all the dishes or clean off the walls.

Yes, she says, but just five more;
And then when I realize that I am bored,
I crawl up the stairs and turn out the lights,
And finally, at last, I tell her good night.

Connor Guthrie, Grade 9
Bonneville High School, ID

Brothers

We always fight
Whether day or night
Somehow we just might,
Be two peas in a pod

We like to play outside
'Cuz our mom won't let us inside
Whether or not we abide
Some how we just might be two peas in a pod

We like to hit each other
That is 'cuz we're brothers
And we both love our mother
Some how we just might be two peas in a pod

We like to play games
With all sorts of names
Sometimes we go crazy, and need to be tamed
Some how we just might be two peas in a pod.

Titus Hardison, Grade 7
Sky Vista Middle School, CO

Baseball

As the pitcher pitches the ball,
I hear it come swishing towards me
WHACK!
The bat goes crack
My feet hit the ground as I run to 1st base.
Stomp, stomp, stomp.
As the 1st baseman goes for the ball,
I cannot catch my breath.
Cough, cough, cough.
I step on the base and squish.
I'm safe!
YEA! The fans cheer me on.

Riley Skinner, Grade 7
McKinley Middle School, NM

Heart Breaker

Don't let my actions push you away
I was inconsiderate, I had to have my way
You were everything to me, you had to be mine
You see you were my sunny weather, my valentine
I would dream of the day our lips would meet
When our hearts would occupy the same seat
After a while it became clear to me
We couldn't be one, you wanted to flee
You made me cry, left me in despair
You turned my blue skies gray
my sweet dreams, nightmare
You took a dagger, pierced my heart
We'll forever be apart
I must move on, there are other fish in the sea
but I'll never forget you, you were everything to me

Alexander Mitu, Grade 8
Komachin Middle School, WA

The Truth

He broke your heart, oh yes he did
With all those things you thought he said
You hurt yourself,
Badly too
But did you think his words were true?
Deep down inside you knew they weren't
The things he said the words that hurt
So please stop cutting they soon will get deep
And soon enough I will not sleep
I hope you know these words are true…
Dear friend,
I LOVE YOU!

Breana Riggin, Grade 7
East Valley Middle School, MT

People

Mom and Dad
Teach me good from bad
Keeping what we've had
I will always love you

Darren the pain
Power you try to gain
You are the center or main
I will always love you

Jayden just born yesterday
In your parents' arms you lay
Grow up well you may
I will always love you

Grandma Peanut
You are always a nut
You give me so much even though I am a butt
I will always love you

Brandie Beeten, Grade 7
Sky Vista Middle School, CO

Hallway

Hallway
Long and narrow
Racing, tripping, mixing
Hallway to hallway, class to class
Alley.

Adrian Norris, Grade 8
Place Middle School, CO

The Perfect Rose

A red ready rose,
Ready to remain,
Ready to rot.
Rejected and resting, the last rose.

The rose feels ready.
Feels soft and smells,
Like an entire garden
Of the finest kind.

It knows it's ready.
But, it knows it doesn't look,
Like it could be,
The finest of all.

The rose felt sorry
It wasn't picked.
But now it's in
The vase as
The Perfect Rose.

Jacob Zamba, Grade 7
Leading Edge Academy - Gilbert, AZ

Beautiful

There are these days,
When I feel like I'm shattering,
Like the Earth beneath my feet is gone.

But I fake a smile anyway,
Like a mask upon my face.

But when I see those eyes,
So beautiful,
No mere man can capture them,
It's like they see right through me,
They cannot see my body or my face,
They look right into my heart.

And when I'm with you I can't lie,
For you don't see the act I put on,
You see me.

And as trepidating as that used to be,
I've never been happier,
Ever in my life.

Megan Avila, Grade 9
Carson Valley Middle School, NV

The Threshold

Stand on the threshold between Life and Death
Roam through the empty gray No-Man's land
Feel the warmth of Life and the chill of Death
Stare into the ever-shifting skies.

Flee into the freedom of Life and the sanctuary of Death
Touch the tips of the cool swaying grass
Wonder in the concealed secrets of Life and the bare truths of Death
Listen to the heavy wind's whispers.

Walk softly on the well worn path of Life and Death
Follow the winding track
Allow the final closing of the Door of Death
Step through with no return.

Nina Myers, Grade 9
Lakewood High School, CO

The Blooming Flower

My struggles, my fears, and my dreams that slowly have been crushed,
But what if the world became a blooming flower and actually unfolded
And wanted help from the beaming sun?
We all could help each other open our petals,
We can become a part of the picture God painted from the very beginning!
Our selfish ambition has taken hold.
But let's be like the flowers.
Unfold and let your beauty show until there is nothing left to show.
When there is nothing left to show, only let that be the beginning!

Kylie McVey, Grade 8
Albuquerque Christian School, NM

Doors

Lots of doors that have key holes
Not knowing what door to enter through
All the doors go into different rooms
But you only have one chance to go into the right door — only one shot at life!
I feel lost, confused, lots of doors in different colors
"Which door do I go through?" would be crossing my mind
Scared to go through the wrong door — scared to mess up your life!
Keys trying to fit into the various doors,
The sound of keys and locks would be all around me!
Trying to hear the sound of people talking
The banging, banging of doors!
The doors are like soldiers
Guarding what is behind the doors
Not letting you go through to the other side.
In 50 years this picture would look the same
The doors would still be locked and closed
People can get in just not with a key, they need help from the inside.
"Why are you always closed?
How come a key can't open you up?"
People standing up, posed
Waiting for the door to open up!

Marisa Broersma, Grade 8
Sunnyside Christian Elementary School, WA

Summer

Warming up from rays of sunlight
   Taking a dip in the pool
Laying on the dark green grass, getting a tan
   Sleeping in until noon
Staying up 'til one in the morning
   Man! I wish it were summer!!

Sheena Newland, Grade 8
Round Valley Middle School, AZ

The Missing Piece

I looked into his glassy blue eyes
They were confused and full of dismay
"Take care of your mama and baby, son."
Holding back tears I told him, "Okay."
He stood up tall, looked down for awhile
Gave an empty smile, then walked away
If he was on our side, fighting for us
I don't know why I felt neglect and betray
They years procrastinated, dragging on
As things fell apart one at a time
A cloud full of melancholy stood over her grave
Just me and mama, with no more than a dime
Four long years, four million fallen tears
And finally a letter received
"Sorry no time to write, be home in spring."
Mama and I were blissfully relieved
In April of 1865, a figure stood before our street
As an inevitable smile crept onto my face
Here was my soldier, who fought for me
That missing puzzle piece finally found its place

Maddie Cramer, Grade 7
Colorado Academy, CO

Valentine's Day

I know about this day,
It is filled with love,
Passion,
And
More.
Do you know what this day is?
You get flowers
Of all different kinds.
How about now?
Lots of chocolates.
Dark,
Milk,
White.
Have you figured out what day it is yet?
Well you also may get lots of love
From family and friends.
You may find out about someone who likes you.
If you haven't figured out what this day is, I will give you a hint:
It starts with a "v" and ends with "day."
Valentine's Day!

Kachine Goodwin, Grade 8
Knowledge Quest Academy, CO

Dance

Dancing is my life
I love to do it day and night

when I dance I can express my feelings.
when I dance I know it is right.
I wouldn't be able to live if I could not dance.

it can be hard
it can be fun
either way I love to dance.

I'm always learning something new
I'm always focusing on learning the new moves.

Dance is amazing
you should try it too.

to dance is to live
to live is to dance.

Sydney Beckwith, Grade 7
Molasky Jr High School, NV

The Gang

One day my brother
left with another
to join a gang
he was called The Fang
his name was painted on a wall
I guess he thought he would never fall
I was sad
to think he was so bad.
I saw something one day in the news
that made my heart cruise,
a gang member had been shot
then left to rot.
My father told my mother
so sadly…it was my brother
his name on the wall was crossed out with red paint
it's too bad he wasn't really a saint.
Some people cry
"why did he die?"
So now I pray
for gangs to stay away.

Joel Schwarz, Grade 7
Round Mountain Jr-Sr High School, NV

Calla Lilies

Calla lilies are long and sheik,
They are used at weddings and look very sleek.
Ancient Romans used them for a fiesta of light,
During dark times they made their lives bright.
Its soft calming beauty gives life to everyone,
Calla lilies are always the one.

Kalla Madrid, Grade 8
Round Valley Middle School, AZ

The House

It feels like I am in a house. Pitch black no light to be found. Trying to make my way through the house. No windows nothing but harsh sounds sometimes soothing. It's a memory house. A past, present, and future house. Meeting someone you love makes you walk into a house. Getting closer with them, you make your way through the house. An obstacle house. Sometimes entering a room, you reach your hands out. Waiting. Waiting to reach some type of clue. Reaching. Reaching. Reaching until your arms hurt and nothing. Reaching but grabbing nothing. Nothing. Surprised you keep reaching. Anxious to grab something, anything. Walls being built between you and your obstacle to get through the house. It gets harder. Walls closing in. Heavy breathing. Deep breaths. Walls closing. Air escaping. Reaching. Reaching. Walking but getting nowhere. Breathing heavily to stay alive in this house of love. Waiting for something to happen. Waiting. Finally in this house you reach, touch something. Something cold. Metal. No, wood. Cold wood. A pole. Rail. You kneel and feel carpet. Wall. Wood wall. Straight up. Gap. Follow the wood. Over. Up. Over. Up. Stairs. Climbing. Up. Slowly climbing up. Almost to the top. Slip. Falling. Falling. Down, Down. Splat. Ouch. Hitting the floor. Smack. Off the stairs. In no room. By the door. Still in the house. Walking. Running. What happened? Running. Getting nowhere. Trying to regain what you had. Nothing. Trying. But nothing. Giving up. Grab the handle. Twisting. Twisting. Nothing. Nothing. Getting angry. Shaking the handle furiously. Screaming "let me out." Stuck. Trapped. Like a bug. No windows. No lights. No furniture. Nothing. Walls closing in. Air escaping. Thinking you would die in this house of love. Not leaving. Not escaping. You are still in love, but they are not. Stuck in this house. Trying to let go, but can't. In this mansion of love.

Amanda Chapnick, Grade 8
Helena Middle School, MT

I'm a Big Girl Now!

Responsibility:
To be able to follow through on a promise.
To be able to take punishments without arguing.
To be able to do your chores without whining.
To be able to care for yourself and others.

Independence:
To be able to go to college and not cry for your parents.
To be able to tie your own shoes.
To be able to walk to school by yourself.
To be able to not belong to another.

Freedom:
To be able to not have to work for another.
To be able to pay for your own groceries.
To be able to not rely on others.
To be able to walk out the doors of your school and know that you won't be back for 3 months.

Marriage:
To be able to love your spouse.
To be able to trust your spouse.
To be able to share interests with your spouse.
To be able to share beliefs with your spouse.

I grew, I grow, and I will grow some more.

Cortney Mabry, Grade 7
Lincoln Jr High School, CO

8 Ways of Looking at Poetry

1. It's words flowing out of your heart, down onto paper, and then into other hearts.
2. Prose thickened by emotion, read and reread; a memorabilia of the past.
3. Edgar Allen Poe, Emily Dickinson, William Shakespeare, or nature with a calligraphy pen.
4. Little bouts of insanity springing up from your brain.
5. A sensation, quite like that of a fanatic.
6. Somewhat like a song, but rhythm and rhyme exists underneath.
7. Tender blue lilacs sprouting from underneath, creating a garden of greens.
8. Attraction to a pen and paper.

Kaixi Huang, Grade 9
Las Cruces High School, NM

Blue

Blue reminds me of blueberries
Their rich sweet taste
When they're just picked in the summer
Blue makes me think of the summer's warmth
It reminds me of a tulip as well
When it blooms in the nice warm summer
The color you see when you look at the ocean
Blue is one of my team colors
In my perspective blue is the coolest

Caleb Hance, Grade 7
Sky Vista Middle School, CO

I Don't Understand

I don't understand
why people kill
why people lie
why some people always do crimes

But most of all
why people judge
why people are always so mad
why birds fly away when you get too close
why cats and dogs don't get along

What I understand most is
why people smile
why some people help one another
why some people care
why girls do their hair

Jessica Ramirez, Grade 7
Dunstan Middle School, CO

Nearly Anesthetic

The air was still, the night was cold
All breath was silent, all troubles told
It wasn't perfection I lusted to see
It wasn't Amazement I strained to achieve
Yet the gaze of your eyes burned deep to my skull
The pulse of your heart rapped strong in my soul
I knew it existed — desire so bright
I felt it uplifted — this sorrowful night
An ambiguous waltz of sweet passion and pain
Like the swift tears of clouds that we like to call rain
Poured over my being and halted a song
That would've continued, had it not took so long
For recognition of a desperate attempt
But it meant naught to you as a sly, cunning tempt
I'd leave this uncertain, forgetful remorse
But not by my will, it would take me by force
If I just reminisce on that one scrap of hope
Through all the turmoil I knew I could cope
As you always run back to walk by her side
As a slave to the past I'll always abide

Marisa Janke, Grade 9
Mead Sr High School, WA

The Meet

I grip the edge
My heart racing in anticipation.
A buzzer sounds. I jump.
I hit the water — hands first.
Almost sighing as the liquid envelopes me.
I kick, kick, kick.
My arms form an hourglass beneath me.
Propelling me forward.
Farther and farther they push me, until, SPLASH!
They explode out of their liquid coating.
I lift my head and breathe quickly.
My head and arms become one as they
Plunge smoothly back into the water,
Ready to repeat this never ending process.
I kick, push, breathe. Kick, push, breathe.
Again and again.
I touch the wall.
I am finished.
I have won.

Alexa Hubert, Grade 9
Canyon View Jr High School, UT

Where Has Your Heart Been?

Where has your heart been, I don't know
Where has your heart been, I miss it so
Are you hiding it from me, does it have dents
Where did it go, did it jump the fence
Let me see it, let me fix it
Does it need a patch, let me fix it, let me fix it
Where has your heart been, I don't know
Where has your heart been, I miss it so

Alysa Derks, Grade 7
Oberon Middle School, CO

Susie's Story

Said Susie Kelf
I don't care what others say
I will be myself
All along the way

But later in life
Her so called "friends"
Stabbed a knife
In her opinions

Time wasn't at end
Susie met Jill Neff
She met a new friend
A real BFF

Jill showed Susie many things
About this monster inside
Jill gave Susie repaired wings
She showed Susie her own heart, spirit, and mind

MacKenzie Ward, Grade 7
North Middle School, CO

The Apple

The yellow, firm,
Juicy apple
The fruit of all fruits,
The representation of education
The apple.
There is a shiny, sweet,
Smooth apple
Laying upon this desk,
looking at me, tempting me,
The apple.

There is a sweet, crunchy,
Round apple
Tempting Adam and Eve
Causing "the fall"
The apple.
There is a sugary, sour,
Starburst apple
Just laying there
Looking at me, tempting me,
The apple.

Cate Welch, Grade 9
Xavier College Preparatory School, AZ

Enigma

I am a rather tricky fellow
And wear the color of blue and yellow
Adorned with hair as black as night
To confuse is my delight

At the end of my remark
I place a simple question mark

Riddle me this
Riddle me that
What is the name
Of the big black bat

Batman you say?
Why you do know how to play

So you answered my riddle
You played the game
But…can you guess my name?

Alexandra Christensen, Grade 9
Timberline Middle School, UT

Skate All Day

I like to skate all day
It is my favorite thing to do
When I learn a new trick
I get very excited
It's one more thing to do
That's why I skate all day

Nestor Bencomo, Grade 7
Somerton Middle School, AZ

Day and Night

In the morning, clouds move and the Sun rises.
Morning skies are full of surprises.
At that time, it is peaceful, soothe, and bright.
Skies are appealing, up and down, left to right.
Then comes the afternoon where all of God's amazing creatures start to appear.
Most of the animals you don't have to fear.
After that comes sunset.
You will be fond of it, like you and the Sun last met.
Finally, the Sun will fade away.
You can see the exquisiteness the next day.
As soon as the Sun is gone, it becomes night,
That's one of the times to see the Northern Lights.
You may see constellations, planets, and stars.
One of the superb planets you may see is Mars.
Don't worry, the night and day will never die,
But right now, it's time to say good-bye.

Dinah Toolie, Grade 8
Hogarth Kingeekuk Sr Memorial School, AK

Love?

Love is a strange feeling I can't explain,
It's just that my feelings for you cannot be tamed.
I once heard that love is friendship on fire,
But you're the person I mostly desire.
I didn't ask for this to happen, I didn't know it would.
I don't want to love you, I never even should.
You don't know what you're worth to me,
Some other girls would sell you for free.
I don't know what you've been told,
But for me you're worth more than gold.
Days passed, and when you left me you took a piece of my heart,
After that I fell apart.
I am through with pretending, I just can't do it anymore, you know it's true…
I AM MADLY IN LOVE WITH YOU!!!
Keep this in mind, love is pain,
Love is a feeling I can't explain.

Rebecca Mojardin, Grade 7
Somerton Middle School, AZ

Friends Forever

There is no word to describe, the love I feel deep down inside.
You show me what to do and how, and in the end I make you proud.
I cherish the time we spend together, in the snow or sunny weather.
I make you laugh, I make you smile, I make you act just like a child.
We dance, we sing, you hold my hand, both together with pride we stand.
You're smart and strong.
You're more than right, you're never wrong.
When I get scared I'm in your arms, you let me know I won't be harmed.
Indeed you are my inspiration, succeeding with an education.
You make me chase my wildest dreams, and all these other crazy things.
The love we share is unique and bold, even after a heartbreaking scold.
Day by day I miss you so, in my heart I keep you though.
I'd never have known what fun would be, if you were not so great to me.
You're my sister this much is true, and like I said, I sincerely love you.

Rebecca Rogers, Grade 7
Heritage Middle School, ID

Life Is Like a Rose

Life is like a beautiful red rose.
It is elegant, smell it put it up to your nose.
It sits there day after day.
waiting to be put in a beautiful bouquet.
It blooms in the morning and sleeps at dawn.
Give this rose to the one you love before she is gone.
Love it cherish it do whatever you can.
Hold it tight and grasp it in your hand.
Fight and stand
don't let anyone come between you and your rose.
If you do it will become out of hand.
Just remember your rose is your life
that's why you have to hold on tight.

Kayla Trujillo, Grade 7
21st Century Public Academy, NM

Live for Today, Dream for Tomorrow

Live your life to the fullest each day
Remember good times, and forget the bad
And learn from the challenges that come your way.

Enjoy each day
For what is happening in the present
Not for the future
Not for the past.

Only dream for the future
And remember the past
Live life to the fullest
And never look back.

Christie Harju, Grade 9
Coal Ridge High School, CO

War

Boom…Boom…BOOM!
The sound of impending doom.
The sound makes a baby cry,
Making you feel like you want to die

The constitution says, "All men created equal"
But why do we create a sequel,
Of all the lies of the past,
Why can't this war be the last.

I know of the sacrifice of men,
Who signed for war, then
Were lost in a blaze,
Leaving America in a daze.

Violence is not the answer
But people today act like they can't master
Their impulses of violence and rage,
Opening up another page,
Of the history of war in America!

Katie D., Grade 8
Diamond Ranch Academy, UT

Life 'n Love

Life can be depressing,
life can be sad
Life can be horrible,
life can be bad.
But the best thing is,
that life is full of love.
All around you there is love.
So find your love and
live life to the fullest!

Riley Hatch, Grade 7
Knowledge Quest Academy, CO

Forever

Water swirling,
Tickling at my ankles,
I look down
There is a sparkling white shell at my feet,

I look to my left,
There is a clear bubble on the sand,
I realize it is a man-o-war,

I start back to dry sand
As I walk I take photos of the stunning water,
I take in a long breath,
Then I wish I could stand there forever.

Anna Zwolinski, Grade 7
Mandalay Middle School, CO

My Devotion to Basketball

My talent so great,
I rise above.
My quickness blinding,
No time to act,
Once you've noticed,
You're done for sure.

Practice and hard work
Makes a team
No matter what,
We will improve.
To be the best,
We must not test,
The wisdom of our coach.

It's game day now,
My heart is racing,
Over anticipation of the score.
We're ready now,
I know we can win.
But no matter what,
My devotion to basketball
Will show through.

Ismael Robles, Grade 7
St Elizabeth Ann Seton Catholic School, AZ

Dogs

Dogs love to run.
They are a lot of fun.
Some dogs love to play.
Some dogs sleep all day.
A lot of dogs are really big.
Other dogs are shaped like twigs.
Jamison Williams, Grade 8
Place Middle School, CO

Hot

The heat
The hot
The hottest hot I've ever felt
So hot
So hot
Like the center of the sun
Hot hotter hottest
Singed and burnt
I live to tell the tale
Jordan Jarvis, Grade 7
Elk Ridge Middle School, UT

My Crush

Every day I see you
I break down and want to cry.
We used to be good friends
But now we're far and wide.

You mean a lot to me
And you will never know.
The feelings that I have for you
I can never show.

I'm afraid that you will laugh at me
I'm afraid that I will cry.
I'm afraid that you won't like me back
And for that I must continue to lie.

You will never know the feelings
I have locked inside my heart.
I guess I'll keep it in me
Until I slowly fall apart.
Ashley Fuller, Grade 7
Mandalay Middle School, CO

Fog

I'm Fog
I sneak like a snake.
I'm never heard but I'm seen.
I stay in the depth of night.
You think I'm nothing,
until I blind you, and cause you to crash.
Then morning comes and I sneak away
Like nothing ever happened.
Kodi Watson, Grade 7
Eagle Point Middle School, OR

Summer Fever

I wish school was out,
And I could be at home,
Getting ready to ride,
The range I love to roam.

But here I sit,
Thinking and hoping,
School will be out,
And we'll get to roping.

Finally the bell rings,
At last school is out,
Running out the door,
Kids scream and shout.

The summer will go fast,
But I will have fun,
Riding and working,
Under the warm summer sun.
Ross Wahlert, Grade 8
Pawnee Jr/Sr High School, CO

The River

Rushing down a narrow path,
Crashing, and spilling over the top,
I put my hand into it,
The water is icy cold against my fingers.
I pull out my hand with a jerk,
As a little purple fish swims by.
Splashing, sloshing, sleeping,
Finally emptying into the ocean,
Ending with a small still breeze.
Sara Williams, Grade 7
Barnette Magnet School, AK

Basketball

Orange as the sun,
she bounces high.
Reaching for the basket
and diving in.
She flies to each player,
waiting to make the next dive.
As she's tossed in the air,
she smiles with pride,
her team won the game!
Amanda Amodemo, Grade 7
Mears Middle School, AK

King Kong

King Kong
Giant, hairy
Fighting, loving, scaring
Battling for his blonde lady
Ape.
Pablo Chavira-Nieto, Grade 8
Place Middle School, CO

Love Is Weird

One day I fell in love with this girl.
So I bought her diamonds and pearls.
Then we went to the park.
And she started to bark
So I went home to pack.
And I never came back.
Olajuwan Johnson, Grade 8
Place Middle School, CO

Listen to Running

The sweat was
running down.
My heart was pumping,
as fast as it can!
My leg muscles growing stronger,
as the heat beams down on me!
I'm kicking up dirt as I run,
my shoes hitting the floor.
The finish line is close,
the leader in a cheer.
One, two, three people
zip past the finish line!
I stop running,
I can hear my heart pounding.
The winner is announced,
as I walk up to get my silver medal.
People cheering and shouting my name,
but all I hear is my heart still pounding!
Ashley Bencomo, Grade 8
Mesa Middle School, NM

A Teacher

Countless teachers I've seen
there's one in particular,
Mrs. Zhang,
she's the best I've ever had.

She is very special to me.
Like the sun to a plant.
She opened the doors to my knowledge,
she led me to my success.
She taught me things,
I'll never forget.

Mrs. Zhang,
she helped me when I have given up,
her life is like a candle,
she lights herself on fire,
to chase away the darkness,
to light our heart with knowledge.

Thank you,
Mrs. Zhang.
For devoting your life to teaching.
Fran Li, Grade 8
Sylvester Middle School, WA

Clouds

They are fluffy;
Like cotton candy
That floats in the sky.
It feels like a mist
That gets you wet.
They taste like water
Refreshing your mouth.
They are chilly,
Especially when
They are about to snow.
You could hear the wind
If you flew in them
Without being in a plane.
Too bad you can't!

Andrew Hansen, Grade 8
Cedar Park Christian School – Everett Campus, WA

Beauty of the Forest

On my way back
Home
Oh what a joy
But then
I stopped
For the beauty
Was right there in front of me
It was a cold morning
But my heart was as warm as a fire
For the mysterious forest
Was upon me
It was very calm but my mind was buzzing in imagination
With the snow heavy
And the sun shining
The sparkles were like a million
Little Christmas tree lights
For when I reached home I took one last look
At my beauty
The forest
On Christmas morning

Wyatt Anderson, Grade 7
Terry 7-8 School, MT

Half-time Show

BEEP, BEEP, half time bell.
That means it's time to go out
and give the performance of my life.
As I walk out to the center of the court,
thinking about my routine,
trying to remember to get my kicks higher,
and spins just perfect.
All eyes are on me, watching my every move.
The music starts,
I smile and I'm on stage.
Let the show begin.

Taralyn Cruz, Grade 7
Mandalay Middle School, CO

The Stars

The stars above…
I wonder what they're made of.
They really shine
Way above the pine.
They don't give off much light,
But they're still bright.
I love the stars
Up there with Mars.
What if they were to disappear?
I would live in fear!
My favorite is Orion's Belt;
When I look at it, I simply melt.
The stars can get through anything,
Yet are as silent as an owl's flapless wing,
Whenever I need a helping lift,
They're like a silent, calming gift.
Wherever I go,
I will always feel their glow.

Emily Kinsey, Grade 8
Canfield Middle School, ID

That Night

You told me that fatal night
That it would never run out
It would last longer than time itself
Those words have kept me strong through the years
I love you
It's the best last sentence ever
And I love you too

Sadie DeCent, Grade 7
Eureka Middle School, MT

Friends

Sometimes they're there,
    sometimes they're not.
You always seem to finish
each other's sentences,
    but you can't figure out why.
You wonder how long you'll stay friends
or how long you'll be in an argument;
however, you never seem
    to
        know.
You try not to get mad,
or you try not to get sad, but it just happens.
You try to be happy like the memories from summer,
but you know,
    it's not going to happen.
You miss those days playing,
screaming,
    just having a blast
But you know things are
    different
you try not to admit it.

Vanessa Otamendi, Grade 8
Walt Morey Middle School, OR

Soft Magentic Night
The twirple sticks were bustling
The dum-lum bush was rustling
But, me and you were hustling
On the soft magentic night.

The vrum-vrum cats were vrooming
The noisy whistlers tuning
But, me and you were swooning
On the soft magentic night.

The lim lime clouds were fading
The clumal trees were shading
Now, you and me are dating
On the soft magentic night.
Betty Neils, Grade 7
McKemy Middle School, AZ

My Plane
Ever soaring, never dying plane!
Always flying, never sinking.
Always swooping and diving.
Colored yellow and black
Without propellers
It's engine whirls
The plane glides
It's fast
Cool!
Robert Long, Grade 7
Beacon Country Day School, CO

Ever Changing
What's to come who's to say,
Not knowing what will blow your way,
Strongly believing you're always right,
Keeping in mind you are not to fight,
Leading a life you've yet to find,
Never letting go of what's left behind,

Another day has come to find,
Love is leading life so blind,
Broken hearts from silly boys,
Emotions fill life with noise,
Girls confide with music and laughter,
All together it's another chapter,

Knowing there's more years to come,
We come together and remember,
There can't be fear nor jealousy or hate,
Life's too short to keep a full plate

Having faith when laid to rest,
The thought of life at its best,
Wanting to keep the journey alive,
Leaving our trail left behind
Samantha Winters, Grade 9
Mesa Ridge High School, CO

Love and Hate
Love and hate are different things sometimes you can confuse
Hate is something you'll have forever and love you'll sometimes lose
No matter how strong you love someone you might feel some hate one day
They might have hit you very strong or most likely what they say
You'll learn to keep the hate inside and never let it out
But when they tick you off so hard it'll make you want to shout
So love and hate are different things you'll think over every day
But when you find that perfect one, forever you will stay
Diana Gonzalez, Grade 7
Somerton Middle School, AZ

Book…
If I were a book I wouldn't shove you full of knowledge.
I'd be so darn interesting you couldn't put me into storage.

You would read me 'till the sun came up and your eyes would bag and sag.
And your mother would come and she would nag and nag.

"How could you stay up? So very, very late?!
I told you to be in bed at exactly 6:08!"

And what could you really say to her? That you couldn't put me down?
'Cause if you said that she would spank you out of town!

But she would wait for an answer and tap her fussy feet.
And all that you could say was "Gee I dunno Ma! You really got me beat!"

So then she would ground you for a whole 'nuther week.
But you wouldn't complain, no you wouldn't even speak.

'Cause you would have stayed locked in your bedroom anyway,
Reading that fantastic book you just couldn't put away.
Graciela Fierro, Grade 7
21st Century Public Academy, NM

Courage*
It is not the courage to become a father or to be a doctor,
it is the guts to stand up for what is right,
and become a soldier, that put their lives on the line to save another's.
It is a courage that nobody can change or take away from you
and is kept until death, and even after death.
Some military families, even pass down the Honor and Glory to their children
that they may join the military to keep the tradition going.
We may tell war stories if others ask, "What is war like?"
or "How can you stand the memories of war?"
But only those that have been can tell us what it is really like.
Courage is not to be chosen, given, or even commanded to have.
It is something that is earned, and should not be taken away unless lost.
To all the soldiers out there serving, wherever you may be —
please remember to be safe, and we support and love our troops,
and we want you to come home soon and safe.
Chelsea Blanchard, Grade 9
Bonneville High School, ID
Dedicated to all of the soldiers

Springtime
Like the wind, the tide, the dawn, and the hurricane,
It comes bearing new life among the old.
Like being unmasked from the haze and the rain,
A new light is shown from beyond the cold.

Springtime sheds light back on old memories,
Memories that come like a flash, flicker or flare.
Springtime is like new breezes up in the tall trees,
Trees that had just recently no life there.

Like the wind, the tide, the dawn and the hurricane,
It comes quickly but not without being seen.
It brings joyful memories that can ease any pain,
The springtime brings love, hope and grass that is green.
Shannon Donnelly, Grade 9
Tempe Preparatory Academy, AZ

He Will Not Run from Me
He will not run from me today
For he is sick
And rolled too long
We did not see for we were sleeping
Your head hung low
For that morning there were tears
You were the one I had trusted for so long
As I had feared today is the day we must part
This shall be our meeting place where one day I will lay aside
As I look into the sky I shall see you and no one else
But my companion, my friend and most of all my horse.
Morgan Taylor, Grade 7
LaMotte School, MT

The Dream of a Buckle
I picked out a big black 4-H steer,
And hoped that this would be my year.
To win that big round golden buckle,
That would make my big brothers chuckle.
My first task was to give him a name,
Hard work together would bring us fame.
Bubba is the name that came to me,
Cause he's so big and easy to see.
Washing, feeding and time for fair,
Bubba has grown lots of hair.
We are now in the show ring,
Good luck to Bubba and I, this will bring.
The judge gives me a serious look,
He better put me in his book.
And sure enough I am first in line,
And I am feeling very fine.
I have the buckle in my hand,
And I hear the crowd cheering in the stand.
It sure was a great day,
Now Bubba looks at me as if to say,
We won…now where's my hay????
Hayley Allen, Grade 8
Torrington Middle School, WY

From the Start
You are like a star, stunningly designed,
Luring me away from the cold stillness
That lingers in my raw, deceptive mind
Freeing me from this distressing illness.

Even though you can save me from this hell,
I can't help but question if you are true.
If you are not, release me from this spell
So I can save my tortured soul from you.

Still, I long for you to fulfill my life,
And show me what it is like to feel love
Without twisting in pain and spiteful strife,
But wishing upon the bright stars above.

So, my dear, protect my once shattered heart
For I have always loved you, from the start.
Renatte Mecozzi, Grade 9
Tombstone High School, AZ

How Are You?
If someone you love seems to be slipping away,
I believe that they'll be fine.
But the question that's on my mind is,
how are you?

I prayed for you the other day.
I prayed that you'd pull through the sorrow,
and bravely face what might happen tomorrow.
How are you?

By day, a clear sky may be empty,
save for the wandering sun.
But come night, come thousands of twinkling stars,
who's number will never be one.

Grieving alone is too much to bear.
So pretend you're a star in the sky.
Never alone, never neglected, and never afraid to ask "why?"
How are you?
Shannon Ludeman, Grade 8
Arbor School, WA

A Real Friend
May a smile always reach you when your day's gone wrong,
And the birds always be there when you need a song.
May you always have strength to go another day,
And never a sibling who gets in your way.

Now, keep this in mind when your day's going well,
'Cause for right now you might be feeling swell,
But in the future you will see
That a pesky sibling is just what you need.
Haley Kight, Grade 9
Portland Cornerstone Academy, OR

Hershey Kiss

I sit and look longingly at it, as I am about to encounter a passionate experience.
All I can do is just focus on it, it's too good to waste.
Just waiting for the perfect moment. There it sits in perfect proportion, untouched, sophisticated, fragile, and delicate. A whiff of the smell of heaven and taste bud perfection, wrapped in a thin layer of foil.
It taunts me, I am at war with myself, questioning when is the right time. I start to unravel it, the thin layer of tin foil slowly tears and starts to crumble. All I know is, once it's gone, it's gone, and there is no going back. I just watch and see a glimmer of light bounce off of it, making it shine, to glorious perfection. There it is, with a little name tag crumpled by its side, like a best friend or companion. I touch it, it is so smooth that my finger slides off the side of it and onto the cold table. The aroma is so intense, I can't explain it. I hear it just talking to me, telling me to come closer, it's taunting me. Finally, the temptation is too much, I give in, I can't take it anymore. I pick up this delectable treat and place it, slowly, into my mouth.
My taste buds come alive, savoring the sweetness as it breaks apart in my mouth, melting evenly on my tongue, it starts running down my throat, trying to make what I have left in my mouth last. I live for these moments,
I will never forget them, every time I taste the world's famous Hershey Kiss.

Jennifer Bruni, Grade 7
Sky Vista Middle School, CO

Texting — Can't Live with It, Can't Live Without It

Waz up? IDK? LOL! Sometimes it seems like I'm under a spell! My feelings about texting are so intricate to explain, but you'll find them credible because I'm sure you feel the same if you're a teen who loves texting, but has to pay for your own phone and you're not old enough to have a job of your own. My plan makes me pay 10 cents for each text, and when I ponder on the bill that I'll have to pay next; my mind diligently tries to think of ways to defray for the superfluous conversations I've had day to day. I wish I could free myself and believe me I've tried, but then a friend will text me and I'll hurry to reply to their question or forward or just random remark…soon I've been texting for over an hour! I've done it while eating, doing homework, and even in the shower! Self control is all I need, I'm really not that bad, my bill compared to most my friends is really not that sad. But to quit it all together…oh, I know that I can do it! But I'll feel so cut off from the world…oh, somehow I'll pull through it! — 1 Hour L8R — Wow! I think I've overcome it! I haven't touched my phone in ages, I was so silly to think I couldn't quit! My mind now fills with possibilities to spend my money, since I don't have to pay for texting my days will now be sunny! In my daydreams I've already bought out the mall with all my newfound dough…oh! Hey, was that my cell phone? New message! Got to go!

Celicia Howard, Grade 9
Bonneville High School, ID

Contentment

I am contentment
Everyone should have me and want me
Although I rarely want
I am happy with what I have
And don't often wish upon getting more stuff
Like video gamers who think
They need all the new games
People who have me
Normally are very cheerful
Like a small child
At the fair for the first time
They are also very optimistic
Looking at life half full

Unlike a COW F
                E
                N   Who thinks the GRASS is greener
On the other side of the C
                E

I am contentment
Happy with what I have
Always looking on the bright side

Alex Brouwer, Grade 7
Sunnyside Christian Elementary School, WA

Winter Snowflakes

The snow was beautiful
So so beautiful
The snow glistened like a pearl
As the snowflakes fell like a summer's rain

I played all day in that pearl
And laughed as those snowflakes fell on my tongue
I had so much fun as they fell on my tongue
But it soon became dark and my dog started to bark
So I had to go inside

Alie Meisinger, Grade 7
Mandalay Middle School, CO

Live for Highs and Lows

The best song is written by you,
Because you can sing it when you're lonely and missing,
You can sing it on those long walks home,
And you can sing it in your sleep because then…
You can sing it to him.

The worst kind of list goes on
And on
And reminds you that you don't have time
To just be silly and act like you're seven again.

The best person doesn't give up easily,
They honestly care about what you're trying to say,
And if you say it's hard to explain,
Their only response is "try."

The worst unsettling thought is that maybe
The footprints I've made in this life
Are just like snow,
Only here until the next big storm.

Laurel Williams, Grade 9
South Jordan Middle School, UT

Family

Your heart, your soul, your weakness.
The people that support you and are important to you.
Ones that care and that are cautious.
Your heroes.
The ones you might like or hate.
The ones that tell your secrets.
Your best friends they can be.
They are the family that loves you.
The family that you love.
Ones you would cross the world for.
Your family, the ones that will be with you till the end.
The family that you should cherish.
Because in the end you will lose them
Anyway
Any day.

Mark Bernal, Grade 9
Queen Creek High School, AZ

You

Twisting my feelings and thoughts, you came
Tearing through me like a tornado
Running and turning my life upside down
A twisted soul you are
Who gave you the right? Not me

Hidden thoughts like a cloudy day
lies were told until now
The honesty of a full moon shone through you
You said your feelings for me have changed
I was no longer to be in your life

You taught me never to love again
Fear, pain, and loneliness was caused by you
No longer will I trust as I used to
A blaze of fire burned through me
As my hate for you reflected in my eyes

Rachel Vice, Grade 7
Sky Vista Middle School, CO

Winter

The clouds put blankets of snow everywhere it goes,
The snow is soft and fluffy to everything it touches,
It baths the land in a soft pure glow,
You look to see a desert of white cold snow,
The sky is gray and the land is white,
You look and try to find green trees,
Everything is asleep right now,
But just wait until spring.

Brianna Johnson, Grade 8
Enterprise Middle School, WA

Basketball

Basketball born from the street and up.
Basketball isn't something you know…
It is taught or told.

Basketball hear the swish of the net.
Hear the buzzer…and swish

Fresh orange ball on the court.
10 players on the court.

Sweat rushing down the necks.
People screaming your name.
Can't miss the shot.
People, fans, teammates counting on you.
Got a lot of time.
Jump see the ball in the air.
Nothing but net as it glides in the rim.

Basketball from the street.
To the gym.
To the NBA.

Kimani Julious, Grade 7
North Middle School, CO

Your Face

Your face is beautiful
Your eyes are blue like the ocean
Your lips are red like the roses
Your nose is beautiful and little
You hair is yellow like the gold
And that is your face

Andrea Herrera, Grade 7
Somerton Middle School, AZ

Roller Coaster

Tack, tock, tick
The track went click
Suspense took over
I needed a lucky four leaf clover
If I ever survive this
I will praise God for this bliss!

Tack, tock, tick
The track went click
Clutching my handlebars
My hands were turning into tar
I'm scared of this big toy
Oh boy oh joy

Tack, tock, tick
The track went click
Here we go
Get ready to go from head to toe
I opened my mouth
But all that came out was
AHHHH!!!!

Alicia Andrew, Grade 7
Sky Vista Middle School, CO

Winter Is

Walking through a snow-white castle,
Like drifting through a clouded sky
Peaceful, serene beauty
Surrounding every inch of land.

Wildlife indulging
Lively, joyful creatures
Still, quiet movements
As if nothing's there.

Fluffy ice lay beneath me,
Soft and enchanting
The crunch under my feet;
A calm alluring sight.

Freezing weather
Dropping snow,
Winter is
My favorite show.

Gillian Jackson, Grade 8
Valley Academy Charter School, AZ

Waiting

The dog silently waits on the second stair as she adores her toy
A round, yellow object most often seen flung through the air.

There are many of them, she knows, hidden
In a box in the wall which she cannot open.

Only her masters can, and her masters are gone,
A routine she has become accustomed to
Yet still, she is lonely.

She knows her masters make her toy fly the farthest
In her favorite game, But her masters are gone,
So the game cannot be played and the only thing left to do is wait.

MacCoy Smith, Grade 9
Mountain Ridge Jr High School, UT

Untitled*

The day you died was no ordinary day.
It was the day that I had lost you.
It was the day I knew you weren't going to come back.
The day I heard the news it just blew me away.
I wish I could take back what happened to you.
But there just isn't.
I wish I could go back in time, to say I love you one more time.
I wish it was something else and not you.
I want you to be here to help me through things.
I want you to be here to walk me down the aisle on my Wedding Day.
But most of all
I want you here so I can say "I love you" without a tear.

Morgen Shoemaker, Grade 8
Fort Morgan Middle School, CO
*Dedicated to my father Richard Allen Shoemaker 1975-2001

Dream World!

I am from the state of arches and red rocks,
Where all people are free and kind to one another.
Utah is where I live and where I want to be.

I am from a loving and caring family,
Who is always there for me when I need help.
They always make sure that I am safe and that I stay out of trouble.

I am from a big family
Who loves one another and always has fun together.
My family gets along like peas in a pod, or at least they do most of the time.
I love my family and my heritage.

I am from a school that believes we are all equal
And should be treated equally and with respect.
My school is full of kindness and laughter.

I am from a world full of amazing things
With plenty of things to do and see.
The world I live in is full of hopes, dreams, and many wonders.

Anna Parry, Grade 7
Our Lady of Lourdes Catholic School, UT

The One

She gets my attention like purple silver haze
She makes my days brighter than my happy days
I miss her she makes me smile when I'm with her
I wish we could run away and I have a nice life with her
I call her every night yes she so dear
I call her every night and wish she was here
She my sun and my moon light
I might be going blind because she's so bright
She's more than perfect you can't explain her with words

I can imagine her being my wife
Just me and her for the rest of my life
There isn't anyone else she's the love of my life
She's not just a person she's not just a girl
She's very special to me she's my whole world
I always knew this love was meant to be
This life will soon end but our live will forever last
It will continue on even when we have past

Daniel Andrade, Grade 8
Cimarron Springs Elementary School, AZ

Prison

I lay on my brick cot
All sweaty and stained my sheets are
Night sweats drain me when I'm hot
I'm stuck between these metal bars
Day and night men have attitudes
Barking and punching
Shows no gratitude
The sounds of their bone crunching

Alone in your chambers
Nightmares come alive
Pitch black means danger
Trying to escape alive
Some prisoners want freedom
Some awake from the alarm
Some go to God's kingdom
And if you are an eagle you mean no harm

Prison is living in fire
Eagles are not the picture
Everyone is a liar
Everything is a mixture
Prison

Miranda Whitfield, Grade 7
Sky Vista Middle School, CO

Football

Football is so fun you should try it
If I can't play it, I'll have a fit
I hate to be indoors
I want to play some more
So go outdoors and just go play it.

Jordan Andreasen, Grade 7
Thomas Edison Charter School - North, UT

Weather I Enjoy: A Story

Two of my favorite kinds of weather
All tied in together
To create this literature art
That I hope will touch your heart
Don't run off and play with a toy
Just sit back, read, and enjoy

It whips around all of creation
Over every continent, every nation
A whirling breeze on a hot summer's day
It moves around the trees or hay
And everything is still
But suddenly, you get a chill
It is wind

Shining down on your face
As hot as someone's eyes filled with mace
Go play in the ocean or the lake
But don't forget the sun screen for Peter's sake
Your skin might turn golden, or as we know it tan
Or it could get red like the cheeks of that Santa Claus man
It is the sunshine

Kaitlin Marie Kitchens, Grade 8
Cedar Ridge Middle School, OR

Alex

Alex is a goofball, a weirdo at that too!
She's real good friends with everybody
And enemies…JUST a FEW!
All she does is laugh — never does she cry
More and more people like her
As every day goes by
Everybody trust her, now that you can see
She's pretty good at everything
Especially being a friend to me!

Marina Duran, Grade 7
St Catherine of Siena School, CO

Alone

I wander though the tall leaning trees
Whose limbs are drooping and saying please
Quit spitting these heavy weights
We want to raise our limbs with ease

I trudge through the thick deep snow
Who is tugging at my feet and screaming no
Do not leave a footprint in me
Leave me untouched, let me be

The wind is screeching out clear
It's biting at my face and giving me no cheer
I keep wandering, wondering if I'll survive
It seems as if this forest is alive

Lindsay Stickel, Grade 7
Terry 7-8 School, MT

How Long Is Forever?
How long is Forever?
How long shall we say?
Does Forever last a lifetime?
Does it even last a day?

Does it stretch into eternity
Like a rose toward the sky?
Does it rise up like a little bird,
And spread its wings and fly?

Is Forever ever-changing,
Like the tree leaves in the fall?
Does Forever know when it shall end?
Does it know anything at all?

Is it different for every person?
Does it live as long as they?
Does it have a heart that loves and feels?
Does it only know the day?

Perhaps I am forever,
Perhaps you are, too,
Perhaps it knows the things we know,
And all we ever knew.
Katie Taylor, Grade 9
Sehome High School, WA

What It Takes to Be a Real Cowboy
Running through the streets they played,
One the cowboy,
The other the Indian,
Bang bang went the fake gun,
Thwang thwang went the fake arrows,
'Til suddenly they stopped,
Towering above them,
There was a real cowboy,
Their eyes were saucers,
They shook like an earthquake,
Shyly one spoke,
"What does it take,
To be a real cowboy,"
The cowboy grinned,
"True grit son,
True grit."
Dylan Karr, Grade 8
Eugene Christian School, OR

A Bird's Sweet Spring
I am a bird hear me tweet
I am perched on a branch
Eating my cherry blossom treat
I feel the wind so cool and sweet,
But when it's gone
I feel the heat.
Mackenzie Lawrence, Grade 7
Eagle Point Middle School, OR

The Darkness
The darkness has seen my heart
I hope from you I will never part
The closer to me this darkness becomes
The more pain everyone sums

I have to part from you
I can't believe what I'm saying is true
But I don't want to see the pain hurt you
For I love you, can't you see?
When it hurts you, it hurts me

I have a quest I must overtake
I'd never thought I'd see such a crime
Like hurting my lover, my valentine

We shall run towards the light
Far from the darkness sight
There are many things that we have seen
And because of that, you are my king
Beth Poling, Grade 7
Shadow Ridge Middle School, CO

Ode to My House
It sits and waits
for me to arrive.
I sit inside and
watch the cars drive by.
It shelters me when it's
raining or snowing.
We chill outside
and hear the wind blowing.
We always look at the stars
sometimes we see Mars.
We never fight.
When it's dark we say goodnight.
Joseph Barrio, Grade 8
La Plata Middle School, NM

Yellow Orbs
The bright yellow orb
still wears an elfish-like chapeau
yet in the house, how rude?
Tiny light brown freckles
speck the sphere.
Star-like mark darkening
the underside of the orb
jubilant tastes, watery, yet crisp;
smooth as marble
aroma wavers off into sweetness
freshly unique
Making Mother Nature proud
Behold! A yellow tomato
Beckons someone to masticate it,
thoroughly.
Erica Masters, Grade 8
Cedar Ridge Middle School, OR

Caring Family*
When I was scared, who dared to care?
My one and only father.
When I was sick, who was by my side,
and when I cried, who dried my eyes?
My one beautiful mother.
When I am bored, who cheers me up?
My one bratty brother.
When I was in my hospital, who
came to visit me?
My Loving Family!
Amy Beagles, Grade 7
East Valley Middle School, MT
*Dedicated to my whole family

Curiosity
Curiosity is that one sweeping ghost
That swarms through your mind
For it's the parasite and you're the host.
It's asks in a way, so kind,
Whisper's in your listening ear,
"Don't you really want to know,
For what do you have to fear.
Your wanting really does show."
"My wanting for what?" you demand
Aware of the peculiar accusation.
"You're questioning where I stand.
I strongly sense your hesitation."
Replies the taunting voice,
"What will come of one little peek
But the satisfaction of your choice
That you followed what you seek."

The real question is what will you do,
Will you walk away or will you give in.
Lacey Reece, Grade 7
21st Century Public Academy, NM

The Inkworld*
In this story the inkspell has been spun
For beware the story has just begun
The father is dying
The mother is crying

The Prince of Sighs
He has finally died
But do not cry
His son did not die

As the story moves along
The war shall move on
The evil king will die
For the White Women are nearby
Michael Trepanier, Grade 8
Pomerene School, AZ
*Inspired by "Inkspell"
by Cornelia Funk

High Merit Poems – Grades 7, 8, and 9

Hate

The trap to destroy humans is hate,
The seduction of revenge is the ultimate bait,
It was intended to be our fate,
Designed to destroy,
All the care,
That exists to this day.

He was not prepared,
For the Son who dared,
To save all for whom he cared,
From the devil's greatest sin,
Against love,
The devil could not win.

The devil did not have foresight
To see that Christ's saving light
Would bring back all that was right.
He did not expect an offering
Of the Lamb of God
That would save everything.

Keenan Emery, Grade 7
Holy Family Academy, OR

The Ways of Nature

Rain jiggles as it jumps into a puddle
Rain splashes on my face like a dog giving me kisses
Rain falls like a lullaby just getting sung. I like rain

Stars sparkle in the sky like the shine in someone's eye
Stars fly across the sky like a little man in a canon
Stars dance in the moonlight. I like stars

Snow falls like a date on the horizon
Snow melts like a finger just getting burnt
Snow tastes like a sweet lollipop I enjoy. I like snow

Mary Brehon, Grade 7
Eaton Middle School, CO

The Gridiron

I believe in the greatness of football
The love of the game
The fire that runs every player
The joy of victory
The tears of defeat
Blood, sweat, determination
But I don't believe in saying I can't
I believe in running the ball to the house
I believe in passing to victory
I believe in the friends you make
Laughter, tears, victory

And I believe in the blood that gets you there,
the struggles along the way, and the pride in victory.

Paul Eayrs, Grade 7
Terry 7-8 School, MT

Humanity Crying

Tell us it's over, our struggles, our pain
all we want to hear, is you calling our name.
Tell us it's over, hear our screams, hear our cries,
because all we've received, is bitter lies
Tell us it's over; don't let us die here, alone
and through our lips escapes a haunting moan
Tell us it's over, take us away from this lonely place,
where all we're seeking here is your face
Tell us it's over, as the blood runs down our wrists,
tell us the lovely truth, that some have missed
Tell us it's over, suicide, and cyanide
is how most of the human race died
Tell us it's over, the lies, through this world consumes us
we still remain, greedy with lust
Please tell us it's over, we grope blindly through the black
though the enemy may attack
Tell us it's over
why are we dying?
why is humanity crying?

Jonathan Alden, Grade 7
Eagle Point Middle School, OR

Moon and Sun

The Moon and Sun were in a fight,
Because Sun wanted to be in dark and Moon in light,

But Sun couldn't stay awake till night,
And Moon thought day was too bright,

So Moon stayed dark and Sun stayed light,
So up to this day they are still in the fight!

Sierra Carlson, Grade 7
Shadow Ridge Middle School, CO

The Winds of War

Alone, alone in a dying land,
I sit and watch the final fall.
Alone, alone in a war-torn land,
The winds of war reign over all.

The land was once alive and strong,
T'was thought it would stand evermore.
Now it has fallen, dead and gone,
Fallen to the winds of war.

Hate caused the pain, the fear, and the death,
Hate and envy caused the fall.
Hate caused men to breathe their last breaths,
The winds of war have long stood tall.

If it could be started, started again,
There might have been a better mend.
If all could live in peace again,
The winds of war would meet their end.

Jack Despain, Grade 8
Mountain Ridge Jr High School, UT

Always Loving You
My heart always skips a beat,
Just because you are so sweet.
You hold the key to my heart,
So we will never part.
All I want to do,
Is forever love you.
You always make me smile,
And it goes for a million miles.
I want you to always hold me tight,
Even after we fight.
Our love is always strong,
Even when we don't get along.
When you're gone I always miss,
The warmth of your every single kiss.
We will always be together,
Even longer than forever.
Jessica Pettingill, Grade 9
Shelley Sr High School, ID

The Fireflies' Dance
Rain beats the ground
Like a steel drum

Each drop forms
Part of the continuous rhythm.

Fireflies dance
To the soft
Pat, pat, pat.

A crack of lightning splits the sky
As the calm beat
Turns to a million guns.

The fireflies fly away
From the harsh
Splash, splash, splash
And wait 'til the dancing of tomorrow.
Erin Norsworthy, Grade 7
LaMotte School, MT

Star
The stars in the sky
Dancing with the big bright moon
Add life to the night
Kayla Promes, Grade 7
Mandalay Middle School, CO

Lost
Lost
Motivated by fear
Needing guidance
Overly dramatic
Why am I alone?
Devin A. Debowski, Grade 7
Sedona Charter School, AZ

Brothers Are…
A ggravating and annoying **b** oring, don't do much
C aring, not, they really don't care **d** umb, don't do much right
E mbarrassing, they yell out who you like **f** un to make fun of
G reat for nothing **h** alf-hearted is how they do everything
I nsane, they have no brain **j** okers, they love to make you laugh
K ind when they want to be **l** oud never quiet
M ean but are rarely nice **n** ot the greatest people
O verly obnoxious **p** ersistent, never giving up
Q uite loud **r** ude have no manners
S tupid, have no brains **t** oxic, it's easier to live without them
U sually annoying **v** ery dumb
W eird attitudes **x** citing to be around
Y our worst nightmare **Z** any, but you've got to love them
Kierston Waliezer, Grade 7
La Center Middle School, WA

A Current World Problem
This thing I've heard, it breaks my heart.
I can't stop thinking of it, so harsh and cold. I cannot stop this start.
It burdens me with pain and sorrow,
So sad, so bad, oh the horror!
But this feeling I know
Oh I wish it would go!
This thing, it scares me to the core.
I heard 'bout it today, and it's like a sore.
It's called slavery, and it happens still.
More than one has met it's kill.
Oh, thank you, Jesus, for where I live.
Oh, help me stay faithful and give
To the missionaries who help these people!
Let them find a way,
And I'll still pray,
Ah, Lord God, please help them find that way!
Stephanie Mitchell, Grade 9
Arlington Christian School, WA

Cruelty
The teachers have an evil plot
that will put us in turmoil
they'll say *this field trip is postponed until next Friday*
but I know what they mean
they are actually saying *it'll never happen* until we go insane.
These thoughts all reek inside my head
like dead rats and spoiled milk.

It's hard to not believe
something that actually happens.
I've tried and tried and tried again
to listen closely for that van
but when that van is nowhere in sight
my head hangs low.
I try to hold tight.

Josh Burdi, Grade 7
Sonoran Science Academy, AZ

Cousin to Cousin*
Well, cuz, I'll tell ya:
Life for me ain't been no diamond road;
It's had bumps in it,
And cracks,
And holes,
And places where there are no lanes —
One way.
Yet all the time
I'se been drivin' on,
And turnin' corners,
And makin' those U turns,
And sometimes goin' down the wrong lane,
Where there are no signs.
So cuz, don't give up.
Don't you stop drivin'
'Cause you think it's kinder hard.
Don't stop now —
For I'se still drivin', Cuz
I'se still goin',
And life for me ain't been no diamond road.

Jayson Ige, Grade 7
Mears Middle School, AK
Patterned after "Mother to Son" by Langston Hughes

Basketball
Basketball is my fave;
It is the sport I crave.

My mind always wanders back to the game
When school is boring and way too tame.

I like the fast action
Much better than math fractions.

I like the slam dunk
Much more than music funk.

I like to dribble
Much more than English scribble.

I always want to play
School just gets in the way.

That is why basketball is my passion
It will always be my fashion.

Ashley Kroeger, Grade 7
Coronado K 8 School, AZ

Autumn Leaves
The autumn leaves did a dance of their own
Circling the earth and its people
They swished and swirled, thanks to the wind
Autumn will leave and come again
To do a dance of their own

Jordan Lowe, Grade 7
Sagewood Middle School, CO

Childhood Memories
Trying to hold sand in cupped hands in vain,
Childhood slips away with each tiny grain.

Trying to hide behind rustling curtains,
So I don't have to clean my room, again.
Trying to explain that it didn't go as planned,
Though I know Mom just won't understand.

Stones skipped across the glassy pond,
Each ripple forming a circle beyond.
Swimming with my brother in a freezing lake,
Tadpoles following in our wake.

Scaring Mom with slippery frogs
Then trying to keep them from the dogs.
Spinning in circles in the dying grass,
Then running to the door, slamming into glass

Always finding a reason to complain,
Just to drive my mother insane.
Moving dining room chairs to make our fort grand,
Telling Mom we were only trying to expand

To hold on to childhood is to try to hold sand,
You can't always keep it in your hands.

Sara Matsumoto, Grade 9
Tempe Preparatory Academy, AZ

If You Try
If you try, when all is lost around you
If you believe at the hardest point, as others cower beside you
If you can be disciplined, while disgrace is of the essence
Or not give in to what is easily taken

If weakness is a trait, but is not easily accepted
If perfection is shot for and just not imagined
If the option to quit is hovering above you
And cover is found
While doubt has been achieved, yet you reject it

If control is in the pocket and you can patch the hole
Then check the ground and clean it
To show others you can obtain an important role
If strength is just on the horizon and you can pay the toll
To keep achieving when nobody is watching
And stop when you've passed perfection

If you can accept a challenge without cracking
If being knocked down does not disturb your composure
If you are among greats and have mentality of a normal
If you can move as a whole, but work alone
What lies within is a path
Which people of whom talent is a virtue can only travel

Justin Rowsell, Grade 7
Sky Vista Middle School, CO

Love

Love is like a burning flame that never dies out, like a shining star in the night sky. Love is a good thing it comes in many ways once you find this love you feel all warm inside. It tingles and tickles you want to speak but can't it's tucked inside until you finally get the courage it will escape and you will feel this so called love.

Angie-Marie Palafox, Grade 7
Elk Ridge Middle School, UT

A Place Called Home

I am from empty, dirty paint buckets, bunches of silver and bronze medals, several decks of red and blue playing cards, aluminum baseball bats, and brown leather baseball mitts
In my yard, you may see a tattered homemade pitching device, a large, green four wheeler, ladders encrusted in multiple colors of paint, many noisy wind chimes, and my grass-covered lawnmower
I am from the spacious Culver Park, 'The Store,' a very popular store, the homes of my friends, the plain school grounds, and my favorite restaurant, the Round Butte Inn
Descendant of my my Debbie, my dad Michael, my only living grandpa Don, and my two grandmas, Grandma Shirley and Grandma Cason
I constantly hear "Were you born in a barn?" "You smart aleck," "That music is too much for me," "If it were a snake, it'd have bitten you," and "We aren't paying to heat the garage."
I am from big bowls of Jell-O, bunches of bags of chips, tasty strawberry shortcake, perfectly cooked cheeseburgers, and sweet cherry cobbler
My memories are in boxes in my closet as well as at my mom's house
That is where I am from

Michael Porter, Grade 8
Culver Middle School, OR

No Sunlight

In my world of creativity and expression no walls no windows lighting does not appear with the touch of a switch no sunlight exists in the air but with a sprinkle of imagination and a pinch of magic and fun you then create your own doors of success windows of love and friendship and your own special sunlight of inspiration and ideas then when I open my eyes it's a guaranteed sight of the world I live in where things are handed to you and everything is taken for granted I wish that people could see life and excitement through my attitude and live in my world where everything is created with your mind's eyes and hard work even just to create a door to open success or sunlight to see your inspiration and ideas

Taylor Porras, Grade 8
Mandalay Middle School, CO

Love

I'm trying to figure out what love is supposed to be about
In the beginning you're always so nice but in the end, you're as cold as ice
In the beginning you would never think that they could be so mean in a simple blink
I told you once I told you twice
That when you love you pay the price
You feel so empty cold and blue
So stressed out and so confused

The one who made you so happy and glad
Is the same one who is making you sad
When one tries to talk about wanting them to stay
The other just turns and walks away
You're just trying to hide your pain after you realize that love was a mistake

Once you realize they're gone you ask yourself what you did wrong
Your heart starts going insane from all their pain you ask yourself how you're gonna stay the same
Your heart keeps tearing because, you're the only one caring
You try not to care
You try to get away, and you try to convince yourself that you'll be okay

Vickie Roberts, Grade 9
Buhl High School, ID

Mad Scientist:
A scientist going quite mad
He was depressed and even sad
He slipped and fell into a machine
Then became very clean
It washed away the good and
Then came the bad.

David Olson, Grade 7
St Anthony of Padua Catholic School, AZ

Adolescence
My pride is my camouflage;
Not a soul can gaze upon my thoughts.
I can live each day as someone new
For my pride would be my disguise.
The melodies of life
That only I can play.
People see nothing in life —
That material is reality.
Unleash, break through the mask
Everyone whimpers behind.
Like scents of lilies so sweet
Vibrant colors of the flowers,
One sees innocence in each petal.
But no more than the eye can draw.
Permanently staining pollen
Hidden beneath the blossoms.
Such stale, surrendered substances
Are not seen, luckily.
Undiscovered, unknown, and even ignored,
Forever the flaw stays unseen.

Angel To, Grade 9
Lakewood High School, CO

Always There
Twisting and turning,
Down a road you're not sure of.
And the help you need,
Is from the Lord God above.

These different paths,
Take you this way and that.
But you know He will be there,
To get you through the gaps.

This path you are on,
Can take you to places
With bumps and bruises,
And lead you to different faces.

With all the struggles and strife,
You don't know how you will get through.
But your Heavenly Father is always there,
On this path of life.

Ashley Harmon, Grade 7
Leading Edge Academy - Gilbert, AZ

Who Is He?
Who is he?
The man I once knew changed over years.
He's almost like a stranger when I see him.
Who is he?
Sometimes I have flashbacks.
I remembered he used to be my best friend.
Who is he?
I remember he lived in my house.
I remember I called him daddy.
Who is he?
I don't know who he is anymore.
I think he's my daddy.
We know nothing about each other.
How can it be he is my daddy.
Who is he?
He's my daddy.

Gracie Chavez, Grade 7
Sky Vista Middle School, CO

Heaven
What is heaven like?
Heaven sounds like a perfect place,
Where there are no problems of hate,
I dreamt of heaven in a dream,
Beautiful rays shine down like beams,
Angels dancing to the gospel sound,
Little angel babies flying around

Is heaven way, way up in the sky?
Is heaven up above outer space?
Or is heaven sitting on the brightest cloud,
While Jesus Christ is smiling down

Will I ever visit heaven one day?
Or will God send me far, far away?
Is heaven a non-sinful place?
Or is it just like the world is today?
I dreamt of Heaven in a dream,
I know that Jesus Christ is smiling down on me

Wonderful behavior on Earth will get me through
The gates of heaven that shine gold and baby-blue,
I can hear God's voice telling me what I need to do,
To go to heaven in the sky that's a beautiful blue.

Charmaine Fructueux-Bocco, Grade 7
Shadow Ridge Middle School, CO

Garden Hose
Gushing down the enclosed elongated cylinder pipe
Comes the ice cold plant energy drink
This quenching pick-me-up jets down the tube
Releasing its intense juice
The long rubber worm spits and slobbers
The plants quiver with bliss

Katherine Kamas, Grade 9
Grand Junction High School, CO

War

The men dress up and go to battle
The swords and spears shine in the light.
You look and see scared faces.
The horn blasts; the charge comes.
The battle begins.
The war is on.
The men come.
Fighting
Death.

Trevor Gaffney, Grade 8
Beacon Country Day School, CO

Baby Girl

Baby Girl never
Smiles, or grins
Laughs, or plays
Because her mom is not around
But when she sees her mom
Baby Girl always
Smiles, or grins
Laughs, or plays
because her mom is around
She loves her mom

Ashley Carpenter, Grade 7
Cody Middle School, WY

Tree

I am a tall beautiful tree.
My lean powerful roots branch from me.
Seeking water streams in the ground,
For me, heavier than one pound.
Creatures make me their lovely home.
A kindly nest after they roam.
As majestic as a mountain,
Shade pours from me like a fountain.

Helen Vaughn, Grade 7
Annunciation School, NM

The Big Trip

Going up the stairs
on my way to math,
I suddenly tripped downward,
My feet flew from their path.
I didn't see this coming
as I twisted tumbling 'round.
I tried doing something
but by then I'd hit the ground.

I slid a few steps back
scraping up my knee,
then I quickly looked around
to see all who could see.
And what I saw were cackling kids
pointing straight at me!

Leah Porter, Grade 7
Eagle Point Middle School, OR

Lies of the Wind

I was standing all alone scared and had no clue.
No clue where I was, no clue what to do.
I started walking down the leaf blown river.
And I felt a blow that made me shiver.
I stood up and looked around.
But I didn't hear a peeping sound.
"Who are you? Where am I!
I do not wish to die!
Just tell me where I am, and away I will go."
I felt it push me for the way it would show.
But, I looked at my compass and said, "For me, this is not the best!"
"I am supposed to go east not west!"

It tries to push me again.
"No, you will not win!"

It pushes me down with a hardy thrust.
I lie there cold on the earth's crust.
So I lie on the ground with tears filling my face.
I have nowhere to go; I have no hiding place.

Liz Thomas, Grade 7
Sterling Middle School, CO

That Rosemary Candle*

As I look at this candle,
I think of love.
Just gazing at the blinding, yellow flame,
I can remember my husband's comforting hugs.
That rosemary scent that I can smell miles away,
Makes me relax and think of the smile he gave me today.
The bright, crimson color,
Reminds me of the strawberries we ate on our first date last summer.
Then after we ate those berries,
Inside I began to freak,
For he planted a soft kiss on the side of my cheek.
And after our date was finally through,
I was thrilled to hear him whisper the words,
"I love you."

Andrea Northup, Grade 7
Sterling Middle School, CO
**From a newly wedded wife's point of view.*

Life

Life is like a game of basketball
You're always going back and forth
You're either winning or losing
When you're winning you're happy
When you're losing you're sad
Missing a shot makes you angry
Making a shot makes you glad
But when it comes down to it
You're down my two and it's a it's up to you
To shoot the three and watch the other team walk away in misery
Life is like a game of basketball

Jon-Mikal Aranda, Grade 7
21st Century Public Academy, NM

I Promise

I promise I will never leave your side
I promise I will take care of you when you are sick
I promise I will never be shy around new people
I promise I will always love you
I promise

Lorrin Jamison, Grade 7
Mandalay Middle School, CO

I Am

I am a smiler, and a thinker
I wonder what my future will bring
I hear the rain
I see my puppies playing
I wish someone would make a real Candy Land
I am a smiler, and a thinker

I imagine a beach, and sun tanning
I feel happiness
I influence my little sister
I worry time is going way too fast
I cry when I see the days go past, having to say goodbye
I am a smiler, and a thinker

I understand the world has problems
I say that there should be peace
I dream of my aspiring career
I try to be serious more of the time
I hope I will always have fun and be happy
I am a smiler, and a thinker

Amanda Rojo, Grade 7
Shadow Ridge Middle School, CO

To Fly

I awake to the wind in my face
For on a cloud I must stay
Yet the winds make me sway
To never succeed in taking me away
So I watch them go day by day
As one by one they go away
My bonds too strong
So I wait to grow
From insignificant to ravishing
In a chorus they will sing
When the wind comes to take me away
But not yet my cloud is still too small
So come for me when I'm to big to hold back
So my wind oh my wind
Take me away Take me away
To your kingdom
Take me to great heights
And never let me fall
Take me flying with you but not yet
For I can't bear to tear away from the bonds yet
So wait for me wind Wait for me

Kelby Gutkosky, Grade 8
Cimarron Springs Elementary School, AZ

Annoying Sister

My sister is annoying
My sister is annoying to me
Even more than a bee

She slammed her door
She slammed her door in my face
Without any grace

At the end of the day
At the end of the day she got hit with a sun ray
And really did pay

Courtney Snyder, Grade 7
Bethel Christian School, OR

Lady Hope

'Twas midnight when she came;
Through the open field she swayed
She brought with her a feeling,
One I'd never felt before.
When she stilled, she came to me and cried,
Come with me, oh, king, be free!
Forget your worries, forget your troubles.
Be free, be free, be free.
The morning after I felt anew.
I was happy, calm, and fearless.
'Twas then I realized the lady
Who had swayed in my dreams
Was the Lady Hope,
Who had taken my troubles with her
And left me with her touch.

Lisa Jensen, Grade 9
Bonneville High School, ID

Everyday Joys

Everyday joys are laughter, and friends.
Shared pain phone calls and humor that mends.
Sometimes I wonder what my grades might be
But there's everyday joys in spite of me.
I live for glamour, friendships, and fashion
The everyday joys don't depend on my passion.
Some things are gloomy and or depressing to know
But everyday joys shine from my puppy's wet nose.
I am all about fabulous can't wait till the end of school.
But everyday joys remind me what's cool.
Smiles and hugs from my brother's grateful embrace
Phone calls, and friends, and a smirk on my face.
Everyday joys
Radiate beyond blues
I am quick to find happy and slow to ruin moods.
My everyday joys are many and bright
They happen so quickly I stay in the light.
Blessings and dreams lots of hope
In between everyday joys simply lock out the noise.

Tae Young, Grade 7
21st Century Public Academy, NM

Basketball
Up it goes,
Off the board,
In the hoop,
The basketball goes,
Down the court,
Between the legs,
Three minutes left to go,
As the whistle blows
Austin Gonzales, Grade 7
Shadow Ridge Middle School, CO

How I Love the Snow
Lightly falling from an endless sky
White as the clouds themselves
Frozen tears from an angel's cry
Light as air itself.
Oh, how I love the snow.

Tiny fairies falling from above
Turning the sky to a sea of white
Blanketing the ground with a coat of love
Everything becomes radiant.
Oh, how I love the snow.
Michael Sanchez, Grade 7
McKinley Middle School, NM

Bad Breath Beaver
Have you ever wondered
Why Beaver's breath stinks?
But not nearly as bad
As the six toed lynx

Instead of brushing
His teeth before bed,
He picks his nose
And scratches his head

He wakes in the morn'
Pickin' his bunions
While he munches his bag
Of month old "Funyuns"

So if you've wondered
Why Beaver's breath stinks,
Just be thankful it's not as bad
As the six toed lynx
Jessica Kirn, Grade 8
Poplar 7-8 School, MT

Spring
At last winter is melting away
Spring is finally coming
The lack of mud
Could surely do us some good
Amber Hanley, Grade 7
Pagosa Springs Jr. High School, CO

The Land of Twilight
In the Land of Twilight,
Not the Twilight Zone,
It's always a bright night,
And never a dark day,
You'll never find a bone,
Of people passed away,
In this calmly spooky place,
The people float around,
In this place you don't weigh a pound,
Don't worry cause you're safe,
There are no schools,
Everyone's born with knowledge,
Here there are no pools,
On reality's edge,
There are no conflicts here,
Nor is there any fear,
Near is the realm of dreams,
Only divided by a sea of gleams,
And yes you heard me right,
In the Land of Twilight,
A realm of eternal night
Parker King, Grade 7
Oberon Middle School, CO

I Am a Book
I am a book
Half my pages are read
My thoughts are the words
On all the pages
My future is the blank pages
At the end
The story is my life
Each chapter has a different story
Just like every day of my life
The dedication is my parents
When they let me free the first time
Each chapter is every minute
Of every day
And the pages are every second
In every minute
of every day
Aimee Ledall, Grade 7
Eaton Middle School, CO

Rachel
Young, pretty, happy, loving
Related to Mommy
Who cares about me
Who feels stress
Who needs to be pampered
Who gives everything
Who fears nothing
Who would like to see me grow up
Resident of my heart
Tyler Hook, Grade 7
Sedona Charter School, AZ

Soccer
They come in
Everyone is yellin'
They got defenders
There are vendors
He passes the ball,
and scores a goal.
Cristian Jimenez, Grade 8
Place Middle School, CO

The Fall
Down she fell to her doom,
Down into her dreadful tomb.
No one around to give assistance,
No one noticed her absence.

But then he did but hear,
Her dreadful cries with his ear.
Down the stairs he went,
He sought her out as if hell-bent.

And when he did draw near,
Her time of death was here.
He took her hand,
Now, she would leave this land.

She was gone forever,
He would get over her, never,
He stood up and looked at her.
His life would be forever, a blur.
Josiah Booth, Grade 8
Academy Charter School, AK

Pain Is Here
See the world falling apart,
no turning back breaking hearts.
Soon to be gone in a short time,
darkness is coming.
When you lose a heart,
yours withers away.
And the pain is there to stay.

Wars are starting, people crying
no more peace.
People dying, horrific sight.

See the world coming together,
everyone can help.
If we keep going it'll stay forever.
Share the love, everyone needs some
no matter how happy one is.
Forgive and forget,
love and lose,
on this Earth
of which we choose.
Kelsie S. Wilson, Grade 7
Diamond Fork Jr High School, UT

Yucky Gum

I am the gum that sits upon every desk. I sit and sit all day long.
Wondering what I will smell like after the day is over.
What color will I be when the sound of the bell rings.
How much longer will I have to be here?
Kids and teachers always touching me, telling me
"You can do it."
O how I hate school days, having to wake up so early.
Gosh when is this day going to end?
All the kids leave and I am just sitting here,
waiting for another day.

Melissa Sandoval, Grade 7
Eaton Middle School, CO

Reminisce

Recall tucking me in every night
Scratching my back before I sleep tight
Going fishin' at the park
Watching our dog bark
Do you remember? Do you remember?

If you had one chance would you come back to me?
Would you make me the prettiest girl you ever did see?
You took me to that magic place
With the big ears and the funny face.
Take me back…take me back

You and Dad were always mad
You left and that's too bad
Crying, hiding, it's just not the same
Who's to blame?

Who would I run to?
I knew you were through
I miss you…

Katelyn Driggers, Grade 8
Bogle Jr High School, AZ

Music

Violin, viola, cello, and bass
Music is very unique and great
It has exquisite elegance and grace
And nobody can dislike music or hate

Music is much more than just notes and rests
There's feeling and emotion behind it too

Clarinet, flute, trumpet, and trombone
Music is different than anything else
And it doesn't have any sort of clone
Music gives you a high pulse

Music is much more than just notes and rests
There's feeling and emotion behind it too

Jessica Hibbert, Grade 7
North Middle School, CO

Solis

Center
of attention.
It rises from the gloom.
Stretches across the sky
Shedding light on the awakening population of the world.
It brings heat and life to plants and people alike.
It returns to the dark depths
Of the amazing starlit sky
As we spin out of
Control.

Max Bennett, Grade 7
Sagewood Middle School, CO

Wild

When you ride you feel like you are flying.
The feeling like the wind beneath your wings.
The one thing you want to do when you are dying.
It's a beautiful sound that your heart sings.
The power it always holds is beautiful.
Its mane moving like the blades of grass.
The power it holds is very spiritual.
It's clear like looking through a piece of glass.
Its hooves feel like they never touch the ground.
Flowing with the horse's long and fast stride.
Feeling like you don't even weigh a pound
Feeling the horse's power from inside.
When you become one with the horse its wild.
Then nothing you could do can make it mild.

Lorrin Peters, Grade 9
Clark High School, NV

Snow

Oh
How I wish it would snow
But it never snows in Oregon only for a few seconds
Then no more

Oh
How I wish it would snow
Snow like white feathers
Falling from the sky
Little by little as it goes by

Oh
How I wish it would snow
I miss the time when I use to go outside
Play snowball fight
Until night
Built a snowman and called it Bob

Oh
Play with the snow until it melts away
Wait until next time to play with you snow
I'll be waiting for more snow

Daisha Begaye, Grade 8
Walt Morey Middle School, OR

Across the Green Glass Sea

A silver ship sails,
With a mast of gold
Across the Green Glass Sea.
A silver ship sails,
With a crew of the dead
Across the Green Glass Sea.
A silver ship's crew
Spies a storm of black
Across the Green Glass Sea.
A silver ship heels
In the waves that crash
Across the Green Glass Sea.
A silver ship turns,
And tries to run
Across the Green Glass Sea.
A silver ship sinks
In the deep black storm,
Across the Green Glass Sea.
A silver ship sits
On a bed of silt
Beneath the Green Glass Sea

Cassandra Edmund, Grade 7
Holmes Middle School, CO

As I Look at My Computer

As I look at my computer
My computer looks at me
We stare upon each other
Until I have to pee
I get back to my chair
I smile at my friend
He smiles back at me
I feel as if I'm free
We make a new meaning
Out of fun and games
As I look at my computer
My computer looks at me

Aaron Miller, Grade 7
Eaton Middle School, CO

A Special Feeling

a feeling
the one when you feel weird
like if you have butterflies
in your stomach
the one where you're too afraid to
 talk to him
 every day there's always
one person on your mind
and you can't think straight when
 you're near him
you want to be his friend forever
the feeling you get when you're in
 LOVE

Karina Arguello, Grade 8
Culver Middle School, OR

Brandi My Best Friend

B stands for bright.
 She is very helpful and always willing to succeed.
R stands for respect.
 Whenever I am sad or just need someone to talk to she is always there.
 Also she never talks bad about anyone,
 Whenever they aren't there,
 Or even if they are there.
A stands for acting.
 Ever since she was nine or ten years old she has been acting in plays.
N stands for newbie.
 She loves to play computer games and be a newbie.
D stands for daddy's little girl.
 She loves her dad.
I stands for idol.
 She is my hero.

Genny P., Grade 7
Diamond Ranch Academy, UT

Fish

Fish are entertaining and fun to watch. They can be exciting!
Angels, Oscars and Jack Dempseys are my favorite and quite inviting!
Fresh water, saltwater, they live in them all.
You can find them in a mall or maybe mounted on the wall!
Swordtails, mollies, guppies, tetras
To all they bring joy, etcetera.
Fish can live in a tank or out in a lake,
No matter where you enjoy them, smiles they will make.
Some are for watching and some for eating,
The pleasure you get from both is never fleeting.
Whether they are big or small,
The joy they bring makes me love them all
When feeding them with flakes or bait,
Every minute I spend with them is always great.
Fish are beautiful in how they glide through the water
But when I fish at Avondale, it's like a slaughter!
Fish are great to watch in a tank,
But give me fish and chips, and I'll take it to the bank!
The fish in my tank are always so hasty
But the ones on my plate can be ever so tasty!

Tanner Cox, Grade 8
Canfield Middle School, ID

Opposite of Perfect

I am not a perfect girl
My hair is never in place,
I spill quite a few things, I'm pretty clumsy, and
 sometimes get my heart broken.
Me and my friends sometimes get into fights, and
 some days just don't go right.
but when I think about it and take a look at how everything is going,
I remember how amazing my life truly is
and that makes me like being unperfect.

Jordan Fernandez-Fisher, Grade 7
Molasky Jr High School, NV

The Hunt

Crisp air, dried, leaves, cool breeze,
walking, walking, walking through the trees.
Being weighed down with backpack and gun,
waiting, waiting, waiting for the fame to come.
Crushing frosted snow, traversing the ravine,
checking, checking, checking the compass that you bring.
Fresh tracks, droppings…all the signs,
evidence, evidence, evidence that we're close behind.
Camouflaged, unseen, quietly waiting as time goes by,
searching, searching, searching nothing still.
Suddenly, movement catches the eye — slowly turning
cold barrel of the gun against my cheek,
as I sight in the animal.

Sydnee Johnson, Grade 9
Bonneville High School, ID

Alone and Unwanted

I am alone and unwanted
I wonder when I will get out from under the bed
I hear children laughing and playing without me
I see myself in a child's arms again
I want to be loved
I am alone and unwanted

I pretend I'm needed
I feel pain in my heart
I touch the dust that's piled up on me over the years
I worry I will never see light again
I cry knowing no one remembers me
I am alone and unwanted

I understand I'm too young for you now
I say you could still love me
I dream I'm asleep in your arms
I try to get your attention
I hope you'll find me one day
I am alone and unwanted

Rebecca Long, Grade 7
Dunstan Middle School, CO

Just Because

Just because things changed for the worse
Don't treat me differently,
Don't cry for me,
Still ask me how I am.
Just because things changed for the worse
It doesn't mean you can avoid me,
It doesn't mean I can't play again,
It doesn't mean things won't change again.
Just because things changed for the worse
Still accept me for who I am,
Still embrace me when you see me.
Just because things changed for the worse
doesn't mean you can't try to make it better.

Kate Schwartz, Grade 9
McMinnville High School, OR

Fools Rush In

You promised me you would be there for me.
So far, I've been left with empty arms and an empty heart.
Then I was used and brokenhearted.
I was such a fool to think you would really love me.
Was this time just another one of your stupid lies?
You can never trust a liar; I learned that the hard way.

Emily Cocchiola, Grade 7
Albuquerque Christian School, NM

Childhood Reminiscence

I've seen adults and older folk
Sit around a great big oak.
Some sit there who want a smoke
Their inner child had not awoke.
Some think their lives shortened and dulled
Their inner child long since culled.
Their days of frolic and play long since passed
And now distant memories of their past.
Forgotten is the fell of sand and ocean breeze,
Lost is the feeling of swinging from trees.
Never more shall fly the ships mast,
That long ago voyage was its last.
Ancient fights forever frozen in time,
Villains never to be punished for their crime.
But still I laugh and joke.
On cigarettes I'll never choke.
Upon these memories they have forever mulled
Into boredom they have been falsely lulled
They think their lives short and dulled
Their inner child long since culled.

David Wibel, Grade 9
Tempe Preparatory Academy, AZ

The Truth of the Beginning

Following through my words,
On paper white as snow,
With poems as strong as steel,
And words that never grow old.
Life is going crissed-crossed,
Lies are being told.
Falling for the one you love,
Never becomes easily told.
Throughout my writing,
Stories are being told,
Memories are being shared,
Feelings are coming from our soul.
Expressing our emotions,
Crying from our tears,
No one really knows what has disappeared.
Wishing on a star,
For all this to go away.
Allowing my feelings and ideas to be shared,
With the truth being told.

Kelsey Engle, Grade 8
Shadow Ridge Middle School, CO

Soccer

The lush carpet of grass dances with the wind as I spring. Kicking the black-and-white patterned ball, the yell of the crowd reaches my ears, I kick, dust leaping into my eyes from where the ball was. The goalie, beads of sweat dropping from his face, leaps for the ball. He misses, score! I run to my place with the wind in my face feeling like a hero.

Brandon Green, Grade 7
Mandalay Middle School, CO

The Man in the Willows

The man in the willows sings a soft tune. He sings about great loses that touch the deepest soul and when he plays upon his pipe, the trees weep with remorse. He sings about great battles lost and won about the tragedies of love!

The man in willows plays his pipe and unravels the secrets of life! And when he plays the forest is still not even a mouse stirs until the tune is complete. Then he gets up and turns to the nearest tree and says, "Now you have heard my tale and my life is done. I have done what I meant to do. Take my pipe as a gift from me to you, and remember me as the Man in the Willows."

And with that he left and never did come back. No one knows what happened to the Man in the Willows, but passed the story down to their kin. Never was the song ever sung 'til one day when they saw a Man in the Willows.

Kathy Myers, Grade 8
Elton Gregory Middle School, OR

Thoughts of the Heart

I never realized how much you meant to me until you were gone and now I see that life pretty much sucks without you in it...
I wish I could take back what I did to you and if I could go back and have a do-over, I would change it all in a heartbeat.
For the past month I haven't been able to love anybody 'cause it felt like I couldn't get you out of my heart or my mind...
I tried a couple of times but no one could fill your place or maybe for the simple fact I didn't want them to.
I love you and I don't think that will change but I don't know.
You say you have forgiven me and when I look at you I see that you love me but I don't understand how you can forgive me...
After what I put you through...After everything people said...After all the lies...
And after I saw how much it hurt you, I realized something...
I still loved you during every second of it.

Alyssa Bellamy, Grade 8
Sheridan Jr High School, WY

The Compassion Within*

Your physical scars will heal with time, but your mental scars will remain with your memories.
I struck your heart with words of pain as sour as lime without realizing how much it hurt.
I destroyed your soul and treated you like a toy
without a single regret, nothing but full of cruel joy.
People around me did nothing but laugh, laughing at you,
but deep in me, a silent voice screamed.
That voice remained unheard until I saw emptiness in you.
No amount of apologies would take back my harsh words to you.
No amount of helping you would make you forget the bitter action.
No matter what I do, no matter what I say,
the scars I created with never fade away.
But that is untrue
The sight of your crying face, the sound of your "I'm sorry,"
brought back kindness once known to me.
The words I waited so long from you were spoken with regrets and compassion.
I knew someday you would be able to hear that voice.
I forgive you for your actions,
and also those of murders, dictators, and anyone who has done wrong.
Can you also give forgiveness to those you had hated?
Because I'm sure one day, those who have done wrong would also be able to hear that voice —
the voice of regrets and compassion.

Jennifer Xian, Grade 7
Sterling Middle School, CO
*Written from the point of view of first the bully and then the victim.

Home

Home is were the family is.
Family is supposed to care.
And be there for each other.
But my family is broken!
Nothing, but hate and misery is left!
All that I know is gone.
Nothing makes sense,
Everything and everyone is different.
My home is torn apart by one person.
That person is you!
You not only ripped me apart, but my family as well!
Nothing can replace what you've done!
My home is now lost forever.
The pain I feel will never leave me.
Now all I hear is the deafening sound of silence.
Home.

Jodie Knowlton, Grade 8
Mario C. Jo Anne Monaco Middle School, NV

A Horrible Sin

The undercover cop responded to a call
When he pulled up, he saw his friend fatally fall

He did not see the shooter's face
But in a flash he was on the case

He looked on the video tapes of the lot
But there was one thing that the gunman forgot…

They clearly saw his face wide open
When they tracked him down he was hopin'…

That nobody would really find him
Committing such a horrible sin

Patrick Kenney, Grade 8
Zia Middle School, NM

Conscience

it's like there's always someone there
   telling you what's right or what's wrong
screams out GUILT!
   will not leave you alone until
you just decide to give up,
   and just say it all
you know you did wrong and
   that there's no turning back
   you need distractions to relieve your thoughts
but in the back of your mind it's all stuck there
   does not wanna let you free
it's better just to let it go
   cause the guild will remain there
you're thinking as time goes by you'll forget
   never, there's no bit of hope

Jasmin Corral, Grade 7
21st Century Public Academy, NM

Music Attitude

Music is a symphony of sound
A bending of different notes
Creating a music to the ears
Never same, always different

Rock music
Always has a hard beat
Blues music
Good for the soul
Jazz music
Dancing with spirit

Used to rest the mind
Used to tell emotion
Used to express feelings
It's the music attitude

Julian Remirez, Grade 7
St Elizabeth Ann Seton Catholic School, AZ

Jacob

Hair blonde, green eyes, concession
Sibling of Nick and Sam
Fan of football, skateboarding, and music
I feel happy, tired and sad
I fear kidnappers, clowns, and slow cars at night
I need water, food, and air
I give money, clothes, and games
I would like to see China, Bigfoot, and the super bowl
Resident of Casa Grande AZ
Rogala

Jacob Rogala, Grade 7
St Anthony of Padua Catholic School, AZ

The Future

I am the one out of a million.
I wonder if I will make it to the pros.
I hear the crowd chanting my name.
I see the crowd jumping out of their seats for me.
I want to make that last second shot.
I am the one out of a million.

I pretend to be the toughest kid.
I feel the hype of everyone in a pressure situation.
I touch the smooth ball in my hands.
I worry that we will lose.
I cry when I'm sad.
I am the one out of a million.

I understand that you win some and lose some.
I say "whooo" when we have just won.
I dream of hitting the game winning buzzer beater.
I try to learn from my mistakes.
I hope to be an all-star.
I am the one out of a million.

David Lenz, Grade 7
Dunstan Middle School, CO

Empowered

I'm ready to take on the world.
At me, many things are hurled.
I can do this,
Just watch me.

Waves will keep crashing,
But I will keep dashing,
For the finish line,
It will be mine.

You can come along,
We'll turn this life into a song.
We'll sing out loud,
Unto the crowd,
We will be strong.

I will make it, so will you,
We can pull each other through.
Don't give up, the sun will shine,
And we'll all be fine.
I promise.

Brittany Spruit, Grade 7
Shadow Ridge Middle School, CO

Meg

There once was a girl named Meg
Who accidentally broke her leg
She slipped on the ice
Not once but twice
Take no pity on her, I beg.

Jacob Mendez, Grade 7
La Center Middle School, WA

Apples

Apples are sweet.
They make a good treat.

Juicy and red.
I eat them on my bed.

Crunchy and tasty.
Good as a pastry.

With stems and seeds.
As perfect as beads.

I like red apples the best.
They're juicier than the rest.

Green apples are sour.
I eat them by the hour.

They're found in stores.
Please get me more!

Carly Mairose, Grade 7
La Center Middle School, WA

Mother Nature

Luscious green, so unseen, is this natural wonder?
Sky blue, so true, in the sky, young fly.
Am I in a paradise?

While the course sand flows through my hand, a hermit crab scuttles in the land,
Why oh my, I raise my hands to praise, what Mother Nature has to offer.

Suddenly, I catch a glimpse of what seems like a lively tree,
raising its leafy arms to pray, in true sweetness, thee.
Then, comes the sway of the wind, which brushes thy course, tree arm,
and drops the last acorn, for a squirrel to keep warm.

Of course, it is truly lively to bear Mother Nature's path,
almost, though in significance, in magic, from start.
The glorious works which are displayed from her is only for one sense,
to take care of her children on Earth, in true contempt.

As the sun sets before the horizon, I see the night fall,
But slightly I can hear Mother Nature's call.
I answer, "Mother Nature, I will back one day,
to see thy glorious works, work in marvelous ways."

Alisha Barik, Grade 7
West Valley Middle School, WA

Places

The empire state building reaching for the sky
Park Avenue on Christmas time with a blanket of snow
The busy streets of New York filled with the honks and beeps of cars
And me, sitting in the middle of the humid rain forest admiring nature

Ivette Mosso, Grade 7
Sunset Ridge Elementary School, AZ

I Am

I am a sensitive guy who believes in the Bible.
I wonder what heaven will be like.
I hear a chorus of angels.
I see good vs evil.
I want to see the Lord my God.
I am a sensitive guy who believes in the Bible.

I imagine rejoicing in the presence of God.
I feel the warmth of His embrace.
I touch the pearly gates leading into heaven.
I worry what the world would be like without God.
I cry when I think about the way
the terrorists think they have to kill to please their God.
I am a sensitive guy who believes in the Bible.

I understand that the Bible is God-breathed and completely true.
I say that Jesus will return soon for His church.
I dream that I will go to other countries and win people for the Lord.
I try to read the Bible every day.
I hope to be an example to everyone I meet.
I am a sensitive guy who believes in the Bible.

Nic Paredes, Grade 7
Sunset Ridge Middle School, UT

If I Had a Million Dollars
If I had a million dollars,
I would be a very rich man,
I wouldn't be greedy,
but buy anything I can.

If I had a million dollars,
I would help out my family,
I would buy my parents a mansion,
I would buy my sister a new Camry.

If I had a million dollars,
I would help out others,
I would donate to charity,
I would help out my fellow brothers.

If I had a million dollars,
I would help out my school,
I would donate to the community,
If I had a million dollars that would be really cool.

Michael Romero, Grade 8
La Plata Middle School, NM

Global Warming
Exhaust, hair spray, and harmful fumes,
almost everything we do is destroying our Earth.

It's getting unbearably hot
and our ozone layer is getting bigger and bigger.

Winter is fading away and temperatures are spiking.

Our cars are slowly demolishing Mother Nature,
and bikes and running are becoming more and more useful.

Those who cannot afford to lose time
by biking or walking are kickin' it with hybrids.

New inventions are coming in the hope of new weather,
global warming is coming from China to Antarctica.

Alexander Calvelli, Grade 7
St Elizabeth Ann Seton Catholic School, AZ

Memories
Cascading slowly from calm white clouds,
Airily drifting downward,
Persistently falling slow and proud,
Throughout the night, arriving from the sky.
In the morning when the sun is recovered,
Vehicles and houses alike are covered.
All pure white as if under a curtain,
The world is a dove.
In every land the children remember,
Never forgetting the snow from above.
Generating memories never to be left behind.

Davis Hilton, Grade 7
Heritage Middle School, ID

Paradise
Loud voices in the hallway of her home,
Images of her past keep her awake.
Nobody's there, unsafe and all alone.
Then she's taken away from her safe place.
Praying for a way out, she can't break now,
Asking herself, "why can't I just go leave?"
Parents fighting, no more will she allow,
The pain, too much, can't stand, and can't believe.
No place to escape, she's empty inside.
In her safe place, where no one can come in,
A safe place to go, a safe place to hide,
Everything's perfect — finally I win.
Different parents, new life, all is nice,
In her own little world called Paradise.

Stephanie Siguenza, Grade 9
Tombstone High School, AZ

The Beautiful Tower
I'm a beautiful tower
In the night I am very bright
I'm like a glossy, shining star

I am one of the highest and prettiest
I'm in a city where people don't sleep
They stay awake all night
Just to see my lights flash in the moonlight

People travel miles and miles to me
They love watching me glisten in the night sky
There are animals, kids, and adults

Many times I'm in pictures or paintings
I look like a huge triangle
Watch for me

Do you know who I am?
Take a guess
I'm the Eiffel Tower

Mariah Hays, Grade 7
Eagle Point Middle School, OR

Classroom
The chalkboard was dusty as the chalk lay still,
Many sat quietly looking like a lion on the kill.

Those who shout loudly were the first ones to go,
The other eyes watched as the bodies walked — they know.

The teacher continued with the lesson of the day.
The students never paid attention as they lay.

What a day, what a day, for those students today,
A day in the classroom is one to pay.

Kimberly Russell, Grade 9
Cedar Park Christian School – Everett Campus, WA

Moon

The moon,
Glistening in the night sky,
Acting as my guide,
for the new path ahead,
Leaving the old one behind.
The moon,
Is an old guide,
With cracks and crags,
Showing his age,
helping me turn another page.
The moon,
Acting as my guide.

Morgan Kuntz, Grade 7
North Middle School, CO

If I Were a Pro Skater

If I were a pro skater
I'd skate all day
And skate all night
And have good spots if I may.

If I were a pro
I would demand a good salary
Plus if I were a pro
I'd skate hourly.

If I were a pro
I would have a good board
Plus a good house
And I'd live life on a cord.

If I were a pro skater
I'd skate up the town
I'd be really popular
And wear a big green crown.

Brody Cook, Grade 8
La Plata Middle School, NM

Love

Love at first sight.
Is it really true,
or just an expression for you?

Love for you is here.
Yet I still wait to be
a girl with a loving future
as I may wish.

Love, love, love.
Tell me what do you
know about love?
It is an emotion
or a mental thought?
What is true love?

Eva Lopez, Grade 7
Somerton Middle School, AZ

The Only Dance

Snow as white
Wine as red
Tears were glass
And as we danced
The floor became a sea
No music could bring us back
The sorrow in this act was far too much
The moon was as full
As the slimmest crescent
And it was dark
Yet still we walked this floor
The blackest of arts
For as we wept
We were afraid to speak
All of us
And all we knew
Were the steps
To this endless dance

Taylor Tracy, Grade 9
Lakewood High School, CO

If I Had No Homework

If I had no homework,
I'd read a book or sing a song,
I'd lounge around the house
Or take a nap that's really long.

If I had no homework,
I'd watch a show on TV,
I'd paint a brilliant picture
Or maybe climb a tree.

If I had no homework,
I'd splash around in a lake,
I'd play a game or two
Or bake a scrumptious cake.

If I had no homework,
It's a silly thing to say,
'Cause I'll always have homework
No matter what the day!

Katie Valentine, Grade 9
Silver High School, NM

Death

Death is a never ending black hole.
A melancholy stream of sorrow
Death is cold and dark,
A kind of dark no light can interrupt.
A sorrow and dejected feeling
Death is a bridge on top of a mountain.
Nothing on this earth can reach the end
Death is an alleyway
No one wants to walk.

Stephen Zamora, Grade 7
McKinley Middle School, NM

The Season of Love

With each new season,
With each new verse,
We cannot deny,
What we must learn.
Love is turning,
Ever so slow,
We may not notice,
But it changes and grows.
We must learn,
What our forefathers have,
That love has seasons,
That we must have.
Without the seasons,
Without the time,
We are lost,
Without a sign.
We must learn to take the seasons,
With no complaint,
With no aggression,
For there are seasons of love,
That we must follow.

Tanner Morris, Grade 9
South Jordan Middle School, UT

Charles

One man,
One woman,
Could have prevented this,
But didn't.

One man,
One woman,
Could have called a cab,
But didn't.

One man,
One woman,
Could have drove them home,
But didn't.

One man,
One woman,
One lifeless teen.
And all because of...
One drunk driver.

Alyssa Putnam, Grade 7
Shadow Ridge Middle School, CO

Little Puddle

My spirit is a little puddle,
gentle, and quiet.
Still, and easily disturbed.
It is a life line for a small animal.
Yet once again alone and still.

Samantha Hackworth, Grade 7
Lone Rock School, MT

Fairy Tale Princess

I don't wear a crown or a big expensive dress,
I'm not perfect or made to impress.
I play in the mud, I play in the dirt,
You can't do any of that in a skirt.

I come from Montana, rugged and tough,
Play poker with me, and I'll call you bluff.
I can defeat what you think, and beat it all,
I be'cha I can catch that fly ball.

Don't underestimate me, I'll prove you wrong,
These girls, my friends, we're all pretty strong.
We've been through fights and broken hearts,
We know our town, and all it's parts.

I'm all me, not one part is fake.
Though when I do make a mistake,
It usually creates quite a mess.
I'm not a fairy tale princess.

Katelyn Ward, Grade 8
East Middle School, MT

If It's

If it's postponed it's a disaster,
there's no telling what may happen.
In life there's a pilot and a captain
if there's not captain
there's no rules.

If there's no pilot,
life will be a disaster.
Without these
there's no point to landing.
It's like seeing hell with your eyes wide open.

Myles Palmer, Grade 7
Sonoran Science Academy, AZ

Me, Myself, and I

Yuri
Awesome, pretty, creative, clever
Sister of Sherry Kim
Lover of my family, friends, and chocolate
Who feels bored, hyper, and happy
Who find happiness in playing the violin,
hanging out with friends, and being with my family
Who needs love, care, and shelter
Who gives help, love, and happiness
Who fears death, bugs, and ghosts
Who would like to see my cousins, old friends, and outer space
Who enjoys laughing, smiling, and having fun
Who likes to wear blue, green, and pink
Resident of Las Vegas
Kim

Yuri Kim, Grade 8
Fertitta Middle School, NV

I Am

I am: smart and stunning
I wonder: why there is war
I hear: the applause when I graduate high school
I see: my self in college for technological purposes
I want: to get a 4.0 grade average
I am: smart and stunning
I pretend: I'm snow boarding whenever possible
I feel: like a BIG celebrity
I touch: the universe
I worry: that I might not get a cell phone
I cry: when people and animals lose there lives
I am: smart and stunning
I understand: e=mc2
I say: fighting without cause or purpose is wrong
I dream: of snow boarding always
I try: to become a good skater and snow boarder
I hope: we will have less racism and hatred in the world
I am: smart and stunning

Tyler Herring, Grade 7
Oberon Middle School, CO

Missing You

I've tried for too long to remain your friend
But now I'm tired and it's time to end
Calling you and writing you and in return
You've left me with only pictures to burn
I thought all along I'd always have you
But you are one friend who's remained untrue
So I'm letting go and walking away
It's up to you if you want me to stay.

Melessa Starbuck, Grade 9
Coal Ridge High School, CO

Shasta

Your golden fur that was constantly shedding.
The way your ears perked up when you smiled.
Your steady pacing at night,
being sure that everyone was in their place.
The way you licked your paws before each nap.
How your name is actually Salsa.
The way you were so sensitive about your nose.
How you constantly begged for food.
But always spit out celery and apples.
The hope that would fill your eyes
as you chased ducks along the edges of the lake.
Always forgetting that they have a secret weapon; wings.
How you knew when something was wrong.
What I would give,
to hear you lick your paws,
to see your sunburned nose,
to feel the comfort when you stood on guard,
to look into your deep brown eyes,
just once more.
Just once more.

Sarah Parks, Grade 9
Canyon View Jr High School, UT

Yum

There once was a pumpkin,
Thought he was really somethin',
He was chopped and he cried,
Made into a pie,
A meal for a country bumpkin.

Devon Mann, Grade 8
Round Valley Middle School, AZ

The Thought

The thought of you
Is always there
In my head
I want to get it out
To make it leave
To end it forever
I still wonder why I'm stuck on you
It feels like it will never end
Morning, afternoon, and night
You are always there
Do you think of me the same way
I think of you?
Do you get the butterflies
When I walk in the room?
Do you think of me before you drift
Off to sleep?
I do
And I feel as though
It will never end
Do you?

Alina Cibicki, Grade 8
Cashmere Middle School, WA

A Mirror of Her

A demon, an angel
A sinner, a saint
The dark, the light
Always there to help
Always there to destroy
Days go by
Nothing ever changes
The way she is
Is how she was meant to be
She is a mirror
Acting as good and evil
She is equality
Healing the broken
Breaking the corrupt
She stands by me
Always stealing my pain
She's been everyone's demon
But she was her angel
She knew her better than anyone else
And for that I envy her
In a way I hate her as well

Xanadu Trevino, Grade 8
Kepner Middle School, CO

Call Skiing…Life

Call the skis the tires on a race car, shifting left and right at every stroke.
Call the poles the pencils on a test, helping you finish.
Call the tracks the roads on a map of life, leading you where you want to go.
Call the turns the speed bumps, making the roads more interesting.
Call the down hills the reward for working hard all day long.
Call the finish line the start of a new adventure and the end of a great memory.

Marion Woods, Grade 7
Mears Middle School, AK

Me, in So Many Words

This is who I am, this is what I do
Now I'm going to share who I am with you
My friends are always there for me, through oh so thick and thin
I try to do the same for them, it's how it will be and always has been
Time is usually on my side, and when it's not, I tend to freak
But somehow still, I usually last another day, another week
My mind is always racing at warp speed through the air
My friends like to comment on how much they like my hair
My passion is for singing, and dancing is my game
When I'm bored I tend to exercise, the endorphins keep me sane
I'm obsessive compulsive about keeping my room neat and tidy
On occasion, I consider my knowledge high and mighty
I live for the theatre; it's my one true vice
Though listening to music often will almost suffice
My legs are my favorite asset, though not lean or long
They help me walk and run and dance, to my favorite song
My future worries me, like the coming of each day
I know what I want, and need and hope for
But for now that's all I can say

Emma James, Grade 8
Kenmore Jr High School, WA

When Darkness Falls Before Me

When it's dark
My body lies into a deep sleep, like I've been hit from behind
Then everything goes quiet
I wake in the ocean where Nemo and Dory swim in front of me
I'm breathing water in though I have no gills, nor oxygen tank

When it's dark
I'm in the sky looking down seeing everything
I also see myself getting hit by a car, but standing up a second later to tell my tale
I see world peace, where if you forget to lock your door
You won't be worried of something being stolen or someone demolishing your house

And when the light returns
Reality hits me, the hate and cruelty in the world returns
The pain that people feel
All this overwhelms me to see all this in our world
I wait to see the change, but nothing, so I fall into my room and go under the covers
I hope for the darkness to return to take me back into the dream
The dream of a world of peace and of happiness

Fred Oaxaca, Grade 7
Sevilla West School, AZ

The Edge

There she stands
There at the edge
The edge of the world
The edge of the universe
The edge of the cliff
She stands there hoping, yet, hoping
Hoping that nothing or no one pushes her
Not a thing or she will fall
Fall? Fall into what? What's at the bottom?
What does she look at when she looks down?
Oh yes, the worst thing
Death
She holds on hoping
Hoping that no one or nothing will push her
She holds on with all of her strength
She is on the edge
The edge of the world
The edge of the universe
The edge of the cliff
The edge
The edge of life

Reyna Harris, Grade 9
Queen Creek High School, AZ

The Time of My Life

Coloring pictures, making designs
That sometimes don't resemble anything but lines.
Running, jumping, and playing
It goes without saying.
Confidence brewing, making new friends
It sometimes seems the fun will never end.
Bubblegum, candy, and treats
Are only some of the marvelous sweets.
Skipping through flowers with a smile on my face,
Feeling great pleasure from the bright sunny rays.
Hide and seek, tag and fun
Wonderful games I won!
Dress-up, make-up, and modeling
What else can childhood bring?

Kristen Amy Grant, Grade 9
Timberline Middle School, UT

Life and Death*

A never ending cycle of the human race,
Most have died and some are alive.
Those who are still alive weep for the deceased.
And beam for the new life.

And no matter where you are,
Or how old you are,
You can never escape...
Life or death.

Tori Yoshida, Grade 7
Mandalay Middle School, CO
*In memory of Takao Komaru and Herman Yoshida.
May you both rest in peace.

Colorado

From the great plains
To the rolling valleys
And to the tall mountains

Hot in the summer
Cold in the fall
Freezing in the winter
And wet in the spring

Filled with all kinds of animals
From deer, elk, bear and moose in the mountains
And antelope and coyotes in the plains

With all kinds of sites to see
From the Rocky Mountains to the Royal Gorge

Nick Farquhar, Grade 7
Shadow Ridge Middle School, CO

Wrestling

W ork wheeze weary we were, winners we are
R ound roman ring for roughneck rascals
E ager energetic engagement endure to end
S trong skilled scrimmage soldier
T ough tussle tilting ties t.k.o
L ethal like the leading lawbreakers
I ndividual independent indestructible identity
N ever knocked never known
G rim gruesome a grappling game

Cade Mortensen, Grade 8
Round Valley Middle School, AZ

Save Me

My scene begins, a little girl is crying
The light in the hallway is dim
She leans back, and thinks of a reason
Why nothing she does falls into place.
She gets more and more curious with every day
More furious in every way, she screams out loud
"Why's this happening to me?"
The answer is, it's meant to be
She's on her knees and begging "Please!"
She wonders if there's somebody out there
Who will save her save us...save me...
From this place they call home
Though we feel like mere gnomes
Standing in the background where they hear no sound
Of our sadness save us...save me...
Everything here is wrong all we see is their talk
Of the better world, where they hear
There is no meaning to our tears
Deaf may be peaceful, but will someone make it meaningful?
To be with us, with me
Save me...save us...

Justine Smith, Grade 9
Cedar City High School, UT

Painful Situation

There I stood, sad, over you.
Thinking about all the fun stuff we used to do,
You with that same T-shirt the color of Navy Blue,
Reminiscing all the fun times that now just seem like they just blew,
As you act like if I'm some piece of gum you spit out after you chew,
Hanging, going out with other girls when we were going out, leaving me with no clue,
If only you could see my point of view,
But yet I felt me and you were 2 pieces of paper stuck together with glue.
You get older, tougher, cuter, and more of a ladies man, now hat you grew.
Talking to the girl that was once my best friend and that you never knew,
I know now that those words "I love you, more than anything and anyone." I come to know sadly they weren't true.
Six last words I really want to tell you, Is "Thank you, and I did love you."

Roxanne Landin, Grade 7
21st Century Public Academy, NM

Where I Am From

I am from a family, who has tried so hard
My father who has made me strong
My mother who has showed me how to be free
And of course my sister who has showed me how to share.

I am from a time where any nationality can be friends
Where white, black and any other color can be what they want to be
A time where everybody is your friend.

I am from a time of great technology
Where there are iPods, cell phones, and even cable TV
Of where you need to be smart, successful and interested in everything.

I am from my friends who nobody can take.
My friends have helped me, listened to me and have shaped me to be me.
Without my friends, I am nothing but an alive corpse. I could not deal with being alone.

I am from all my teachers who have made me as smart as I am.
The people who are smart enough see the interesting future hand.
The ones who know the future is us, the kids
The ones who see me for who I am.

Emiliano Mendez, Grade 7
Our Lady of Lourdes Catholic School, UT

Gift of Rain

I sit alone under the darkening sky.
Masses of clouds veil the sun.
The sky, once blue, now turns a harsh gray, like a blanket just covered the world, but only to make it cruelly colder.
The rain begins to fall, gently, creating puddles everywhere, rippling my reflection.
The aroma of fresh water fills the afternoon air.
Raindrops fall on me — cold and wet.
Thunder roars vigorously, like angels bowling.
Trees dance with a swift breeze, as careless as children.
The raindrops strengthen, tapping at the ground.
Lightning arrives and briefly illuminates the sky.
The rain is my company on this lonely day, providing me completeness no other can give.
It hides the tears and shields from pain.
Such a gift it is — the rain.

Ahdriana Abuliel, Grade 7
Ernest Becker Middle School, NV

Sentimental Freedom
I was trapped in a thunderstorm,
Trapped all alone,
With nothing but my own,
And just as I was feeling myself being drawn to isolation,
Raindrops came pouring down and opened my sensation.
They fell so lightly,
So gentle,
That they freed my soul,
Forever lulled,
In a place of harmony.
Forever known together,
That the rain set me free.
Lauren Kosydar, Grade 8
North Star Charter School, ID

Once
I used to have dreams and once I had hope
My spirit was strong and I never gave up
I loved to imagine and had many ideas
The wind whispered to me and her voice I could hear

Then something happened and everything changed
A cloud blocked the sun and there it remained
My spirit is gone the wind had died down
I no longer dream I let myself drown

I have been taken and tortured and bound
I don't have my life I don't hear the sound
Of laughter and joy or anything else
I don't feel the touch of my dreams, of my hopes

I am just a shell I have nothing left
I am as empty as an old bird's nest
I may continue to breathe and my heart still beats
But my soul is gone I am incomplete.
Abbigail Jones, Grade 9
McMinnville High School, OR

Greed
Picking up puny pennies, and it grows
Nicking some nifty nickels and it grows
Grasping for grimy greenbacks and it grows
Snatching shimmering silver, and it grows
Grasping for glittering gold, and it grows
Pleading for precious platinum and it grows
Diving for devilish diamonds and it grows
Lusting for lottery luck and it grows
Fishing for fabulous fortune and it grows
Praying for presidential place and it grows
Pushing for planet power and it grows
Handling heavenly happenings and it grows
What is next you ask
Perish a poor prince
Jordan Connell, Grade 7
Oberon Middle School, CO

Fallen
Tears fall from my eyes
They've been falling for so long now…
I brought my sorrow, I brought my pain.
I fell in love. I'm still at the bottom.
Betrayal never hurt so much….
Especially to the one who betrayed.
The look on her face was that of a broken and bleeding heart.
Since then I have felt the ever coming darkness.
I hate love. I hate her.
I hate myself more than anything.
I have fallen. Fallen from the graces of all.
Of those I respected. Of those I loved.
Now I understand the melancholy of love.
I understand because I feel it now.
I know what people mean when they say love hurts.
I understand more then I ever did before.
I hate love. I hate her. I love her.
I betrayed her. I need her.
I have fallen.
Hannah Barton, Grade 9
Kamiakin High School, WA

Humans
Self-destructive,
Self-proclaimed.
A quest for power,
A quest for fame.
Waging wars,
Far and vast.
Peace emerging,
From their bloody past.
Mortals live to conquer,
They die for fame.
Mortals fight for freedom,
They fight for pain.
Personal vendettas,
Personal shame.
Heroes and villains,
All the same.
Like animals on the hunt,
They take down a beast,
And have a great feast.
Humans are certainly,
Self-destructive.
Michael McIntyre, Grade 7
St Elizabeth Ann Seton Catholic School, AZ

Black
Black is the color when the lights go off
Black is the color when all hope is lost
Black is the color of the lurking shadows
Black is the color of the fog at the gallows
Black is the color of the undiscovered sea
Black is the color of me
Michael Hayward, Grade 7
21st Century Public Academy, NM

Friends
They stay with you
They laugh with you
They cry with you

They are with you forever
They take pictures with you
They share with you

If you have real friends
Make sure you are with them
Don't let them go
Breanne Humphreys, Grade 7
Mandalay Middle School, CO

Patience
A slicing lash,
A gleaming flash,
Only for a snip of time,
I felt the tightening of the line.
A tiny pull,
And then a lull,
The seagulls sigh,
And so do I.
We've been outsmarted once again.
The day is coming to an end.
Like a ballerina, a graceful dance,
Teasingly, tauntingly, he flips to chance.
Back tomorrow we will be,
Quietly and quickly, that's the key.
Tasha Timm, Grade 8
Pawnee Jr/Sr High School, CO

The Hot Dry Desert
In the hot desert
Cacti crave for water
In the burning sun.
Aj Sanders, Grade 8
Round Valley Middle School, AZ

Re-Sewn
A broken heart re-sewn
Is never the same
What you did to me
Didn't leave me sane

What you took from me
Can never be repaid
You're in debt to me
That's why you didn't stay

My heart is dead
It always was
What you said
did not help
Cayla Christensen, Grade 7
Cedar Ridge Middle School, OR

Please Don't Go
The day has come my grandpa is diagnosed with cancer
In the beginning it was not so bad
Now it's gotten worse
You tried to stay active but the cancer just spreads so fast
Now we can't go to the ranch and play with the loaders
Now you just get tired so fast and you have to go lie down and sleep
You have lost a lot of weight
You made it to your anniversary
Now I pray you make it to my birthday
You have your days when you are weak
You have your days when you are strong
But you will always be the grandfather who taught me everything I know
You gave me your horse and saddle
You tell me to take care of Nana when you go
But you're not gone yet
You will never go in my eyes you will always be alive
Never dead just on a trip to heaven with no return
Daniel Chavez, Grade 7
21st Century Public Academy, NM

Animals
Brilliant colors of orange and black streak across the sides of the tiger.
As it stalks its prey through the tall grass, I can see its muscles ripple.
Its intimidating size puts fear in the eyes of its opponents.
The cunning and powerful tiger rules the land.

The hyena laughs maniacally, seeming out of touch with reality.
The owl watches from its perch, judging intently away from the action.
His dog is loyal and his best friend, never leaving his side.
The lazy pig lounges in the hot sun, rolling in the mud pit.

The butterfly symbolizes new life and change.
As it emerges from its cocoon, it begins to live again.
The dove symbolizes peace and tranquility.
Its color is pure, its sounds are quiet and its movements are graceful.

The cow grazes gleefully on the grass growing from the ground.
The snake slithers silently and steadily across the slippery slope.
The cat purrs and playfully pounces on its perplexed prey.
The dog delightfully dances during dinnertime for a drop of dim sum.
William Moyer, Grade 7
Leading Edge Academy - Gilbert, AZ

Love
Love is the sight and feeling of two people getting married on the most wonderful day
Surrounded by the people they care about,
Love is a mother giving birth to a child being brought to earth,
Love is having a pet to play with on a sunny day,
To care for in time of need and to have a friend when no one is around
Love is the most powerful feeling anyone could have,
It overrules sadness and anger and beats happiness by a wink,
Love is the bond between a mother and her child that cannot break,
Love is friendship, love is earth,
Love is the feeling everyone gets to keep for the rest of their loving life
Lluvia Cano, Grade 7
21st Century Public Academy, NM

High Merit Poems – Grades 7, 8, and 9

Great Grandparents

My life was at the end
My path hit its peak
My leaves are falling off my tree

When you came along
My life started all over
My path came to a clear section
My leaves are growing more greener than ever

You might be my great grandparents
But you helped me a whole bunch
My dad still hasn't talked to me
But I will always know I'll have you by my side.

Alexis Johnson, Grade 7
Coronado K 8 School, AZ

Not Me

Voices buzz in my mind.
An incessant drone, will it ever stop?
They make no sense.
They're always awake, they never rest.
Can they stop?
This is your fault.
The voices become one;
I blame you. It's your incessant drone,
Your never ending buzz you made me this way.
Nothing I write has rhyme anymore,
And the rhythm has left my thoughts.
Your yells drove me to the brink,
Your hits made it hard to breathe.
Everything you've done has made me not me.
And now your screams plague my mind,
And your constant blows pound through my head.
I struggle to regain control, but I am no longer me.
You pulled the rhymes from my thoughts,
And took the rhythm from my lips.
I am cold and thoughtless.
I am not me, there is only you.

Miranda Christensen, Grade 7
Zion Lutheran School, OR

River and Willow

Oh, the river blue, and the willow green,
The fish in the stream, the bird of the tree,
It can be said for the tree of the river,
A beautiful sight beheld day by day,
One thing can be said for the river,
It has the tree as a friend.
One thing true will always be,
The river blue, and willow green.
If the river be blue and the willow not green,
Or the willow green and the river not blue,
Something is wrong in nature to be.
Oh, the river blue, and the willow green.

Chase Morgan, Grade 7
Hendrix Jr High School, AZ

Sunsets

Pink, blue, and purple
are the colors of the sky just before night.
Sometimes the colors are hidden by clouds,
but other times they are the only things that shine.
What makes the sky turn
pink, blue, and purple?
You might know, but I do not,
the only thing I know is that
they are beautiful, whether or not.

Kourtenay Hoefft, Grade 7
Eagle Point Middle School, OR

Somebody Cares

Taken away from my family
crying, shouting for my mom
split up, separated.
New home, new family, new friends

Hoping to do something, something to help
a couple weeks pass
not liking it much.
new home, new family, new friends

Wishing to do something, anything
to help her, but I can't
a couple years pass
just getting settled in.
new home, new family, new friends

We're together now
my siblings and I
we're doing great
we have been adopted
and it's nice to know
somebody cares.

Rita Dalrymple, Grade 7
Sunnyside Christian Elementary School, WA

I Remember That Summer

I will always remember that summer:
It was the last time I spent it with you.
Every smile was true, all jokes clever;
Every day the sky above was blue.
We loved to look for the oddly shaped clouds;
We would play tag and race on bikes all day;
And for fun, we'd scream "Fire!" in big crowds.
We lived the day, keeping troubles away.
'Course, we knew that summer wasn't endless,
But then, we were always good at pretend.
With summer's end marked the end of "us";
That September day, I lost my best friend.
We sat on the roof and talked all that night,
I swear I still remember that twilight.

Miwako Schlageter, Grade 9
Clark High School, NV

I Hate

I hate the way we used to see.
I hate the way we used to be.
I hate the way you made me cry.
I hate the way you wanted to die.
I hate the way I loved you.
I hate the way I saw you.
I hate everything we used to be
everything we used to see.
Everything about the word we.
Bethany Hernandez, Grade 7
Sequoia Village School, AZ

Baseball

Pitch, hit, throw
Hit, throw, out
Throw, out, pitch
Out, pitch, hit
Pitch, hit, HOME RUN
Hit, HOME RUN, run
HOME RUN, run, score
Run, score, win
Score, win, happy
Win, happy, hero
Happy, hero, party
Hero, party, famous
Party, famous, immortal
Johnny Greulich, Grade 7
Dunstan Middle School, CO

Friendship

It's something you feel,
It's something you say.
But most — what you do,
In your own special way.

It's something you give,
And specially received.
It grows with the ease,
Of each thank you, and please.

It's beauty, and wonder,
Excitement, and joy,
It's kindness, and fairness,
And times to enjoy.

There's a time to laugh,
And a time to cry,
A time to think,
And a time to sigh.

It's something you need,
Hard living without.
It's something real special…
That's what friendship's about.
Larisa Jones, Grade 7
Centennial Middle School, UT

The Archer and the Prince

The archer lived a once fragile life
In the land of fame
Until the day
The royal carriage came.
The prince stepped out
And lent a feeble hand
To the young archer
Of his land
The archer stood and bowed,
Like a man should do,
But this archer was a woman
Mind you.
The prince laughed at her poor attempt
Of showing him respect,
So he waved her away
And continued to a circus tent
The archer fell to her knees
And at once began to weep,
For she loved the prince
And he loved she,
But neither would again meet.
Emily McNair, Grade 8
Creekside Middle School, CO

My Lovely Lady Sweet

You remind me of everything good in life
leading me away from strife
every time I think of you
nothing in my life is blue
and when and if I get the chance to
I'll spend my life right next to you
it seems like when I talk to you
my problems just melt right through
your voice seems a subtle dove
sending me right into love
our love is kind I never knew
my mind is free because of you
I think at night while on my sheet
about only you, my lovely lady sweet
Euripides Westfall, Grade 8
Bridger Middle School, NV

Love Life

You should love life,
not end it with a knife.
Don't be sad all day,
and don't care what people say.
Some people won't like you;
don't pay attention, do what you do.
Love life
even if life don't love you;
it will loosen up and run to you.
As far as you know that all is true:
love life and it'll love you.
Alexis Trevizo, Grade 7
Sonoran Science Academy, AZ

Missing

There is something missing
The way your eyes sparkled
Your laughter
In this emptiness I call home.
There's always something missing
Missing always and forever.
Alyssa Stock, Grade 8
Grand Canyon Middle School, AZ

One Summer Day

I walked to the park
I stood there and waited
The grass was green
There was life all around me
I waited till the sun set
The clouds turned pink like cotton candy
The glow of the sun beamed on my face
The warmth touched my heart
On that one summer day
Maitreya Leeuwenburgh, Grade 8
Lyons Middle/Senior High School, CO

Adrenaline Rush

Runners to your marks!
I crawl into my blocks
Get ready!
The crowd dies d
                o
                   w
                      n
My heart thumps
The silence lasts f o r e v e r
BANG!
The gun goes off so do I
  running
    fighting
      finally cross the finish line
    crowds roaring
  adrenaline rush over
Taylor Sandy, Grade 8
Culver Middle School, OR

I Love You

Love is red
Hot and passionate
It is always there, always kind
Kisses and hugs
Never letting go

But then love is gray
Hurtful words and screams
Lying and no trust
It hurts when no one loves you back
Love goes both ways
Faith Montoya, Grade 8
Zia Middle School, NM

Baseball

The crack of the bat gets me high,
As the ball elevates into the sky.
I drop the bat and head for first,
Racing down the line with a burst.

I like to run around the bases,
It puts smiles on my family's faces.
The sound of my cleats digging in the dirt,
Sliding into home leaves stains on my shirt.

William (Blaine) Vierthaler, Grade 8
La Plata Middle School, NM

The Last Goodbye

A fallen tear, a wilted rose,
Some broken glass you can't see through.

A silent scream like a shadow in the dark
She tries to hide her broken heart.

A final glance, the last goodbye,
She turns her head and starts to cry.

You've slipped away for the very last time.
She can't sleep you're on her mind.

She won't let go. The memories remain.
She closes her eyes and sees your face.

It's here in this place she can smile again
But when she opens her eyes it's a cruel reality.

Megan Cotter, Grade 9
Diamond Ranch Academy, UT

The Legend of Might

Of all the heroes of the earth,
One stands above them all.
Like a roaring lion,
With endless strength,
And the wisdom of a scholar.
He was called Might, the great wolf slayer!
Fire swirled about his being.
In his fist,
Was a blade,
Bright as the sun.
Upon an arm he wore a shield,
A serpent engraved on it.
For like a serpent, he was cautious,
But struck as swiftly as misfortunes,
With the fury of a bear.
Demons fell!
Enemies trembled.
Might brought peace to our lands!
Let his name be praised forever!

Lane Hawkinson, Grade 9
Grand Junction High School, CO

I

I am intelligent and funny
I wonder why life is hard at times
I hear people in my ear telling me what to do
I see myself growing into a better person
I want happiness and joy in the world
I am intelligent and funny

I fear my future ahead
I feel like flying away far
I worry about the health of my family
I cry when my life goes wrong
I am intelligent and funny

I understand that this world is cruel
I say there is always a bright side in life
I dream of growing up one day and becoming who I want to be
I try to do my best in whatever
I hope life has something magical for me
I am intelligent and funny

Maritza Quiroz, Grade 7
Sunset Ridge Elementary School, AZ

Stars

Stars are nice stars are pretty,
when it's night they light up the city,
I love them so
because they glow,
they are so BIG but yet so small
but it's just because they are tall,
they look upon my every night,
and I say to myself…what a wonderful sight.

Dulce Haros, Grade 7
Somerton Middle School, AZ

Alone

The wind scrapes against my cold face
The snow sparkles with beauty
The children's laughter punctures the silence
The footprints slowly start to disappear

The snow falls a bit faster
The laughter stops and turns back to silence
I stand, soon I am alone
The snow quickly covers my sight like fog

Soon, I cannot see through the darkness
night has fallen
I am still alone in the silence
I cannot speak

The moon has a faint light, leading the way
down the road, I follow the light as if it is calling me
The snow stops, the moon darkens
I can no longer see the light.

Kelly Sobe, Grade 7
North Middle School, CO

The Desert Floor
On the desert floor
A snake slithers through the sand
In the summer sun
Wil Hoppe, Grade 8
Round Valley Middle School, AZ

The Test Taker
It was called forgetting,
I forgot to study,
I was unsubmitting,
to myself

I was devastated,
on my grades,
I was only being suffocated,
to my own pain

She glides the paper on my desk,
It was a thrill,
It was a mess,
all because I was forgetting

I don't know the answers,
and you know why,
I'll never get my masters,
because I never tried

But now I wanna change,
I wanna start right,
at least before I age,
I think I'll start tonight
Gabrielle Giesbrecht, Grade 7
Heritage Middle School, ID

Open Your Heart to Jesus
Open your heart to Jesus
There is something you're missing,
you are not sure what;
Open your heart to Jesus
and He'll fill your empty spot.
The days seem dark,
and murkiness surrounds you;
Open your heart to Jesus
and He'll light up your days.
You always seem bored
and have nothing to do;
Open your heart to Jesus,
you'll find your part to do for Him.
Later you might notice
that nobody wants to accept you;
Open your heart to Jesus,
He'll be your Friend and will accept you.
Open your doors to Him,
for He died for you and me.
Alena Razinkov, Grade 8
Valley Christian Secondary School, WA

A Real Friend
A real friend is someone that listens without judging appearances,
if you are wrong, if you are good or bad,
and help you defining your thoughts and guiding you.

When you talk things about yourself,
a true friend remembers all the good things that are in you,
and all the things that you forget about yourself.

When you share with your friend,
the decisions are more happy
and the problems go away.
A friend likes you for what you are,
not for what you do.
Whatever part you go a friend will always remember you
in his/her heart, if he/she is a real friend.
Norma Uribe, Grade 7
Somerton Middle School, AZ

Helpless
I sit helpless as I slowly watch the world pass on by.
I hear the voices, the rumors, they're all just a lie.
I walk through the angriness, the red smoke
and I realize it's just a joke.
Everybody is always watching, but nobody ever cares and nobody exactly knows,
they have no idea what's expected or what's hiding behind all the petals on a rose.
Lyndee Zelenka, Grade 9
Coal Ridge High School, CO

The Melody of My Life
My sheet music is the melody of my life
A collection of emotions expressed in the language of tones
Some pages crumpled and yellow with age and use
— Old and familiar friends
Some crisp and white with new radiance
— That I've just met

Thumbing through the pages,
A soft and soothing harmony
Like the lullaby of a summer rain
A mysterious sonata, whispering
Like the moon enshrouded by clouds
A brisk, familiar tune singing of joys
Like the sun-warmed sand between your toes

I play the poetic expressions lovingly, gently turning pages
Taking time to feel their deeper meaning and hear their soulful messages
Then returning them to the cabinet until I have an hour
To spend time with friends again
Their melodies always with me
— Influencing my feelings
— Defining my thoughts,
Graceful. Timeless. Profound.
Mikelle Pyne, Grade 9
Mountain Ridge Jr High School, UT

Broken Heart
We've been through a lot.
You know who I am more than anyone else.
You've seen me through sadness and tears,
You've seen me through the happiness and the giggles.
So it breaks my heart to tell you it is over,
We can no longer see each other.
No more making me laugh, boy,
I can no longer love you.
All those years we were our immature selves.
It's time to move on.
I won't ever see those tears you'll cry when you read this,
I won't see you laugh when you think this is a joke.
Maybe this will make you a man,
Because the boy you are just isn't right.
So I have to say this is goodbye,
I will never hear your voice again.

Amanda Stevens, Grade 8
Colorado Connections Academy, CO

The Flower
I walk through a field of innocence.
I feel renewed.
I feel as though I am safe,
No one and nothing can harm me.
Time has stopped.
I take a breath.
Everything disappears.
I feel white and clean, renewed and welcome.
I close my eyes, I feel innocent.
I open my eyes and see…
A flower.

Kaylene Ross, Grade 7
North Middle School, CO

Jealousy
Jealousy, a strong emotion
You want something someone else has
Something you feel you need
Jealousy, also called coveting
The Bible says we shouldn't do it
Yet we do it anyway
Jealousy, it's a big dark hole
We run into it without wanting to
And we begin falling, falling, falling
Jealousy, nobody likes it
Especially our friends
But only if they still are your friends
Jealousy, it's a terrible trait
To others you seem as dark as the night sky
Yet you don't realize it until it's too late
Jealousy, a horrible thing
You shouldn't do it
You must stop before it's too late
Jealousy

Danika De Groot, Grade 7
Sunnyside Christian Elementary School, WA

The Highway Man
I saw him standing in the rain.
Once a rich man, now a shame.
He destroyed many lives, now his own.
Once held champagne, now holds pain.
His heart corrupt with greed.
Waiting for money so he can fill in his final need.

Max McCafferty, Grade 7
21st Century Public Academy, NM

Tapity Tap Tapity Tap
Tapity tap, tapity tap
Woodpecker drumming on house
Wood splitting
Sleeping parents tap back
It would seem the woodpecker's goal is to annoy the family

Tapity tap, tapity tap
Tap, tap, tap

Bird and man fight back and forth
A battle is waged

Tapity tap, tapity tap
Tap, tap, tap
Tapity tap
Tap, tap, tap

The family won
The house is theirs…
For now

Trenton Hoshiko, Grade 7
Lyons Middle/Senior High School, CO

Greatest Diamond
They say diamonds are a girl's best friend
And the greatest one is usually around the bend.
No matter where you live, or where you're at,
This diamond holds a ball and a bat.

The baseball diamond is where it's at,
The ball, the bat, and maybe a baseball cap.
A day in the Bronx or behind a green wall,
This diamond can hold it all.

Jeter, D-Train, and David Wright
All great players, day and night.
They hit 'em far and wide, right and left,
And no outfielder has been a theft.

However great a field may be,
The diamond is worth coming to see.
You can't wear it on your hand, neck, or foot,
But it's always worth giving a look.

Dylan Culwell, Grade 9
Lake Havasu High School, AZ

My Grandma's Cooking

I was at my grandma's house. Grandma was cooking. She was making fry-bread and pudding. Then all of the sudden a cloud of steam tapped me on the shoulder. After that I realized what the smell was. It was the pudding. After about 15 seconds the cloud of steam went away and the smell soaked into my hair. Then in about a minute another cloud of steam came to me. I smelled it. It smelled like fry-bread. Then that smell soaked into my hair. It was time to eat. A whole bunch of my cousins came in the door. Everybody knows when Grandma is cooking because you can smell the sweet smell of the steam from twenty miles away. When I get older I want to be just like Grandma. I love my grandma.

Haylee Jo Pretty Weasel, Grade 7
Pretty Eagle Catholic School, MT

Alone

Sitting all alone, it's cold and lonely.
Nothing to grab onto, nobody to hold me.
Today is the day where all the dreams are blown away.
This is the day when your worst fears become your worst reality.
If this is the worst day could it be the worst night, week, month, year?
No it couldn't be so much I want to do, so much I want to say.
Yes everything has gone cold.
The future's to remake itself only to get messed up again.
I wonder if this pattern of good and bad ever really ends?
I don't feel even in the deepest place in my mind, body and soul that I can trust anybody.
Because everybody that I've trusted has done me wrong.
Then the clock ticks with the faintest sound, and I suddenly realize that I'm all alone in the cold and lonely.
Nothing to hold onto, nobody to hold me.
Everything is dead, I'm only breathing.
Shake me please,
I must be dreaming.

Sunday Sanchez, Grade 8
La Plata Middle School, NM

The Land of Me

I am from the Virgo super cluster: a massive group of galaxies,
An expanse far beyond my home (by far I mean reeeealy far).

I am from the planet Earth: a blue, green, and white ball floating in space,
The only planet we know to have life.

I am from a place called the U.S.A., where people of many races mix together,
But has had its reputation diminished by bad leaders.

I am from Utah: a land of arches dry as bone,
But where the settlers said, "This is the place."

I am from Salt Lake City: the place that boasts the greatest snow on Earth,
A place where the mountains are like great cones.

I am from lineages of moldy Washingtonians and rusty Midwesterners,
But I am a freeze dried Utahn.

I am from places beyond that too: where the countryside glistens with dew (and picnickers),
Where the glaciers carve paths anew,
Where their chocolates are like sugary goo.

I am from a great family: completely adventuresome and knowledgeable people.
I am from great friends, crazy to the soul.

Erik Poppleton, Grade 7
Our Lady of Lourdes Catholic School, UT

Love

My love has my heart, and I have his.
By just exchange one for another given:
I clasp his dear, and mine he can't miss,
There never was a better deed driven:
My love has my heart, and I have his.

His heart in me keeps him and I one,
My heart in him his thoughts and senses guides:
He adores my heart, for once it was his own,
I cherish his because in me it bides,
My love has my heart, and I have his.

Desirable, beautiful, one of a kind,
If only you were here to hold and keep,
Forever on my mind.
If you ever let me go I would weep,
My love has my heart, and I have his.

Erica Russell, Grade 9
Shelley Sr High School, ID

Tea in the Woods

Not long ago, where the plum trees grow,
And blossoms blow to the ground like snow,
Where water warbles and fireflies glow,
Something happened I'd like you to know.

As I was walking by, you see,
I felt that something was following me
A young little bluebird it turned out to be
"Would you like to have tea?" She sang unto me.

I just had to say yes, so down we sat
We ate tiny bird bites, and had a nice chat.
Looking up from her snack of crackers and sprat,
She said right to me, "Are you going to eat that?"

Michael Busse, Grade 8
Eugene Christian School, OR

Round 4

Punch by punch
Staggering across like a dizzy child
One fell swoop could knock him down
Yet he retaliates with his own
Exchanging blows for what seems like hours
Only one will prevail
The true victor
Rounds and rounds later
He finally goes with a thump
He lies there unconsciously
They take the necessary precautions
He gets up with one less fight
Only one will prevail
The true victor?

Jesse Kibel, Grade 9
Grand Junction High School, CO

Craving

A craving lingers for moments on end,
Never dying, always growing inside.
They say this feeling will gradually mend,
That time is key and she should step aside.
But, hearing your voice, her heart skips a beat.
Now, your tongue does nothing but cause her pain.
You're gone and she's suddenly incomplete,
For months she's attempted in staying sane.
The memories she is trying to drop,
Everything she's given, now she regrets.
Your face brings all forgetting to a stop,
She persists thinking about you instead.
She prays that she will make it through each day,
"I miss you" is something she will not say.

Anita Kuo, Grade 9
Clark High School, NV

Perspective

Life was but a walking shadow.
A poor player strutting the stage,
then heard no more.

It was a tale told by no one,
where none listened and none were heard.
Life was but a walking shadow.

But then,
       Hope.

A new perspective came into view.
Life should be lived in the moment.
We hope and dream a better future,
though not everything is as it should.
The saying "seize the day" is what it is.
Learn from the past,
worry not the future.
Focus on today.
From my dark shroud, I turn over a leaf,
and begin anew.

Ralph DeLeon, Grade 8
Walt Morey Middle School, OR

Out of a Crowd

She sits there not wanting to be seen.
She will say any lie
All she wants is to get high
She's addicted to crystal meth
At the end all she'll get nothing but death
She was kicked out of her house
Forgotten by every one no help was afforded
The things she does just to feel that feeling
She loves so much in her arms her lungs and her nose
Alone and sad
Never to be glad

Aracely Vizcaino, Grade 7
21st Century Public Academy, NM

My Favorite Thing to Do
B laze
A lways
R acing
R ight around
E very
L eft and

R ight
A lways racing
C oming
I n
N ow
G oing again
Micheala Botts, Grade 8
Round Valley Middle School, AZ

Dogs
Dogs Loving Family Adorable
Playing Barking Running
They have a big place in my heart

Always wanting attention
Playing Barking Running
They have a big place in my heart

Always there for you
Playing Barking Running
They have a big place in my heart
Danielle Kovac, Grade 8
Sedona Charter School, AZ

I Wish I Had Seen
I wish I had seen
His eyes before he left
I wish I had seen
The hair across his head
I wish I had seen
A smile from him to me
I wish I had seen
Him having fun with me
I wish I had seen
Him giving me a hug
I wish I had seen
From him to me
LOVE
Lisha Smith, Grade 7
Sky Vista Middle School, CO

A Spider Named Billy
There once was a spider named Billy
who was talking to the one eyed Willy
he went home to check on his kids
all he found was wigs
but you know he was just being silly
Tori Bunts, Grade 8
Round Valley Middle School, AZ

This Person
Am I still there?
I really don't know
When I started I was normal, without thought or need to change
With my own ideas and opinion,
No one else but me.
Then I stepped out the door.
"Her pants are lame."
"She looks like a boy."
Tens of thousand people judge me,
I'm on longer alone but looking through others eyes,
And the thought of no sex appeal starts to scare me.
Then I step into a school.
"Your writing isn't clear enough."
"That wasn't the point of the lesson."
Now the point is to strive to please someone else and their opinion.
To argue and show I'm right to be shot down with a wrong.
When I am back in the safe haven called home,
I look in the mirror and see someone.
Am I still there?
I really don't know.
Jasmine Wood-Jenkins, Grade 9
Roosevelt High School, WA

Blue
Blue is the only color that makes me feel true.
Blue reflecting day through night.
Blue in the big sky, blue in somebody's eyes.
Blue is cool especially in your neighbor's swimming pool.
Blue is my favorite color and, I will never change it for another.
Blue in the ocean, blue is like my feeling and emotion.
Blue in my shoes, blue in the neighbor's pool,
Blue on my folder, blue on somebody's face when the temperature gets colder.
Blue still being my favorite color as I get older.
Gabriela Valenzuela, Grade 7
21st Century Public Academy, NM

Dream into a Promise
It's a dream, I am dreaming.
It's the same one I had every day and it never ends.
Red snow, a world stained in red.
A small child is crying, almost eclipsing the sunset.
I wanted at least to wipe the tears away.
But my hands wouldn't leave my side.
And the tears rolling down his cheeks disappeared into the snow.
All I could do was watch, it was frustrating and sad.
"It will be all right, don't cry, I promise."
I can't help but to wonder whose words those were.
They seem too far to be mine.
And as I lay here looking at the sky.
I see a girl running into a light.
But I soon fall into a deep, deep sleep.
A dream fades into a distant color,
It fades,
Into a Promise.
Stephanie Gaona, Grade 9
Lakewood High School, CO

Childhood

Run and play
Sing and dance
I love to open that imaginary door
To my childhood past

Having no worries
Of work or tasks
Just being able to stay home
To play and relax

Clothes and trends
Nails and hair
None of that mattered
If your friends were there

My childhood door
Will always be there
To daydream back into
The anonymous elsewhere

Cheyanne Franke, Grade 7
St Elizabeth Ann Seton Catholic School, AZ

The Cycle of Spring

The first of the blossoms, like glorious delights,
That churns soil round, sends bees into flight.
The first of the leaves makes its journey to green
As dandelions bask in the light of the scene.

But winds are a howlin' and beasts are a prowlin'
As many an animal flees.
The branches are fallin', like wounded a crawlin',
From uprooted juniper trees.

The storm in its passing has left many clasping
To anchors they luckily found.
And if we look closely, small scale n' remotely,
We see tiny buds on the ground.

During the thunder, while land's torn asunder,
New life makes its way to the top.
However we act there's no changing the fact:
The Cycle of Spring never stops.

Kevin Wilkison, Grade 9
Tempe Preparatory Academy, AZ

Friendship

What is friendship?
Friendship is:
A good friend to lean on
Always there when you need it
Laughs with you, until you both start crying
Poke each other and occasionally pinch each other
Doing crazy things that people would think was weird
Friendship is a piece of gum who's flavor never wears off.

Gabriela Varela, Grade 7
St Anthony of Padua Catholic School, AZ

The Train

The train is going all through town
With its wheels going 'round and 'round.
The train is hissing, "I think I can!"
While the conductor is talking to a short, funny man.
The cargo is going side to side,
And children are laughing with mothers close behind.
The train stopped running,
The laughter is gone,
But this adventure has only begun!

Liza Vernon, Grade 7
Ernest Becker Middle School, NV

The American Flag

The American flag was always there,
it was very dear to us.
Red, white, and blue
will always remain true.

We held it high above our head
through difficult times we showed it proud.
We honor those who live by it
we hold it high raised far as the eye can see.

When the flag goes by hold it high,
take off your hats to those who died.
It's there for our nation
for those who gave their lives.

So stop and stare and ponder,
what a wonderful thing the flag is.
We remember what red, white, and blue,
means for me and you!

Kyle Blundell, Grade 7
Leading Edge Academy - Gilbert, AZ

Dog's Life

Me and my family
are a bunch of stray dogs.
We try to survive
but there's always a trap
that gets in our way.
We try and try
but everywhere we go
there's another trap.

One day, one day,
oh God, please, one day!
We poor dogs,
why can't we have a good time?
When, God, when
can we have a good,
relaxing day?
Oh God, when? When?

Anthony Avila, Grade 8
Mario C. Jo Anne Monaco Middle School, NV

Life
Life is good, but also bad.
Life makes me happy and mad.
Everyone's life is like a treasure chest,
But out of all, mine's the best.
Bethanie Hokanson, Grade 7
Peoria Horizons Charter School, AZ

Sunset
Winter petals rain
gently upon the flowers,
Beauty never masked.
In oceans of wine
the skies are dark, (in the streets)
Where? Trees once flourished
in a darkening world,
unveiled by the colored snow,
left to die alone.
City in the rain, clinging to
squares of concrete "reason,"
Is one the other, fusing together?
Artificial or natural?
Is there a difference!
Petals from the dawn,
falling, failing, in the snow,
can they survive past winter?
Center of the town,
Do trees stand high as clouds?
Is it lost, never found?
Does anyone know?
Spencer Barringer, Grade 9
Lakewood High School, CO

Darkest Hour
This is my darkest hour.
My heart can't find the light,
Like walking on a pitch-black night.
My heart aches with sorrow,
And is submerged in darkness.
Tears run down my face.
As I plunge into my darkest hour,
I grab for a hold,
But I cannot reach.
The circle of light grows smaller,
And smaller,
As I dive into my darkest hour.
Slowly my body has been eaten,
Eaten by the darkness,
Like a ravenous bear.
As I fall, I'm covered in darkness,
As it invades my heart,
I feel I am not the same.
I'm not me anymore,
Because this is my darkest hour,
And the darkness dwells inside me.
Celine Stefanich, Grade 8
Glide Middle School, OR

Sundae
My dad is the cup
He keeps us together and protects us

I am the bottom ice cream
I am the youngest and smallest

Viri is the middle ice cream
She is the middle child

Myrna is the top ice cream
She is the oldest

My mom is the fudge
She protects us all

Foxy is the whipped cream
She is as sweet as whipped cream

Bonita is the nuts
She is nutty and fun!

Menoush is the cherry
He thinks he is the king
Jenifer Banda-Torres, Grade 7
La Center Middle School, WA

Green
endless forest
fresh evergreen air
stream flowing gracefully
gentle breeze
pine tree's bite
beautiful place
Megan Mahrt, Grade 7
Valley Academy Charter School, AZ

Abuse
Always yelling
Always fighting
Can't get along
Always hitting me

Bruises across my face
Even on my legs
I can't do anything right
All they care about are themselves

They never care if I come home
They don't care if I sleep in a field
Never agreeing with me
Why is life so hard?

My friend's life is so much easier
Why can't mine be?
Cody Huckabay, Grade 7
Shadow Ridge Middle School, CO

Rose
Flower of passion and love
Red as blood
With a drop of dew, it is a benign calm
With a purple rage, it is intense fury
Seeing it makes the heart beat faster
To the beat of the rain that falls upon it
Fury
Love
Passion
In one single flower
Its dew sparkles in the sun
It drinks the rain of spring
Until
It is picked from the ground
For one's true love
Rose
Nola Basey, Grade 7
Lyons Middle/Senior High School, CO

Natural Disasters
Tornado,
Dark, ripping,
Twisting, twirling, taking,
Kansas, beast, New Orleans, monster,
Growing, destroying, ruining,
Horrible, ending,
Hurricane.
Emily Blake Hamblin, Grade 8
Round Valley Middle School, AZ

Fire Red Roses
Bumble bees buzzing around
The fire red rose
Fresh from last night's rain.
They blaze in the
Noonday's rays,
Casting long shadows
From the fire red roses.
A symbol of love,
And the color of fire
Burning in your heart
With the deepest desire
For the fire red roses.
Michelle Wilfong, Grade 8
Round Valley Middle School, AZ

Elk
An elk,
As big as can be,
Traveling through the woods,
As beautiful as I see,
Bugling for cows,
To know where he could be,
Fighting for his territory.
AJ Tafoya, Grade 8
Round Valley Middle School, AZ

Best Friend

While going through stress and strife
Somebody to run to, is all I need in life.
Yes, you are the one
I call you my best friend.
And even when we say "we're done"
Our times will never end.
The two of us have been through it all
That's why I'll always catch you,
right before you fall
We have shared every special moment together.
Every tear…
Every smile…
Every wink…
Every laugh…
Yes, we are like two "peas-in-a-pod"
and that is not a lie,
I will love you forever
Up to the day we die!

Amber White, Grade 8
Sequoia Village School, AZ

Skiing

The ski blends with the smell of pine tree
The snow is an old friend, waiting to be cut free
The white blends perfectly with the blue
I hit the first morning powder and glide through
Catching that jump, I can feel myself soar
At the end of the day, I want more!!

Brian Kampfe, Grade 7
Luther School, MT

Time

One breath, one sigh,
one rose, one lie.
Each drop of blood, each tear shed,
is just another moment wasted away in the end.
Sing a song, weave a plot,
don't forget that time cannot be bought.
Spin some gold, whisper the time,
listen to your man's rhyme.
Tell me something that's worth more than gold.
Show me a place that's sweeter than a rose.
Give me a scent that's denser than fog.
Sell me a workout that's better than a dog.
Don't cry, don't lie. Don't sin, don't win.
I'm sick of the rules and tired of the slang,
tell me, give me a reason to do good; to do as I should.
Write me a song, read me a book.
Look me in the eyes and tell me you're not the crook.
One pistol, one dagger,
one bullet, one stab.
Each man dead, each soul lost,
are just more tears wasted, wasted, and then forgot.

Rowan Quirk, Grade 7
Sagewood Middle School, CO

Always Say "Can't"

Livin' the age of limitation.
Told to build a structure without a given foundation.
Our futures you tell us to try 'n see.
While blinded by doubts given so unbelievably.
Like tellin' a child their friend is in their head,
And the boogie man lies beneath their bed.
And the magic that lies within each legend and story,
Has been wiped clean of all its wonder and glory.
Cast in a movie of black and white,
Hung by a rope of wrong and right.
Our unlimited creativity you have deceived,
All just because you yourself have never once believed.

Christina Flores, Grade 8
Foothills Middle School, WA

Childhood

Every childhood is not the same.
Some really exciting, some just lame.
Scratches, bruises, anything but tame
Running around, people screaming your name
Hide-and-seek is what we play.
But let's play something different today.
We are young and free.
You wouldn't care about a scratch on your knee
Play 'til the sun goes down.
Once it's black, back to town
When the sun goes down all is lost,
Everything will come back though at no cost.
Games stop; need to be put on hold
We must run fast, it's getting cold.
Run home, maybe fall no shame.
Get a cool scratch and here comes fame
Get home, jump under the covers, that's the way
Time to cool down, just lay
But up bright and early right away
Run out of the door, no need to stay.

Alex Smolenski, Grade 9
Tempe Preparatory Academy, AZ

Prison

I sit here alone in my cell
Poor decisions I have made
No time to dwell
I look out the window and watch the sunset fade

Trapped and scared, its getting colder
Wanting to be free as an eagle
I'm dying inside, and have become much older
All because I chose to do something illegal

The morning sun has risen
I put on my orange pants
Another day in prison
I kneel and pray for a second chance

Marissa Aguirre, Grade 7
Sky Vista Middle School, CO

The Last Snow Cold Kiss
The wind blows cold
On my bare skin
And it reminds me that
I'll never see you again
The color of your eyes
Embedded in my mind
Another reminder
That you left me behind
These are the thoughts
That drive me insane
The memories
That have caused me pain
But none are as painful
As the sound of your name
Another pawn
In this mind game
And if I win
Does that mean that you'll stay?
To hold me
For one final day?

Sara Story, Grade 8
Fertitta Middle School, NV

Summer
Summer day, summer night,
I find myself filled with fright.
As I'm trembling with fear,
I shed a little tear,
for the summer's end is closely near.
Year by year summers go.
I say the dreadful word that is NO!
Summer's gone school is here
no more time to run and cheer,
no more pool or flying kites.
Now we have to go to sleep at night.
Summer day, summer night.

Amber Nolte, Grade 7
Coronado K 8 School, AZ

Potatoes
Potatoes are good
Potatoes are curly
Potatoes are food
Now make them in a hurry

I love the potatoes
I do, I do
Hurry up and make them
One, two, one, two

Potatoes are good
Potatoes are delicious
Potatoes are over
Now wash the dishes

Raul Ortiz, Grade 7
Somerton Middle School, AZ

War
It was the beginning of the end as I feared on the bus.
The clouds were as grey as the cement beneath my feet.
The air smelled of fires and bodies so rank as I walk down the war torn street.
Only two blocks away, the former army had lay.
The cracks in the road held rivers of blood.
I could see where there used to lay buildings,
But in the buildings' place I can only see mud.

My squad walks behind me.
They've no fear in their eyes
Nevertheless they will soon cry to the mercy of war, why?
Because all I see in them is nothing but lies.
No training, no guns, nothing they have,
Will protect them from an invincible man.
That man so dangerous yet easy to find.
Is right underneath the skin of the man that is so vigorously blind.

The objective's been reached after an hour less journey
I suited up and walked to the chopper
I thought to myself is it worth it again?
As I look at the faces of the young men and women
I know that to be a commander
One boy must fall and one man must rise.

Taylor O'Harra, Grade 8
Fertitta Middle School, NV

How Does Love Die?
I thought we were forever, I thought our love was true,
But then he went behind my back and played me for a fool.
He said he'd never hurt me, he said he'd never make me cry,
I guess the words he was telling me, were nothing but white lies.
But now my heart is broken and all I do is cry,
Every time I think about it it makes me wonder why.
I think of all the memories, still held deep inside.
I wish I could forget but it's really hard to do
I loved him with all my heart and now suddenly we're through,
He said I was his shining star and his sun in the sky,
I never thought it would end like this how does love die?

Ariana Madueno, Grade 8
Cimarron Springs Elementary School, AZ

Mysterious Sky
Watching with an ever penetrating gaze
with a charcoal abyss ready to engulf the teetering minuscule stars
with a smoky gray hanging listless and seemingly dormant
with the lightest of blues moving like silken raindrops
with the bone aching rumble and roar ripping itself from the dark mountains
with night's perfect imperfection gliding and darkly radiant
with moonbeams arcing to crest the dense black velvet
with electric blue fields gracing the horizon until only a memory
the sky ever watching
in all its mystery

Forrest Rhinehart, Grade 7
Salt Lake Arts Academy, UT

In the Middle of the Night
In the middle of the night,
The sounds you hear,
The sights you might,
The night is near,
As you hear the cries,
In the middle of the night.

In the middle of the night,
The blanket of dark falls over the sky,
The hours pass
This night says good-bye,
The sun wakes up,
In the middle of the night

In the middle of the night,
It's warming up and the night is growing closer,
The blanket covers the river with ice,
In the middle of the night.
Kayloni Holm, Grade 9
Shelley Sr High School, ID

Passion
His eyes are the fire
Burning a hole through my skin
When he stares
I look away
Frightened by the love
Coming through his eyelids
I taste the teardrops
As they role down my trembling cheeks
There he is
Wiping them away
Shining in my life
Like sunshine seeping through the clouds
The past is haunting
But we fight through the pain
Hand in hand
Sweet candy kisses
Dancing on my lips
Like rain on my window
I watch as every single drop falls down
Melissa Schrand, Grade 9
Queen Creek High School, AZ

Don't Judge Me
You say I'm too small, too dumb, or too skinny
My hair is too short, too curly, too long.
Or I'm ugly, because I'm not blonde.
My skin is too dark, my skin is too light.
It makes me so mad, I want to get up and fight.
I want to cry, I want to scream.
What you say is so hurtful and mean.
I want to speak up to reveal,
That this is how I really feel.
Alina LeDuff, Grade 7
Peoria Horizons Charter School, AZ

I Am a Daughter
I am Sammi.
I hear chirping birds.
I see the countryside.
I say we should all stay positive.
I cry about him — not being here.
I am Sammi.
I am a daughter.
I feel strong.
I try to think everything will be fine.
I dream about seeing, smelling, and hearing him again.
I am a daughter.
Sammi Jo Gibbins, Grade 8
Sacajawea Jr High School, ID

Poison Spring: A Geothermal Feature of Yellowstone
P oisons animals big to small
O nly accessible with a ranger
I nnocently stands off the trail
S ilently bubbling
O minous and hypnotizing
N ice little spring off to the side

S imple but amazing
P eaceful and deadly all in one
R ight for looking, bad for drinking
I n Mammoth Springs area
N ever touch or breathe the water
G o with memories
Angela Henrich, Grade 8
Cody Middle School, WY

I Am Proud to Come From…
I am from my mom,
Beautiful and strong,
Smart and brave,
And been through things I can't imagine.

I am from my grandma,
Strong and proud,
Giving and grateful.

I am from my sister,
Tough and smart,
Outgoing and competitive.

I am from my aunt,
Wise and smart,
Traveler and social.

I am from the state with the greatest snow on Earth,
The Grand Canyon,
Sego Lily's,
And Ute Native Americans.
Aundraya Dain, Grade 7
Our Lady of Lourdes Catholic School, UT

The Pool

When summer comes, the pool's the most popular place in town. As you come in, chaos surrounds you. Smelling the chlorine and tasting it too. Hearing the "splash!" of the children jumping in. Their screams fill the small enclosed space. Looking right through the blue transparent water as the lifeguard blows his whistle and it's time for a break.

Taylor Grimm, Grade 7
Ernest Becker Middle School, NV

My Piano

My piano is beautiful, like a memory calling to be remembered.
Its old surface and rigid keys are not unsightly, but beautiful, whispering of the sound waiting inside.

The strings resonate deep within like valor called upon in danger.
It whispers peace and warns of oncoming peril like the eye of a storm.
Its keys clank and clatter jazz like a peddler's cart on a dusty road.
Its music laces together, weaving in and out like the whispers in a wind.
It sounds out as soft as a wet, polished stone on the bottom of a river.
It is a patient friend, lifting me on hard days, begging to be played, a friend to soften my soul's sorrow.

The keys remember my fingers; recognize old songs I haven't played in ages.
My emotions flow through its keys and they bleed my joys and worries.
It forgives when my hands come crashing down upon the ebony and ivory in frustration.
Its speech is music, a splendor of passion: a splash of ego.
It is not to be mastered, but loved.

I will exercise it daily, for I know it loves to work.
Tenderly I will polish its surface.
I'll allow my fingers to fly across the keys, ask them for a dance.
Introduce new music, and reunite with songs almost forgotten.
Smile in thanks at the happiness it gives me.
My piano, you are loved.

Chloe Mehr, Grade 9
Mountain Ridge Jr High School, UT

Life Never Ends

Most people have had a loved one die
Have you; maybe you; I have of all people
You never think that death will disrupt your family,
But watch out for it will strike you when all is going well and when you least expect it
My beloved grandmother, died at a young age she did,
She knew how to love and got the chance to live a little
She never knew that her time was coming. Nobody knows really how much time they get
Live a little is what I say or soon you will regret
She was a Christian woman and loved very much at that. Who could tell her that she had cancer?
She was a sweet lady with sparkling eyes. Nothing she did made her even deserve to have this horrible disease
We came one day to that deadly place that smelled of rubber and meds to visit our loved one and find that she had gone
That day Gwen's life went and when she'd gone we all knew that she was at
Heaven's Gates rejoicing and praising in God's name, singing with her beautiful voice and breathing with her angel's breath
That one last look was all I could bear. She had no more life, for her soul had gone away.
My one last wish was that I could see her smiling face,
To hear her laugh or cry, or to hear her voice yet one more time
One last moment with her was all I wanted
But not on this Earth will I ever see her.
In Heaven that is, where all of us belong
Although her life may be over, it never truly ends
For she went to Heaven, and Heaven is where she stands

Allyssa Dunn, Grade 7
Sunnyside Christian Elementary School, WA

Life

When you are young and don't know why
you're here on earth,
you feel like a speck of dust.
But when you start growing up,
you get stuck in the middle of the ocean and
don't know what direction to go.
And when you are all grown up and
you know what you're here on earth to do,
you feel like a beautiful flower
that doesn't know when to stop going
in the right direction.

Alexandria Olguin, Grade 7
St Catherine of Siena School, CO

Hide

I hide behind these masks and faces,
Because I don't want you to see the real me,
The person who loves to read,
I hide behind these masks and faces,
So I never feel any pain,
I don't want you to see me cry,
I hide behind these masks and faces,
To live the way that's expected,
No one wants to see the real me,
When the "REAL" me is already known,
I hide behind these masks and faces,
Because I am not comfortable with myself,
I hide to feel as if I am wanted,
Wanted for the "REAL" me.

Kara Giorgi, Grade 9
Yerington High School, NV

Red, Silver, and Green

Red as fierce as a lion
Its flame grasping the edge of the forest
Fading away the color of reality
Only soon to flee over the mountains

Darkness now covers the land
The silver face who rules the night reaches out his hand
Transforming the forest into a soothing array of peace
Only soon to flee over the mountains

The silver face vanishes with the blanket of darkness
Red charges out from its hiding spot
Brilliantly shining bringing a new day with him
Only soon to flee over the mountains

The luscious green of the forest
The trees watch the two great faces silently
Waiting for one to conquer
Though the trees will never figure out
They are always soon to flee over the mountain

James Turner, Grade 7
St Elizabeth Ann Seton Catholic School, AZ

Shadows

I want a moment, just a moment in
time to take for myself. I am not one
of those girls, your girls, who can stand in
your shadow, the girl to whom you will run.
I will not stand waiting, searching, my eyes
trained above; hoping for you, just you.
My calm will not waver, fed by these lies
of something greater, to those who are true
to your word, your book, to those who will learn.
Is it love that can hate, shun, and despise
us, for our love? Now empty, I will yearn
to abandon your ways, my wants unwise.
You took him away, in trade for this pride;
Now behind this colored curtain I hide.

Katherine Laveway, Grade 9
Clark High School, NV

Nightmare

The girl stood with a silenced mind,
The sky mocked me with madness,
I stood with steady movements.

The sky was crumbling down,
Lightning struck hard with hatred,
Everything was torn up and then disappeared.

The sidewalks went up,
Kids went down,
Sounds destroy souls.

I woke up,
It was all just a nightmare,
My body shook with no control,
I realized I was trapped,
Nowhere to go but in a hole.

Nikayla Shaw, Grade 8
Circle Cross Ranch K-8 School, AZ

Vincent Campbell

Vincent
Crafty, nice, funny, playful
Son of Kris
Grandson of Betty and Sue
Who wants to sleep every day
Glad to be alive
Afraid of being alone
Who fears spiders
Being different
Being ungrateful
Who would like to go to Hawaii
Spends more time with his family and pets
Drawing
Resident of a little town in Montana
Campbell

Vincent Campbell, Grade 8
East Middle School, MT

Nature, Simple

A gentle sunset,
glowing in the horizon,
calm tranquility

Mighty tree forest,
colossal giants of old,
watching silently...

Benevolent sea,
beautiful beyond belief,
untamed and wild

Wilson To, Grade 7
Ernest Becker Middle School, NV

The Street

When all is silent in the night
People start to fight

Not believing my sight
Standing in fright

Seeing all the light, standing in the street
They're going to start throwing heat

I want to get out of these feet
And run down the street

Vance Grabow, Grade 7
Timberview Middle School, CO

The Footsteps That Made America

The footsteps that made America
Came from no one man we know,
But from brave and weary soldiers
Leaving bloody footprints in the snow.

The footsteps came from men
Holding their flag up high,
Fighting for liberty and justice for all
And for that many would die.

It's amazing after all they did
Their names? We hardly know any.
Yet the number who died for us
Is such a very great many.

The brave soldiers who died for us
We must never forget.
In the freedom of America
We are forever in their debt.

I wonder if those soldiers knew
Weary and battle laid,
That the "Footsteps of America"
Were the footsteps that they made.

Shannon Babcock, Grade 7
Idaho Distance Education Academy, ID

Perfect

Being perfect is nonsense,
Whosoever wishes to be, might spend their life on a fence,
Constantly placing a toe on either side,
Not knowing how to cope with what's inside,
Perfect is a word that should not exist,
Because I've yet to see anyone or anything,
That goes along side of it,
Being perfect is such nonsense,
You can't even describe,
When trying to be perfect you're in for a wild ride.
There are some people who try but they have their flaws,
From gently breaking a simple rule or a big time law,
Perfect is a word that should not exist,
For some it's only a veil that covers up zits,
To be perfect is such nonsense,
There will always be something wrong in each point of view,
Because the label of perfect is nothing new.

Abigail Gonder, Grade 9
Arizona Agribusiness & Equine Center - Paradise Valley Campus, AZ

Basketball

Basketball brings a feeling I can't describe.
If you are a player all you can see is the basket
And eyes filled with doubt or determination.
You can smell the odor of jerseys drenched with sweat.
You can taste nothing but dryness in your mouth.
All you can hear are the bleachers filled with roaring half-crazed fans.
And thunder of twenty feet going up and down the floor.
You can feel the rough, but gentle leather of the ball.
To live is to experience basketball.

Kylie Kielbasa, Grade 9
Duchesne High School, UT

Fuchsia Is Power

Fuchsia is strong. It controls the minds of everyone who sees it.
Fuchsia is passion in a color form.
Fuchsia is rebellion, against the unfair and unjust.
Fuchsia signifies happiness found during hard times.
Fuchsia is the plastic beads hanging from a hippie's van door.
Fuchsia is the clouds at sunset, awing and spectacular.
Fuchsia is the color of the head band, tied across every freedom-fighter's head.
Fuchsia is freedom.
Fuchsia is playful.
Fuchsia is a work of art.
Fuchsia laughs along with you.
Fuchsia is the color of the words spoken for justice.
Fuchsia is the jump ropes that little girls skip.
Fuchsia is the feeling of accomplishment, doing something, and doing it right.
Fuchsia has overcome the hardships of the '60s.
Fuchsia is when you've won the right to do something.
Fuchsia is the smile on someone's face when you've helped them.
Fuchsia is chuckles, not snickers.
Fuchsia recharges you.
Fuchsia...is power.

Julia Jahanpour-Burke, Grade 7
Ernest Becker Middle School, NV

An Ode to Summer

Summer is the time of year,
When children's hearts fill up with cheer.
The close of school is growing near,
All worries and thoughts just disappear.

The sun beats down shining Oh, so bright,
Everyone's spirits are happy and light.
There's swimming and playing and ice cream too,
Winter's once gray sky is now deep blue.

As summer's warmth begins to fade,
It brings an end to a great crusade.
Winter's cold is returning fast,
Summer is over, too soon it has passed.

Tanner Ellison, Grade 8
La Plata Middle School, NM

Her Hair

Her hair shiny as the sun
All tied up in a pretty little bun
It's as soft as the moon
With a rubber band wrapped around it like a typhoon
When she takes it out and shakes her head
You can't help but stare
She looks like a star
She is not very far
To your heart she will travel
To be with you in your dreams
You love her you know you do
You're so proud to call her your buggity boo

Rachelle Hahn, Grade 7
Sky Vista Middle School, CO

Big Brother

It happened at Lake Valley
It happened at lunch time
Our school had an alley

My brother played basketball
I was going to the bathroom
Down the hall
I finished, I turned around
I noticed four guys looking and smiling
They all tackled me to the ground
They dragged my head
To the toilet bowl
"This is funny," one of them said
I was so scared and sad
They were all making fun of me
My brother burst in mad

He took me to the principal
Who talked about me on the loud speaker
It took away 1,000 souls

Matthew Kee, Grade 7
St Bonaventure School, NM

The Apple

Thump, as the apple falls from the tree,
I sit and admire the golden gift from God.
As it stands out from the fuzzy green grass,
My mouth waters reminiscing,
The sweet pure taste.
I pick up the distorted circle,
And flick it to hear the vibrations
Travel through the slush hidden treasure inside.
My tooth breaks the unique red skin protecting it
And as the sweet inside enters, my heart pounds in excitement.
How a simple thing makes me appreciate what I have.

Elaine Mahoney Casap, Grade 9
Xavier College Preparatory School, AZ

Sharon

So strong, so beautiful
Yet so stubborn, but so am I.
My mom says I look just like her.
I know when she goes to visit Jesus,
It will hurt, it will hurt so bad!
My one angel,
She will be my guardian angel
And she will protect me.
She once told me,
"The ones you love never really leave you."

Rayven Reese, Grade 8
Bessemer Academy, CO

Snowy Memories

The wind hard against my face
My feet connected to my snowboard
My legs sore from falling
The feel of your hair blowing in the wind
As you rush down the steep slope.

I feel high up on the lift
My snowboard glides on the icy sheets
I feel a sudden rush come
Through me as I speed down
The snowy, ice of the rocky hill

My cousin speeding and jumping like a pro.
He grabs me by the hand
And teaches me step by step
Like a little child learns to walk
We glide down the hill on our snowboards
I see the pine trees everywhere and the snowflakes drifting.

Soon the day has come to an end
I am so exhausted from falling and picking myself up again
I watch movies with my cousins and sleep
Now the day is over and we head home
That trip I will never forget.

Celeste Perkins, Grade 7
St Elizabeth Ann Seton Catholic School, AZ

Tree
Standing peacefully,
Watching over animals.
When it rains and snow,
The animals find safety
Underneath its large branches.
Aliyah Montgomery, Grade 8
Place Middle School, CO

I Am
I am Nick Mitchell,
I hear a good tee shot.
I see the ball in the hole,
I say it's in the hole,
I cry in joy,
I am the greatest golfer.
I am Nick Mitchell.
Nick Mitchell, Grade 8
Sacajawea Jr High School, ID

A Snow Fall at Night
House grows cold, silent
Snow drifts, innocently
Roof changes, green to blue
Slowly piling against clear window
Inside flannel sheets bundle
Soft breathing, otherwise still
Trees, not moving, snow covering green
The hush of night snow falls.
Arbor Dykema, Grade 8
Luther School, MT

A Monster Hiding Within an Angel
In the middle of the midnight trees
Lies something no one sees.
Hiding secrets in the dark
Is a monster hiding with an angel
Waiting in the midnight trees.
I step closer just to see if I can find
The person that I lost a long time ago.
Her personality is lost in the wind,
All that is left of this person
Is a monster hiding within an angel.

I want to see my friend again,
But this friend is no longer a friend.
She is a monster hiding within an angel.
I see no resemblance,
She has lost her dignity,
And is filled up with rage.

In this forest,
The purple moonlight shining in,
Is the last time I will ever see
A monster hiding within an angel.
Sarah King, Grade 7
Sagewood Middle School, CO

No Matter the Weather
A little sack just filled with sand.
What fun can that be?
How bland.
Up and down the little ball goes.
Where it stops nobody knows.
A jester, a stall,
Or even a rainbow,
Are some of the tricks
If you just learn how.
It may go twenty feet up
Or stay on your shoe.
It's very unpredictable
But what can you do.
Up in the air.
And around your back,
Pretty amazing for one little sack.
Gravity forces it down.
Like a lifeless feather.
Around the leg,
Stuck on your hat.
No matter the weather.
Jordan Stocks, Grade 9
Bonneville High School, ID

The Russian River
Combat fishing of the
        t
      s
     e
    h
   g
  i
h
kind
People as far as the eye can see,
This place is shut
d
  o
   w
    n
because of brown bear sometimes.
good luck
get there early
and you might get lucky
at the Russian River.
Dominic Monson, Grade 8
Culver Middle School, OR

Clock
Clock
Clock is ticking
Clock is ticking, quietly
Is ticking quietly, quickly
Ticking quietly, quickly, never ending
Ellen Fiori, Grade 8
Sedona Charter School, AZ

I Can't
I can't think of a poem that will rhyme
I feel like I am wasting my time
My teacher says that its easy
But poetry is making me queasy.
Patrick McBride, Grade 8
Recluse Elementary School, WY

Hunting
Hunt
fast, powerful
pulling, exciting, bugling
compound bow, elk, fly rod, lure
winding, spinning, turning
sharp, long
Fish
Brychan De Money Gross, Grade 8
East Middle School, MT

I Am
I am nice and curious
I wonder why school is so long
I hear splashing
I see shells on the beach
I want school to end
I am nice an curious

I pretend I can moon walk
I feel soft pillows
I touch the snow
I worry about my fish
I cry when I see an onion
I am nice and curious

I understand why there is night and day
I say friends can help you
I dream about riding rollercoasters
I try to help my parents
I hope for a snow day
I am nice and curious
Nick Schott, Grade 7
Dunstan Middle School, CO

Snow
Snow is like a bombshell.
When it hits, where does it go?
Snow touches your hand,
but when you look, no snow.
"Snow is harmless," people think,
but an avalanche would kill them
before they could blink.
If you want to avoid it now,
my friend found out how.
So be like Theodore,
and move to Ecuador.
Randy Satterthwaite, Grade 7
Sequoia Village School, AZ

Friends
She did not!!!
Why did you do it?
I didn't.
YES!!! You did.
What did I do? Honestly???
No one knows…No one cares…

Feeling alone. Day in day out.
Being lied to without a blink of an eye.
Covering your own back and no one else's.
Not thinking about who you step on as you go.
Why?

That's not nice.
It's not fair…it's never fair.
When will it be fair? Soon? Not soon?
When?

It's not all their fault. It's mine too.
I play into it; I go so far sometimes I could almost drown.
Luckily I always seem to find my way out.
Lying, cheating, accusing, smashing their way through,
Everyone for themselves. Everyone. EVERYONE!
Except one real friend, and you know who that is.

Anna Walling, Grade 8
Riley Creek Elementary School, OR

Shock of the World
A calm, peaceful morning
Everyone doing their usual thing
Then, family and friends call each other
Turning on the TV
As the world turns to a new light
They watch in shock and terror
As two tall towers crumble to the ground
Some families weeping
Some families yell
As the world awakens to a new darkness
Men and women giving their lives
To save their loved ones
Those people with ordinary lives and died
Those are the true heroes of 9/11

Ryan Ebert, Grade 8
Liberty Baptist Academy, NV

Football
The football spinning in the air.
The QB swinging his arm.
The kicker kicking his leg.
The runningback's getting tackled and hurt.
The receiver's running for the catcher.
The linebacker's yelling for help.
The coach screaming for corrections.

Austin Peterson, Grade 7
Eagle Point Middle School, OR

Trees
As I walked into the woods one day,
I thought I heard a tree say,
"Turn back."

I thought this quite strange indeed
That a tree could talk, "Maybe, too, can a seed!"
I wondered.

I searched for a seed, sadly alone,
And cried for a friend to help,
When then a sapling oak jumped at me
And grew eyes out of its trunk!

Crash! He moved his legs, or uprooted them rather,
From the ground.
So scared was I, that I fled without a sound.

Let this be
A lesson to thee,
To never talk to trees

Shelby Blackburn, Grade 8
Eagle Rock Jr High School, ID

Come Home to Me
I lost you once,
I was such a dunce.
Come home to me
I left you waiting in the park,
If only I could hear you bark.
Come home to me
I went to get some ice cream,
Me and you are such a good team.
Come home to me
I went on home and left you behind,
Sorry I wasn't more kind.
Come home to me
You are a homeless person wandering, waiting,
And now I'm blindly stating,
Please come home to me!

Cheyenne Trujillo, Grade 8
Round Valley Middle School, AZ

Nature's Orchestra
The coolness surrounds me
Giant trees guard the woods
Protecting nature's orchestra
A flute perches on a naked tree
She starts to play
Then some trumpets land on a big oak tree
To join in the symphony
I listen for a while
Then the spotlight begins to dim
I have to leave the woods for now
To go back to the hustle and bustle of my home.

Wesley Birch, Grade 9
Alliance Charter Academy, OR

Summer Days
The hot summer days are full of life.
Beautiful flowers bloom and grow
As they dance in the warm winds.
Children swim in the lakes.
Diving all the time
Bright and happy
Always glad
Summer
Days

Madeline Cordier, Grade 8
Beacon Country Day School, CO

Penguins
Penguins are awesome,
They can swim but cannot fly.
But, they eat fish, GROSS!!!

Jade Singleton-Reich, Grade 8
St Catherine of Siena School, CO

Basketball
The hard wood is a player's office.
Their job is to give it their all.
A team wins scoring baskets.
The action is intense
It takes commitment
Will and hard work.
Stakes are high
This sport
Job

John Michael McArthur, Grade 8
Beacon Country Day School, CO

Suffering
Hard to believe
So much hate

Ways they treated
Disturbing

Being punished for doing nothing
Innocent

Each passing day
Getting weaker
Color fading
Deprived of everything

Tomorrow
Eyes open
Last day
Still alive

Taken away
Never to see them again

Joseph Perez, Grade 8
Barcelona Elementary School, NM

Hope
Hope,
This is such a simple yet confusing thing,
Everyone thinks others have it, this mechanism to cope.

Who gets to decide the standards for this feeling?
It's just another drug to numb the pain,
Just another way to avoid confronting things that aren't appealing.

When do we stop living in ignorance?
When do we realize no one has a reason to live,
We can't continue living in negligence.

Just taking a stronger dose,
To avoid dealing with our responsibilities,
To avoid taking more degrading blows,

Blows of reality,
Each one is worse than the last,
We all act in such formality,

Maybe that's what's wrong,
We can't let down the barriers to show what's really hurting,
Can we start now, or have we been too closed for too long?

Kayla Garcia, Grade 8
Albuquerque Christian School, NM

That Boy
I lay down in my bed, the stars twinkling overhead.
My brown hair curly and soft,
Falls gently over my ocean blue eyes.
As I drift off to sleep,
The feature film of my dreams stretches before me.
I see a boy who loves to act, run, play soccer, and write.
I see a boy with the ability to change his shape.

First he is a vine, long leafy tendrils branch out wide,
To a selection of friends and acquaintances.
Then, he is a lion, free and in control, a feeling he loves.
In a second, he is an ant. Constantly surrounded by friends and family.
Next, he is a cell phone, a consequence of his incessant talking.

The boy is walking along a warm sandy beach,
The surf playing hide and seek between his toes.
He flips his brown hair out of his eyes,
A trait he picked up somewhere along the timeline of his life.

The sunlight streams through my open window.
the sweet smell of waffles swims tantalizingly through the air.
I think back on my dream,
A grin stretches across my sleepy face.
That boy was me.

Kyle Downs, Grade 8
Miller Middle School, CO

Life

Life is a taxi cab driver
Taking you wherever
You want to go
Keeping you along the right path

Telling you great places to visit along the way
Life is a lump of clay
Pieces taken pieces
Forgotten, and pieces
You'll never get back
Always starting out as
Nothing but a hopeless thought
And ending up as something that you will
Never forget
Life is a beach
Dirt can be cracked all around and you can be sunburned

But it's always worth waiting
For the breath taking
Sunset in the end
Life is a dream
Waiting to be fulfilled but
Yet so hard to grasp

Mikaila Chavez, Grade 7
21st Century Public Academy, NM

Love

Love is not just a saying nor is it a game.
The person you are with will always say the same.
Even if they are lying deep down inside.
When you hear the truth, you want to run away and hide.
So don't fall in love too quick.
Because all those lies and manipulation will make you sick!

Kayla Terrell, Grade 8
Place Middle School, CO

Imagination

Imagination is complicated
These are a couple of words that describe
It is in your mind you created
This is the one for the big juicy bribe

It is colorful, vivid, bright, happy
Also dull, colorless, dark, and mournful
It's also contagious and very sappy
It can also be sort of delightful

It can be evil or destructive
It is also very energetic
It can be very, very disruptive
It can also be very ill or sick

British nation and then Russian nation
Well, this is called your imagination

Jackson Douglass, Grade 8
Thomas Edison Charter School - North, UT

When I'm Ready

When I'm ready to grass dance,
I really move my feet
with the rhythm of the drum.

It takes me back to when I was a little grass dancer.
I had my bells and plumes flying in the air.
My red roach flying with my plumes.

My feet can control my dancing,
my dancing controls my mind.

Merval Phelan, Grade 8
Pretty Eagle Catholic School, MT

My Garden

A garden for all.
For those in need,
For those who just need a boost.
No matter who you are,
This garden is yours.
Bright, colorful, flavorful, rich.
Trees with oranges brighter than the sun,
Watermelons more pink than a baby's cheek.
Pineapples with juice sweeter
Than sugar after molasses,
Strawberries more red than blood.
Bright flowers coating the ground like
The icing on a cake.
Red, pink, yellow, orange, purple.
The rainbow at its best.
The place where you can come
Grab a little something to eat.
No charge.
Just come try it.
Eat, talk, relax.
This is my garden.

Sarah Hatch, Grade 9
North Layton Jr High School, UT

The Pain of Exhaustion

Exhaustion is too hard to overcome.
Your body is telling you to stop it,
But your mind says, "Come on, you lazy bum.
Go! Keep it going for a little bit."
The pain, it hurts, give it up, take a rest,
No, keep it going and work hard for once.
If you want it, earn it by doing your best.
I'm so tired, I have no endurance.
I need a break and I need some water,
No, I need to move, don't stop now, fight on.
I don't think I can be any hotter,
I need to stop, I've been running since dawn.
All I want is a drink that is frosted.
I don't know, but I know I'm exhausted.

John Sheehan, Grade 9
Clark High School, NV

My Life

I hate my life because of my school. All my friends make fun of me because I'm in a special needs class. Actually I have no friends. I don't know why I don't have any friends I only have one and he just likes to use me for my stuff. But I don't care because he is the only friend I got. No wonder no one likes me because I am in a needs class. That's why I hate my life because every time I raise my hand the teacher never picks me and when I shout out I get in trouble and there's like five people shouting out.

Cameron Valdez, Grade 7
Shadow Ridge Middle School, CO

My Great Dream

In my dreams I am a great inventor. Standing in a dark room I felt objects flying past me, the sound of jets, helicopters, submarines, boats, motorcycles and go-carts. I could not believe my ears. I am a great inventor. The dark room suddenly becomes my workshop, I invented things that made people happy, like vehicles that don't use gas and can run on air, boats that can sail across the sky. I am a great inventor. The room is getting brighter and my dream has come to an end. I am a great inventor.

Ronald W. Lee Walker Jr., Grade 7
Dunstan Middle School, CO

The Fight

Crying Yelling that's all you hear
All the things come out of fear
I hide under the desk nowhere to go
Wishing Dreaming that it would all be fine
Whipped Spanked Beaten that's what I hope does not happen to me
Hoping everything is fine in the other room
I take a peak Zoom there goes something my dad threw
Crying Yelling that's all you hear
Bing Bang Boom
That's what you heard in the other room
The walls tell me what is going on in the other room but I'm too scared to listen
My brother walks in looking scared like a beaten dog but he acts like he's strong and tough
But he's a puffy cloud in a fierce thunderstorm
He is like an angel that came to help me
All of the crying and yelling is coming to a close
The tears have left my eyes for the last time
I know the war is over there is no winner or loser
The sun has broken through the clouds the day is ending
I know my parents love me they know I love them
We are all back together and my parents love each other

Dylan Szalwinski, Grade 7
Sky Vista Middle School, CO

I Am...

I am from the fun little toys, the huge and heavy TV, and the wonderful pictures of my family members, the exciting footballs and the dangerous guns we hunt with.
I am from the crazy dogs in the yard, the tall creepy barns, the plain hay fields and the refreshing pool, my fast and sweet dirt bike.
I am from a huge mansion and the lazy cows, the restless horses and the grazing helpless deer, also the helpful and grateful people.
I am from my great great uncle Conway Twitty and my great strong loving grandpa Reed, my slender frail grandma Nonnie and my strong brave cousin Phillip, and also my cool cousin Ty.
I am from the saying "take your time but be quick about it" and "you aren't the parent," "are you 18?" and "if it ain't yours, don't touch it," "did you buy it?"
I am from the delicious turkey at Thanksgiving, wonderful biscuits and gravy, the soft, homemade banana bread, also the homemade ice cream at hunting camp my grandpa makes.
I am from wonderful Brightwood, and the busy streets of Sandy, also the fun loving Culver, and at last, the wonderful snowy Mt. Hood.

Ryan Kasch, Grade 8
Culver Middle School, OR

Swords

In many different shapes and sizes
In battle it quickly falls and rises
Sharper than a needle's point
Penetrating through a joint

Faster than a human can flee
Filling the sadistic with glee
Seeing foes drop onto their faces
Before getting two paces

Blades raining upon a head
Soon the enemy is dead
All of this brought about
By swords invented by some despicable lout

Yet survive forever they cannot
Soon battles with guns would be fought
Swords take place as relics of history
No longer wielded by an army

Brice Muniz, Grade 8
Academy Charter School, AK

Enchantment

My sad eyes glisten as the stars beam through,
I see in my heart a glimpse of sweet hope.
A song plays throughout, bringing thoughts of you;
I find refuge, and words I could not grope.
My mind is a safe place, where we exist
A sanctuary I will not lose twice;
I know life, and this one I can't resist.
Spare me your worries, keep your doubts concise.
All is all right now, please don't make a sound
This moment is more than we could have sought
It needs not to be perfect or profound
This enchantment is the best God has brought.
We've made it here, there's no need to be coy
I'll love you and save you, my sweet star-boy.

Beth Selshi, Grade 9
Clark High School, NV

Forgiven

She sits on the ground sad and alone
No one hears her cry; no one hears her moan
She fakes a smile as others exceed
Out of this misery she wants to be freed
Her thoughts reflect on the things she's done
The mistakes she's made are hard to shun
She has nothing left; no one to love
All she can hope for is a new life above
Surely her day will finally come
Sadness surrounds her; she is cold and numb
To her surprise forgiveness He gives
Finally she's content; with her redeemer she lives

Anna Werner, Grade 7
Sterling Middle School, CO

The Orphans of the World

Children all around the world suffer today
They have a voice and have something to say
They are the souls we always forget
People who need the most
The ones we have never met

They are just like you and me
They have a family
They always have a smile on their face
The ones who love the most
The people with a heart of grace

These souls are in Africa,
The Americas, Europe, and Asia
These children who suffer a horrible fate
People who've lost the most
Kids we must save before it's too late

John Gearhart, Grade 7
Timberview Middle School, CO

My Friends

Friends are there for love and support
They come when you need them
In just the nick of time
Just like when falling they'll be by your side

Friends give you someone to
Share all your secrets with
And laugh about all the funny things
And cry about all the sad

Friends guide you through the good times
With laughter and fun games
They carry you through the rough
With a shoulder to rest your head

Friends teach you when you're confused
And they know you do the same
Lord please bless all my friends
And guide us Your way

Alyssa Thompson, Grade 7
St Elizabeth Ann Seton Catholic School, AZ

Shadow

It's a spy,
As silent as a thief at night.
It's every person's personal stocker.
It sees and knows every thing you do.
It can grow and shrink in minutes.
It's a faceless shape staring at you every moment.
It mimics your every move.
Even in pitch black when you think you've escaped from it,
It will always show back up at the first sight of light.
It's your shadow.

Joshua Taft, Grade 7
Timberview Middle School, CO

Summer Nights
The sky is dark and full of stars,
There is no sound, no passing cars,
The warm breeze caresses my skin
I open my eyes and breathe it in.

I smell the sweet dew covered grass.
Shooting stars twinkle as they pass
Swaying beside a deep black creek.
My hair lays across my cold cheek.

Supported by nothing but strings,
I think of joy and happy things,
My mind is clear, my body is calm,
I fall asleep hand to palm.
Rachael Versey, Grade 9
Shelley Sr High School, ID

Relatives
Showing up at holidays,
Someone's birthday,
Or the occasional Thursday
You love them, you hate them,

Driving, flying, running in
Only one relative will win
The others act like it's a sin
You love them, you hate them,

Crazed
Amazed
Lazed
You love them, you hate them,

Tornados of hugs and kisses
Each other throwing disses
After threats and hisses
You love them, you hate them.
Austin Ivey, Grade 7
Sky Vista Middle School, CO

On the Shore
He finds himself staring at
the calm, glassy lake.

Picking up a smooth rock, he
lets it go, thinking of
how he let his wife's hand go.

He watches it hit one,
two, three ripples formed,
getting wider and wider.

He sits down on a cold shore,
watching the ripples grow.
DJ Ferran, Grade 8
Mount Jordan Middle School, UT

Yesterday
Swirling angry clouds, dark like the ocean's abyss
Suffocates my heart
Yesterday for you I yearned.
Breathing doesn't come easy, as I think of us from the start.
The smiles ripped away
Our laughter mocks me like a broken record.
A gap is left where you once stood.
Yesterday for you I yearned
My heart writhing and squirming from your lost presence
Your addictive smoke fills up my lungs,
Fating me a slow, painful death
Our happiness reminiscing each day the love of Orpheus and Eurydice
My love, you are with me like an unforgiving splinter
Is there no way to get you out of my heart?
Yesterday for you I yearned.
Kaxee Her, Grade 7
Mandalay Middle School, CO

K-9 Loyalty
They guide us through life and wilderness,
White as snow, through black as night,
When we sleep their ears are up,
When a masked man comes, they bark and growl, get out of the house,
They live to play, please, and protect,
They have been with people for thousands of years,
Whether it's rescuing someone from a fire,
Tracking down criminals, or just helping a seven year old with a meltdown,
They are always by our side.
Danni Henson, Grade 7
Sky Vista Middle School, CO

A Walk in December
Snowing lightly, the sky grows cold.
"Stay inside!" we are always told.
But unlike most, I choose this day to take a walk in the frozen solitude.
The wind blows quickly, yet softly, trying not to be rude.
My face feels the damp, icy air clinging to my skin.
Some get sad in weather like this, but I wear a grin.
The Blue Spruce along the path are covered in shimmering white.
Oh, the scenery of this snowy land is a beautiful sight!

Chills are pulsing up and down my back;
The cold tiny hailstones falling upon me are sharp as tacks.
The moon is out shining ever so brightly.
A snow covered bench I find, I sit upon, only to rest slightly.
Each breath I take nips at my lungs.
The stars come out and night has begun.

I slowly stand and take a look around.
I turn and walk home; my footsteps in the snow never make a sound.
Retracing my steps, I hear the chittering of the animals of night.
They scamper here and there, playing with each other in delight.
For the rest of my life I will clearly remember,
When today I chose to take a walk in December.
Emily Adams, Grade 9
Bonneville High School, ID

Food

Food of variety is absolutely good,
I would eat all the food if I could.
Foods of all kinds are positively yummy,
I love how all food satisfies my tummy.
Food is delicious wheats, meats and more,
But it's the desserts that I adore.
Food is tasty, favorable and good,
I would eat all the food if I could.

Samantha Puente, Grade 9
Lakewood High School, CO

Sunflower Brown

The brown of a sunflower worn and old
walked with me 'til the last trice.
Sunflower brown thrown all around my waist,
lending me strength, strength needed for prospect,
strength used to shoulder royal heritage.
Sunflower brown held out a hand until
tossed away to a close family member.
Sunflower brown lives out life constantly
holding out her hand and lending out her strength
Now when I see a sunflower tears come
to my eyes and memories flood my heart.
Sunflower brown stays after having been
blown in the wind many a long hour.
Sunflower brown you hold me in your debt.

Makelle Jenkins, Grade 9
Mountain Ridge Jr High School, UT

Halo

As I sit in my seat
I watch the other players reach defeat
It's a great big fat comfy chair
I see my opponent just right there

Just right there I am blasted off my feet
For a second I thought I would be the one to reach defeat
As my brother came in my room
He tried to hit me with a broom

I told him get out! Get out! Get out of my room
Then took 1 more swing with the broom
As he finally went on his way
I knew I should have taken that broom away

Although I was about to complain
I just looked at the TV with lots of shame
The score was 49 to 50
I thought this guy was quite swiftly

After all was said and done
He was laughing and I was shunned
As I sat there in my seat
After all I was the one to reach defeat

Isaiha Martinez, Grade 7
Shadow Ridge Middle School, CO

His Protest

When looking upon that old bench,
I remember — that one day.
It was frozen, cold and a macabre display
Of what to come —
Death, that day.

For October it was frigid, weathered
Autumn's first snow
Frail crisp under his leathered shoes.
His weapon sealed
Beneath his coat noir.
He neared the bench kneeled.

With his weapon he struck
That old bench.
And stayed so stuck,
Against his rival.
That tower from which he now stood
Watched the foe's survival.

Christopher Regnier, Grade 9
Lakewood High School, CO

A Detail Unnoticed

The darkness crept in the night
as the lightning struck with fright.
The moon rose high
like a diamond in the starlit sky.
A piece of velvet, a shining moon
the piercing cry of the loon.

The silence wore down by morning's light
the lilies opaque, crescendoing in height.
As the moon leaves the sky
it bids the world its goodbye.
Pay notice the sunlight, the time is at hand
and the orchestra starts of the morning band.

Bailley Ferguson, Grade 8
Sacajawea Jr High School, ID

Missing You

The years have passed,
Oh how they fly!
We are both so different now
You and I.

I remember you then,
Merely a boy of 6
And how we used to fight and play with sticks

You are a lasting memory
Stuck to me like dog doo,
Always there haunting me,
Because I miss you.

Lacy Henry, Grade 7
Colorado Connections Academy, CO

chores
i hate taking out the trash
it smells really bad
i would rather just crash
then i would be glad

i hate being
where i have to be cleaning
what i have bean eating

i pull the weeds
at a very slow speed
i mown the lawn
from dusk to dawn

i hate cleaning my room
while i'm using a broom
my closet's a mess
like one of my sisters ugly dress

this is what i do
but i really don't want to
Jose Cueto, Grade 7
Artesia Zia Intermediate School, NM

Death
Death,
The dark abysmal end to life,
Death,
Leaving nothing unseen
Death,
Separating soul from body,
Death,
Staining a mark on loved ones,
Death,
The chance for new opportunities,
Death,
Seeing your effect in life,
Death,
Meeting your predecessors,
Death,
Eternal freedom,
Death,
The inevitable end.
Perry Knowles, Grade 7
Henkle Middle School, WA

Books
There are many books around
Just choose one and abound
From literature to biographies
Then history and geography
There are spelling books
And books with "hooks"
Dive into the land of books.
Ben Petrie, Grade 8
Aurora Academy, CO

The White Sun
Sparkling like stars,
a burning intensity
brightens the sky.
With a whitening glow,
it shines
when the angels take flight
in the world.
This burning light
blinds the stars
with intense light.
Its brightness
shocks the human eye.
Kurtis Wooten, Grade 7
Cedar Ridge Middle School, OR

The Way I Feel About You
I love you.
This feeling is very true.
When you're gone
I can't wait till the crack of dawn.
Just to see your smiles,
I would walk a million miles.
But when I see you
It's like my life is brand new.
You're the star I see at night,
Even after we fight.
When I say I hate you,
I really mean I love you.
When I see you sad,
I feel really bad.
I know you need a big hug.
And you're going to get a big hug.
All I want you to know.
Is that I'll never say no.
Because I LOVE YOU!!
Ashley Bradford, Grade 9
Duchesne High School, UT

Realist
I am a realist
Even when life throws
You a twist
You've got to come back up and
Not be a pessimist
Life is like an ice cream cone always
Sweet and not postponed
Even when life is held on a
Tiny thread
You have to look at life and
Come ahead
Life is like a giant see saw
Even though life has a flaw
You just lift up your spirit and
Just yell hoorah
Gabby Garcia, Grade 7
21st Century Public Academy, NM

The Moon
Trying hard to sleep,
The moon closes his big eyes,
Giving rest to all.
Sydney Cooper, Grade 7
Mandalay Middle School, CO

Forest
The ground slopes up
Into mountainous terrain
And into towering buildings
Of emerald leaves
Each tree is a hotel
No vacancy though
For every tree is filled
With chattering guests
Of birds and squirrels
Davion Irons, Grade 8
Wiley Jr/Sr High School, CO

Monsters
Monsters
They creep in the shadows
They hide from the light
You can feel their eyes on you
Watching your every move
There is no use hiding
I promise they will find you
Monsters
Alexandra Nevarez, Grade 8
Zia Middle School, NM

The Apple
When seen it's
bruised
freckled
aged
leathery
smooth
shiny

When felt it
snaps
drips
crunches
squishes

When tasted it's
sugary
sour
sticky
refreshing
quenching
Tree of Knowledge
Adam and Eve
Brittany Mints, Grade 9
Xavier College Preparatory School, AZ

Dolphins

Some dolphins are blue,
Some dolphins are gray,
Although dolphins can't chew,
They do catch their pray.
A dolphin is kind,
And very unique;
He can always find
Whatever you seek.
So ask your dear friend
For a little surprise,
He'll be true to the end
He will tell you no lies,
But he'll bring you the best of the best he came find,
Because he is a friend that won't leave you behind.

Nadia Fedchun, Grade 8
Valley Christian Secondary School, WA

Heartbroken

I lost a guy,
And I don't know why,
What went wrong?
I'll love him for so long!
I thought we'd be happy,
Loving you seemed so right,
You broke my heart,
I felt all the pain,
And all the tears…
They never went down the drain,
You put me through troubles it hurt oh so much!
I just wish I can go back to your soft gentle touch!

Samantha Bañuelos, Grade 7
Somerton Middle School, AZ

My Angel

To dropping rose petals
On the big black box,
I stare intently
As a friend strokes her locks.

Standing there completely still
And overwhelmed with feeling numb,
The people pass by my hip
A congregation starts to hum.

Waters fill and pour from my eye
The line no longer stirs.
A speaker starts to whisper
And soon my vision blurs.

My memory begins to fade
Her loving smile I cannot find.
As the big black box begins to close
I look at my mother's angel face for the very last time.

Emily Smith, Grade 9
Stapley Jr High School, AZ

Whisper of the Wind

I hear the wind howl as it shakes the trees
Forgetting its place as a slight breeze
It screams as it rakes at her leaves
It whirls and twirls until a tangled web it weaves
What is it that makes the wind so mad?
As she shakes her head, her song so sad
She drives little children to their nest
Snuggling warm near their mother's breast
But not I.
I hear the whisper of the wind
By tearing the trees she has not sinned
Through the forest she dances
Blowing rain kisses, she prances
The rain laughs gaily as it splatters the ground
The drops so cool, large and round
And yet the wind whispers, "hush, hush, hush,"
Her lullaby to the world, laying in sleep, is lush.

Abigail Joy Borneman, Grade 9
King's Jr/Sr High School, WA

Wal-Mart: No Love for Sale

Love is something good.
It gets you in a good mood.
You can love a girl, a pet, or a plant,
but love is something special.

Sooner or later, you'll experience it.
It will be something you'll never forget.
Love comes from inside your heart.
It's not something you can buy at Wal-Mart

Deybin Rodriguez, Grade 7
Phoenix Preparatory Academy, AZ

Be Smart

It was for a boundary that I faced
with a huge vicious kid in face.
With a big force of power
with the palms of this man, all I saw was carpet.
Mrs. Mariscal was out in the hall,
and with my smartness, I was a flower waiting to bloom.
When my teacher came back to the room,
the bell rang, with some of the kids laughing
some helping, I still felt bad.
After school I went to the dean,
I told one teacher and he did not do one simple thing.
I thought to myself, "Nobody is helping me.
I'm going to fight him that will do something."
The next day all I did was pray saying
God give me the strength to beat this kid.
When I got to school I said no this isn't right,
then right before my eyes I saw a fight.
It was the guy I wanted to fight beating this kid.
I walked away and then he went to the dean and got expelled.
And I said I'm smart.

Donovan Dykes, Grade 7
Molasky Jr High School, NV

Love

Love is so powerful;
it can tear us apart
but yet it is wonderful,
we can get shot with cupid's dart.
But love is a trap
that we can't get out of,
until we finally snap,
and God gives us a map
that we must follow
until our heart is so full
that it won't ever be hollow.

Ashley Dunn, Grade 8
Canfield Middle School, ID

The Marathon of Life

Life is like a marathon,
always racing,
sometimes leading,
other times falling behind,
sometimes having trouble,
other times enjoying the moment,
sometimes looking behind to the past,
other times looking into the future,
not knowing what will happen next,
but no matter what,
always heading toward the finish.

Cody Thomas, Grade 7
North Middle School, CO

Colorful Rain

The rain beats like a heavy drum,
Plop, plop, plop, plop,
As it hits the boats waving sails,
It rains on and on,
And when the rain finally lightens,
The sun comes out,
And the knots in the clouds unfold,
Colors of the sky emerges,
Shining brightly,
In the form of a rainbow

Brooke Yordy, Grade 7
Les Bois Jr High School, ID

Kiss a Frog?

Is a frog really a prince
in green disguise?
Heck, I don't know,
but I thought I'd kiss one
and find out.

Better judgment prevailed
and I changed my course.
"Hey, girl," I thought,
"are you out of your mind?"

Demi Garcia, Grade 7
Phoenix Preparatory Academy, AZ

The New Fallen Snow of Today

The snow started to fall
The blanket of snow covered the ground
Four-wheelers defiled the clean, white, perfect snow
Business workers delineated the demographics of the town,
Looked outside, worried their car might get icy
Kids outside were indicting each other about who threw the snowball
Some kids were abdicating their snow forts
Inside people were watching the pandemic spreading throughout Northern Asia
Some watched politicians denounce and contradict other politicians
Some of the viewers said the democracy that is the U.S.A. is falling apart
But in the minds of the children the only thing that mattered was
The new fallen snow of today

Ryan Boucher, Grade 7
Lyons Middle/Senior High School, CO

Still That Flag

Bright and worn, bullet torn, still that flag stands through the war.
War and fear, still are near, still that flag stands through the war.
Bombs resounding, flames bright howling, still that flag stands through the war.
Victory nearing, dignity bearing, still that flag stands through the war.
Dawn is here, do not fear, still that flag stands through the war.
Sun's bright ray, through the grey, still that flag stands through the war.
Hope's bright light in soldier's eyes, still that flag stands through the war.
Now our freedoms we enjoy, 'cause still that flag stands through the war.
Remember it always, honor the day, still that flag stands through the war.
Don't forget its legacy; or we shall be but history, still that flag stands through the war.
We shall stand, strong and proud, still that flag stands through the war.

Heather Merrill, Grade 9
Timberline Middle School, UT

The Truth About Childhood

Childhood is a time filled with false hopes and broken dreams,
when people find that nothing's quite as simple as it seems.
The inexperienced child will always try for the extremes,
and standing out makes one the butt of other people's schemes.
They try because society says that all of mankind
will help them on the way to anything they wish to find.
Consider this: a young child walking home from school one day
discovers a one-hundred dollar bill along the way.
He turns for home, but meets a man wearing a long black coat
who says, "I'll give you an ice cream if you hand me that note."
Of course, the child agrees; he trades the cash for frozen treat
and brags of the nice man to anyone that he may meet.
Blind to the fact he's being greatly underpaid,
he's slaked by the dreadful, yet short term satisfactory, trade.
And worse off still is the poor child whose sheltering parent deems
that it is right to teach kids life is full of that which gleams.
Such children have no clue that all the road of life is lined
with dangers, lurking all around and creeping up behind.
Imagine what a shock awaits for such a child who finds
that not all people on the earth are caring, loving, kind.

Gabriel Martin, Grade 9
Tempe Preparatory Academy, AZ

My Love

My girl so young so beautiful, a perfect 10
I wish that I could talk to her again and again
She makes my heart skip a beat
When I go to school I'm in for a treat
Every time she looks at me
She always seems to set me free
One day I'm going to ask her out
And she's going to say yes without a doubt

Taylor Dao, Grade 7
Dunstan Middle School, CO

Boom!

It was a beautiful morning
I say bye to my parents as I leave for school
I catch up with my friend
I say "hey"
As we go to cross the street
I was the first to cross
I do not see the car, and Boom!
I get hit with such force I fall to the ground
My friends run to help me, but there is nothing they can do
As I seem to be awakening, I see angels all around me
It is such a beautiful sight
I realize that I am dead
I start to cry
An angel flies to me and says "it is not your time"
I wake up, to see my mom holding me
I hear her say "my baby, my baby you are alive"
I get carried away by a stretcher
As I remembered that it was the angels who helped me
I tell them "thank you, you have given me another chance"

Angela Gallegos, Grade 7
Pagosa Springs Jr High School, CO

I…

I am smart and prepared
I wonder what walruses do
I hear the cries of the past
I see the rims of my glasses
I want life
I am smart and prepared

I fear death
I feel that I will do something important in this life
I worry for my friends' sanity
I cry because of the death of others
I am smart and prepared

I understand why I'm here
I say live to the fullest
I dream of a bright future
I try to escape fate's stranglehold on me
I hope I can forget the past
I am smart and prepared.

Jairo Gonzalez, Grade 7
Sunset Ridge Elementary School, AZ

Performance

My heart is beating; my mind is racing,
With all these thoughts of reverie.
Though I'm anxious and nervous too,
I think I'll do all right; I hope I do.

When all at once, in that moment, I step out on the stage.
My heart begins to soar!
I imbue myself and everyone else,
With the soft, sweet music I play.

I never once thought I could beat the nervousness inside me.
Then finally, flushed with excitement,
And hearing the roaring crowd beneath me,
I leave the stage with no grief at all;
But the good feeling of accomplishment in that concert hall.

Kailey Bird, Grade 9
Bonneville High School, ID

Writer's Block

It is simple to see I have writer's block
for this poem is as plain as chalk.
I have nothing to add to this chain of simple words
because the letters fly away like a flock of birds.
So I write the rest of this poem in invisible ink
but instead it comes out a silvery pink.
And here I am staring at my cat
who seems amazingly fat.
And again my words have come to an end
so I say goodbye and try not to offend.

Kayla Worthington, Grade 7
Colorado Connections Academy, CO

The Journey

Shocked, tired, and drenched in sweat,
I wake up fearing regret,
knowing what I have to do
will help me start my life anew.
All those years of planning
All those months of doubt
All those days of constant raining
waiting for an easy out.

Knowing it will never come
forgetting all those days of fun.
Soon I know the sun will rise
as I sit here on my cozy bed.
Tomorrow holds me no surprise,
my thoughts have gone from hate to dread.

My journey there will start today,
out on the dock, overlooking the bay.
Everything from my past life gone —
as I sail away to prove them wrong.

Vianka Rodriguez, Grade 9
Arizona Agribusiness & Equine Center, AZ

If I Could Show You Something, Teacher*
If I could show you something
I'd show you how you've done so much more, than you ever thought possible
If I could show you something
I'd show how big your seeds have grown
How those little kids you used to teach now have a life of their own
If I could show you something
I'd show you all the young minds that have expanded so far
If I could show you something
I'd show you how you warmed their hearts, and now they're warming others
I'd show you how big of a role model you've been, I'd show you
How many of us kids want to be just, like you
If I could show you something
I'd show you the positive indention you've left my heart
I'd show you how much of an effect you've made on me, and my life
If I could show you something
I'd show you how much you need to know that you're the greatest value in the world, to me
I'd show you how much I truly appreciate you, and love you
If I could show you something, teacher
I'd show you how you've done so much more
Than you ever thought was possible, for me.

Shantel Kilkenny, Grade 9
Capital High School, NM
*Dedicated to Mrs. Segura you're my hero

The Elephant That Goes to the Circus
A n elephant was going to the circus, **b** ut he was a little nervous since it was his first time.
C ircuses were very scary to this elephant. **D** inner was just served to him, which made his stomach uneasy.
E verybody clapped as he walked by and made him blush, **f** or this elephant was a little shy.
G reen tents, circus people, **h** elicopters riding by.
I t was all a little intimidating. **J** oking, laughing, it was all so scary.
K eeping the circus animals in cages. **L** ions, tigers, bears, flamingos,
M onkeys, gorillas, camels. **N** o one should be treated like that.
O n and on he walked to the show, **p** eople were lining up ready to go.
Q uack, quack the ducks said, **r** oar, roar the lions screamed and the elephant
S huddered at the sound of that. **T** hey finally got to the show.
U nder the tent, **v** ertical banners hung on the ceiling.
W ater is what he drank before the show. **X** ylophones started as he walked to the ring.
"**Y** ahoo" is what the crowd screamed. **Z** ap, zap, zap is how the show started.

Alexa White, Grade 7
Ernest Becker Middle School, NV

The Fields
As I opened the door, I couldn't believe my eyes. The wonderful scenery felt like I was ready to fly. The beautiful nature springs spread throughout the land, it looked liked the ground was held by God's hand. The lands and the fields made me feel safe, as I walked through the trail counting the steps of my pace. As I sat under the high mellow tree, I looked up and a great mountain I see. The great white winter seasons, and a bright light shines on it for a reason. That the world is so great, and I will say, this day is truly a Fate.

Cecilia Youkhana, Grade 7
Chandler Preparatory Academy, AZ

A Picture
A silent brush of air rattles the plains in a soft wave. The sun sets a golden haze across the earth. Birds chirp the last of the morning songs, the crickets lull the creatures to a sleepy trance. As the night's creatures creep into a glowing day, as the age of night goes by, the sounds blurt out and eyes stare at the candlelit moon.

Annie Jensen, Grade 7
Diamond Fork Jr High School, UT

The Shadow

The shadow casts across the sky,
Butterflies swarm through air,
The rainbow stretches far and wide,
Searching the world with pride,
And me I don't know where.

The geese swim to and fro
My cousin with blonde hair,
She walks with cold wet feet that are bare,
She reaches up and touches the sky,
And me I don't know where.

Victoria Curtis, Grade 7
Mandalay Middle School, CO

True Friend

We sign our cards and letters "B.F.F."
You have millions of ways to make me laugh.
You're always there for me when I take a fall,
When I feel depressed, I give you a call.
It's so good, to have you around.
You're a true friend,
You're here 'till the end.
You pull me aside when something ain't right,
Cover me now and into the night.
No need to pretend
I love you dear friend.
You're a true friend

Andri Kleinman, Grade 8
Sequoia Village School, AZ

My Fantasy Love

Remember the times we had together
Remember them as I do
Remember the sights we saw together
Remember them through and through

Let the good times roll as an old projector plays
Let the memories set in place
Let the motion of the swing set as it sways
Let me never forget your face

You were the world to me
You were so attractive
You were my everything
Your heart was always active

In your spare time you pondered of me
In my spare time I was dreaming of you
I craved for the time you'd come set me free
I always knew you loved me too

The only regret to this poem is this
I will never see your face you don't even exist

Derek Wilson, Grade 9
Shelley Sr High School, ID

Hope

Hope is a candle
that leads our way through the darkness,
if only for a little while.
Hope is the wings of an angel
soaring high into the sky,
but held down by the gravity of reality.
Hope is the crazy little voice inside our heads
that tells us we can overcome anything,
no matter what the odds.
Hope is blind optimism.

Maggie Graham, Grade 7
Les Bois Jr High School, ID

The Silent Shadow

You came to me in the middle of the night
A silent whisper blew out my candle light
A single touch, a gentle voice
Curled up beside me in awed rejoice
He said to me "my child you've grown,
Now see the ones who are lost and alone.
They seem ok, all perfect outside,
But deep inside their pleading cry
Screams out to those who've got it all,
The love from my everlasting call.
Now would you go one more day?
If you knew my love was here to stay
And fill your heart with surpassing joy?
For a new day awaits you choice.
Get up and go to spread the word
Of the gleaming shadow that circles our world."
And with a swish of his hand
My candle lit up
And he left me in a silent hush.
I watched as my dreams and fears became true,
The revolution will start with me and with you.

Caitlyn Berry, Grade 9
Soroco High School, CO

My Man

He wasn't only a man
He was my man.
He was my knight in shining armor
When I called he came running
When I said I need space he left,
I would cry and his shoulder was always there
to catch my tears
I would laugh and his eyes would gleam with joy
When he smiled, oh when he smiled,
Everything wrong just disappeared
His opinion was the only one that mattered
So why didn't he listen?
Nobody's heart should be broken this bad
He wasn't only a man,
He was my man.

Madisson Goody, Grade 7
Sagewood Middle School, CO

Poem

Amazing.
Flexible and fantastical.
A dog playing with a ball.
A man at work inside a hall.
Love is like a rose.
A little kid with a garden hose.
Something original.
Something unique.
Something you think of when you sleep.
Don't let it go.
Be like Edgar Allen Poe.
Write a poem.

Jamie Cannon, Grade 8
Kenmore Jr High School, WA

Spread Silver Wings We Soar

Opening of the page
A new sensation takes hold,
One once remembered
When life seemed so bold;

Out here in this thinking,
Where dreams seem to lie
Beaches formed of sands color,
As again the door swings wide;

On the voyage goes
As an ocean carried sigh,
Unlocking of secrets pertaining
The whisper in the ride;

Onto another's daring
We dare to explore,
Seen by currents action
Spreading silver wings we soar.

Miranda Correa, Grade 8
Villa Montessori School – Phoenix, AZ

An Ode to My Teddy Bear

You cuddle with me
Close at night
You keep the
Boogeymonster
Under my bed
Your soft brown
Fur
Warms my
Heart
You are my
Guardian Teddy bear
Though your name is
Simple and plain
You're always my friend
Teddy bear

Shelby Rushing, Grade 7
Cedar Ridge Middle School, OR

Me

My brain is as slow as a turtle,
My body is as old as a myrtle,
My eyes are as huge as a whale,
While my hair is as black as the night,
My skin is as sweet as a brownie,
My mouth my teeth and my smile are like a clown they don't go together,
My personality is like a monkey but less relaxed.
And my face is as soft and delicate as silk.
That's me!!!

Luis Yanez, Grade 8
Round Valley Middle School, AZ

I Don't Want To

I don't want to spend my life waiting for him,
waiting for my chance for him to be mine again.
Friends constantly telling me I'm obviously missing my baby
and I guess it is pointless to spend every day wishing for him.
He, in my eyes, was a man, not a boy.
Calling me "beautiful" when I didn't look it,
kisses when I didn't deserve them, hugs when he saw I needed them.
The last thing on his mind was ever disappointing me.
Pointless to see all of that could disappear as fast as it came,
hopeless to fight, and hopeless to cry.
Nothing I can ever do can change the fact that "I loved him"
no one, nothing, no person, no feelings can bring him back,
no matter how much I want to be with him.
It was a hopeless fact and let's face it,
"He was all I ever wanted, all I ever needed, everything I dreamed.
He was all the things in the world, and he was and still is everything to me."

Kendra Ojeda, Grade 8
Torrington Middle School, WY

Sanctuary Fair

I sat peacefully, passively under yonder tree
With the sun-bit morn and the dewy grass, and the sharp wind to greet me,
My one place to hide from all hurt and pain,
My one, my only one true sanctuary fair.
The birds were singing as though possessed, their beautiful music rent the sky
And the squirrels were dancing, chattering, living free,
Free of fear, for fear they knew not, and nor did I.
Never could I guess my one, my only one true sanctuary fair could fall.
But deluded was I, for fall it did, and withered and died.
Charred by flames, biting flames, destroying flames
Destroying my one, my only one true sanctuary fair.
Devastated was I, no will to move nor will to not.
Then I looked to the heavens to ask why, but no help came, so I wept and cried.
I told myself, to calm, to ease, anything to escape that horrible pain,
That it was God's fault because He had sent my sanctuary far beyond,
Exposing me to all the world's want and strife.
But again, deluded was I, for as I fell in bitter tears
And pressed my hand in the dying land once fair,
To my amazement, a seed was there in the palm of my hand
To grow my sanctuary again from the land.
My one, my only one true sanctuary fair.

Harlan Brichacek, Grade 7
Eugene Waldorf School, OR

Victoria

V ery lovable me
I n case you didn't hear
C ats are my favorite animals
T etherball is me
O r maybe,
R oller coasters make me scream
I n case you didn't notice
A wesome grades are totally me.

Victoria Acevedo, Grade 7
Emerson Edison Jr Charter Academy, CO

Puzzle Piece

Hidden behind the living room couch,
Or down the cushion's side,
I am the missing puzzle piece,
For the puzzle you failed, but tried.

Worn down to brown over the years,
It seems like no one cares,
Except for that little puzzle girl
Who runs around searching in tears.

Whenever my puzzle is taken out
I pray I will be found,
But seeking and searching comes and goes,
And still I lie on the ground.

As dust gathers on my skin,
I realize as I cry,
I'll remain the missing puzzle piece
For the puzzle you failed, but tried.

Augusta Milford, Grade 7
West Valley Middle School, WA

Love Has Wings

If you ask me about love,
My reply will be:
Love is as common as the waves in the sea,
As they come back and touch us again.

Love sings,
Love has wings,
It flies around,
Never dropping low enough to touch the ground.

Love is within us,
If you can see us,
Love travels among us,
Even through me.

Love lives life,
Living long enough,
For the Lord to linger in our love,
As the love lives long in our hearts.

Emily Schroeder, Grade 7
Leading Edge Academy - Gilbert, AZ

Southern-Comfort

The South is what I like,
From the Florida Swamps
to the Louisiana Bayous.
Everywhere you go there's something new.
Stop in for a crawfish pie,
Or some down home Bar-B-Q,
No matter where you go,
Try the Gumbo it's so good,
Then again have some shrimp Etouffee.
So come to the south
And try some of our treats,
And they'll be sure to take care of ya'll!

Justin Swearingen, Grade 9
Bonneville High School, ID

Pain

when someone you love with all your heart leaves you
it's like they are leaving you in the dirt to die
to suffer in your worst pain possible
you're left there in the cold night
all alone and there's no one there to help you
through all your pain and suffering
you'll once find someone that can help you
knowing you're not going to try loving someone
you have to trust your heart that this one
won't let you fall to the ground
trust everything that you have
you can believe in them with your whole heart

Danielle Bennett, Grade 7
Kingman Academy of Learning, AZ

Far Out to Sea

Far out to sea,
An island awaits,
For two worlds to sit upon it
Only the ocean knows,
About this luxurious island
For the ocean tide pulls,
The other world in,
To join them in island paradise
Soft, white sand and sea shells
Fill the ocean depths
Of a foamy, green sea
A palm of a hand,
Strokes the ocean floor,
Causing ripples of waves,
To crash on the moist, seashore
Dolphins jump and sea birds fly,
While, the sun slowly sets on the mountain
A slight wind blows through the air,
While the salt of the sea fills your senses
Peace and happiness fills the world
Far out to sea.

Brianna Ragels, Grade 7
St Elizabeth Ann Seton Catholic School, AZ

Sky
I look at the sky and it is blue.
I look at the grass and it has dew.
The sky gives me a very good view.
The clouds can be many or be few.
The rainbow has a very bright hue.
Each day I look up the sky looks new.
When I look up, I think about you.
Jacob Smith, Grade 7
Timberview Middle School, CO

Love
My loneliness is an eagle
All I need is a ladybug to love
Can he help me?
He can give me a hug
I'll blossom up on a tree
But will it last?
My confusion is a bat

But he
Gives me that kiss
Butterflies will flutter again
Or could it be hate with thorns
On the side of the rose?
Why?
When I see the smile of happiness
On his face is a flower

But if…
He walks with another girl the jealousy
Acts as a dragonfly
But my sadness
Is still a
Droopy flower
Heather McWain, Grade 7
Sky Vista Middle School, CO

Never Forget You
I miss my friend,
Always there through thick and thin.
I can't keep you out of my mind,
Trying to forget you is a sin.
You were a hard worker,
A great honest man.
You fought all your battles,
Problems came but you never ran.
I miss the days spent with you,
You're my best friend.
I'll love you forever and ever,
You're in my heart until the end.
I'll miss you more and more,
My days keep turning blue.
Sitting here thinking about how,
I will never forget you.
Katelyn Duggan, Grade 8
Pawnee Jr/Sr High School, CO

Un-cliché
I don't have a trick up my sleeve.
I'll hide it
in the trick itself.
That way they'll never find it.
They might look
near the banana across from the marker
and behind the cantaloupe.
My trick is
if you want to divide by a fraction
flip the second fraction and multiply
or
i before e except after c.
Without education
the trick may never be found.
Mason Holloway, Grade 7
Sonoran Science Academy, AZ

I Want My Windows
I don't like this place.
There is no sun.
I can't get my work done!
This room is so depressing…
It's caressing my thoughts
With dull images.
Yuck!
I can't think here.
When is it over?
I Want to go home.
And get away from this dark cover.
I want my windows…
Summer Pruett, Grade 7
Artesia Zia Intermediate School, NM

My Brother
He wakes me up every morning
Ready to leave for school
He runs downstairs and ties his shoes
While I lay in bed and drool

Playing soccer, baseball, and football
While swimming and surfing in the sun
His everyday motto suits him well
He says "Let's all have fun!"

He never complains he's tired,
He has a strong self-esteem
He brightens the day with his smile
And never says anything mean

I'll never be quite like him
Though I'll always aspire to be
He has a bright happiness within
And he will always inspire me!
Jenny Pattison, Grade 9
Mueller Park Jr High School, UT

Stranded on the Sea
Some days life is dull upon the sea
And some days are more horrific.
Miles and miles of open sea
Feeling much deserted
Yet, one's hope is there
Waiting, longing
Strength fading
Stranded
Live!
Tristan Seawalt, Grade 7
Beacon Country Day School, CO

Nature
Oh, the birds and the bees,
And the wind in the trees.
Do you ever hear nature?

Oh, the fish, swimming in the creek,
And butterflies, nectar they seek.
Do you ever see nature?

Oh, the pollen and the mountain tea,
Not to mention the rosemary.
Do you ever smell nature?

Oh, the grass around my feet,
And the coolness of the stream.
Do you ever feel nature?

Oh, the apples and the pears,
And other fruits up in the air.
Do you ever taste nature?

I know I do,
But how about you?
Kristen Rhodes, Grade 8
Eugene Christian School, OR

People
People who love discipline,
love knowledge.
People who look for good,
find good.

Cheerful people,
make joyful faces.
Gloomy people
make darkening sounds.

People throughout the world
are different.
Not even one
the same!
Angelina Gorkovchenko, Grade 9
Colorado Connections Academy, CO

School Time

It's time it's time
School has started!
I love it sometimes it's fun
You learn and learn so C
            O
              M
                E on and
Work! Work! Work!

Amy Lopez, Grade 8
Culver Middle School, OR

Soldier

They protect us from war
They give their lives for us
They are ready to die at any time
Fighting for our freedom
Sometimes we take it for granted
Much blood is shed
Many tears are dreaded
For many don't come back home
Their families will miss them
Their loved ones just wish to see them again
Their hearts will hurt
But knowing that they are there for a cause will help
Being a soldier is rough
You have to have tough skin
A brave heart
Or you will be torn apart
For that is the life of a soldier

Alexa Higbee, Grade 7
Albuquerque Christian School, NM

Sitting Home Alone

Sitting home alone
all alone
no one to hold
sitting home alone
no one knows how it feels
what it's like to have no one care
all alone in this world
sitting home alone
all alone listening to that sad song
that song that used to mean something
sitting home alone singing that sad song all day long
waiting for him to come and knock at my door
until then
sitting home alone
all alone
no one to hold
listening to that sad song that once meant something
singing it all day long
waiting for him to come knocking at my door
sitting home alone

Shantell Guyton, Grade 8
R A Brown Middle School, OR

Lonely Bird No More

Somewhere a lonely bird soars
Such long lonesome hours he has at wing
Lonely bird is flying and flying without a rhythm
Disembarking here and there to rest his wings
Lonely bird has nothing to do, nowhere to go, no one to talk to
So lonely bird takes flight, hoping to find another bird
Hours, hours, and hours lonely bird journeys
Lonely bird suspends and perches on a bell tower
"Peep, peep." calls a female bird
"Peep, peep." the lonely bird calls back
The female bird soars off
The lonely bird follows
Now the lonely bird, is lonely no more

Kaeleigh Hugill, Grade 7
Colorado Connections Academy, CO

When the Dream Bank Runs Dry

When the dream bank goes empty, then so does your soul.
It's just like drinking instead you scrape the bottom of the bowl.
The lights flicker off and the candle snuffs out,
What's left in life but to sit down and pout.
It seems like no one's your friend and life's not fair,
Now you just deal with the little things that get in your hair.

You feel like you're lost or just spinning around,
You either can't say a word or you're singing aloud.
You wonder where you're supposed to be, or whom to be with.
You wonder if they really miss you or if it's just a myth.
Were there ever really dreams or were they just a lie,
You're afraid of the world, and feel as pathetic as a fly.

Dominic Allen, Grade 9
McMinnville High School, OR

Cops and Robbers

It was the dead of night There was no fright
We ran in and stole the candy the Tandy yelled "the cops"
We ran away and got a car we only drove so far
Then we crashed and got road rash
Then we got busted and our car got rusted
We were took to jail and traded places
Then the other team was the bad guys
Then we were cops and busted the robbers
Then we ran to my house to turn on the fan

Tyler Bylbie, Grade 8
Cimarron Springs Elementary School, AZ

Horses

Horses are like the wind,
so fast and mysterious.
You never know when
they're going to come,
You'll never know when one,
just one horse
will come and capture your heart forever.

Sarah Darst, Grade 7
Sequoia Village School, AZ

The Apple

Limy and sticky,
It sits on aisle 12,
The smell of gardens' and farms'
Produce wafting through the air.

An apple, the simple fruit,
Ages as humans would.
Bruised and wrinkly,
Waiting 'til it's decay.

Crunchy and dripping,
Smells of citrus and fall.
Warm with brown leaves,
Falling from the autumn trees.

An apple
So innocent, can be something
O' so evil, as in
The Garden of Eden and temptation.

Its firm, leathery touch,
Makes a thud as it falls
To the ground
And lays there for the rest of its life.

Elise Hulsey, Grade 9
Xavier College Preparatory School, AZ

Shadow

Shadows following after me
Where I go, have no need
Watching, waiting 'til I leave
Jumping, climbing with me.

Shadows walk up and down the street
I see her in the mirror
When the day can't be any clearer
When the rain comes we won't meet.

Shadows play on a sunny day
They parade in the beautiful way
Climbing trees and dance all day
When night comes it all ends

Shadows, oh shadows come out to play
Hello you again, come to play
On this bright sunny day.

Eryn Lamb, Grade 8
La Plata Middle School, NM

Jell-O

Jell-O makes me giggle
I like the way it jiggles
I like it lemon, I like it sweet
I like to giggle every time I eat

Noemi Cordero, Grade 7
Somerton Middle School, AZ

Wrestling

Slam! Thud! I feel the earth shake, quake, and break
I hear crashing and pounding
The houses are rumbling
The streets are vibrating
All is calm, is it over? Or is it like the puma waiting to attack?

Slam! Thud! It strikes again
More violent and powerful
Twisting and turning
The crowds falling like waves on the beach
All is calm, is it finally over? Or will the puma be back for more?

Slam! Thud! There is screaming and yelping
Like a plea for freedom
I see blood dripping and eyes watering
I hear pain and suffering
All is calm, is it over yet? Or will the puma be back again?
I see an uprising before another

Slam! Thud! Is there more, or is this over?
Ding, ding
"Good job out there guys."
"Shake hands and go to your coaches"
"Will the next wrestlers please come to the ring?"

Chris England, Grade 7
Sky Vista Middle School, CO

The Tide of Life

Coming closer to the ocean
Becoming more visible, the warm yellow-golden sand
Soaked at the shore by the waves in motion
Now I can see the details of the delicate shell in my hand

As the waves crash around me
I wonder how they can be so cruel
But another part is key
There is a sanctuary in the water, glistening like a jewel
The ocean has many mysteries some will never get to see

Out, farther away, the water looks so still
With only the rolling waves
But the lively dolphins come out and the ocean seems to fill
The once soothing waves are now parted by the trail the dolphins seemed to pave
They head toward their destiny, nobody holding them against their will

Against the vibrant and colorful sky
Where the setting sun is burning gold
Is where the day's memories lie
The warm day water turns cold

And tomorrow is full of promises

Nicole Milstead, Grade 8
Our Lady of Lourdes Catholic School, UT

Evil

Holocaust
It was evil
How hateful can a person be?
Psycho, mentally sick
Hitler destroyed people's lives
Murderer
Evil
Ignorant, stupid, and psycho
He wasn't any better then anyone
He was nothing

A little short man who thought he had the right to take a life
If anybody deserves to die it was him

He ended families
People
He ruined childhoods and ended them
Evil
Such an evil man the world couldn't be how he wanted it

Rebekah Chavez, Grade 8
Barcelona Elementary School, NM

Soldier

Strong, trained, lethal, loyal.
Related to a worried family.
Who cares deeply about flags and country.
Who feels ready to serve his country.
Who needs order.
Who gives his life.
Who fears the enemy.
Who would like to see home again.
Resident of tent 356.

Mateo Oramas, Grade 8
Sedona Charter School, AZ

Memory*

I saw your face in a dream,
as my mind slowly dissipated,
my anger overcame me,
and I can't convey my guilt.
You would not recognize your son,
his eyes have gone cold,
his heart too slow to beat.
The countless times that you told him,
you loved him,
have been forgotten in his memory.
I ask God why you left.
Was the choice only His?
Was I not good enough?
My pain is too real for this life that I lead.
My heart too slow.
And as I sit here writing my dreams,
all I have is memories.

Michael P. Diltz, Grade 8
Diamond Ranch Academy, UT
*Dedicated to my mother, Ellen C. Diltz

Families

families are forever
families are wherever
when in doubt
families are better
families laugh together
families play together
your friends my be cool
but families are cooler
when you laugh at them
they laugh back
when you yell at them
they talk back
but when you let then know you love them
they will love you whenever
that's why, families are forever!

Kayla Settle, Grade 9
Shelley Sr High School, ID

Inspiration!

Words of inspiration fail certain people
Living in a world full of knowledge
Sometimes people need a little encouragement
You need confidence to get through hard times
Inside every person there is brilliance
When you least expect something, good things will happen
It is okay to be alone sometimes
When nobody is around sit still and listen to the silence
If you look deep enough inside yourself,
You will always find those words of inspiration!

Mailee Benedetti-Peters, Grade 9
King Kekaulike High School, HI

Just Listen

In school I just listen
to the boring teacher talk about science.
Blah, blah, blah
is all I hear. I ignore her.
I think that I will never need this information
so I just sit and draw weird figures.
Years late
I'm going to wish I had heard my teacher
because now in high school
is when I need the "science information."
Gosh, I feel so stupid,
everybody is raising their hand
participating, answering questions
except for me.
Ohhhhh my how embarrassing
how I now wish I could go back in time
and listen to that boring teacher
instead of drawing figures,
how I wish I could go back in time:
I could've paid attention.

Alejandra Hernandez, Grade 8
Sonoran Science Academy, AZ

Why Can't I Be Just Like Everyone Else?

Why do I have to see different, look different, talk different, walk different? I hate being different from all the 'normal perfect kids.' They always have to tease me just cause I seem different but I'm still a human, that does not mean that I don't have feelings, that doesn't mean I don't react to all the things they do and say to me. If I were given a simple chance, I would be the same like everyone else so I would be treated like a normal person would but no I'm nothing but a monster, I can't even stand having people look at me cause I don't look like them or what they might think of me. If they hate me so much then why don't they just rip out my heart and shred it to pieces, but they wouldn't need to do that cause they already hurt me enough. I won't let it happen to me anymore. I wish they could just accept me like how I accept them for being themselves. I guess, I always feel my eyes water when I think about all those times those judgmental people hurt me. They're monsters not me, but why do I feel like I am? Every day that comes and goes, I always ask myself 'Why can't I be just like everyone else?'

Tyonna Green, Grade 7
Molasky Jr High School, NV

A Kitchen's Persona

The cooking is now in session!
I love this time of day!
The clacks of my pans, the clicks of the wooden spoons,
the light whisper of thin smoke coming up from my creations — it's just so exhilarating!
The smells always get me giddy too.
I adore that sweet sensation when my food comes bursting out of the oven,
and that great smell of anticipation from the hungry people.
When my work is completed, I always have that savory taste of a job well done.
I, the kitchen, have finished my mission, feeling warm and joyful that my customers are satisfied.

Alex Katz, Grade 7
Ernest Becker Middle School, NV

In Stone

Carved in stone the words were wrong, from anger to jealousy the rage beneath set free. I am my own worst enemy. I can't control the feeling when the fight is being fought but I can feel the pain left over when I've given all I've got. My time here to mend my wounds is a process that takes time, and all I have to give is what's on the inside.

Ashley Horne, Grade 9
Pueblo County High School, CO

An Autobiography

Vast assumptions stain the lens
Faded realizations of everything that was taken for granted litter the momentum
Mistakes follow the perspective in ownership, I rejoice myself
Displaying the mediocrity along the way
Abundant mentalities assist the facade that conceals what is overwhelming
Excuses used to solicit themselves to the unknowing
Delusional and contradicting states add to the ambiance of us all
This is what I asked for, an environment of endless possibilities
I conform to the hierarchy that I view from my vantage point
Respect ensnares my decisions and leads me toward what is now justice
The bleak horizon used to contrast with potential
Now I stand again with others, this time leading them
Empathetic moments collide amidst the confusion
A realization overcomes the ungratefulness of my adolescence
An act brings awareness to the undeserving
Comprehension of the culture was able to create some sort of appreciation for what we have
And no longer a need for what we want
Today is a continuation of the pendulum of us all
A collaboration of peace and persistence directs life down an anxious path
Purposes and acceptance create the climactic beginning of my story
But the moral still creases down the frames of all my memories.

Nicholas Hutchinson, Grade 9
Sehome High School, WA

Everlasting Snow

Snow melts away
But I have everlasting snow
Standing in a snowstorm
Can you see me glisten?
Looking around you can see where the snow lazed and rolled
This snow is everlasting
This snow will never melt away
For this snow lives in many people's hearts
This snow has changed many people's lives
You ask what kind of snow this is?
This snow has a soft, warm, white body, four legs
And a huge loving heart
My snow is my horse Misty

Kayla Artman, Grade 7
Eagle Point Middle School, OR

Welcome to the Present

We are here — now —
Here where we stand, sit or lay
Here where each day becomes our
New present — every last second — our past
Our future, never ending, always changing
Our past — frozen
We cannot change our past
So we try to form a better future
Our lives are what we make them to be
So…hello tomorrow —
Goodbye yesterday — see you soon —
Or not at all —

Haleigh Shotts, Grade 8
Walt Clark Middle School, CO

First Impression to the End

10 seconds pass, 11 assumptions about you.
Most of them wrong, a first impression.
Time stretches more judgments are made
For you to prove, right or wrong?

When you know each other long enough,
And you make a mistake,
Why do people judge for what you've done
And not what you've become?

When you walk and the glances you get.
Trying to ignore, is it worth it?
Don't stop to consider who I am inside.
Just look through hate's eyes.

People can't see through
Unless they strain to.
Then they see
The flawed beauty
Of my soul.

Savannah Dixon, Grade 7
Mandalay Middle School, CO

Moon

The Beginning
The moon is a flashlight arising from a hand.
The moon is a white ball arising in the sky.
The moon is a light,
That lights up the streets of the world.
Midnight
The moon is a lonely light up in the sky,
Awaiting for a new place to shine.
As its journey ends here,
It continues on the other side.
Morning Coming
The moon is a small hero,
Making it clear to walk in the streets.
The moon is a cherished miracle,
That awaits the sun to takeover.
Morning
The moon is an old light,
That comes back every night,
As you stretch out your arms,
The moon slowly disappears.

Cindy Guzman, Grade 8
Ernest Becker Middle School, NV

Bullied

I see his hope get beaten and battered.
From the sidelines where I watch,
I step into the ring.
I ask him to sit with me.
I compliment him.
He smiles wanly, and I grin back.
He has found a friend.
Then I open my eyes.
I look down at my clenched fists
And am slapped awake from my daydream.
I am still in the circle watching.

Nicola Morrow, Grade 7
Fairhaven Middle School, WA

Traffic

You want to be free,
with cars zooming and whirring past you.

You want the wind to blow through your hair.
But instead you're stuck in traffic.

You want to be anywhere but there. Anywhere!
And you will do anything to get there. Anything!

You want to be at home with your family.
Having a nice conversation over a home-cooked meal.
But you're stuck in traffic.

Finally, the traffic clears,
and you're moving forward with your life.

Hayley Theriault, Grade 7
Lyons Middle/Senior High School, CO

All We Have Ever Had

The world is nearly shattered
With all that's wrong today
The economy's down
The temperatures up
And the clouds keep
Getting more grey

In Africa, Children die
Northern ice caps melting
Polar Bears fry

Fuel gets burned
More and more
Gas prices so high
We are all poor

The Media twists it
All I see is the bad
Come on, world
Get better!

You are all
We have ever had

Nathan Fletcher, Grade 8
Century Middle School, CO

Harvest Moth

The white moth leaves
A trail of sparkling dust
As it flutters through
The night air with the full
Glowing moon shining orange beams
Upon white wings.

Stars pulsate with energy
As trickling breezes
Filled with cosmic breaths
Of night gently carry
The sparkling dust through open
Windows to coat dreams within.

Daniel Goughnour, Grade 8
Sweet Home Jr High School, OR

My Heart Flutters

My heart flutters
whenever I see him.
His eyes blue as the summer sky.
Warm sweet smile.
He gives me butterflies
when he kisses me.
Our lips like puzzle pieces
lock together perfectly.
My heart flutters
when I'm with him.

Brittany Byrum, Grade 8
Lyons Middle/Senior High School, CO

Imprisonment

Scared in a dungeon, with everything insecure,
Your good thoughts all gone, and mean threats being thrown at you.
You're all alone in the night, which is unsteady enough already,
And those nights you get terrible frights,
Hoping that they'll get better soon with glee.

Then in your dream you see an eagle soaring,
With a bright orange eye that gleams,
In the sunlight it is king, and when night falls, it peacefully dreams.
You don't want to wake up, worried you'll feel trapped,
But you do, and you wish that time could just stop,
Fear comes over, and sadly you feel all wrapped.

Remembering the peace in your dream,
You try to touch the softness, warmness, and comfort,
While trying to battle everything else like cream,
And despite all this, the eagle brings you power.
Using this power you become a knight, no fear approaches you,
And a good soul deep within, flying and floating like a kite,
Having a shielding courage, which is as soft as a coo.

Grace Lee, Grade 7
Sky Vista Middle School, CO

I Wish

I wish that everyone was treated equally.
I wish that no one was judged by what they look like.
I wish that the war would end and we could bring the troops home.
I wish that some things weren't taken so seriously.
I wish that people would try their best to help others.
I wish that our world wasn't in such need.

Shannon Florio, Grade 7
Sky Vista Middle School, CO

Parents

They come in the most unusual pairs —
And we don't get to choose them
We get what we get
For them it's unconditional love and admiration
For us it sometimes feel like constant
Strife and frustration!
Can we ever be good enough for them?
To them, yes
To us it sometimes seems it's a question.
They have so much responsibility and pressure
And they still work so hard,
To give us what we want
But yet at times we take it all for granted
They love us, feed us, and teach us to one day be like them.
They are our examples of the adults we someday will be,
With their guidance and knowledge —
We hope to fall close to the tree.
We know without a doubt, they are always there to guide us on our way
So even though we didn't choose them —
In the end we should be thankful for what we got.

Mitch Berry, Grade 9
Bonneville High School, ID

Sis

Every day I see her,
I always will remember,
All our trips to Coffee Bean,
Every special memory.
Next year she will be leaving,
I wish that I was dreaming.
She is very important to me.
She is my sister as you can see.
We fight, we laugh, we cry together,
No matter how far apart we will be sisters forever.

Christina Angarola, Grade 8
Fertitta Middle School, NV

Banks of Knowledge

Have you ever wanted to unlock them,
The banks of overflowing knowledge?
They hold so much,
All you have to do is read.

Open up your mind;
Pick any book you can find.
Start now, don't waste time.

Choosing a subject is fun,
But truly learning is better.
And if you're ready for any adventure somewhere,
Let a book take you there.

Derek Sanchez, Grade 9
Lakewood High School, CO

Bones

Ghostly ghouls lurking in the night
Zombies putting up quite the fight

Ghosts will come without warning, BEWARE!!!!
You best prepare yourselves for quite the scare

Snakes come for a quick bite
You better run into the light

What is the purpose of running you say
The purpose is surviving okay

Your skeleton begins to quake
You begin to tremble and shake

"What's wrong with me?" like you don't know,
Careful now, don't let your bones show!

Time is upon us it's almost midnight
The time of running scared in the dark of night,

Oh no it's coming, sunrise
People are in for a big surprise!

Christian Arredondo, Grade 7
Shadow Ridge Middle School, CO

Let

Let the snowflakes tickle your nose
in the mid-February breeze
Enjoying every minute for soon will blossom a rose
Let the raindrops kiss your cheek
in the stormy lot
For soon when summer comes a raindrop you may seek
Let the wet sand massage your toes
on the beautiful summer shore
Soon the warm gentle water won't flow
Let the newly cut grass cushion your play
on summer break
Soon it will be the end of May
Let the breeze sway your every move
in the afternoon
and let it relax you and be soothed

Emylee Anderle, Grade 7
Eaton Middle School, CO

Not Knowing

I see her standing
She's all alone
Does she know I've been with
Her all this time?
Is she just standing there
Not knowing anything
Not knowing people were watching
Not knowing that someone cares
That I care
That I love her
I see her alone, not knowing

Tyler St. Pierre, Grade 7
Arts & Communication Magnet Academy, OR

Yeah, I Was Thinking

In 1809, he was born in Kentucky.
And later moved to Illinois.
Self-educated, I'd say he was lucky
Was this tall, awkward looking boy.

He became involved in politics of his day,
And fought to make his world a better place.
Many didn't like what he had to say.
"Freedom to all, regardless of race."

War between brothers, whose way was right?
Blood ran again in Liberty's name.
To break the chains of bondage, did they fight.
Righting the wrong of our Nation's shame.

This war changed the face of our nation.
Which makes me wonder, yeah I was thinking.
We will always respect the Emancipation Proclamation,
And keep alive, our late President, Abraham Lincoln.

Alesha Cain, Grade 8
Montezuma Middle School, AZ

My Little Sister

You may be just four,
However, I know when you walk in the door
That even more
There is a mess coming

I love you so
And you're not a foe
But a sweet doe
But a tornado hitting our room

I sometimes may be tough
It may not always be enough
And you may sometimes be rough
To handle, but I love you so

You are so cute
I might wish, at times, that you were mute
And you might not have learned that cute isn't kute
But you are my sister and I love you so

Crissy Hill, Grade 7
Sky Vista Middle School, CO

You're Not Alone

I want to hold you close and steal your pain,
listen closely and hear what you're saying.
Just forget about everything that's on your mind,
only look forward and don't rewind.
Wipe those tears cause I'm here for you now,
I'll do whatever it takes just teach me how.
This isn't really you cause you let them take your best,
be strong and confident, don't let them take the rest.
I know that you've given up and that you've fallen to the ground
and when I tried to pick you up, pieces were all I found.
So please don't give up, you only have one chance to live,
just give it all you've got, and everything you have to give.
I am here forever and forever with you, I'll be.
We walk this Earth together, for always you and me.

Chelsea Symons, Grade 8
Elton Gregory Middle School, OR

Goodbye Dear Sanity

Roads roam from near to far
Watching wondering he sits quite up
Driving by drivers drive quite down
Carefully closing his emerald blue eyes
Everything enclosing him tight 'a tough
Holding on in hard desperation
The raging road screaming below
Fingers fumble losing control
The raging road screaming below
Watching wondering the man closes his eyes and sings aloud
Losing again all behold
The battle inside of the raging road

Haley Morrell, Grade 7
Eaton Middle School, CO

Nostalgia

There is always a yearning for the past,
wishing that time would rewind to before.
The love I once had from you went by fast.
I was happy then, but now I feel sore.

If only I am still seen in your eyes,
perhaps things would have turned out different.
But now my world seems to be full of lies.
Presently, I'm left with discontentment.

Hiding behind a fake smile isn't tough,
but sometimes I wish you would see through me.
I lock up my feelings, I've had enough,
but you are yet to realize and see.

I'm waiting for a sign so helplessly,
standing on the side watching hopelessly.

Jeanne Lin, Grade 9
Clark High School, NV

Warrior

His spear stands high and has claimed many lives,
His shield is glinting and has blocked many arrows,
His breastplate is spurred and has withstood many blows,
His sword is gleaming and has severed many heads.

One could be fooled that this is an impenetrable unit,
But when facing his enemy his face is drenched,
His heart is beating at a constant high rate,
He knows that one mistake could mean death.

But then, a flash of lighting speed.
The warrior is unleashed.
He has shown himself to his enemies,
And will not go down without a challenge.

But what could cause such a warrior's life?
It's simple: his lack of aid.

Chris Turner, Grade 8
Wiley Jr/Sr High School, CO

Now the Pastures Are Empty

The mares stand alone in their stalls.
Those who've lost their foals
For the first time, paw the hay,
Sniff for something familiar.
Moments before, the barn full of shrieks
And neighing, a dark truck back firing.
Ruffian dug her tiny feet into the hay,
Tried to nuzzle her mare, her long legs black
As the bones of cherry branches.
She was born as the petals opened,
Stood close to her mother in the shade,
Is gone before light comes.

Gilana Martin, Grade 7
St Bonaventure School, NM

Kitty Treat

So small and black
She sleeps on her back
When she awakens and slinks
We know what she thinks
Her soft fur shimmers in the morning light
Her eyes gives off a sparkly light and bright
She makes her way
Her tail a-sway
She sits by the dish and stares
With her paws in pairs
So with a blink she asks her question
Out comes a meow and there is no reaction
She has to eat
But kitty wants a treat.

Maia Lang, Grade 7
Lyons Middle/Senior High School, CO

Colors

Everyone knows their blues and greens,
This also includes their twos and teens.

From the mixes of red and yellow,
To also see if you read and be mellow.

Some also have pinks and purples,
Which you need inks and maybe turtles.

There's also the dull black and white,
You see only blacks and it's all right.

You all might like the orange and browns,
And it could be orchard and sundown.

There's also grays and gold's,
Which some are graceful and bold?

If you all like the colors of the rainbow,
Then you cannot play the banjo!

Gregory Knowles, Grade 7
Shadow Ridge Middle School, CO

Mind Movies

A person dreams and dawdles on,
Reaching for the starry sky.
Tinkling bells in your molting mind,
Inspiring what happens ticking in time.
Starting to wonder why,
Tiring thoughts are there, like…
If mermaids are weaving through your hair.
Creative can your mind be,
Only you can let it free.
No one can dream quite like you,
Exceptional daydreams is what I love to do.

Hanna Karas, Grade 7
Eaton Middle School, CO

See in Me

Look at me,
What do you see?
Just another girl or the unique person I am?
Am I like a fierce lion or a precious lamb?
What do you see?

Most people don't really see me,
I hope you see what I see.
I'm not perfect, but I do what I can.
I'm a girl who loves being tan.
In me, I hope this is what you see.

I look in the mirror at me,
And I'll tell you what I see…
I'm like a boat on the river's path.
Someone who loves a hot bubble bath,
This is what I see.

I seem to always wonder why me?
But then I realize it's just what people see.
Silly, simple, smiley, and sweet say a lot.
I am a ray of sunshine that is easily taught.
I want you to see this in me!

Michelle Fowler, Grade 9
Shelley Sr High School, ID

Rejection

This aching pain
Is so insane
Sometimes I wonder
What he sees in her

And why he doesn't see
What's happened to me
'Cause of his betrayal
Should I really try to unveil

How much this pain actually burns
'Cause of his love that quickly turns
To hatred very easily
So his rejection may very well scar me

Victoria E. Simmons, Grade 8
Desert Sky Middle School, AZ

Love That Lives On

Just the sight of you brightened my day.
Just the sight of you made me smile.
Even though we may not have liked each other in the same way,
The time spent with you was still worthwhile.

The loss of you still fills me with grief.
My time with you was so very brief.
The loss of you still makes me blue,
Because I still have love for you.

Zachary Lepkoske, Grade 7
Mandalay Middle School, CO

Found
Strip and colors
Pleated satin
Beautiful soft velvet
Rough edges
Felt
Simple tie
Sierra Zikmund, Grade 8
Ontario Middle School, OR

Home Rodeo
Oh I dread the day,
When I have to walk my steer.
I take him by the barn and hay.
Then I am struck with fear,
When he just would not stay.
I try to hang on,
But I trip over a rock.
I get control of him again,
Oh dear, he takes off!
He gets away two or three more times,
Oh man, I am ticked.
I grab the rope one last time,
And BAM, I get kicked
I would have had control,
If he wouldn't have been so dumb.
He drug me left and right,
And nearly broke my thumb!
I cleared some dust from my eyes,
And it almost made no sense.
It was flat out not good.
We were headed for the fence!
Brandon Nicoll, Grade 8
Round Valley Middle School, AZ

Insomnia
Bloodshot eyes
Heavy head
Lost in a daze

No sleep
Can't sleep
Dilemma stuck in my head

Toss and turn
Staring at the ceiling
Thoughts talk to me
But I can't speak back

All of this frustration
After you left
Overwhelms with tears of dark

Next night
Starts over again
Hannah Sealock, Grade 8
Falcon Middle School, CO

Look Beyond
Look beyond that girl in torn jeans, what do you see?
I see a need, a want…for a better life to live.
Look beyond that boy dressed in black, what do you see?
I see a wounded soul, a cry for help…in the scars on his wrists.
Look beyond that couple in love, what do you see?
I see a broken bond, a feeling faltered…in his reaction to her affection.
Look beyond that teenager's smile, what do you see?
I see a secret, one they cannot confess…by the blank look in their eyes.
Look beyond that bitter old man, what do you see?
I see a young man's devotion, his love…for the woman he lost.
Look beyond that crippled, what do you see?
I see a heavy heart, an artistic means…to run wild and free.
Look beyond that beautiful girl, what do you see?
I see her hurt, her cuts and bruises…because she's her daddy's punching bag.
Look beyond that wall, the one covering the truth
The wall that separates what we see…and what we look for.
Look beyond that dress, it's not brand new
She lives with her mommy, but her daddy moved
Look past material things, the gossip and lies
So that you may embrace the honesty…and forget the disguise.
Carli Restivo, Grade 8
Ashton Ranch Elementary School, AZ

Pitching
When you pitch your heart starts to pound, you begin to get really nervous,
you hear a bunch of people cheering you on hoping to get a strike, you get in
you wind up, hoping not to mess up then you let go of the ball and everyone stops.
Then your heart starts to pound again.
Ezekiel Deleon, Grade 8
St Catherine of Siena School, CO

If
If you can be nice and kind with an open mind
If you can be honest and trustworthy you may be worthy
If you can act like a good friend it will never end
If you can always be there for them they will always be there for you

If you can't lie to them you would rather die for them
If you are always loyal your friendship will never boil
If you do not use them you are sure not to lose them
If you don't betray they might save your day

If you help them in their time of need and do not show them any greed
If for them you stand your friendship will be as tight as a band
If you do not let jealousy take over you'll be as lucky as a clover
If at night they lay in fright you will be there for them to talk all night

If you need advice you can trust they will be nice
If a partner is in need you can count on them indeed
If you let them lean on you they will have your back too
If you stand by them till the end then only then will you be a true friend
Jamie Goodwin, Grade 7
Sky Vista Middle School, CO

Turtle

Slow, green, afraid, sheltered
Related to the snapper
Who cares deeply about the environment
Who feels like a display
Who needs attention
Who gives a dance for fish
Who fears the audience of people
Who would like to see the ocean once again
Resident of the Zoo

Kelly Franck, Grade 8
Sedona Charter School, AZ

Do I Not Deserve This Freedom?

I may appear to look like a mere wild animal,
But I carry this role as a dog,
Chained to this world, my home.
I'd rather run like a stray and never be caught,
To live on my own.
I feel as if I'm wearing a mask,
With a leash connecting to my collar.
"Do I not deserve this so-called freedom like everyone else?"
Is what I think true or is it a lie, like myself.
Do I not deserve a free life where I can roam free,
With no chains, no rules that bind me.
Why do I live this part, as a house-owned pet?
Is that all I am?
Why? Did I do something wrong?
If I did, will someone tell me?
I ask myself these questions,
Not knowing how I got in this mess.
Oh, how I hate this longing to be set free
In the wild where I belong.
I sit in my solitude and think,
"Do I not deserve this freedom?"

Naomi Price, Grade 9
Bonneville High School, ID

The Greatest Sport Ever Made

Football...
   my life!
  action-packed
    feeling great
      on a touchdown score!!
When you're in a game,
  got that excitement and
    butterflies in your stomach.
When on the line,
  whether offense or defense
    and the quarterback yells "HIKE,"
      for those thirty seconds or less,
    I'm free.
   Feels like I have no problems
    Or anything to do
     I'm just free.

Gabe Bolton, Grade 8
Culver Middle School, OR

Jews

World War 2
Everyone is dying
The one person didn't like Jews
Jews can't walk on sidewalks
Can't do anything
SS would kill

This was sad
Jews were killed for no reason
Jews getting run over
Jews had to shut down their own buildings
Jews were sent to be slaves
Unhealthy Jews were killed

Disabled Germans were killed
Hitler wanted to be a perfectionist
Germany was turned into a police state

Wilson Suen, Grade 8
Barcelona Elementary School, NM

Life

Life is an engine blowing up.
At first you start with a bang and then another.
Life is a twisted road.
It has you going in all different directions.
But then it has you going up a mountain.
Then you hear the car crashing down.
But at the last minute you think what you could
  have done to make your life better.
Then you find yourself at bottom of the mountain
  you find yourself in a cemetery, in the ground.
But it is not over yet.
Then you see that it is all a bad dream that has come to life.
Life is a weed that has been cut.
You see the weed starts to shrivel to a brown
  unwanted stump in the ground.
So live life to it's fullest of joy or this will happen to you.

Jacob Wonder, Grade 7
21st Century Public Academy, NM

Waves Upon the Sand

Listen to the waves crash against the sand,
playing its sweet song of the band.
Hear birds sing like never before,
as they fly in the sky and land on the shore.
Feel the cool wind blowing on your face,
and open up your arms in embrace.
Look at the clouds, never in one place,
and then lay down your towel in your own little space.
Walk along the beach and look for shells
then listen to the stories people have to tell.
Enjoy this moment while you can,
have no regrets and hope you get tan.

Emily Falk, Grade 9
Stapley Jr High School, AZ

White

White feels like winter
Like a baseball flying into your glove
Like clouds floating in the sky
White is excitement.

White sounds like Christmas
Like songs flowing through the air
Like paper rustling in the wind
Like a dog barking in the night.

White tastes like snow
Like delicious mints
Like drinking milk after a rough practice
Like ice cream on a warm summer day.
Adam Garrison, Grade 8
La Plata Middle School, NM

The Struggle

One battle lost
But not the war
As life goes on
We'll lose much more
Although it hurts
It's not over yet
And we will live
To feel the regret
Lise Welch, Grade 7
Les Bois Jr High School, ID

What Is a Friend?

A person whom you like,
someone who is kind.
A friend until the end.

Someone you can talk to
who will be there for you
when you need a shoulder to cry on.
Someone you can depend on.

Someone who will listen
when you have a problem.
Someone who will understand
when you need a helping hand.

A friend is someone you can love,
someone you can hate.
But in the end, is loved without mistake.

A sister, a brother
a man, a woman
a child, an elder
who will be there till the end.
That is what a friend is.
Kourtney Correll, Grade 7
Yucca Middle School, NM

Thinking of You

Sitting in the sun,
I am thinking of you
Standing in the rain,
I am thinking of you

Oh, sorrowful I feel!
When you are away
I can almost see your face
When I am thinking of you

The things I would give
To return to you again
For I feel so lonely
When I am thinking of you
I am thinking of you.
Mathia Lam, Grade 9
Abundant Life Academy, UT

Why?

Tell me you love me
Please don't hurt me
Tell me forever
Please don't torture me
Tell me you need me
Why?

Give me the hug I've wanted
Help my heart heal
Don't treat me like I'm haunted
Give me the love I need
You're begging for me to suffer
Why?

You said you loved me
I know you did
But you just hugged me
And said 'I'm sorry.'
Why?

I know why
Love hurts
Keep on fighting
Love is a mysterious wonder
Stephanie Handy, Grade 7
Sky Vista Middle School, CO

My Best Friend

She's been here through all the years.
Through all the laughs,
Through all the tears.
We've been friends for so long.
She was here,
and now she's gone.
Kaylee Kauffman, Grade 7
Sequoia Village School, AZ

Lost Summer

Brittle leaves shake
In chilly breezes
Like dried shriveled clumps.
Summer is lost and gone.

Rose petals lie like faded tissue
Alone near the fence
Separated by icy gusts.
Summer is lost and gone.

I miss the sun,
The lush colored flowers.
Summer is lost and gone.
Fall has invaded the air.
Eric Lash, Grade 7
Reid School, UT

Cell Phone

I passed my number to a friend
Who passed it to a girl
To my surprise
It passed throughout the school
Which put me in the hands of chaos!
Then, by the end of the day I was saved
When my number was finally changed.
Adam Brodie, Grade 7
St Bonaventure School, NM

Life

Drowning,
Sinking
In my despair.
Easier,
Simpler
Just to give in.
Just to stop caring
Just to give up.

No one cares,
No one knows
What I feel.
What's the point anyway?

But…
A pulsating light
Draws me up,
Gives me strength
To continue my fight.

I won't give up
And I won't give in
'Cause it's my life,
And I want to win!
Mary Peterson, Grade 9
Timberline Middle School, UT

Rainy Night

I'm walking outside
DRIP! SPLASH!
The puddles big and wide
I feel like I am in nature's shower
But Daddy said "You need an umbrella."
So all that I get wet is my squeaky rubber boots
I never want to go inside.
It's late. Daddy is yelling at me,
"You're going to get sick"
BOOM!
The thunder is here.
I run inside.
I sneeze a few times.
Dad was right!
I am sick

Danielle Lewis, Grade 7
McKinley Middle School, NM

She Is Rain

Drip, drip, drip
She races down from the sky
She drops, down, directly under my feet,
She is rain
Rain, rapidly, rushes down to the earth.
Plop, plop, plop
She drops into a puddle as she hits the ground,
She is rain
Splash, splash, splash
Kids, carelessly, crash into her.
She is rain.

Luisa Tago, Grade 7
Eagle Point Middle School, OR

I…

I am unique and imperfect
I wonder what the future is going to be like
I hear all the words that are spoken
I see the conflicts around me
I want the world to be a better place
I am unique and imperfect

I fear getting in trouble
I feel love along with hate
I worry about what will happen after I do something wrong
I cry when things go wrong and nothing is okay
I am unique and imperfect

I understand few things
I say what I believe
I dream of what I want
I try to do my best in everything
I hope that after all, everything turns out all right
I am unique and imperfect

Andrea Pizano, Grade 7
Sunset Ridge Elementary School, AZ

About a Teacher!

When I came to school ready to kill
you broke me down.
 Now I see you didn't do that out of anger,
you did it because you cared.
 When I was younger I thought caring
was something you did out of anger.
So I wouldn't let anyone care for me!
 Now I understand when someone cares about you
they do it out of love.
 Even though we went through our ups and downs
you ALWAYS stayed by my side.
 Thank you for giving me
the TLC I needed.

Brianne Thompson, Grade 7
Sylvester Middle School, WA

I Want You Back

I felt exposed when you left me in the hall
All alone in the shadows of darkness
You knew at that moment you could have it all
But you left me there feeling loneliness

I felt heartbroken when you told me you had to go
Not knowing when you were going to be back
For me to tell you that I would disagree and say no
Empathy for me is something you lack

Now you made me sit here and ponder my decision
Oh how I could make you see
That my eyes are watery and I have no vision
But I'm here now to pay my fee

I want you to know that you have been missed
Come to me and start to unpack
All the love and passion you gave when we kissed
If you haven't noticed, I really want you back

Ryan Liljenquist, Grade 8
Arrow High School, UT

Yes

Purple forests calmly ending
Lights and trees all bending
Come and go
Stop to say hello.
The sun set low in reverse
Like a summer sky
Just stopped before speaking
The soft skin bled
As fire was the sun
Smoggy rain falls down upon the city
And life calmly stops at a standstill to be issued insanity
"Come again"
"Come again"
The soulless voice echoes from a speaker

Sean Senogles, Grade 7
St Mary's School, OR

Art

The canvas screams
For the beauty of the soul
Who cries back,
The canvas is not alone

The ink flows
From the heart
A river flooding the banks

The color splashes
From the eyes
A rock thrown into a lake

The calamity ends
And order is restored
What is left,
Something to be adored

Garrick Lemley, Grade 9
Grand Junction High School, CO

Poor Jane

there once was a guy named Earl
he really wanted a girl
her name was Jane
she acted so plain
well now he wants Pearl!

Sandra Gallegos, Grade 8
Round Valley Middle School, AZ

True Love

True love isn't a game
You want to mess around, then go away
Don't play with her heart
Do you want to tear her apart?

She can't stop thinking about you
She wonders if you feel the same way too
True love isn't a game
You want to mess around, then go away

She can't explain how she feels
Will it ever heal?
Can it really be love?
Or was it just fate from above?

True love isn't a game
You want to mess around, then go away
So many feelings run through her head
She lies awake thinking in bed

Then he calls
She starts to fall
He says, "I love you"
She replies, "I love you too"

Makeri Richardson, Grade 7
Shadow Ridge Middle School, CO

Love

Sometimes love is like the Northern Lights,
So mystical and bright
It takes you on amazing flights
And soars you up to tremendous heights
With beams of joy so bright, in every single sight
That sweep you up so fast, you don't have time to fight.

Other times love is like an earthquake.
It leaves everything crumbled and cracked —
Broken
With people devastated and confused.
And it may be painful and take awhile,
But you have no choice;
You begin to mend the cracks,
And pick up the broken and shattered pieces of once treasured things,
Trying to mend the open wounds,
Just hoping that it never happens again.

Alaina Hawley, Grade 7
Mears Middle School, AK

True Friend

True friends are people who care and are always willing to share
People who notice when you are sad and are always trying to make you glad
True friends know the feelings you have inside
True friends are the ones who help you decide
True friends hug you extremely tight
Before they ever leave your sight
If you think you have someone that will last till the end
Make sure it is your TRUE FRIEND!

Wendy Malta, Grade 7
Somerton Middle School, AZ

Horse

I am a horse
I have a white mane and tail
I have polished hoofs and a colorful brown and white body
I love to prance and run with my friends but I am also calm
When I run you can hear my hoofs beating on the ground and me nickering
I feel the wind
I feel the saddle on my back and the cold bit in my mouth
I feel the flies on my belly and the water running down my back when the rain falls
I see the grass blowing in the wind
I see animals playing
I see men by the trees
I smell the sweet new fallen water in my pond
I smell the winds passing scent
I smell other horses walking in the green pasture
I'm known for roaming wild
I'm known to be a carrier in wars
I'm known for showing for the prize and racing for the money
I'm scared of trainers
I'm scared of mean things
I'm scared of being whipped
I am a horse

Heather Haasl, Grade 7
La Center Middle School, WA

Riding My Dirt Bike

Riding my dirt bike is like nothing else
It's fun even by yourself
The thrill of it all
The stillness of it all

The joy of flying through the air
The feeling of the wind in my hair
It's fun being way up high
It's like you could reach the sky

The fun of riding with your friends
It's like nothing you could comprehend
Riding for me is just a dream

So it seems…

But when I wake up I see
That it is more than what even I could see
Riding my dirt bike is just my dream

Dallin Loveless, Grade 9
Queen Creek High School, AZ

The Life of Our Flag

I once was a flag of red, white and blue,
On a stand proud and tall as I waved so true;
My colors were steadfast, bright and bold,
As I stood for justice and freedoms untold.

I waved to everyone as they passed by,
Some held their hearts, others started to cry;
I saw joy and laughter, and tears of pain,
I was there for disaster, saw victory and strain.

I remember celebrations, dedications and birth,
I even flew strong, high above the earth;
I've welcomed the sunshine and even the storm,
I've hung in cathedrals for those who mourn.

But now my dedication and job is through,
I've become weathered myself and tattered too;
So now I'm retired in one little dash,
Thrown into the fire and returned to ash.

Joshua Manning, Grade 8
Grace Lutheran School, UT

Tulips in the Wintertime

Left out in the bitter cold,
The bunch that was neither gathered nor sold.
Yes, they are the tulips in the wintertime,
Yearning for the warmth of summertime.
Photosynthesis has been delayed,
The tulip's petals fall or become frayed.
The petal's colors become bland and sigh,
For the flower has yet to die.

Ludmila Malakhov, Grade 8
Jefferson Middle School, NM

The Guy of My Dreams

His smile is marvelous
Those eyes are like shimmering emeralds
If he looks at me…I freeze!!
He's like an angel sent from Heaven
    Just for me!
When I hear his name
    My heart STOPS…
    I Love Him!

Georgina Mendoza, Grade 8
Culver Middle School, OR

Waiting Until Saturday

I can't even think about what to put on the paper
I keep thinking I'd rather do it later
Sitting here in my seat so very bored I could weep
What makes it bad is the very way
They keep us here 'til Saturday

When finally I am sprung free
To run and play and mostly ski
When I get up to the mountainous hill
Where I speed and race and fall on my face
It is such a joy, so much fun indeed
To shoot down a run with blistering speed

And when I see the setting sun
And realize my day is done
I'll ride home all tired and spent
But still excited for tomorrow's ascent

Reid Edwards, Grade 8
Luther School, MT

Walls

As I sit here
In front of these
Silent falls
And white complex walls.
The agony pounding
Waiting…
The perilous call.
Fear of answering
What might occur
Needing the touch to reassure.
Sitting in haze
Nothing…
A lifeless gaze.
Eyes wide shut resisting the tear,
Closing them, what will appear?
Blinds are open, no sun shining through,
Oh dear God just give me my cue.
The reason to smile, though very few.
Now bid farewell, anxiety stalled.
Up from the fall, these white complex walls.

Olivia Smaciarz, Grade 8
Komachin Middle School, WA

Fishing Lure

It swims through the water attracting other fish pretending to be something that it is not. It's danger in disguise. It dances in the water like a newborn minnow. A snap, a bite, it has done its job. It works today, will it tomorrow? It floats on the water pretending to be a bug. As it skips across the water, there is a splash and it is out of sight.

Sean Earley, Grade 7
Eaton Middle School, CO

Remembrance of a Friend

A good friend or actually a family member. To be specific my dad. The one who helped me give birth. The one who was there so much and so happy too. So close but so far away. Just a memory for now on running, jumping, screaming but now forever sleeping, and resting good times now dissolve like the water in the air. Soon I hope to find you in the after life but until then I drown in my sorrow. I feel as if there was so much for you to finish in your talented, strong, and big hearted life. But whatever you left behind is now ours to cherish and reminisce on. I will always remember the scent you carried. The love you showed my mom, my brothers and me was priceless. But I would give any price to bring you back into my life. But until my death you will always be A REMEMBRANCE OF A FRIEND.

Dustin Gillard, Grade 7
Sky Vista Middle School, CO

Just Prove It

Think is to learn.
I think about you,
But I am not learning.
I want a guy that can prove to me you aren't all butt heads that think about just yourselves.
You say I'm hot, wow,
Doesn't mean much to me.
Yeah it makes me happy but it's not something that will brighten my day.
Tell a girl she is beautiful.
She will be happy all day.
That's exactly what most of us want to hear.
I wish that you could just prove that you aren't like those other guys.
So far you are about as cheesy as them.
You try to be romantic but it's not working.
Don't try so hard, be yourself,
Then you might prove that to me you aren't just another one of those jerks,
By just being yourself.

Erin Rockey, Grade 8
Rock Springs East Jr High School, WY

The Nameless Man

The hardest part is the beginning, where the wind has blown and the rain not fallen.
Where you must start from new, amongst unfamiliar faces crying for your mother screaming for your sanity.
Where you cannot be touched and cannot be broken, destroying yourself.
Collapse from the sorrow and cry out for the pain.
Scraping the ground calling my name, surrounded by shallow water that seeps through your belonging,
sacrifices emotions only one can hold.
As old as day, but as wise as youth passing slowly accepting the truth,
quaint thoughts cross and leave and paradise as come,
but inside release you emotions, the life is done, look up truth spoken, thoughts let out.
Strength leaves, lives close. Keep them near.
One flame gone, one side cold, with heat return.
The nameless man cry's, do no mock him at the corner.
Do not pity him at sight.
Treat him as us, but understand why.
Walk two steps behind and watch his feet.
Watch the two pairs of prints become one.

Quinton Owens, Grade 9
Buhl High School, ID

Cherry Blossom

Sun fades into darkness,
Leaves begin to fall.
A strong winter blizzard blows in,
Like a thousand white frosted shards.

As the day went by turned to months,
The last storm passes.
The sun shines once again,
Through trees, flowers, and frozen chandeliers.
The snow melted disappearing in thin air.

Flowers bloom, leaves were as green as the ground.
Cherry blossoms dance through the air with the wind,
Until the day fades away.
but it does not stop there.

Fireflies sparkling in the skies like stars,
The trees and leaves played with the wind,
Finally the cherry blossoms stayed in the tree.
Showing the beautiful faces they have.

Knowing one day,
They have to repeat this perfect paradise once again.

Anthony Rivera, Grade 9
Queen Creek High School, AZ

Runaway

She wants to run away
To get out of this town
She's running away from her dreams
Away from you
And what you used to be
You must be blind
If you can't see
How much she means
But she can't turn back now
She's gone too far
And she left thinking you'd chase after her
But you just sat there
And let her go
So she kept going
And now she is gone boy
And you will never catch up with her now
And soon you will realize what you let go

Paulina Dennis, Grade 8
Orangewood Elementary School, AZ

Laughter

Laughter has fingers that tickle your heart
She whispers every giggle
And she sings every chuckle
She lives in everyone
Just waiting for her solo

Jessica Fontaine, Grade 7
Mears Middle School, AK

The Classroom Is Like a Bird's Nest

The classroom is like a bird's nest.
The teacher a mother bird teaching hatchlings to fly.
A classroom is the nest,
The place to learn,
When it is time,
For the fledglings to fly,
It is time for the students,
To use what they've learned,
The birds make their own nest,
The students make their own future,
And learn new lessons in a much larger world,
And a new classroom is formed.

Cody Cottrell, Grade 9
Grand Junction High School, CO

Waiting in the Wind

Red stripes against a white background
Blue cornered with white stars
Hangs in every classroom
Reminding us what we really are

We are free
Like the flag that waves to everyone
Who walks by
Watching, waiting, whistling through the wind

Every day
In every way
Telling us what to be
One nation united and free

Never is our nation nothing
Always living in peace
Take a flag as a symbol
Of freedom ringing

Ashley King, Grade 7
Leading Edge Academy - Gilbert, AZ

New Years for All

On December thirty-first, Times Square is full,
Of people all waiting for midnight to make its toll,
The ball finally drops! It's a brand new year,
Fireworks and screaming you can hear.
Parties with champagne are happening now,
While the Chinese are having their own pow-wow.
There's dragons and dancing with family and friends,
The Chinese never want it to end.
With feasts and renewing,
It's all their own doing,
They will all celebrate until they can take it no more.
Red and gold decorations light up the streets
Children get money to buy new year's treats!
Our celebrations may be different you have to admit,
But we all like to party, and everyone knows it.

Samantha Lawlor, Grade 7
Dunstan Middle School, CO

Gasoline

Gasoline is dangerous,
it can explode,
that's why I use it,
to burn down my clothes.
Gasoline can burn,
it really smells,
when I am out,
I go to Shell.
For my big truck,
it costs lots of money,
for my toy car,
I use the Energizer Bunny.

Andrew Doiron, Grade 7
La Center Middle School, WA

Left Overs

Left overs are gross,
all sloppy and cold.
But we still eat them,
when they're five weeks old.
I don't like old tuna,
spinach or macaroni.
And even when heated,
it just tastes so phony.
We try to hide them,
but we always fail.
And in the end,
Mom always prevails.

Jennifer Reynolds, Grade 7
La Center Middle School, WA

In My Head

C an't stop my imagination
D on't try, you'll always fail
E very time I'm in my head
F airy tales come to life
  With dragons, and pixies,
  and so much more.

Amelia Jerome, Grade 8
Heath Middle School, CO

The Wrath of Tybalt

Warlike fiery eyes,
To ones surprise;
He wields a sword,
Off evil he will ward.
Only to protect his name,
His family hath no shame;
Though for his family to remain,
There must now be pain.
To protect his good lord,
Their blood his reward;
Hear his battle cries,
His warlike fiery eyes.

Brandon Neely, Grade 9
Fremont Jr High School, AZ

Who I Am

I'm the girl who falls head-over-heels for a guy
But she can never say the right thing to make them even stumble
The one who everyone sees as "Katie's" little sister
The one everyone sees as only a friend
I was never popular
Every grade I got was for hard work
I have to work extra to be good at anything
But one thing I know
I am original I am me and I can take it
I have been to heck and back
I would love to see someone break me

Crysta Robinson, Grade 9
Havre High School, MT

What Is It?

I saw something today, while I was walking home.
Something that caught my eye.
Not quite what I see every day.
But yet something I hear about a lot.
When seeing this, I came closer…waiting to feel this strange object.
It felt so…smooth…like air…yet…not quite.
It smelled so pure…just like rain…but, yet swampy in a way.
It tasted so rich and clean…like newly fallen rain.
It sounded silent, with occasional sounds of "trickles."
Something very confusing at first glance.
Something so very simple in a way.
Then I realized…after a while…it is a pond.

Shania Hill, Grade 7
Sterling Middle School, CO

Childhood

Running, jumping, trying to fly,
Flinging from swings, rising so high
A little fishpond holds the color of the sky
Bouquets of cotton candy slowly pass by
Cramped in the corner stands the little tool shed
Its splintery pieces were once apple red
Dinner with friends on the deck out back
Is that the tenth humming bird? It's too hard to keep track
The tall shady maple opens her arms to me
I catch a glimpse of her large trunk. She is a magnificent tree
I sit on the porch eating my ants on a log
Celery, peanut butter, raisins, worries without a fog
Warm humid summers, cool breezy springs
Warm browns in fall, waiting for what winter brings
I think I am invincible. Never to ever die
Secretly the thought of death brings a tear to my eye
When the stars begin shining, I skip to my bed
Now to the land of dreams I will soon be led
I waken. Still with the thought of growing old quietly bringing dread
Washing that from my mind I must happily look ahead.

Natalia Hankins, Grade 9
Tempe Preparatory Academy, AZ

I Believe

Life is a highway
Be brave enough to ride it
Never ending, not knowing where you'll end up
Life is a roller coaster
Being brave
Not knowing what's going to happen next
Up or down just get through it
I believe that
You don't follow your dreams
You can chase them
Live life to the absolute fullest
Life is a bucking bronco
Trying to knock you off
Just hang on
Life is like biting into an apple
Not knowing if it is sweet or sour
Just living life
Where ever you may end up
In the end
You will be rewarded

Celina Day, Grade 7
21st Century Public Academy, NM

My Christmas Day

There I was waiting to open my presents
With all my family waiting 'til 12:00
Seeing the presents anxious to see
Hearing the music sounds of Christmas songs
There I was waiting 'til 12:00
Before getting some presents and unwrapping them all
Sitting there seeing the brightness and the lights
Of my wonderful Christmas tree

Yesenia Sanchez, Grade 7
Somerton Middle School, AZ

I Am

I am an English rider
                      I am a Western rider
          We ride
I trot
                      I jog
          We ride
I canter
                      I lope
          We ride
I wear breeches
                      I wear chaps
          We ride
I use a crop
                      I use spurs
          We ride
I ride English
                      I ride Western
       We both love horses

Shelby Hughes, Grade 7
Elk Ridge Middle School, UT

Friends

Friends will be there till the end.
They will stick together side by side.
Friends will never fade or bend.

We love each other as sisters.
Friends will help you in times of need.
Friends will be there till the end.

They go to the park and hang out.
They laugh and have fun.
Friends will never fade or bend.

Friends will trust you.
Friends will love you.
Friends will be there till the end.

Friends will bring you soup when you're sick.
You will give them food if they have none.
Friends will never fade or bend.

You can talk or gossip with them.
You can trust them and share your secrets.
Friends will be there till the end.
Friends will never fade or bend.

Emily Lovern, Grade 8
Cedar Park Christian School – Everett Campus, WA

The Sun

Can you move? The sun is in my eyes
No because it looks so beautiful in them
The sun is like me
Here forever assuring you a new day has risen
Saves you from a world of darkness
Not capable of leaving for too long
The sun's like you
Sending happiness throughout the world
Shining beauty upon all
Giving life to many things
The sun is like us
Strong, bold and willing to shine passed any obstacle
To be defeated by nothing
But to be cherished every moment it lasts
The sun is like us

Brittany Borré, Grade 9
Queen Creek High School, AZ

The Ocean

Whoosh goes the waves, splashing on the shore,
Ouch, the sand is hot under your feet,
Hey look, a seagull that plunged into the crystal clear water,
Ohh I found a purple shell; it smells of the salty sea water,
A girl dives into the cool ocean waves,
Laughing, laughing, having fun in the ocean.

Deryn Cattaneo, Grade 7
Ernest Becker Middle School, NV

Snowflakes

Snowflakes
Intricate, small
Drifting, floating, soaring
Creating massive mounds of snow
Crystals

Torri Duncan, Grade 7
Sky Vista Middle School, CO

Boxes

You sit here, wanting to leave,
but time won't allow it.
Too much responsibility
and too much weight.
All this sitting on you,
so your shoulders
BREAK.
But thank God for the music.
The way it seeps
into your brain and into your soul.
It glides effortlessly
weaving together tattered ends.
It's like you have boxes.
And they're all empty
with pain,
with sorrow.
But the music fills them.
The lyrics lock them up.
So you shove them aside
and pretend to only hear
safety.

Samantha Burkett, Grade 9
Roosevelt High School, WA

Childhood

Toys laying all on the floor,
Crayon drawings on the door.
All subjects I must explore,
Above the sky my mind did soar.
Always asking "how?" or, "why?"
Wondering, "must I comply?"
My sleep time was always eight,
'Cause 9 o'clock was just too late.
Sleeping, running, breathing, playing.
"let's have fun!" was our one saying.
Pink ice cream with jellybeans,
Birds and ponies in my dreams.
Having playtime all day long.
School was just all fun and song.
But soon older, we grew more.
Not as fun as life before.
Our minds never again soared high,
And nonstop fun was soon to die.
When childhood leaves, we all must sigh,
And to our past we say: "goodbye!"

Pooja Nair, Grade 9
Tempe Preparatory Academy, AZ

How Can I Know?

How can I know that you are really there for me?
How can I believe you when you say you love me?
How can I know that you will really miss me when I'm gone?
How can I know that you believe in me?
How can I know that you trust me?

This world we live in has come to even the closest friends
not even knowing if they love each other and can trust each other.
In fact we are taught by society that we can't.
Our world has taught us that believing in someone
will lead to disappointment and loving someone will leave us brokenhearted.

The truth is that to live life to the fullest you must always trust,
always believe, and love someone with your whole heart.
You can never live life to its greatest unless you do this.
Leave a legacy that is worth being remembered for,
there is no way to know how it will turn out,
but you just have to believe in yourself, in each other and in Christ,
that is how you will know.

Jessica Reinert, Grade 7
Albuquerque Christian School, NM

Importance of Family

my family is like a tool box
my dad is like the hinges of the tool box keeping us all together
my mom is like the hammer as hard as nails
my brother is like the wrench fixing all of the mistakes
my cat is like the paint of the tool box always messing the house up
but this is a very strong tool box that will always be together
these tools will never be separated and will always be together
as our family will never be separated and will always be together

Christopher Wojtowitz, Grade 7
Molasky Jr High School, NV

Friendship

When you told me I was your best friend I jumped for joy.
I thought I could tell you anything and it would be safe.
I thought wrong.
When you said I was your best friend I took it seriously.
I was there when you were sad,
When you were happy,
Crying and depressed. I listened to it all
When I didn't agree with you,
When it didn't matter to me. I listened because for once I was a best friend
I knew it was a lie.
When I spilled out my problems and you didn't listen,
I knew it was a lie
When I did something you didn't agree with and you walked away.
You walked away and left behind a best friend.
But that's ok.
It doesn't bother me now.
Someone new calls me a best friend
I know it's real because I say back to them:
You are my best friend.

Chantel Romero, Grade 8
J O Combs Middle School, AZ

Television and Life

I don't know what it is,
but every time I look at it,
it brings back memories of
happy and sad thoughts,
hardships, and laughter,
hatred, joy, and fear.
The television.
The thing about the television is
it's a tool of emotions.
Sometimes it's funny and
sometimes it's dull and boring.
Life is also.
It can be wavy,
or be turning, never knowing where
you're going to end up —
Wondering if you're ever going to get past the commercials.
TV,
life,
can be interesting,
you just need to know the right channel for you.

Danny Bakken, Grade 7
St Pauls Catholic School, ID

The Distant Light

There is a light a beacon on the shore
its light has guided many sailors on the sea
Through mist of storms
it still can be seen
The distant beacon on the shore

It's light stands scenic and majestic
in towering buildings and monuments
In ancient times the mariners
went from sea shore to sea shore
knowing a harbor was safe
and that the lighthouse would guide
them safely to their journey's end

The ships flag flapping in the breeze
the groan of the ropes and the wood
the sound of the scurrying and shouting
as the ship slips from view
It will be back in a year full of goods and riches
as homesick sailors descend the gang plank

Dallin Vance, Grade 9
Mountain Ridge Jr High School, UT

Giraffes

They come in yellow and brown,
They come with extremely long necks,
Making weird noises and making people smile,
Being lazy and eating greens,
That's just how they roll.

Sarah Francisco, Grade 8
Round Valley Middle School, AZ

Untitled

There, on mountain high,
Beckoning sadly,
Let out mournful sign
Those of old
Doomed forever to wave on tired souls
Their wings unfold,
They take to the sky
Banished from the world of mortals,

Tears fall from the diamond eyes of the ethereal
Wings point towards the firmament
And feathered scales drift to earth
A last memento to the hopeless.

Jenaya Fowler, Grade 9
Home School, ID

What Would I Do Without Mom?*

She gets us out of bed,
Makes sure we're all fed,
Oh the many books she has read,
What would I do without Mom?

She uses the army-tank of a washing machine,
And makes sure all our clothes are clean,
And has not a streak of mean,
What would I do without Mom?

She packs me every day a lunch,
And keeps a house with this big bunch,
And when we have a bad day, gets that "mother's hunch,"
What would I do without Mom?

She opens her arms into a loving hug,
And picks up each one of us little bugs,
And shows a smile when on her apron someone tugs,
What would we do without Mom?

Tayler Knudsen, Grade 7
Sky Vista Middle School, CO
*As a thank you for all she does

Memorable Wounds

The memories I have
of you aren't enough.
The cold mornings you wake up to.
The color blue is your favorite color.
I loved you so much, but this
is how you repay me.

You've moved on,
but I still wait for you.
I visit you every day
and leave flowers where you rest.
When you left, you took my tears with you.
I'll leave but won't come back.

Eric Labra, Grade 7
Syringa Middle School, ID

Outside

Monkeys in trees
Lions in bushes
Bears in caves
And dogs on leashes

Sitting on the porch
Waiting for the wind to blow
Cats hiding
Dogs barking

What a wonderful place to be
Cars are screeching
Kids are having fun
Parents waiting for the day to be done

The sun is setting
The kids are yawning
Parents falling asleep
Still a wonderful place to be

Ciara Snyder, Grade 7
Shadow Ridge Middle School, CO

Snowboarding

It's the funnest sport in the snow
when it's choppy I go slow

It's no fun when it's icy
It's no fun when it's dicey

It's a lot of fun when there's powder
when you go faster you scream louder

When you hit trees
you fall on your knees

If you hit a jump
you hit your head and get a lump

When you're going down the mountain
You could really use a Gatorade fountain

When you're in the air
You can see people everywhere

Michael Marugg, Grade 7
La Center Middle School, WA

Pride

Basketball
Is the best sport ever
Playing it
Gives me a sense of pride
On the court
Running, shooting, blocking
Working hard.

Rex Hamblin, Grade 8
Round Valley Middle School, AZ

Shine

Some wear strings of gold to show they are important.
Others rely on intelligence, for their hearts are full of arrogance,
to the fools you can be sure.
I'll seek for a better heart full of love and life and more.
More strength to show a better way,
more love to soften hearts,
more time to take to do your life's work,
more time to laugh and play.
The selfish hearts of others are buried in their pits.
They waste away their closed off lives when it could be full of this!
So while you preach your love and care I'm walking in your wake,
I'm following right behind
because I seek for a better life.
It's not a waste of time.

Shannon Jones, Grade 8
Brockbank Jr High School, UT

I Dance

In the hollow of the August moon,
Where birds fly in the lights of June's past.
The breathing of dawn brings the dance of life,
The see is reborn, the ray of the sun is dancing upon the Earth.
All that lives is born again and the dance will continue.
I breathe, I dance, I live, I am what I am.
I am music, I dance, I dance, I dance,
I dance with rhythm the soul of Earth,
I dance with joy for when some can't.
In the circle of life there are animals everywhere and we are one.
For if we fail to connect as one.
We all were made for loving and being helpful to others
Even whales and even otters.
I love us all! I pray for us all!
Amen!

Annatje M. Haner, Grade 7
Lied Middle School, NV

Dream Gone

Have you ever had a dream gone
 Or does it rise at the crack of dawn?

 Does it itch like a piece of hay
 Or does it simply just go away?

 Does it build like a child's blocks
 And then slowly fade away like chicken pox?

 Do you say "I want this"
 And they say "No" and give you a kiss?

 Do you come back in hope of more
 Then they say "Leave it be, dear Cor."

Cora Marrama, Grade 7
Dunstan Middle School, CO

Flight

Up! Up! Up! We went like gravity didn't exist.
It was like magic as this giant metal bird took off to the sky.
I looked through the window upon the busy city.
I gazed upon the clouds.
I stared at the wide open plains.
And I was in awe at the beauty of the sea.
I felt as if I was flying myself.
As if I was a bird.
Then I remembered I was still on a plane.

André Lang, Grade 9
Lakewood High School, CO

The Life of an Apple

The golden speckled apple crunching in the distance,
Sour yet sweet you can barely use resistance,

It's almost round but not quite,
It's size, not too small but just right,

With sleek, fresh sides,
Its solid body can't hide,

You feel its soft skin in your hand,
Nearly everyone is a fan,

You take a large, refreshing bite,
Now the round apple must say goodnight.

Amanda Bull, Grade 9
Xavier College Preparatory School, AZ

Not Playing

I first practiced after that joyful day
On the blacktop
Hoped to be there all day

Now I've moved indoors
Much nicer courts
Also I'm safe, when the rain pours

Still spend most of my time there
Practice and play
Even if it hurts, wouldn't rather be anywhere

They tell me I'm good
But to be great
I have always worked as hard as I could

Said I could make it to the top of the game
I can only not make it happen
So everybody will know my name

Going to fight every mile
I am not playing
Because it's a lifestyle

Jacob Stein, Grade 7
Lincoln Jr High School, CO

Burned

I stealthily opened the screen door,
Careful not to breathe or make any sudden sound.
I just had to catch him in the act.

My little eight year old self questioned why
I hadn't known this in the first place.

I crept on to the deck,
And there, slouched in the corner,
A dragon stood

Puffing out rings of smoke.

Daddy?
The dragon turned, blue eyes fiery,
Face softening.

Hi, baby, it whispered.

Eva Hall, Grade 7
Mandalay Middle School, CO

Dawn

Dawn is beautiful
The fog outside the window
Downy flakes falling.

The roads are slushy
Covered with the wet mixture
Everything is wet.

The flakes keep falling
They fall very wet and large
Blanketing the trees.

Chris Teglas, Grade 9
Coal Ridge High School, CO

Basketball

Crowd screaming
Players positioning
The game begins with a tip

Sweat falling
Scores rising
Their hearts pounding hard
Like thunder on a clear day

Warm blood boiling
Jersey blowing
The ball is snatched by a winning teammate

Hearts beating
Players crying
Only the best will win the game.

Hannah Palmer, Grade 9
Timberline Middle School, UT

Back Stabbers

The pain in your back
The blood spills out
The pain draws tears
The thought makes you shiver
You crawl into your shack
You sit and whine and pout
You look at him with wrathful leers

Happiness sadness
You give them no thought
Who could guess?
There is a traitor who we fought

It takes you back
Cruel reality gets you
Go to your shack, make plans for battle
Bid him adieu.
Estes Weeks, Grade 8
Zia Middle School, NM

Ocean of Red

Love is like an ocean,
An ocean of red.

It loves to take motion,
And is small like a thread.

Love seeks everyone,
And everyone seeks love.

It goes by the sun,
And is soft like a dove.
Christopher D. Oldeschulte, Grade 8
Rim Country Middle School, AZ

Colors?

Lime green isn't my only favorite color
   There's
Hot Pink
   Neon Orange
     Light Blue
Eccentric
   Always on your toes
    Let's Party and
      There's always more

Not only are there colors to define you
   There are friends to remind you
     So let your colors shine

Maybe his!
Maybe hers!
Maybe mine!
Brittney Toms, Grade 8
Culver Middle School, OR

Painful Situation

Seeing you blue and purple
watching you lay in that hospital bed
now you're gone
now I'm
wishing upon the moon that
one day I'll be able to see you soon
I loved waking up to see your face
but now you're gone
in a better place
you're not suffering anymore
I love you so,
it seems like yesterday
when you left us all
now you're watching us from above
Brianna Garner, Grade 7
21st Century Public Academy, NM

High School

Take a look around,
Appreciate what you've got
You won't win every championship
You won't pass every test
Sometimes it seems like no one cares
But all you need to do is open your eyes.
Life is short, but high school is shorter.
They say live life to the fullest,
So live high school the best you can.
It's just a phase to start your life,
So give it all you've got!
Rebecca Peatross, Grade 9
Duchesne High School, UT

Cats

My favorite pet is a cat.
Sometimes I dress them in silly hats.

I go to bed with them at night.
When I wake up I see them in sight.

Cats have always seemed to love me.
Even when they need.

Even when they die I look for love.
All I have to do is look above.

Some are orange, some are white,
When they get scared cats hide.

Cats are dumb, but sometimes smart.
Their cousins are above the food chart.

Once again cats are my favorite pet,
Cats are the greatest, that's my bet!
KC Johnson, Grade 7
La Center Middle School, WA

These Days

These days,
I hear constantly,
Of the evils in the world,
I hear of murder,
And war.
Death,
And deception.
Loss,
And failure.
I question,
Is there any good in the world?
Is life worth living?
I look around,
I see a family,
A mother,
A father,
A sister,
And a chubby little dog.
Love seems to emanate from them.
Is there any good in the world?
I think there is.
Connor Holbert, Grade 7
Villa Montessori School – Phoenix, AZ

Just Because I'm a Guy

Just because I'm a guy.
I'm not lazy.
I'm not barbaric.
I'm not a pig.
Just because I'm a guy.
I don't love racing more than anything.
I don't love war.
I don't love leaving the toilet seat up.
Just because I'm a guy.
Why should it matter.
Is being a girl that much better.
What is life without guys.
Daniel McKune, Grade 7
Dunstan Middle School, CO

Memories

shards of thought
meanings of dreams
memories
parts of life
good or bad
memories
times to share
times to hide
memories
a soft touch
a burning flame
memories
Preston Court, Grade 7
Sky Vista Middle School, CO

Beautiful Loneliness

People always tell me I'm beautiful,
I want him to see the real me today.
Being beautiful is nothing to him.
Beauty means nothing if I can't have him.
Loneliness is beauty, lovely blue
sadness creeping over to swallow me up.
Eyelids like blushing lotuses, beauty to the beholder.
Look at me, only me, see…
Drawing me in toward your lips, kiss me.
Love, I don't understand teach me, please Amor.
My untidy heart beats louder when you come,
in my eyes your beauty not me
Hold me tight to your heart…close.
I'm a new fledgling with these feelings inside of me, flying.

Melisa Ramirez, Grade 9
Clark High School, NV

Hurt

I feel it in the pit of my gut.
Hate, Vengeance, and rage all riddle my head.
Annoying like a tiny paper cut.
Plotting ways to get back for what she said.
I don't understand how she could do this.
And I loved her with all I had.
With our relationship in complete bliss.
I didn't think it would make me this mad.
I really tried to hold back all the hate.
She deserves everything and has to pay.
I can't help it with being so irate.
There was nothing more she could do or say.
Thank God it's all over now.
It's time to let go; I'm just not sure how.

Jesse Gage, Grade 9
Clark High School, NV

Black

Dark
Depressing
Yet subtle
The night sky's hidden trait
A Halloween's night
Bad luck's national color
Splendor as well
A wall to hide
With those who thrive
On the deep, dark, depressing, satisfactory poetry of all colors
That lives within the skin of all of us
The fresh, clean, deep, emotion
Feelings of expression
Filled with hatred
My color,
Black

Tatiana Carrier, Grade 7
Sky Vista Middle School, CO

Love

What's love?
Beating heart
Sweaty palms
Sighs
Affectionate glances
Unexplainable feelings
That's love

Mackinzi Taylor, Grade 7
Sedona Charter School, AZ

Sadness

Sadness shows when something's wrong or broken
Sadness is showing someone that you care
Sadness is a tear falling off a young girl's face
Even though no one is noticing
The girl keeps a smile
Sadness is love for someone that's dying
And doesn't want to do anything to stop it
Sadness is a little child's face
Sitting on the floor, crying

Sadness is the look in the little girl's eyes
When she looks at you
Sadness means what the other person feels
When they see something is wrong
Sadness is meant to show
But only when that person wants to show it
Sometimes people cry,
Others just hold it in, waiting to burst

People need to know when to let it out
And others to keep it in
Sadness needs courage to make it better
If no one knows, how can they help?

Autumn Peterson, Grade 9
Granite High School, UT

White River

Dear River,
You have seen me in the state of joy and filled with sunshine
You have carried me down your white waters
You have endured my anger
And caught my rocks, boiling with rage,
Gently in your rapids
You have been frustrated with my behavior
And fought back
Scraping my knees with your knives made of stone
Your beaches have welcomed my muddy feet
And your thorny twigs have moved aside for my toes
You have shown me your deer, fish, and bugs
Providing me with hours of interest
You have given me a place to swim with your fish
You have given me a doorway
Into your secret paradise.

Erin Flagg, Grade 7
Rosemont Ridge Middle School, OR

Hayti

Swishing corn leaves
under our eves

Quiet fields of corn
and field of grass
for cattle and horses

I will never forget
the sound of swishing corn
and a car horn
the mooing of cattle too

Grasses swishing
we are wishing
that our time here
will never end

Cornstalks bend
time we spend
with work and play

We are yet to harvest hay
from the seeds we planted in May

Stacey Talaro, Grade 7
La Center Middle School, WA

Wondering

Sealed with a kiss,
but never sent
never around,
but always missed.

All that's left is a dent,
a dent in my heart
always being drowned,
by the loneliness within.

Never being apart,
not knowing when to love
or even where to begin
so very much confused.

Being pushed and shoved
leaving pieces of my heart bruised
not finding out how I'll be treated.
Love is undefeated.

Cynthia Binetti, Grade 9
Queen Creek High School, AZ

Love

I wonder what love is.
What is it supposed to mean?
Is it a feeling, a joke, a tribal ritual?
Is love a word to say or…to feel?

Sandra Mendoza, Grade 7
Phoenix Preparatory Academy, AZ

The Mountains

I can see the sun glistening off the mountains,
making it look like diamonds shining everywhere,
I could hear the trees swooshing in the breeze, as if they were making music,
You could hear the waves of the rivers,
They sound like fish are making bubbles and they are popping in the water,
I can sit on the side of the mountain and watch the sunset,
it looks like fire blazing down into the ground ending a perfect day.

Destri Pena, Grade 8
Round Valley Middle School, AZ

Dusk

It's cold
Around me falls golden leaves crippled and old
They twist through the darkening wood
Whose biological aspects are rarely understood
Through the bare skeletal branches the sun takes fleeting glances
There is a soft crunch as a trespasser takes willing chances
A sudden sound silence seems to hold a breath
As a small heart is heard alarmingly distressed
Shrill cry
Quick fly
Make haste for soon will come dusk
With hope of a fresh taste
A string is released
Now it is dark
The day is no more
For it has hit its mark.

Leticia S. Wilson, Grade 7
Davis Middle School, WY

The Night Is Long

The night is long the morning is very well expected
I'm tossing and turning in my bed way more anxious than I detected

The house is still dark everyone's asleep
I'm wide awake but must not make a peep

It must be at least 6:30 I look at the clock
It's 2:00 a.m. Wow that's really early

I fall back asleep sugar plums are dancing in my head
I'm dreaming of the perfect Christmas suddenly my brother pulls me off my bed

It's 7:00 the sky foggy, but bright
My nerves are screaming "Time to open presents, all right?"

I see colored wrappings of presents all dolled up and pretty
Big ones and small ones now my head is dizzy

Christmas morning is so much fun
To tear open presents until everyone is done

This Christmas morning as you wake up remember the true meaning
Which is Christ's birth and the sincerity of his giving

Whitney Slade, Grade 9
Stapley Jr High School, AZ

What Is Red?

Is red a rose with a smell so sweet?
Or is it the blush that colors your cheeks?
Maybe it's your beating heart
Or the blood pulsing through your veins.

Is red just a color, or is it something more?
The flowing blood, the pain and the hurt.
The ruby set in the gold ring.
The dress for the Latin dance.

Does it make you feel alive?
Is it romance and passion?
Or is it nothing but a pigment
In the evening sky?
What is red?

Heather Shulsen, Grade 9
Preston High School, ID

My Pet and My Friend

Best friends are always there for you
And they comfort you when you're not well.
A person can have many best friends.

One of my best friends has the qualities of many others,
And I love him like he's family;
But I guess you could say he's different
From some other best friends.

This one friend in particular,
He chases after his toys I throw,
And those he also chews.
His ears are real soft like a newborn's skin,
And his tail would wag in circles like a race car ready to win,
Showing his joy to be home.

This best friend of mine is my dog,
With spots like freckles climbing up from his paws
And sprinkled all upon his back.

They say that "man's best friend is his dog"
And this can be considered true;
But my best friend dog is like family too.

Mary Semon, Grade 7
St Elizabeth Ann Seton Catholic School, AZ

Taste of Freedom

The moon shone the brightest in the night sky.
Fireflies rose from their dwelling and flew high
The tiny yellow lights under the luminous light
But something was wrong, something was wrong
A brighter light came closer to them
These flies went into a jar guided by a lamp
They were trapped.
Freedom was now long gone.

Shung Chai, Grade 7
Les Bois Jr High School, ID

Unspoken Emotions

You are in my head each and every day.
I dream and think about you in my sleep.
I'm afraid to tell you, what will you say?
There are feelings here that lay very deep.
Three words to describe how I truly feel.
Three easy words, but they just won't come out.
These words that will make my broken heart heal.
These emotions are real; there is no doubt.
Emotions that only my heart can tell.
I want to tell you, I want you to know.
It is hard to say, you must listen well,
I want to hold you and never let go.
Every time I see you my heart falls through.
I am just trying to say I love you.

Janice Bautista, Grade 9
Clark High School, NV

Dreamz

I fall asleep, sound asleep and dream.
Dream of days on the beach, and nights
on the
town.
Dream of
people and
cars,
of slaves
working hard.
Of dancing
in the
rain
and watching
stars
go by.
I dream
and dream
until I wake.
I go to school and play with friends, but I can't
wait 'til night. To see where my dreams will take me…

Cali Heber, Grade 7
Diamond Fork Jr High School, UT

Wild Wonder

Leaves the color of charcoal,
Branches as arms reaching for stars.
Undergrowth entangled like a spider's web,
Pools of water surround all.
Splash, splash.

Oak tree stand tall,
Wind calm down.
Yet another day awaits.
Mighty oak forest be still.

Kassi Spinnie, Grade 8
Chehalis Middle School, WA

Love

Love, what is this so called emotion that so many have experienced, and yet, so hard to explain?
This indescribable emotion that so many have driven into madness, obscurity, and rarely happiness.
Flourishing at moments unknown,
Causing actions in a surprise…
Given a burden to some, and a flash of serene bliss for others
Pushing them through a darkened cave of love,
And in conclusion,
Is where the true feelings are shown.
The veil that's hidden,
Seeing nothing but transformations and despondences of this emotion.
Transformations that leads to torture,
Despondences that leads to despair…
Hoping that anything could pull us through this time of depression
While the beholders reach the ending of this so called hole,
Veils are lifted, the love one flies
And love? Well isn't so much love anymore until we find ourselves a new veil to fall under.
And for those few lucky people whose veil has never been lifted,
Who have encountered that unconditional love,
Where they have each other,
"To have and to hold, from this day forward, for better or worse, in sickness or in health,
to love and cherish, till death do us apart."

Sandra Luu, Grade 8
Cimarron Springs Elementary School, AZ

The Battle Between Friends

This battle ground, the constant shooting,
It's from the rise to the set of the sun,
Beginning in the day and continuing, throughout the night, never stopping
This battle began many moons ago.
I stand caught between the shots fired
Now a choice is left to me: pull the trigger, or let them go,
Run out between them and suddenly show
The friendly bond they both once had
I took a deep breath and ran into the mist of the bullets
But one shot was fired from the side I knew best; they never felt bad.
It hit me without warning, the pain was a shock, not once were they sad,
The side that had shot was so easily fazed,
For I left the middle with ease,
And through this day and this thick haze,
They witnessed me leave them forever and they were amazed,
One shot, one careless shot, from someone I knew so well,
Hurt me more than once, and once is a lot.
I went to the side with their weapons down, and stopped every shot
No more did the side I'm with shoot, but the other did with anger and rage,
They thought I had been stolen from them, and so they shot.
No more did we worry about their shots. We turned and left, and that was the shot we shot!!

Dallas Kelton, Grade 8
Grangeville Elementary/Middle School, ID

Dark Cell

I spend endless time shackled in chains in a pitch black cell with nameless terrors, and no one to keep me company I could hear prisoners talk about the dark cell and how guards stuff men into the cage, when I stood up I knew it was over I couldn't breathe the harder I tried the faster I panted I'd lost the power to calm myself I'm fighting to control my terror I've kicked walls, and cried "I can't breathe."

Loren Thomas, Grade 7
Somerton Middle School, AZ

Truth

Forever lost in the words of the people around me.
Trapped in the lies of my so-called friends.
If only to free this caged angel from the fiery hell that awaits.
Can't wait till I am the words trapped in your sentence.
Don't let these tears consume you,
Although they have consumed me.
Lost in the mixed emotions of myself and everyone around me.
Doesn't anyone love me?
Left here to fend me,
How could anyone understand a girl like this?
This angel is forced to be strong enough for everyone,
Lacking the power to be strong for myself.
I, she, we,
We're all just a face, a voice, a name,
forced to be anything,
but me.

Cassie Anderson, Grade 8
Mountain Ridge Middle School, CO

Endings Create New Beginnings

Terrible scene of destructive fire,
Burning human flesh as fuel,
Peaceful eye of the horrid tornado,
Gives you hope before tearing you down,
Rumbling sound of feared thunder,
Reminding you of the lighting strike before,
Fierce shaking of Earthquakes,
Smashing everything we hold dear,
Seeing water recede knowing what will come,
Too many bones ache to move to high ground,
High waves crashing down upon the land,

Taking everything it touches back to the sea.

Lauren Bobo, Grade 9
Canyon View Jr High School, UT

Conscience

The small voice in your head that tells you what's responsible
Has been there through it all.
From your smallest mistakes,
To when you're struggling at the side of the road.
It's told you how well you've done in the past,
And how strong you can be in the future.
When you take that voice for granted,
It's like you've disowned a relative,
Or like being lost in a forest
Or having no one there to comfort you.
When you listen to that voice,
Everything seems obvious.
The problematic becomes simple.
When you listen to that voice,
You are listening to God.

Melanie Vande Brake, Grade 7
St Pauls Catholic School, ID

Into the Sunset

I have a young Arabian mare
with a winter coat as soft as cotton
her mane blows with the wind
as she runs like a leopard
stalking its prey
the half moon on her forehead
shines like a star at night
I slide in the saddle on her
and she knows
it's time to work not play
she neighs like a child
who doesn't want to go to school
she tries to fight away from me
when I try to put the bit in her mouth
when I mount her it feels like nothing matters
just she and I
riding away into the sunset
wondering what tomorrow will bring

Paulena Martinez, Grade 9
Menaul School, NM

Grandma Terri

I remember my grandma Terri
I remember her being my best friend
I remember going to Kohls and Chilis
I remember her sleeping over on Christmas
I remember her leaving on October 11, 2006

Ashlyn Hoffman, Grade 7
Sagewood Middle School, CO

In a Perfect World

In a perfect world,
There would be no pain,
No hurt, no shame, no sin.
There would be smiles,
Laughter, friends, and perfect families.

But instead we have a world with war,
With each other, within ourselves.
Some wars have death and grief.
Some are just mental,
And we must fight to travel the path which is right.

But that is not the point,
The point is that our world is not perfect,
Neither are we.
But we can smile, laugh, and seek pleasure,
To make the world better.
So if all we think about are the bad things:
War, grief, pain,
Then that is all we'll see in this world.
Yet if we focus on the good things:
Smiles, laughter, families,
That is what our world will be.

Bethany Piehl, Grade 7
Evergreen Middle School, WA

Love

Love is a wonderful thing,
It always makes your heart go ding.
Though I don't know why,
It feels like you want to fly.
Don't even think to compare,
Because you never need to prepare,
For what love can do to you.
Love is like a star
It is an open book
Very far.
Love is the color red,
So this color has to be fed,
Love can always be found,
No matter how many pounds
That are in mounds
Of perfect love.

Jacqueline Wrobel, Grade 7
North Middle School, CO

Family

My family is an ocean
My dad is a shark
He is strong and protects my family
My mom is the clown fish
She makes my whole family laugh
My sister is a crab
She is always trying to hurt me
My dog is a sea turtle
She seems to always be a tired, shy dog
I am a dolphin
I am always happy and jumping around
My family is an ocean

Sallie Croissant, Grade 7
Eaton Middle School, CO

Remember

As the sun sinks low in the fiery sky,
I think about my life,
and how it's quickly gone by.
Just yesterday I was a little girl,
spinning and playing
without a care in the world.
And as the years went by,
stress was added on.
Sometimes I wondered,
if it was worth going on.
But along with the bad times,
there was also good.
The love and hope,
that surrounded me day by day,
From my friends and my family
caring for me,
in every,
possible way.

Rachel Egging, Grade 8
Shadow Ridge Middle School, CO

I Wish

I wish someone would have told me about you,
I wish someone would have told me not to trust you,
I wish someone would have said you will be my friend then forget about me.

I wish someone would have told me about you,
I wish someone would have said not to look up to you,
I wish someone would have said that to you I mean nothing.

I wish someone would have told me about you,
I wish someone would have told me that you really don't care,
I wish someone would have said not to trust you with my deepest darkest secrets.

I with someone would have told me about you,
I wish someone would have told me not to take your advice,
I wish someone would have told me that you were going to lie to me like that.

Danielle Waller, Grade 9
Buhl High School, ID

Bird and Fish

I am a bird

    I am a fish

I fly in the sky

    I swim in the sea

I lay eggs

    I lay eggs

I am higher than everyone

    I am lower than everyone

I soar through the air current

    I speed through the sea current

I am an animal

    I am an animal

I have wings

    I have fins

The sky is my home

    The sea is my home

Devon Harvey, Grade 7
Elk Ridge Middle School, UT

The Window

She looks outside the window and sees the cars pass her by
She looks outside the window and sees a dog roaming the streets
Can the people that are passing by see me?
She looks outside the window and sees the mailman go by
The mailman looks right at her but he doesn't even smirk
As if she wasn't even there
She looks outside the window and sees her mom's car pull into the drive way
Her mom walks into the house and she just walks on by
The girl says "mom" but the mother did not respond
Her mother starts to cry so the little girl followed her wondering what was wrong
Her mom goes by a family portrait and underneath it there is a picture of the little girl
It says "R.I.P. Hailey" The little girls looked up at the picture and then to her mom
The little girl walked to the window
Hailey looked out the window her final last time.

Chelsea Barzee, Grade 9
Shelley Sr High School, ID

Flowers
A friendship is a flower.
It grows as you water it.
But what it grows into can be
Rather different from what you imagined.
You must shower it with love.
Because if showered with the wrong thing
Like envy and anger,
It will surely wilt and disappear.
Sometimes it's a rose, beauty on top
But danger underneath.
When you take off the gloves
Of fascination,
And discover the thorn that is there,
The flower wilts.
Happiness turns to pain.
Other times the flower is choked
By a weed that is another's vision of a flower.
The weed deceives and ruins the flower
That was beauty.

Christie McKernan, Grade 7
St Thomas More Catholic School, CO

Unknown
Outer-space is a place that we do not know.
A place that many will never go.
With all its stars that shimmer and show.
But what is it that we know?
That the night comes and goes?
That the sun follows the moon every day as if its foe?
That is about all we know.
The rest is as the unknown.

Chelsea Woodrum, Grade 9
Crow High School, OR

The Circle of Life
My life is the entire food chain in one
My hopes and dreams are a hunter,
Striving to lie me down into an eternal slumber

The spear of pain and strife the hunter carries
Tortures me by discouraging my soul
to go after what I want

My ambitions are the buffalo,
Strong, but vulnerable
They are disintegrated by
what I try too hard to achieve

Am I stressing for what I don't want?
If so, I have cheered for the opposing circle of life
I have gone against my very being

The potentially permanent damages frighten me.
I will never be the same again.

Austin Prichard, Grade 7
Eaton Middle School, CO

Grandpa and the Moose
Yellowstone has its tricks,
But Grandpa and moose don't mix.
Walking along with his sack of granola,
Grandpa stopped to rest beneath a canola.
He threw his pack loose,
And was snorted at by "the moose."
The moose tore for him, roaring like the sea.
Grandpa turned to flee.
The only place was the tree.
The rest is history.
Yellowstone has its tricks,
But Grandpa and moose don't mix.

Jacob Seely, Grade 7
Tahoma Middle School, WA

Death by Homework
I worked long and hard until it was very late.
As the hours passed by, I realized my fate.
My fingers were cramped, and I could do no more.
Homework made my head oh so very sore.
I could feel the end drawing near,
As I took my last breath in fear.
Homework had done me in for sure.
For this problem there was only one cure.

Emily Kortan, Grade 8
Round Valley Middle School, AZ

What Poetry Means to Me
The world of poetry
Is a dazzling array
Of colors,
Pictures,
And endless words,

Endless words that can entangle your mind in a spider's web,
Or caress you as you would a child's cheek,
Words that open the door
To an ancient and unexplored world,
Or bathe your mind in glowing rays of sunlight

Words that hold the peace and silence of a summer lake,
Or the comfort of a meadow breeze
Poetry can be an escape,
From the world of do and don't,
Can and can't

Poetry is a lavender bubble bath
A kiss in the rain,
Timeless as gold,
And beautiful as the glistening diamond,
Poetry is light and peace,
That is what poetry means to me.

Makenzie Head, Grade 9
Mountain Ridge Jr High School, UT

Disneyland

A trip to remember
Was in mid November
When all the trees
Had no leaves
And only a week until December.

I would miss my home,
And my dog T-bone,
But when we got there
I didn't care
For I got an ice cream cone.

I got to hold Mickey's hand,
The time we had was all so grand,
We even saw my big mean sister smile,
But only for a little while,
I really do love Disneyland!
Cassie Hamilton, Grade 8
Chehalis Middle School, WA

Outside

As I walk outside
Into the cool, calm air
The grass seems to be
Slowly swaying without a care
Then comes the giant, glowing sun
He spreads his warmth by
Using the big, bright sunlight
But then as the sun
Slowly begins to set
And the last whoosh of wind
Goes by my face
I take one last breath of
The cool, calm air
And look at swaying grass
I walk home remembering
This was all outside.
Sho Talmadge, Grade 7
Eagle Point Middle School, OR

Thingamabob Whatchamacallit

It's a thingamabob, a geegaw
whatchamacallit, knickinket.
It's one of those things
where you go "Kabloom!" and
you go "neehawhaw!" and
"zooboom!"

It's a thingamabob, it's a rockuttle,
it'll take you to the moon and back,
with a zip, zap, zup, zoom!
Now, here's the count down...
10, 9, 8, 7, 6, 5, 4, 3, 2...1, blast-off!
James Callaway, Grade 7
Mandalay Middle School, CO

Winter

As I ride, I slow to savor,
The beauty, snow still lightly falling
World stopping before my eyes
Snow crunching under my feet
Squirrels running to and fro
Rabbits hopping here and there
Deer nibbling at the bark
Ah, it must be winter here
Ah, it must be winter here
Tyler Forcella, Grade 7
Terry 7-8 School, MT

Lonely Son

The night was dark,
Most dogs barked,
I was alone,
With no home,
I was scared,
Most people stared,
Then I ran,
To nowhere,
It was cold,
Shivering cold,
The night was freezing,
Like an ice cube,
I felt warm,
When I heard,
A voice,
Calling me,
And saying,
Come home,
Boom,
It was a dream,
A great dream.
Tony Hoang, Grade 8
Ortega Middle School, CO

Austin Much

Austin
Strong, handsome, adventurous, funny.
Son of Eric and Brandi.
Friend of many.
Who feels lucky to be alive.
Lucky to have a family.
Lucky to have friends.
Who fears nothing,
Nothing at all,
Nothing in the world.
Who would like to have a great career.
Travel more.
Be famous.
Resident of Butte, Montana.
Much
Austin Much, Grade 8
East Middle School, MT

Hockey

We get to the rink ready to go
Excitement and nerves growing large.
We go outside to warm-up
Then we put our gear on.
Game plan is explained.
We start warm-ups.
Butterflies
We cheer
Win!
Madison Nikkel, Grade 8
Beacon Country Day School, CO

Ode to My Grandma

The smell of her was very unique
she was one of a kind
She said I was her pride and joy,
The reason she lived.
She always gave us hugs as if there
was no tomorrow.
Thinking of others was her specialty.
She could never stop with loving,
always hugging me or kissing me.
My grandma and her brooches,
She loved wearing different ones.
She loved seeing our smiling faces.
The way she held me was a fantasy
she was like a huge teddy bear
that you always wanted to hold.
Ode to my grandma,
May she rest in peace.
Hunter Null, Grade 8
La Plata Middle School, NM

Lost Friend

May you finally become
In others' eyes,
What you are to us.

May you enjoy life to the fullest,
Even if it has been
The cruelest of all
Cruel things,
To you and to us.

May you be blessed
With care
And understanding
From the world around you;
The people, the items,
And all the cruelness
Turning to care
For you,
My dear friend.
Monica Muncy, Grade 7
Syringa Middle School, ID

I Am

I am sweet and funny
I wonder what I will do when I'm older
I hear music playing
I see animals at the zoo
I want a new cell phone
I am sweet and funny

I imagine a peaceful world
I feel happy
I touch my 7 year old brother, Colten
I worry about my sister
I cry when my family leaves or goes away
I am sweet and funny

I understand friends lie
I say there should be peace on earth
I dream to have a big house in New York one day
I try on my school work
I hope to get a great job and make lots of money one day
I am sweet and funny

Emily Thompson, Grade 7
Shadow Ridge Middle School, CO

Hunting Season

The lonely and desolate woods.
The adrenaline rushing, and nerve tingling season of hunting.
The break of dawn.
The rattling of buck's antlers.
The chirping of singing birds.
The scuffling of sprinting chipmunks.
Cautious does.
Hyper squirrels.
Love to camp out when tired.

Coltan Butler, Grade 8
Culver Middle School, OR

Chocolate Bars

Chocolate
The chocolate bar melts into a puddle
Chocolate bars melt like snow in the summer
Sweet, softness
Chocolate
A small girl unwraps her chocolate
Like it is Christmas again
Yummy, deliciousness
Chocolate comes in different kinds
White chocolate, dark chocolate
Chocolate mixed with rice crispy
Long bars with 10 pieces
Small 1 piece chocolates
Chocolate
Mmmm!

Alexa Busby, Grade 7
Lyons Middle/Senior High School, CO

To Get the Perfect Poem

To get the perfect poem,
You must write in purple ink.
Write only on pink paper,
Drink lemonade to help you think.
You must make it as long as possible and longer,
So your poem sounds nice and smart.
Print it in your best handwriting,
Or if you're typing, use word art.
You must write this poem in a tree,
With orange glasses,
(So you can see)
Plus don't forget to bring those lucky socks.
And if you question my advice,
Thinking maybe it's not true,
Maybe not, but I sure have found it helpful,
Haven't you?

Natalie Mecham, Grade 9
Roosevelt High School, WA

Dress Up Mess Up

Looking back on the simpler times
When I couldn't wait 'til I turned nine
I only wanted a Barbie for Christmas
Now it's all about getting prom dresses
Don't you ever want to go back
To when you got your first knapsack
Time after time I want to go back
To when I was as tall as a small haystack
Now all I hear is welcome to the real world
But all I want is to stay in the fake world
I'm just a dress up mess up
Trying to get my first job
Remembering when all I wanted was a doll
Everyone telling me I won't succeed
Is that something I need to believe
Don't you ever want to go back
To kindergarten and take another nap
Now I'm watching my daughter grow up
Cleaning up her diapers, growing into pull-ups
Playing with her friends outside
She can't wait 'til she turns nine

Lindsey Boshes, Grade 8
Bogle Jr High School, AZ

Tree

I am swaying in the breeze
on a cool spring day
watching the squirrels play.
I should have a long life,
but my confidence has wavered
after seeing my kind cut down
and made into toilet paper.
Humans, they envy our long life.
At least the environmentalists are on our side.

Isaac Sampson, Grade 7
Lone Rock School, MT

Daytime:

The faint
glow of the sun,
ever so distant was
leisurely strolling above the
hillside.

It was
around midday,
with the sun as high in the
sky as it was going to get
today.

The sun
rolled gently down
the horizon into
an inevitable blackness
of night.

It is
now dark and the
loneliness is starting
to creep into my thoughts without
a sound.

Dylan Whitaker, Grade 7
West Valley Middle School, WA

I Am

I am…
I am a sister
I am a daughter
I am a friend
I am tired of drama
I am different
I am not perfect
I am a person and not a joke
I am faithful
I am inspired
I am smart
I am chaotic
I am lost in the world
I am misunderstood
I am shy and yet outspoken
I am me and that's all I expect of myself
I am Chelsea

Chelsea Dozsak, Grade 7
Mandalay Middle School, CO

The Ocean

The many wonders of the ocean
Millions of sea creatures
Filling the ocean's waters
From the small starfish to the big sharks
The vast ocean's water
Continue for miles and miles

Alyssa Tegtmeyer, Grade 7
Sky Vista Middle School, CO

I Love You

If I don't call, it is because I'm waiting for you to.
When I walk away from you, follow me.
When I push you away, grab me and never let go.
When I get angry with you, kiss me and tell me you love me.
When I'm quiet, ask me what's wrong.
When I ignore you, give me your attention.
When I pull away, pull me back.
When you see me walking, sneak up and hug my waist from behind.
When I lay my head on your shoulder, lift my head up and kiss me.
If I don't answer for a long time, reassure me that everything is okay.

When I miss you I'm hurting inside.
When you break my heart the pain never really goes away.
When I say it's over I still want you to be mine.

Alma Merino, Grade 8
Reynolds Middle School, OR

I Want/What If

I want to love you, what if you don't love me?
I want to hug you, what if you don't want to hug me?
I want to kiss you, what if you don't want to kiss me?
I want to see you, what if you don't want to see me?
I want to walk by you, what if you walk past me?

When I think about it my body quivers as I know you're thinking the same,

You want to love me, what if I don't love you?
You want to hug me, what if I don't want to hug you?
You want to kiss me, what if I don't want to kiss you?
You want to see me, what if I don't want to see you?
You want to walk by me, what if I walk past you?

I want to talk to you,
You want to talk to me,
Why don't people just let me be?

We love each other that's it that's all
It doesn't matter what people say when were walking down the halls

Don'Jhanae Austin, Grade 7
Denny Middle School, WA

Determination

I believe in determination
The fact that it is possible
The light that will shine brightest
The right to do and accomplish the goals you have set
The many obstacles that stand in your way
Strength, positiveness, idealism
But procrastination will consume you
I believe in determining you can
I believe in you and I
I believe in devotion to that one goal
Dexterity, devotion, zeal
And I believe in strength, strength that will break you free, free of all the negativity

Andy Henry, Grade 7
Terry 7-8 School, MT

B-Ball

Swoosh, as the ball flies into the net
The whole team cheering and some start to sweat

The game is tied twenty to twenty
"Water the coach yells you better drink plenty"

You are fouled going for the lay-up
Now you get two shots, if you miss you can't make up

You're concentrated on the shot through the hoop
Suddenly you miss and the ball goes swoop!

Now that it's all up to you
Your body numb, your face turns blue

You shoot and jump up into the air
Your mind suddenly turns very clear

Your team is cheering as the ball goes in
Suddenly you realize that you win!

Kaleb Bakel, Grade 7
Shadow Ridge Middle School, CO

America

America is home to freedom.
She is a shelter for you and me.
She lets us dream big and achieve our dreams.
She grants us so many of our desires.
America is our protector, it is sure and strong.
America is our mother, she leads and guides us quietly along.
I love America and what she does for me.
Do you love America and the opportunities she gives you?

Julie Christiansen, Grade 9
North Cache 8-9 Center, UT

Everyday Thrills

To me life is a thrill ride
Every day new and exciting things happen
New friends are made
Family members are born
To me life is a thrill ride
Everyday you always have something happy to say
Whether it's something happy
Or sad
Or something funny your dog did
Everyone has a story to tell
To me life is a thrill ride
Every day is the beginning of a new adventure
Going to your grandparent's house is an adventure
To me life is a thrill ride
Every day you're never alone
Just take a look to your left or your right
You'll always find someone there by your side
To me life is a thrill ride

Janae Jaeamillo, Grade 7
21st Century Public Academy, NM

Vanished

Knives and blades piercing her dreadfully within;
Strangling her as she struggles in her cage;
It seemed as though she was cursed with a sin;
Confused and clueless she burst into rage;
She collapsed at news of father's tragedy;
Positive thoughts kept her hanging above;
Surroundings kept her alive through comedy;
She could not help but to forget her love;
Back and forth the painful memories swept;
Like an illness that she'll carry forever;
Twenty-four hours and seven days she wept;
A lifetime experience she'll look after;
At last she decided she should let it go;
Suddenly her heart opened like window.

Jing He, Grade 9
Clark High School, NV

Elephants

We are elephants the intelligent nomads of the wild
Brave and strong
But know right from wrong
Taught to us by our moms
The enforcer of discipline and right from wrong
Along the way if our traveling family
Finds another all alone
Without a home
We proudly take them in
And treat them as if they were one of our own

Jared Meade, Grade 7
La Center Middle School, WA

New Life

The life I used to live
Was not made for me
Now I am trying to show responsibility and give
I knew that the life was not meant to be.

I used to hide in the dark and lurk
Now I'm showing improvement and work
That life I used to live is history
Now I'm standing here with love and glee.

I love my family now and forever
And how they used to tell me never say never.
I go to school, and show up every day
I even have time on the weekends to play.

I'm doing fine, and it feels so right
I'm even no longer afraid of the night
The days I used to live weren't so fun
Now I'm happy to share the new days
With everyone.

Ramsey R., Grade 9
Diamond Ranch Academy, UT

Student

Turn the other way, I beg you please don't look at me
Don't look into my eyes for I fear what you may see
Oh, believe me, it's not easy to keep in me all these lies
I try to tell you, I really do, I try to do what's wise.
But when I stand before you, I am a forgetful old fool
I simply do not have the brain power to remember what happened in school!

Trust me, it's very easy with one bell after another resounding in my ears
To get caught up in thinking, how many more days? How many more years?
Will the fear ever end? Will the work ever cease?
Should I really waste my life doing all this pointless work?
How will calculus help me when I'm old and married in New York?
It's simply your fault for you don't comprehend
That I have many other problems besides learning the name of Mr. Julius Caesar's best friend!

Priyanka Gaba, Grade 9
The Meadows School, NV

Papa

Always called me "sweet pea" and held me with strong olive arms. Brown steadfast eyes would follow my motions and there was always a strength and presence to rely on. My defender when in trouble, my grandfather with advice, my friend always, the only man in my life.

Time eventually came and took him away. I'll never understand why things have to be this way.

Brianna Bartholomew, Grade 7
Mandalay Middle School, CO

Nature

What do you hear? Do you hear the wind whispering? It says…
Listen to the waves lapping hungrily at the shore as they say,
"We come, we go on and on, we come and go"
They say in a whisper to you.
What do you hear? Do you hear the wind whispering? It says…
Listen to me as I swish and swoosh through the trees and bushes,
even the grasses on the moor,
I say, "Come, young one, come to the wild where you belong,
come back home, come back," I whisper.
What do you hear? Do you hear the wind whispering? It says…
Listen as a thunderstorm comes in, it says, "I come with thunder and lightning.
Even now I bring rain to the forests, moors, and marshes for a summer storm," the storm says.
Before going on, "I block out the sun, the moon, and even the stars.
I bring thunder and lightning; rain and hail.
When I leave, I am taken away on the breeze."
What do you hear? Do you hear the wind whispering? It says…
"I must move on while the moon is bright and the forest is alight.
I will remember what has been said here.
Before I go, you must know that if you listen to the forest, the moor, and the marshes,
you will find they are talking to you."

Kendall Setser, Grade 7
Sagewood Middle School, CO

Friendship

Sometimes friendship is like a good book, you want to keep reading and never stop, every time you turn the page there is something new and fun to discover. Other times friendship is like a torn out page, you sit there and wait for something good to happen, but all you can read is that torn out page, you never get to go on with what you want.

Cheyane Rider, Grade 7
Mears Middle School, AK

Autumn

Autumn leaves falling down
Dancing until they touch the ground

Red, yellow, orange, and gold
Are the colors these leaves may hold

Their naked branches dance and sway
To the music the wind may play

Now the wind has died down
So the dance is no longer shown

Their moaning has stopped
And the trees now settle down and take a long nap

Megan Rogers, Grade 7
Shadow Ridge Middle School, CO

I Am Me

I am smart and witty
I wonder why I'm me
I hear horns honking
I see the grill of a BMW
I want to be the richest man in the world
I am smart and witty

I pretend I'm the richest person in the world
I feel funny
I touch people's hearts
I worry I'm turning retarded
I cry when someone dies
I am smart and witty

I understand people are smart
I say God is one
I dream I'm the ruler of the world
I try to do my best at things
I hope I have patience
I am smart and witty

Cullen Madrid, Grade 7
Dunstan Middle School, CO

It'll Just Be Me

I love him, but he doesn't know,
he says he loves me,
but all he's doing is putting on a show.
To show his friends how bad he can make fun of me.

I love him, but he doesn't know,
I show him, but he doesn't see.
Every time he walks past me he never knows.
And this time around I know we'll never be a we,
It'll just be me.

Tessie Dominguez, Grade 8
La Plata Middle School, NM

Comedy Central

Comedy Central is the best TV channel,
I watch it every day.
From *South Park* to *Futurama*,
And people making jokes about your momma:
It's so hilarious.

There are standup comedians,
Like Dane Cook and Larry the Cable Guy.
Sometimes they make me laugh so hard
It almost makes me cry.

I love watching Comedy Central,
It gives my day a little zest.
It has so many funny shows,
It really is the best.

Ronald Hickey, Grade 7
St Elizabeth Ann Seton Catholic School, AZ

Exhaustion

The endless days of work
Leave me suffering from fatigue
Longing for Saturday consumes my mind
So when it finally comes I can truly unwind

The weekdays filled with homework
Leave you frustrated and tired
But to do well in school
It is absolutely required

Projects, quizzes, and tests never cease
It's just one after another
The constant studying is quite stressful
Even though it helps me perform better

Despite the monotony
Accomplishing it leaves me content
Regardless of how exhausting
I try not to relent

Durin Uddin, Grade 8
Fertitta Middle School, NV

Love

What does the word love mean?
Being true to those we care about,
Or caring for those we hardly know.
There is no cure for love.
It just comes and goes and maybe some day
We will know what it means.
But for now we must guess maybe
We won't know what it is or even what it means
Even though we all have our own definition on what it means.
Some say it is something made up
Others say it is a part of life.
What does love mean to you?

Juli Cartwright, Grade 8
Douglas Middle School, WY

The Old Dirt Road

I sit by an old dirt road
Watching people pass by,
And I notice how fast
Time can fly.

But I have no wish to
Travel this road of life.
For, although with happiness,
It brings strife.

I see many people pass,
Both old and young.
Weary old travelers,
Their song sung.

The young and fair
Wave and smile at me.
But I don't wish to go,
And I stay where I be.

But then an old friend
Helps me stand up,
And we set off together:
I drink from a new cup.

Mikayla Murphy, Grade 7
Valley Academy Charter School, AZ

Freedom

He fights for freedom every day
O, how he fights for freedom every day
He fights for freedom in a different way

He fights for those he doesn't know
O, he fights for those he doesn't know
Just for his friendship to grow

He just can't wait to leave
O, he just can't wait to leave
So he just waits and believes

Brian Daugherty, Grade 8
Bethel Christian School, OR

Soldier Sings the Blues

Another base is taken
Oh, another base is taken
Now we sit in the sun, bakin'

The supplies are gone
Oh, the supplies are gone
And it is the break of dawn

Another life is lost
Oh, another life is lost
And it did not go without a cost

Jacob Buck, Grade 7
Bethel Christian School, OR

Extraordinary Mother

My mother is as calm as the moonlight
Her eyes glisten like the starry night sky in the summer
Her love as warm as the sun's light that shines down on both of us
Letting our halos glow

She's the butterfly in the light flying high
Keeping her spirits high with the wings of a butterfly
May she fly in peace
To a place where there's silence

Hugs soft as the puffy luminous clouds
Comforting as a mother's encouragement
Her cry for me is like the rainy day tearing up
Just to say I love you forever as long as I live

The beating of her heart
Fragile like a vase filled with water and delicate flowers
The voice I hear in the distance
So gentle like a baby

I am the lucky apple
That did not fall far from the tree
Because she was there to hold me up

Kelsey Sorensen, Grade 9
Queen Creek High School, AZ

If...

If you have determination, confidence, and commitment
To keep your strength when in doubt
If you can fall in front of those to impress
And make the thought one to live without
If you can learn from every mistake
And have the might over those who can't
If you can see the competition
And come upon the meaning of their catchy chant

If you can glue your eyes to the ball
And follow its shadow
If you can tolerate the aggravating shorts and the necessary kneepads
If you can still find time for your other favorite sports
If you can look at your arms after your first practice
And not let that be the influence of your desire
If the smack of the volleyball becomes a distinct sound that'll never tire

If you can serve ignoring the pressure of the audience in the stands
If you can find triumph on the face of the ball
And victory in the palms of your hands
If you can look at the score and discover attainment no matter who's in the lead
Then you know that you have the attitude and confidence
To be a volleyball player who will succeed

Taylor Ackling, Grade 7
Sky Vista Middle School, CO

Holocaust

A boy sneaks over the fence;
The fence that separates his world from theirs.
He throws on the striped pajamas.
He walks along with his friend,
Thrilled to venture through the unknown.
There are only two versions of this side of the fence.
One is of families huddled together.
Tears roll down their graying cheeks.
Their hair is shaven off.
The other part is of soldiers,
Laughing, taunting, and threatening the others.
The boy does not like this side of the fence.
Gunshots ring in the air.
The boy has to trample over lifeless bodies.
Soldiers begin to push the group into a room.
The room smells like tart,
Yet the fumes are unbearable.
The boy grabs onto his friend's hand,
Refusing to let go.
More gunshots, fusions, unbearable screeching.
And then, all is silent.

Rachael Kroeger, Grade 7
Villa Montessori School – Phoenix, AZ

Lonely Man

Limping…
Limping like a poor dog that lost a leg
Trying to get to his destination, the bus stop
With only one support, his crutch
His lungs exhausted and weak
Two flat tires are his lungs
Only filled with smoke
A cigarette in his hand
Taking another week away from his life
His mind only grasping the image of a family he could've had
A sad face
With only the warmth of a woolly jacket he's had for years
And a cold pair of torn jeans
Lonely…
Thinking…
And gone.

Alec Ortega, Grade 7
21st Century Public Academy, NM

Me

Mercedes
Short, cute, talented, sister of Tiffany.
Lover of dancing, talking and texting.
Who feels happy, hyper and talkative.
Who needs to keep her grades up, to have a vacation and sleep.
Who fears spiders, guys, and snakes.
Who would like to see Alaska, Europe, and my room cleaned.
Resident of West Jordan.
Vosgerau.

Mercedes Vosgerau, Grade 7
Elk Ridge Middle School, UT

True Love

I think I have loved you from the start
You are the purest thing in my heart

When you are with me you make life better
It is like I am cold, and you are a sweater

You make life worth living longer
When I think of you it makes me stronger

Every moment with you is worthwhile
It helps a lot when you smile

Life without you, I could not bear
Every dream without you is a nightmare

Life without you just would not be
I think you could say you complete me

I hope you believe me when I say all this is true
The only thing I can say now is I love you!

Sadee Ballard, Grade 8
Eagle Rock Jr High School, ID

Flight of the Sparrow

Swooping, soaring, spiraling
Through the wide open noon day sky
Wind rustling through its open wings
It sings a song of pure merriment and joy
Dashing, Diving, Dipping
Wind currents lift him
To unimaginable heights
The small and fragile sparrow
Knows no limits
The sky is his home
Free to go wherever he wishes
Nothing can stop his flight
Nothing
But a juicy worm upon the ground

Hayley Huntsman, Grade 9
Mountain Ridge Jr High School, UT

Love

Love is when you care for someone,
love is when you would do anything for that someone.

Love is like a drug,
it is very addicting,
because if you love someone you'll never stop loving them.

Love is also a special thing,
and everyone deserves someone to love,
so just wait, because love is worth waiting for.

Nalani Walker, Grade 8
Wendler Middle School, AK

The Ocean

Crashed against me,
Pressed against me
In and out it moved me,
Submerged me,
Until I ran away,
Onto the silvery shore.

Kiah Mott, Grade 7
Juneau SDA School, AK

Jail Cell Blues

Wearing orange in my cell
I feel so trapped
I can hear the death bell
Every time I'm slapped.

I'm scared of the guard
That watches my every move
While doing time in the yard,
He is out, and has nothing to prove.

My biggest fear is when I cry.
Everyone here wants to say good-bye.
I want to see that eagle fly,
And never relive this day until I die

I'm alone in my cell
With only the cuffs and chains.
Don't get me started about the smell
And how surprisingly it heals my pains.

I want out
I want to leave
It's my chance to sprout
It's my time to achieve!

Nikki Duresky, Grade 7
Sky Vista Middle School, CO

Me and You

Don't you love me I love you
Don't you wish it could just be
Me and you?
I do
When we're together I feel happy
Do you?
When we're together I can do anything
Can you?
Don't you want it to be
Just us
Together
Forever?
I do
I wish it could be
Just me and you.

Chris Oswald, Grade 7
St Olaf Catholic School, UT

The Sunset

It happens every evening
but it is better all the time
with orange, pink,
purple, and violet.
The clouds reveal
its wonders, and colors.
It is disappointing
when a storm is coming through
for its darkness ruins its pride
but the sunset
is the last wonderful thing
of the day.

James Schermerhorn, Grade 7
Eureka Middle School, MT

Life

Sometimes life is like spring
The sun might shine
The wild flowers might bloom
Many different shades
Of reds, blues, greens, pinks, and more
The skies might gray
The rain might fall
But that's okay
Soon they'll clear
So do not fear
The weather changes
All the time

Kristin Warner, Grade 7
Mandalay Middle School, CO

The Painting

The lighting
the color
softening the faces or the hair
showing the emotion
they seem moving alone
but there is no motion
they look at home on that wall
made by so many, signed by them
passer-by looking if any
passing by the hem of the painting
on the wall
made with oils and paints
colors of all sorts
like splashed by the saints
sent to all ports
to be sent to my wall
it will stay there forever
unless someone bought it
I hope it will never
though someone else wants it
to put it on their wall

Carolyn Nowak, Grade 7
Timberview Middle School, CO

Dancer

Beautiful hair
Amazing costume
Shoes slide on
As my heart races
I am ready to go
The spotlight shines
As the audience awaits the show
The music plays
As my feet move
The crowd cheers
And the curtains close
Who knew. I DID IT!

Tiffany Jones, Grade 7
Oberon Middle School, CO

The Forgotten Candle

As the clock strikes twelve
A forgotten candle sits
waiting, waiting, waiting.
Until a silver moth
drifts to the candle,
its wings illumined from behind.
Then suddenly it leaves.
Leaving the candle
waiting, waiting, waiting.

Chance Losee, Grade 7
Les Bois Jr High School, ID

Lacrosse

The whistle blows
Face-off begins
Clamping the ball
No one in sight
I scoop the ball into my net
Cradling down the field
Spin and bull dodging
Heading towards the goal line
Stop, set, step
Shoot…
The whistle blows again

Bryce Garcia, Grade 8
Connect Charter School, CO

Monsters

Carnivonies are scary,
And hufflelumps are hairy.
Bed creepers drool,
While shades act cool.
The dark thing growls,
And the werewolves howl.
A vampire named Gary,
And a troll named Terry
Went to a public pool.

Korinne Aguero, Grade 8
Round Valley Middle School, AZ

High Merit Poems – Grades 7, 8, and 9

Never Look Back

She gripped her memories and held them tight
Not knowing what the future would toss into the fight
The struggle to be someone in the end
Though what would life be without the occasional bend?
She'd lost that excitement that had once been
She knew it would leave, but not quite when
The moment had arrived at this exact time
A last word to a poem that doesn't rhyme
A longing for change hid deep within her soul
The bell to alter her life rung with a loud toll
The chance would come sooner than she thought
Thrown at her, she knew that it must be caught
So she packed up everything
Anxious for what this new life would bring.

Casey Harlow, Grade 8
Miller Middle School, CO

Reflections

Summer comes and goes
Like a rose pedaling on a rose
You know it's gone once the alarm clock rings
Just like the jingles on the Christmas springs
Finding hope in every corner
Is as hard as juggling life without order
Wanting an adventure without enthusiasm
Is just as humans without hearts
What to do with the summer blues

Amber M. Moore, Grade 7
St Mary's School, OR

Sunrise Awaiting

As the springtime rain begins to cease,
and welcoming the summer heat
I feel the smile in your sweet voice,
the one I've grown so accustomed to
and I can picture us so vividly
your skin melting into mine
and the way the summer stars collide
with my anxious heartbeat's
all I want is you and me
I'd choose our fate; eternally
let's slow time down for a moment or two
see, our lips mold so perfectly in place
and your hold upon my waist
tonight, tonight is love
but midnight is soon upon us
so rest, my heart, till morning
I'll never fail to return to you
on winter nights of shattered moons
the love we share is just so true
so sunrise still awaits us
sunrise always awaiting us.

Danielle Pastier, Grade 7
Timberview Middle School, CO

The Girl Born from Ink

She was born in the midst of black frock coats
Ink stained hands passing quills and lined paper
The pages soon filled with bleeding black quotes
Souls pinned in ink, they fade and they taper
Polished black shoes on the cobblestone street
They pound and they flash in a corporate beat
Blank paper, white paper, without a written word
She wrote her soul on that paper, the girl born from ink
And broke free from those pages

Shay Christine Larsen, Grade 9
Preston High School, ID

The Battle

Creeping through the brush under the brown wood
Looking for my great and terrible foe
My friend beside me, who can think no good
Sword in hand, striking enemies much woe

Quickly, they are ambushed, the battle starts
Swords and shields clash, the enemy falls back
This fight shall be won by great smarts
Under our huge assault of sword and axe

We pressure them to the verge of retreat
One by one the fall of the enemy
As the battle races on, they are beat
The fall of our rival, archenemy

They have given up, and run for the hills
Numbers erased, by our efficient kills

Ben King, Grade 8
Academy Charter School, AK

Ten Little Seagulls

Ten little seagulls had a paper to sign
One didn't know, and then there were nine.
Nine little seagulls found some fish bait
One got hooked, and then there were eight.
Eight little seagulls found a boy named Alvin
Alvin took one, and then there were seven.
Seven little seagulls ate some Trix
One choked, and then there were six.
Six little seagulls ran into a hive
One lay slain, and then there were five.
Five little seagulls in the sky had to soar
One went too far, and then there were four.
Four little seagulls had to pay a fee
One didn't and then there were three.
Three little seagulls watched *The Who*
One got scared, and then there were two.
Two little seagulls were having some fun
But one went to heaven, and then there was one.
One little seagull felt he was done
He signed off, and then there were none.

Samuel Honeycutt, Grade 7
Beacon Country Day School, CO

Just Because I'm Young

Just because I'm young
Let me go with my friends
I promise to check in still
I won't talk to strangers
Just because I'm young
I won't mess up
I won't screw it up
Don't worry so much
Just because I'm young
Don't have low expectations
I'll still be home by curfew
I'm not a troublemaker
Just because I'm young —
Still give me freedom and independence

Berit Beckner, Grade 7
Dunstan Middle School, CO

My Bestest Friend

Sweet as honey from the hive,
loud as a rockstar at a concert live,
tasty as a juicy burger at the Super Bowl,
cute as a baby wolf curled up in a hole,
we'll be together until the end,
you'll always be my "bestest" friend.
We go together like dogs and frisbees,
skiers and races,
it's us and our smiling faces.
I hope we'll be together forever,
I won't ever forget you. Never, never.
We will be together until the end,
you'll always be my "bestest" friend.

Chandlar Schubel, Grade 7
Sequoia Village School, AZ

I Never Give Up

I never give up.
I never say die.
It's never over
Till it's over.

I'll never surrender;
I'll show you what I've got.
I've died and
Never been reborn.

Too many times I've been told
To meet their expectations.
It's going to take an army
To hold me back.

Nothing will stop me
From accomplishing my dreams
Because I know what it means,
And I'll never give up.

Johnathan Petreman, Grade 7
Syringa Middle School, ID

Voice for Our Protector!

An invisible guard high above the Earth,
A life saver some fifteen to fifty miles away,
Protecting us from the deadly heat of the Sun's rays,
A thick layer in the upper atmosphere, the Ozone layer!
Absorbing enough of the burning heat,
And allowing the rest to warm the crust below,
Without it, planet Earth will be boiling, melting away under the fiery Sun.
A serious damage to this shield and that's the end for all of us.
Every day's pollution, is a slow destruction to our protector,
A slow doom to planet Earth and all that lives on it.
Chlorofluoro carbons and dangerous greenhouse gases,
Gushes out of dense smoke from factories and vehicles,
Resulting in a thinner and much feebler ozone layer.
Harmful ultraviolet rays leaks through, setting a slow death for Mother Earth,
Arctic and Antarctic bares the scars already,
Penguins and Polar Bears are sweltering!
Harmful effect as bad as Global Warming!
Behold humans! Heed the warnings, burn fuel responsibly,
Work your share to save Mother Earth!
For a start, less than a mile or more,
Let's use school buses for us all!

Sarmishta Diraviam Kannan, Grade 7
Union Middle School, UT

The Kid in You

Remember all of those memories?
Back in the day when boys had cooties
And when no one was afraid to get dirty.
No girl ever needed to be flirty.
All what we did was play
That was our schedule from day to day.
Nap time, cookies and ice cream,
A perfect world is what all of that seemed.
And now everyone is growing up fast,
And they think that if they act like kids then they'll be an outcast.
Everyone is afraid to get dirty.
Girls are one hundred percent flirty.
Everyone tries to bring that kid down
When he gets out, they make sure that no one's around.
But we shouldn't be ashamed of the kid inside,
It's something that we should not hide.
Remember, no matter what you do,
That little kid will always be in you!

Ulianna Pavlova, Grade 9
Early College High School, OR

My Place

Some call it a soccer field, but I call it my haven.
As I walk from the parking lot I spot a huge sea of green blades.
The swish of the grass as I kick the soccer ball on it.
I smell the freshly cut, green grass, and feel the wetness from the water settled.
The hot boiling sun beats down on my head.
I taste the sweetness of the gatorade splashing in my mouth.
Some call it a soccer field, I call it my palace!

Gabie Turner, Grade 7
Ernest Becker Middle School, NV

The Snow

The snow
Covered the place
Like a blanket

It made the place
Sparkle
With white, clear, crystals

It came and left
Like a person
A cold it gave
The sickness it left
The snow it drops
The warm
And summer days it stole.

Trey Bryant, Grade 8
Shonto Preparatory Elementary/Middle School, AZ

Fluff

Silent, dark bliss,
Quiet, not a thought on your mind,
What? What's this?
It's still dark but you're awake,
There's velvet on your face,
It's hard to breathe,
Tiny fibers bristling your face,
You reach your hands towards your head,
A minuscule "me-ow" escapes this furball,
A cat! A sweet, cuddly creature,
You pull it towards your body,
A sudden purring noise fills the room.
Warm, misty feeling disperses throughout your body,
This time you fall asleep with happy thoughts.

Sierra McComas, Grade 8
Eugene Christian School, OR

Crocus

Crocus challenging his frosty foe
Hoping only to escape the treacherous snow
Although the icy liquid slush persists,
making it hard to resists it's deathly cold

It's blooming blossoms fight with the chilly wind and ice
Never giving up, never losing their spice

Like a warrior deep in battle
The crocus triumphs over the constant rattle
The wind eventually gives up the fight
And winter ends, up springs the light

The sunny rays comfort the crocus
And the bunnies come into focus
The joy is back to the world
Nothing lacks

Alina Perez, Grade 8
Sedona Charter School, AZ

Transitions

Some fury arouses inside of me,
Feeling true, pure, hatred within my soul.
This emotion of anger and envy,
Leaving my heart with a giant black hole.
Cruel, yet bitter words slip out of my mouth,
Anger is trapped in me like a potion.
This feeling should just leave me and fly south,
It is tough coping with this emotion.
Suddenly, cheerful thoughts rush in my head,
Excitement causes dimples to appear.
Now there is happiness in me, no dread,
Gladness is surely here, rage is not near.
Delightfulness and joy build up in me,
Emotions go quickly as one, two, three.

Paulette Reyes, Grade 9
Clark High School, NV

The Light of Hope

The sun's luminous arms stretch through the sky.
Distant storm clouds evanesce into haze.
Morning light paints daybreak pink with their dye.
Light collects into pools of lustrous blaze.
Effulgent rays jolt me from deep slumber,
My mind caught between the real world and dreams.
Seeking for more rest is too much cumber.
Shadows withdraw, shrinking from the sunbeams.
A new day starts without hesitation;
A day of hoping for new achievements,
Scorning stress with my firm proclamation,
Of banishing thoughts of vile bereavements,
Shortcomings are but a chink in the wall,
Determination will guide me to all.

Vivian Zhou, Grade 9
Clark High School, NV

I Wish

I wish I could fly far away,
I wish I didn't have to stay.
I wish I didn't have to live with this blame,
I wish I could have remained the same.
I wish everyone would just be kind,
I wish everyone would leave their differences behind.
I wish innocent people would remain safe,
I wish this world was a better place.
I wish we all could help the needy and poor,
I wish everyone wasn't so selfish anymore.
I wish the hungry could be fed,
I wish that they wouldn't rather be dead.
I wish I could run wild and free,
I wish everyone could understand me.
I wish no one started to lie,
I wish all my sorrows would go away and die.

Holly Adams, Grade 8
La Plata Middle School, NM

Sigfried

"Listen to my story," thus said the old sage of King Sigfried and Queen Bertha before the Golden Age.
Sigfried, with glimmering armor and sharp blade went down to the river to make sure the Cyclops was slayed.
Fair Princess Bertha was enchanted by the evil Cyclops's spell to sleep with unending nightmares which was her Hell.
A man appeared and he implored Sigfried to take with him an old sword, saying it was the only way to defeat the land's evil lord.
Sigfried then walked into the monster's den and saw his beloved lying on the floor at the cave's end.
Then came the evil lord, Sigfried seeing him unsheathed his sword.
The Cyclops noticed the sharp blade and with its hands took it away so he won't be slayed.
Sigfried hopeless, took out the old sword hoping to slay the frightful lord.
Then with one hit did it go to the eye, causing the cyclops to scream and then die.
The princess awoke from her cursed sleep; to be in the arms of her beloved again made her weep.
Then the old man appeared and revealed that he was actually the guardian of a powerful jewel in the cave sealed.
The man then gave Sigfried the jewel and then said, "The jewel recognize you as king so now you can rule the land."
Sigfried and Bertha ushered their nation into a golden age. "Their descendants ruled wisely," thus said the Old Sage.

Lorenzo Badiola, Grade 8
St Anthony of Padua Catholic School, AZ

The Grim Face

I lay awake late at night against the cold hard chill that blankets me in and out shivering against my will as I can't do nothing but just sit there in that cold frigate room and wait till it's my turn to fall asleep never wake up hoping it will soon so I can think of daisies rubbing against my face until I close my eyes and see me curled up in the corner sleeping never waking up then I look around and see a grim face looking at me holding his hand out and said little girl come with me to a happier place and run in the field of daisies that you wish that you dreamed of and I said no when it's my time I will come with you and he vanished I woke up not cold but the warm sun beaming out the holed of the tin house and a warm feeling inside and a tear dripping from my face and a form of hope covers me

Jayce Arnold, Grade 7
Eureka Middle School, MT

Hockey Stick

The roar of the crowd encourages it, they never get mad at each other, they're either against or with each other,
Their strength puts the puck to a scream, they always think before action, they never take blame nor credit,
There's always a place for them with a fan or player, yet they always want to play, their hearts are only broken when they are

Daniel Melusky, Grade 7
Eaton Middle School, CO

If

If you could care or be willing at the least
And be able to bare the pounding from the beast,
If you can play fair without being ceased,
If you can work in a pair, then you've been increased.

If a team player is what you want to be, hard work and practice and you'll see.
If motivation is what you need, then find it and you'll succeed.
If defeat pulls you down, then through victory you'll wear the crown.
If you are strong and relentless in what you do, then determination will pull you through.

If you can block, run, throw, or catch, then it is likely you'll win the match.
If you are fine to sit or play, then your job could be to do this all day.
If you can endure the pain, then give it back and win the game.
If you get a fumble that causes a frown, come back for the touchdown.

If you listen to your coach, the recruiter will approach.
If you encourage a teammate, a winning atmosphere you will create.
If you remain loyal even in the soil and persist in what you do,
Then my friend football is the sport for you.

Anton Latta, Grade 7
Sky Vista Middle School, CO

I Am

I am the hot sun
  Looking down on the earth
    Hear the wind "whoosh,"
      And whistling through the watchful town.
    I watch all day long
      Looking down.
        When I come up over the horizon
      I am glistening with giggling excitement
        People are hiding from my harmful heat.

Branden Wilson, Grade 7
Eagle Point Middle School, OR

Stars

Night

Night so still and steady
With stars so brightly shining
Night without light
And stars shining with all their might.

At the Top

So wonderful and gleaming
No sound at all and no movement
"Nothing at all" I feel
Wonderful but still overcome
By sadness not light at all
"No nothing, nothing at all."
Just by myself to enjoy the stars
Just all to me and only for me to enjoy,
Nothing to me is more gorgeous
Then the steadiness and the stars
So quiet and the darkness of the night.

Cintia Gonzalez, Grade 8
Emerson Edison Jr Charter Academy, CO

Dark Hill

It's when the moving lights pass by
Over the dark and forgotten hill
Her tired heart relieves a sigh

The years she's lived
Doesn't show on her face
But forever will she count the ways

Never taught the simplicity
The joy of living
She'll forever stay missing me

It's when the moving lights pass by
Over the dark and forgotten hill
Her tired heart remembers what she used to be

Samantha Wiltz, Grade 9
King Kekaulike High School, HI

Arches National Park

Once upon a windy road
We headed on a journey
Across the vast and open terrain
We started on the adventure of the rain
First to Utah we sojourn
Of awesome wonders we do learn
Amidst the arches we did hike
At times we wished we'd had a bike
We had never seen such lightning and thunder
As kings fighting for great plunder
Flash, Flash, boom, boom,
The sound and smell of rain and lightning
Was actually very, very frightening
Flash flood! The rain is pouring
Gushing water, the sound is roaring
Down the mountain, across the road
Every crevice the water exploring
The colorful sign of God's wonderful promise
Did suddenly appear
And quickly alleviated
All our fear

Kara L. Den Hoed, Grade 7
Sunnyside Christian Elementary School, WA

Dream

Seeing you is a dream
with a love of heart
looking across a stream
and never wanting to be apart

I never met nobody like you
and I know you are the one for me
jus' the thought of being without you makes me blue
without you who would I be.

I wouldn't want it any other way
you are my life, my heart, my everything
these are the things I want to say
to you my love I will sing.

I promise to give you all I have to give
I'll do anything for you as long as I live.

Calandra Charlie, Grade 9
Sargent Jr/Sr High School, CO

The Ancient Spirit

Wind is a spirit
It's only air but you can hear it
Invisible and cold
Telling about times of old
Howling and moaning before age
It's not something you can keep in a cage
Spiraling into a hurricane
It's much more deadly then fire and rain

Samuel Magaziner, Grade 8
Sedona Charter School, AZ

After an Awful, Horrible Terrible Day

Nothing could make your day worse
But what could make it better?

A soak in the tub or a nice hot shower
Let them wash your troubles away

The shoulder of a special friend
Drain your sorrows

A nice comforting hug
Embrace happiness

And a good friend to talk to
And laugh with

And when the day's done
Crawl in your warm bed

And drift asleep
Tomorrow will be better.

Allie Fischer, Grade 9
Lakewood High School, CO

Friends

Buddy, pal, ally, chum
These are synonyms for friend
It doesn't matter what they're called
They're with you to the end

True friends are hard to come by
But once they've befriended you
They're there through thick and thing
They'll last your whole life through

My friends are like a rock to me
They keep me down to earth
I make new friends and keep the old
Some who I've known since birth

Without my friends I'd probably sink
I've said it once and I'll say it again
Buddy, pal, ally, or chum
They're with you to the end

Forrest Moffat, Grade 9
Queen Creek High School, AZ

War

We are fighting an endless war
Now our enemies are very poor.
They lured us in
But they will never win
There is no fun
Because we have to use guns.

Roman Moyle, Grade 8
Place Middle School, CO

I Am From

I am from the land of arches.
I am from the land of red rocks.
I am from the land of tall, snowy mountains.

I am from the place where religion is a big part of the community
I am from the land where the biggest sporting event was held.
I am from the land of the Utes.

I am from the place with the best snow on Earth.
I am from the land of a great salty lake.
I am from the land of a great mine that is seen from space.

I am from the bee state.
I am from the place where a great basketball team plays.
I am from the place where the Japanese were once held in camps.

I am from the land of the fastest flats in the world.
I am from the land where a golden spike joined two rails.
I am from the place where brine shrimp only grow.

Christian Graham Feldman, Grade 7
Our Lady of Lourdes Catholic School, UT

One in Everyone

Childhood is sucking your thumb till you are eight
Childhood is climbing a "mountain" just to sled down it
Childhood is getting up at four to watch cartoons
Childhood is shoving everything under your bed
and saying it's clean so you can get your allowance
Childhood is training your dog to eat your vegetables
Childhood is an extra scoop of ice cream because you lost a tooth
Childhood is a forever Kool-aid stain on the carpet
Childhood is Band-Aids on both knees
Childhood is striped pants and a plaid shirt
Childhood is a purple popsicle
Childhood is wearing two different socks
Childhood is picking "flowers" for your mom
only to find out ragweed isn't a flower and that you are deathly allergic to it
Childhood is the craziest and most fun time of your life

Hannah Baldwin, Grade 7
Sagewood Middle School, CO

Mom

Mom,
Opens her heart whenever I need the extra push,
Warmth of hope knowing I can do it,
Warmth of her skin reminds me of my comforter coming out of the dryer
Smelling like vanilla lavender,
To have the feeling someone loves you is like, your favorite movie or dinner,
I love my mom because she kisses, hugs me good night,
I will always know she will be there for me the rest of my life.

Alycia Roetting, Grade 7
Komachin Middle School, WA

The Falcon

By the stream I slowly ramble.
To trust one's ears is a gamble.
Oh so faintly I hear a scream,
Vague but vivid, just like a dream.
Racing into the sky so sly,
Like black smoke that smoothly blows by,
Dark and dastardly, wild and wise,
Into the darkness, the falcon flies.

Liam Hallada, Grade 7
Annunciation Elementary School, NM

The Bird Calls

Chirp, chirp, twitter, twitter,
Bird call after bird call,
Harmonious and true,
Yet cacophonous too.

Flitter, flitter, flap, flap,
And away they fly.
Their calls stop for a moment,
Startled, they relent.

Tweet, tweet, chitter, chatter,
The symphony begins again.
The melody rings across the sky,
The birds do not seem at all shy.

Scritch, scratch, scribble, scribble,
There is another being in their midst.
Writing lines in a piece of poetry,
About the bird calls, as plain as could be.

Monica Pan, Grade 7
Fertitta Middle School, NV

At the Pond

The glistening blue water,
That I stare at with my father,
Reminds me of something that I can't describe,
I can feel it on my tongue, practically by my side.

And then I see a bird's reflection,
Soar over the water with affection,
That bird shows hope, love, and peace,
The thought makes me so weak I fall to my knees.

I close my eyes and breathe in the air,
As the crisp coldness whips through my hair,
And there sits the pond waiting and waiting,
What a hush of patience it is creating.

There is a deer on my left and a rabbit on my right,
But they did not run in their fright,
Yes, miracles happen by the pond,
Everything is hooked together in an unspeakable bond.

Ashleigh Feather, Grade 7
Sterling Middle School, CO

The Wrecked Pickup Truck

Clang went the two trucks.
Boom went the power poles.
Crunch, my driver-side door is closer than before.
Drip, my truck is dripping antifreeze.
Ring went my ears as the trucks hit.
Squish went the passenger side of the truck.
Puff went the airbags as they deployed.
Screech went the tires as I applied the brakes to stop.

Daniel Brazil, Grade 9
Buhl High School, ID

Ode to My Daddy

He is my life, my heart and soul,
The one I could count on with no doubts,
If he were food, I would have bowl after bowl.
He is very dedicated and hardworking,
If he only knew how much he is appreciated.

Without him,
My life would be a mess
And all I would be going through is stress.
He is simply the best Dad ever!
My love for him would be always and forever,
For he is a part of why I want to wake up and see tomorrow.
Without my daddy, I would have nothing but sorrow.

My daddy is my man,
My angel and protector,
He means the world to me.
For he is what I have always wanted to grow up to be.

Brianna Ortega, Grade 8
La Plata Middle School, NM

Freedom

I see that same door in front of me
I don't know what lies on the other side
My friends and others open the door,
Pass through and close it behind them
Why can't I go and be where they are?
Where did they go?
How do I get there?
I hit the door as hard as I can to break the lock
A voice said, "Stop! Turn around!
Close your eyes and imagine where you want to be.
Imagine what you want to be…"
When I did, I heard a loud creak and moan.
I turned around and opened my eyes
And there it was, that same door,
But this time it was different.
It was open! The way it was meant to be!
Finally I am free…
FREEDOM

Madison Medina, Grade 8
Our Lady of Lourdes Catholic School, UT

Skin Deep
Cool and clean
As the water in a stream
My looking glass
Does it show my hair
Skin so very fair?
My looking glass
No, not true,
It reveals what's in you
My looking glass
Wispy, airy souls
Full of nothing but holes
In my looking glass
Am I to blame?
Am I the same?
My reflection in my looking glass?
My opinion of me seeps
In the dark, it goes to sleep
After all, in my looking glass…
Beauty is only skin deep.
Erin Stephenson, Grade 7
Heritage Middle School, ID

Worthless
I am sad.
I feel as if a hundred eyes
Are just staring at me,
A hundred mouths opening
And telling me that I am worth nothing,
That I am horrible,
That I deserve to die.
My heart yearns for love,
Which seems
To run away from my touch.
I grow bitter,
Thinking that they
Are telling the truth,
That I do deserve to die,
Until an angel comes
And saves me
From the horrors,
The pain,
The suffering
In this world.
Kathleen Pahissa, Grade 8
Wind River Middle School, WA

Baby Boy*
Boy
Sweet and carefree
Lovable and cuddly
With a fat belly and short legs
Baby
Taylor Leonhardt, Grade 7
Dunstan Middle School, CO
*Inspired by Aiden, my nephew.

Flakes
Snow
Floating down from the clouds
Covering the ground
A thick blanket of white
The world seems to stop turning
As the delicate flakes fall
Celie Hull, Grade 8
Academy Charter School, AK

The Boy Who Broke His Arm
There once was a boy
who broke his arm.
When his parents saw
they were in great alarm.

To go to the hospital
they got in their car
they drove very fast
because it was far.

Soon they were there
they waited with great intent
eventually to the doctor
he was sent.

The doctor looked at his arm
he had to get a cast
It was so uncomfortable
Once it was off, he cried, "At last!"
Brevin Barney, Grade 8
Pomerene School, AZ

Feelings of Them
The history is depressing
Poems make me sad
Written by a dead person
Strange feeling
Eerie feeling
Poems tell the harsh reality
What people felt like
Also angry
Feeling the need
To beat Hitler to death
The pleasure
Saving millions
The children
I don't know
At the camp
I am sad
What they had to go through
Such a process
Witnessing death
No escape
Joseph Quintana, Grade 8
Barcelona Elementary School, NM

A Call for Help from the Every Day
I'm trapped in the ordinary
Banging on the walls,
Trying to find a way out of these
Solitary halls.

Just a window will brighten up my day,
Just to see a difference so my
Mind doesn't have to stay,
Just to know what I may find.

But here in the ordinary,
I feel so blind,
This place was fun just years ago,
But for now,
This is all I know.
Kristin Bloomingdale, Grade 7
Harbor Ridge Middle School, WA

The Blackbird Mute
There once was a small black bird
But its voice could not be heard
It tried shouting loud
But still there was no sound

The other birds mock
As he tries to bock
The little bird cowers
As the squawks grow louder

He tries to sing
But there was not even a ring
The little bird tries as hard as he can
To let out a note to a man

But still nothing came out
As he tried to pout
He tries cursing his luck
To friendly duck

That duck tells him a hint
With his eyes having a glint
That hint changed the bird's life
For now he can talk to his wife
Cody Krollpfeiffer, Grade 7
Shadow Ridge Middle School, CO

Rain
Look at the rain, dancing in the sky.
Rain hits the ground without a care.
It will soon be all together.
Together tonight turning to mud.
Together tomorrow leaving in time.
Together forever repeating over time.
Zach Styer, Grade 7
Eagle Point Middle School, OR

My Retainer

My retainer is sparkling like the rippling sea
Sparkling like the hopeful stars in the sky
Sparking like diamonds!
It's beauty succeeds all beauties imaginable
Glittering in an abyss.

My retainer has ridges like the mountains.
It is like the land and the sea.
Half of it emulates beauty,
The other half shows majesty and authority.
The shape brings comfort.
Its white air-pocket areas are like the crashing waves.
Its upward posture is like a saint, ascending into
Heaven,
It resembles Poseidon.

I will wear it all night,
With my toothbrush I shall drive away germs.
Let them infect some other neglected retainer;
The toothpaste suds belong to me and my retainer.
Bask, my retainer in the suds; I am here
To guard you with my toothbrush.

Sarah Brunsdale, Grade 9
Mountain Ridge Jr High School, UT

What Once Was/What Is Now*

As I walk, I hear you
It's hard to say
That one day…

I will find your true place in my heart
I may not know you as mother
And I may not know you as friend
But know this much is truth
I still love you

As I walk, I hear you
Now knowing your true place in my heart
It soothes my soul
To hear your voice
And just to keep your delicate words alive

I pray to God
That one day
I will forgive you
And all my pain will drift away

Thinking back now…
On all my past hurts
I can know in my heart
That I no longer blame you

Mandy Ballard, Grade 7
Knowledge Quest Academy, CO
*Dedicated to my mother, Melissa!!

Nowhere to Go…

The clouds opened up,
Threatening to grab him.
He Looked around for help,
But no one could save him.
The water poured from the sky,
Attacking him.
There was no where to go,
so he sat there and let the heavens attack him.

Savannah Douglas, Grade 7
Foothills Academy, AZ

The Sounds of Nature

In the distance I could
hear the wolves howling.
In the distance eager
cricket's chirp.
In the distance trees
surrender to the wind.
Nature itself can be
one big song.
This makes me wonder
who are we to disturb it.
All the hums and the
whistles sound through the night.
And all we do is
destroy it.
Who knows how nature
would sound without such interruptions.
We can only hope that this will change.

Owen Proctor, Grade 7
Aurora Academy, CO

Without Love

We hear love all around
But I myself, have never found
"It feels like, a million just got won,"
"And it's so sensitive, unpredictable, and fun."
I heard all these words in songs, books, movies galore
But I'm not screaming I want anymore
Don't feel pity for me, or for him
We just broke up, and it feels like a win
We stop talking on the phone,
We never shared our first kiss
But honestly I didn't feel we missed
I got stabbed with knife,
Right straight in the heart
It had not been love,
So we had to part
He was cute, handsome, and sweet,
Smart, nice indeed
There walked through the door on his noble steed
You've heard it thousands of times
I feel in love with him
This very rhyme

Paige Ward, Grade 9
Buhl High School, ID

Spring

Spring is a beautiful season,
rain pouring from the sky,
flowers springing from the ground,
in the spring the sun shines high.

In spring you can take long walks,
there is loud, beautiful thunder,
you can hang with friends, and talk,
spring is a blooming flower.

Alli Luft, Grade 7
Sagewood Middle School, CO

Epidemic

Small pox and measles,
Yellow fever and black,
All of these illnesses,
They keep coming back.

As humans we fear them,
Block them away,
But as cunning as a fox,
It finds it's way in.

Bioterrorism we fear,
The fate of us all,
The epidemic has struck,
We are left to fall.

Defeated by none,
It lies,
Awaiting the day,
When the poison is uncovered,

Creating
An
Epidemic.

Lizzy Nagle-Heim, Grade 7
Oberon Middle School, CO

Seasonal Colors

White is the new fallen snow
When temperatures are down low.

Black is the stark night
Filled with stars of white.

The forest is brown and green
So peaceful, so serene.

White is the color of a dove
Bringing peace from above.

The leaves from autumn are red
Falling from branches overhead.

Jessica Schneider, Grade 8
Fertitta Middle School, NV

True Love

My mother, my mentor, my best friend
The one who has been there for me through the roller coaster I call life
An inspiration to all women
She shares her love with all of us, her five kids that is
She mentors me, and keeps me on the right path
Teaches me many things, and never keeps a secret from me
Even though she shields us, she also gives us room to learn and grow.
Support and love is what she gives me most
I can cry on her shoulder, and she can cry on mine
We can watch a movie together
And although sometimes we fuss and fight,
We'll be best friends 'til the end
My mother is number one
She tries hard to take care of us
And has taught us we need to stick together, and love each other
Friends may come and go but family will stay with you until the very end
Although there are four other bedrooms in the house I always sleep in hers
It soothes my soul that I can say there is no love like a mother's love
And when she's gone I'll remember her for everything she has done for me.

Amber Rollins, Grade 8
Komachin Middle School, WA

A Friend

What happened to you it's only been a day,
And just yesterday we were the same.
But you got sad and lonely, depressed and really scared,
You felt like no one loved you, the truth is no one was there.
You hated everything in your life, you hated who you were,
You never gave yourself a chance to see what good could occur.
You shot yourself and now you're gone,
We'll never forget you, we'll never move on.
Suicide wasn't the way to go and now I'm sad and regretful.
But I will find the hope and strength to make it through the rest of the day.
I miss you so much, even though it's now the end,
I want you to know that this is from me,
A friend.

Brittany Henry, Grade 7
Ranch View Middle School, CO

Never Again

May I always glorify You and Your name,
Forever shall it ring through the halls of history.
It shall be carried on the wind the same
As the breath of God is so clearly.
Never again shall you be violated o Zion,
Never again shall exile rule your lives o children of Abraham, our father.
For you are the light among all nations, o lay on
Your backs no more bring the jubilation to the King forever.
Bring us back to You, heavenly judge of goodness.
Let us sit before You in judgment of our actions.
Everything shall be counted and judged in righteousness
And so we live with what we did in our factions.
    Make ready the path for Him to bring us back,
    Only through our unity shall we be judged white and black.

Parker Bottlemy, Grade 9
Lakewood High School, CO

Secret Admirer

Beautiful to the eye
Outgoing but also so shy
Love that no millionaire can buy
Fragrance is sweet like a homemade apple pie
Gives me the feeling that I can fly
Also can make me want to die
All I hear is a simple hi.

Angel Antonio Ung, Grade 9
Fremont Jr High School, AZ

Why I Couldn't Write My Poem Book

I couldn't write my poem book because I was in the hospital
Well actually I glued my fingers to the wall
Oh, and did I mention that my dog also ate it?
It doesn't matter, I hated it
My hands were stuck together,
Because of the freezing cold weather
My puppy got sick,
Because it ate a tick
My computer blew up
Because I spilled orange juice in a cup
I fell down a hill,
And my mom made me take a nasty pill
I also had the flu,
And I think I got it from you
My printer broke,
As soon as I awoke
I forgot about the assignment,
Because to the dentist I went.

Laura Olsen, Grade 7
Ernest Becker Middle School, NV

Tree of Friends

Friendship is like a tree
The roots are your foundations
Your relations with God
The trunk is the one friend
The perfect one, Jesus
Because of Him, your trunk
There are branches reaching out
Representing how you reach and hold your friends
And the fruits and flowers
The nuts and acorns
Are all the friends
That you are getting to know
Will know, do know
The leaves are the friends
The ones you knew already
Each flower and nut will change
Some will fade
And some stay strong
But all in all what matters most
Is that you love each one
No matter what

Kyrie Fuchs, Grade 9
King's Jr/Sr High School, WA

Life Is Like

Life is like a journey
You explore and have loads of fun
Life is like a candle
All your worries and troubles melt
Life is like a flower
All your dreams grow bigger and bigger
Life is like a shopping mall
You find some good things and you find some bad

Life is like a dance marathon
You have great rhythm and tune
Life is like a pot of gold
You find great riches and make the best of life

Life is like a thought make the right choices
Life is like an eye
Don't blink or you'll miss the special moments
Life is like your heart very fragile and delicate

Life is like the sun very strong and powerful
Life is like a bottle
You have to open it to your happiness
Life is like a speed limit
You have to old on and chase your destinies and dreams

Shante Ortega, Grade 7
21st Century Public Academy, NM

Daddy Come Back

Watching them fight
I'm hiding and plugging my ears
Why can't they get along anymore
I try to hold back my tears

As he steps out on us
He hugs me goodbye
He says, "I Love You Baby" and leaves
She lets out one last cry

As us girls sit on our steps
She turns to say, "We'll be a family again"
When she leaves I watch my daddy drive off
She says, "There are other men besides him"

My daddy came for me a month later
I missed him dearly
I wish what my mom said was true
I felt so blue

Daddy told me no more Mommy and Daddy
It would be just Mommy until the weekends come
He wipes away my eight year old tears
And listens to me play my frustration on my emotional drum

Myriah Troussel, Grade 8
Shadow Ridge Middle School, CO

Makeup

Makeup's my life,
Can't live without it,
Tryin' to get the best fit,
Keeps me lookin' good
While I'm in the 'hood,
I'm always wearin' it
From simple lip gloss
To high-fashioned eyeliner,
With makeup I look finer.
Makeup — I could go on about,
Without it I would pout.
I love my makeup,
All you other girls
Just need to wake up!

Isis Cuellar, Grade 7
McKinley Middle School, NM

How to Live Long

It is said
that
an apple a
day
keeps the doctor
away.
I have to
disagree,
I believe that
laughing
a minute each
day
is the key
to
living a long
life.

Amelia Rust, Grade 9
Oak Canyon Jr High School, UT

These Are the Signs…

The whispering of the leaves,
The silence of the trees,
These are the signs of fall.

The blankets of white,
The snowball fights,
These are the signs of winter.

The fresh cut grass,
The kids out of class,
These are the signs of spring.

The water fountains, and
The luscious green mountains,
These are the signs of summer.

Samantha Steeves, Grade 7
Eagle Point Middle School, OR

Pain

A blinding darkness,
my heart still beating,
bound in the corner,
with pain that keeps bleeding.

Water runs down,
from the tips of my eyes,
with feeling that hurts,
and all I can do is cry.

Tied to the wall,
with the iron metal chains,
bound hand and foot,
and no way to escape the pain.

Run from my fears,
run from the changes,
I don't know what way to go,
but the darkness is still a hurting pain.

A shining light,
a whisper of comfort,
gives me the feeling that I'm not alone,
in the dark pain of one broken soul.

Nikki Pierson, Grade 7
East Valley Middle School, MT

Basketball

Bounce, bounce, bounce
You can hear the ball hit the court.
Bounce, bounce, bounce
Bright orange flies through the air.
Bounce, bounce, bounce
You can see the crowd roaring.
Bounce, bounce, bounce
Players shoot and make the shot.
Bounce, bounce, bounce
Cheering when your team wins.
Bounce, bounce, bounce.
This is basketball.
The ultimate sport.

Adam Huntsman, Grade 7
Eagle Point Middle School, OR

Me…

Daughter, sister, niece.
Loud, fun, crazy.
Granddaughter, and friend.
Obnoxious, ditzy, amazing.
These are the things that describe me.
At the end of the day,
that's all I can be.
And that is perfectly fine with me.

Shianne Hale, Grade 8
Sequoia Village School, AZ

The Rado

The Rado
The Rado is Colorado
The home of the 303
Where everyone is a G.

The Rado, the Rado,
The Rado stands for Colorado
Home of the snow
Makin' us glow
We don't need light
Because we're so tight.

The Rado
The Rado is Colorado
People doin' their deals
And makin' their bills.

The Rado, the Rado
Stands for Colorado
Someday we'll be on top
Watching everyone drop
As the moon glows off the snow
We'll be ready to go.

Scott Nolan, Grade 9
Hinkley High School, CO

The Tiger

That white tiger
Has a lot of anger
Its dinner
Is ginger
Its stripes are dark
And it also imitates a bark!

Esmeralda Lopez, Grade 8
Place Middle School, CO

Raspberries

Red as blood
taste as gold
look as plain
yet so good
sweet as sugar
tart as wine
juicy as water
with texture of silk
seeds that crunch
they grow in bundles
many in one
with rich flavor
this fruit
gift of God
raspberries raspberries
destroy my hunger.

Steve Gulliksen, Grade 7
North Middle School, CO

Babies

Babies always cry,
and I ask myself why?
They slobber when they cry.
It gets annoying, and then I sigh.
The best part is when they go to sleep.
I tiptoe on my feet, and try not to make a peep.
When a baby is born, it is so cute,
they can be small, chunky, tall.
But what eva day look like, I love dem all!

Jessica Oliver, Grade 8
Place Middle School, CO

Relationships

It starts with just friendship
The sunshine that warms life
The sunshine that is wonderful
But will burn you if you get too much
Then it becomes a feeling of love towards each other
Life's bouquet of roses
The sweet aroma of romance given off
Then it becomes a commitment
One where you combined yourselves into one marriage
It is the single rose you both become
Then slowly your rose of marriage withers away
And all that is left of the once beautiful relationship
Are the thorns of divorce
Those small pricks that invoke much pain, anger, and sorrow
Then in some cases but not all
That once passionate rose of love
Withers away in the burning fires of hatred
Towards one another
All that pain and joy started with the sunshine of
Friendship

Sarah LaBonde, Grade 7
Sky Vista Middle School, CO

The Crystal Telescope

To contemplate infinity,
That there exists divinity,
No coincidence that all this was created.

The perfect balance of life on earth,
The miracle of death and birth,
"Does god exist?" This question so debated.

Do you really think that it is chance?
That living is merely happenstance?
Of the billions of planets this one can live and thrive.

This wonderful gift that's been given to me,
It's surprising how little people really do see,
Why do I exist? It's a miracle that I'm alive.

Jason Gottfredson, Grade 9
Timberline Middle School, UT

If the Sun Didn't Come Out Today

If the sun didn't come out today
If it didn't want to play
If it just wanted to hide away
And not be part of our average day
Well, that wouldn't be okay.

If the sun didn't come out today
It would be gloomy and dark
There would be no one in the park
Dogs would be more likely to bark
If the sun didn't come out today.

If the sun didn't come out today
Someone would have to pay
Their bottom dollar that they bet yesterday.

So if someday
You feel the need to wish the sun away
Stop to think of a day in gray
Without those beautiful rays
And be glad the sun came out today to say
'Have a great day!'

Erica Elias, Grade 8
Cashmere Middle School, WA

Silent Winter

The snow floats gently to the ground
The snow does not make a sound.
The snow so soft and so mellow
It greets you as if saying "Hello."
And when the snow is all done
The kids come out and have fun.
Their minds don't want to concentrate
They laugh, they play, throw snow, or skate.
I love this season, not spring or fall
For winter is the best of all.

Keaton Turner, Grade 7
Wiley Jr/Sr High School, CO

Hey, Mom

She doesn't think it matters to her kids,
Whether or not they like the guys she dates,
In my mind, the past is still so vivid,
I cannot let her make the same mistake.
She claims that she's not going out with him,
But I feel that she is not speaking true,
There is no way to get rid of that imp,
And the thought of him makes my anger fume.
She doesn't seem to know how much it hurts
To see them even exchanging a hug,
Ev'ry time she sees him, she starts to flirt
With that disgusting, irritating bug.
He calls her every night on the phone;
Why can't he just leave my mother alone?

Amy Jones, Grade 9
Clark High School, NV

Sk8boarding
Skateboarding is the best
better than all the rest
all kinds of tricks
Olie over sticks

Don't get bored
There is no end
Some people are good
Some pretend
Do It with a friend

Transportation
So here you are
Skateboard and you can go far
If you're lucky
you won't get a scar

There's vert and street
Amazing board
Wheels under your feet
So take a seat
Watch some pros
Then go and skateboard
With your bros

Charles Schweizer, Grade 7
Shadow Ridge Middle School, CO

The Man with the Dream
He had a dream, Martin Luther King.
He left us with a heavy sting.

A lot he had lost,
So now it's time to pay the cost.

Clyressa Hollingsworth, Grade 8
Place Middle School, CO

Basketball!
Basketball is so fun
even when you play in the sun

Exercise and energy
will be more beneficial to me

Running can be so fun
especially when you run, run, run.

In practice we do the Hollywood too
it makes me have to tie my shoe

Shiny blue jersey and shorts too
it rocks so much 'cause I love blue

The coaches are the best
They push us hard then let us rest.

Jackie Boyce, Grade 7
La Center Middle School, WA

An Ode to My Computer
My computer entertains me when I'm confined to the four barren walls of my room
My computer is my link to the outside world
My room, like a prison,
Shuts me away from the world
My computer, acts as my man on the outside
Every key I strike,
Is like a piece of freedom shooting through me
My computer contacts Pizza Hut delivery
When my stomach roars with hunger
But more important than any of these
When condemned to silence
My computer brings me a far greater treasure:
Music
Heavy metal riffs pumping me up for the big game
Throw on a bit of Marley for the times when hope seems lost
Red Hot Chili Peppers slowly lower my anger level
A magical song helps me get the girl of my dreams
Accept it or not music rules our lives
Go ahead and try to argue I'll prove you wrong
But that's for another time
For now, this is my ode

Cory Johnson, Grade 9
Menaul School, NM

My Grandma's House
Every year at the start of summer, we fly to my grandma's house.
As we drive along the long, winding, dirt road through the desert to her house,
I start dreaming.

I see the century plants and purple sage blooming,
And prickly pears tangled together.
We pull up to the tiny white stucco house, and I hear the dogs bark wildly.
We unload the bags,
The smell of fried okra hits us as we walk in the door.
My grandma hugs us all and the coolness of the house feels calming.
But the lake keeps calling us.

I drive the truck with everyone piled in the back to the lake.
We frolic and splash in the water until the sun glows.
We drive back to the house and I walk down the trail to the lake.
I grab my camera and snap beautiful pictures of the sunset.

As I walk back up the trail to my grandma's house,
Ready to enjoy the fried succulent catfish she has cooked,
I remember all the magic I have experienced at her house before.

And in the dead of winter, I lie down on my bed, close my eyes
And imagine myself at my special place, deep in the desert;
My grandma's house.

Trevor Cook, Grade 8
Cody Middle School, WY

To Mend a Broken Heart
To mend a broken heart,
So sad and broken inside.
You can't hide the pain.
To make the pain stop,
I have to stop loving you.

To mend a broken heart,
I need to move on with my life.
I need to open my eyes and see,
There's always someone there for me.

To mend a broken heart,
That will only be the start.
I will start to get over you,
But there will always be a place in my heart.

Jazmine Ramirez, Grade 8
La Plata Middle School, NM

I Believe...
I believe in friends that are real,
In taking a break from life,
In having random fun,
But not in betrayal, suicide, or illegal activities

I believe that make-up is evil.
I believe Barbie® is a giant fake.
I believe that life is a journey;
It gives me good times and bad.
It's up to me to decide how to make
Something of myself.

Stacy Dalley, Grade 9
Preston High School, ID

The Wink
How many times have I seen this thing,
when both of the eyelids meet,
with eyelashes soft as a butterfly's wing,
something often known as a blink?
So why does hers strike me so differently?
Instead of both eyes, only one,
it's pointed at me quite directly,
and with the blink of an eye, it's gone.
Her eyes caught mine, just for a second,
and she silently stared right back,
and with her gaze she beckoned me,
Oh my lungs! Their breath did lack.
Feeling lightheaded, my heart suddenly fluttered,
and I knew just what to do,
I looked at her, with her face sweet as butter,
and gave her not just one wink, but two.
Then she did something that made my heart sigh,
and I felt the need to dial,
a chariot to take me straight to cloud nine,
for right then and there, she gave me a smile.

Cynthia Judd, Grade 8
Villa Montessori School – Phoenix, AZ

Chocolate Chip Cookies
Hot and ready
enjoyed with my best friend Betty

Fills the air with a chocolate smell
enough to make everyone yell.

The taste of sugar and spice
makes your mouth fell like water on ice.

The beat of the blender
makes the dough feel tender.

When making cookies I sneeze every hour
only to find, it was just the flour

The chocolate chips add the perfect touch
that makes my family's happiness clutch

All golden brown
look I deserve a crown

Kellie Marcle, Grade 7
La Center Middle School, WA

Baseball
Waking up and putting a purple jersey on
Knowing that you will compete
Deciding what to do
As the day goes by
It's a flying jet
Before you know it you're on the field
Like a battleground
You go up to bat
With a feeling in your stomach
But after the game you regret
But the only thing left to do
Is be strong and let the past go
For there will be another chance
Not only to be a champion
But to show everyone you can!

Omar Mendoza, Grade 9
Queen Creek High School, AZ

Life's a Journey
Life is a journey
You can choose to go all the way
Or you can choose to stop

There will be short cuts
But not all short cuts lead to great things.
The farther way is always getting to be the harder way.

Life's a journey.

Johnny Wilkerson, Grade 7
Eagle Point Middle School, OR

Ode to a Friend
There he is watching WWE,
While he is there his eyes are glued,
To a turned on TV.
This man that I know,
Goes by the name Leo.

Leo is fun and works two jobs.
He loves my grandma's cooking,
Gee, who doesn't?
This man that I know,
Always makes up funny names.

This man that I know,
Is dating my aunt.
This man that I know,
Wow, I hope he doesn't have to go.
Nathan Jackson, Grade 8
La Plata Middle School, NM

Emotions to the Heart
We laugh, we cry
We live, we love
Give gifts of the heart
Share memories
Express opinions
We know each other's lives
We argue, we fight
We play, and give advice
On the meaning of life
We're best of friends
But we're also sisters
Tara Atwood, Grade 9
Grand Junction High School, CO

Gymnastics Meet!
I am flippy and springy.
I wonder how I jump.
I hear the crowd roaring.
I see my mom and dad cheering me on.
I want to win a medal.
I am flippy and springy.
I pretend to not be scared.
I feel wonderful.
I touch the floor.
I worry I will mess up.
I cry when I fall.
I am flippy and springy.
I understand I am not perfect.
I say sorry to my team.
I dream of winning a gold medal.
I try to imagine.
I hope my team will forgive me.
I am flippy and springy.
Brittany Jacobsen, Grade 7
Dunstan Middle School, CO

Black Cat
Her green eyes glow,
Her black fur glistens,
In the light of the moon
Against the dark sky.

With a wave of her tail,
And a flick of her ears,
She disappears in to the shadows,
Leaving just a single hair behind.
Anna Teadtke, Grade 8
Astoria Middle School, OR

My Thoughts
I wish the world would be at peace,
I wish there were no more wars,
I wish that everyone had food.
I wish everyone would be happy,
And I wish happiness would spread.
I wish that everyone could fly,
And fly to peace at last.
I wish that everyone laughed,
And kept that laugh forever.
I wish that everyone came together,
And forgot about the hatred.
I wish that everyone would get along,
And that happiness would go around.
Rebecca Nan, Grade 7
Sky Vista Middle School, CO

Third Eye
My third eye sees everything
Every mistake I make
Every step I take
It watches me
Everything I talk about
Taking pictures of my life
Making every moment special
And recording it in the book of my life
My third eye is like God
Always with me and always there
Alexis Cardona, Grade 7
Sky Vista Middle School, CO

The Star Race
Speeding down the oval track
Shooting past its opponents
A shooting star on a road that's black
Winning the game in moments

Snapping photos and a great applause
A star gleaming in the crowd
Looking perfect with no flaws
He accepted his prize and bowed
Summer Moss, Grade 9
Oak Canyon Jr High School, UT

My…
My dear friend Rick
You laughed and laughed
The joy in your voice
The joy in your life
You were great
Until you smoked
Now a scratchy voice
A tired face
You still laughed
But not the same
Now that you are gone
I miss you so
My Rick
Juliana McDonald, Grade 7
Mandalay Middle School, CO

Peter Pan
A boy that never grows up,
But never messes up.
He lives on a tree,
Nice and neat.
His friend is a fairy,
That is never getting married.
He flies around the clouds,
Nice and loud.
Stole Wendy from her house,
To show her a paradise!
Adriana Medina, Grade 8
Place Middle School, CO

Imagination
Imagination is the key
to unexpected unity
It thrives on a world of unknown
and transforms our life into stone
If life is key
then life be told
then all minds will unfold
Stephen Betts, Grade 7
Sequoia Village School, AZ

Have You Seen Me?
You've seen me laugh
You've seen me cry
You've seen me in pain
You've seen my spirits die
You've seen me at my best
You've seen me at my worst
You've seen me mad
You've seen me in love
But have you seen me?
Not what I can be
But what I am.
Shayla Givens, Grade 9
Duchesne High School, UT

When Someone Passes Away*
When someone passes away
you feel pain,
you feel that someone stabbed you in the back,
you feel that you are heartbroken,
you feel that your world is over,
but when you bury that person,
you know that you will never see him again,
you'll have to live with the pain inside you
and that's when you feel you're dead.

Jacqueline Fuentes, Grade 7
Somerton Middle School, AZ
In loving memory of Marco Antonio Figueroa Quintero

The Picture
I looked into the picture it seemed to speak to me,
It said, "I have a lot of memories," it seemed to say to me.
I used to live in the White House
I was in the Oval Office
Now I hang here in the museum,
People see me every day,
I sit here and they say;
"There is Lincoln"
They take pictures
And then they walk on by,
They leave me
But forever I will stay in their mind,
Full of memories.

Koby Rohr, Grade 7
Wiley Jr/Sr High School, CO

Standing Out
You walk step by step
Maybe if you were prep
You would just fit in
All you want is a twin
Maybe they would understand
Even though you wear an arm band
You're still like them
You can still party and have fun
There is no such thing as being normal
You're not what they say; you're not paranormal
But again, why not stand out
Who cares if everyone pouts
Ignore all the glares
You shouldn't care if anyone stares
Why not dare to be different
Let everyone else worry about you being indifferent
It doesn't matter if you're tall or small
People should like you for you above all
Show your talents instead of hiding them
Don't be afraid to shine like a gem
It shouldn't matter if you stand out

Bryan Gonzales, Grade 8
Fertitta Middle School, NV

Another Dream
When it's dark
Small noises become big
Time seems to stop
It's like the world no longer spins

When it's dark
Imagination becomes reality
Fear becomes me
Silence overpowers me

When it's dark
Uncertain thoughts run through my head
My mind goes wild
When it's dark my mind is free

And then the lights return
And all is what it seems
And once again imagination is just another dream

Jazmine Hernández, Grade 7
Sevilla West School, AZ

Rosa Parks
After a day's hard work,
Rosa Parks sat on a bus.
She would not move for the white man who was a cork
Even if it meant there would be fuss.
The police were called.
They threw her in jail.
If there was a bail,
No one recalled.
Finally, she was released.
She continued her fights,
For the Blacks civil rights.
There was eventually racial peace.

Hailey Stockton, Grade 8
Academy Charter School, AK

The Ultimate Sport
Bull riding is the ultimate sport,
You bounce and you bounce, and you bounce
and then you come off
and worse, you tumble and roll and you get stomped
OUCH THAT HURT
and then someone comes and rescues you.
The bullfighter, he's my hero
I am the bullfighter I am here to protect.
I will save you from harm,
and then you get up and run to the bucking chute,
that is where you are safe my friend.
Safe from harm
and when it's all over, you go up to the announcing booth
and collect your reward.
And that is my favorite part of bull riding
Like I say, "It's the ultimate sport."

Coleton Curtis, Grade 7
Eagle Point Middle School, OR

Beautiful Day

Watching the blue green waves
Racing on the sandy beach.
While the watermelon sun,
Comes rising up from the earth,
As a phoenix,
Rises up from its ashes.

You can feel the cold breeze,
When it hits your face.

As you lye there,
Dreaming
Of a beautiful dolphin,
Jumping over the clear blue sea.
The simmer of the water,
On their long bodies,
I softly close my eyes.

Smelling the salty sea;
Hearing the waves,
Crashing into one another.
That's —
What makes a beautiful day.

Cory Rice, Grade 9
Queen Creek High School, AZ

My Good-bye

I was lost when you guys were gone
It hurts to weep
Why did this have to happen?
Trying to still remember the memories
I had with both of you
I miss you
It's hard for me in some ways
To let you both go
I was not able to say good-bye
So this is my good-bye
I love you both
Rest In Peace

Rosie Caballero, Grade 7
Grand Canyon Middle School, AZ

The Beautiful Sky

The blue sky is beautiful
Just like the ocean and the sea
It can be seen by anyone
Including you and me
The clouds in the sky are beautiful
Like the cotton in the field
The look of them makes you yield
The bright sun is beautiful
Like all the stars in the sky
It makes you look at life
And wonder why?

Kenzie Peery, Grade 7
Sagewood Middle School, CO

Bubble Gum Yum

I like bubble gum.
Yummy yum yum.
I blow it up like a balloon.
Until it's as big as a monsoon.
It takes me up, up, up real high.
If it bursts I think I will die.
My big bubble takes me to space.
Where I see an alien with an ugly face.
The bubble takes me up past the moon.
I don't think I will see any one any time soon.
I hate this gooey green gum. Why did I chew it?
I'm so dumb. The bubble takes me up to the sun
Well, this isn't going to be to be very fun.
Pop!! Oh no, my bubble has burst. This just
couldn't get worse.
But, then a miracle happens. I land on a space ship
with a star captain. He gives me a drink and tells me to sip.
He takes me back home and I tell him, "thanks Mac."
When I go in my house, the first thing I do is get a piece
of bubble gum which I begin to chew. I like bubble gum yummy yum yum.

Josh Salazar, Grade 7
Shadow Ridge Middle School, CO

Guess My Color

Do you know what color is the best of them all?
You can see it at the mall.
You can see it in a zoo and anywhere in between.
It's the most colorful of all colors.
It's the color of love.
It's the color of warmth.
It's cozy and wonderful.
You can see it at night; it lurks in the shadows of your room.
It's the color of the ink that wrote my name at the top of this page.
It's the color of joy.
It's the color of life.
You may disagree but look around how many black things can you see?

Erin Wild, Grade 7
21st Century Public Academy, NM

Broken

I breathe you in like the humid air at sea. My only wish is that you would just love me.
I can see the tears that run down your face. Our love is like an unsolved case.
Glances slowly come together, I need to hold your hands forever
Water fills my dark green eyes knowing of those untold lies
You're throwing my heart down on the floor me only thinking that I want you more.
We were sewn together like strings on a quilt finally now you're feeling the guilt
I need your love, your touch, your smile. Please please just stay awhile
We've been growing apart during these frazzled days trapped, like in a cloudy maze
My heart forever beats for you oh how I wish we could peruse
You're like an angel disguised our trust, my feelings you did despise
Will you stay awake for me? Forever as our initials carved on that tree
I may be sad but I'm not weak this situation is bleak
You're under my skin like a horrible sin
It is time to close our eyes and say goodbye, yes yes go ahead and cry.

Morgan McCaleb, Grade 9
Mountain Ridge Jr High School, UT

2006 Blizzard

The grass was covered, a white blanket of snow,
It had climbed to the top of my house. Did you know?

The door was shut tight; we were trapped in our house,
But I knew I'd be right, we would never get out!

Still I pushed and I pulled, but the door wouldn't budge,
Were we stuck in there forever? You be the judge.

The next day I woke up, and I looked at that street,
And that snow piled up, to more than six feet!

And day after day that blizzard kept going,
I couldn't believe that it wouldn't stop snowing!

Even though it was boring, I'll still always miss,
My white winter's break in 2006.

Zoe Asztalos, Grade 7
Mandalay Middle School, CO

Faded Memory

I wanted to go to that one place.
The place where I first met you,
First saw you.
I wish I could see your face again.
But I know I can't.
I wish I could have stopped it.
But I can't.
Now you're gone.
Every time I see your picture…I feel mad and sad.
Now your voice has left me as well.
I feel so cold without you.
You make me warm.
Nothing left.
Just the painful memory of you gone is all I can feel.
Sadly enough,
You're just a faded memory.

Charlene Carrero, Grade 7
Ruch Elementary School, OR

The Stallion

The stallion plows through the mellow fields
of excitement and wonder.
He flaunts his coat and shows his skills.
He is happy.
Then he comes upon a creature with two legs.
This creature holds up a stick.
It stings.
It burns.
The pain…goes away.
He dreams of extraordinary lands
and has a wonderful sense of going home.
The stallion plows through the mundane fields
of potatoes and barley.

Christian Sagers, Grade 9
Mountain Ridge Jr High School, UT

Me and Myself

I looked in the mirror and this is what I see
A confused, complex version of me
Why am I like this, why am I here?
Why must I have this awfully deep fear?
Of what you ask, and why do I fear
I fear the times that are so very near
I watch my reflection, staring at what I see
Is she as I am or is she mocking me?
Mocking at my worries, mocking at my mistakes
He has me thinking that my life's something fake
I swiftly step back afraid of myself now
But when I look back she gives me a bow
Is my reflection perfectly content for what I am
Does he not care for the thoughts of them
Maybe she doesn't mind, maybe she doesn't care
Maybe he thinks that life is perfectly fair
Perhaps I'll look at this view and continue my life
And pretend that it's not stabbing me like a knife
Pretend it's not broken, pretend it's perfectly fine
For time is life, and my life is mine

Adrianna Harrison, Grade 9
Alma D'Arte High School, NM

Everyone

Quilt blankets, patchwork done,
Stitch by stitch everyone.
Enjoyed at picnics very long,
Carol singing, campfire song.
Watching the sun set or watching it rise,
We will always remember these special times.
Colors colliding as years go by,
Time goes so fast it almost flies.
Now our time is almost done,
We are all happy everyone.

Taylor Rose, Grade 7
Centennial Middle School, UT

Broken

You broke up with me yesterday
and ripped my heart in two.
I never thought I'd hurt this much,
I couldn't stop crying over you.

I do not feel complete anymore,
A part of me is missing.
I loved the way you used to play with my hair,
When we were on your bed, kissing.

You are the man of my dreams.
I wish we could be together.
Now I know that it's just not possible
But I want you to know that I'll love you forever.

Mallory Greybull, Grade 8
Poplar 7-8 School, MT

The Moon

I was walking down the street
When suddenly the moon was dancing
With the stars up in the sky.
I knew I was late
So I ran up the street to my house.
The time went by fast.

Junior Zuniga, Grade 7
Deamude SDA School, UT

Pops

When my pops passed away
It was a really sad day.
Everybody felt bad.

And time passed
It hasn't been a blast.
It is really quiet
Now the cat looks like it's on a diet.

We have lots of memories
Lots of photos
And many of his mottos.

But,
Now he is gone.

Conztancia Loretto, Grade 7
St Bonaventure School, NM

The Dark Dream

As I close my eyes
I begin to dream
Is it all lies?
My heart begins to scream

I saw the orange moon shining bright
I was left all alone
It was a starless night
There was an eerie tone

Locked in my cell
I felt trapped
There was a horrible smell
Overhead the thunder clapped

What do I hear?
I am so scared
I could sense someone was near
I only stared
I can taste the fear

Let me out!!!
Like an eagle flying
Fearfully I will shout
Every day I keep trying

Quianna Demaniow, Grade 7
Sky Vista Middle School, CO

In Loving Memory

Always like summer shining in the sun ready to greet people; adding lots of fun
She smelled of flowers; tall and strong with a sweet soft voice, smiling face
Nothing seemed wrong

She was like a second mom, even a sister to me
Long eyelashes and nice curved blue eyes
Softly framing the dimples on her cheeks
And my favorite part
Her long dishwater blonde hair, shining and full of laughing curls
That suddenly disappeared into happy memories

She had a great life before it hit — that dreadful disease
It crept up behind her in secrecy
Like a knight in shining armor, she would sit high on her horse
To fight the big, spreading monster
Then — it would fall off only to haunt her
With sword in hand, she fought to the end
Until — in weakness, there was nothing left but to surrender
To that mean, ugly ogre

But even that monster cannot conquer me
Because now I hold dear all those great memories

Kim, Sweet Kim

Kalinda Reed, Grade 7
Redlands Middle School, CO

Peace

Peace on Earth, I think we've wanted it from birth.
All this war, we can't take it anymore.
Guns and violence, there is no silence.
Lives are lost and there is a big cost.

Peace on Earth I think we've wanted it from birth.
There's no need to guess, this Earth can be mirthless.
There is so much stress, yet we dress for success to impress,
We all want progress to possess.
Nevertheless some can't confess.
Dirty deeds crash to the ground and no one can pick up a sound.
Missiles launch from the ground and no one can say that's profound.

Peace on Earth, I think we've wanted it from birth.
TV, you don't need this mindless entertainment.
You can watch but it keeps you in containment.

Peace on Earth, I think we've wanted it from birth.
countries don't fight, everything shall be all right.
The next generation will overcome segregation.
Peace on Earth, I think we've wanted it from birth.

Myles Thompson, Grade 8
Villa Montessori School – Phoenix, AZ

High Merit Poems – Grades 7, 8, and 9

New Life*
Oh precious new life welcome home,
Take in the world with your baby blue eyes,
Now with your family you'll never be alone,
We'll be there during your midnight cries.

I love your little hands and feet,
Small, soft, sweet smelling, and clean,
But I know they won't always be so sweet,
If you know what I mean.

Life has been so full of despair,
You're the bringer of hope and joy,
You're our breath of fresh air,
You're our precious baby boy!
Hannah Natwick, Grade 9
Tanalian School, AK
*Dedicated to Noah Jesse

Tool Time
Tools are clamorous, screws do spin,
Hurry and grunt and let the building begin.
Hold not thy outrageous sound,
Your creative ideas are now to be found.
First you start with a baby screw,
Fire up the nail gun and see what it can do!
Then you build a runty toy,
That's good for girls, and not just a boy.
Next thing you know you're building a doll house tower,
While coughing up all that saw dust powder.
You're way hyped up from this entire racket,
Since you have wood chips from foot to jacket.
Now you see your tools are hot,
You want to create and never stop!
All this power flowing through your veins,
Just to generate these discovery pains.
It is time to master this design,
The plan is perfect and eager to shine.
Now it's through and the tools are wasted,
AT LAST! It's time to clean what we have tasted.
Kapri Evans, Grade 9
Shelley Sr High School, ID

The Hot Warm Sun
I am the sun.
I'm bright, beautiful, and blasting colors
of orange, yellow, and red.
I'm like a heater that warms the earth.
Or a blanket that warms you at night.
When you drop a little bit of water on the sidewalk.
I heat the sidewalk.
With my radiant rays.
It becomes heating hot for people to touch.
Cecilia Figueroa, Grade 7
Eagle Point Middle School, OR

Electric Wiring
If I were the electric wiring for this school
Nothing would get done
The lights would flicker
The fire alarm would go off every minute
And if you tried to replace me
You would receive a lethal shock

In the winter the cooler would blow
In the summer
The heater would never go off
The phones would dial themselves
To call the cops for a swat standoff
The microwave would explode
People would think it is the end of the world
The computers would receive viruses
And delete all saved data
The televisions would never work
The DVD players would not play
The VHS players would destroy the tapes
The school would be a disaster zone
That is why I am glad to be a student instead
Of the electric wiring for the school
Andrew Culp, Grade 7
21st Century Public Academy, NM

You and I
You and I,
me and you,
one love,
two hearts,
carved names in a tree,
promising we'll always be,
trust and love,
we're soaring like a dove,
ups and downs but we're invincible,
haven't I told you we're inseparable,
kisses and hugs for eternity,
our love reaching as far as infinity,
seeing your face just may brighten my day,
I will always run your way,
I love the way when we kiss your cheek brushes mine,
will we possibly ever run out of time,
our time together may not last forever,
but our love will never die.
Amber Herbert, Grade 9
Wasson High School, CO

Love
Love is sometimes crazy,
Love is good but hazy.
Love can be an escape,
But if your heart breaks you can't use tape.
When it breaks it can heal,
If it's love why don't you kneel.
Edwin Thomas, Grade 8
Place Middle School, CO

Broken
I am broken and jealous
I wonder what my soul mates doing?
I hear his voice calling
I see his picture
I want my baby back
I am broken and jealous

I pretend I'm beautiful
I feel lonely
I touch out to you
I worry about Justin
I cry over him, too
I am broken and jealous

I understand love
I say I love you
I dream of him daily
I try not to fight
I hope he's with me forever
I am broken and jealous

Justina Gill, Grade 9
Buhl High School, ID

I Love You Because…
I love you because,
when I look into your eyes I feel
so free, so beautiful, like a turtle dove.
I love you because,
when I see you
my stomach starts to churn,
and shivers run up and down my spine,
and when I hear you speak,
there are no words for how I feel.
I love you because,
when you walk into the room,
it just seems to light up,
like nothing was, before you got there.
I love you because,
even though I try and try,
I just can't stop.
You seem to be a drug,
I am addicted to,
for I can't live without you.
I love you because,
life just wouldn't be without you.

Tedra Kay Spencer, Grade 8
Mount Adams Middle School, WA

Love
I know I love you
I know what I feel for you is true
I can't stop thinking about you
That's all I do
I hope you feel the same too

Javier Celis, Grade 7
Somerton Middle School, AZ

Mysterious Cloud
What is a cloud?
Is it a calming ball of white fluff,
Or a relaxing wonder in the sky?

What is a cloud?
Is it a big white thing dropping fun,
Or a huge dark mass bringing terror like the bully at our school?

What is a cloud?
Is it a peaceful addition to the sky,
Or a thick gray fog like a blind covering a window?

What is a cloud?

Collin Sanger, Grade 7
Sterling Middle School, CO

I Am
I am short and athletic
I wonder how they get the filling in the Twinkie
I hear music
I see chocolate chip pancakes
I want to be a combat pilot
I am short and athletic

I imagine getting straight A's
I feel confused
I touch my family
I worry that people will find out that I wet the bed, Oops, did I just say that.
I cried when the 2007 Broncos lost, now I'm out of tears
I am short and athletic

I understand that $2 + 2 = 4$
I say cookies rock
I dream I grow 3 inches every day for a week so I can be in the NHL
I try really hard to make sure I don't wash my iPod again
I hope I can see the Avalanche win The Cup
I am short and athletic

Colton Wiles, Grade 7
Shadow Ridge Middle School, CO

One Friend
There is this friend, who is a different in a sea of all sameness.
There is a friend, who is hiding when I'm seeking one who does not exist.
There is a friend, who says things when I don't want them to
but when I need them to.
There is a friend, who lets no one in her heart
unless they earn it.
There is a friend, who makes the best out of the
upsetting situation.
There is a friend, that can never frown
can always make me feel as if I wear a crown.
There is a friend, who loves cake as much as I
There is a friend, who sometimes sits in the corner.
But she always tells me we will be best friends forever.

Stephanie Norton, Grade 8
Canfield Middle School, ID

Weather

Windy with rushing water
Cool and colorful colors
Igniting into intense sound of rhythm
Falling far from the sky
Bold as brass beating on the windowpane
Overtaking with ominous sweeps
Jubilant joy brought to us
Terrifying yet tolerant all together

Lindsie Snyder, Grade 7
La Center Middle School, WA

Fort Collins, Colorado

I always enjoy spring the most
I can see the early blossoms
And feel the semi cool breeze
It's the end of winter
And I can feel it like none other
I can smell the start of summer
Fresher than ever in the moist air
I can taste the fun BBQs waiting for me
And the long nights hanging with friends
I see the new colors of the precious flowers
And see the bushy trees cast shade
I can eat my favorite foods all the time
And enjoy the wind whipping through my hair
I can sit on the front porch
And read my favorite book
And those are only some of the reasons why…
I enjoy spring the Most!!!!!!!!!!

Olivia Damge, Grade 7
Lincoln Jr High School, CO

Sports

In track everyone sees my back
Eats my dust when I bust
For that finish line even they can't even whine
As I cross into the great divine
In tennis my serve's so fast
It practically whips the sweat off their backs
As the ball bounces down the court
They watch out so they don't get hurt
I got my racket at value village
But it doesn't matter because I've got skillage
In water polo I can win solo
With the help of my team
We can cut through the defense like a laser beam
As I swim down towards the goal
It's like I'm tunneling through the defense like a mole
In basketball I can touch the rim
And my skill ain't just a hymn
When I play the game
I can make it rain
My downtown shots are sick
But they ain't the same as Michael Vick's

Wesley Boyett, Grade 9
Shorecrest High School, WA

Returning Discovery

Weeping willows and wandering worries,
Caress their way into my mending heart,
My thoughts turn into something quite abstract,
Making any ounce of sense, struggle to start.

Whispering winds and dancing daffodils,
Profound and sparkle in my hazel eyes,
And welcome back the dimples settling in my cheeks,
As everything becomes undoubtedly realized,
Making any arrogance near me, weak.

Elated tears embedded within my quavering questions,
Have begun to shift gears.
Life, is the silver lining on every cloud.
Even the dullest can become sheer.

I now peacefully play along with the swaying leaves
Graciously accepting the effervescent fact that…
I have found me.

Andrea Minster, Grade 8
Shaw Middle School, NV

Clouds

I am a cloud, floating with loneliness, in thought, in denial,
As I gently follow the breeze,
I see the world with jealousy that I too can't be there,
Feelings so detached, from love from longing,
But maybe if I scream you'll hear my pain.

Alexandria Yoo, Grade 7
Dunstan Middle School, CO

Blue

Blue is the color of the sky,
Blue is the feeling of bouncing way up high.
Blue is the color of the ocean,
Blue is the feeling of a motion.
Blue is the color of a scorching flame,
Blue is the feeling of winning a game.
Blue is the smell of a wonderful dinner,
Blue is the feeling of getting thinner.
Blue is the feeling of accomplishment,
Blue is the feeling of knowing you're important.
Blue is the taste of frozen ice cream,
Blue is the feeling of a wonderful dream.
Blue is the feeling of gladness,
Blue is also the feeling of sadness.
Blue is the color of the Iris carnation,
Blue is the feeling of relaxation.
Blue is the feeling of sleeping in late,
Blue is what makes me feel great.
Blue is the sound of a rushing water fall,
Blue describes it all.

Jacob Roberts, Grade 7
Ernest Becker Middle School, NV

A Long Lost Friend

It was love at first sight; I wanted to hold him with all my might.
His green eyes looked up at me, as I help my shaking puppy.
His floppy ears hung there, like the pedals of a flower.
His cute little paws — looking at him made your heart pause.
His fur was so soft, like a cloud aloft.
It looked like the coat of a bear, brown, with a hint of black hair.
Then it hit me, his name would be Grizzly.
As he grew, my homework pile did too.
I watched him play outside my window, not being able to play with him made me sorrow.
Then that fateful day came, "Grizzly bit my dog!" my brother claimed.
After hours of discussion, my parents came to an accusation.
Grizzly was to go, he would live on my uncle's farm in Idaho.
Apparently, my life was too busy.
I see him once a month or so, on that farm in Idaho.
He's still soft to the touch, though he's grown so much.
And when I look into those eyes, I wonder if he remembers when I
Held him, and first loved him.

Catherine Woolston, Grade 9
Mountain Ridge Jr High School, UT

Fire Sounds

The fire crackles brightly and purrs like a tabby cat
The wind suddenly howls like a wolf on the hunt
Whipping trees as he passes and they groan in agony

The wolf once more howls and whistles and with glee charges the fiery feline
The tabby spits and sputters then growing a long mane
And enlarging in size the tabby now rivals the howling wolf of wind as a lion of fiery proportions

The lion roars out a challenge the wolf howls in acceptance
The wolf charges once again howling and roaring fills the air
The wolf wind only feeds the lion the wolf then howls out a summons

And to his aid comes a soft pitter then a patter, a drizzle and finally thunder
The lion can only spit and sputter at this and tries to escape
Only growing weaker and smaller

The wolf sits still watching the end
And only intervenes when the lion is no more and the wolf blows away the ashes.

Caleb Gerdes, Grade 9
Buhl High School, ID

Soccer

The light shines onto the grass tickets get sold out way too fast
Crazy fans run through the streets just to see professionals with a ball at their feet
All stores are closed in town you can hear the home team's stadium song
You can hear the sound of the cleats on the ground players ask for the ball as they pass it around
You hear the whistle blow when the ref calls a foul the defender yells at his teammate loud
Corner kick is called and the ball is in the air the goalie dives out as you see the sweat off the forward's hair
A penalty is called and he is about to kick one step two step then he slips
He gets the ball back and shoots right at the post he missed about an inch he was just so close
The midfielder crosses it in the box his own player scores everyone is in shock
The team takes the lead the other team must not give up they must proceed
The game is over and they are in defeat there is only one winner and loser this is the game of soccer.

Ryan Benavente, Grade 8
Fertitta Middle School, NV

Build Me a World

I feel nothing in this world,
I experience nothing at all.
I go through no emotions,
even as tears begin to fall.

Can't you hear my cries for help,
or the pounding of my feet?
Can you describe the way it felt?
The way my young heart would beat…

Could you fill this world with people
who won't talk about you from afar?
People who won't ignore you
for whom you really are.

Build me a world that's worth the emotion,
a world where we can be free.
Build me a world I can escape to,
a world where I can be me.

Mara Almanzor, Grade 8
Mattson Middle School, WA

Because of You

Because of you I stand here today
Because of you I grow and play
I watch the choices and changes you make
Sometimes they may be a mistake
You turn things around and make them great.
There is no dad in the world that could ever take your place
There is no one who has quite your taste
You're all I have to win the race
Life is hard but I'll make it through and it's all because of you

Makala Cox, Grade 7
Philomath Middle School, OR

My Language Arts Teacher

In the beginning of fall
I met a teacher who was quite tall
After a few days, I thought, this teacher knows all
From the easy punctuation to the difficult and precise commas
My teacher rubbed out all the fuzz
That my brain had, I understood
I actually thought I could
I could write a story without the horrible, awful mistakes
That I had made in the past
I put apostrophes before almost every s
Making my whole paper a mess
But now I can rest assured that will happen less
Stories come to my head as fast as lightning
Thing is, they come so fast, I never get around to finishing
I have never learned more about language arts
Than from my language arts teacher with her smarts

Laura Doroteo, Grade 8
Cedar Ridge Middle School, OR

Baby Cheetah Slippers

Baby cheetah slippers are as soft as a pillow.
Baby cheetah slippers purr when you wear them.
Baby cheetah slippers love you and you love them.
Baby cheetah slippers are fun to wear.

Ricardo McCrary, Grade 7
Grand Canyon Middle School, AZ

Love Has No Sympathy

to care about your love
you need to treat it like something you love
treat it like something you care for
but you must find it
and not let it slip out of your grasp
but to keep that love you must cherish

because love has no sympathy
not even for me
love will leave everyone heart broken
and
if you try to rush love
it will leave you in tears
to let you drown
in your own depression

later and later
you start to forget
but
you won't forget your first love
because love has no sympathy
so hold on tight, and never let go
enjoy the ride, and the show

Matthew Thompson, Grade 9
Hendrix Jr High School, AZ

The Ocean

Waves are crashing, bish, bash
Fish are swimming, splish, splash
The wind is blowing, swoo, woo
The clouds are rolling in too

The stars disappear one by one
the moon is gone, as is the sun
the sky is a mix of green and grey
how will the ship find the bay

But then the wind stops its blow
The water starts to slow
The clouds begin to move away
all that is left is a slight spray.

Sometimes it is quite dreadful
other times, it is quiet and simple
For how large and frightening, the ocean may be
It is still part of nature filled with beauty.

Hillary Peterson, Grade 7
Aurora Academy, CO

Program Life

Program life can be quite tough,
Rules, chores, all that stuff.
Accountability galore,
Schedules, and much much more.
Some of us will stay here longer,
But all of us will leave here stronger.
And on our graduation day,
The newfound confidence we display
Will be with us for our whole lives;
We'll see the world with brand new eyes.

Thank you, Diamond Ranch Academy,
For changing my life.

Chris Makaron, Grade 9
Diamond Ranch Academy, UT

Summer's Day

I can feel the grass beneath my feet,
the wind through my hair.
Days like this are calm and few,
days like this are rare.

My feelings are all mixed and matched,
on this summer's day.
Eventually the truth comes out,
but in my own special way.

Elsa Homann, Grade 7
Mandalay Middle School, CO

The Spring of Life

sun shining brightly
tress swaying in they wind
hair blows in my face
happily dancing around
the spring of life is in my step

Gem Boehm-Reifenkugel, Grade 8
Sedona Charter School, AZ

The Dead

I am sitting in a graveyard,
listening to the dead.
All other people hear the silence,
but I can hear them speak.
Most say how they died,
others tell about their lives.
All of their whispers and shouts
seem overwhelming at first.
But after you hear them all
in one single verse,
you wait and wait for the next hearse,
bringing another story to hear.
The next time you go to a funeral,
listen, and you will hear
the dead as I do.

Ellery Wagner, Grade 8
Zia Middle School, NM

The Evil We Call Violence

I'm gonna talk to you about how to be a friend,
So you don't have to learn that when you are pushed you are alone,
But rather that when somebody starts messing, you can talk it out on the phone.
We are brothers and sisters, we don't need to fight or pretend,
We can all hear you; we know that it's true, that we must make amends.
So that when you ask you will receive and though no words can retrieve
What has been lost in this "war" you can replant your core.
You can start over anew, the only one stopping you is you
So, if you dare to stand up nice, strong, and proud,
Will you say "I will stop this violence someday!" and yell it out loud?
Do you dare to be different? Do you dare to be strong?
Do you dare to make a movement that says violence is wrong?
Can you be who you are, and say what you say?
Can you stand up right now and make a change today?

This is to those, who are willing to fight,
For those who know the difference between the wrong and the right,
If you are that brave,
If you know who you are right on this day,
Then let's take up this nation,
And stop this violence today!

Danielle Little, Grade 7
Martin Middle School, NV

Memories Aren't Always What They Seem

As I walked back through the lanes that I had walked before,
Ambled cautiously through briars, cut my heel 'gainst a stone.
I realized a secret hiding in the woods under heath, and lore,
As I trudged along the path that I trudge along alone.

Lo, soon my quarry showed its face, letting out a soft sweet sigh,
Unparalleled epochs of absences, distractions kept me from this place.
As the chains that bind it to its stationary spot let out a creaking cry,
I wept for joy, for shame, for me, and adolescence showed its face.

Dark timber, rustic iron, and pure joy my niche was made of,
Untouched by time or human hands a valley of beginnings.
Memories that rushed through the soul reminded me of love,
As the babe cries to its mother so to did these to me, so I sat upon my swings.

A lasting remnant of childish amour, forever captured moments,
I recalled a single memory that sprouted in midair,
I swung as high as chains would fly then released all earthly claimants,
'Tis a place to cry, to say goodbye, to kiss, to love, and share.

Soon the frame of remembrance shook me from my lofty perch,
A weakness in the cornerstone rattled the ancient metal beam.
I dropped with nought of dignity or valour from my reminiscent search,
It was only then I recalled that fault; memories aren't always what they seem.

Emma Anderson, Grade 8
St Mary's School, OR

High Merit Poems – Grades 7, 8, and 9

Pencils
Could be sharp, could be dull.
Always used by all.

It's sitting on the cold stone desk, all alone.
Just waiting for someone to pick it up.

A girl picks one of many for the test.
Could this possibly bring good luck?
The test begins and she starts to write.
Does it hurt the pencil?

The test is done and she gives it to the teacher.
The pencil is alone again,
Alone on the stone cold desk.

It's waiting for a gentle hand to pick it up once again.
But no matter how many times it may be used,
It's always left back on that stone cold desk.
Isana Urquidi, Grade 8
St Pauls Catholic School, ID

Little Seed, Big Tree
Here's a little seed,
lonely and cold.
It's forgotten there in the dirt.
No one will talk to it; no one cares.
Everyone ridicules it
because it is so small.

Who could guess that someday
it will be tall?
It goes through good times, and bad times.
It survives the seasons — alone and afraid.

But, one glorious day you stare
up, up at that grand, great tree
that sprang from one tiny seed.
Will Lane, Grade 7
Phoenix Preparatory Academy, AZ

War
War is the thing no one wants
Death is everyone's fear
Life is what everyone wants to keep
Going to war is letting life loose to do as it pleases
For some it just runs and plays
For others it jumps off a cliff and dies
For soldiers in war their life is standing on the edge of the cliff
Some jump, some don't
It's not our choice, it's God's
They never know when they're gonna go
They don't want to leave loved ones behind
They don't want to leave family and friends behind
This is why people fear war and most of all death
Derek Buttram, Grade 8
Round Mountain Jr-Sr High School, NV

On the Stage
Backstage, last minute preparation.
Opening night, the house is full
Of crying babies and sleepy old people.
The lights flicker, time to start.
We sing LaLa and dance to the beat.
The audience claps.
It's my scene now.
I fight my way through the crowd of actors to the stage.
Bright lights beat down like the sun.
I feel a bead of sweat through thick makeup.
The soft piano builds up to a loud drum.
I sing LaLa and dance to the beat.
The audience claps.
My smile reaches up to my ears
It's curtain call now.
Thunderous applause still ringing in my ears.
I walk out to the theater into my parents' open arms
Back in the warmth of the dressing room
The smell of flowers sweet
I'm thrilled yet tired.
Tomorrow we start again.
Emily Van Loan, Grade 7
St Elizabeth Ann Seton Catholic School, AZ

Flight Sonnet #1
Wings spread to catch the ever upward stream
Shove off and slide through the cool light blue sky
My mind and my wings will work as a team
I feel like spirit when I'm up this high
I soar above clouds and through them too
The scintillating plane of aqua light
Now I wheel downwards, feeling fresh and new
My feet hit the water — cool, fresh, and bright
And then the patchwork world way down below
Next, a tempting array of city lights
I cannot stop and I know I can't slow
This is not the most of important flights
But some things just cannot be delayed now
And some day I'll be there, one day, somehow
Jessica Hale, Grade 8
Eagle Rock Jr High School, ID

Comforting Fog
The fog has already set over the plains
I sit on my porch with my coffee in hand
I snuggle myself in my comfy blanket
I just sit there thinking about those days you are gone
But then I think about those times you are right by my side
The fog reminds me of you
I just sit there with you right by my side
Even though I might not see you
You are in the fog looking over me
Nathan Hall, Grade 7
Sterling Middle School, CO

In the Dark
Sitting in the dark,
just you and me,
escaping the world.
Just sitting there face to face.
Not speaking,
not knowing,
not understanding,
just sitting.
The wind blows in our hair,
cold, yet calming.
It whispers to us,
softly, still, and full of hope.
Still not speaking,
we sat and waited.
Stephanie Walker, Grade 7
Lowell Scott Middle School, ID

She
If you loved her
Maybe then you would've saved her
Made her a little braver
She would've felt a little safer

She walks silently without a sound
Thinking "Do you see me now?"

Her tears hit the floor
She can't take this anymore
She's lost her soul
Her heart's become cold
Her feelings she holds

There's no love in sight
She hates her life
Every day she's filled with fright
Emily Smedley, Grade 8
Molasky Jr High School, NV

The Cotton Field
The cotton field.

A place where birds nest,
a home for ground squirrels,
a sea of white puff balls.

Picking time comes around.

All the birds fly away,
the squirrels find new homes,
all the puff balls are gone.

No life in the cotton field.
A forest of twigs.
Byron Ollerton, Grade 7
Villago Middle School, AZ

Ode to Chocolate
Oh dear chocolate,
Here's to you!
Foods that compare,
Add up to few.

Oh dear chocolate,
You make me melt.
You also act as a gift,
That is meant to be heartfelt.

Oh dear chocolate,
You taste so divine;
And when I see someone else with you,
I wish you were mine.

Oh dear chocolate,
If I had to choose,
Between you and other candies,
You would never lose.

Oh dear chocolate,
So delectable and pure,
I will be eating you soon,
That's for sure!
Madelyn Sander, Grade 7
Sterling Middle School, CO

Dreams
My dreams are not large,
My dreams are not small,
But I do dream after all.

Some come in packages,
Some come in sleep,
But dreams keep on coming,
Like growing wheat.

I do need to dream,
I do need to try,
Otherwise, my life will be dry.
Nick Low, Grade 7
Dunstan Middle School, CO

I Don't Want
The place I never want to be in
Where we have to wake up early
They make me do math homework
And we actually read
I just want to sleep
Hope it ends soon
The last day
And then
Summer!
Dezmond Lewis, Grade 8
Bessemer Academy, CO

My Girl, Adrian
Adrian is my girl,
With whom I spend my time.
If looks could kill,
She'd commit a crime.

She has long, dark hair
With the body of a goddess.
But don't let that fool you,
She is very modest.

Her dark brown eyes,
Are truly to die for.
Her legs are long,
Oh, by the way, there's four.

What kind of girl,
Would look like this?
The kind of girl,
You don't want to kiss!

Where is this girl of mine?
She's in the barn, of course!
I brush her and feed her,
Adrian is my horse!
Andrew Pullara, Grade 9
Pueblo County High School, CO

Soccer
Soccer is fun
Soccer is awesome
I like to kick the ball,
I like to kick the ball to the net
And scream GOAL, GOAL!!
Francisco Villegas, Grade 7
Somerton Middle School, AZ

Voices
Look at the trees,
the leaves, the grass!
How beautiful they are,
with their heart-touching voices.
Voices that fit who you are,
That love you and stay with you,
comforting, soothing, wild voices

No longer are they wild and free.
A lust for power and domination
Destroyed them, leaving only
few alive.

We still have them, those
sweet, loving voices, in our hearts;
All we need to do is listen.
Melyzjah Smith, Grade 7
Aurora Academy, CO

Rock Band

A one…a two…a skididlydoo
The band rocks in fear.
Youngins rock till they drop.
Security tires from pushing the fans back.

The lead singer is about to drop from dehydration.
Guitarist fingers are about to fall off from guitaring.
But me I rock till I can't rock no more.
The concert ends every one is sad.

Trenton Spillman, Grade 7
Shadow Ridge Middle School, CO

Loneliness

I spend most of my time in solitude.
This loneliness is because of my fears.
This fear is showing my feelings and moods.
I try not to show anyone my tears.
I try not to have or make any friends.
Because of my distress of losing them.
The agony in my heart has no ends.
I reserve myself because of my hem.
I guess people would call me an outcast.
Since they would see me appearing forlorn.
I was never a "Loner" in my past.
But I guess my destiny is just torn.
So this is what caused my forsaken life.
And also why I live a lonely life.

Yolanda Li, Grade 9
Clark High School, NV

Gathering Dust

Lost in a world with only hate
I can't get out
Behind closed gates.
In this world
All love is lost.
Many paths never crossed.
The sky is gray,
Holds no hope.
Tragedy strikes.
Impossible to cope.
There are wishes for color,
In this helpless world.
But, the gray only swirled.
I feel like I'm looking,
From the outside in.
I try to help.
They won't listen.
One day,
Emotion will show.
Bringing with it
Color and glow.

Hayley Dahlhauser, Grade 7
Our Lady of Lourdes Catholic School, UT

Awake

After a long slumber,
Everything comes awake.
They look around trying,
To think of what to make.

There's an endless possibility
But sooner or later they'll know,
Of what to make for that year
After the season of falling snow.

They have many ideas to choose from
Because of earlier years
Dark green leaves or drooping blue flowers
Which sometimes look like tears.

After a long slumber,
The plants come awake,
They look around trying,
To think of what to make.

Katrina Shumway, Grade 7
Terry 7-8 School, MT

Childhood

Childhood is a chunk of plain, fresh-bought clay,
Never before shaped in any way.
Sometimes I wish my childhood would stay
A cold hard slab, forever gray.
Never to be heated, molded, or pressed
By worry, knowledge, shame, and stress.
Before, I envied Peter Pan,
Being able to do something no one can.
Always staying a kid that can fly.
Now, I remember that time with a sigh.
I realized that I was very scared
Of growing up and becoming white-haired.
I saw everyone leave to be on their own
But I didn't want to be left all alone.
My childhood is a piece of candy.
Sour, sweet, it's all up to me.
Once it was gone, I knew I was wrong.
Now, with life, I just have to go along.
If our childhood is good, it's a sweet song.
If not, it will temper us to be strong.

Breanna Tai, Grade 9
Tempe Preparatory Academy, AZ

When My Best Friend Moved Away

Looking back at that day,
Feeling empty inside,
How could she leave?
I felt so bereaved.
She said that we would always be very best friends.
I knew it was coming but,
So soon? The pain never ends

Claire Rader, Grade 9
Lakewood High School, CO

My Sister
Sister, Sister
Oh how I love to hug and kiss her
We spin like a twister
That's my little sister
Oh what you've taught me!
My sister
Your smiles that shine
Your eyes that twinkle
Your hair that glows
Oh what you've taught me!
My sister
When you come into my room
When you give me a hug
When you "hold me tight at night"
Oh what you've taught me!
My sister
When you fall
When you crawl
You always get back up again
Oh what you've shown me
Sister, sister oh how I love you!
Andria Monks, Grade 7
Sky Vista Middle School, CO

I Wanna Fly
I wanna fly
I wanna fly like an eagle
I wanna run
I wanna run like puma
I wanna fight
I wanna fight like a hungry lion
I wanna win
I wanna win like a super bowl player
I wanna be a leader
I wanna lead like a chief
I wanna party
I wanna party like a rock star
I wanna have pride
I wanna have pride like a rooster
I wanna be happy
I wanna be happy like a baby
I wanna be honest
I wanna be honest like God
I wanna succeed
I wanna succeed like my dad
I wanna fly
Juan Palacios, Grade 9
Shelley Sr High School, ID

Clouds
I like to compare clouds to airplanes,
they move so fast but yet so slow
when it hails it is like bombs
and when it rains it is like bullets.
Alex Inscoe, Grade 7
Dunstan Middle School, CO

Ode to My Goldfish
Oh, no! My fishie! I think that he is dead!
He's floating still at the top of his bowl and I think he's underfed!
    I fed him well this morning,
        And I think the day before.
            Oh, I'm not sure, but I need a cure 'cause I miss my dear Fred!

Oh, no! My fishie! He has left me now!
I'm so sad, I'm a nervous wreck and Mom's gonna have a cow!
    I just replaced him Monday,
        And twice the previous week!
            It's all a blur, but I need a cure 'cause I miss my dear Fred!

Oh, no! My fishie! He has gone away!
Well, I guess he's in a better place than he was the other day!
    He always had fresh water,
        And his bowl was somewhat clean!
            Oh, I'm not sure, but I need a cure 'cause I miss my dear Fred!
Chelsea Fletcher, Grade 8
Marshall Ranch Elementary School, AZ

Black and White
Your father taught you it was right to wear the pointed hat of white,
I see the ashes track their front yard you torched,
Into the grass the letters are scorched.
But soon green will return,
To leave no trace of the words you burn.
But forever there will be, someone we can't see,
Because of who you chose to be.
The crosses points as sharp as knives, show me you took more than lives.
The jurors pale faces hold no concern,
I hear them yell that court's adjourned.
Your cruel words slipped through your innocence plea,
You said you had a heart but you can't convince me.
Your heartless mind is not to blame,
Your dad can hold his rightful claim.
The young know only the hate you teach,
He took because it was the only thing in reach.
Despite the battles that were fought,
We believe what we are taught.
Wrong is the same as right,
In this world of black and white.
Elspeth Jensen, Grade 8
Enterprise Middle School, WA

My Friends
My friends are an endless track of paths.
Taking one way leads to another and ultimately a dead end.
Find the right way, the right path is like walking through a maze in pitch black.
If I choose one friend I lose another, back at a dead end.
I'll go with a friend that I know and trust, the one I know will go for the gold.
Meeting new people along the way, others looking for a way out as well.
Helping others, others helping people, working together.
Ultimately a way is revealed to the outside world.
Devon Browitt, Grade 7
Eaton Middle School, CO

Indiana

The cold breeze rushes through the trees
making noises like creatures from books
and pushing the creak onto rocks

A bright sun pops through the clouds
and splotches of light can be seen through the brush

Deer trample down flowers, birds sing in the skies
you can smell the sweet bark smell
and feel the heat of Indiana

White puffy clouds float high above
and the sky is like an ocean

Hay is growing all around
all yellow-golden and smelling good
the grass sways to the wind
and seems to be a sea of green

The stillness stays and lasts forever
until the dark skies come

Michaela Vining, Grade 7
La Center Middle School, WA

Love

Love is unconditional
Love is true
Love will make you smile
Even when you're blue
Love is precious
And oh so dear
Someday for me it will appear
And when it does
My arms will open
My heart will fill
And I will give it my everything
To make sure that my love does not just stand still
But for now I am too young
So I will wait
For when it comes
I surely hope it's not too late

Anisa Ann Archuleta, Grade 7
Mandalay Middle School, CO

Falling

I love the way she makes me feel.
She gives me butterflies whenever I think about her.
When she looks at me I feel like I'm floating.
The first time I heard her voice I thought
it was the most beautiful thing I'd ever heard.
When I see her it's like time stops.
Her beauty glows like she's looking down from the sun.
I'm falling for her and she's the only one
who can catch me.

Pyper Goodro, Grade 9
Mount Jordan Middle School, UT

Baseball

I love to play baseball in the springtime.
It is more about hanging out with friends.
We don't often make time for each other.
It's always hard to put everything else aside.
But we make time to play baseball each year.
Some coaches are nice and some yell a lot.
Sometimes I listen and sometimes I don't.
And I love to play the game, in the field mostly.
I try not to get mad, good call or bad.
I always eat a hot dog and drink a Coke.
Baseball in the spring means summer is near.
The weather is getting hotter each day.
Soon I'll be putting away baseball gear.
I love to go fishing in the summertime.

Kahner Cunningham, Grade 9
Clark High School, NV

Grandma Judy

You're like my good luck charm.
In Iowa you live by more than one farm.
You would never do anyone harm.
You are my Grandma Judy.

You play golf both miniature and big.
From my soda you always take a swig.
In your garden I still help you dig.
You are my Grandma Judy.

Even though you live a million miles away,
You can still save my day.
In the soccer tournament you watched me play.
You are my Grandma Judy.

I have spent every Christmas with you.
You are the angel I always knew.
Without you I wouldn't have a clue.
You'll always be my Grandma Judy.

Zachary Goodenow, Grade 7
Sky Vista Middle School, CO

Drenched in Homework

As I sit doing homework
I wish I could chillax
My brain is spinning like a top
I have a ginormous page written
But still only halfway done

As I snack on my grapple and craisins
An idea came to mind
I'll just write about the trouble I'm having
Now many ideas are coming to mind
Too fast to even write them down

Ryan Sinclair, Grade 7
Mandalay Middle School, CO

I Wish

I wish I was there with you
I wish we could be together
I wish the drama would just fly away
I wish other guys didn't get in the way
I wish I could just fall into your arms
I wish I never cried
I wish you weren't the one to make me cry, yet the only one to make me smile.
I wish I was playing the sport I love where I want to be, because my time is done here
I wish everything was the way it should be
I wish you absolutely loved me the way I think I love you
I wish I knew what I want
I wish I knew that we will be
I wish you were mine
I wish other girls never interfered
I wish when I look in your eyes I wouldn't just melt the way I do
I wish I didn't get a huge smile on my face when I see your name on my phone
I wish my stomach didn't fill with butterflies when you call my name or I hear your voice
I wish, I wish life was simple!
I wish I didn't love you! Sorry.

Haley Nichols, Grade 8
La Plata Middle School, NM

What You Call Volleyball

Call a spike a knife — always sharp and on point
Call a volleyball a pogo stick — bouncing from place to place always trying to get around
Call a serve a tennis ball — has to always get over the net
Call a net a bridge — you'll eventually have to get over it
Call a set a trampoline — gently bouncing you up
Call a uniform a business suit — you always have to wear it while at work

Jordan Lewis, Grade 7
Mears Middle School, AK

The 2nd Most Perfect Man Alive

His skin as white as the sparking snow glinting in the sun
Hair as blond as the bright, warm sand next to the rolling waves
　　Smile as fresh as the sweet morning sunrise
His heart as melodious as the peaceful strum of the vibrating strings
　　Of a well-loved guitar
His spirit is one with Zeus, energetic, mighty, yet compassionate
The stars twinkle in his silky blue eyes like diamonds on a baby-blue feather
Hands smooth as a worn pebble, gentle as the calm running water in a stream
　　Laughter is his shadow,
Sunshine is his friend, following him like a dog does his master
Every room brightens in his presence, every flower grows stronger, every tree stands erect
He is a happy buzzing bumblebee forever undisturbed on a bright, sunny afternoon
　　Polite, sensitive, like a lamb softly chewing on a green wad of grass
Amusing as a young, adorable child. Hilarious as a well-known comedy.
His walk, shuffling like a duck, confident, yet reluctant
　　Voice as the rolling, crashing, rumbling of thunder
Bright and clear covered with dripping honey-sweetening dew, yet still undefined in its grace.
I will catch every drop of dew
　　Cherish it with all my might. Treasure every moment
Hold on to every word, every memory,
Every laugh, every tear.

Sydney Heyrend, Grade 9
Mountain Ridge Jr High School, UT

Mountain Road

I went for a hike, just me and my dog Butch,
We started at the mountain house,
We ended at the meadow,
We headed past the chicken coop,
The goat pen and the outhouse.

We saw white clouds in the sky,
An abert's squirrel upon a rock,
Golden aspens, green pines,
And a bluebell flower in its periwinkle smock.

The sights around made us elated,
And oh so free,
Butch leapt around in joy,
The mountains too, stirred the joys inside of me.

Brinna Ammons-McCarron, Grade 7
Mandalay Middle School, CO

I Hate How You Are

I hate the way you walked to me.
I hate the way you talked to me.
I hate the way you made me cry,
And that every time I saw you a little more I died.
I hated sitting waiting for your call.
I hated how you didn't think of me at all.
I hate how my heart was just a way for you to play.
I hate how you didn't even care to stay.
I hate how you think I'm ruined.
But, I love how you built me up.

Frankie Lane, Grade 8
Shaw Middle School, NV

The Beauty of Nature

A fawn ran to me and asked happily,
Do you know where my family has gone?
I said I'm sorry, I don't and the fawn ran from me
To the beautiful, rising sun

Smooth, solid stones give me a seat,
I watch wavy water flowing downstream
Little lilies lay by my feet,
As the breeze passes by, all of them beam

I see majestic, green trees
Wave a friendly hello,
Birds that fly in the breeze,
Their colors not mellow

Though the world is full of beauty,
This poem means much more
God gave us a simple duty,
To take care of the Earth from crust to core.

Michele Spangle, Grade 7
Leading Edge Academy - Gilbert, AZ

Dear Cecilia

My dear Cecilia,
I'm far away.
For a ruler of what I rule
It's funny 'not' to say
Uncreative realistic indifferent fools
love isn't a game and when all of hell cools
I'll be waiting in the dark,
I'll be waiting in the day
But even if the day is dark
The light will fade away
Your tinted wings and pastel eyes
(Can't) can ask onto the sky
But after a long while of heartbreak and ache
You (can't), can fly
And of the love in my heart
Of the feelings deep in my core
Oh, My dear Cecilia
I could offer nothing more.

Sara London, Grade 8
Colorado Academy, CO

I'm Not Who You Think I Am

I'm not who you think I am
I know what I am doing, I think for myself
You think I am a good person
But you don't always trust me
You get mad when I speak the truth
And you get mad when I tell a lie
You say something about me
And when I tell you you are right, you explode
I don't know what to do to make you happy
So I hide away in my room to avoid the situation
I'm not who you think I am
I can tell right from wrong
I know what I should do
And what I shouldn't
The people I am with shouldn't matter
You should know I will do right
No matter what is happening
I will be who I am and will do what I know is right
I can be foolish and stubborn, but that's just me
So no matter what you believe
I am not who you think I am

Preston Sample, Grade 9
Buena High School, AZ

Accident

When I crossed the street I saw
screaming cars coming at me with great force.
My bones cracked.
I couldn't get up, the pain was enormous,
I just lay there with no movement.
But I still remember that car slamming into me.
I have been afraid ever since then to simply cross the street.

Kelsey Knox, Grade 8
Cedar Park Christian School – Everett Campus, WA

Scenes of Shells
I see dazzling colors
I smell salty sea
I hear whispers of the ocean
I feel a curly touch

The colors are endless
The salt is strong
The ocean calls to me
The spirals are stories of their own
Michael Chidester, Grade 7
Sky Vista Middle School, CO

Life
Flowers die, so will I
So truth be told, I'll just live my life.

Petals fall, petals grow
Life will go on, even if you fall.

Pain hurts, with sorrow and grief,
Love's happy, as a belief
So bright and pretty
'Til the clouds roll in
And your pain comes once again
To hit you in the soul
'Til you fall with no love.

So you have no love,
You're all out
'Til God raises you once again
In the shadows of the deep.
You rise as a flower
And break with no love
But just as a single flower.
Kylie Cecil, Grade 9
Granite High School, UT

Troubles
Have you seen the world today?
All the violence,
all the crime.
Everybody says,
"just give it some time."
How long do we have?
Till our bones waste away in the wind.
Does any of it matter?
Our accomplishments, our sins.
I don't see the answer
to the questions I seek.
Things are never true,
never as they seem.
Should we try to redeem
or just give up,
on life I mean?
Cody Gibbons, Grade 8
Stapley Jr High School, AZ

Celebrations
I am a rose, helpless, weak, tender, and pure.
I turn my head towards the sun, for the morning, warmth's cure.
The white blanket that has held me falls to the ground,
to join the ocean of snow…without a sound.
I watch as the sun rises up in the east,
to melt the snow on the ground, sun's springtime feast.
The other flowers come up as the snow disappears,
the sun melts the snow, and it falls down like tears.
The birds all chirp in celebration of spring,
it's like they're laughing to hear the springtime bells ring.
Grace McPhail, Grade 7
Ilwaco Middle School, WA

School
It's Monday morning at 7:01, I am half-asleep.
I'm having a bad hair day as I begin to freak…
I just remembered the homework from last week!
Even though school starts in an hour, I am now just starting my shower.
Screaming now, the water is cold, I soon find out my cereal has mold.
Searching now for bread and butter, I cannot find one or the other.
Now school starts in a half-hour! How am I to make it?
As I sit here wondering, maybe we have bacon.
My stomach starts rumblin', and then it starts achin'. My ride to school's a comin'.
Putting on my shoes, Watching *Winnie the Pooh*
Brushing teeth, combing hair, contacts in, off to school, nothing forgotten.
How was I supposed to know my apple was rotten?
When at school, classroom is cold…The thermos heater was sold!
It's Monday morning at 8:01. How was I to know school just begun?
Alyssa Schmidt, Grade 8
Canfield Middle School, ID

Across the Trail of Tears!
We are at home running free
Along the trail through the tall tree

Then the long knives came what a difference they would make
Our lives were changed forever not for a good sake

The trail they took us on, long and hard
Through the blistering heat, left all our memories scarred

Many are gone, left on the trail
Since we have moved far on to take our land they did not fail

Our long journey has ended, although our lives aren't far from the end as well
They put us in a canyon, little food they give us, it tastes like gel

Me and my love will make a run tonight
No matter how it ends, somehow we'll be all right
Brooklyn Neubig, Grade 8
Bethel Christian School, OR

The Roman Coliseum

The Roman Coliseum is rusted tan.
   It sounds like the cry of the dead.
   It feels like the weight of the world.
   It smells like human bloodshed.
   It tastes like milk, soured by hundreds of years.

Kayla Laywell, Grade 8
Zia Middle School, NM

Passion of Music

it vibrates in the air
the sound makes you feel happy every day
the sound is like the rain coming
down to water the plants and flowers
the passion of playing
as you touch the key it's cold
pushing down the key to make music
the key is like cold ice as you push
the passion of playing
reading notes to make a song
fun, fantastic, funky song to play
moving your fingers slowly or fast
the passion of playing
on stage you bow to the audience
pulling the chair towards you
you start to play
the passion of playing
everyone enjoys and listens
as you're done it vibrates in your
ear and through the air
the passion of playing

Dolly Lor, Grade 8
Walt Morey Middle School, OR

Childhood Memories

Childhood quickly came and went
But all those memories represent:

Playing dress up and darting around
Dizzy twirling 'till you hit the ground
Tottering on a "tightrope" in a tutu
River dancing like there's none but you

Hanging on Mommy, crying, "Don't go!"
A big little heart filling with woe
But then one thing will make you be brave
— The thought of a spectacular day

Backyard camping in a plastic tent
Finger-painting a sunset event
Carrying the barbie that you adore
Building sand castles on the seashore

I wish I could have billions more
Memories lasting forevermore

Kayla Beene, Grade 9
Tempe Preparatory Academy, AZ

If Dreams Came True

If dreams came true there would be no cancer,
No one going through chemo, looking for an answer
No child would cry over a slice of bread
Because there is not enough food to eat before bed
If dreams came true no young girl would think she's ugly
Because a cruel girl looked with a glare and said she's pudgy
No math whiz would get turned down
At the prom, by the beautiful girl wearing the crown
If dreams came true no child would hope and pray
That daddy would come back from the war one day
No one's heart would ever get broken
By the words that were never spoken
Look at the world in a positive way
And it will bring hope and promise to each and every day
It's very true some things cannot change
But if you try hard some can rearrange
There's never a dream too big, so take a chance
Reach for the sky, let it loose, and just dance!

Jamie Christensen, Grade 8
Grantsville Middle School, UT

Life, Do You Want to Make Something Out of It?

I can only tell you why we have to suffer.
Why there is pain,
Why there are bad things that happen to us,
Like death, sorrow, and cruelty.
The only thing I have to say, IT'S LIFE!
We all go through bad things but guess what?
The things that keep us together are
LOVE, RESPONSIBILITY, and HAPPINESS!
So, when you think you got it tough,
Just think of what you got and
MAKE SOMETHING OUT OF IT!

John Macias, Grade 8
Kepner Middle School, CO

Ode to the Lord

Whenever I am in His house
I know that I am safe
I never feel like I am small like a mouse
My protection is always in His place

Three men traveled far to find this King
In His presence they sit on bended knee
And they are soon surrounded by protective wings
Wings of grace I depend on entirely to guide me

Though sometimes in life I may fail
He never hesitates to forgive my mistakes
At His side I walk easily and sail
Over the mountains that He makes

Sara Anderson, Grade 8
Heath Middle School, CO

Space
I see the stars all around me
I hear the emptiness surrounding me
I smell the stardust in my nose
I taste the nonexistent air inside of me
I feel the planet's light embracing me
I know that I am one with the galaxy
Claire Pearson, Grade 7
Sedona Charter School, AZ

Butterflies
Flutter fly
Soar through the sky.
Like the beautiful butterflies
That they truly are.
Like them
Love them
read all about them
They're peaceful
They're gentle
They sometimes come in a bundle
Then they flutter away
In their own little way.
Cassie Page, Grade 8
Culver Middle School, OR

Sunrise, Sunset
Sunrise, Sunset,
The sun goes up
And then it rests.
It lights the day,
Then fades to gray,
The same as life
It comes to say,
"Now I'm over,
But I won't betray,
For tomorrow
Is another day.
I'll rise up to the heavens
And into the sky,
Where all of the other sunsets lie."
Savannah Lyle, Grade 7
North Middle School, CO

The Forest
Dead leaves drooping,
Living leaves cracking,
Thorns poking trees majestically,
Spiders laying eggs with grace,
Trees, homes to animals,
Roof to forest floor,
Some swaying some straight,
Some struggling to survive,
All worthwhile to the forest.
Devon Merriman, Grade 8
Chehalis Middle School, WA

Mrs. Drew
Fun, nice, smart and always right
Inspiring, interesting
She never yelled
She never sighed

She was never mean
and always right
It's easy to be right in Kindergarten
but she was right in a different way

She was sincere
She was caring
She pushed us to try new things
She inspired us to be our own us

She was always
and will always be
my favorite kindergarten teacher
and favorite teacher all around
Ellen Scribner, Grade 7
Sylvester Middle School, WA

School and Heaven
School
misery, hopeless
boring, tutoring, disgusted
black hole, darkness — white hole, light
helping, caring, loving
cool, nice
Heaven
Jakob Adams, Grade 8
Round Valley Middle School, AZ

Panther
Darker than the night
Wandering through the shadows
Alone without fear.
Shelby Leiba, Grade 8
Bessemer Academy, CO

Noah's Ark
One day God was a so mad
Because the people were being bad
So He threatened to send a flood
And there was some blood
Then He told Noah to build an ark
Then it became dark
After that it started to rain
Then it caused pain
It rained for forty days and forty nights
Some of the animals had some frights
Then Noah sent out a dove
Which symbolized love
Hans Eklund, Grade 9
Shelby High School, MT

Just Because…
Just because I'm tired,
Don't give me less work.
Don't say, "Don't come to work today."
Don't treat me differently

Just because I'm tired,
It doesn't mean that I can't do it.
Doesn't mean I can't play anymore.
It doesn't mean I don't care.

Just because I'm tired,
I feel like I'm as awake as day.
I can still help out with things.

Just because I'm tired, please trust me.
Katrina Baker, Grade 9
McMinnville High School, OR

My Angel
Come live with me and be my love,
For you're an angel from above.
With our rings you can't betray it,
And our love we will display it.

And then we'll sit upon the beach,
As we count the clouds each by each.
With all of our toes in the sand,
I will sit there and hold your hand.

Then to tease you for just a sec.,
I might kiss you with just a peck.
With that peck our grip gets tighter,
The glow on your face gets brighter.

It's more than love a state-of-mind,
Our true love is one of a kind.
For that I say you're in my heart,
Your figure is a work of art.

When we lay your cheeks get rosy,
We'll go to bed and get cozy.
For your my angel from above,
Come live with me and be my love.
Ricky Brito, Grade 9
Basic High School, NV

The Machine
It sputters and spouts
as the noise comes out
The machine starts to smoke
and the driver starts to choke
It's what every sixteen year old fears
it's the family Oldsmobile
Jacob Hays, Grade 7
Mandalay Middle School, CO

Anger

Anger sounds like a loud car,
It tastes like blood,
It smells like tar,
It feels like a thousand needles poking you all at once.
You cannot get away from something like this.

Anger is red,
It's loud and it's mean.
You're so denying,
You feel frustration,
You sound like you are growling.
You smell like you're burning.

Anger is hot,
It burns like fire.
It feels like your skin is made out of steam.
It's caused by damage to anything dear.

Anger is red,
It's big and it's horrible.
You cannot escape it,
You're devastated, heartbroken.
You are out of it.

Meagan Moore, Grade 8
La Plata Middle School, NM

I Miss You

I look up at the sky and think of you
I hope you know that I miss you
I wonder if you think of me too

A shooting star goes whizzing by
I make a wish for you and me
I look up at the sky and think of you

I miss you so much it hurts inside
I wish you would come home
I wonder if you think of me too

Come home to me; I miss you so
I hope you're safe and well
I look up at the sky and think of you

I love you so, come back please
Without you I'm lost in the snow
I wonder if you think of me too

Come home, I miss you so
Come home to the warmth is all I can say
I look up at the sky and think of you
I wonder if you think of me too.

Erika B., Grade 8
Cedar Park Christian School – Everett Campus, WA

Hurt

How could you leave me?
What did I do wrong?
Didn't you see I loved you?
Too late…cause now you're gone.
I'll never forget that treachery from you,
Someone I thought I could trust,
And no longer do.
You left for reasons unknown to me.
Tell me why you left…truthfully.
Is it because of what they said?
That someone was better?
They're messing with your head!
She never loved you more than me.
Honey get your facts straight,
It's not true!
Don't you see?
Tell me why you left me,
Or I'll be haunted forever more
Please, won't you tell me?
You can't hurt me anymore…

Larkin Griffor and Tanys deDecker, Grade 9
Tombstone High School, AZ

Mother to Daughter*

Well, daughter, I'll tell ya':
Life for me ain't been no flower garden;
It's had weeds in it,
And thorns,
And plants torn up,
And places where the sun can't reach —
Dark.
But all the time
I've been a-plantin',
And a-waterin',
And a-weedin',
And sometimes a-prunin',
Where there ain't been no growth.
So girl, don't you stop a-plantin'.
Don't you take a break
'Cause the ground's too hard.
Don't you give up now —
For I'm still plantin', sweetie,
I'm still tendin'
And life for me ain't been no flower garden.

Emily Goodrum, Grade 7
Mears Middle School, AK
*Patterned after "Mother to Son" by Langston Hughes

Pig

There once was a pig
Who wore a wig
Because he thought he would get attention
But really all he got was detention
It was his own grave he did dig

Mariah Smith, Grade 8
Round Valley Middle School, AZ

Living Lie
I am always lonely
No one tried to know me
I just don't belong
I just have to be strong

Chorus: I am tired of being an outcast
I want to change my life
But I am never noticed
I just want people to know that I exist

I am tired of pretending
That I am okay
No one seems to know I am there
And they don't seem to care

Chorus: I am tired of being an outcast
I want to change my life
But I am never noticed
I just want people to know that I exist

I hate going to school
When I go I am alone
I feel like I am living a lie
With everyone passing by
Riley Greer, Grade 8
Bogle Jr High School, AZ

Ode to Erasers
Pink and gross smelling,
You get rid of my mistakes,
Thank you very much.
Shelby Ambrose, Grade 8
Bethel Christian School, OR

Dad
Even though you're gone
I felt you all along
Even though you're gone
I still love you dad

When I'm gone
I won't be left all alone
I know we will meet again one day
I miss when we used to play

Even though you're gone
You're still in my prayers
Even though you're gone
I still love you dad

Even though you're gone
It has felt so long
Where have you gone
I love you dad
Aaron Casados, Grade 7
Sky Vista Middle School, CO

Simplicity
Simple is interesting to me.
I am the rope that coils around the old cowboy's hand.
The maple that stretches out its branches for tired birds.
The marvelous spider web that glitters with dew in the early morning.
The red and white Christmas wrapping on the present.
The Indian's woven reed baskets.
And the black satin that wraps around the night sky…
This is what I'm made of.
Ciera Wilson, Grade 9
Park City Independent, UT

Friendship
Friendship can be many different things
Maybe a business partner
A good friend during camp or through the summer
Or just a pal that you know through your parents
But then there's that special friend that is always by your side

A friend can last a lifetime or maybe just a week
But you should always pick the one that's by your side when the world walks out.
They can be a fake but that is just a mistake that we all can make
You just always have to remember that a friend watches you cry
But a true friend has a wet shoulder when you're done crying.

Friendship is one thing in this life you have to experience
The bad times and the good times
Yes, we all make mistakes and pick the wrong ones but that's just life
We got to keep God by our side to help us find the true friend
Because one day we all will. =]
Sarah Swinehart, Grade 8
Sunnyside Christian Elementary School, WA

Where Would We Be…
Where would we be if we looked past the color of people's skin,
And treated one another as if they were kin.

Where would be if we didn't choose war,
And instead choose a different door.

Where would we be if we didn't lie,
And told the truth day and nigh.

Where would we be if we weren't violent,
And cherished every moment together we spent.

Where would we be if we didn't tear down one another,
And lifted each other up like they were our sister or brother.

I'll tell you where we'd be,
And that's a world in peace and harmony.

Though this message is simple at best,
Be kind to one another and let good actions do the rest.
Dillon Papenfuss, Grade 9
South Jordan Middle School, UT

High Merit Poems – Grades 7, 8, and 9

A Game No One Wins

Her shining eyes gazed back at me,
As I stared across the emerald sea.
Would I ever see my love again
So beautiful and lusted by many men?

Remembering the first time we ever met
Our memories I cherish and won't forget.
As I look into my angel's eyes
The moon comes up and the sunlight dies.

My heart beating hard, out of my chest
I walked away hoping for the best.
There wasn't a chance or even a prayer.
All I could do was stand there and stare.

I stood there for hours with a saddened grin
For love is a game that no one can win.

Jackson Barney, Grade 9
Oak Canyon Jr High School, UT

The Lightning Storm

A big, bright, blue light goes across my roof.
The thunder crashes against my ears like a drum and she says,
"You see my light, I'm coming towards you. Get ready for me."

She is so self-seeking she makes people shaky.
We come with Mr. Rain's Revolution.
rich smell
can't taste
in the end, the tree is now gone.

Ashley Roberts, Grade 7
Eagle Point Middle School, OR

The Last Leaf

The last leaf has fallen,
Winter is here.
Well not quite,
But it is very near.
All trees are bare,
Not one leaf remains,
Soon snow will start falling,
Like weightless white rain.
The time of fall is done,
Soon winter will come.
Goodbye to the color,
Here comes the white,
Soon snow will start falling all day and all night.
Now it is here,
The blanket of white,
The day is now shorter and longer is night.
The snowplows are here,
The chains have come on,
I know it is winter,
Because the last leaf is gone.

Erik Ruehl, Grade 7
Desert Hills Middle School, WA

The Marines

The Marines always in camouflage.
Always creating a montage.
Never leave a man behind.
Always looking to find.
Nothing really can go wrong.
They'll execute their strategy without a flaw.
It kinda makes you want to say oorah.
Being in the Marines may cost some fees.
So show us what you're made of out there, at ease.

Andrew Hines, Grade 8
Place Middle School, CO

Wild Horses

Hooves beating against the Earth
Like drums from an ancient forgotten
Song
Coats in many colors
Glistening in the sun
Running, wild and free
Untouched, unridden and no name
Running free but…
Forced to hide in a land
Where he once stood
With pride
And with no fear
Big and strong
Now only a few stand on the Earth
Wild horses
All around the world

Raudell Nez, Grade 8
Shonto Preparatory Elementary/Middle School, AZ

The Looking Glass

Through the looking glass I see,
People staring back at me,
Staring at me with unhurt eyes,
I guess the glass mutes my cries,
I need to know I'm wanted,
But I have the feeling that I'm haunted,
You're staring now, at me through the glass.
I hoped this would never end but always last,
Our romance just begun,
And we only wanted to have fun,
To prance around a windy beach,
And never listen to our parent's speech.
Now I'm trapped in this little glass box.
And people fled like I have pox.
Through the looking glass I see,
You sharing tears and staring back at me,
The glass breaks and falls away,
And our love will soar another day.

Courtney Laning, Grade 9
Hendrix Jr High School, AZ

Musik

The black and red scorpions with soft shells
take me to the light beach still warm from the recent sun's set
the moon arises in a crescent over the Island
whose cool inhabitants who were, themselves, gods of the infested mortals
the demigods of the muses were once our calm, degenerate musicians of irrationality
But the island has aura: the sun takes its rest within the central volcano amid no other competing peaks:
the sun's deep red rays circle lethargically as vapors and others among the vacuum of air
the moon creates its new self with the dimmer stars pervading the collective cosmicity
Luna y Estrellas
blackness as a blanket of cottonous corduroy reveals in streaks and perpetual lines the firm bodies of the scorpions
they glow green in the light's blackness, you know in minor keys the miniature arachnids control me
D amasses a guitar and I play a slow symphony of sitars
the crabs dance, the water bubbles, and that kind blanket lifts revealing surreal geometric universes
my hard-shelled scorpions cause all the sublime greatness as they travel somehow in step with calculating randomness
I contentedly watch as they join those gods and deities for my peaceful and dramatic message has transversed.

Kendra Lund, Grade 9
Grand Junction High School, CO

Becoming

I lifted both feet and started to fly
I flew up and up, 'til I hit the blue sky
My arms flapping uncontrollably like those of a bird
And that's when I started to feel absurd.
Suddenly my nose turned into a beak!
I looked down and had no toes on my feet!
My hands no longer had fingers
But now two huge wings begin to linger.
I felt my eyes growing smaller and smaller
And then felt feathers growing out of my collar!
My shirt started to rip, with feathers bursting out of it!
Flying over lakes, rivers, puddles, and streams
Oh me, oh my, this must be a dream!
All of the sudden I stopped, falling on the ground and rocks.
Next thing I knew I woke up in my bed
Why, it was all just a dream floating around in my head.
I looked at my toes and I felt my hair
Everything was normal, until I felt my chest, there was one huge white feather still there.

Shannon Lowrey, Grade 9
North Layton Jr High School, UT

As I Sit Here Thinking

As I sit here thinking, I think about you. The way that you smell and how your hair was. The way you skated and how you looked. When you fell down and acted like nothing ever happened.

As I sit here thinking, I think about you. The way you would wait for me. The way you would sit with your friends and look bored. The way you would motion me, I would say "no."

As I sit here thinking, I think about you. The way you would look bored like you didn't know what was going on with the day. How people would bump you on the shoulder and tell you what is going on. I would sit here and think about what you were thinking about.

As I sit here thinking, I think about you. The way things could be different. I wish that things would go back to the same instead of how they are now with us as "just friends." I wish we could do things differently than the way they were. How we used to hang and laugh about things that were just funny to us. Everyone would just sit there staring at us.

Samantha Lucero, Grade 9
Hinkley High School, CO

What Will I Be?

As I sit in my chair, I think of what I will be,
Will I be successful? I'll just have to see.

Will I work at NASA, and see outer space?
Driving a spaceship; a large challenge to face.

Will I create video games; the perfect job for me?
I could create a Playstation, or Nintendo Wii.

Or how about Disneyland!? Oh, quite a fun place!
I could dress up as Mickey, if that was the case.

I could print comic books, I'd love that you see
I could make Spiderman, scaling a tree!

A job in computers! Won't need a fast pace
I could just sit there and copy and paste!

As I sit in my chair, I discover the key
I don't need to know what I'll be!

I still have many years 'till I'm outta the house,
So I'll chase my dream, like a cat on a mouse!

Aaron Tomlinson, Grade 8
Desert Sky Middle School, AZ

Winter Beauty

The snowy slopes are white and light,
The fox hunts for an evening kill.
Crystal ponds are tranquil and bright,
The snow falls light and still.

The mountain tops are sharp and still
The wind is singing in the night
This is the weather crisp and still;
Crickets chirp in the night.

The wind whistles in the cold night.
A moon rises big, round and still
Shadows cast in the starry night;
The weather crisp and still.

Snow tickles the end of my nose,
And the world is all around me.
Wind kisses the ends of my toes,
Whirling all around me.

The earth is still but I still breathe,
Mother Earth comforts me in the dead of night.
I sleep little with ragged breath, thinking
The earth's too much for me.

Madison Keyshae, Grade 7
Petra Academy, MT

Family

They always bug me
They never let me be
And even though we disagree
They'll always be my family

They never leave me alone
Even when I'm on the phone
But I just want to make it known
They'll always be my family

They never know what's mine
They act like I've committed a crime
They won't just let me sit and rhyme
But they'll always be my family

They make me want to fly away
Yet their love is like a musical play
With them I'll never be in the gray
Because they'll always be more than my family

Alyssa Arbuckle, Grade 7
Sky Vista Middle School, CO

Football

Shower, pads, jersey
Pads, jersey, cleats
Jersey, cleats, helmet
Cleats, helmet, water
Helmet, water, ball
Water, ball, car
Ball, car, drive
Drive, game, win
Game, win, undefeated
Win, undefeated, championship

Audie Shrum, Grade 7
Dunstan Middle School, CO

An Unknown Friend

One summer day
I went out to play
I could feel the warm grass between my toes
When I heard a sound
Just faint enough to notice
I looked around and saw a cat
She was as thin as a stick
I went in to get some food
When I came out she came
And ate from my hand

She soon became ours
And after some love and care
She began to grow
Big and strong
But no longer does she frolic and play
She just sits around all day

Justin Altmiller, Grade 8
Eugene Christian School, OR

Bubblegum

I like bubblegum
But I wish I had some
When I blow a bubble
I usually get in trouble
Bubblegum is the best
And it beats the rest

Carlos Bermudez, Grade 7
Somerton Middle School, AZ

I Miss You, Goodbye

I'm sorry that you left so soon,
I didn't get to say goodbye,
I know you would want me to smile,
But I'm not shy that I cry,
Every once in a while.

I'm sad to say goodbye,
But I know you're in a better place,
I miss you so much,
I just wish I could see your face.

I know that you would want me to smile,
But it's so hard,
I'm going to be sad at least for a while,
I wish I didn't have to say goodbye,
But I guess it's time,
So goodbye Grandma,
Goodbye, goodbye.

Maranda Robbins, Grade 7
Coronado K 8 School, AZ

You

I looked up at you
With your big eyes of blue
Then you smiled at me
My heart never felt so free

Once you grabbed onto my hand
My heart melted like quicksand
The first look at you
I knew you were the one

You make me feel
Like fairy tales are real
It's like I'm in a dream
When you are with me

Blinded by love
Blinded by you
With your big eyes of blue
I would do anything for you

Love is pure
I am sure

Erica Hansing, Grade 9
Queen Creek High School, AZ

Cold and Alone

I'm cold and alone,
With no one to tell.
Why I'm on my own,
Trapped in this scary cell.

Orange is the color I wear,
It must be a sign that I'm bad.
Blue, green, even pink are there any other colors to share,
I am thinking of words to express myself, but all I can say is mad.

I always feel that I'm trapped deep down,
Am I who I want to be?
I feel like a bug and they just smashed me on the ground,
All I want them to see is a different side of me.

I want to be an eagle,
Respected and so free.
Instead I'm just a seagull,
Watched by the sea.

I feel the cold hard floor,
And I want to go back home.
I always wished I had done more,
Right now I wish I'd been that eagle and flown on home.

Aquaila Barber, Grade 7
Sky Vista Middle School, CO

Sky

high above in the pearly grey clouds
the sunset swirls across the horizon,
the setting lonely sun, a ball of glowing flame has lit,
and now it burns, silky, peachy pink, glowing, golden orange,
slashing, scarlet red, a typhoon of vicious color
raging across the sky,
the sun dips and swirls, spinning down
to the ancient silent Earth to dip and fall,
behind high majestic, mountains,
rolling, aqua rivers, swirling, silky seas,
and sweeping, vast and golden plains,
the sun plummets into night,
to velvety blackness studded with tiny diamonds…stars
the moon shining down
on an age old sphere of terra cotta…the Earth,
night spins around the Earth wrapping it in a cocoon of midnight,
and then to light a faint candle,
the weakened fire of the eve before, to light the dawn,
a splash of faint pastels, color the pale sky to light a fiery orb to life,
to day…to light,
the sky

Cori Gianniny, Grade 7
Miller Middle School, CO

High Merit Poems – Grades 7, 8, and 9

As the Sun Disappears

The ocean whispers to the sky,
while it tosses and turns,
trying to sing itself to sleep.

The dolphin cries and whimpers,
as the ocean tosses and turns,
not letting her leave.

And the trees dance in the wind,
begging and pleading to stay awake,
while they laugh and play.

The sand storms laugh in their faces,
he knows what he does, shaking the earth,
and playing with their heads.

Why does the wind whistle and encourage
the trees to dance and the sand to shake,
as it hugs the earth and watches the sun disappear?

Michelle Allen, Grade 8
La Plata Middle School, NM

Darkness

At night the sky darkens with fear
Light is the only thing that blocks the darkness out
Ask and make a difference
Will it show again?
Will we live in fear?
Forever and ever?
Will light show?
Ask and make a difference
Can we save the light?
From destruction
From being consumed
From madness
From us
Ask and make a difference

Lauren Clappisi, Grade 7
Oberon Middle School, CO

The Cool Cling

Do I have to smile in order to hide?
The pain in my heart when I see them pass by
I hear their voices and just one question
My head only chants
How do they feel living like that?
Is it possible to hide the pain they must feel
As they toss the lives like the one they fulfill
Are they really that ignorant to not understand
The results of this scar they produce on the
Ones they embrace
Just close our eyes so we will never again
See their cluster pass by and seize with them
Who we all are inside

Abdi Lopez, Grade 9
Maryvale High School, AZ

I Am a Cloud

As if I were a cloud I go wandering in the world
Bringing rain to those who need it
Passing by those who don't
Flooding some who underestimate
Droughting some who forget
You need me to live
I may roar up unnoticed with a gaining tempest
or give you fair warning from a distance with menacing clouds
Other days protect you from the sun
Don't expect me to go or stay
Don't expect it to snow
Don't expect it to rain
Expect me to change and dazzle
Expect me to go but not stay
Expect me for what I do
Do not tell me to dazzle or change
I will do as I please
You cannot hold or grasp me
Let me go
Let me be free
Free as a cloud

Jasmine Beul, Grade 7
Dunstan Middle School, CO

Invisible

L ove to me,
M eans almost
N othing at all to you!
O h how I wish we could talk
P eacefully in a
Q uiet place. And I wish you knew how I
R eally felt.
S o until
T he day when all is revealed
   I will remain invisible.

Bree Haas, Grade 8
Heath Middle School, CO

Haunting

I ran, I stared into its haunting eyes.
I heard voices or redemption inside of me,
with no apparent surprise.
I felt weak and cold,
freezing cold.
As I collapse on hard ground
I feel an angry soul swarming me
As its haunting eyes come closer and closer,
it becomes bright.
As the bold burning sun rises
Its spirit disappears
all because of a beautiful light.

Wendy McNeace, Grade 8
Aurora Academy, CO

Our Love

What happened to us? Our love?
My love for you was so strong,
But tell me what I did wrong?
Your kisses said everything and
You tore my heart in so many pieces
How come you played a game?
Why didn't you feel the same?
You grabbed my heart and
We went so far
Then you stabbed my heart and
I told you I love you no more
I told you I hated you,
But deep down I can never
Stop loving you.
Dulce Jaime, Grade 8
Grand Canyon Middle School, AZ

The Stars

A home away from home,
Only in the starry night.
Lying on my back,
Watching the stars so bright.

It was my only sanctuary,
Until he came along.
He stole my heart so easily,
Almost like a Cheesy love song.

Turns out he loves the stars too.
They're comforting, you see?
He said his most favorite thing
Was watching them with me.

So whenever I go out there,
He's always by my side.
Now the stars aren't only at night,
'Cause I can see them in his eyes.
Rylee Mecham, Grade 9
Shelley Sr High School, ID

Nature

As the wind
blows through
the trees,

The birds
continually
stay pleased,

Under the
warmth of a
midsummer's
night breeze.
Silas Babilonia, Grade 7
Aurora Academy, CO

Ms. Waistell

Ms. Waistell
Flowing blond hair
Big wise eyes

You help me through
All I do
In your class called band

High pitched flute
Is hard to play
But all you do is coach

You help me get
The best grades
I can ever imagine

As I end this poem
I give you a salute
In honor of
One of the best teachers
That I've ever known
Sabine Glocker, Grade 7
Sylvester Middle School, WA

A Friend

A friend should be loyal,
A friend should be true,
Not back stabbing or mean,
Nor greedy and rude.
They should appreciate you,
And respect who you are.
They laugh at your jokes,
And tell you, "You're a star!"
A friend is kind
And always true.
They'll always be there,
Through and through.
They cry when you do,
And love you always.
No matter what comes between you,
They will care in all the small ways.
Hannah Courkamp, Grade 7
Sagewood Middle School, CO

Poor Pluto

Poor little comet you hover in the dark
Stuck up X put you off the mark
Pluto only as big as me
Charon said why pay this great fee
You and your moon sit and wait
For scientists to end this terrible fate
Pluto and Charon both stand tall
A planet is a planet no matter how small
Jessica Miers, Grade 7
Annunciation Elementary School, NM

Violin

The silence before performing
is the most nerve-racking of them all.
We quietly joke around
to forget there is an audience.
The director raises her arms
to show us it's time to begin.
Graceful notes
fly off the strings of
my gleaming violin.
The song is over.
We stand up,
take a bow,
and go off stage.
Just another day in
the life of a
violinist.
Teresa Leithead, Grade 8
Round Valley Middle School, AZ

I Am

I am a tree
Tall and branching out to all
I am a dog
Loving and loyal
I am a car
Always on the go
My thoughts are the ocean
Deep
Paul Rastrelli, Grade 7
Connect Charter School, CO

Just Don't Care

Caring about what people say
is like watching a puppy die slowly
painfully withering away.
The words will start to eat you.
You won't be the same,
your family will start to lose you,
and one day, you're gone.
So love life
and it will love you.
Mekenzie Goodson, Grade 7
Sonoran Science Academy, AZ

The Heartthrob Tale of Bob

Bob got robbed by an angry mob.
All was taken, even his corncob.
He ran across very bad luck.
He even lost his pickup truck.
Bob is very much like a bug.
Working; getting less than a hug.
Even the trees insult his life.
It's filled with only pain and strife.
Alan Gross, Grade 7
Annunciation School, NM

Justified

They came and herd them like cattle
The walk lasts forever
Loved ones fall
Their life is blown away like a feather.

They are told of happiness and life at the end of the despair
They continue to walk with that promise on the their back
The burden of the lost
They hope that they will get back on track.

All hope is tearing away
The winter chill brings a killer frost
The frozen mountains curve an slope
Is there no hope?

When they arrive they are shattered
Their enemies are not about to share
Soldiers don't even care
All they can do is stare.

Starvation and cruelty take their toll
Many perish before their time
Thousands fall before the mountains
When did murder become a justified crime?

Mitchell McCaw, Grade 7
Bethel Christian School, OR

Beach Walk

The water crashes upon the rocks,
Foamy white reaching toward the sky,
Contrasting the blue
Like bleach on a tattered dish rag.

Low-tide in morning;
Perfect for uncovering the treasures left by sea.
Seagulls scavenging the salty beach,
Picking at the mussels left as tribute from the sea.

The breeze savors the salty scent,
The scent somehow finding my nose.
The salty sea is overpowering to other odors,
But I haven't yet found it overwhelming.

Freedom is the sea.
The ocean is a pendulum of an old grandfather clock;
Its rolling crests of water advancing upon the sand,
Then receding as it may in rhythm.
Advancing,
Then receding,
Advancing,
Then receding.

Cody Holik, Grade 9
Grand Junction High School, CO

Winter's Here

Snow falls as I sit and stare
I stare at silence, lights memorizing my thoughts
I hear the fire, crackling right beside me
Winter is finally here
The Christmas tree is up
There's gifts in all the stores
All we can do is sit and wait for Christmas day

After the season is over
We are served another platter of celebration
The New Year comes at full blast.
All through the year we have four seasons
But it's not the seasons that make the year
It's the love we share with family and friends

I think of the memories I had so long ago
And try to make them grow and grow
Celebrations and traditions fill my calendar.
All the time I daydream away
On the window sill I sit
For so long I've tried to make my winter
Simply the best.

Kimberly Quent, Grade 9
Stapley Jr High School, AZ

I Am…

I am an athletic student who sometimes messes around
I wonder if I'll ever stop loving sports
I hear the teacher telling me to put my name on the board
I see the sweat dripping from my teammates' faces
I am an athletic student who sometimes messes around

I pretend I'm in the NBA playing alongside my favorite players
I feel the deathly glare I receive from my teacher
I touch the smooth grip on the baseball bat
I worry about getting in too much trouble
I cry for the ball as the clock ticks to one second left
I am an athletic student who sometimes messes around

I understand I shouldn't mess around
I say I'm going to do better today than I did yesterday
I dream of having a successful life
I hope my teachers don't think of me badly
I am an athletic student who sometimes messes around

Tyson Wilson, Grade 7
Sterling Middle School, CO

Basketball Mornings

I wake up in the morning,
My room as cold as ice,
I walk to the bathroom,
And brush my teeth twice,
I look out the window and see the bright moon,
And realize that basketball practice is really soon.

Grant Marett, Grade 9
Duchesne High School, UT

Rain

The sweet smell comes,
Rain beats down,
Softly on the flowers.

An early spring morn,
The clear dew is beautiful,
Birds are chirping.

Britany Coil, Grade 9
Duchesne High School, UT

Demise

You stare at me
Through your hazel eyes
Each glance shows
Hatred and demise

What I have done is really sad
But it was for you
The answer is bad
But my feelings were true

I can never explain to you
Truthfully and in depth
But maybe if you tried
You could really understand

Of course you being you
Wouldn't know how it came to be
Because you're always in the spotlight
Surrounded by a crowd

Mollee Gleason, Grade 7
Shadow Ridge Middle School, CO

The Best Thing

F orever fun friends
R eally rad
I ronic imaginations
E ndless exciting entertainment
N ever normal knuckleheads
D efinitely delightful dudes
S orry sounding singers

Alicia Gutierrez, Grade 8
Round Valley Middle School, AZ

Sometimes

Sometimes I feel like a sloth
   that's lazy and tired, motionless

Sometimes I feel like a turtle
   that's safe, snug and cozy

Sometimes I feel like a puppy
   jumping up and down
   with excitement!

Brandon Morrison, Grade 7
Juneau SDA School, AK

Swimming vs Diving

I swim far	
	I jump high
We both use water	We both use water
I dive for speed	
	I dive for points
I don't care how big my splash is	
	I make mine as little as possible
We both dive	We both dive
I love to swim	
	I love to dive

We both love water

Diana Olsen, Grade 7
Elk Ridge Middle School, UT

Bear

I crawl out from my lone winter's slumber,
My past sleep as deep as the roots of oak lumber.
I squint at the bright new season's sun,
With a roar of anticipation, "There's fish to be won!"
My paws pad lazily towards the murky water's splish-splushing.
I rummage in the frigid water, craving some all natural sushi.

I rise like the triumphed moon, sure and strong, from the rapid,
An ill-fortuned rainbow trout my scaly captive.
He duels and wallops and wails, "Let me GO, I say!"
But I am the predator, and he is the prey.

Rachael Lowery-Rowley, Grade 9
Lake Havasu High School, AZ

Wonder

Wonder is the silent, thinking mind
You wonder about everything in a sport about a book

And even on the first day of school
Wonder is the everyday thing
You will always get caught saying "um" or "hmm"
Wonder is a "um, um, um, what happens next"
You even wonder in the doctor's office
You never know what will happen
Wonder is life
Some um's and some hmm's, but that is life

If you play soccer you wonder who the opponent is
If you play basketball you wonder "what if this is a bad ref?"
If you play football you wonder who will make the first touchdown
If you are in gymnastics
You wonder

"Well what if I mess up or trip"
Every sport you wonder
When you are lying down
You even wonder "What will happen tomorrow"
Wonder is life!

Emily Patton, Grade 7
21st Century Public Academy, NM

Victory

It was Green against Blue
We were undefeated and going to BEAT you
The surprise in our eye was WOW!
Look at the score us down by 4.
5 and a half minutes left.
We were at rest. No worry this is our "VICTORY"
"Coach play me" I ask
With 3 and a half past.
"Go in" he mumbles
As our point guard stumbles
But wait just to her luck a lay up,
Now 2 up!
But wait they shoot
I go in with a salute
Shoot once shoot twice
SWOOSH!
4 point and we're up again
Coach proudly screaming
We win, we win!
GREEN once again
My game my victory!

Megan Warren, Grade 9
Oak Canyon Jr High School, UT

The Apple

Tangy and sweet but not always red
Sometimes yellow and shiny and brown
A soft crunch when you take your first bite
The burst of juice comes from the orange stripe
Smooth and sticky to the touch
The refreshing crisp wetness calls to you
Take another bite
Fall harvest always brings a few more
For the simplicity of an
All-American apple pie

The light "snap!" as it falls from the tree
Causes it bruises and leaves it
To become aged and wrinkly
Red Delicious, Granny Smith, or Washington
Are all types of this
Nature made
Juicy
Delectable
Treat
Apples

McKenna Osborne, Grade 9
Xavier College Preparatory School, AZ

Self Portrait

My eyes are like a brown branch growing green leaves
My arms are flexible like sticky, stretchy taffy
My mind is full like a concert arena
My heart holds memories like a photo album

Priscilla Mesa, Grade 7
Sunset Ridge Elementary School, AZ

Snowflake

Soft and puffy,
White and blue,
Soft and lonely because of you.

Peacefully falling,
From the clouds to the ground,
But when you open your mouth,
I think my life will soon turn around.

I'm falling into a pink tunnel with white spikes,
Away from all of my friends.
Then the heat scorches my skin,
As I begin to fall in.

My legs are disappearing,
From my toes to my nose,
Goodbye to my old life,
Hello H_2O.

My life is almost over,
My life is almost done,
But after I am discarded,
I will be vaporized by the sun.

Madie Scully, Grade 7
West Valley Middle School, WA

Baseball

I keep on dreaming about that one day
When I will get to play
The one chance I can be the hero
Or…Be the zero

Hitting the ball ain't so hard
Just like the people on the cards
Hard work will get you where you want to be
My dad said that was just like me

I want to be a pro
Not just some Joe
I love the game
I don't care about the fame

Just one day
Preferably in May
I want it so bad
I would thank my dad

I have learned a lot
But now I want to show people what I got
One day
I hope to play

Jakob Bublitz, Grade 7
Shadow Ridge Middle School, CO

The Lord Is Calling Out to Me

Lying on the hospital bed, I hear my name, Miiiikaaaylaaaa, Miiiikaaaaaylaaa, the Lord is calling out to me
I see a bright light flash before me, the Lord is calling out to me

There is a man with almond brown hair and holes in his hands and feet, the Lord is calling out to me
I feel spellbound as I float toward him, the Lord is calling out to me

Death has opened her doorway to me, the Lord is calling out to me
I look down to see a pale sick little girl, the Lord is calling out to me

Doctors and nurses hastily rush around her, the Lord is calling out to me
A family rushes in, my family, the Lord is calling out to me

The family sheds damp tears over the body, the Lord is calling out to me
I cry a small sad tear, the Lord is calling out to me

I look at the man as I weep, the Lord is calling out to me
Death begins to close her door, the Lord is calling out to me

I cry out my family needs me right now, the Lord stops calling out to me
I drift back to the pale sick little girl, my family is calling out to me

My eyes flutter open and I say the Lord was calling out to me

Mikayla Klas, Grade 7
Oberon Middle School, CO

I Am From

I am from very old green couches that are fluffy and nice, beige chairs that are comfy, new rugs neatly placed on the floor, old photos bring back memories, and old books telling about the past.

I am from old toys rugged and dirty, old china cracked but special, new cars running on expensive gas, old rundown skateboards dirty, and old bikes with popped tires and bent bars.

When I look around I see broken fences bent over dramatically, little kids playing in the street, deserted houses from people who have moved away, and old tall trees high above my head.

I am from Grandma Linda who never liked me, my grandpa Jim who loves me for who I am, my mom and my sister who are my most favorite people in the world.

We love to say "hi how was you're day, what's shaking bacon, what time is it, see you later."

I am from Hershey's from when I went to Hirschberg, pasta when we have someone over we make spaghetti, salad when we have picnics, apples for my church, and cotton candy at the fair.

My historic valuables are in my closet in a very big box, at my aunt's house in her barn, in my room on the walls, on the computer in flies, and in my mom's closet in boxes of files.

Brianna Cole, Grade 8
Culver Middle School, OR

The Sunset

You watch the sun sink behind the mountains. You feel the pink wrap around you in a tight squeeze. You see the array of colors that light up the sky. As you watch the sun sink farther behind the mountains, you start to feel night and dark settle into the sky. Slowly, ever slowly, the chill and dark of night overcome the beautiful colors and fabulous sunset. This makes you think your day's over. You replay the happy moments and they give you that peace you've always wanted. You watch the sun sink behind the mountains.

Deisha Morgan, Grade 8
Sequoia Village School, AZ

It's What Counts

Love is like a rock
It never breaks
But when you drop it it's like losing a possession

Love can be true or false
And sometimes last forever
But when you treat it wrong it hurts

Love isn't about gifts or dates
It's about what you feel inside
And how much you love the person

Love can tear your heart in half
But sometimes make it better

Marcus Derrera, Grade 7
Knowledge Quest Academy, CO

Night and Day

The moon comes out in the dark sky,
glowing because he is tired.
Then the stars come out to help the moon sleep.
They act like the moon's a night-light, shining in the sky.

In the morning the sun comes out to wake everyone,
in the clear sky.
With its bright shinning rays like huge arms wrapping the Earth.

All of a sudden the clouds came to block the sun,
blowing toward the sun.
Trying to make the day a horrible day

Andria Gomez, Grade 8
La Plata Middle School, NM

Team

Walking toward the court, I dream about fame.
Fans' cheers for our team echo through the gym.
The game comes to an end, and we feel shame,
All the shots we made bounced off the rim.

Together on the court, not as a team.
If we lose again, we stay where we are.
Our talent is great, we go to extreme,
We need to win this or we won't go far.

The whistle blows, and the crowd goes crazy.
Bad calls by the ref could cost us the game.
I'm getting tired; my vision gets hazy.
Our games have been bad this can't end the same.

The score is tied — one more shot and we win.
Shot up, buzzer off, championship begins.

Efrain Galvez, Grade 9
Tombstone High School, AZ

My Journey

Most I meet have one thing in common
It is not the tone of their voice
Or the look in their eyes, burning for what they love
But they have found it, their passions
Something I long for
I yearn for my own corner of the universe
Pure happiness
I would be forever grateful
To find it though it is like searching for true love
Never knowing what might happen
Or who it might be
It is a bit troublesome to continue to have a lack of reassurance
Will I find what I am searching so desperately for
Being driven by faith
Grabbing my hand and dragging me through
I will continue this journey
My journey to you

Emily Campos, Grade 9
Queen Creek High School, AZ

A New Day Dawning

The break of day is coming the storm is finally over
The smell of rain reminds me of fresh, moist clover
As the day starts unfolding the clouds start rolling high
They look like rows of golden wheat waving through the sky

The sun's warm rays awaken the playful baby calves
They arise and stretch and give each other baths
They grunt and bump each other tottering and falling
Until mama awakens and they heed to her calling

Eventually the calves will tire and they go back to sleeping
But a new day is beginning so their mama goes back to eating
A day on the farm is full of exciting things to see
These things I discover every day are miracles to me

Billy Housley, Grade 7
Lyons Middle/Senior High School, CO

Night

Night is cool and sweet.
Your bed welcomes you,
As night washes over your tired and aching body.
Night is opposite of day.
Dark and quiet,
Peaceful as your eyes gently close
And your mind drifts into a deep sleep.

Dreams fill your head,
Making anything possible.
Starlight slips into your room and into your dreams,
As air is very, very slowly inhaled and exhaled
Making your body calm and almost immobile.
The crickets outside the open widow chirp a lullaby,
As if saying, sweet dreams.

Jennica Smith, Grade 7
Syracuse Jr High School, UT

My Grandma

I love my grandma,
With all my heart;
She gives me anything,
That I want;
She understands me,
When I'm sad;
She always scowls me,
When I'm bad.

Tanisha Morales, Grade 8
Round Valley Middle School, AZ

Oceanic Love

I sway,
Full of life in the strength of his arms,
Guarded by his shoulders,
And lost in his eyes,
Like a sailor lost at sea
My thoughts engulfed in him alone,
The waves of his hair,
Slowly glide through my fingers,
His words echo through my head,
Like the beat of drum,
This ocean is so dangerous,
Like when a woman seduces a man,
So full of possibilities,
And I'd rather be here than on land.

Tori Sato, Grade 9
Stapley Jr High School, AZ

Silence

Silence speaks a thousand words,
but when that Silence is broken
more words flow through the gap.
Like the rush of a river
tumbling over stones.

Silence means nothing,
except to the people
that know what Silence truly is:
A way of communicating
through looks or feelings.

The love that is shared
between two people.
The happiness that is felt
when a being takes its first breath.
The time that passes simultaneously
from sunrise to sunset.
All in Silence.

Sound creates a thousand meanings.
Love ties a thousand people together.
Life brings a thousand new voices.
Silence speaks a thousand words.

Kate Hruby, Grade 8
Komachin Middle School, WA

My Cool Life

Matthew
Cool, funny, outgoing, and nice
Relative of Dawn Krueger my awesome mom.
Lover of peace on earth, my family who rocks and love for God and Jesus.
Who feels happy from helping others, really excited from riding my dirt bike
    and proud of doing a good thing.
Who needs encouragement from parents,
    friends to hang with, and my dirt bike to ride.
Who fears the pitch dark places because of what might come out,
    getting my neck broken by someone, and being kidnapped by someone
Who gives help to others who need it, clothes to the poor so they won't be cold,
    and give food to the poor also so they won't starve
Who would like to see Tony Hawk, a pro skateboarder,
    Disneyland which has roller coasters,
    and peace on earth so that people would stop fighting each other
Resident of Culver, Oregon, U.S.A., Earth, and the galaxy
Krueger

Matthew Krueger, Grade 8
Culver Middle School, OR

The Glistening Bay

Where everyone goes to end their day
The glistening bay is the place to be
Oh! How it glistens and glimmers look at that sea
To see the people fall off of their boards with such a grace,
go on top of the waves to see the small and big boats in harmony
going to and fro from loading docks
here is the place to be when you feel your feet cutting through the sand,
and you know it will never wash off
When you are interrupted by loads of passersby
When the day is over
There truly is no place like home

Josh Williams, Grade 9
Lakewood High School, CO

Home Sweet Home

Dog claws on the wood floor,
Water running and shutting off,
The quiet squeak of a bird,
A cage rattling around as she moves,
Opening and shutting of a sliding door,
The scattering feet of the dogs running out,
The whining and barking of them wanting back in,
The voice of a boy saying, "You will never guess what I brought home,"
Another voice, "Wow,"
The rattle of a snare drum for five or six beats,
A door shutting after,
Off the bird goes squeaking away,
And the door opens and shuts again.

McKenzie Hardy, Grade 7
Cedar Ridge Middle School, OR

Poems

A poem needs to take you back
Into when times were easy,

Burn
Like a candle in your soul,

Take you places
That are beautiful and hidden, mysterious,

A poem should make you take flight
As a graceful bird soaring,

As peaceful and calming as a paradise
Secluded from the rest of the world,

Flowingly take you away from your stresses
And show you a different way, to forget all.

A meaningful thing,
A peaceful thing.

Kelsi White, Grade 9
Mountain Ridge Jr High School, UT

The Wandering Spirit

The wandering spirit in the dark
Stumbling tripping over my heart

I grieve for you though I may not even know
The sadness you had to behold

I lost you once before
But now I'm here to stay
Now were together again like always

So wandering spirit in the dark
Won't you stay in my heart

Troy Gardea, Grade 8
Round Valley Middle School, AZ

My Love Forever

The choices that you have to take,
All seem so difficult to make.
When you love me I feel just fine,
For I know that you're all mine.

And care about me, I know it's true,
Every breath I take will be for you.
This feeling in my heart will never fade,
Because of all the memories together we made.

The love you give me, please don't lack,
Just take my hand and don't look back.
Forever on, you're my best friend,
The compassion I feel will truly never end.

Kimmy Allan, Grade 8
Desert Sky Middle School, AZ

Under the Shadow of a Tyrant's Rule

I remember when the dark heavens shed their tears,
And the Earth shuddered, sobbing, and turned away,
And the eyes of the rest looked far off.
Best only to ignore. Best only to forget.

And now, all that is left,
Under the shadow of a tyrant's rule:
An ancient city of man.
Many worn streets cross this place,
Zigzagging to nothingness, to sand.
Things that used to come so bountifully,
Are now as distant as the sun.
Things so hard to get,
Are also so easily lost. They come, and are gone.

I saw it form,
I watched it come to be,
I am memory,
I am truth,
I am man,
Now bound, but once free.

Chelsea Baker, Grade 8
Sweet Home Jr High School, OR

Life

Life is how you enjoy it.
Life has new adventures for all of us,
like going to the Bahamas
or going into the rainforest.
Life is like eating food and drinking,
meeting new people and seeing new places.
Maybe God sends us to help people enjoy life
by doing good things or helping them into Heaven.

Lilly Dust, Grade 7
Pretty Eagle Catholic School, MT

One Rider

The Wild West was different from the rest
It was an idea of a horse and rider
Side-by-side through the worst and best
An adventure for sure in a wider
Perspective of understanding between two.
A provocative exploration of the unknown
Hard work definitely, but through and through
Incredible. The sunset falls in a horizontal cone
Shape. Exploring new heights
A lifelong bond forms.
The horse is excited at the sights
The home coming is warm
Different from many; one horse
And of course, one rider.

Hannah Jacoby, Grade 7
Sky Vista Middle School, CO

My Fiery Sunset in the Sky
The fiery red overtakes the sky,
As a mixture of colors gather round.
The breathtaking view makes time stand still,
While the sunset's gaze is filled with such passion,
Such hunger,
It craves for the attention.
As my sunset fades I shed a silent tear.
Wishing, believing, hoping,
It will reappear.
But for now I sit in the dead of night,
Shattered, broken, and traumatized.
My sunset is gone,
But one day it will return.
And by then,
My tears will have disappeared.

Jacqueline Dunnavan, Grade 8
La Plata Middle School, NM

I Am
I am a sports player and funny
I wonder if it's sunny outside
I hear my football coaches yelling at me
I see a football flying in the air
I want to be a running back
I am a sports player and funny
I imagine being in the Super Bowl when I get older
I feel strong like a bolder
I touch my little siblings
I worry that I am getting older
I cry never
I am a sports player and funny
I understand the plays that my coach tells me
I say that I can do anything I want to if I put my mind to it
I dream of winning the championship
I try to sack the quarter back every time
I hope that I could go to the pro football
I am a sports player and funny.

Marcus Moran, Grade 7
Shadow Ridge Middle School, CO

I'm a Poet and I Don't Even Know It
I'm a poet.
I don't even know know it.
I hate to rhyme.
It's such a crime.
It's always a waste of time.
I have no time to rhyme.
I'm in a hurry,
Because I have to go make some chicken curry
This is my last line of rhyme,
So let's go and have a good time.

Harley King, Grade 8
Chaparral Middle School, NM

Brave
I am brave. Yes, I am brave.
Never fear, for I am who I am.
Yes, I am brave, strong as a lion.
Never will I fall, for I am brave.
I am brave to stand up for myself.
Brave to seek new things.
Never will I be discouraged.
I will not be terrified.
I am brave, strong as an iron.
The death of the grave howled.
The shadow of the spirit bellowed.
But alone I stand, for I am brave.
The highest mountain could not
Keep me away from reaching out to the world.
Alone I stand, brave as a lion.
The lights go out, but I'm standing in the
middle without making any sound.
I'm not afraid to make mistakes,
for this girl learns when she makes an error.

Levia Gee, Grade 7
Discovery Canyon Campus, CO

A Fading Friendship
A companionship of two years was formed.
From that acquaintance blooms the best of friends.
Between the children a promise was sworn,
That the friendship would never meet its ends.
Alas, time would not stand still for the pair;
Separation was inevitable.
Although it seemed that neither of them cared,
Isolation made them irritable.
The correspondence between them flourished,
For they much wanted their friendship to last.
Contact ceased, although it was not their wish,
the present now overshadows the past.
Several efforts over time had been made,
To keep the friendship from fading away...

Doris Chan, Grade 9
Clark High School, NV

Parents
Always there to support you
and help you with your struggles
even when times are hard
they help you fight through it
so when your shining in your own
world thank your parents for
giving you the support that you need to
get through your problems such as helping
you with your homework and school work
and when you're done you might have a lot
of free time with your friends or family so
just remember to thank your parents
so then you're safe and sound at home

Clayton Napp, Grade 7
Diamond Ranch Academy, UT

Where I Am?

As I sit among the trees,
Of the most brilliant greens,
The trees that go from red to yellow
And then bow down at winter's breath.
I think…where am I?

As I awake to morning light.
Beautifully bathed by night's sweet shower.
A blade of grass bent in fear,
A dew drop sweet as an angel's tear.
I whisper…where am I?

The waterfall flows lightly down,
A crown among the mountains brow,
Glistening jewels those snowcapped peaks,
Signs of the mountain's majesty.
I breathe…where am I?

A sight this place takes from my breath,
A feeling of peace, of love,
My imagination runs wild and free,
No need to ask where I am,
I'm home, I'm home to my forest!

Chelsea Frisby, Grade 7
Diamond Fork Jr High School, UT

Anger

Anger is a powerful feeling
and has many a shade,
once it strikes out,
the pain just won't fade.

Anger is a fierce volcano,
waiting, dormant, inside,
once you have voiced it,
people won't, can't just abide.

Anger is a raging mad bull
with its sight misted red,
it will blindly charge,
making fireworks in your head.

Anger is a big menacing storm,
it arrives quickly and hard,
no excuses for this,
nothing can stop it from coming, it can't be barred.

Anger gnaws at your insides,
begging to come out,
you'll give in eventually,
and then start to shout.

Irene Allen Dufowe, Grade 7
21st Century Public Academy, NM

Why

Why should we be good?
Why should we be nice?
Why do we need to have good friends?
Why?
Why do we need God?
Why do we go to school?
Why do we have birthdays?
Why, Why, Why?
Why should we go places,
When we don't even know where we are going?
Why are there so many things in the world?
WHY?
Why do we make life so complicated?
When it's not nearly as hard as we think it is.
Why, oh Why?
That is the question.

Ashley Stephenson, Grade 9
Intermountain Adventist Academy, CO

I Believe

I believe in the choice of being who you want to be.
The choice of going to college,
The choice of being a rockstar,
The choice of traveling the world,
The choice of being a soldier fighting for our freedom,
Hard work, determination, success.
But I don't believe in quitting.
I believe in sticking with something and finishing it.
I believe in achieving something you work hard for.
I believe in setting goals and achieving them,
Having dreams, visions, reality.
And I believe in people having choices to become individuals.

DJ Hubbert, Grade 7
Terry 7-8 School, MT

Haunted

You said that you looked at me and saw an angel face
Were we really in love, or was that not the case?
When you finally admitted that you liked me too,
I couldn't admit it, "Did I really like you?"
I guess we'll never know because one day, I moved on.
A piece of me left once you were gone.
Now, I really know that we'll never see.
Were we in over our heads, or was it just me?
You've been gone so long, but I can't forget your face.
It haunts me at night, so I must get up to pace.
After you left, I fled from my song,
But it traveled back after not so long.
Confusion fills my mind whenever I think of you.
I was always mystified with your poetry too.
So now, I wonder: will you ever come back?
Or when you left here, was it your last time to pack?
I'm writing this now to let my feelings burn.
This is for you, if you ever return.

Sarah Tillotson, Grade 9
Custer County High School, CO

Drama Queen

People call her the drama queen
She lives down the block
All her problems are dramatized
That's what makes her her
I'm sure she wonders why people stare
However I don't think she really cares.
Even the buildings stare at her
Everyone whispers as she walks by
Why doesn't she notice
Why doesn't she care
I would care
Wouldn't you
Maybe she doesn't notice
Yea that's it she doesn't notice
But there's a reason
She's blind
She's deaf
How sad
So sad
To be the neighborhood's
Drama queen

Jessica Harbert, Grade 7
Shadow Ridge Middle School, CO

I Try to Find My Spirit

I try to find my spirit
I look above every mountain
I look in every river
I look in a valley
I look up down all around
Then I found my spirit inside of me

Joaquin Ramos, Grade 7
North Middle School, CO

Guardian Angel

Sweet soft fragrance
kissed my nose
lullabies
apple pies
she is here
my guardian angel
her sweet songs
croon my ears
I hum them softly
they come the hear
a sweet secret
of a guardian angel
she twirls and spins
across the sky
my sweet sweet angel
leading me
keeping me
sent to protect me
my dear sweet guardian angel

Megan Frei, Grade 7
Marsh Valley Middle School, ID

Power

Power is a fire burning down a forest,
It is Gatorade that quenches your thirst for the championship game,
It's a cheetah dodging any of its predators in its way,
Power is electricity lighting up the whole city,
It is a friend, who stands up to a bully,
A wave that can sweep away huge buildings,
It is one man, changing the course of history,
Power is the sun energizing everything on our planet Earth.

Audrey Florence, Grade 7
Les Bois Jr High School, ID

Under the Puffball Trees

I cannot tell how far I've come along –
Or how many times I've sung this same song,
But this time it's different, for I've gone along
Those weathered paths long counted gone
Once more. I smelled the puffball tree's pollen
I've picked up the brilliant yellow puffballs that had fallen…
I would put them in my hair, and squish them in my hand,
So that the flowery smell might stain my soul unmanned.
And then I would take that yellow and paint streaks
Across my face, staining the necklace from my "love" (that week)
I would laugh and run in the places from which I wasn't banned,
The small river-wash where small trees clung to the land.
My mother had her headaches so silence she would seek;
I would don her office clothes and my Barbie fixed the leak…
I went once more to the house, a few hours before dawn.
I saw my door, my roof, and my bedroom light was on.
I could almost hear my name as if my mother had been callin';
And all around I could smell the fuzzy yellow pollen.
Yes, I went once more to where the puffballs had fallen;
I held them in my hands and remembered through the pollen.

Anna Wille, Grade 9
Tempe Preparatory Academy, AZ

Ice Covered

I take the first step outside of my house
It seems like a new world, I notice it more than ever;
Aware, alert
I observe the birds chirping, the sun rising, the newly fallen snow

There is complete silence
Asides from my boots crunching through the snow
Then the raven's cawing pierces the dead silence
I take a deep breath but the icy air stuns me

I stop and wait for the bus
Time has almost slowed to a halt
I am completely calm
I look around myself
Everything is shiny;

Ice covered

Hing Poon, Grade 9
Lakewood High School, CO

High Merit Poems – Grades 7, 8, and 9

The Dark Cloudy Rain
The sun is shining and kids are at play.
But a dark evil cloud has arose above them.
They have to go inside, goodbye sunny day.
It is pouring outside and the children are upset.
Curse that evil cloud that ruined the shiny day.
I walk outside the rain is hard;
I look up, the evil cloud is striking above me.
I wait as I sit in the mud;
Wait, here it comes she's coming out, the sun is back.
Goodbye evil cloud, and Hello Sunshine!

Kaitlin Dunham, Grade 7
Sequoia Village School, AZ

The Uplifting Unknown
Love
is your lost red balloon,
suddenly found. It's grand uplift forcing
gravity out of the way, and giving you your
very own tour of the universe. Taking you to new
heights every second of the day. Up and away!
So hard to speak, always stealing your breath.
You're spinning, gliding — flying even!
Your heart swelling with each new
height you defy. But your balloon
slowly deflates. As you
come back
D
O
W
N
Hoping
one day
to find another
lonely
balloon.

Izzy Trinklein, Grade 9
Grand Junction High School, CO

I Don't Understand
I don't understand
Why life has to be this hard
Why we have to fight
Why the cup is considered half empty instead of half full

But most of all
Why we strive so hard and get so little
Why we always have to follow the crowd
Why there are difficult decisions we all have to make
Why some things are just not enough

But what I do understand is
How to hope
How to dream
How to live

Katherine Romano, Grade 7
Dunstan Middle School, CO

War
The more I hear, the more I see,
I begin to realize what war can be,
It's not just a deadly dispute in history,
It's brutal, disastrous, that's what I now see.

It claims so many soldiers' lives,
It's merciless, it heeds no cries,
Of sorrow, as a soldier dies,
That's what I've come to realize.

The thundering missiles the blasting guns,
Think of all those courageous ones,
Who stood and fought, did not turn to run,
Who bore the heat of the blistering sun.

I think of all the soldiers dead,
Who fought courageously, none of them fled,
And now they lie there, the ground is their bed,
We take them for granted, it fills me with dread.

So pray for the troops, keep them in thought,
Remember the ones who for freedom sought,
So many of them have with bravery fought,
Be thankful for everything, and love as we ought.

Bethany Miller, Grade 9
Portland Cornerstone Academy, OR

Murder
This is not what I was made for,
to kill this sweet young girl.
How could someone do this?
I wanted so badly to turn myself around,
to lock my trigger; but I couldn't.
He had control over it all,
as much as I hated it, he did.

Her tears and fear killed me inside.
I don't understand why it had
no effect whatsoever on this man. His hand
drowned me in sweat, moved over the trigger;
he pulled. It was over. He dropped me fast,
screaming and crying as if he regretted it. maybe he did.

He ran to her. I heard nothing.
He returned to me and picked me up,
this time pointing me at himself.
He once again pulled the trigger;
But this time nothing. I was empty
like I thought his heart had been.
He pulled again and again, but nothing.
This is not what I was made for.

Emily Hadd, Grade 8
Mount Jordan Middle School, UT

Artists

Green, blue, pink, red,
How can they all fit in their heads?
Streak, stroke, flick, tick,
Wonder which one they will pick.
Curve, squiggly, scribbles, straight,
To make the things they will create.
Dot, splat, scrape, smudge,
To put on the finish before they judge.
These great ones I'm talking about,
Are the best without a doubt.
Michelangelo, Da Vinci, and Mucha too,
These examples are very few,
Of amazing artists of this world.
So don't take them for granted,
Or you will miss out,
'Cause they are the best without a doubt.

Samantha Barnes, Grade 9
Portland Cornerstone Academy, OR

The World Let Go

moss spiders made of trees
branches with spears
a suspended nest
wooden frogs that guard the entrance
great horned owls standing
hidden among twisted trees
twin stumps
covered in down
looking out on mountainous holes
moles claim the earth
while eagles own the clouds
fungi lead up to the sky
out upon the water
the light splashes down
creating invisible rain
frogs trumpet
welcoming new.

EJ Bridge, Grade 7
Komachin Middle School, WA

Sugar Rush

i pick from the tree a speckled apple
it is golden yellow like the sun
it has speckled imperfections.
the smell makes my nose tingle

its sweet earthy smell.
i find it smooth to the touch.

taking a bite
it has a sweet earthy taste.
i can taste how fresh it is
after one bite i can feel the sugar rush.

Lauren Bigler, Grade 9
Xavier College Preparatory School, AZ

Just Because I'm Athletic

Just because I'm athletic
Don't expect me to win at everything
Don't call me a jock
Don't call me stupid
Just because I'm athletic
It doesn't mean I'm good at everything
It doesn't mean I beat up nerds
Just because I'm athletic
I'm not perfect
I'm not always mad
I'm still a kid
Just because I'm athletic I love sports.

Kyle Sether, Grade 7
Ogden Middle School, OR

Like the Rain

Dark and gloomy thoughts
pounding against our lives,
thoughts not to be said
are said anyway,
many are now crying
from those many a thought,
pounding, pounding, pounding,
Those thoughts a pound,
they patter, patter
like the glistening rain,
they pound, and patter
until one can't hold them in!
You release those gloomy thoughts.
Making…always making,
someone cry.

Brandon Kurns, Grade 7
East Valley Middle School, MT

The Eagle

The eagle is strong.
It fights victoriously.
It fights to win.
It fights because it can.
The eagle thinks it is the best,
But what does it know,
For it is only one.
The eagle was not always this strong.
It worked for strength,
For trust,
For superiority.
The eagle is always fighting.
It knows not of peace,
But the eagle always prevails because
It fights victoriously.
It fights to win.
It fights because it can.
The eagle is strong.

Jacob Anderson, Grade 7
Lyons Middle/Senior High School, CO

Beautiful Rivers

Flowing down stream steadily
In amazement I
Watch it gracefully swagger
Down as it depletes at end

Joseph Finn, Grade 7
Sky Vista Middle School, CO

Today*

Today is a chance.
It's a risk,
It's a thrill.
Today is variety.
It's wind on your face,
It's water off your back.
Today is an experience.
It's snowboarding,
It's surfing.
Today is emotion.
It's love, it's hate.
Today is life.
It's sorrow,
It's joy.
Today is logic.
It's not,
It is.
Today is today.
It's yesterday,
It's tomorrow.
Today is now.

Aaron Mauthe, Grade 7
Diamond Ranch Academy, UT
*Inspired by Nick Vella

Flying

I can't fly
It's just too hard
I'm the only one left
I try and try again
Flying is just too hard
My mother tells me to try again
I'm getting better every time
Maybe I can fly
I get better and better
Day by day
I try and try again
I'm almost there
I think I can do it
I'm ready to fly
I step, and then I jump
And sure enough
I glide with the wind
It feels good to fly
I'm ready to fly away

Tyler Bernards, Grade 9
Mountain Ridge Jr High School, UT

Pain

I learned to break yesterday;
I've destroyed tomorrow.
I've watched each leaf fall off my tree
I've watched the seasons change
Numb to all feelings
(Life in winter's chill)
To feel the warmth in this bottle is useless;
(When I wake up the warmth is gone)
When I wake up the pain all starts again.
Nothing can stop him…
Not even a scream.

Kiera Thompson, Grade 7
Farson Eden Elementary School, WY

Skating the AZ Gem

Rolling up to the big red cope,
Preparing to drop down the slope,
Rolling down and carving with flair,
Soaring out with a front side air.
Coming down and landing with ease,
I looked up to see that the crowd was pleased,
They shouted my name, cheering me on,
I then knew that the pressure was on.
I looked around and then at my feet
As I heard my get called for the 2nd heat,
I dropped back in pulling my best stuff,
Which made the other contestants mad,
Then the competition got tough.
Omar Hassan pulling front side board slides,
And Christian Hosoi indy grabbing as he flies,
I became a little intimidated but kept my cool,
As I popped in and out of the t-bird pool.
It soon came down to the last heart,
And I ripped and shredded up that pool's concrete
I dialed in all my trucks without a trace,
And skating away with a trophy of 1st place.

Zakk Tokash, Grade 8
Cimarron Springs Elementary School, AZ

My Family

My family is important to me
Isn't it to you?
My family is important to me
They help me get through.

Whenever I need caring and support they are always there.
My family is my life
Even when sometimes they are not always fair.

I love my family more than anything
Because in the end they are all I need.

Victoria Kohagen, Grade 7
Molasky Jr High School, NV

Butterflies

Fluttering butterflies
Fill my chest
Whenever I see you, my heart cannot rest
Not knowing what's coming
Which is both bad and good too
You don't know it yet
But it seems I've fallen for you
I so deeply want to tell you
But my mind won't let me go
It's that little voice I hear
That's reciting all my fears
I don't know why I can't, maybe it's just too soon
Or maybe I'm scared that you won't love me too

Kimberly Agron, Grade 7
Mears Middle School, AK

The Life It Takes

The light it shines,
The sounds it plays.
From morn 'til nine,
Through night and day.
The life it takes, so slowly away.
Violence it makes, of kids who stay.
Shall I join the trance,
Or break away?
I'll take no chance, I'll choose today.
Xbox and Wii, Nintendo and 360.
The life it takes, a "juvee" it makes.
The life it takes, the friends gone by.
The life it takes,
A flashing sky.
I'll make the choices, to stay away.
I'll hear no voices, I'll make my choices.
I'll choose what's best, what's right, what's good.
I'll show the rest, the way to go.
Then I'll be good,
I'll know the way.
The good, the best, that's where I'll stay.

Devyn Smith, Grade 8
North Star Charter School, ID

Things to Do at a Stoplight

Eat your breakfast because you didn't have time
or fix your tie so it's sexy like mine
or text on your phone because it's not safe to text and drive
or turn on the radio and listen to the morning show live
or call into work and say you'll be late
'cause you got a flat on the interstate
or check out the weird guy in the car on the right
because he's the fattest thing in sight
then the light turns green and you zoom away fast
cruisin' in style with your foot on the gas
wait you got a flat and your car is dead
ya right you got an excuse so go crawl into bed.

Daniel Miller, Grade 7
Dunstan Middle School, CO

You and I

I notice you
Every day of my life.
You never see me.
Never even look.
I live; in pain
All day, every day.
One day you saw me,
Called me ugly.
I want to live no more.
I have a party,
You come to crash it.
We play spin the bottle.
It lands on you and I.
We go in the closet and you scream.
I run away.
Nobody sees you ever again.
Not a tear in my eye.
Why did you ignore me?
Why call me ugly?
I hope to never know.

Ryan Werner, Grade 7
Eagle Valley Middle School, CO

The Shores of an Ancient River

Have you ever thought
how the shores of a river brought
to life the kingdoms of this earth
to prove humanities true worth?
From the beginning of time
they've stayed just as fine;
the ancient river shores
have always helped us do our chores.
The river itself flows swift and steady
it is always there, always ready;
to fly by the calm shores
never exposing our true cores.
The river shores hold in
the swift fury of what's been;
in the past of our own race
this is where history took place.
If the shores could talk
about those who used to walk,
up and down their feeble rocks
I'm sure there'd be a lot of shocks.
Upon the shores of an ancient river.

Shelby Nies, Grade 7
Shadow Ridge Middle School, CO

Life

Life is a path
Sometimes you get bumped off
Or run into obstacles
But you always find your way back
But we just keep going

Austin Strong, Grade 9
Coal Ridge High School, CO

Life and Death

Life is like a gift certificate, limited,
But to what only you can say,
Life is like a lump of clay,
Born as a random shape,
But slowly evolved and molded into what you become as you age,
Life is like a license plate,
On the outside many look alike,
But it's the number on the inside that really counts,
Life is a long corridor,
Filled with surprises and forks in the road,
Death is a garage sale,
The only thing for sale is your soul,
With the devil's minions racing God's angels to bring your
Soul to pain or pleasure,
Death is a box of matches,
Everyone struck and burnt out is another soul lost to the
Heavens or the underworld,
Life is life, death is death

Many question which is better,
Yet not many willing to find out,
Life is life, and death is death

Brandon Sessions, Grade 7
21st Century Public Academy, NM

Servant

You are a servant.
You always try your hardest to impress the King
but it doesn't always work the way you want it to.
You are always loyal.
You stick to what you are told to do,
even at the toughest times
like pine needles to a tree,
covered in snow.

You are a servant.
You hold back your anger to all the terrible jobs you do
day in and day out.
You are becoming more of a volcano
Building up steam until you erupt
and show how you truly feel.

You are a servant.
Your job is tough
and the only thing you can do is let a rain storm fall from your eyes.
This sadness continues until
you can do something better.

You are a servant.

Christian Towner, Grade 7
Sky Vista Middle School, CO

Grandma

The sweet smell of your hair, the good times we've had
the memories created, you have left me, sad.
Your warm heart, the way you smile
your gratitude for everything, has inspired me all the while.
Your embracing hugs, filled my soul with glee
you made your way through trials, humming every so happily.
Your home was my home, as we enjoyed the cool nights
and walks through the woods, and saw nature's sights.
How I miss you, when I reflect
times we caught fireflies, and other insects.
Finding fossils in the brook, making forts in the snow
shaping objects out of clay, and never saying no.
To the wonders of childhood, the amazement of finding
a whole new world, outside the backdoor, hiding.
Just waiting to be, discovered by someone
who loves to be, at her pine haven.
Now the memories fade, away into the past
for my grandma is in heaven, with her family, at last.

Carolyn Malone, Grade 8
Hendrix Jr High School, AZ

Forever We Are Twisted

My dearest, brilliant, and most mysterious Puppet Master,
I ask that you pull the strings attached on your wrist.
Drag me down upon my knees,
Let me beg and let me plead.
Let me look upon your face and see your utmost need.
Now, Puppet Master, do not lose your face.
For remember now and for always,
I am just a simple toy,
All clad in cloth and lace.

Please, my cruel, darling Puppeteer,
Do not weep, and please do not fret.
For you know this especially well,
I am just a worthless pet,
Entirely clad in blood and pearls,
Your favorite sort of attire.
Attached at your skilled yet mangled wrists,
I will always be for your hire.

I am just your little girl,
Hanging from a wire.

Mary Covington, Grade 9
Bonneville High School, ID

Thank You for Confessing

You just say what you don't want other people to say
To you don't you, but why? That hurts so many people
No one likes a bully and you know that.
Weren't you bullied when you were little?
Then why do you think we like it? Well we don't like it
Just like you didn't so just stop it now it can help…Yes.
Oh okay but why oh I see okay thank you for confessing.

Kimberlie Russell-LaFave, Grade 7
Shaw Heights Middle School, CO

Sleepy Willow

My best friend is a sleepy willow
I can see him from my window
I can tell my secrets and about me
And he just stands there as if he was nodding in agreement

His tree trunk is frail and withered
Of all the things that had occurred
His leaves keep swaying to and fro
They go down so low

It's almost as if he was protecting me
From the world I cannot see
In the bark are encrusted lines
Showing just how wise

After school I run to my friend
I will tell him everything and a shoulder he will lend
I tell my parents not to cut him down
Because a new friend I have just found

He is far from our house but worth the walk
When I need to talk
He's my one friend
And I'll stay with him until the end

Izy Hunt, Grade 7
Shadow Ridge Middle School, CO

History of Humanity

from a baby's first breath, to an old man's sigh
the history of humanity is just a blink of they eye

from an old farm cottage, to skyscrapers a mile high
the history of humanity is just a blink of the eye

from Christopher Columbus, to Peter Budai
the history of humanity is just a blink of the eye

from chariot races, to cars that fly
the history of humanity is just a blink of the eye

from dinosaurs who roamed, to robots, oh my!
the history of humanity is just a blink of the eye

from good home grown cookin', to "fresh" over frozen pies
the history of humanity is just a blink of the eye

from your mamma and papa, to you and me
the history of humanity is not quite what it seems

from saying hello, now to saying goodbye
the history of humanity *was* just a blink of the eye

Hallie Venaglia, Grade 9
Lakewood High School, CO

The Boy
The boy was different.
He was special.
Husky and deep singing voice,
As deep as the ocean.
Hearing his voice was
A heart monitor
Keeping me alive, yet
Ready to let me die.
Tall as a sycamore tree,
As tall as Goliath
Far away as heaven
Close to touch as my own mouth.

I will wait for My Boy —
The Boy
Because he is not mine.
But I will wait
Until the end of the earth,
As if time grew on trees.
Time cannot separate me and
My Boy.
Abrie Lunt, Grade 9
Mountain Ridge Jr High School, UT

Winter
It is a cold, snowy day
The wind is blowing
It is freezing outside
With their backs to the wind
Because there is a breeze
The trees are bent
My face is frozen
My breath is a cloud
I can see my breath
It's so cold, I can hardly breathe.
Dakota Lewis, Grade 7
Wiley Jr/Sr High School, CO

My Dreams
In my dreams I see a doctor
In my dreams I see a dancer
I see a mother
I see a future

In my dreams I see a friend
In my dreams I see a supporter
I see an encourager
I see a woman with success

I hope to become these people I see
Each and every one

In my dreams…
…I see me
Grace Anderson, Grade 7
Dunstan Middle School, CO

As the Crowd Was Clapping
warming up, thinking note after note
feeling so nervous my stomach seemed to float
my partner says time to go
I seem to hold back, wishing I could say no
I walk on-stage, as bright as can be
always looking down, hoping no one can see
I pick up the stand, pull it up near to my eyes
my face hides my feelings, it acts as my disguise
oh the urge to hide my face
wishing I could be in another place
then danyelle says go; I start without a flaw
holding tight to my ombasure so much it hurts my jaw
the song soon ends and I don't mess up
we take a step to the left, bow, show off our flutes like big golden cups
we turn and start walking
as our hearts start beating
we walk, amazed, surprised, the crowd was clapping
Kesha Lowe, Grade 9
Duchesne High School, UT

The Best of Friends
It's only been two years and we're the best of friends
we share secrets and we always keep them.
Lately you've been so sick
and I just don't know what to do
I came over you said you were fine
but deep inside I knew you were lying.
You say you're okay but I can hear
the silent screams your body is making, crying and suffering
I pretend I'm okay and try to be strong
but my sadness is deep as the oceans.
I saw your face that terrible day
pale purple
your lips bluish gray your sad eyes,
you tell me you want me to go with you
to the hospital but they airlift you.
We all rush to meet you,
there you look so much better
I don't know what I would do without you. I love you,
all the nights we've stayed up laughing and telling stories,
I can't lose that. You've helped me so much now I will help you,
I would give up my breath just for you.
Jessica Fenstermaker, Grade 9
Queen Creek High School, AZ

Life
Life is like a maze.
You take turn upon turn not knowing where it is going to lead you,
Going into one dead end after another.
Seeing a trap and having to avoid the trap.
It is like a search for a pot of gold.
You want that perfect life.
And when you find that pot of gold your options are unlimited.
Andrew Zeigler, Grade 7
Mandalay Middle School, CO

High Merit Poems – Grades 7, 8, and 9

Memory

Thoughts about the day, wait for it to come.
Excitement, dreams about it, smiles, family.
12/11 we watch and listen, similar, not a movie.
Drive home, sleep in the back,
Have a dream that your on a roller coaster.
Your head hits back and forth, what's really the cause?
Woken up to a voice if we're all ok.
Blue, red lights, flash all around.
Arguments to one another, sister on a stretcher.
On earth or heaven was the question.
With greatness of an angel, no serious injuries.
Together we are all again on 12/11.

Amber Coca, Grade 8
Shadow Ridge Middle School, CO

Friends

Friends are the ones who listen
their attention is drawn to you.
Friends are the ones you're missing
when you have to move schools.

They are the ones you look for
when you're lost in afar.
They are the ones you adore
for the people that they are.

Friends are the air you breathe.
They are something you can't live without.
Friends are like the grass that is green.
They are something that gives no doubt.

Friends are the ones you want around.
They'll be there for you
when you're looking down.
Being a friend is something to do.

Angela Jednat, Grade 9
Queen Creek High School, AZ

The Perfect Treat

I trade my dollar for a cool treat,
Something to help me escape from the heat.
Ice cream would be great, nice and sweet.
I could finish a cone in just one heartbeat.
Or maybe I should get some orange juice,
Or maybe a cake, covered in mousse.
These are all snacks that I could use,
But ice cream is what I cannot refuse.
I feel the ice cream flow down my throat,
But I must eat fast, or it'll drip on my coat.
So remember that if you ever have a sore throat,
Eat some ice cream, it is the perfect antidote.

Tiffanie Chu, Grade 8
Valley View Middle School, WA

Childhood

My childhood, filled with sweet memories
And some not as sweet nor quick to please.
I remember camping in a forest of trees
And traveling around the country with ease.
Sometimes we'd go camping with family and friends.
With my grandparents, I hoped it would never end.
I remember at Ellen's cabin we'd stay;
And when Miranda fell of the stairs a long, long way.
We kids would go hiking all around.
We saw a rock, thinking it was a dinosaur newly found.
I remember going to get flavored ice.
During the hot summer it was always nice.
"Simon Says" was the game we would play;
I would win sometimes on a really good day.
I remember riding on my little trike
And dancing in the rain as a little tike.
I remember when the huge tree fell on my house
And my first dress, a Princess Jasmine blouse.
I have many more memories whirling in my head;
Too many, I wish they all could be said.

Melissa Bevilacqua, Grade 9
Tempe Preparatory Academy, AZ

We Are the Future

Tomorrow's leaders,
Today's believers,
We are the children of the future.
Athletes, singers, writers, and all,
We all make mistakes, we rise and we fall.
Together we walk, we run, and we play.
We are all equal in our own way.
We the children beat as one heart.
We beat together looking toward a new start.
Through big and small, or thick and thin,
We may lose or we may win.
Tomorrow's leaders,
Today's believers.
We are the future,
The children of the future.

Brittnie Avila, Grade 8
Fertitta Middle School, NV

I Love You

Ever since you came into this world
You became a part of my heart,
Now I can't stand to be apart.
I'm glad for all the time we spend together,
I wish those moments would last forever.
Every time you go away,
I get sad because you don't stay.
When I look into your eyes I see love,
That makes me feel like I'm floating above.
You are like my precious treasure,
That gives me that unique simple pleasure.

Priscila Ortiz, Grade 7
Somerton Middle School, AZ

Basketball

From one side to the other
we run hard up and down
passing the ball back and forth
making it go in the net

we win together
we lose together
when one is down
the other helps you up

we are a team
we do everything together
you can't win without a team
you can't lose without a team

Ty Summarell, Grade 7
Duchesne High School, UT

The Bad Day

Darkness fills my spirit,
As I trudge through the gloom.
Everything I touch,
I fill with hopeless doom.
Suddenly I see a light
The shadows fade away.
Your kindness and your smile,
Brought some sun to my bad day.

Phoebe Frerichs, Grade 7
Villa Montessori School – Phoenix, AZ

What I Miss

I miss so many things,
Though I am not old.
Am I, with my hopes and dreams,
Not allowed to remember?

I miss stomping in puddles,
In my big plastic coat.
When subtraction was a muddle
That made my head float,

I miss make believe play
When friends were forever,
And enemies only a day
'Cause I like friends better.

I miss Mother Goose,
And our friend Dr. Seuss.
Because these friends of mine
Don't care about the grapevine.

I miss ribbons in my hair,
When everything wasn't strange,
And I didn't have to care
About life, friends, and everything.

Darlene Thompson, Grade 7
Vancouver Home Connection, WA

September 11th

I was young when it happened, I didn't quite understand,
Everyone was sad, but I wasn't, I was just a small, little lad.
When I grew older, I saw on TV,
What a terrible thing, they did to our country.
They highjacked the planes, they flew at top speed
They smashed into our buildings, what an awful, mean deed.
The towers collapsed, they crumbled to dust
People were blinded, people were crushed.

Some people cried, some ran away,
Some were in shock, some stayed there, and many breathed their last breath of air.
And then, there was the other plane,
It crashed into the Pentagon, without any warning,
It was definitely remembered, as a very bad morning.

Another plane was highjacked, but the passengers on board,
Defended their country, they put up a fight,
Made the plane crash, they saved the White House, from turning to ash.
I see the event today, and tears fill my eyes,
I can't believe what happened, but we have to recover,
And next time be wise, don't let people carry knives.
Now we're in war, Americans are dying, politicians are fighting,
But hopefully one day, this country will be okay, and that's the way it should stay.

Zachary Taylor, Grade 7
Coronado K 8 School, AZ

I Am…

I am from an amazing family of seven.
I have two awesome sisters and two wonderful brothers
We all have at least one thing in common and many differences.
But no matter what we like or dislike, we will always love each other.

I'm from the beautiful Rocky Mountains;
The greatest snow on earth;
The beautiful salty lakes; the state of the Arches.

I live in a cute, blue house,
Where the sun always shines,
And the flowers always bloom.

I'm a girl who loves and always will love Barbie dolls and playing dress up.
One who is obsessed with Winnie the Pooh and Tigger.
Loves anything that gets her heart pumping;
Plays all sports especially basketball.

I am from the days that you could wear anything
And it wouldn't even matter if it matched or not.
I am from the only planet with life.
I am from someone who cares about me.

Clarissa Avila, Grade 7
Our Lady of Lourdes Catholic School, UT

Seasons

Spring flowers bloom in the warm air,
Gentle winds whisper in one's ear.
The bright summer sun shines down on frolicking kids' hair,
Cool water on a hot day washes away all worries and cares.
Falling leaves fill the autumn air,
Peaceful colors just seem to appear.
Fluffy, white winter snow falls down everywhere,
Carolers spread holiday cheer.

Nick Sewell, Grade 7
Albuquerque Christian School, NM

Not Yet Out of the Rain

The memories play over in my head
They play back like movies as I lay in my bed.
No matter how painful they may be
I can't stop thinking about these memories.
Just when I think they're gone
They pop back up into my head

Not yet out of the rain.
Not far from that ray of sunshine.
Life takes you in
Whether you're ready or not

The past is in just that
There's no changing what's already happened.
Death. Pain. Sorrow. Unhappiness.
All you have left is the memories
However painful they may be.

I wish the clouds would go away
And let me have that little sunshine ray.
Let me have that Hope, Laughter, and Happiness
But no, not a chance
I am not yet out of the rain.

Elizabeth Jane Kettles, Grade 8
Fertitta Middle School, NV

Soon

Soon is coming near,
It may be sometime this year.
I don't really want it to come,
Thinking about it makes me glum.

But then again it means moving out of the nest,
Where I have a choice of doing my best.
I get to choose where I fly,
And to my parents, I say good-bye.

Out in the world I go,
With a lot of things to learn and know,
Soon has a lot of things,
And when it comes,
It'll be like being a bird and spreading my wings.

Julietta Sheng, Grade 7
Lincoln Jr High School, CO

Endurance

As I know there's only one more lap to go
My horse's tiredness starts to show

If I can complete this last jump I might win
But I don't know where my mind has been

We have only made five of the ten jumps
And my horse keeps slipping on all of the bumps

I don't see anybody anywhere
My ambition is starting to tear

Sometimes I get the feeling that we might be first
But also the feeling that we are the worst

This feels like an everlasting race
Until I can see the winner's face

I slowed my horse to a stop
When my jaw started to drop

As I went to retrieve my second place prize
I woke up in my bed, quite surprised

Ariel Marinetti, Grade 7
La Center Middle School, WA

Life Is a Wrestling Match

At the beginning
You might start out unharmed ready for anything

With a few hits and disappointments
You think you can't go on
And just want to give up
But you have to go on until it finishes.
With one good hit
You might get back in the game.
But there is always going to be a miss in a punch
And you get mad because it didn't work out just like you wanted

There might be a time when you have to decide
If you are going to punch or kick

One will come out to win you the match
And the other to miss
But you don't know which one will work out for you
You have to make a choice on which one
To do because you can't stay there
Just standing until they beat you.
So you have to go on because
Life is a wrestling match
And you have to keep going until it's over

Emmanuel Castillo, Grade 7
21st Century Public Academy, NM

Remember When...

Remember when we didn't care about hair, makeup, when we could run around in a diaper and not care?
Remember when we could go out in our pj's and not be judged?
Remember when we could make best friends in two minutes of knowing them?
Remember when it was all a simpler time, no consequences for your actions just sorry and all better?
Now if you say something politically incorrect you could get in trouble.
Now we must conduct ourselves in polite fashion.
We are supposed to know etiquette and junk.
When all we are, are large kids when you hit a certain age you shouldn't be expected to be an adult,
You should come to that gradually and on your own.
Remember when we wanted this to come? For example, "I can't wait until I am older."
Remember when the little things that we have now meant so much,
But at least we didn't have to go through when you turn seven or eight you lose your best friend because of their ethnicity.
Remember?

Aryssa Brantner, Grade 7
West Valley Middle School, WA

Place Unknown

I am in a place unknown, my friend is at my side, we are both now on our way, there's nothing left to hide.
We left without them knowing, much to their surprise,
our families will be searching, but we were long gone by sunrise.
The days seem like they're longer, the nights even more,
every minute I think of my decision, I feel that it was poor.
This place is terribly lonely, my friend and I do nothing,
we sit under a tiny tree, only dirt that we are touching.
There is nothing much to eat here, only garbage on the ground,
we don't have many choices, I long for the food we haven't found.
I think about the place we left, the people we surely hurt,
all it took was one decision, now I'm alone out in the dirt.

I start back to the place I left, nothing in either hand,
I was getting closer, leaving the dirt and stepping towards the sand.
I walk up to the ocean, but there's no one to be found, I am at the place I love, yet not the slightest sound.
A quick knock on the door is my final attempt, I hope to hear someone come,
I slowly twist the doorknob, and my fingers start to numb.
I tiptoe through the hallway, and walk quietly up the stairs, I call out to my family, yet I feel like no one cares.

They must have left; what has come of this? I need my family, just a hug or a kiss.
Back down the steps, and across the beach, I have searched for my family, they are nowhere within reach.
I ran away from home that day, and now I'm all alone.
My teardrops trickle down my cheek; I'm in a place unknown.

Carley Schmidt, Grade 7
West Valley Middle School, WA

What I Come From

I am from crusty rosin covered ropes, western pictures, and squeaky saddles, from riding in the rain to cattle eating hay.
I am from apples falling from trees, shady front porches and a garden bench, from green crisp grass to lazy dogs.
I am from tractors plowing fields, horses running through the wind, cows grazing in the field, hay barns full of hay, and a cemetery across the street.
I am from my adventurous grandma Louise, my grumpy old papo, bus driving granny, and pops our grandpa Mel.
I am from "lock 'n' lode time to go," from "I brought you into this word and can take you out," to "I love you."
I am from Grandpa's barbecued ribs and Grandma's apple pie, the famous mashed potatoes and gravy, chicken fried steak, to Grandma's biscuits and gravy.
I am from the chest under the bed, the walls of our house, photo albums, secret story books and journals.

Jordan Hanslovan, Grade 8
Culver Middle School, OR

Poetry Is

Poetry is a quiet, small whisper
That shouts so loud that images are invisible.
Poetry is a faded, soft blanket
Waiting to enfold you.

Poetry is as familiar as your hand,
But as foreign as your 1st lover's
Poetry is a sweet escape,
But the return is always bitter.

Poetry is a smile —
Both a sad smile and a joyous one.
Poetry is a ripple in a pond,
But on occasion the water is drained.

Poetry is a red rose,
Sweet to the nose, prickly to the finger.
Poetry is love
Poetry is hate

Poetry is a path
Waiting for a traveler.

Jen Swindler, Grade 9
Mountain Ridge Jr High School, UT

The Wooden Dragon

With painted wings and broken heart,
It looks forlornly into the dark
It cannot move; 'tis carved of wood
A statue doomed forever to brood

Of what it would be like to live and breathe
To live a life of pain and ease —
But no! 'Twas brought into the world
With wings that it could ne'er unfurl

Alone nearby, inspired one sits
At last knowing what it is
That they must draw and write
That they shall show the world that night

At long last finished, the author sighs
And, to the shock of plastic eyes
Upon the pages lays a tale
And a picture, a marvelous portrayal

With painted wings that seemed to soar
It did not matter anymore
That it could not move, for 'twas in that night
The carved dragon received a seed of life

Jessa Kraus, Grade 7
Mandalay Middle School, CO

I Know My God

I know that the Lord is by my side
I know that He is here to guide me.
He can make the blind see
  And He can make the deaf hear.
The Lord is my creator till eternity.
Lord you are all I need.
Lord you're all I need to succeed.
Every day and every night
I know that You are by my side.
I've trusted in You all my life, all my life
  And I believe that You were sacrificed, sacrificed.
There's nothing greater than your love for me,
  Nothing greater than your love.
I've trusted in You all my life, all my life
  And I believe that You were sacrificed, sacrificed.
I know that the Lord is by my side.
I know that He is here to guide.

Alexis O'Leary, Grade 7
Yucca Middle School, NM

You Are…

You're sitting on the park bench,
But only for a moment or two,
You're always standing close for when we make a sudden slip,
You stay close only for that reason,
To catch all close calls,
You are…Mr. Gordy,
You tell us all we want to know,
But one thing remains a secret,
This secret you don't tell is a secret inside itself,
Why is it only us that can see you for who you REALLY are,
Even though they don't, we do?
You are…My. Gordy,
Even in the silence of our forts,
Or the screaming on the playground,
You, but only you, respond to our silent calls for help,
You hear these calls,
When no one else does,
You are…Mr. Gordy,
We see as our friend,
But an imaginary one at that,
You are…Mr. Gordy.

Mikayla Christenson, Grade 7
Sterling Middle School, CO

Spring

The flowers are in bloom,
And my mood is no longer full of gloom.
I see their beauty everywhere,
Nothing else can compare.
Roses of red and pink
Make me stop and think.
I want to look at the world and really see,
Open my eyes and just be me.

Aurora Hurlburt, Grade 8
Cut Bank Middle School, MT

The Treadmill

Life is a treadmill,
It keeps going,
And going,
With the end in sight,
Although it cannot be reached.
Life, too, has settings,
We may choose how far
And fast we run,
Even as we know
It can be hard or easy.
Life is difficult and some
Choose to take the easy route.
But those that find the easy way,
Are seldom satisfied with life.
The treadmill is our choice,
And we know,
To run faster,
Harder, longer,
Steeper, is the only way
We get the best results.

Kamron Medina, Grade 9
Grand Junction High School, CO

Transform Life

The harsh words answer questions
Neighboring allies criticized
Atomic energy agency halted

Transform Life   0 deaths

Past government announcement
Strategic studies tank
Limited ballistic missiles

Transform Life   100 deaths

Leaders judicially approve punishment
Nuclear aims to campaign life
Vigilant ministry spokesman abuses right

Transform Life   10,000 deaths
War equals death

Joshua Scott, Grade 8
Walt Morey Middle School, OR

Books

Books are filled with knowledge,
However thick or thin,
The chapters can be long or short,
With many pages within,
Despite the size of a book,
There still are things to learn,
So now or then a book or two,
Wouldn't be hurt to be read.

Nathan Burk, Grade 8
Round Valley Middle School, AZ

Childhood

Childhood is spilling cereal everywhere while you eat.
Childhood is having your dad check your room for ghost before bed.
Childhood is turning on the night light before you sleep and dream.
Childhood is cracking open the door before you sleep.
Childhood is watching *Barney* on the weekends instead of the news.
Childhood is going to Mom and Dad's room when you get scared at night.
Childhood is getting oatmeal baths when you get the chicken pox.

Spencer Moreno, Grade 7
Sagewood Middle School, CO

You Are

You are My sunshine.
You make my frown turn into a smile.
Every day I hold you it's like I feel a phase.
I need you in my life while we grow older.
You are my friend as well as my Daze,
In daze I mean my Lover.
You make my heart discover so many feelings, it's a shame.
The way I feel for you is for no other.
There are no words that can express the way I feel for you.
You can say you don't love me no more, but there will be no other
to love you like I do.
The words I say now mean that
You are my boy and I am your girl
You are my world you are my star.
You are my outer space.
You are my Jupiter, you are my Mars.
You are the reason for my seasons.
You are the twinkle in my eye,
and the Giggle in my laugh and the reason of this is because,
You are my sunshine.

Tatyana Dupree, Grade 7
Fertitta Middle School, NV

If

If you can keep your head held high, even when your losing it all,
If you can encourage even when all are down,
If you can listen to coach you can learn the game,
Or move your feet, or drive the puck, then you will make the cut,
If you can work and make a difference,
If you can stay positive,
If you can be one with your opponent and play aggressive, but not too mean,
If you can bare the pain of your screaming lungs and burning legs,
Or watch the other team score, but get it back without evil revenge,
If you can leave all your distractions behind you come game time,
If you go out there with full heart, and start the game strong
If you can be a good team player on and off the ice,
You will become a good friend and therefore a good teammate,
If you can teach and instruct, the younger level players,
If you have no hard feelings with your team, nor the other teams around,
If you can forgive the unforgivable
If you can keep your word and not lie,
If you can skate your shift and sit your turn out, you will make a good hockey player.

Becky Helgesen, Grade 7
Sky Vista Middle School, CO

'Tis the Day of St. Patty

'Tis the day of St. Patty and all through the town
An Irishman's cold glass of guinness soon went down
The bright green clothes were donned not sparing an inch
In dire hopes to avoid a terrible pinch

O'Shea, O'Malley, O'Donald they all came
For stories of leprechauns sure weren't very lame
Although these traditions may seem simple and old
We always search for that special pot of Irish gold

Rhett Gutierrez, Grade 7
Mandalay Middle School, CO

The Flow of Time

Through the swift long passage of ancient time,
The innocent and the wicked are born.
And pure new life slowly begins to chime,
While death comes and people voicelessly mourn.

Events unfold as father time moves on,
Famines and long, deadly, blood world wars.
Using innocents as the useless pawn.
While others lose those they deeply adore.

For most people will break, kill, and destroy,
Causing harm to the land they come to love.
They seemingly tend to greatly enjoy
Watching all birds fall, even the beautiful doves.

For the ancient flow of time never stop…
There will always be showers of teardrops.

Kelly Smith, Grade 9
Tombstone High School, AZ

Songbook

Have you ever known
how important being you
can really be?
Have you ever tried
to be someone else
and regretted it?
Have you ever met
someone you really like
and found out they were a bad choice?
Have you ever decided
to be something else
and cried over the consequences?
Don't make my mistakes again.
They're bad enough the first time through.
Looking back at my life
my book of songs guides my way
A new song has entered my book.
Is it a mistake? I won't know.
Was it for the better? I don't know.
Until I look upon this again and finish it.

cade beck, Grade 9
Lakewood High School, CO

Grounding

Grounding is no fun
Grounding hurts my bum
I get grounded when I do something dumb
Like deliberately disobey
I am stuck in my room almost all day
They say I need to learn from what I did
Any kid would say it's so unfair
And we feel like no one would care

When I am grounded
I am always cold
And wherever I sit
I get sore

When I am grounded
I can't wait for school
So I can talk to friends
Play some ball
And study in class

When I grow up I'll never ground my kids
Because I know what it's like
And how grueling it is
I don't like being grounded.

Ricky Driesen, Grade 8
Sunnyside Christian Elementary School, WA

'Twas the Night Before Soccer

'Twas the night before soccer and all through my head
I lay there dreaming of a soccer field to tread.
My shin guards sat ready all set in my bag
I had to be ready or my mom would nag.

The whole team was asleep all snug in their beds
While visions of soccer balls danced in their heads.
And Mama in her dreams and I in my pjs
Had just settled my brain for a long stressful daze.

When on my dresser arose such a rumble
I sprang from my bed my body was a jumble.
Away to the clock I shot like a rocket
Hit the button, my game was on the docket.

The sun reflected off the bright green grass
Gave shimmer to the morning of games with class
When, what to my excited eyes should appear
But a small team, and I realized I should not fear.

Being our last game, playing badly is a sin
I knew in a moment it must be a win.

Lindsay Block, Grade 7
Mandalay Middle School, CO

Night
The stars are shining brightly
an owl hoots softly in the night
and the moon is my light
Hailie Conover, Grade 7
Elk Ridge Middle School, UT

As the Wind Pours In
As the wind pours in
I grab my dreams
While pulling them close
Frowning upon the sin
Of the air coming in

As the wind pours in
I think dreams might be mine
Standing there like on a line
Putting on a smile
As long as two miles

If the wind pours out
Then I could play
And follow the people that say
"Let them go, they will never be
your way"

If the wind pours out
I won't cry because I know
That if I chase them down
Like a dog by the snout
They would be mine someday
McKenzie Purdy, Grade 9
McMinnville High School, OR

Freedom?
Sitting in the dark
There's no light here
My heart cries out
but I show no fear

Will they ever let me out?
good Lord I don't know
But I will tell you sir
I sure hope so

The sun will shine again
but will I ever see?
All I know is 4 stonewalls
that are surrounding me

Nothing much to do right now
except plan for the day
When freedom rings around the world
and I can shout hurray!
Rachel Christensen, Grade 8
Kenmore Jr High School, WA

I Wish
I wish so bad that you were here
But now I know that you'll stay there.
My only thought is to see your face
But now you're gone without a trace.
If only you could see what I've become
You would see that special someone.
I love you now and I will forever
But that empty space is close to sever.
I wish so bad that I could see you
But that wish won't come true unless
You start pulling through.
And that is why I have to say
I think about you every day.
Vanessa Bilodeau, Grade 7
Bradshaw Mountain Middle School, AZ

Don't Know What to Do?
I love you
But I don't know what to do?
You're nice, you're kind
You're perfect for me,
But I don't understand.
Acting all bad.
Being in gangs
But you don't realize
In what gangs you are
Smoking that stuff
Whenever you want
You should do something else
Not doing all this bad stuff!
Maricruz Cirila, Grade 7
Phoenix Preparatory Academy, AZ

Death
Standing still in a fast moving ocean
The towers from above oh so close
He's standing there in a battle
Where no soldier is to be found
His shield strong but weak
His sword sharp but dulled
The enemy's curse
The curse of death
Death is coming with the towers
They're coming fast
Doors open wide
Waiting for you to fall
When you do they take you in
No hope of coming back
Doors locked tight
Don't fall
Don't go in
Don't let them take you away
Stay please just stay
Amanda Navolynski, Grade 7
Toledo Middle School, WA

My Homework
To the tune of twinkle twinkle little star:

Oh my homework big and thick,
you can see it from Mudlick,
it will sit there till it's due,
social studies and math too,
oh my homework big and thick,
you can see it from Mudlick.
Brooke Solomon, Grade 7
Ernest Becker Middle School, NV

Hunting
Walking slowly
So I hear sounds,
WAIT!
I hear something.
I follow the sound of twigs breaking.
I heard it start to run.
I find tracks from it.
Start to listen.
I follow it to a meadow.
It wasn't just one.
A herd of them!
Lots of cow elk.
But, two BIG bull elk.
Aim my gun and
BANG! I missed.
I shoot again and,
Got him!
He ran for a hundred yards.
I walk up to him.
I see his huge antlers.
It was a nice five by five.
Jordan Jones, Grade 8
Culver Middle School, OR

What Poetry Should Be...
A wild horse running free,
The calm before a storm,
Raindrops against your face,
A sunset,
Or a waterfall,
The colors of the rainbow,
A song,
A story,
Or a tale,
A friendship that will never end,
A memory,
A gust of air,
The wind rushing through my hair,
The first signs of spring,
All things both wonderful and terrible,
That is what a poem should be.
Kyrsten Woolstenhulme, Grade 9
Mountain Ridge Jr High School, UT

High Merit Poems – Grades 7, 8, and 9

The Land of Chocolate
I went to the land of chocolate
I ate everything in sight
I ate it all from telephone pole to street light
I even ate all the mail
For that I went to jail
I ate myself out
Then went to the river for some chocolate trout
I heard an earthquake
I felt my little tummy shake
My day is finally done
Tomorrow I go to the land of gum
Ray Barkis, Grade 7
Red River Valley Charter School, NM

Everyday Joys
Watching movies until the end of the night
Seeing the bliss of the morning light
Shining through my window is quite a sight
Eating Ben and Jerry's ice cream
Until the container is completely clean
After I eat all that sugar it is quite a scene
Soaking in hot bath after a harsh game
While talking on the phone with friends
About things like who is fame and who is lame
Reading a book on a rainy day
Joys happen everywhere, every day just sit back and play
Kandice Baker, Grade 7
21st Century Public Academy, NM

Why?
I love you but I also hate
But yet I want to date
What did I do wrong
I wanted it to last so long
You do a great job making sure I hurt
When you are being a flirt
You make me so mad
You make me so sad
You make me want to cry
But why?
My girls say forget
But that will make me regret
Remember the day you asked me out?
I wanted to shout
You're a skater
May I add a hater?
You treated me so wrong
So why did I want it to last so long?
I am now over you!
So Shooooo! That means I don't like you
Demi Chavez, Grade 7
Shadow Ridge Middle School, CO

I Am
I am a middle school student and a football player
I wonder if I will make it to the NFL
I hear the fans cheering
I see the football field
I want a million dollars
I am a middle school student and a football player

I imagine the football field
I feel happy
I touch my friends and family
I worry about losing my mom and my brother
I cry about when I lost my grandma
I am a middle school student and a football player

I understand life can be hard
I say never give up
I dream to be rich
I try to score at least two touchdowns a game
I hope life will get easier one day
I am a middle school student and a football player
Jordon Sidenstick, Grade 7
Shadow Ridge Middle School, CO

A Tribute to My Grandma
The day had come.
I watched her struggle,
As I said my last goodbye.
She took her last breath as I watched her die.
I hated to see her lose energy so fast,
But that was when I realized it wasn't going to last.
My heart was breaking in two,
and I didn't know if I could make it through.
I sat at home with tears in my eyes,
I really wish she wouldn't have died.
My grandma was in heaven where she had wanted to be,
A place without sickness, hurt, or disease.
Although I'm very sad to see her leave,
Because she's in heaven I won't have to grieve.
Emily Benton, Grade 7
Coronado K 8 School, AZ

Dear Anonymous
I wish you were more present in my life.
If only you somehow knew what you miss:
Church
Parties
Barbecues
You will never know how this feels.
I wish you had open ears and arms.
It's like all of my weight is on my heels.

I love you so much.
And nothing…
Nothing in the world can change that.
Tayler Stoker, Grade 8
Cedar Park Christian School – Everett Campus, WA

Nature

Sunset
I sit at sunset
Watching the blood fade away
Darkening my eyes

Water
Watching the water
Sink down hill disappearing
Into the white snow

Clouds
White clouds are fluffy
Filled with peace, joy and calmness
Help me sleep at school
Phillip Edwards, Grade 7
21st Century Public Academy, NM

Forest Paradox

Oak forest
    Drainage area
Crinkle of leaves
    Honking semis
Droplets of rain
    Shivering spine

Wind rushing
    Compost oozes
Trees stand strong
    Cars rush
Water splashing
    Spiders creep
Tingle on my toes
    Frozen hands
Nature is pristine
    Filthy
Never want to leave
    How much longer
Sophie DeBolt, Grade 8
Chehalis Middle School, WA

Little Yellow Airplane

The little yellow airplane
Soared through the angry air
It whirred this way and that
Diving and skimming
Through the grass
Humming gracefully
Through the clouds
Drawing puffy lines in the air
Dodging trees here and there
Then when the engine
Purred to a stop
It hit the ground
With a gentle plop
Brian Grubb, Grade 7
Lyons Middle/Senior High School, CO

Clock

The clock ticks so slow
I wish that the writing would just flow
As the clock tics by as if it has nothing better to do
The clock haunts me because I have nothing better to do

If I write the words will just come for when you write time goes fast
Now the time is flying past
tic tock is the sound the clock makes when I am stumped
I wish that I could just go home and be a lump

My eyes seem glued to the clock
As it goes tic tock
The clock is laughing at my pain and misery
For of me it makes a mockery

The thing is that when the writing flows
Time isn't so slow
When I look up at the clock
It seems as though time itself has slowed to just t-i-c t-o-c-k

If summer was this slow
Nothing would flow
Now it is time to go
To a place we do not know
Kylie Swenson, Grade 7
Shadow Ridge Middle School, CO

Home of My Bones

I see the faces of ones I once knew
To say hello would be a delight
The sad truth was my mouth stuck shut
A wave?
No, stiff as a board
Once in the black dirt though
The maggots gave me company
In return I let them feast
To see them oh I wish
Once the wooden door closed
The inside turned dark as my eyes
Oh no they're almost done
How sad
Soon they'll move on
To the next tasty meal
And in the end it'll be me and the dark
My new home is quite sad
I want to leave
Please, I beg you
Until then I'll sleep
Maybe my bones will turn to dust and create a smile on my face.
Ashlee Sysak, Grade 9
Chatfield High School, CO

My Letter, I'm Going to War
A horrid fear; loss and hope.
That shining sign of strength and cope.
I find myself sitting alone…
Has the sun got scared; it has not shone.
He went away to reveal this scene
That sharp eyed boy that's upright keen
Receiving a stunning letter one day
Upset and confused about his display
His uniform was on dignified and proud
His country was now his respected crowd
That flag waved with passion and his arm raised high

That was his disclosing way to say *good-bye*
Tiffany Hardy-Gonzales, Grade 8
Shadow Ridge Middle School, CO

Invisible
Invisible to see
You're invisible to me.
I know you're there,
Just…somewhere.
Nowhere yet everywhere.
You are waiting for me
To return to you eternally.
I can't wait to meet you for the first time.
I'm waiting for you to drop me a line.
You're setting up your kingdom above.
You will forever have everlasting love.
You've given me a sense of peace
When I think of you my troubles are released.
You paint the broad blue skies
You are truthful and tell no lies.
The heavens above unleash your glory
As the stars' horizon opens before me.
And yet, you are still invisible to me,
But hardly impossible to see.
Invisible.

Jecelle Fetzer, Grade 7
Sterling Middle School, CO

Meeting You
Meeting you has left its print.
I never thought I'd open my eyes again.
But then you came along and showed me,
that there was more than darkness and despair.
You have left a print on my life,
I wish you had never left.
Life was wonderful, life was grand,
    but,
now you're gone.
I will never forget you.
You have changed my life,
Now it's bright.
Meeting you left me with a print on my life.

Amber Pagni, Grade 9
Coal Ridge High School, CO

Deceit
A good friend's embrace, welcoming and warm,
Can deceive the eye from a rightful truth.
Back stabbing, betrayal, 'tis this the norm?
To lies, we listen, wasting our own youth.

Hearts broken and tossed upon the cold floor,
Wanting to wrong you was never my aim.
It flares as it fails, each moment a war,
Why is it life always seems like a game?

Feelings of digression, I will not show,
The just of my life is not what it seems.
The break of our friendship a fatal blow,
All of this hatred, it seems like a dream.

A friendship destroyed by another's word,
Why was it only their lies that you heard?

Stephanie Woodland, Grade 9
Clark High School, NV

King's Court
Trumpets announcing her royal grand entrance,
The queen, adorned by gems, silks, and furs,
Glittering below a dazzling diamond chandelier,
Scents of strong perfumes lingering in the atmosphere.
Voices grow as the lively music swells,
Champagne glasses tinkling.
As the scent of roast meats rises from the long decorated table,
Guests brushing up against each other,
Then the king rises to make an announcement,
Everyone falls silent in respect.

Erin Bauer, Grade 7
Wiley Jr/Sr High School, CO

There Is No Second Chance…
I asked you that question for a reason.
You said, "there would be a second chance,"
You didn't put it that way,
But that's what it meant to me,
I asked that question to see,
If you were really trying,
To see if I would be trusted once again.
I know it was "too good to be true"
I didn't want to get my hopes up,
So I didn't put them up there,
I asked you.
I got scared when I got nothing.
That's when I knew they were just words.
You got quiet so fast.
There are no second chances…

Clarisa Nevarez, Grade 8
Phoenix Preparatory Academy, AZ

Stepping Up

You came into my life without asking or pleading. Not knowing how you could change me. You were the one who stepped up and filled in the position that couldn't be filled. Making others happy and me complete. Still you know we have some work to do before we can be whole. Our roads are still bumpy but together we can fix our pot holes. You helping me and me sheltering you. When the road got rough you liked a challenge. You didn't take off and hide, instead you took the hit and kick. You were man enough to be a man instead of being a boy. You actually knew what was coming still, strong as a tree, you stood through the thick and thin, lost one or not. Instead of real you were fake replacing the part that was missing. When the best was useless you weren't even playing the game but you still stepped up. You were neither love or friend, hate or enemy you were an angel sent to me when my other angel was in lust. There are never enough words to express how I can ever thank you or tell you how I feel. You'll never know how I could ever feel if you were to leave me. Let's work together and build this relationship. You know I love my step father of mine.

Felecia Estevan, Grade 8
Laguna Acoma Jr High School, NM

Different

You say you want to be different, you want to swim against the crowd
the lies struck from their societal perch, the greedy and manipulative broken down
you say you march for peace and justice, and trust me friend, I march there too
but lies a thick wall between us, it's the difference between me and you
the colors explode a breath from your face
you're tripping past control
you feel as though you have found a place
but soon twisted addiction will take its toll
you start slipping, tipping, falling hard
losing your grip of the life being stripped from you
you soon want to quit but your mind is scarred
there's nowhere to turn, you look for a sign of what to do
you're going dead broke, due to your habit
you go to sick extremes just to have it
the world around has been transformed into a disturbing hell
you're thinking that you want to die, well
only after you do it one more time, because it's worse to go without it than to die
but if you look through my eyes you will find, that you have long been dead on the inside
you say you want to be different, but you're just like all those other thugs
because it's hard to live a life of justice and change the world when you're bound to drugs

Emily Michel Pahl, Grade 7
St Mary's School, OR

The People I Admire*

The people I admire are the fallen soldiers who have given their lives for this country.
After visiting Washington, D.C. and Arlington National Cemetery;
After seeing all of the fallen men and women who have given their lives for this country.
SEEING acres and acres of white stones; it can bring a tear to a grown man's eye.
Appreciate, honor what they died for,
BECAUSE THEIR SACRIFICE IS WHAT KEEPS US FREE.

Seth Jayne, Grade 7
Sequoia Village School, AZ
*Dedicated to the fallen soldiers

Moon

She grabs the sun with her magic hands and drags it down behind the mountain tops.
She pushes off the ground and rises to the sky, letting out a shimmering glow, lighting up the earth.
She reaches out with her hands and places each star in their spot.
She is the almighty moon!

Janelle Feller, Grade 7
Mears Middle School, AK

Comfort

As night falls, water droplets can be heard.
The dark and loneliness changed the feeling.
Speechless, there weren't a single spoken word.
I can feel that your inside is aching.
Your tears roll down your soft cheeks, secretly.
I was clueless how you endure this pain.
As you finish telling me your story,
I've realized your emotions were all feign.
It hurts me knowing this is how you feel.
Let's end this together with a breakthrough.
I promise you that your pain will soon heal.
Just remember that I'll be there for you.
After the rain, I'll be your bright sunlight.
And at night, I'll be your glowing moonlight.

Lilian So, Grade 9
Clark High School, NV

You*

You give me love,
You give me peace,
You always stay with me.
Even if I don't deserve Your true love and care
You're always there for me.
My family, friends and everything You give to me.

Even when problems come
When I'm with You day and night they seem like nothing
But they are always hard.

Some people think my life is perfect
But in the end I'm just like them.
And for Your grace and loving care
I survive this dirty and unkind world.

Karina Marin, Grade 7
Sterling Middle School, CO
Dedicated to my only true loving friend, God.

Froggy Day

I'm sitting here in the misty, cold fog
Just waiting to see the mighty bullfrog
I can smell the fishy, wet moss
It sort of reminds me of my boss
Fish are what I hear jumping for food
I seem to be in a really good mood
Then, all of a sudden I hear this, "Ribbit"
I turn my head and quietly pivot
And there he is right before my eyes
Just sitting there eating some flies
Before I knew it he swam away
So I went back home and called it a day

Macy Kiel, Grade 7
Sterling Middle School, CO

Perfect

Are things ever really perfect?

Not usually,
Perfectness twirling and swirling,
Perfectness sliding and combining,
Appearing as we think they are,
But turn out they're not.

Although, sometimes they can be.
Perfection on the outside,
Perfection on the inside,
Even though it doesn't usually happen that way.

Or does it?
There's no telling.
Sometimes it's half and half,
It may look perfect but it's not,
It may look imperfect but it turns out it is.

So what really is perfect?

Rachel Gilbreath, Grade 7
Coronado K 8 School, AZ

Sparkly Speckles

Little, white specks float gracefully down,
From the bluish-gray sky
The specks start to cover the dead yellow and brown grass,
Formulating a glittery white blanket
The snow swirls as the wind gently stirs it
It looks as if the snow is cookie dough,
In a mixing bowl
When the snow stops
The ground looks like a big fluffy cloud

Samantha Bullock, Grade 7
Cedar Ridge Middle School, OR

My Sport!

Hot and sweaty
High-spirited and ready
The spiker hits it hard
But the digger's on her guard

The rush she got when she dove for the ball
But now it's up and ready for all
The setter gets it
It goes to the spiker, ready to hit

She spikes the ball
She blows them away
They just don't know what to say
The "ref" makes the final call

This is my sport
This is volleyball!

Kristine Hayes, Grade 8
Desert Sky Middle School, AZ

Journey

Sailing off into the sea.
Sailing, my buddy and me.
Sailing from my home.
Sailing to a place unknown.
Sailing off into the blue.
Sailing off to find something new.
Sailing to catch a great big fish.
Or to do anything I wish.

Hayden Stegman, Grade 7
Wiley Jr/Sr High School, CO

I Am a Bird

Sometimes I pretend I am a bird
flying high.
I wonder how it would feel
to soar in the sky.

Sometimes I pretend I am a bird
feeling the wind in my face.
I wonder how it would feel
to spread out my wings like lace.

Sometimes I pretend I am a bird
soaring above all the people.
I wonder how it would feel
to make a nest in a church steeple.

Even though I pretend I am a bird
I like being me.
Now I wonder how it would feel
to buzz like a bee!

August R. Ferree, Grade 8
Fertitta Middle School, NV

I Am a Skater and a Kid

I am a skater and a kid
I wonder what it's like to be famous
I hear loud music
I see cute boys
I am a skater and a kid

I imagine the beach
I feel happy
I touch my family
I worry about my friends
I cry about fighting
I am a skater and a kid

I understand responsibility
I say love is strong
I dream I will be famous
I try to do well in school
I hope I'm loved
I am a skater and a kid

Breanna Drumright, Grade 7
Shadow Ridge Middle School, CO

I Am

I am the child the world depends on; the child of happiness and excitement.
I am the child of sorrows that the world has never seen before.
I am the child of mischief that is sly, quiet and loving.
I am the child that is the mother's loving son.
I am a child of God.
I am also the child of hope.

John "Miles" Ellis, Grade 8
Our Lady of Lourdes Catholic School, UT

Chocolate Melting Cake

Light, fluffy chocolate cake,
slightly toasted on the outer rims,
with powdered sugar sprinkled on the top.

When sticking the spoon in the center,
the cake collapses falling into
an ooey, gooey melted chocolate puddle.

After filling the spoon with a mesmerizing, marvelous, mixture
of cake and melted chocolate,
dip the spoonful into a bowl of vanilla ice cream.

As the spoon enters your mouth you will instantly experience
a combination of warm and cold while the taste
envelops your taste buds with a rich, dark, chocolaty excitement.

Swallowing this sensational sweetness is like
slipping into dessert heaven!

Teal Schnurr, Grade 7
Mandalay Middle School, CO

Friendships

The world is filled with noisy quarrels.
But, friends are there for no betrayals.
I have a friend, who is always there,
Through times that sometimes give me a scare.
She is my best friend no matter what,
She's the one that I can always trust.
We all can make a friend to love and to hold.
Relationships with friends stay very bold.
Our lives. Our world. Our friends.
We will stick together till the very end.
Anger, frustration, and emotions twirl through my mind
Like a spinning ride spinning around and around.
But friendship and life keep my heart and my mind sincerely sound.
Friendship is the condition of being friends.
It is a friendly relationship that we can always mend.
Finding a friend that you will always care about is a journey throughout life.
And once you find that special friend, your life will be without discomfort and strife.
Without the relationships and friends we have,
Our life would seem to be very bad.
Together as friends we can make our lives very pleasant.
And keep them as new as a birthday present.

Olivia Laos, Grade 7
St Elizabeth Ann Seton Catholic School, AZ

Natural Perfection

Perfection is a twisted tree
Lovely in its misshaped state
Know that nature made no mistake
The twist was meant to be

Perfection is a thriving forest
Glorious in all its moments
Know that nature didn't recreate
The beauty is originality

Perfection is an earthen mass
With a variety of harsh and friendly faces
Know that nature is well designed
The test was to adapt

Perfection is a dying sphere
Beautiful in its final condition
Know that nature will stay majestic
And know that nature will fix OUR mistakes

Natalie Miller, Grade 7
Mandalay Middle School, CO

In the Air

In the air snowflakes are flying everywhere
Snowflakes falling from the sky like little cotton balls, and
Snow is on the ground that looks like powdered sugar,
Ice on the ground looks like frozen crystals

Hot chocolate smelled like Grandma's cookies
My boots were as warm as a bear hug
The bitter wind is cold but comforting
The air is frozen like my ears

Maggie Hodge, Grade 7
Mandalay Middle School, CO

The Knight of Camelot

The Knight had a fear that
he thought was quite queer
That the Knight would prevail
but somehow may fail
and be swallowed by teeth
but alas he pulled his sword from its sheath
and to his despair
the Dragon did not care
for he sent him flying through the air
The Knight hit the ground
with a very loud sound
As the knight ran away
a ray of fire
hit the Squire
and to this day
the Knight runs away
from the Dragon
that almost put the knight in his grave.

Zac Murphy, Grade 7
North Middle School, CO

Hail

I am Hail, hear me C
                  R
                    A
                      C
                        K
                          L
                            E
And P
     O
    P
See the ghastly gray sky above me,
I'm nothing like the soothing sound of snow, I B
                                          O
                                             O
                                                M
And C
     R
    A
   S
  H
I have all my fun, then the sun chases me away.

Sara Lloyd, Grade 7
Eagle Point Middle School, OR

I Am Me

I am the youngest child of three
I am the only boy of loving parents
I am Greg
I am the best son I can be.

I am a believer in God
I am a student who loves to learn
I am a fan of many teams: Bears, Utes, and others
I am a player of many games like golf and baseball
I am Greg

I am a resident of Salt Lake City, Utah
I am from a beautiful place where a lot of people are friendly
I am like a kindred spirit flowing through the wind
I am the best me I can be

I am a reader of many books
I am a person who could handle a little change
I am a person who reflects on their day
I am a person who tries to see the positives in life
I am me.

I am a person who loves his family
I am a funny person who makes people laugh
I am the only me I know.

Greg Archuleta, Grade 8
Our Lady of Lourdes Catholic School, UT

My Leaving Late Valentine
On this Valentine's Day,
When I heard you were leaving,
I went to get you something special,
And almost stopped breathing.

And since you're the love of my life,
The center of my heart,
You need something special,
Before you depart.

So I found you some chocolate,
I hope it will last,
So that the memory of me,
Won't fade so fast.

Happy Late Valentines!
Ian Wright, Grade 9
Union Middle School, UT

Crazy
As crazy as it SEEMS,
this might shock your HEART.
that night I heard some SCREAMS,
and that was just the START.

I was creeping up the STAIRS,
and I know this might sound LAME.
I looked over at the CHAIRS,
It was just my dad watching the GAME!
Jessica Bacon, Grade 8
Aurora Academy, CO

Home
Sand between my toes
Wind through my hair
Sun on my nose
Salty smells in the air

I love the beach

Chapped lips
Looking way down
Mountains, snow on the tips
Shh! Not a sound

I love the mountains

Curled up in bed
Music softly playing
Look out, a clear view of the flower bed
But what I'm really saying is

I love my home
Katie Church, Grade 7
Lyons Middle/Senior High School, CO

Life from Death
I was in a sea of green,
walking oh so gently,
Admiring the little breeze
that fluttered by so gracefully.
Amid the shade and beauty seen,
an ugly sight
stretched before me.
The sea of green turned into black.
And nothing but heat
bore down upon me.
The wind was hot
and nothing bloomed
All there was gloom and doom.
Nothing moved and there was no sound,
In what seemed like sacred ground.
In the middle of it all, was one blade
of grass so tall and strong.
So I did come away
with hope and new perspective
that life can come from death.
Becca Brunner, Grade 7
Aurora Academy, CO

Falling Fall Leaves
Falling fall leaves
dancing in the air
swivel and swerve without a care,
colors like a rainbow
as if putting on a show,
rake a pile here,
rake a pile there,
even though they fall everywhere,
they're all different shapes
and sizes,
go watch
as the sun rises,
for the next day
it will start again.
Kurissa Bustamante, Grade 7
Timberview Middle School, CO

When It Was the Two of Us
We used to have fun
Always played in the sun
So many things we would do
And I would do them all with you
so many things we did back in the day
did what we want, had our way
you were the sparkle in my eye
for some odd reason I can't say why
after all the things we do
I still wish for it to be me and you!
Jazmine Salinas, Grade 8
Alfred F Garcia School, AZ

The Morning Comes…
The morning comes with
Drops of dew,
That falls from every tree.
The morning come with
Light from east,
Till westward takes it down.
The morning comes with
Song from bird,
That sings the day to end.
The morning comes with
Life that lives,
Beneath the sun so warm.
Lori Hofer, Grade 8
King Colony School, MT

The Apple
Sweet crisp air surrounds me,
Engulfing me,
Like a warm blanket.
Juicy temptation to satisfy my hunger,
Snap!
Thud!
Its flushed
Brown freckled face,
Lands in my palm
Dimples smiling up at me
Shining and new
Yet wrinkled and bruised with age.

Crunch!
Tangy sweetness,
Rejuvenates my energy
Sticky residue
On my finger tips
Was all that was left,
Of
The apple.
Evelyn De La Cruz, Grade 9
Xavier College Preparatory School, AZ

Plaid
Plaid
Skirts, pants
Red, green, yellow, blue
all colors
like a rainbow of fabric

Plaid
squares, lines
orange, purple, white, black
checkered
like splattered by paint
Jules Byers, Grade 7
North Middle School, CO

Euphoria

Great big smiles donned upon their faces,
A bright light in their eyes that shows their joy.
They're in one of their favorite places.
Happiness is among the girls and boys.
A feeling of pleasure and contentment,
Cheery and joyous and carefree.
Not showing one small bit of resentment,
One of good-fortune, well-being, and glee.
Euphoria, a feeling so intense;
It's a great feeling of achievement.
When you experience it, it makes sense.
It's not something that you have to buy or rent.
It's not the easiest feeling to find it.
But once you reveal it, you're in a bind.

Sarah Riscen, Grade 9
Clark High School, NV

Sunrise on the Beach

Salty, icy, spray is in my face
My toes buried in the warm, soft sand
Gusts of wind playfully toss my hair
The rising sun greets with its golden hand

The waves crash against its beaten shore
Slamming the sand with all of its might
Tropical fish swim without a care
Pearly, pink shells lay with crabs out of sight

I can't contain myself anymore
Running full speed towards the water's edge
I fling myself into the ocean
Every evening I make this pledge…

Danielle Mathieson, Grade 7
Coronado K 8 School, AZ

Determination

Determination is what I do have
Failure is not an option in my mind
People may put you down but that's the past
I grow strong and don't waste time, I'm fine
Leadership is what I desire and need
Courage is something that comes natural
The knowledge can help me think, learn, and read
You can't mess up that's unacceptable
Success is what you must strive for today
Do not let judgment put you down and weak
Let nothing get in your way and it's your day
Never be weak gain all your energy rise thy feet
Determination is what I do have
People may put you down, but that's the past

Antonio Riley Jr., Grade 9
Clark High School, NV

Heartbroken

My heart is aching
My knees are shaking
I haven't been fairly treated
And I know I have been defeated

I have an awful fright
That I might cry throughout the night
So, I'm sitting alone on my bed
And there are no thoughts of you running through my head

All the pictures in the fire
Tell me that you were a liar
I have moved on now
And isn't it funny how

I was strong
And you were wrong
I'm not aching
Or shaking

My heart is mending
And this misery is ending
I'm the lucky one that he has chosen
And I will no longer be heartbroken

Megan Powelson, Grade 7
Shadow Ridge Middle School, CO

Might

A mighty stallion,
Galloping past prickly bushes,
At the crack of dusk,
In a field of swaying grass and blooming blossoms,
Because of fear and of darkness.

Billy Chung, Grade 7
21st Century Public Academy, NM

Mistakes and Misjudgements

A chance had not the taken life,
To go to college, have a husband or wife.
No opportunities to have fun,
For life was taken away before begun.
No Legos, big toys, or paint,
Or running around 'til they faint.
No life to lead,
Or Mother's Day presents made of beads.

The incident was an accident and a huge mistake,
But there was no turning back after they had wake.
Mommy and daddy were too young of age,
And couldn't afford nearly anything with their wage.
So down the stairs she reluctantly fell,
Before daddy had a chance to yell.
Losing their child left them in a trance,
Because they knew there was a life, and now no chance.

Savannah Reinhardt, Grade 8
Chehalis Middle School, WA

Space

I stare into space
Thinking of you.
In space I see
An ocean so, so blue.

I see the fish
And a whale and a dolphin,
And I think how can this
Be a situation you can't win.

I see us sitting on a beach
Not very far away.
We're talking about many things
Including that day!

Then we stare into space
As the sun goes down,
And I see my face
With a smile, not a frown!

Paula Moreno, Grade 9
Coal Ridge High School, CO

Coming and Going

Seasons come and go,
just as the river might flow.
Winter comes, autumn flees,
on a northern breeze.
Friends come and go.
Only true ones seem to stay.
The bad ones will make you pay.
The world is like a top.
It might just spin till it stops.
Just like the river, as it goes.

Alan Fry, Grade 7
Miller Middle School, CO

Winter's Closing

The snow is melting
and the water still draining
clouds straining to rain

Tanner Lewis, Grade 9
Duchesne High School, UT

Teardrop

Teardrop
Tear from soul
Weeps of sorrow
Shed tears of all my pain
Cries for all my suffers
Agony from deep inside
Sadness for all my mistakes
Distress for the ones you love
Happiness and joy for one another
Droplet

Britney Gutierrez, Grade 8
Heath Middle School, CO

Temptation

Today is the day that my son will come home, my son, the King of Kings.
I hear now the trumpets of his coming. Fleeting hoof steps are ever nearing
with my son, the King of Kings.
I see now many horsemen, with banners held tall, trying not to let them fall,
for my son, the King of Kings.
And now I see the one who comes with love so great and divine,
that none on this earth has greater love than His and Mine.
Behold! My Spirit dances with joy at the coming of my son, the King of Kings.
But what is this I see: a man cloaked in evil and dressed in black
has stopped my son's company on their way back.
In a sly voice of evil and sin he spoke:
"Come, my king, renew your selfish hope.
I have something that is a treasure; some food would make you better.
I have these stones here which you might turn into your heart's delight."
But my son said in a peaceful tone: "Man does not live by bread alone.
But rather by my Father's words as He sits upon his throne."
I had to smile at that remark, but on the stranger's face, anger had sparked.
The stranger's name was Satan, that evil serpent of despair and hate.
Two more times did he tempt my son, the King of Kings?
Yes, it is true. But my son, Jesus, has wisdom beyond any evil of that kind,
for He is the Divine, my son, the King of Kings.

Paul Ashby, Grade 9
Hope Christian School, NM

My Parents

My parents are my everyday heroes.
They are always there when I need them.
Seeing their smiling faces brings me joy.
And their love for me and my sisters is greater than the whole universe.

My parents sometimes get angry or just like any other child,
they make me do chores, even though it makes me have a frown on my face.
But, I know that they do this for a reason.
They want their children to be the best people they can be.

I thank my parents for who I am today.
They taught me many lessons and things.
They keep teaching me how to get ready to explore this big world and who I am.
They are like angels with a mission
to help their children become better persons.

My parents had always been there for me,
in both the good and bad times.
When I had tears falling all over my face like a waterfall,
they would give me a hug and console me with their kind and truthful words.
When I had a smile across my face, they would celebrate my joy.

I love my parents a million times more than the whole wide world.
And, my sisters and I are their greatest treasure of all.

Jennifer Gongora, Grade 7
St Elizabeth Ann Seton Catholic School, AZ

High Merit Poems – Grades 7, 8, and 9

An Ode to a 2009 Dodge Challenger
Dodge Challenger, oh how your engine roars
Every time I hear it,
My heart nearly soars
425 Horsepower under your hood
Oh how it sounds so good
Your sleek body design
Is very, very divine
You have an old-school look
Except with a few changes

Your leather seats are so soft
And your engine scares the birds aloft
Your gauges are like eyes
They stare at me glowing and unchanging
You are so, so fine
Oh how I wish you were mine

Brandon Broersma, Grade 7
Sunnyside Christian Elementary School, WA

A Lesson in War
Like the snuff of a candle a life is gone
We see that they're mortal another mom's son.
People say that it's worth it they say we are faultless
It was never our choice the enemy brought this

With every drop of blood we spill
Humanity dies and yet we fight still
Every war is a foolish thing
Fought for glory by tyrant and king

Look into your enemy's jaded eyes
And tell me what you find
Unveil all shadows; hopes of disguise
And try to glimpse his mind
This my friend
The only purpose you'll see
Is that in the end
He might be free

Lindsey Greenwaldt, Grade 9
Oakridge Jr/Sr High School, OR

What Miracles Are
Miracles are when God chooses to remain anonymous.
Mountains are miracles,
Trees bud in spring and plants explode.
The Balloon Fiesta glows in the early morning
And the State Fair rides light up the Fairgrounds.
Yellow leaves sway in the fall.
Giant snowflakes flutter in the winter.
These are all miracles.
Snowstorms in July and 80 degrees in December are miracles.
Everything is a miracle.
They are all around us.
Just look around.

Henry Lockhart, Grade 7
McKinley Middle School, NM

Sorrow Redemption*
I didn't mean what I said,
And what I said I didn't mean,
But it's too late; I said what I said,
But didn't mean,
I have said a lot of things,
Doesn't mean I mean it,
What it means is, I love you,
But it's too hard to show it,
From the time I've spent with you,
And the time you've spent with me
I know you and I won't always be,
But we are brother and sister from here, to the sea,
All I want to say is, I'm sorry,
And give you a key to my heart,
And hope you'll forgive me, before you part,
Because brother and sister we shall always be,
Hey even if you don't like it,
I love you and I hope you love me,
For I will always love you forever and ever,
Until it's my turn to flee,
From this bottomless sea.

Jordan Juan Sisneros, Grade 8
Centauri Middle School, CO
*Dedicated to my sister Steph

One Chance, One Choice
Think of a day,
When you wanted to
Sail away

I've had days
Where I could sail away,
Across the oceans blue

Still further more,
I've crossed small streams,
Large lakes
even a skinny straight

I soar across the stars,
Pass the planets of blue
Even out of the universe one time or two

To return to Earth
Away from the stars
From the heavens above

To be with you,
Because I wasted my lifetime treasures
For one day in exchange

Haley Fobia, Grade 8
Cimarron Springs Elementary School, AZ

Ocean Waves

I am sitting on the sandy beach. Waves coming up from the sea to tickle my toes. I soak in sunshine. My smile is brighter than snow in the morning and I listen to the music played by the ocean. The foamy ocean gently covers a crab and splashes a seagull who landed to play. But, when I walk away I promise to return to my love, the ocean.

Hailee Williams, Grade 7
Mandalay Middle School, CO

Dreams of Fairies

When you were a child what did you dream of?
Was it a land far away where no one could stay?
Was it of a giant so tall and so hungry so gruff?
Were you like me and dreamed of a fairy?
Nice so small and sweet did she wear pink or blue flowers or a dress that was made of silk?
Did she have long flowing hair or short like a boy was it brown, black or golden?
What was your fairy like only you know and you don't have to tell, but I choose to tell you mine.
She had long flowing hair as golden as the sun.
And a dress made of thread that she got from the wind, water and sun.
Her wings had all the colors of the rainbow that when she flew they left a trail behind.
Her name was Rose a simple rose but in one way oh so extravagant.
She flew around by day and night giving gifts of hope and sight.
She gave me a gift, a gift of sight so now that I can see.
I can see the wonders and beauty of the world that is all around me.
So I am writing this poem today,
As a simple thanks to a fairy.
A figment of my imagination who gave me the sight to really see.

Sarah McMinn, Grade 7
Bright Light Academy, AZ

My Lacrosse Stick

My lacrosse stick is black and white like life and death.
Its deadly blow brings cries and blood.
Its perfect accuracy causes shouts of victory, and dismay.
The shaft of my stick is like the moon, stronger than steel but hanging weightless in my hand.
The head of my stick is pinched tightly to keep the ball from defenders that swing and hack.
My stick is like a weapon of mass destruction, leaving the field full of battered and bloody bodies.
The sight of my stick causes fear and doubt to enter the minds of its enemy.

My stick needs no protection or comfort,
Its sight scares off most.
All that my stick needs is someone skilled like me to wield it.
Together we will dominate the field.

Brennan Clement, Grade 9
Mountain Ridge Jr High School, UT

Love in a Dream

I'm awake or is it all a dream? Does this mean it's for keep or just to see what I could never have in my life? Does he really love me or does he just want me to feel what he knows I would never get close to? Is this what I always dreamed of? A man to love me for me and to be with me for eternity? I've never felt like this. I look up to the sky and ask God why.

Why does this have to happen to me?
I see that thy eyes cannot.

All this pain is what is called love? The hurt goes away, but the pain will still stay the same. This is like love in a dream where anything could happen. In a dream you can wake up, but in life you cannot. This is love in a dream.

Bella Tello-Gonzalez, Grade 8
Cedar Ridge Middle School, OR

High Merit Poems – Grades 7, 8, and 9

There Is Beauty

I see the flower, the perfect flower,
Blooming
Every ruby petal, every sapphire of dew,
Every emerald leaf, catches my eye

I see the flower, the lovely flower,
Blooming
My eyes leave the flower, the beautiful flower,
And gaze at the wonder around it

I see the grass, the crooked grass,
Sprawling
But I gaze at the grass as I did the flower,
I breathe its fresh scent,
There is beauty

I see the tree, the gnarled old tree,
Rotting
But I gaze at the tree as I did the flower,
I touch the soft moss,
There is beauty

As I walk from the meadow,
I gaze all around…
There is beauty.

Lauren Pope, Grade 7
Centennial Middle School, UT

Melody of Life

The grip of winter's hand,
Shall be cast out, now leaves the land,
Without a backward look,
The day rejoices, leaps abound,
Life is back anew —
With its cadences of blue,
No fraud can cheat,
Life's great feat,
Induce such loving care,
The bear of winter's witness,
As life blows through the air,
Hurries its time away!
The sacrifices of nature's maze,
Bring communions in the summer's haze,
As death doth wane to dust,
Life, o joy, o sombers none,
Bring us thy eternal sun,
Sweet caress of life,
Hear nature's plea,
Our eyes to see,
Death no more, now life.

Melissa Boyer, Grade 9
Evergreen Jr High School, WA

Fight

Remember when you used to have a life,
One without the stress and strife,
Then your friends came in
Like a spider bite.
You've lost your pride and might,
You always listen to your friends and give up all your rights.
You might learn
To be yourself and tell your friends good night.
I hope you don't give up your fight.

Thomas Rose, Grade 8
Grand Canyon Middle School, AZ

Leadership

Leadership is standing up, when it's hard,
When you're scared, when you're young,
When you just want to have fun, for what is right.
Standing up takes courage and strength,
But you never know, it may just change a person's way.
You may feel small, but don't let that stop you at all
Because as soon as you're up, you can't go back down
You must speak your mind, or else they may forever stay blind.
A leader stands firm, through the good, through the bad,
Through the happy, and through the sad.
A leader is a listener, a leader is a friend
One that's always willing to help, no matter when.
A leader is not perfect, but they do their very best
To fix the world's problems, and put evil to a rest.
A leader gives a hand, helping as many as they can
Whether rich or poor, strong or weak,
It does not matter, everyone is for keeps.
Leadership isn't just a passion, and it isn't just for fashion
But you have to be an illustration to civilization
To be a true leader without any limitations.

Tracy Garrett, Grade 7
West Valley Middle School, WA

I Can Feel It

I feel it in my soul,
Even though sometimes I feel like a fool.
Days go by and still I can feel it,
I know there's no escaping it.
I feel it in my soul

I hear it in my mind, just to find,
That anywhere anytime it can go,
I know I can hear it but can I see it.
Nobody really knows but I do.
I hear it in my mind.

Now it's time to finally find,
that every little part is in my mind.
Now I understand, it doesn't take a lot you just have to listen,
And when I hear it I know what it is,
I feel it in my soul.

Christian Scott, Grade 7
Shadow Ridge Middle School, CO

Big Brother
Thirteen years of teasing each other
Standing up for one another
A brother, a hero, a friend

Where did time go?
We yelled and cried
Laugh and played

Off you go to college
Getting your degree
Making something of yourself
Out of your dreams

No more fighting over the computer
Or helping me with homework
And no more big brother advice

Good luck with your dreams
Have fun while you're gone
Come home soon
So we can get back to the bickering
Anna Sabin, Grade 7
Shadow Ridge Middle School, CO

life
life is like holding a dove
hold it too tight
and it will die
hold it too gentle
and it will leave you
Cody Ropp, Grade 8
Round Valley Middle School, AZ

Kicked Out
The day begins so warm and bright,
Shining with the sun's yellow light
I head into the morning sun,
I can't wait until the day is done
Heading home from daily deeds,
Must take care of all my needs
Getting home to a shock,
Finding all the doors are locked
I can't get into the house,
Man I wish I was a mouse
We got kicked out of our home,
Somehow I don't feel alone
We're headed to a freaky inn,
I want to kick someone in their shin
I am now really mad,
But not all things are really bad
Living with my mom's best friend,
I wonder if it will ever end
This is a blessing in disguise,
It's time for me to shut my eyes.
Heather Blaine, Grade 7
Shadow Ridge Middle School, CO

Neglected Heart
Young love seeks this day,
Though days ahead are cloudy above,
Blinded by fate's pathway to say,
She is a beautiful angel or dove,
His mind wonders and wonders,
Listen or to forget,
Cupid's arrow struck him like thunder,
He chose to choose the one he thought his life was set.
Deceived by Gerti herself,
His life was sent crashing down,
Locked his heart away for her on that shelf,
With the name inscribed there for it to drown,
The Great Poseidon couldn't have seen this coming,
All what was left was his heart without the love it needed to be living.
Timmy Lee, Grade 9
Shorecrest High School, WA

School
Going to school is a real bore
When you sit down in class you can't help but snore.
Seven periods a day; Five days a week
It's no wonder the world's going to the geeks.
Math is just about the hardest class
You'd be surprised at how many people don't know how to add and subtract.
Geography is up next and ready to go
You learn everything is going on around the globe.
Why go to school when you can stay at home
That is exactly where I wrote this poem.
Logan Parker, Grade 9
South Jordan Middle School, UT

My Heartache
Excruciating heartache pounding on my chest to free itself of captivity.
Every pulse every pump was a devotion,
But it has trapped itself inside showing no emotion.
My heart aches for more, but it's falling every second.
My heart is kept in captivity to be guarded and be watched.
It's like a ticking clock waiting to go off!
I ache for love, I ache for hope, my heart is at a loss.
My pain, my pleasure, my hate, my love,
Is becoming one sick prison.
Locked behind these bars I bang,
But no one listens out to hear my scream.
I cry, I weep, every fear and insecurity is another tear!
I'm scared, I'm alone, but I hold on, but does that last forever?
I need some help, but I can't do this by myself!
My voice is running out!
Is there anyone there,
To save me from an excruciating heartache?
My heart hurts because it's love is forcing it to forget,
Every Good and Bad I've ever had!
To protect itself from a catastrophic heartache!
My time is running out!
Courtney Jones, Grade 7
Sky Vista Middle School, CO

High Merit Poems – Grades 7, 8, and 9

About My Cat Hokey
Oh my pet Hokey, I do wish him luck.
He fights with mean cats in the dark nighttime.
At times, he also fights with my cat Buck.
Oh when will he stop fighting and stop crime?

When I hold him tight he always claws me.
Every time he comes in he wants more food.
He lays on my bed and I let him be.
He'll live a long time because of his mood.

When he was a kitten, he did like me.
But now he is a cat and he hates me much.
I give him food and I just let him be.
When he is hungry I give him his lunch.

Oh when will he like me too much?
Even now I like him much too.
Duncan Metcalf, Grade 7
Thomas Edison Charter School - North, UT

When One Heart Softens
Every day children witness violence.
Horror was depicted on every countenance
Because all they can do is stand by,
Staring with such eager eyes
Many pleadings go unheard
"Please, Sir, I want some more"
Until one heart softens,
"Take the boy back to the workhouse"
Although some hearts stay the same.
"That boy will be hung!"
Lindsay Gray, Grade 9
South Jordan Middle School, UT

Friends
We are great friends
We are not alone
We looked the same
Till you broke your bone
You may be tall
I may be small
But inside we have the same length of strength
I felt so sad when you went away
What a horrible day
I found a friend she's not the same
She says her mother passed away
I said I'm sorry
She said don't worry
I will be strong till the end
Because you're my friend
And I will be your friends until we find someone more nice
Someone who is worth the price
Friends together
Always and forever
Mireya Ortega, Grade 7
Somerton Middle School, AZ

A Friendly Voice
I walk through the snow,
Teeth chattering,
Feet cold,

The winds are cruel,
As life can be,
I hear a voice and wait,

"Why do you walk,
If God took your boots and jacket,
Why do you walk"

"I walk the road of life,
If I stop I die,
My hope is gone, I am cold but I walk,"

"If you had no hope, I would not be here,
you would be sitting down,
Though cold, you are not alone,"

I look for the old man who spoke and see no one,
I look at the footprints behind me,
And I walk through the snow
Ciera Kieler, Grade 7
Eaton Middle School, CO

Abandoned
The sea lies closer to me now,
sparkling like a freshly polished diamond.
I see the boats go by more often now;
just trying to stay afloat.
The dwelling on the shore belongs to the sea,
but it is always open to someone like me.
Someone there to protect it from everything,
for I am the protector of the house by the sea.

The house does not cost a dime.
But I know that it is worth lots more.
Even though it is pretty old,
it holds an elegance sweet and dear.
And I love this house by the sea.

The house is practically falling apart now;
its walls thin and letting in the cold air.
But this house has stolen my heart
and that I will always remember.

This house may not appeal to you,
But I will always call it home.
Alisa Anhold, Grade 7
Oberon Middle School, CO

Chloe

He felt like my best friend
We would be together till the end
Together we played day after day
He wasn't a human by the way

For five years this went on
Until one day he was gone
My guinea pig was dead
My best friend was dead

Rebecca Leaf, Grade 7
Mandalay Middle School, CO

The Truth About Rain

The rain falls down,
teardrops from heaven's angels.
Angels, why are you crying?
I went to church today.
Angels, why are you sad?
Did one of your relatives die today?
Good angels in heaven,
God wouldn't want you to cry.
So cheer up!
Don't be miserable!
Smile!
And be glad that you are up in heaven,
with God in all His glory.
The rain has stopped,
and the sun shines through.
Dear angels,
There you go!
Wipe your tears away,
and try to make it through the day.

Rachel Gima, Grade 7
Eagle Point Middle School, OR

Apples, Bananas, Oranges

The tasty tangy treats
of apples, bananas, and oranges
jump off the brown broken branches
of the tangled trees
and I retrieve these tangy
tarty, tasty treats to eat
as I take a bit of the delicious
divine, red, rosy apples
it spits scrumptious juice
into my mouth
and as I peel the plaster
off the perfect round oranges
it decides to make itself
into 10 to 13 pieces
but whatever fruit I eat
it slides down my throat willingly.

Emily Peck, Grade 7
Lyons Middle/Senior High School, CO

Life to Me

L ife to me is endless possibility,
I nfinite possible paths.
F ollowing them is like getting lost,
E xcept when you stop and think.

T o think of things bigger than
O ur own egos, our own problems.

M eaning of life is just one theory,
E ndless possibility, truly that's life.

Roshell Hesler, Grade 8
Sacajawea Jr High School, ID

Midnight

Midnight darkness
Midnight light
Many feel a fright
In the midnight blackness
 To me
It is a warm cloak to conceal
So you cannot see
The tears I shed unceasingly
I will cry and laugh
No one will know
Or care enough
To wonder
Who is that shadow like crow
No one cares
No one fears for my sake
Or in the dark what might take
 Me
So I shall stay there
Hoping to become
Part of the darkness

Kira Collings, Grade 7

I Don't Understand

I don't understand…
Why people don't have money
Why people don't give
Why people won't help

But most of all…
Why we don't get along
Why we give up
Why people don't feel safe anywhere

What I do understand is…
Why we have homes
Why we get rain
Why we love
Why we dream

Kristen Romano, Grade 7
Dunstan Middle School, CO

Love

Every time I see you
my heart starts to beat.
When I do not see you
I feel weak.
When you sit by me
I feel like if you are here
to protect me.

I wish you were always with me
so I could have the strength
to keep on living.
Without you I would not exist.
Please do not leave me,
my love, I love you so much
that without you I would not exist.

Ilse Aguirre, Grade 7
Somerton Middle School, AZ

Rivers of Blood

Rivers of blood,
Winds of death,
I gasp in their hold,
Searching for a breath.

Rain of poison,
Wind of curse,
I'm drenched without mercy,
I try to quench my thirst.

Lightning of fears,
Thunder of goodbyes,
I scream and I run,
I'm terrified.

Grass of evil,
Dirt of spirit,
Slice goes the knife,
And no one else hears it.

Scarlett Hernandez, Grade 7
La Center Middle School, WA

Silence

The madness lasted
Only a moment,
Only voices,
Hopelessly in the dark night,
I did not know men ever cried,
Harsh, painful, despairing sobs,
The world had lost its boundary lines,
The night was silent now,
But the room was too
Crowded with fear.

Kaelina Harris, Grade 9
Colorado Connections Academy, CO

The Chosen Path

I find myself torn,
between the path I choose,
and the path chosen for me the day I was born.
To follow the latter would be to lose
all that I've thought to dream.
Meaning to lose all my heart's desire, my wish.

Do I follow the path, the stream,
already in motion?
Do I follow the song pulsing within my heart?
Or do I end up hurting my parents in part?
Causing a stir, quite a commotion.

I've come to the fork in the road, is it time to part?
Time flies by,
With a heavy heart and confused mind,
I see someone's hopes and dreams die.

Struggling with decisions, I fight my binds,
Then with a sudden surge, enlightenment erupts.
My way is shown, nothing left to corrupt.
I sigh in thankful relief,
And we settle with little grief.
And walk the chosen path.

Corrie Evans, Grade 9
Bonneville High School, ID

Heroes

A treacherous snake of natural desires
betrayed a man of virtuous thought
he who embarks on an impossible quest
seeks virtues of the gods to aid
and aid the gods did impart
slumber in a sanctuary of illustrious grandeur
imaginings of gods and prophecies of glory
a golden bridle placed before him by mysterious hands
spoke insight to him to support his mission
to slay a monster nigh untouchable with fiery breath
given a steed of magical breed
more than beast of divine
caught and tamed to do his bidding
slew that terror which roamed the land
and gained reverence and admiration
but hubris insinuated breeding deep within
proceeding without thought or reason
had stormed the keep of the mightiest gods
and thought that steed who felt his pain
punished shall he who in hubris
believes himself to be equal to the gods

Kenneth Tseng, Grade 9
Shorecrest High School, WA

Picture

It's looking down at me.
I want to move but I can't.
It's glued me to the ground.
It's reached out its arms and has taken me in.
I'm cut off from the world,
Time has stopped.
It's attracted all of my attention.
Then it released me.
I looked around.
Only to be caught once again.

Ryan Caylor, Grade 8
Kenmore Jr High School, WA

Blizzard

I am a blustery blizzard
I have many fresh, flakes of falling snow
Snow is falling,
      down,
         and
           down
onto the heads of children
My horrifically howling wind — "whoosh"
is making my snow fly about
while many people complain and pout.
They don't want a blizzard,
they want it calm,
that's too bad,
I'm here to stay,
here to stay,
until I pass away.

Eric Radcliffe, Grade 7
Eagle Point Middle School, OR

Childhood Sucks

I chuck a baseball through the trees,
Grimy leather makes hands sweat with ease.
Mom, can I have a popsicle, please! Please!
I take a bite, preceding the brain freeze.
Awwwww, headaches making senses null,
Beating drums making drum roll.
On the playground, sliding, climbing,
Sandy hands, I slip. Missed my timing.
Crash! After seconds of free falling
I come to the ground, head ringing, eyes bawling.
Slip. Splash! Down the drain with the keys.
Uh-oh! Dad's coming! Lock the door! Privacy please!
Too late! It's hard to drive without keys you know.
Where are they? I confess! I dropped them in the bowl.
As you can see childhood is no game.
It's a time of "whoops!" a time of pain.
Many bruises and bumps, a trial and error,
What works and what doesn't, couldn't be fairer.
He catches the ball, throws it back, I shriek like a foal.
I panic, thump on head. Passed out, lump on skull.

Ryan Gould, Grade 9
Tempe Preparatory Academy, AZ

Rain Puddle
snow
white, cold
falling, sticking, freezing
rain puddle, rainbow
pouring, chilling, splashing
wet, gentle
rain

Maitreya Carmen, Grade 7
Sedona Charter School, AZ

Friendship
The joyous laughter of your voice
Makes me smile and rejoice.
When you take me by the hand,
It really helps me take a stand.
I often long to see your smiling face
When I think of you in a righteous place.
The ring of friendship shows to all
When we go and play some ball.
The love we share goes round and round
While we whisper with no sound.
We sing a very merry song…
…Of our friendship all day long!

Ashley Mooney, Grade 8
Glide Middle School, OR

My Peak
It stands up there all day and night,
waiting to be noticed,
and appreciated,
through rain, snow, night and cold.
Just waiting
makes mornings beautiful,
pictures worthwhile,
nights, not so lonely,
I don't know why it's waiting,
I notice it,
I appreciate it,
through droughts, sleet, day and heat
I am personally,
glad it's staying,
waiting.

Jessie Berndsen, Grade 7
North Middle School, CO

The Train Station
As the train came charging in
It squealed and squeaked and groaned
Swarms of people came and left
Going about their business
Then the train pulls away
Leaving smoke and steam
Wishing it's already there
And puffing as it goes

Michael Harlan, Grade 7
Les Bois Jr High School, ID

The Girl with the Violet Dress
The months turned into years as she waited for him to return,
From that wretched war far away in the east.
She waited in the fields behind the orchard.
And as her violet dress flowed wistfully into the breeze,
Her deep emerald eyes gazed to the horizon.
The sheer blue scarf wrapped around her neck wandered into the wind.
Her mind raced as she ran her fingers through her chocolate brown hair.
"Where is he? When will he return?"
The wind began to pick up, screaming at her,
"He is gone! Never will her return!"
Her yellow hat flew off of her head, stolen by the wind.
Her heart began to break,
The tears began to flow,
He is gone.

Megan Deaver, Grade 8
Miller Middle School, CO

That Person
That person I saw, not too very long ago, he had dark brown eyes,
so obvious he had hidden so much lies.
Not even a smile to enhance his face.
He only talked once or twice, when you talked to him he seemed a little nice.
He'd never boast, I knew his life had always been enclosed.
I always knew he had a secret identity, even though he was so friendly.
That person I saw will always be anonymous, to my eyes and to everyone else's.

Paul Gallegos, Grade 7
21st Century Public Academy, NM

Ms. Saffold — 6th Grade
When I walked into your classroom,
I didn't know what I was going to do.
Another grade, a different teacher,
everything was new.

You said "hello" with a smile, I said "hello" back,
kindness, was definitely something you didn't lack.
You became my favorite teacher,
class was fun, you sometimes swore, thank God you're not a preacher!

You're more than just a teacher, you were a friend.
The type of person who helps others soar, even if they are poor.

You are like a shooting star,
only getting brighter, and telling us to be true to who we are.

So, to finish up my thanks, I would like to say
that because of you, my dreams are coming true,
throwing us into the world but saying
I know you can do it, I believe in you.

Kayla Olson, Grade 8
Sylvester Middle School, WA

I Am Sorry

My feelings are bad
And I can't sleep because of it.
My conscious echoes through my mind;
It cuts through me like a knife.
It makes me feel like I have done something wrong.
I can't remember what it was,
But I think that I was at fault,
And that I should say I am sorry
For what I might have done.
Will you forgive me?
At the time it felt right,
Even though I was wrong.
I'm sorry that it has taken me so long.
I can't run from these feelings any longer.
I hope that you can see
That I am being honest
When I say that I am sorry
For what I have done.

Will Robertson, Grade 9
Bonneville High School, ID

Camping

Soft, fluffy birds and animals in herds,
deer grazing in the meadows.
They are such friendly fellows.
How I love camping, it's so relaxing.
Crickets sing, owls hoot, wolves howl at the moon.
How I love camping, I can't wait to go soon!
I love nature, don't you? I love to hear the birds.
Now, it's time to go. I bid you goodbye.
Maybe you can come some other time.

Crystal Lewis, Grade 7
Molasky Jr High School, NV

My Crutches

As I walk into the courtyard
I meet the people that I call my friends
They've been with me through thick and thin

They smile as we greet
The long known
And the shortly met
Are just as great to me

I trust them with my secrets
Of who I might like or don't
I tell them what makes me frown
Or who might turn my frown upside down

My friends are as wonderful as my family
Greatly loved and amazingly strong

They are part of my crutches in life
Holding me up when I am too weak to myself

Kendra Navarrette, Grade 9
Queen Creek High School, AZ

Choose Your Path

Three paths lay ahead of you, with a beast on each one.

At the end of the first is a beast
terrifying and powerful, rearing its ugly head
and brandishing a two edged sword, but it's completely benign
On the second path is a beast
small and sad, residing in your heart
and slowly killing you from within. It's easily misunderstood.
At the beginning of the third is a beast
seemingly a blessing, letting you weave your own web
and leaving you to your demise. It's the deadliest of all.

We take these paths every day
and see these beasts as often as we wake to the morning

The first is the path of honesty,
its beast, reality, wielding its potent weapon, truth.
The second path is the path of silence,
its beast, remorse, with its powerful weapon, guilt.
The final path is the path of deception,
its beast, secrecy, with its deadly weapon, lies.

When choosing your path
remember these words,
Choose wisely.

Maureen Baker, Grade 8
Winslow Jr High School, AZ

I'm Sorry

Through the snow to camp you go
Snow,
Snow falling like feathers
I'm not rain, I'm not hail
I'm snow
You look at me with solemn eyes
You look at me with solemn eyes
Why?
Do you not want me?
But…through the snow to camp you go
Snow,
Snow falling like autumn leaves…in an autumn breeze
I'm cold, not warm
Is that why you look at me with solemn eyes
I'm not the sun shining
I'm not the hail hitting
I'm simply snow
The silent wonder
Still you go…
Through the snow

Bailey C. Myers, Grade 7
Eagle Point Middle School, OR

I'm a Puppy

I'm a puppy not knowing what to do time after time. Sitting in my bed being bored just sleeping and eating all day. Waiting until someone comes home to play with me every once in awhile. Finding a toy to make me entertained. Jumping away from everything that scares me. Biting at things that make me mad or in my way. Not caring what people think of me or tell me. I'm a person that is jumpy and can get mad without warning. I'm a person that loves to see people that hates being alone.

Jessica Shepard, Grade 7
Eaton Middle School, CO

Hosts

Poetry is me. Is magic, is all
Poetry is spun tears, heartbreak, fears
Poetry is a crooked path, hanging in the balance of aftermath
Vaguely apprehended rhythm in a uniform, shadowy half formed thought
Poetry is unsaid — said
Poetry declares the soul not dead
Liquid air, sunlit hair, a baby's sweet cry. Poetry is live, poetry is die
Poetry is warning, rejoicing,
A sunrise bold or pastel traced across a translucent egg shell: Mortal-derived-show-and-tell
Poetry encourages, brings out
Poetry is longing, poetry is skipping. Poetry is calling, dancing, tripping.
A foggy day, the difference between jittery hopefulness and ashen expectations
Emotions responding, forming revelations
Poetry is what has been lost then found — in long forgotten pockets.
A medium for things beyond
A medium that makes you. Breaks you. Pulls you. Gives you glances of omnipotent knowledge.
Poetry is an unheard of book, the most ancient classic. That somehow gathers all to take a look.
It weaves instinctively, spinning a spell, until you have a story of your own to tell
Poetry is purpose, poetry is. Poetry is raw entity. We capture it and write it. We are hosts.

Crystal Larsen, Grade 9
Mountain Ridge Jr High School, UT

Horse-Back Rider

If you can keep your patience when the horse doesn't listen to you
And your instructor is yelling and all eyes are on you
If you can persevere when no one listens, but make room for their criticizing too
If you can sit straight and not have your back hurt, or be tired from kicking
Or be laughed at, don't get upset and yet don't brag about success nor never make room for improvement

If you can feel free and not leave reality forever
If you can show power and still have balance
If you love through hatred and failure and overcome these two obstacles
Treated as an underdog for not controlling a horse,
Or watch all your hard work fall to pieces and stack and build 'em up with worn out tools

If you can care about the horse's needs and feelings
Understand what they go through, stop without getting mad when they need a break
And never overwork your friend and companion
If you can want to ride, live, and dream and hold on when they leave your heart
Except the will which says to them, "Keep loving!"

If you can encourage your horse and not be impatient
Or ride with champions, nor lose your confidence
If neither horses nor people can break you
The Earth is yours, and which is more, you'll be a horse-back rider, a champion.

Hannah Barry, Grade 7
Sky Vista Middle School, CO

Blonde Ninjas

There once were four blonde ninjas.
They met at the park,
Dressed in all black,
And waited for the sky to get dark.

At night they run around the neighborhood
As quiet as they possibly could,
Running on the tips of their toes
But Janea was a klutz and tripped over a pile of wood.

They run around sneaking up on people,
And making them jump ten feet in the air
Then they sprint away laughing,
As people they haven't scared just stare.

One night they were walking around the corner,
And BAM! Janea fell on her face!
Ashley, Rachel, and Hannah tripped over her
With very little grace.

Ashley Zugschwert, Grade 7
Shadow Ridge Middle School, CO

Back to Simplicity

And she sat there at her desk
staring into space
hoping the stars would take her back

Back to a time of simplicity
when everyone dreamed of being a doctor
and melty popsicles were her favorite food

Before things got complicated
when friends turned into fakes
and boys lost their cooties

She wants to take a ride through time,
bring back that day of first triumph
from riding a bike or losing a tooth

For her, growing up made it harder
to know what was going on,
secrets became more lies than truth

She wants decisions to be easy again
and for feelings to not be tangled in webs;
growing up was supposed to be about readiness

But she just wants to go back
to those childhood years, simplicity.

Samantha Zachary, Grade 9
Lake Havasu High School, AZ

That Girl

There's a girl at the school, really bossy and mean.
Everyone likes her, but not me.
She has giant blond curls and big beautiful eye lashes.
I wish I was her, but I don't think I could.
She's the queen of the school and has herds of friends.
During lunch she pushes and shoves.
She throws paper at my head in class.
She tells me that I stink.
She trips me in the hallways.
She tells people mean things about me.
It's hard to avoid her when she's stuck in your head.
Her giggles and laughs all day long,
You can hear them from a mile away.
Everyone likes her I don't know why.
A fact that's true, I don't think I do.

Terani Engstrom, Grade 7
Shadow Ridge Middle School, CO

How Different We Can Be

I am from a family
My family you see
You could not imagine how different we can be.
My sister who is a smarty
My sister who is funny
My dad who is stuck in the past
And my mom who hates to be sassed.

I am from Boston
A very busy place
Where all of the people are in haste.
I am from Ireland
Where my ancestors came from
Here, they could barely afford a crumb.
I am from Utah
Where I can ski to my heart's content,
Or I can bike down mountains on a steep descent.
I am from all of these people and places
All of which have familiar faces.
They make me who I am
Those who try to deny who I am,
I tell them to SCRAM!!!

Patrick Sullivan, Grade 7
Our Lady of Lourdes Catholic School, UT

Etch-A-Sketch

How you draw my ideas on your face,
How I twist your knobs and command your fate,
How I use you to draw my plans,
Of evil and destruction and conquest over the land,
Who gives me joy when things turn out right,
And must shake you down to conceal my fright,
You are the place of my own,
To create the things that were never known
Thank you dear Etch-A-Sketch

Ryan Leman, Grade 7
West Valley Middle School, WA

Rain

Rain is fun
I love the rain
Rain is cool
It brings me no pain

I have rain boots
A coat too
I play in the rain
Till I get the flu

Where does it rain
it rains at home
It rains at the park
The rain is free to roam

I play in the rain
Till my pants are wet
Till my lips are blue
Yes that big puddle is where I sat.

Ashley Hook, Grade 8
Sedona Charter School, AZ

Stress

So uptight, just like a dress,
doesn't feel right,
I hate the stress.
Here, there, it's everywhere,
at work, at school,
I feel like I'm drowning in a pool.
I want the stress to go away,
let's start fresh, from yesterday.

Vivian Alvarez, Grade 7
Peoria Horizons Charter School, AZ

Raspberry Bake

There once was a raspberry shake,
It went in the oven to bake.
The baker named Bob,
Had just lost his job,
And discovered a raspberry cake.

Little did Baker Bob know,
The oven his shake would go.
He then told his boss,
Who took back his loss.
Creation makes a big show.

Merrisa Woodbury, Grade 9
Mueller Park Jr High School, UT

The Pencil

So much depends upon
A child's green pencil
The gray lead breaking
On the coffee table

Kayla Knights, Grade 7
Lone Rock School, MT

The Waterfall

As I sit there watching the waterfall
I see the water crawl along in narrow rivulets and gushing flows
I watch it laugh as it tumbles downwards and lands with a thunk
Then it rumbles away.

Then I glance at the boulders just squatting there out in the open
They echo the fall of the water
And bask lazily in the sun
They look welcoming and seem to call and say "come on"

I see the golden sun shedding its light on all of these things
The water is making its rays jump around
And the boulders cast lovely shade welcoming me further still

All of the rocks and the water call for me
The sun also sends out a beacon of welcome
Though I wish I could stay it will have to be another day
For I must leave this place

Peter Valentine, Grade 8
La Plata Middle School, NM

Loneliness

Loneliness is a cactus all alone in the desert
It's one flower by itself in one pot
Loneliness is a hole of emptiness with no one in it
It's train tracks in the middle of nowhere
It is an empty room with jail bars on the window
Loneliness is small mouse in a big forest
It's having a bright red flame turn off in seconds in the midst of darkness

Marissa Villamor, Grade 7
Les Bois Jr High School, ID

Summer!!!

Summertime! The best season of all four!
Seeing all the colorful flowers burst out like pom poms.
Jumping into a pool on a long hot day.
Sleeping in till one in the afternoon.
That is what summer's all about.
I love going outside feeling the fresh summer breeze fly by.
Going to my friends house every night for a straight week.
Having fun and feeling free.
That is what summer's all about.
No homework to do or teachers to yell.
Having fun is what summer's all about.
Sitting in the cool grass at the park hearing all the children scream and shout.
That is what summer's all about.
Staying up all night and day, wanting to sleep all the next day.
Going on road trips and vacation.
Rolling down the windows for the sweet summer air go through my hair.
Sitting outside drinking an icy cold lemonade.
Watching my nephews run and play.
That is what summer's all about.
I'd love to have summer FOREVER!

Jessica Lara, Grade 7
21st Century Public Academy, NM

Dear Brother

Dear Brother
How are you
Over there
Across the sea
Fighting for something that I know not
What's it like
so far from home
With only letters, pictures,
and this poem
I miss you so much it's hard to bear
Promise me you'll be safe over there
Fighting for something of which I know not

Michelle Fulford, Grade 7
Lewis and Clark Middle School, ID

Never Really Gone

People come, and people go.
But that doesn't mean they really leave.

I had a friend,
Whose life had shortly come to an end.
When she met her fate,
I was filled with hate.

But she has taught me something
In the time I had to spend with her.

Even though she's gone,
That doesn't mean I won't see her by dawn.
She's in my heart forever,
And she'll never leave me EVER.

Yesenia Yepez, Grade 7
Somerton Middle School, AZ

Seasons

Birds chirp, flowers bloom,
A brief reprieve from winter's gloom.
Spring surmounts.

Sun shines, plants grow,
School adjourns, winds blow.
Summer triumphs.

Leaves drop, vines climb,
Weather auspicious, a beautiful time.
Fall prevails.

Temperatures drop, snows descend,
Icy waters, year's end.
Winter conquers.

Spring, summer, winter, fall.
One season supplants the next, life's credible rhyme.
Transforming, revolving, connecting…carrying time.

Arissa Iglinski, Grade 9
Bonneville High School, ID

Friend's Betrayal

Friends are Friends,
Enemies are enemies,
Sometimes I wonder what a world we live in.

I started thinking…
When a friend became an enemy.

So why do we live in a world
that some people betray others
to get to the top to be number one?

Then I wonder what does the next generation will bring?
Will it bring happiness or sadness only time will tell?

I think life is a precious thing.

If we can come up with something better to fight about.
Something to end drugs.

I am still wondering when people will end fighting.

I wonder why we can't live in peace and be kind to others.

I think it would be nice to have no more enemies.

No more war in this world.
No violence.

I believe that the future will bring great things in this world.

I have one question…
What will the next generation bring to us?

Lawrence Muldoon, Grade 7
St Elizabeth Ann Seton Catholic School, AZ

Dinosaur Day

I met a dinosaur way up on the moon.
He had a long tail,
and one missing tooth.
I asked him his name and he said it was Pong.
We became good friends,
and played all the day long.
But once it got dark
I had to say goodbye.
I hopped on the plane,
then we started to fly.
I got back home,
and went straight to bed,
but couldn't get to sleep with the thoughts in my head.

Kaeli Wiltbank, Grade 8
Round Valley Middle School, AZ

I Am
I am a daughter and loved
I wonder if love lasts forever
I hear music
I see sunsets
I want my mom to live forever
I am a daughter and loved

I imagine my house
I feel sad and happy
I touch my uncle and cousin
I worry about death
I cry for my mom
I am a daughter and loved

I understand we die
I say we need love
I dream easy life
I try hard in school
I hope for love
I am a daughter and loved
Destyni Apodaca, Grade 7
Shadow Ridge Middle School, CO

Crush
I have a crush,
I won't tell who,
But here's one thing,
It is not you.
He is sweet and kind,
A lucky find,
He's not too tall but not too small.
He smiles through every day.
There's one more thing I have to say,
I wish that you would GO AWAY!
Rachel Ponath, Grade 9
Duchesne High School, UT

White Feathers
God's beautiful birds,
Glide through the bright sky,
Their wings at perfect balance,
All is peaceful in the air.

They move in lines,
As if on a thin wire.
Yet some move in V's
As if stretching out.

They lay their little eggs,
High up in a tree,
Always to return,
Giving those little doves a happy family.
Tyler Karcher, Grade 7
Les Bois Jr High School, ID

Cleaning
Cleaning, cleaning
it is such a bore
cleaning my room
and sweeping the floor.

Cleaning the kitchen
is like looking for a shoe
you can't find one
and you don't know what to do.

Next is my room
how lucky am I
I'll just skip it
because I am a guy.

Last is the bathroom
only the worst
it's like poking a balloon
and watching it burst.

Now I am finished
what a great thing
I get my allowance
so I start to sing.
Josh Gonzales, Grade 7
Artesia Zia Intermediate School, NM

These Thoughts
These thoughts weigh me
Down into the ground.
Sometimes I wish I could
Just blurt it all out,
Maybe then I wouldn't
Have to carry them around.
But I'm afraid.
I'm afraid of things
I can't even explain.
Rossa Wright, Grade 8
Centauri Middle School, CO

Friends
Tall, small
Talented or clumsy
White, brown, black or just really tan,
Popular or nerdy,
Smart or not so smart,
Shopping, hanging out,
Secrets on notes or texts on your phone,
Anybody, anywhere
Seven years or seven months
Someone to make you smile
On those dark and gloomy days.
Chelsie Metzentine, Grade 8
Culver Middle School, OR

The Past
Never shall I accept
The fact of defeat.
I've set goals in my life
And those I must meet.
Never will I let negativity hold me down.
Always think positive
To keep me around.
Never shall I dwell on things in my past.
Bad thoughts come,
But never do they last.
Isaac Ngirachedeng, Grade 8
Bessemer Academy, CO

The End
There once was a man named John Allen
Who punished a boy named Dallen
Mr. Allen turned bright red
When Dallen made fun of his bald head
Then there was no more Dallen
Dallen Ashcroft, Grade 8
Round Valley Middle School, AZ

Fire
Fire's tail wags
As it leaps from log to log
Destroying all in its path
Fire loves to dance
Letting flames lick the ground
As it eats the air
Catherine Baxter, Grade 8
Enterprise Middle School, WA

Snow
Snow goes to the rhythm
of the air
and the beating
on your window pain.

Bundle up
from head to toe
to stay warm
in the cold, frozen season.

Snow is like
a giant white quilt
covering the
ginormous earth.

Get out a steamy cup
of hot cocoa
and sit in front
of a burning fire.
Harlie Ricks-Scanlon, Grade 7
Emerson Edison Academy, CO

High Merit Poems – Grades 7, 8, and 9

Dreams

Once again in the dark
All alone with my black heart,
Tear drops falling down
Not just from me but from the clouds,
Heavy winds toss and turn
Trying to sleep undisturbed,
Sitting out on the lawn
Is the fox that's been there all month long,
Hair plastered around my face
Make up running the wrong way,
Opening up to the midnight breeze
Wishing it could just take me,
Tearful eyes and a broken heart
Just waiting to fall apart,
Nothing helps me fall asleep
Cause I keep staring at my dream,
Thrown on the ground
And crushed beneath my manicured feet,
In my room in the dark
Just waiting for my mom to ring,
And come wake me from my awful dream.

Barbara Conner, Grade 8
Colorado Connections Academy, CO

Just Me

Have you ever felt as if something's wrong
That you just don't belong
Have you felt just not yourself anymore
Because there is something inside of you just telling you no
Well I've felt as if I can't be myself around others
And I've lost just who I am

And even if I finally find myself
Society is not the forgiving type
So it seems I just need to wipe
All the things I know away
And then just forget myself when I live my life

I just don't understand why we can't see
That everything is going astray
So I'm going to break this habit
Before I get too far away from where I should be
Somewhere where I can just be me

I need somebody's arm to hold onto
But every time I reach out no comfort can I find
Please somebody save me
I need somebody to understand me
Somebody that loves the me that's just being me

Matthew Jackoski, Grade 8
Bogle Jr High School, AZ

Election Year

Election year, lend me your ear,
More choices, hear their voices.

We could have our first black,
Would that set us back?

We could have our first woman,
Would she be as good as Truman?

We could have a former prisoner of war,
Would our country be better at the core?

The political process is quite intriguing,
The American way keeps us believing.

We choose a president to find an antidote,
Don't be lazy, use your power and vote!

Landon Howard, Grade 9
South Jordan Middle School, UT

Just Because I'm a Girl

Just because I'm a girl
    Doesn't mean I can't play football
    Doesn't mean I can't play hockey
    Doesn't mean I can't skateboard
Just because I'm a girl
    Doesn't mean I can't play video games
    Doesn't mean I can't be in the marines
    Doesn't mean I can't wear hats
Just because I'm a girl
    Doesn't mean I can't build stuff
    Doesn't mean I'm not strong
    Doesn't mean I can't play the drums
Just because I'm a girl doesn't mean I'm a wimp
So boys must accept the fact
That I am better at some things than they are.

Amanda Harris, Grade 7
Dunstan Middle School, CO

School Days

Up in the morning and out to school.
The teacher was teaching the golden rule.
American history, practical math,
I study hard and work to pass.

Working my fingers down to the bone.
The kid behind you won't leave you alone.
Ring ring goes the bell,
The food is ready to sell.

You're lucky if you can find a seat.
You're fortunate if you have time to eat.
As soon as three o'clock rolls around,
You finally put your burden down.

Michael Archibeque, Grade 8
Desert Sky Middle School, AZ

Letter to God
God, do you remember me,
I know it's been a while,
But take some time to listen,
To me your broken child.
Please Lord let me let go of him,
And move on with my life
Mend my heart and save me
From this agony and strife.
I know he doesn't love me
I know that much is true,
But I do know I still love him
Something I wish I didn't do.
It's not that I hate him,
Just the opposite of that,
But my days of mourning are all used up
I need a different path.
I know you're very busy
Being in charge of the world,
But take some time to hear the prayers
Of this broken, crying girl.
Zoie Sammons, Grade 7
Sagewood Middle School, CO

A Season's Change
The wind sweeps all the leaves away,
The trees are bare and ugly.
In the dry grass the children play,
The cold is frightful and smugly.
Winter comes and summer goes,
Snow drifts down from the sky.
The waves of the ocean flows,
And the birds, they do not fly.
The chill of the night is so cold,
The smoke from the chimneys rise.
Colors of the leaves are so bold,
And the smell of homemade pies.
The winter will leave with a song
'Til the summer comes, it won't be long.
Melissa Montoya, Grade 9
Temple Baptist Academy, NM

Hero
C haracter who became a
H ero by
A ccepting the call to
S ave a life.
E ven though he did what's right.

P ay attention all
O r you might not know
W hen your family teaches you
E mergency numbers
L isten to them carefully
L earn to save a life!
Chase Powell, Grade 8
Culver Middle School, OR

Snowboard
The snow, blowing in my face.
The speed, overwhelming.
The adrenaline, addicting.
The hill, steeper than hell is hot.
The trees, waiting to absorb my momentum, hoping to steal my speed.
The board, a tamed monster growling under my feet. Barely holding on to being civil.
My hands, shaking from the excitement and desiring to be flying through the air.
My mind, trying to remember what to do as I get ready to trick.
I fly into a flip. For a split second, gravity has no say over what I can and can't do.
My mind, blank. Waiting for impact.
Bending my knees, staying low, keeping my balance up, I stick the landing.
Another job well done.
My prize:
Satisfaction and a sunset in the mountains.
Awesome.
Kat Moon, Grade 7
Oberon Middle School, CO

Books
B elieve me when I say, books are "imagination stretchers,"
O ver and over you can read a book and it will never lose its joy,
O verly read by some, and under read by most,
K ept as a treasure is how they should be,
S o many fail to realize the greatness hidden in between two covers.
Amanda Warren, Grade 8
Walt Clark Middle School, CO

Freedom Fighters
My heart is pounding;
Like the drummers drumming, strumming, strumming,
Keeping the beat for the soldiers' feet,
Left foot, right foot, left foot, right.
Why must we fight?
We fight, we fight, all day and all night,
Praying we never will feel the cold lead's bite.
We sneak through the night
For the enemies' base we have in our sight.
The fervently awaiting enemy so near,
A shadow of doubt comes over my soul from fear,
My brothers in arms who are so near.
Do I have the strength to save the ones I love from a lifetime of fear?
"Charge!" Yells the general as a few men fall,
"O fight for the days of freedom for all."
This fight we must fight,
For our freedom and right,
Upholding peace throughout the land
We are the deliverers from injustices' hand,
We are the bullet biters,
We are the Freedom Fighters.
Brian Griffith, Grade 9
Bonneville High School, ID

I Walk into the World
I walk upon the world,
Like snow surrounding a puddle.
I'm speechless.
As snow falls upon the puddle more and more,
The puddle begins to freeze.
And grows to be stronger.
I try to leave the world now,
Like rain falling upon the puddle.
I'm shaking now.
As more and more rain falls upon the puddle
It seems to grow weaker.
I'm crying now.
I walk through the puddle,
Hearing its ice crystals breaking and shattering,
I now feel enchanted and in a dream of good spirits.
I wake up and see no rain nor snow,
But just the sun now.
While the thick ice chips still lie next to me.
Leah Best, Grade 9
Superior High School, MT

Life
Live! Live life to the fullest, I dare say
But try to do so without any foul play
Let life come slowly, but jump when it reaches you
Make life like a book.
Worth reading through
Make sure to look
to the Heavens for true
adventures that may come your way.
Take every hardship with a deep laugh
For surely one day that hardship shall pass
Like a threatening wind in the grass.
Live life to the fullest
and your legacy will live on
forever and a day!

Hannah Grim, Grade 8
Round Mountain Jr-Sr High School, NV

Where the Green Grass Grows
Where the green grass grows all around
It is such a happy place
It is quiet and peaceful
And calm as the summer sky

You can lay there watching the clouds go by
As the sun shines bright like a lamp
You sit there thinking about the time that flies by
And then the sun sets

As you leave the frogs go ribbit!!
You climb in bed and you'll never forget
That such a wonderful place
Where the green grass grows
Denys Hanytskyy, Grade 7
Mandalay Middle School, CO

Me and My Friends Have a Saying
Me and my friends have a saying
That saying is very dear
We only repeat it when we're mad at each other
It's a very special saying

Me and my friends have a saying
It's are own special verse
We think about it every time we're lonely
It always cheers us up

Me and my friends have a saying
We made it up one day
You may be wondering what that saying is
Well soon you will know

Me and my friends have a saying
That saying is
Good friends don't let other friends do stupid things alone
That is our very special saying

Me and my friends have a saying
You may be saying it's stupid
But it's very special to us
So please don't make fun of our saying
Heather Lopez, Grade 7
Shadow Ridge Middle School, CO

Jews Couldn't Hide
History is sad
Hitler was mad with all his power
Jews were flies for Hitler
Thousands of flies died every day
Jews couldn't hide
If boys and girls
Men and women were Jews
And if they rebelled they died
Jews couldn't hide
Blue eyed humans
Would just laugh at the Jews
If only they opened their eyes to see the world
If only they knew what evil Hitler caused
Some helped them out but
Jews couldn't hide
Nazis confused
Humans killed humans
Why kill each other
When we are all the same
But Hitler found the Jews and killed them and…
Jews couldn't hide
Jonathon Acosta, Grade 8
Barcelona Elementary School, NM

He

He walked.
He walked 7 miles.
He walked 7 miles to find his city.
Destroyed.
Kate Zeigler, Grade 7
Mandalay Middle School, CO

Rejection

Her beauty is like a radiant sunset
Hot like a summer day,
The kind of day never found in May
Walking down the street is where we met

The taste of failure is bittersweet
Her face wet with tears
Feeling stabbed with spears
This is the ultimate defeat
Ryan Cooper, Grade 8
Eagle Rock Jr High School, ID

The Woods

Walking down a silent path
Aromas wash over me like a bath

Pine trees give off sharp scents
Following where I went.

Clear cool wind blows my hair
I spot a lake over there.

Pebbles poke out from the ground
Hurting my feet like loud sounds.

Squirrels cavort in the trees
Trying to eat the swirling bees.

Seeing my cabin up ahead
I look back at the woods I dread.
Andrew Barlow, Grade 7
Reid School, UT

I Wish It All Could Happen

I wish I could have it all,
Whether it be laughs or love.
I wish all could happen,
Money, fun and forever.
I wish it would come together,
Life, family and friends.
I wish people would listen,
Parents, family and all people.
I wish life would not fall apart,
Like an amazing toy you just got.
I wish life was more perfect,
But nothing can ever be.
Jessica Culmer, Grade 7
Sky Vista Middle School, CO

Every Morning

Every morning, I pull myself out of bed
'Morning came again' is what runs through my head
The pillow is damp, from last night's tears
However they did nothing, nothing to calm my fears
I shiver as the outside air hits my skin
The air is cold and bitter, like it's always been
I step into the scorching hot shower
And stand inside for what seems like an hour
The sound of the water drumming
The pain I once thought would go away, just keeps on coming
I wish that the heat of the water would drown this feeling
There is something about the wound you left, that just keeps it from healing
I go through the day, a fake smile plastered on my face
My shield from the world is sorrow's embrace
No one knows, no one can tell
Alone in my thoughts is where I dwell
How am I supposed to cope?
When I have lost all of my hope.
Annie Shearer, Grade 8
Kyrene Middle School, AZ

People in the World

There are good people and there are bad.
I prefer the good people because they help you out.
There are more bad people in the world well at least that's what I expect.
Imagine there's no violence and we can live as one at the end.
I wish there was a good reason to fight and no guns to find.
I hope one day there is no violence
And we can be normal with no one getting angry to another one.
Bryan Fornelli, Grade 8
Barcelona Elementary School, NM

Just Another Memory

Tear drops fall from her eyes,
As she lays there in her bed,
It all caught her by surprise,
And she couldn't rest her head.
It was just another moment,
In another endless day,
And in that very moment,
She heard her heart say.
I thought you loved me,
Like you never did love before,
I though you knew me,
But I just don't know anymore.
So why did you hurt me,
I've been hurt too many times before.
She felt something very special from someone she hardly knew,
But something held her back right then and there was nothing she could do.
But he made her laugh and smile,
And he wiped away her tears,
But what she couldn't understand,
Was how he took away her fears.
Andrew Heitman, Grade 9
Glacier High School, MT

Cycle

I was lost
And he found me
My life was nothing
But he made it something
I was left in the dark
So he shined his light
And made me bright

I told him "I love you"
And he took the light away
Then took away his love
And left me dark

Now I'm sitting here
With no one to care for me
Back to the day that way
Except this time my
Heart was confused
Beat up and bruised
Left cold and used

I strive to make it but I can't take it
And my mind erased it while another replaces
Me with joy, peace, Pleasure of LIFE

Jasmine Menefee
AZ

Elegant Ocean

Night sits on the lonely land,
silence beating across the sand.
Splash, roar.
Do you hear that?
Strong, overtake.
Do you smell that?
The blue tide hitting the shore.
Eyes shut, imagine it more.
It cannot escape, it won't escape.
It'll never leave, my elegant ocean.

Its soft cold beats my skin,
all of my troubles recede with the wind.
Swoosh, pound.
Do you feel that?
Salt, grit.
Do you taste that?
Coldness is the blue that hits my soul.
The warmth it brings cannot be ignored.
It shall not escape, it couldn't escape.
It'll never leave, my elegant ocean.

Selyna Moczary, Grade 9
Southwest Secondary Learning Center, NM

Cinderella Dress

At five years old
it's the cute boy with the blue lunch box
chasing you around the playground
in your Cinderella dress
When you turn fourteen
it's getting caught sneaking out
just to see him one last time before the sun will rise
Now that you're twenty
it's wondering if he's the one
you might spend your whole life with
At twenty-two
it's the way your heart pounds
as soon as you say I do
sparks flying when you kiss
When you're forty
it's trying to get through rough spots
watching your kids grow up
At sixty-six
it's gazing in his eyes still feeling like
he's chasing you around the school's playground
in your Cinderella dress

Jen Finkbeiner, Grade 7
Les Bois Jr High School, ID

My Grandpa

My grandpa was a very nice person,
He used to tell me a lot of stories.
We used to walk around under the sun,
Or sometimes we would sit under the trees.
It was a lot of fun to talk to him,
But he passed away a few years ago.
I won't forget how he taught me to swim,
Or all of the fun we had in the snow.
I miss all the times we spent together,
And all of the things he taught me to do.
I used to think he'd be there forever,
Now that I'm older I know that's not true.
I will always remember him in awe,
And I shall never forget my grandpa.

Shawna Phan, Grade 9
Clark High School, NV

War

War has hands that reach down and tear out your heart
He holds his head high, ignoring those he hurts on the way
War leaves you alone, injured and cold
Then he'll laugh at your being and spit where you're bleeding
He will taunt your loved ones
And trample your friends with his shattering footsteps
He is everywhere, not only in politics
But in public, school, and family
And if you search hard enough
You can catch a glimpse of his harsh cold stare
Looking back into your eyes

Peyton Johnson, Grade 7
Mears Middle School, AK

In the Night
Just when your day ends,
Another adventure is just beginning.
Creepy crawly critters slither out,
To start their quest.
They prey on those,
Who have just started to slumber.
But when the light touches earth,
They go back to hiding.
Like they never existed,
And you don't even know they are there.
Hollie Richard, Grade 8
Round Valley Middle School, AZ

Joy
Happiness,
Elation,
Heart soaring,
Emotion cascading through me
Like a rippling, bubbling brook
That turns into a roaring waterfall!
Every fiber of me sings,
And
Tears
Of pure joy
Fill my eyes.
No sorrow or stress reaches me,
Love for life and
Everything
Bursts forth from deep within me,
And I am filled with
Joy.
Peter Despain, Grade 9
Mountain Ridge Jr High School, UT

Only Human
I'm only human
I'm nothing more
I cannot run
Before Death's door

And so I live
My sad, doomed days
To the fullest
In my own ways

But nothing's right
There's nothing real
I sit and wait
But I don't feel

My view is distorted
Through my little portal
I've given up
Forever Mortal
Dallin Richardson, Grade 9
Mountain Ridge Jr High School, UT

Heart Secure
Would he keep my heart safe, would he protect it?
He runs away from my love.
Makes me feel uneasy, and used.
If my heart isn't broken yet, would you break it for me?
I do concede to the fact that my feelings are ill at ease.
Destiny brought me to you.
Was I searching or did you come save me from my misery?
You are the one who simmers my heart in the love I run to,
while you compete in emotion's race.
My feelings are in a state of war, and my heart is my soldier.
My mind takes me to my shelter, and blinds me from the light.
Your pride is held by your heart's consent, and is never let down.
Your confidence is triggered by your desperation.
It is held together by your feelings, and torn apart by fear of your heart.
You have mastered your intense depression, and let it all run free.
You lock your sadness in your eyes, and never let them see you cry.
It takes much strength to look at him.
Though he does not look back.
Is he the one for me?
Let your heart decide.
This is a job for your feelings but don't just let them hide.
Jennifer Constable, Grade 7
Hyde Park Middle School, NV

But Only in Winter
In summertime
You can eat a juicy, green, sour lime
Or swim in a cool refreshing pool during the daytime
But only in winter
You can spend time with your loving family that will last a lifetime

In fall you can play football or go to study hall
But only in winter
You can throw a cold, round snowball
During a light breezy snow fall

In spring you can glide on a porch swing
Or get a painful bee sting
But only in winter
You can spread the sound of Christmas carols
Singing "Hark, the Harold Angels Sing"
Only in winter
You can roast fluffy white mouth watering marshmallows on a campfire
While cuddling, close to your admirer so the time doesn't expire

Only in winter you can find time
To have a wonderful snowy mountain climb
But only in winter
You can spread the joy of happiness to enjoy
Felicia Roberts, Grade 7
21st Century Public Academy, NM

My Best Friend

Always there when I am sad
Holding me back when I am mad
Comforting me through all my tears
Telling me to have no fears
Giving me confidence I never had before
You are a person I absolutely adore.
Staying up late, just talking, some nights
Having only 32 second fights
Making me smile in each and every way
You truly brighten up my day.
Supporting me in everything I do
I can even tell you my secrets, too.
You are a person I can trust.
Kind, honest, and just
We have a connection that nobody will ever break.
We're practically sisters for goodness sake!
You are my rock,
My sanctity,
My best friend,
And forever you will be.

Magin Hall, Grade 9
Lake Havasu High School, AZ

8-13-01

August 13, 2001, a time when no one had fun.
It started off good, smooth like a car hood.
A car pulled up at our house.
My sister sat there and I listened like a mouse.
My mom said, "Go to Grandma's across the street!"
We ran across in our bare feet.
In the blink of an eye — we started to cry.
An ambulance pulled up, I dropped my cup.
My mom came out and she cried, without doubt.
A body came out behind her.
As the body came through the door,
I just wanted to drop to the floor.
Next thing you know, on the floor I see my bro'.
Wrapped in a white cloth, I moved slow like a sloth.
I knelt down beside him and I looked around,
I saw people, all wearing frowns.
My grandma walked in, she couldn't believe her eyes.
She couldn't breathe and started to cry.
My only brother lay there dead.
Oh, how I miss his sweet and wonderful head.
Good bye, brother.

Malorie Nieto, Grade 7
Cochiti Middle School, NM

Volleyball Dreams

In my dreams…
I bump, set, and spike the ball.
It bounces off my arms, and my finger tips.
I run and spike the ball…
"Point goes to Grantsville, Aimee Linton with the spike!"

Aimee Linton, Grade 8
Grantsville Middle School, UT

Ode to Friends

Friends —
Sister, best friends for life
Whatever you call them
Friends are with you till the end
Friends
No matter how many fights you have
No matter what you go through
Always count on them
Friends
You know each other like a book
You know each other's feelings without taking a look
Because friends got each other's backs
Friends
Never telling secrets
Going to movies, having fun
Best friends love each other
Friends
Stick together
Don't leave each other
No matter what the weather
Friends

Satarra S. Chavez, Grade 7
21st Century Public Academy, NM

Sachi and Otto

They were so cute and fluffy
Their fur was blond and puffy
They were little eight week old puppies
They chewed up everything, even toy duckies

Then they grew bigger and bigger
They grew quicker, quicker and quicker
It was kind of sad
But it wasn't too bad

I played with them a lot
and when I petted them on the right spot
they shook their legs up and down
They definitely would not frown

Then they grew to full size
It was such a surprise
That in such a small time, they could grow so big
Now they can fetch a big twig

They are the best dogs ever
In any kind of weather
They are loyal, that's their motto
My dogs Sachi and Otto

Alli Groninger, Grade 7
North Middle School, CO

Daddy Don't Go

Daddy don't go, as I said in that first sentence so long ago Daddy don't go.
It almost broke my heart when you left knowing, if I get the chance to see you again, it won't be until next October.
I haven't known you more than two years, but now you are part of my life and if you die I would cry.
I wouldn't hide it.
I would let myself fall apart.
Not wanting to be strong anymore.
If you die part of me would die with you.
You have changed my life more than anyone in my life.
Daddy don't go to the other side when we still need you.
Sure, we can't be with you now.
You will go off to war soon and we will be hoping and praying that you won't die.
Like all those other people who did.
Who had lives, they had families, they had friends, they had wives, they had children.
I plead Daddy don't go.

Jessica Thacker, Grade 8
Bonneville Jr High School, UT

Fast Forward

When you looked me in the eyes it felt like I was dreaming. Like it wasn't real. It went by so fast one second you're looking me in the eyes, then the next second you're walking away. It's like somebody pressing the fast forward button on a universal remote control. When you hugged me I didn't want to let go. When you hugged me I felt like nothing could hurt me. It felt so right for you to be there with me. But then you let go and I was unprotected all over again.
I caught a glimpse of heaven. I found my paradise when you held me tight like you were afraid that if I leave that you might not ever see me again and that you wanted me to stay with you forever. Even if it was a dream, it was sure beautiful like Cinderella, but better.

Heather Heupel, Grade 9
Oakville High School, WA

"If" the Boxing Tournament

If you can bounce your body from left to right, ducking and hitting with mighty speed,
If you can feel the hard hits you will receive, throwing them back as a payback
If you can look at the fierce face of your component, and him looking back at you with no doubt
If you can walk forward with no care
If you can take the first hit and keep knocking him out, till he's no good

If you can swing and bang those hard fists around, into the fierce body of your component
If you can see your component suffering on the ground trying to get up in pain
"He's up, he's up" the crowd yells in excitement
If he can come toward me as a man swinging his fists left to right in my face.
Wrapping and coiling our bodies together, and taking no more

If you can hit and not be tired of hitting,
If you can think and make a move quickly,
If you can keep your head up throughout the fight
If you can dream, dream of being a champion,
If you can force yourself a knockout, giving him a blackout till he's down to the ground,

If you can risk it all on one good hit,
If you can fill the hit on one good minute,
If you can trust yourself to knock him out,
Bang! Bang! The crowd roars
Beginning the countdown until 0
And the winner is in the black corner.

Nataly Soiza, Grade 7
Sky Vista Middle School, CO

Grandpa

I remember playing on Grandpa's lap,
tumbling around the living room.
Going fishing in the pond behind his house
And catching my first fish, an inch long sunfish.
Getting lost in an acre of corn,
The long rows of tall stalks.
Roasting the ears over an open campfire,
Having fun with Grandpa.

Then the cancer came again,
Making Grandpa weak and sick.
The chemo made him bald and sick,
With tubes in his chest.
We visited him every summer in the hospital,
Then at his house in Iowa.

One day in August,
The day before his anniversary,
Grandpa didn't wake up.
The cancer had taken his body,
But his soul fought to the end.

Kyle Fritz, Grade 7
Lincoln Jr High School, CO

Shadows of the Dark

Shadows of the dark,
They stay hidden,
Not wanting to appear in the light,
Hoping not to cross paths with shadows or solids.

Shadows of the dark,
Each value their shadow the smallest,
When it is not true,
Groups of solids make the shadows smaller.

Shadows of the dark,
Some may disappear soon,
Because they have become too small,
Other shadows may take a violent stand against solids.

Shadows of the dark,
To be seen,
They need help to step into the light,
But no solids dare to venture into the dark.

Shadows of the dark,
There will always be dark,
But there can be fewer shadows,
Shadows of the dark.

Matthew Fischer, Grade 7
Lake Oswego Jr High School, OR

Light in Darkness

Night, waiting lonely for sun to ascend,
Daytime, pensive thoughts running through my head,
Exploring in darkness for the way hence,
Blood pulse diminishes as the heart dread.
World slipping away as disaster race,
Ocean waves surged towards shore as it led.
Rain dripped down like falling tears upon my face,
Sheer windows reflect clear blue sky instead.
Clouds from the dusky sky gradually fade,
Sun rays shone upon sparkling drops of dew,
The flowers bloomed with vivid blushing shade,
Gentle breeze across time it swiftly blew.
Golden sun glows beamingly as it may,
Light thrives to brighten the drab world today.

Zhiyin Qin, Grade 9
Clark High School, NV

The River

My favorite place to go is the river
when I feel the wind blow it makes me shiver

At the river I love to fish
then turning those fish into a delicious dish
oh how I love the river.

Out on the water my boat and I
speeding across the water at a fly
as we approach the launch I sigh
for I have to slow down and no longer fly.

The river winds through valleys and mountains
picking up speed like water from a fountain

The rivers used to run wild
but since the dams, they're like a tame child

The river may end in the ocean
but it will last on like a sacred potion
oh how I love the river

Joshua McNeal, Grade 7
La Center Middle School, WA

Who Are You?

Are you the sand?
Between my tiny terrific toes
Are you the waves?
Crashing among the beautiful beach — whoosh
Are you the wind?
Covering me gently
Are you the salt?
I taste when I breathe
Are you the seagulls?
Silently soaring over me
Are you my guardian angel?

Alisha Earle, Grade 7
Eagle Point Middle School, OR

Do You Miss Me, Too??
I probably shouldn't write
This letter to you,
But I had to know
If you miss me
Just as much as I miss you.
My heart aches for you,
My soul cries out for your presence.
Do you miss me, too?
Will you still talk to me once in a while?
Do you see why I had to write this?
To know if there was
Any part of you that
Could still love me,
To know if you were feeling
The same anguish I was feeling.
So do you? So are you?
I really do miss you.
It hurts really bad,
Deep down inside.
Will you come back
And heal the hurt?
Natalie Keller, Grade 9
King's Jr/Sr High School, WA

Friends
We're born together
Do everything together
Friends until the end
Go shopping until the end
While driving to Downtown Denver
Alexis Cortez, Grade 7
Shadow Ridge Middle School, CO

Importance
Just another nameless, faceless teenager
Who roams this dusty hall.
Someone of no importance
Whose name we never call.

Feet shuffle along the weathered floor
Eyes searching, probing, down.
Someone of great importance
Head heavy with a crown.
Taylor Malowney, Grade 7
Explorer Middle School, WA

I Love Pizza
Pizza is the world's food
It tastes good with any mood
The yellow cheese is as bright as day
It can be eaten in any way
Forwards, backwards, upside-down
When I see pizza I never frown
Pizza makes the world go around
Sean Palizzi, Grade 7
Mandalay Middle School, CO

My Guardian
You are the one who sees me through
Because I'm always around you
You taught me everything I ever knew
You are the rock on which I stand

You taught me how to kick the ball
To keep my head up when I fall
You helped me through it all
You are the rock on which I stand

You always keep me laughing in the middle of the day
Because you blurt out everything you say
I wouldn't have you any other way
You are the rock on which I stand

You showed me persistence when you took the real estate test 7 times and never quit
And hand cuffing inmates when they're having a fit
You're one I'd never forget
You are the rock on which I stand

You could push the clouds away in my rain
Because you are the light in my time of pain
I'd say this over and over 10 times again
Mom, you really are the rock on which I stand
Briana Compton, Grade 7
Sky Vista Middle School, CO

From the High Snowy Peaks to the Dry Desert Valleys
I am from
The high, snowy peaks of the Salt Lake City mountains,
The high, rocky hills of Moab,
The very long ride of the Jordan River Parkway.

I am from
The Great Salt Lake,
The clear, blue waters of Bear Lake,
And the dark blue, murky waters of Lake Powell.

I am from
The small town of Sugarhouse,
The streets of 21st South,
And the walkways of the Gateway.

I am from
The concrete skate parks,
The smooth ride around Sugarhouse,
The steep and fast ride from 18th East to 6th East.

I am from
Our Lady of Lourdes, the school that has gotten me this far,
Judge Memorial High school, the school that will get me further,
And my parents, the people who got me through everything.
Zachary LeMon, Grade 7
Our Lady of Lourdes Catholic School, UT

High Merit Poems – Grades 7, 8, and 9

If I Were Her Man

If I were her man
I would love her so much
She would be my only
I would thrive at her touch.

If I were her man
I would never hurt her
She would never cry
I would see her and my feelings would start to stir.

If I were her man
I would love her till the end
Our love is a flower waiting to bloom,
But never to bend.

If I were her man
I would give her all my love even after I die
Like in the vows till death do us part
I would say now it is time to say good-bye.

Michael Garcia, Grade 8
La Plata Middle School, NM

Cats

Feel their velvety fur
Hear their golden purr
They affect your heart and mind
They will not leave you for all of time
When enraged or depressed
They'll make you feel better while you rest
In many peoples eyes cats are the best

Amy Jeane Stafford, Grade 7
Oberon Middle School, CO

Third Time's the Charm

Childhood makes me laugh with glee
Because I'm often hurt, you'll see.
Though I've never been stung by a bee
I've broken everything 'cept my knee:
My ankle and pelvis a long time ago,
And my wrists three times, I should know…
I've had stitches three times on my chin
Three times on my small fingers' skin.
It seems like the third time's the charm,
But to me it invokes plenty of alarm.
The third time's always been the worst
Though often it was a joke, at first.
But little did I know it would evolve
Unto the problem I know I must solve.
But hopefully now that it's three times three,
I'll be done with this hurting-myself spree.
Yes that's the answer to this unlucky woe,
I'm all done with the pain that I self-bestow.
I was ran over, eight years ago
But I know that's a once-in-a-lifetime show.

Travis Rozich, Grade 9
Tempe Preparatory Academy, AZ

the apple

alone in the shade,
sore from the fall
with all but a snap and a thud,
a firm body
splashing in morning's dew.

alone in the shade,
the tangy scent
stale in crisp autumn air,
with sour tears
upon its juicy frame.

alone in the shade,
simple and sweet
bruised yellow skin,
wrinkled with age
spotted by the sun.

alone in the shade,
once a smooth perfection of leathery skin
now rotten from days left unnoticed,
untouched, uncared for.

alone in the shade.

Lauren Bailey, Grade 9
Xavier College Preparatory School, AZ

Sorry Mom

When I was a baby I saw her.
I saw the woman that gave me the world.
I just saw her.
She was there.
She looked at me and said
"This is the happiest day ever!"
But
When I was older, I just messed it all up!
I talked back to her, I didn't listen to her,
I didn't realize what I was doing.
But one day she looked at me,
She asked with a sad face why am I so mean
That moment.
All I did was cry and understand
Her life with me
So I said "This it it,
I'm sorry Mom!"
She heard me
A tear fell, she hugged me
With her heart
She forgave me!

Alexis German, Grade 7
Phoenix Preparatory Academy, AZ

Wooden Storytellers

A walk though the forest
An Adventure it would be
Stepping over rocks
When I saw that very tree
A tree so tall
It could not be despised.
Wish to see the top
Now with your bare eyes.
I walked up to the tree
And wrap my arms around.
I hold my head close
And hear a faint sound.
I open my eyes
And see World War II.
The tree's memories brew
A gust of wind
Blows me to that spot
Where I hugged that tree
That had started to rot.
From a war that was wet and gory
Every tree has their own story.
Kiera Florence, Grade 7
Aurora Academy, CO

Sun Bird

Perched upon
A branch
Nibbling and gnawing,
On a flower.
Blending in,
No one seeing
The beautiful bird.
Tress Whitfield, Grade 8
Academy Charter School, AK

Winter's End

Winter's dreary gleam,
Is slowly fading away.
The white sparkle of Spring,
Now on Winter's doorstep.
Snow is now melting,
In the presence of the sun.
And leaves are now growing,
Where they once begun.
Grass is growing greener,
As temperatures are rising,
And wildlife is returning.
Spiders spin their delicate webs,
Rabbits dig their hiding holes.
Life is now returning,
As the force that sent them away,
Is slowly dying off.
Candace Martin, Grade 7
Sky Vista Middle School, CO

Falling Apart

Falling apart
I was falling apart
Into pieces until I found you
You picked me up
And helped me love
You make all my dreams come true

Your smile
Your touch
Your precious love
The way you hold me tight
The way you say you love me
And everything's going to be all right

Falling apart
I was falling apart
My dreams they seemed to fade

You always stayed strong
And helped me along
Your love, it saves the day

You are everything to me
My love and my dreams
Thank you love for everything
Jessica Pardos, Grade 7
Colorado Academy, CO

Music

There's a beat in my heart
It's been there from the start
It's something I can't ignore
Like it's knocking on my door

I try and I try but I just can't deny
When I try to say, "Goodbye." to thee
I tried again but it was a dead end
My heart, my soul, and my mind I lend
I hope to hear you soon again

I feel music in me
I feel it all around
I feel it from my head
To the very ground

It's in my head
It's in my heart
It's been there since the very start
I hear it
I want it
I love it too
Say dear, what about you?
Brittany Scheer, Grade 7
Shadow Ridge Middle School, CO

Read Me

If you look
Inside me, deep
Read me, a strange book
My heart would seep
Out onto pages
Through ebony ink
And a strange story unfold

Not like your average
American teens
If anyone could gauge
My strange genes
They might go and break
The tool you used
To measure me.

The music no one knows about
The dance that no one can see
These both stretch throughout
This large thick volume called "me"
Can you read this book?
Full of complex emotions
Joys that no one knows?
Ashlene M. Silva, Grade 7
Lincoln Jr High School, CO

The Pursued

Across the prairie we fled,
And the hot dry winds pursued us.
Across the rivers we flew,
And the hot dry winds pursued us.
Over the mountains we climbed,
And the hot dry winds pursued us.
Through the valleys we hid,
And still the hot dry winds pursued us,
And still the hot dry winds pursued us.
Mai Samhouri, Grade 7
Samhouri Home School, CO

Life Leaves

I sit behind my lonely tree,
A place where I can just be me.
I sigh to all of my years past,
Yet only find what I did last.
My heart aches to see me free,
Only beneath my lonely tree.
And as we're told what we can be,
Most of us just hide and flee.
We're racing through our life too fast,
Instead it could be large and vast.
What we *should* do is watch and see,
What our life could truly be.
Nicole Copeland, Grade 8
Miller Middle School, CO

I Don't Deserve

I don't deserve to speak a word.
I don't deserve to have a name.
I don't deserve to hear or be heard.
I'm the only one to blame

We don't deserve beauty when treated like waste.
We don't deserve to be given a new birth.
We don't deserve to live in a beautiful place.
Why is it then we dwell in Earth?

You don't deserve to stand when you fall.
You don't deserve to have a free will.
You don't deserve to be loved at all.
Yet, you still deny that this is real!

Do I deserve to let my lips speak?
Do we deserve respect when we just quit?
Do you deserve strength when you are weak?
Do all of us deserve any of it?

There is but One who can answer these thoughts.
One holds and burdens our labor,
To a price that was sold or bought.
The answer…is our Savior.

Rowee-Jane Swank, Grade 8
Valley Christian Secondary School, WA

Expression

People say you can learn much about a girl
Through the contents of her purse
But it's much better to look at
Her MP3 player first
Led Zeppelin Green Day Jethro Tull
Queen The Beatles Bush
The music soars
It swells
Guitar chords consuming all
Fast tempos release
A flurry of energy
The notes sway
Sad songs
Pull at heart strings
Music is my world
My means of expression
You can keep
Your hip hop and rap
I listen to songs
From a time when
Music could change the world

Sara Stavile, Grade 9
Lakewood High School, CO

Passion

As I shift my weight onto my toes
Performing a song everyone knows
I have to be quick to hit the pose

Performers in make-up like layers of cake
There's a word for that and it's called fake
In this game there's no room for mistakes

When will they call me, when will it be?
I'm waiting at back where they can't see
Hoping they don't see through me

Dance is a passion that burns deep inside
It's a spark of fire that's considered in my life
Here I go, it's do or die
I step out of line and into the light

Viviana Aguilar, Grade 9
Queen Creek High School, AZ

Advice

Okay people,
Call me the advice master.
I'm going to give advice on girls.
Girls are cool to hang out with,
but they aren't always fun to be with.
Boys, when you're around them,
you do dumb things to try to impress them
and you make yourself look like a fool.
They are nothing but trouble —
Most of the time.
Weird thing is —
I, the advice master,
LIKE girls.

Joseph Manuelito, Grade 7
McKinley Middle School, NM

I Am…

I am a cheerleader
I wonder why stars sparkle at night
I hear lots of new things each day
I want to see my Tia again
I am a cheerleader

I fear clowns and death
I feel happiness when I'm with my friends
I worry about the world coming to an end
I cry when I think about my past
I am a cheerleader

I understand my friends when they need me
I say I am a good friend
I try to be a good student
I hope I have a great life
I am a cheerleader

Alyssa Fimbres, Grade 7
Sunset Ridge Elementary School, AZ

Life Goes On

The sun sets on life
As the moon rises on night
Along comes summer, fall, spring
And winter white as an angel's wing

Andrew Hanover, Grade 9
South Sevier High School, UT

Gentle Eyes

I stand next to you
Your curly hair sways
As you turn upon me
Your soft hands glides out to meet mine
Our hands touch with simple passion
Our eyes meet as one
Eyes blue and kind
Show the internal love within
You pull me towards you
I feel your heart against mine
As your lips brush on mine
I feel your sweet breath on my face
Our lips meet
We slowly pull away
Your eyes on mine
My face grows warm
I feel overjoyed
That even I
Can have true love
As I look into
Your gentle blue eyes

Kayla Galloway, Grade 9
Flathead High School, MT

Just Watching

On this dark and lonely day
while the bees are humming
and the bears are snoring
walking outside
getting hit by a gust of wind
sending chills up my spine
the smell of fresh air
making it a beautiful day
while the clouds are clearing
bring out the boiling sun
now the birds are coming out
from the leaves of the tree
getting older by the day
thinking to myself
what a beautiful day
for when I was just 15
now I'm 80
lived long enough
to know what's inside
while I sit here just watching
for the world to pass by

Andrew Phelan, Grade 9
Queen Creek High School, AZ

Journey to Heaven

You plunge into the darkness and suddenly you see
A place of light and laughter, peace and harmony.
Here there are no worries — your fears are far away.
The only thing on your mind is cherishing this day.

You have no regrets, no reason to feel down.
Here you see old friends from that distant town.
It seemed so long ago when depression hit you hard.
That long, pitch-black ribbon stretching so, so far.

Suddenly a miracle hit you, falling from the sky.
There was no reason for this darkness, no reason for the light to die.
You felt like you had been reborn into a life of happiness.
You tried so hard to keep it up and started to progress.

Soon your effort was worth it all — your friends had helped you through,
Your family always by your side, all your goals — fulfilled.
After that streak of light came the suspected dark blur.
You always knew this day would come, as it had to so many others.

Finally, that darkness passed, you were greeted at the gates.
To a joyful, happy kingdom, congratulating your faith.
You came far from where you started. You have lived your life well.
Welcome to a place of peace, far away from Hell.

Andrea Majkowycz, Grade 8
Valley Academy Charter School, AZ

Time Waits for No One

The days fly by, time ticks away,
In a seemingly straight line, or does it?
It moves like school girls playing hopscotch,
Jump, jump, jump, skip forwards and hop backwards,
It doesn't only move forwards, no matter how much we tell ourselves it does,
It ebbs and flows, it fades and sharpens in the calming mists of the universe.
Time isn't straight so,
What would you give up, if you could go back and fix it?
What would you give up, if you could make it all better?
Time, caught in between,
Jerked backwards, thrust forwards,
Yet in this I've lost what I held, now ensnared in the web of time.
Though no defense is perfect,
Time is perforated, punctured with lies.
Soon we begin to wonder,
What stories were lost, changed, and replaced to fit the false truth behind the textbook,
Time tailored to fit those lies.
When the sun rose on the blood scattered fields of times past,
And people thought the sun would never rise again,
Yet the sun will always rise tomorrow,
But the sun only rises once on this day.

Katelynn Raney, Grade 8
Jefferson Middle School, NM

Crushed

Every time you walk past me
I wonder if you see me.
Any time you talk to me
I can barely breathe.
Whenever I see you
I can't help but smile.
Whenever we're together
I don't know what to do.
I'm crazy about you
And I know you like me too.
Any time you're near me
You're redder than the sun.
Whenever you talk to me
I can hear you tremble.
I see you staring at me
In class, and in the hall.
Every time I turn around
You're there, gazing at me.
So admit it; you like me.
It's not that hard.
Because I like you too, more than you know.

Tynesha Long, Grade 9
Ogden Preparatory Academy, UT

Clouds Go By

As I watch the clouds go by
I also watch the seasons change
Time's flying away
And I don't know what to say
The weather's getting colder
As I am getting older
The more I know the more life seems to unfold
I can't help but notice what a beautiful world I live in
And I'm so thankful for all I've been given
I couldn't have made it this far
Without you
And with that I would just like to
Thank you

Caroline McInnis, Grade 8
Red River Elementary School, NM

Animals

They bring us such delight,
With the grace of a hawk,
To the power of a Great White Shark,
To the sleepiness of a sloth,
The size of a Gray Whale and the brains of a dolphin,
The strangeness of a platypus,
The courage of a lion,
And the many disguised forms of an octopus
To the ugliness of a tarantula,
And the secrecy of a puma,
All these animals bring joy, awe, and fear
To the awesome beasts!

David Fumagalli, Grade 7
21st Century Public Academy, NM

Talk

Talk
Tell me how you feel
Open up
Sit down
Let it out
I want to know what you're going through
We are merely one half of one person
You and I
As most twins are
When you go through pain so do I
When you cry so do I
Can't you see
I care for you
You need to tell me
So I can change
Let it out
Sit down
Open up
Tell me how you feel
Just please
Talk

Elizabeth Grace Mayer, Grade 8
Fertitta Middle School, NV

Love

Love is like a chainsaw,
Breaking your heart,
Ruining your friendship,
Making you all sad.

Love, love, love,
Can you ever get over it?

Love you stab me in the back,
Making me sad when my girlfriend breaks up with me,
Golly will I ever get over you?

Love, love, love,
Can you ever get over it?

Love will eat your heart,
Crying in your sleep,
I just can't get over this relationship,

Love, love, love,
Can you ever get over it?

Love is like a chainsaw,
Ripping you apart!

Jayce Mangum, Grade 8
Kenmore Jr High School, WA

My Family

My family is the best, we all stick together.
Even if it is through all kinds of messed up weather.
There is my brother Caesar and Adrian, too.
They stick together like a mama and her baby kangaroo.
There is my mom and my dad, they love me no matter.
Even if I went psycho and killed the Yankees' batter.

Then there is my brother Angel, who looks down on me from up above,
I know God took him for a good reason and now he soars up above just like a precious beautiful white dove.
I know I have to stay strong, he was like my twin,
He would have even helped me through the time I fell off that wall right into a garbage bin.

Well this is my family, they are all I have. I wouldn't trade them for anything,
Even some solid gold bling bling.
My family is my world, I couldn't live without them.
I love them with everything I have; to me they are a perfect ruby gem.

Sonny Sierra, Grade 8
La Plata Middle School, NM

Under the Reaper's Cloak

The mysterious cloaked woman stiffly walked down the dark damp alleyway. She listened to the talkative wind blow trough the leafless frozen trees as if they were whispering about the sad look upon her face. The fog followed her and surrounded her black knee high boots which made a maddening clopping sound as they struck the wet hard cobblestone pathway. The woman slowly walked up to a weathered wooden door, secretly her arm raised, and she made a hollow knock. From the other side you could hear a deep clink as an old man unbolted the door and stuck his wrinkled face outside. The mysterious woman leaned toward him and mumbled something into his cauliflower ear, something that made him look shocked…She stared deeply in his elderly green eyes like she was staring into his soul. As if he were under a trance, the old man widened the door to let her enter, but before she did so she sniffed the air blowing across her pale face. The woman again whispered in his ear, "the time is now," she swiftly crossed the entrance. Her hood floated across the elder's face, the old man knowing he had just let death in as he saw a metallic blade under her smooth cloak glisten.

James Barker, Grade 7
Kootenai Jr/Sr High School, ID

What Love Is

Love is the picture of two white swans,
Their snow-covered feathers glistening against the deep blue of the calming lake they swim upon.
The moons rays dancing and twirling around them,
the Night enfolding them in its blanket.
Serene, harmonic, perfect and forever.
Love is the scent of a wild rose, right after a rainstorm,
The morning dew enhancing its sweet fragrance.
Love is the sound of the wind, whistling and dancing its way through the trees.
The sound of geese, flying together-as-one
Heading home, to the South.
Compound, intact, together.
Love is the zap! Of a lightning bolt,
Penetrating deep beneath your skin, all the way down to the core of your soul.
So obvious, so strong,
yet so dangerous, so invigorating, so wanting.
Love is the taste of his lips against mine,
like sweet honey, but better
More exciting, more promising.
Love is what I feel for him.

Agata Figurniak, Grade 7
Sky Vista Middle School, CO

A Spark, a Fire, Ice

A Spark,
When Nicole brought you to our table,
You were shy,
Didn't eat much, talk much,
You stayed when Nicole left,
Another funny friend.

A Fire,
When you asked me if I liked you,
I said yes;
When we talked at recess, you made me laugh.
As we passed in the halls
Sharing a smile, a wave,
The glow of your smile
When you stood next to me on a cold day.

Ice,
When you said you didn't see me enough,
That we should see other people,
But that we could still be friends
And I muttered agreement
Waiting to cry until you left my sight,
Then melting into a pool of tears.

Chana Peaker, Grade 7
Shadow Ridge Middle School, CO

White

White is the color of loneliness,
It sounds like breaths slowly taken in and out.
It sounds as if the breeze is crying,
And won't let you out.

It feels like you have been forgotten,
Like no one could ever care.
So you just keep sitting,
And let the soft breeze go through your hair.

It smells like the white paint that is used to cover up your past.
So when you sit alone,
All of the pain comes back into focus.
You just try to slowly breathe,
But when you exhale,
Your life seems to fade away.

It tastes like the blank piece of paper,
That's supposed to be your life.
Just as you were going to leave,
Small snowflakes come into play,
All of the people who once loved you have faded away.

Anelle Brand, Grade 8
La Plata Middle School, NM

If You Could Go Anywhere

If you could go anywhere, where would you go?
Would you go to Alaska or Colorado?
Would you go to L.A. or maybe Monroe?
If you could go anywhere, where would you go?

If you could be anything, what would you be?
Would you be a giraffe or a big chimpanzee?
Would you be a lion or a man in Bisbee?
If you could be anything, what would you be?

If you could do anything, what would you do?
Would you write a new book? Would you go to the zoo?
Would you live in Arkansas or Katmandu?
If you could do anything, what would you do?

If I could go anywhere, I know where I'd go?
I'd go to Australia and Ontario.
I'd go to Hawaii and to Idaho.
If I could go anywhere, that's where I'd go.

Dallin Goodman, Grade 8
Round Valley Middle School, AZ

The Life of a Music Box

Tiny metal hairs,
Tuned and sharp,
A pattern up and down the musical staff.
Each plinked note reverberating.
One wind, to dust the clockworks,
Two to spin the gears,
And three to tinkle a melody.
A lifted lid springs forth a tiny dancer,
The endless pirouette of a minute ballerina.
Each circle so perfect, yet so unreal.
She slows each second;
The melody has gone sluggish.
The tempo long forgotten
As the pins are plinked slowly…slowly
Tink,
 Tink,
  Tink,
   Tink,
    Click.
The life of the tiny box is silent once more.

Mariah Wenzel, Grade 9
Chatfield High School, CO

A Wish

I wish for so many things but if I had to pick only one
I would wish for a daddy.
Someone that will love me and my mommy
Someone who is fun to be around
Someone who is tall and rich
Someone who will be around for a long time
Someone who God thinks is a good daddy for me.

Tewana Altaha, Grade 8
Sequoia Village School, AZ

My Worst Day
Once I fell on my back
Then I figured out that people laughed
I saw a cat that was black
I tripped on a bag of trash
And I accidentally broke a can
Then I saw when I almost crashed
On that day, I was mad.
Jaime Olivas, Grade 7
Somerton Middle School, AZ

Spring
We know spring is here
When all the flowers are near.
The colors shine,
The grass looks fine,
And the kids go out to play.
All the mothers fear
When come around deer
Who like to dine
On their flowers divine,
All in the month of May.
Down come rain showers
Which help out the flowers
To grow big and bright
Getting food from the light;
There is so much fun all day.
When the flowers come out,
And there's never a pout,
Little critters run around,
And eggs are hidden on the ground;
We know spring is here to stay.
Allison Cohen, Grade 8
Canfield Middle School, ID

If I Were to Leave
If I were to leave,
Would you be sad?
If I were to leave,
I don't want you to be mad.

If I were to leave,
I need you to be strong.
As every day goes by,
Though it may be long.

If I were to leave,
I want our relationship to be the same,
I'll always feel the same about you,
My affection for you is not a game.

If I were to leave,
Don't worry we'll meet again,
You have always been there for me,
That shows you are a good friend.
Nicole Medran, Grade 8
La Plata Middle School, NM

Pages
Feeling the pages of my well spent book,
A seat by the café window I took,
A word popped out and so I looked.
The first word, my journey to a new world was commencing.
On and on it flew,
Chapter to chapter like I never knew.
Tragedy and love, both enemies and lovers, staging a coupe
To turn on each other, spiraling the enchanting story into a deeper lust.
Sooner or later I knew it would steal my trust,
But on and on I went past the crust.
When the café manager came to my side it felt as though I would cry.
The story had not ended;
All I wanted now was for its descending.
The time well spent on this book of pleasures,
Now I will treasure it forever.
Brook Saville, Grade 9
Bonneville High School, ID

Decisions
You should always make your own decisions.
Don't fall into peer pressure.
If you don't make your own decisions you can hurt your family and friends.
You can also hurt yourself.

When you make your own decisions,
you can always be yourself.
When you are yourself,
people will want to be by you more often.

If you are not sure your decision is the right one,
then you can ask for help.
Your friends and family are a great source of help,
even when you are mad at them.

If you have no one to go to,
then just stick with what you have.
If you still can't decide after that,
just pick whichever one sounds better to you.
Alexis DeLude, Grade 7
Shadow Ridge Middle School, CO

The Nature in Me
I am a morning stroll on Monterey beach feeling warm in my terry cloth robe,
listening to the crashing surf and smelling the wet sand after a rain.

Noontime I am the oozing hot fudge atop a frosty sundae,
beside the remote as it can effortlessly flip through channels to the volleyball game.

At midnight I am the immense willow tree,
lonesome in the springtime breeze secretly guarding the blooming white tulips.

I am me.
Savannah Lippitt, Grade 8
Fertitta Middle School, NV

Gone in the Night
The night engulfs the sky with blackness
The chilling breeze runs through his spine
The bleak and parched air fills his lungs
The cold wind strikes upon his frightful face
Images and illusions of rescue run rapidly through his mind
His hopes of survival blow away with his senses
He presents his face to the mountainside
For tonight he rests in peace

Jared Moskowitz, Grade 7
Colorado Academy, CO

No Darkness Is Light
The bright blue sky hides behind the clouds
The grass holds me tight
The lilies flow as a I walk down the path
They cry, they smile, they pull yet release

The trees whisper to me secrets of spring
The lake curves and flows while it passes my heart
The crisp brown leaf shudders at the howling wind

My heart beats wild in the trees
More or less for green is shown
No darkness is light all is bright
No darkness can see but what it wants

For all is flourished and found
None hides in shame of the shadows
For the darkness is dark and dreary
None can contain such closeness

Shayna McEntire, Grade 7
Leading Edge Academy - Gilbert, AZ

Regret
Regret is the feeling of disappointment
The feeling of being sorry
For something you have done wrong
Regret is when you know you have done something
You were not supposed to do
When you feel regret you feel sorrow
Regret is when you ask yourself "why did I do that?"
"Why was I such a brat?"
You have regret throughout your lifetime
Regret is in the air
Regret is a nightmare
Some people have it on their outerwear
You have regret when you are in a dentist chair
Or even the E.R. of Urgent Care
Regret can tear your life apart
If you are not smart
Sometimes regret creeps in through your open windows
Regret can make you lose friends
Regret can lead you to a dead end
Don't let regret extend!

Jovena Domingo, Grade 7
21st Century Public Academy, NM

third eye
my third eye
knows what i do
whether it is good or bad
he watches me all day
he watches me all night

my third eye
protects me from danger
he protects me from strangers
he is there for me when i need him the most

my third eye
is my guardian angel
he was there when my mom left us
he was there when we left my dad
he sleeps in a corner all day
he keeps one eye closed and one eye open
so he knows what's going on
he is all gray
from nose to tail
standing on all four
he is there for me no matter what

tom

Amanda Zaeske, Grade 7
Sky Vista Middle School, CO

A Friend
I once called you a friend.
We had a past together.
Talked every night.
When you could see the moonlight.
Talking for hours.
Everything seemed great.
We were just friends,
that was all it could ever be
I wished at one point it was more.
You didn't feel the same way.
One day everything changed.
We had a huge fight.
And no longer were best friends.
It was all okay just to be friends,
you thought I wanted it to be more.
You were a great friend, I miss you dearly.
But it could never go to what it used to be
I hope you know how I feel.
And one day maybe it can be the same,
for now we will just have to leave it be.
Deep down I still call you a friend.

Samantha Chambers, Grade 8
Kenmore Jr High School, WA

My Bathroom
My bathroom can be so messy,
You can't tell it's there,
Toothpaste covers my countertop,
Do you still wanna share?
Kylee Bates, Grade 8
Deamude SDA School, UT

Stormy Night
Wind blew softly
over hills of green
Nothing made a sound
Everything was serene

Everything changed
That one night
A rumble of thunder
Sending everyone a fright

Rain poured down heavily
Lightning hit the floor
Then it all stopped
There was danger no more.

And the wind blew softly
Over hills of green
Nothing made a sound
Everything was serene
Cassidy Mills, Grade 9
Stapley Jr High School, AZ

Steak
Steak
warm, tough
choking, inhaling, Heimlich maneuver
pain, sadness, agony, hurt
medium rare
Derek Stein, Grade 7
Dunstan Middle School, CO

My Friend
You catch me when I fall,
And you help me to stand tall,
You understand the way I feel,
And when I'm hurt you help me heal.
We can laugh, smile and cry,
We can sit and watch the world pass by,
Thinking that time really can fly,
Now it's all we want to buy,
I don't know how long this will go on,
Hopefully we won't break our bond,
I will trust you till the end,
Because you are my friend.
Lanette Laman, Grade 9
Soroco High School, CO

Vermilion Rays
Sneaking up mountain cliffs
The sun peaks over hills
As shyly
As a pup.
Overheard sunlight
Dapples the fields below
Painting leaves with
Flecks of gold.
Day is fading
As the sun catapults
Vermilion rays
Across the sky.
Nigel Long, Grade 7
Reid School, UT

Why Is Love Hard
Love is difficult
It is hard
And yet it's what we do
What we strive almost all our lives to get
But some have met the perfect person
I am one
One of the few
One of the lucky ones
And still I'm shunned for who I love
How much I love her
How long I've been with her
And how un-perfect she is
But I still love her
And that's all that matters
Nicco Fanelli-Poole, Grade 9
Lakewood High School, CO

Hanz
You come into my yard, my life
Uninvited, only, to hurt me
What was your excuse
I was merely a kid
You were the adult,
How could you
Who could do that
Who could hurt —
Someone intentionally, a kid no less
How could you pull out a deadly weapon
To know you were going to
Pull the trigger, to kill,
Kill my innocent guard dog,
In cold blood,
I don't know if
I'll ever get over what you did,
But, I just have one question —
Do you regret it?
Ashlee Steagall, Grade 8
Lied Middle School, NV

My Life
A test in math and science
A project due in geography
My best friends fighting
Since when has the world gone mad?

There's wars going all around me
Fights going on in the back of my head
The economy is not helping
And I'm losing my mind

Teachers don't get it
Parents try to understand
Everything's going crazy
And I'm ready to take a stand

My grades are dropping
No one seems to care
What the heck is going on?
My life is hard to bear
Architha Devati, Grade 8
Fertitta Middle School, NV

Mrs. Shaper
You are my favorite teacher
and you will always be.
You were the best teacher
I have ever had.
You made people see
That they could
learn how to read.
I'm sad you're not
a teacher anymore
but I'm glad
you helped me learn
Shyla Jones, Grade 8
Sylvester Middle School, WA

Rain
Outside skies turn black,
Once droplets turn to rain,
You can never go back,
Just forget and rid the pain

When the streets become bare,
And no one is out there,
Go out and be solo,
Picture everything chromo

When sunshine bursts through,
In your eyes there's light,
You see true virtue,
And now your days are bright
Cody Johnson, Grade 9
Shelley Sr High School, ID

The Beautiful Violin

My violin is brown like the soil of the forest
Brown as a horse of the wild
Brown like the darkest of honey.
My violin is red like the bark of the trees.
Its beauty is as breathtaking as the mountains.

My violin's sound is as rich as the soil of the forest.
As beautiful as the rushing of water.
As rousing as the wind in the trees.
It's sound is warm and inviting
Like a warm summer night.
A beacon to the sad or the lonely
Or those searching for beauty.

Hardly will a day go by,
When those near it will not
Hear it's melodic sound.
I will protect it always;
From the sun, the cold, and the hard floor.
In its little case it calls home will stay
Until it is played again.

Mackenzi Christensen, Grade 9
Mountain Ridge Jr High School, UT

A Day to Remember

The buildings came crashing down.
The love between people buried under the ruins.
Smoke raised in the air.
People darted in every direction.

Fire spread around the disaster.
Sirens blared in everyone's ears.
The feeling of sadness wrapped around.
Tears flowed like rivers.

Emotion mixed in with noise.
Terror rang a bell.
Flags represented hope.
The battle had just begun.

Firefighters tried to save who they could.
Windows smashed and doors flew open.
News reporters announced the catastrophe.
Vehicles roared to life to get out of the street.

Helicopters swooned to aid the injured.
Now we all stand as one nation,
representing love, faith, liberty, peace, hope, and justice for all.
Remembering those with all our heart who died saving on 9/11.

Krisha Pathak, Grade 8
Ashton Ranch Elementary School, AZ

The Sea Queen

There lies a man in a barrel
At the bottom of the sea
Only bone, rotting, algae spreading over his dusty body
When the grand Sea Queen
Shining in a lush gold
Whizzes past him

The Sea Queen must complete her journey
Flying over little blue pebbles
Controlling the ocean with grace
Tall strands of seaweed
Dancing with wavy motion
Block the queen's way
Tail fin swishing in thought
She must continue

An idea strikes the queen's mind and she turns upward
Getting higher, higher, higher
Climbing the ladder of water
The top of the seaweed is reached
The end of the journey is near
The queen dashes, and completes her hearty task
The pet fish arrives at the other side of the fish tank

Remington Aalbers, Grade 7
Mandalay Middle School, CO

I Wonder Why

I like tart lemons and sour limes
Reading Harry Potter books
The color green
And Carrie Underwood's music.

I like smelling new cans of tennis balls
And eating anything minty
And peanut butter and banana sandwiches
And cute little monkeys.

Kim Koerth, Grade 7
St Anthony of Padua Catholic School, AZ

The Richest World

Every time the sun goes down another group moves on
Every person receives four days and then we are done
My time is short I will leave tonight
But others will continue to see the light
No food or water for me — there is not enough
But it is our decision to make things nice or rough
We can build things up or take them down
Wear beggar's rags or king's crowns
With eagles to soar
Or snakes to slither
With rockets to stars
Or nothing to wither
The World can change, but you will never have to
We receive our needs, and who can complain?

Austin Tracy, Grade 9
Timberline Middle School, UT

Racism

Black, white, yellow, brown,
always fighting in this town.
Black, white, yellow, brown
yelling, screaming, full of sounds.

Why can't we get along?
Black, white yellow, brown
in this fast food's little town?

We discriminate.
We incriminate.
Why can't we smile and say,
"Have a very happy day?"

Jose Luis Aguilar, Grade 7
Phoenix Preparatory Academy, AZ

Water Water

Pitter patter
Drip drop
Water water
Tick tock

Falling dropping
Here and there
Water water
Everywhere

Splat smack
On the walls
Water water
Big and small

Faster harder
Huge drops
Water water
Never stops

Maeve Moynihan, Grade 7
Colorado Academy, CO

Versus

Light
Bright, warm
Welcoming, sensing, calming
Cloud, angel, monster, pitt
Chilling, unwelcoming, terrifying
Evil, scary
Dark

Jon Osborne, Grade 8
Round Valley Middle School, AZ

The Beach

Summer is a beach
Glittering like the sun
of a reflection...

Alisha Harding, Grade 7
Elk Ridge Middle School, UT

Playing the Piano

My fingers run up and down the piano
The music so beautiful and sweet
It helps me forget about the things that can happen tomorrow

The notes trickle and flow
Unlike birds who squawk down the street
My fingers run up and down the piano

The music takes away my sorrow
It comforts me while I'm going through defeat
It helps me forget about the things that can happen tomorrow

The sounds that come from a grand piano in a concert hall seem to echo
The music needs to match the rhythm and the beat
My fingers run up and down the piano

While I play the piano, I let go of my worries and focus on a concerto
The soothing music reminds me of ice cream in the summer heat
It helps me forget about the things that can happen tomorrow

I cherish the sound of a piano, just like the laughter of an Orecchio
It reminds me of a special treat
My fingers run up and down the piano
It helps me to forget about the things that can happen tomorrow

Stephanie Lam, Grade 8
Cedar Park Christian School – Everett Campus, WA

Nature: An Epilogue

The sun has risen over the faded black sky of an eerie forest, a lifeless Eden.
The souls of the innocent creatures are now forever lost.
Animals scuttle in fright at the sights and sounds of machines hacking away.
Many a bird coos as it nests in a Wal-Mart gutter.
A rabbit dashes in a maddening heartbeat from its pursuers, the steel giants.
They flourished in the days doing what Mother Nature willed.
But what do they do if they find their life's work crushed?
The fluttering leaves of the past and present danced before the days of metal.
Rainbows shined vibrantly, filling the sky with color and beauty.
Black smoke now clouds this, clean air is a gift.
Nature's deathbed has been made.
Smoking futures lie in wait.
Human kind has stabbed the Earth.
Without change, Mother Nature's child will die, wounded by its own inhabitants.
Another log falls onto the home of an otter.
Another den caves in to the pressure of the drill.
Alas poor children, Mother Nature is old.
She coughs as she is carried to her grave.
She wheezes from the bony fingers pressing into her side from the reaper himself.
And then she passes, not calmly, not smoothly.
Her children weep at the lifeless body of their mother.

Nick Munsen, Grade 7
St Elizabeth Ann Seton Catholic School, AZ

Afternoon Jazz

Proceeding now to the stage
On my stand my music lie
Ready to play, I'm on the page
Trumpet at hand I breathe a sigh

The mouthpiece gently on my lips
I start to blow on the tips
Jazzing it out, we keep on beat
Not just in our heads, but in our feet

First song's done, it's now my chance
To play my solo up front in a glance
Singing now with a saxophone,
Me and her, hit the perfect tone

The stage lit in a cool glow of light
Was left behind as we passed out of sight
The audition was good, that's all I know
Correcting our mistakes we improved our show

Now in our seats, watching, listening
We heard others voices new and glistening
Missing school for an afternoon of fun
The day is over, we had played our run

Josiah Lindow, Grade 9
Oak Canyon Jr High School, UT

Look How Far We've Come

The wind whistled through the trees
While children played by the brook,
Wild flowers bloomed alongside
Birds chirped above
Crickets sang below.
Everyone was together,
Now we are alone.

The wind whistles, but there are no trees.
No children are allowed to play by the polluted stream
Flowers don't live here long
And the birds don't fly;
No cricket would ever live here,
Let's watch the world as it dies…

Erin Quigley, Grade 9
Buhl High School, ID

Grandfather

We watched the stars stream across the sky
As we lay in the grass that august night.
We both knew his time was running short.
For the cancer was back again.
His body was old and weak
But his heart was young and pure.
That night is never forgotten
For it was one of my last with him.

Haley Graham, Grade 8
Chehalis Middle School, WA

Football Mind

Football.
The crowd roars,
Always wanting more,
We bust out the door,
They adore because this game isn't a bore,
The opponents kneel down,
We're ready to stomp them into the ground,
The ball on the twenty yard line,
The ball is hiked,
Tackling to the right,
Jumping the greatest height,
Reading the QB's sight,
Trying to make a game play with all our might,
The light needs to shine on us tonight,
We can't let defeat bite,
Seconds on the clock,
We are all jocks,
The field goal need be made,
This is Super Bowl day,
The ball soaring, the ref's hands are up,
Victory!

Zachary Thompson, Grade 7
Sky Vista Middle School, CO

Winter

Spring seems so far away
Rain pounding the ground
We endure the cold, but with dismay

Already starting their slow decay
Flowers wilt without a sound
Spring seems so far away

Cold winds blast you out of their way
Walking quickly, homeward bound
We endure the cold, but with dismay

Looking for sunlight's scattered rays
Its yellow glow, so warm to fall around
Spring seems to far away

Awaiting the approach of spring and May
Snow gathers now in mounds
We endure the cold, but with dismay

Darkness comes much sooner in these cold days
Frost covers the things it crowned
Spring seems so far away
We endure the cold, but with dismay

Grace Lackey, Grade 8
Cedar Park Christian School – Everett Campus, WA

Live Life

It may be dark and cold, the fear of fun getting old.
There are good things too, like when flowers bloom.
So if it rains, sing or stay inside and have hot cocoa.
If it snows go up to the mountain and get in some good runs before the day is done.
If you cry, cry, it will be all right all those smiles makes life worthwhile.
The colors of a sunset or a rainbow etched across the sky so run and leap and sing, don't be shy!
The exhilaration of being on top of the world, or the giddy excitement of being miles beneath the ocean
is a type of adventure that everyone should experience.
So don't sit down and watch TV, you've got the whole world to see.
Life is short, but not too short, long enough to see what there is to be.
So scream when you need to, because sooner or later you'll be shouting with joy.
If something happens that you don't like, get as much out of it that you can, if you go to the rainforest see a toucan.
So don't sit down and watch TV, you've got the whole world to see.
Life is short, but not too short, long enough to see what there is to be.

Natalie Kirkpatrick, Grade 7
Miller Middle School, CO

A Rose Without Its Petals

A rose without its petals is a gangly little stick. A rose without its petals is a rose that is so sick.
A rose without its petals a very sad plant indeed; a rose without its petals is a plant that is in need.

A rose without its petals is a rose that needs our help! A rose without its petals is like an ocean without kelp!
We need to save and rescue this very precious rose, for a rose without its petals is like a person with no clothes.

Its naked head is in plain view, we need to make it fair anew!
We need to put some petals on, for a rose without its petals is an angel with no song.

I get some glue and scissors, some yarn and ribbon, too. Should I be the beautician? No, I think it should be you.
You take a snip there; you put a dab here, I know that our rosebud friend can't wait to see the mirror!

We add some ribbon, then some daisy, there is one straight up, and I nickname her Maisy.
We add some other flowers, some odd dried stuff too, finally it's all together, stuck with super glue.

I bring the looking glass into her sight, and Rose's bud got as dark as the night.
She doesn't like her new look; no she doesn't like it at all, for a rose without its petals, just isn't a rose at all.

Jasmine Pielemeier, Grade 7
Home School, AZ

Living by the Day

A lot of people live by the day.
Some people look past one day.
For me, I try to look past the day and live for two days or more.
For the soldiers in Iraq they might live by the day or the hour.
They are always trying to stay alive and serve our country,
like the wall between me and the world's harsh weather.
But living by the day can be good.
So say your dog dies one day.
The next day you only see what happened that day.
But if you think you will live for one or two more days,
you might go and blow all your money on nothing but butter and balloons or something.
So living by the day has its ups and downs.
If you use this the right way, you can be set for life.

Skyler Bobak, Grade 9
Shelley Sr High School, ID

Big Horn Mountains

The Big Horn Mountains, tall they stand,
Beautiful, glorious, and grand.
The wind whispering like a sad voice through the trees,
Blowing up a nice cool breeze.
The stream sounds like a sweet melody,
I sit in quiet, and listen happily.
The birds are twittering with a glorious song,
In this tranquil world, nothing can go wrong.
The pine tree smells so fresh, so sweet,
Not like the litter on city streets.
A world so clean upon the hour,
When the rain comes for a light shower.
Oh, the animals, they're so dear,
I could live up there without a fear.
Two worlds separated by a road,
One, an ugly city, the other, a beautiful grove.
Time flies by when you are having fun,
Although the journey has just begun.
The flowers bloom, pine cones fall,
The trees are like giants, and stand so tall.
When it's time to go, I always sigh, I hate, to say good-bye.

Kelsey Frost, Grade 8
Cody Middle School, WY

The Race

Thinking, thinking, betrayed by mind
Waiting, waiting, too much time
Jumpy, jumpy, yearn for chime
Nervous, nervous, has to be sometime.

Bang, bang, sudden start
Scurry, scamper, swiftly depart
Nudging, pushing, stay apart
Hustle, hustle, give it all your heart.

Bounding, sliding, slippery trail
Splooshing, splashing, fighting the gale
Panting, panting, inhale exhale
Fighting, fighting, I must prevail.

Trudging, persisting, fighting raindrops
Give up, give up, can't continue must stop
Keep running, keep running, must go nonstop
Don't give in to the mighty hilltop.

Hoping, dreaming, I'm in first
I see the end and put on a quick burst
I win, I win, I have finished my traverse
I have finally beaten the trail accursed.

Jesse Dahms, Grade 8
Academy Charter School, AK

Moab, a Land Afar

We packed our trunks
We hopped in the car
Then drove to a land
A land afar

We were in a desert
A desert that's cold
With arches and canyons
With a sun like gold

We hiked
We hiked
Till our feet were sore
And when we got back we slumped to the floor.

Kyle Schroeder, Grade 7
Lincoln Jr High School, CO

Sister to Brother*

Well, Brother I'll tell you
Life for me ain't been no perfect basketball game.
It's had fouls called,
And travels,
And charges,
And places where you just want to quit —
Tired.
But all the time
I'se been a playin' on,
And workin' hard,
And sometimes alone
Where there is no one in sight.
So Brother don't quit now
Don't you toss in the towel
'Cause you find it's kinda tough.
Don't you stop now —
For I'se still goin', Bro,
I'se still playin',
And life for me ain't been no perfect basketball game.

Sierra Afoa, Grade 7
Mears Middle School, AK
*Inspired by Langston Hughes

Why?

Why do we ask questions?
What is it that we want to have?
Knowledge
We crave more knowledge.
All the information of the world we wish to possess.
Because of this knowledge,
We can make the world a worse or better place.
We often forget our simple backgrounds,
And leave those who struggle behind.
So ask yourself; Why do we ask questions?
What is it that we want to have?
But also ask; How can you make a difference?

Lauren Bailey, Grade 9
Lakewood High School, CO

Prison Feelings
I used to have a life
and as an eagle I soared
But now my life has been cut by a knife
and I am tethered by a cord

In these walls I feel so trapped
and no one cares for me
It seems like my life has snapped
I feel that I will never be free

In this jail I feel so scared
dressed in these orange clothes
no one seems to have cared
How I feel no one knows

So here I am, all alone and sad
hearing the cries of guilty mates
wishing and hoping we had
a future that promised better fates

Jason O'Dowd, Grade 7
Sky Vista Middle School, CO

Winter's Snowy Days
Two days have passed
My patience will not last
Each flake has hit the ground
Like its own touch down

I throw on a coat
A warm scarf to cover my throat
But after I step outside
There is something for me to find

A couple of footprints
Where do they lead?
Will I be pleased?

Now I have a mission
Around and 'round I go
Trudging through the snow
Stopping only to ask,
Did they get past?

Only to find out they were my own!

Emily Perona, Grade 7
Wiley Jr/Sr High School, CO

Funeral
I see a coffin
I hear people crying
I smell death
I taste sadness
I feel emotion
I know someone is in heaven

Diego Daniel, Grade 7
Sedona Charter School, AZ

Mother and Daughter
Loving and caring, sitting and staring we unite in a heart of joy.
Two sides we share become on on this journey of life.
We share, we fight, but something in our hearts will always be right.
Hazel to hazel, blonde to blonde
We are rambunctious and lively when our heads work as one
Snow boarding to four wheelers we spin and carve
With a crazy crave of adrenaline rushing through our veins.
These are two of our favorite things to do, oh and we love shopping too.

Jade Hansen, Grade 7
21st Century Public Academy, NM

Beaming
Their flag would wave in the wind
in colors green, white, and orange.
Their voices are heard — every word — for it cannot be ignored.
A beaming in my heart brought me to a place only I could see.
More beautiful and stunning, than beneath the greatest seas.
A place where four leaf clovers are the path to good luck.
A place where shining rainbows are the guide to great wealth.
A place where only I can see what lies beneath the water.
A place only as lovely as to make my heart be *mine*.
Beaming is Ireland.
Beaming is free.
A resplendent color in my eye, green is what I see.
Crashing waves now are pure, in my mind.
Church bells ring, in my heart.
A beaming noise I hear.
Ireland is near.
Poverty is clear.
The future is fear.
This is my pledge to my Ireland dear.

Audrey Roberts, Grade 7
West Valley Middle School, WA

Just as Quiet
I smelt, smelled him that day, inhaling, it was so strong,
it nearly made me faint, made me think,
of that old saying, weak in the knees, I got it now,
his pheromones, so strong and just as quiet, radiating
me, attuned, like a clock to time, for me
that smell, I smelt, swept, wrapped me up in a blanket and
took me out to dream, breathing ecstasy, intensity
made for me, made me, nearly faint, attuned
by a smell, pheromones, just as quiet
as powerful, a drink to an alcoholic, an addict
tempting me devilishly with that twisted blanket, over and over
my eyes, made me float, cozily cushioned by air, a scent
made me faint, falling, his smell on my face, on my body, on my hands
you know
I got it, that saying,
weak in the knees, so powerful and
just as quiet, when it cut me down

Camille Ashbaugh, Grade 9
Roosevelt High School, WA

The Greatest Great
A feeling like no other is to run.
When sweat falls down my neck I feel alive.
It's more than a sport, it's what I call fun.
Every runner is great because they strive,
For the wonder that is the finish line.
No matter the distance you wish to go,
If you try your best you will do just fine.
If you are confused, just go with the flow,
For soon you will see what I mean by it,
When I say to run is the greatest great.
So I will keep running on bit by bit,
Even when my legs seem to have deep hate.
I'll ignore the pain and keep running still,
'Cause a feeling like this you just can't kill.

Althea Hicks, Grade 9
Clark High School, NV

Friends
Friends come in many shapes and styles;
Some live close by,
Others live away many miles.

Some are people we just met;
But the best one we have kept.
Some are tall, round or thin,
In doesn't matter what shape they are in.

They are the pals we share our secrets with,
They are the buddies we share our time with;
They are the ones we most want to be with.

We have to talk every chance we get.
It is a must to chat about boys,
teachers, moms and tests.

Friends make our lives complete;
Our parents and teachers cannot ever compete.

Abigail Conklin, Grade 7
Coronado K 8 School, AZ

Purple
Purple is the color of romance
That expresses my thoughts and feelings
It leads me to my hopes and dreams
As it looks like shredded speckles of love.
Purple is the color I turn
When I'm squeezed tightly
It is the color of calmness
As I relax to the smell of lavender
Purple stands out
Like pictures that are hung up on my bedroom walls
Purple is the color of romance
As it looks like shredded speckles of love
But what does purple mean to you?

Anna Long, Grade 7
Sky Vista Middle School, CO

What, Why? I Am!
I am what
moves the grass in its green limbs
that which swirls, unnoticed, above your head.
I am what
brings forth the corn in its
golden leaves of harmony;
and that which feeds all things.
I am what?
Why what?

I am what
seethes beneath you feet,
in every changing motions of heat.
I am what
fish glide through,
the colorless thing that apes others;
never there till the need is dire.
I am what?
Why what?

I am the world,
why, because all things need a home,
and a mother.

Patricia Reagan, Grade 8
Jefferson Middle School, NM

Ode to Imagination
So little things will happen,
So little we can do.
Can we start a journey,
And finish it all the way through?
You can't chicken out,
Bad things could happen to you.

Time, and time again, reaching,
Take a shot.
Jump into a world of non-belief,
Things will happen here, so little you can do.
Everything's a journey in this small world for you.
No scientific explanations,
No more exaggerations.

You've finally realized
This place inside your head
Can be for you, and you, and only you.
For it's your world to hide from the real world,

But soon enough, you have to come back
And deal with what they call the real world all the way through.

Lauren Sanchez, Grade 8
La Plata Middle School, NM

Vampire!!!

Sunshiny days make me afraid!
So I stay in my closet all day long
until the sun is gone.
I try to think of what I can do,
can I please suck the blood out of you?
Sorry for the question, that's just my way
of trying to say please stay away.
I am a vampire if you have not seen…
wow I think I just hurt my spleen!
You made me fall from way up high,
from my closet, from the sky!
Oh no I see a sight, I see a light,
now I think I'm going on flight!

Dani Goodman, Grade 8
Round Valley Middle School, AZ

The Apple

Apples grow on trees
They can be yellow, red, or green
They can be sweet, tangy, or delicious
They can be smooth, firm, or rough
They can be crunchy, chewy, and fun
They can be extremely tasty
Whenever I eat apples I think of teachers
School
And education
But apples aren't always perfect
They can be bruised and wrinkly
They can be too chewy and too soft
They can be sour
Or even freckled
When I look at these apples I think of
Adam and Eve
And the serpent
And the evilness that apple brought
These are the apples that are
Disgusting

Amy Mulhern, Grade 9
Xavier College Preparatory School, AZ

Give Me the Time

Give me the time
Give me the time of your thoughts
Give me the time to write
Give me the time to learn
Give me the time to listen
Give me the time of life
Give me the time for school
Give me the time of sound
Give me the time to hear

Now will you give me your time?

Natasha Loghry, Grade 8
Sequoia Village School, AZ

A Storm at the Beach

The angry sea meets the jagged sand,
A torment of rain descends,
Above, an intense storm looms,
Lightning rumbles in the sky,
Where clouds of black unite,
Deep beneath the crashing waves,
All is tranquil and ordinary,
Atop the sea, the storm rages on,
But slowly and surely,
The winds force the tempest away,
The clouds shift to another course,
And the sea quiets gradually,
Where once was jagged sand,
Is now smooth sand,
Where once were black clouds,
Is now blue sky,
Pink combined with white clouds,
Now frames the sky,
A truly superb day,
Came from a truly wild day.

Rachel L. Baker, Grade 9
Cascade Christian High School, OR

Bird

The Blue Bird sings its sad song
Boldly heading for the wrong.
Trying to find its way out of the craze,
Trapped in the shadows of a maze —
Rays of light shine through
The bird has finally gone and flew.

Adrianna Sanchez, Grade 8
Place Middle School, CO

Life

Life is peaceful in the rain
When the world has no pain
but when someone dies
That is when the earth cries
but when one is born
The world cannot mourn

Dillon Hanson, Grade 7
Sequoia Village School, AZ

Love

My love is like forgotten wings
When touched by love
They spring to life
It helps my heart break free
And it stays like that
Like heaven's pure
A starry void of
Mystery

Darcys Rivas, Grade 7
Elk Ridge Middle School, UT

Maui

a small rock.
nothing to do.
but beautiful.
not as busy as oahu
water as clear as glass.
sun shines bright all year 'round.

Jayme Boonstra, Grade 9
King Kekaulike High School, HI

A Day at the Slopes

As I was riding up the lift
My nose was running so I sniffed
The view below was quite a sight
Fresh powder which was pearly white

As I was whisked to the top
I knew the day would be nonstop
The ride was over so I thought
I turned left and became distraught

Double black diamonds is what I see
If I get hurt to what degree
My tips are pointed to the trees
Gravity sure helps me bend my knees

I am very focused along the way
If I don't the price I will pay
The steepness of the slope is less
And end in sight to claim success

Devin Torgerson, Grade 7
Mandalay Middle School, CO

A House Full

Believe me
when I say that there's…
Monkeys in the dishwasher
and turtles in the tub;
macaroons in the laundry
and feathered turkeys in the sink.
And how can we forget
the Macintosh computers
in the sugar canisters?!
There's green tea in the toilet
and lady bugs in the flour bags;
cucumbers in the vases,
peacocks in the cribs,
and giraffes in the bedroom closet.
Did you see the elephants in the beds?
Or the lions in the mirrors?
With the tigers in the kitchen
I don't think I'll get much help
with this mess!

Lisa Archer-Hostetler, Grade 9
Dakota Ridge High School, CO

Menial

When you cry in your room over some guy
Who left you and your life in a mess
Chin up, stand tall, it's not that bad
There are girls being trafficked for less

When you look at your house or look at your car
And honestly feel very beat
Strut to your door and welcome the warmth
Ugandan children sleep on the street

When you check your watch and tap your foot
While waiting in a line to vote
Just smile a bit and lightly converse
In China freedom is a joke

When you gag on the food that comes from the school
And feel very dejected and hurt
Plug your nose and choke it down
The Haitians eat cookies of dirt

When you gripe about life in general
And on the bad things obsessively dwell
Just ponder some trails that others have faced
And your life will seem pretty swell

Rachel Free, Grade 9
Mountain Ridge Jr High School, UT

What I Love About You

What I love about you, is the way you look at me,
With those beautiful eyes, the ocean,
That I look at and get lost in
A sea of thoughts that churn in my mind.
What I love about you, is your smile,
Your big smile is the sun in my day
It lights up everything
Keeps me warm.
What I love about you, is the way you touch me,
The way you hold me tight in your arms
As if I was going to slip through your fingers,
And wander with the wind.
The way you kiss me with your soft lips,
So gentle, like I was made of porcelain.
What I love about you, are the caring words you speak to me,
The promises of forever, an eternity of love.
Words you speak to me in times of need
Comforting and calming, a voice so soft and sweet.
What I love about you is everything,
Every little thing about you
Makes you my life and everything I live for.

Brittney Russell, Grade 9
Queen Creek High School, AZ

Prototypical Nonconformist

Normal and abnormal,
Popular unpopular,
Oh, how those words haunt.
How those words shape our thoughts and minds.
We all must conform to each other
To be accepted,
To be labeled as "ok,"
To be a run-of-the-mill kid,
Who will grow up to be a run-of-the-mill adult,
Who will have kids that are ordinary,
Kids who will start this brutal cycle all over again,
I've seen it all happen before.
I want my money back.

Arianne Hermida, Grade 8
Villa Montessori School – Phoenix, AZ

Life

Life is full of happiness, and joy.
No matter what race you are,
No matter girl or boy.
It doesn't matter who you are,
If you have a dream follow it you will go far.
Happiness is full of joy,
And joy is full of happiness.
Life is full of all of these,
So these are the key essentials.
Think of these,
When in need of advice,
Look to your heart,
It will tell you what's right.

Adam Horton, Grade 8
Liberty Middle School, CO

The Wonders of Blue

Blue is the field where 50 stars lay.
Blue is the color of the afternoon sky.
Blue is the taste of the ocean.
Blue is the softness of a birds feather.
Blue is the hardness of hail.
Blue is the brightness of a violet.
Blue is the sadness of someone dear.
Blue is the faint ringing of blue bells.
Blue is the greeting of winter.
Blue is the sweetness of cotton candy.
Blue is the warmth of loving eyes.
Blue is the crisp taste of Thanksgiving pie.
Blue is a starry night.
Blue is the gift of a baby boy.
Blue is the start of your wedding day.
Blue is the smell of a rainstorm.
Blue is the protection of the navy.
Blue is the pair of suede shoes in the street.
Blue is that special memory of your childhood.
Blue is the design of the future.

Kira Pitchios, Grade 7
Ernest Becker Middle School, NV

Angry at Me

Everyone's angry
and I don't know why.
They glare at me
So, I feel I want to cry.

My eyes are looking down,
brimmed with tears.
As they scream in my face,
my heart fills with fear.

I know they won't hit me,
but I flinch and inch away.
The tears are pouring now,
I ignore what they say.

They're angry at me,
I finally realize why.
I'm not good enough for them,
and it kills me deep inside.

Shanti D. Bagha, Grade 8
Ontario Middle School, OR

Happy Dream

I woke up
To the voice of the DJ
And the morning sun
The faint memory of a dream in my head

I get up and take a shower
Eat breakfast
And walk out the door
Today will be a good day

Patrick Muljadi, Grade 9
Lakewood High School, CO

Dragons Flying

Dragons flying through the sky
Through the misty mountains high
Flashing scales in brilliant blue
Breathing fire, red shimmering hue
Claws sharp piercing as a spear
Teeth like daggers coming near
Ever soaring towards the sun
Dreaming of past battles won.

Hannah Klager, Grade 7
Albuquerque Christian School, NM

Horses

Horses love to run
They like to have fun
Some enjoy eating carrots
Others like to watch parrots
All will neigh
When they see hay.

Jasmine Lenz, Grade 8
Place Middle School, CO

Secret Garden on the Mesa

The last snowflake has fallen and spring has broken through winter's harsh grip
Melting snow is pooling, and each drop is merging together in the form of a drip
The earth has warmed and loosened and the new grass is showing their tips
Birds are returning from different parts of the earth tired after a long trip

Sweet music on the wind has began again with each bird's stirring song
Starved for a flower all winter long the bees have awakened buzzing along
Magical breeze makes the flowers and grass dance upon the beautiful land
The garden of plenty has began, drawn are the animal, bird and insect bands

Ashley Pharo, Grade 8
CDELA, CO

Rainbow

I look out my window and see a magnificent sight.
A splash of colors painted across the sky like watercolor on blue paper.

They float through the air like geese that landed in a pool of food dye.
They call to me like waffles on a Sunday morning.

Closer and closer, I follow its radiant streams of light.
It is the rainbow in my sprinklers,
Only bigger, brighter, and much more beautiful.

I am only ten yards away and it seems as if I am walking into heaven itself.
But, before I get to this miraculous shower of joy and color, I stop.

I love to imagine I am in the rainbow.
I have never been inside the rainbow and I never will.
I turn, walk away, and think to myself.
I will know what it's like when I get to heaven.

Heidi Bonham, Grade 9
Mountain Ridge Jr High School, UT

Dinka

My puppy is as black as the jaguar fur.
Black like the midnight sky with no moon.
His ears brown like melted chocolate dripping down the wooden spoon.
He is small and fragile like a china pot.
He is speckles of white that shine like the night stars.
A tiny face as innocent as a toddlers writing on the kitchen wall.
As small as a baby bunny.
His small bark is as loud as a waterfall, and as chiming as a windblown chime.
His jump is like the jackrabbit's hop.

I will love him as he grows into a large lion
With a room I will shelter him from the rain and snow
He will always find a home when he is in need.
Rain or shine you are mine,
I will always protect you.

Holly Nufer, Grade 9
Mountain Ridge Jr High School, UT

Love

Love
What is the meaning?
Love
How would you know?
Love
People talk not knowing,
I think I know it,
But how do I know?
Maybe that's the answer
It's not something you should understand
It's something you wait for,
It is something you are privileged to have.
Love
What does the word mean?

Áine Sandford, Grade 9
New Vista High School, CO

Eagle

He leaps from his nest to make his ascent.
Soaring high above the earth he searches for prey.
Zipping through the air his eyes scan the water.
Circling lower and lower until
At last he spots the small target and dives with great speed.
Talons outstretched, his timing precise, the clutch is made.
Struggling with his new catch it slips from his grasp
Irritated but not discouraged
He takes one swift dive
The demanding catch now assuredly safe
Back to the nest he returns — noble and strong.

Miranda Lee, Grade 9
Mountain Ridge Jr High School, UT

They Said You Were Gone

They said you were gone, gone forever.
I don't believe that it's true.
I feel you in my heart.
So that must mean that you're not gone.
You're standing next to me.
I can see you, I can hear you, I can feel you.
I believe that you're not gone.
I have heard them say, you have gone away.
Never to return.
I don't care what they say.
What if it is true.
I wonder why did you leave? Why didn't you stay?
Why did you have to go?
I am lost, in this world, now I have lost you.
Very soon I will join you,
Because I can't go on without you.
When a day goes by, we'll be together again.
Now that a day has gone by,
I will see you very soon, because I love you.
Soon you'll know how I feel, we will stand side by side.
Soon to love again.

Shelby Peppers, Grade 7
Hyde Park Middle School, NV

Life

Life is a chest
That holds our story
Memories of the best
Even 'til we're hoary

But when we die,
The chest seems to close
To seal itself up
For nobody knows

The lock is firm and holds the chest tight
Hoping and waiting all through the night
Dust collects and no one comes near
Waiting and waiting but not shedding a tear

Joyful is the day when someone comes along
Someone happy and singing a song
Though the lock is stiff and firm,
They take a chance and give it a turn
They study and study and never stop
Flipping through pages until they hear 'plop'
Happy is the face when victory is won
And at last the waiting is finally done.

Jessica Hawkins, Grade 9
Oak Canyon Jr High School, UT

Out of a Crowd

The pain he felt,
Standing alone against a tree,
Worried about the ones he left behind,
You see his darken face.
With his eyes covered just like his pain,
You see the cuts that give him peace,
But if you look you see a story,
The way he glares at you,
But he really wants your help,
For he has lost his job, and the ones he loved.

And now there's nothing left to be,
No more smiles laughs or grins,
No more personality that's now a fib,
Cuz now he lives shallow and alone,
No longer living under a home,
You see him here,
And you see him there,
But did you look to see his story,
The story that his face can tell,
The story of his tragic life,
A story you will never forget.

Laura Hernandez, Grade 7
21st Century Public Academy, NM

Just Me

Perla
Funny, sweet, playful, and adventurous
Relative of Gloria, my cousin
Lover of my relatives who are special, music to dance to, and soccer since it is fun to play
Who feels happy when visiting family, sad when we leave California, and delighted when going to Disneyland
Who needs to be close to folks, to spend time with cousins, and to talk more to aunts who are the best
Who fears breaking a bone considering it would hurt, losing my parents who are important to me
    and big, ugly, black rats
Who gives little brothers assistance, help to Grandma baking, and a hand to cousins when they're in trouble
Who would like to see Paris, France and how awesome it is, Lumidee in person 'cuz she is my idol
    and a volcano in Hawaii for its awesome view
Resident of Culver, Oregon in the United States
Jaimes

Perla Jaimes, Grade 8
Culver Middle School, OR

One Human Being

I walk through the forest feeling calm and one with the earth.
There's a stream trickling beside me, birds chirping, a breeze gently blowing in my face,
deer grazing in the distance and chipmunks and squirrels gathering nuts for their dinner.
Just then, I hear a bang and a deer falls to the ground as all the animals scurry away.
The sky turns from a beautiful light blue with no clouds in sight into a dark gray blob of clouds.
Rain pours down on me and thunder and lightning start.
I look at the poor deer that was shot as the hunter walks toward it.
The deer's life is lost, my hair and clothes ruined, the animals scared, my day ruined —
Everything is ruined by one human being.

Marissa June Fox, Grade 7
Upper Columbia Academy, WA

Pappy the Way You*

The way you said your first "hello" to me…
You cried the first time you saw me I know for sure, and was the proudest man ever,
I just know you that good, I know the truth!!!!!
The way you looked at me…
Was so special, that it was the only look you gave to me,
And to no one else.
The way you talked to me…
Was a tone I never heard you talk to anyone else that I have heard,
So that makes me feel like I am your only grandbaby.
The way you walked with me…
Was so slow that we just glided our way through town,
While everyone else moved right on by like they were in a hurry.
The way you said "I love you" to me…
Would make me want to cry just cause you love me so,
Even though you said "little girl don't cry, there's no reason why you should."
The way you would look at the world…
Was that your family was the most important thing in your life,
And you would never let anyone get in between you and your family.
The way you said "goodbye" to us…
You said "if ever I come back, I will be a bird that would carry us back to where we were,"
you were a crazy dreamer and believed in anything.

Kelsey Barksdale, Grade 7
Cholla Middle School, AZ
*Dedicated to Carrol Fred Glover 1932-2001 aka my Grandpa

This Is How I Feel

Every time I look at you
I feel shy and look away
wondering why I feel so scared
when you smile and walk the other way.

I always sit and think to myself
will I ever have the nerve
to ask you out.

I don't know how to ask you
except by writing this poem
please take this under consideration
and don't think I'm stupid for asking you this way
because this is the only way I could think of
to tell you how I feel
without making a complete fool of myself.

Alex Coffman, Grade 7
Mandalay Middle School, CO

Katrina

I wince at the explosion,
Turning my back for safe being;
Pieces of homes fall before my eyes
I am stuck there, dumbfounded,
As a sense of awe washes over me;
How could a place so tranquil become a cemetery overnight?
The voices of leaders guide me through.
The closer I come, the louder the ever growing roar becomes.
Scattered in a frenzied state of being, without food or water.
People scatter, like roaches to the light.
Will this hell ever cease?

Laura Dahl, Grade 9
Crow High School, OR

What Will It Be?

What will it be? I wonder to myself.
Will it be a herself or a himself?
I can't wait to see.
God has given my sister the key, to have a beautiful baby.
The time has come for my first niece or nephew.
The waiting is done and all I can say is PHEW!
What will it be? A football player? Or a ballerina?
Will it be a sweet heart or a hyena?
My sister Sarah is sending a precious package.
My sister Sarah is going through a precious passage.
This child is not an accident, but a wonderful surprise.
This baby will be my flower, my sunrise.
Seven more months till my niece or nephew is here!
It's so far, but to me it's so near.

Elizabeth Q. Anderson, Grade 7
21st Century Public Academy, NM

I'm Sorry

I'm sorry for what I've done
I'm sorry for not being there for you
I'm sorry for not seeing you, I'm sorry

A while ago I fell down
and I didn't think of your smile
from missing me and you I'm sorry

I'm stuck on the bottom with no way up
I'm going to try and use your love
but as I get up I see the terror the true evil

I'm sorry for not helping you
take down the evil in the truth
Now all I have to say is I'm sorry

I now realize those words don't always cut it through
I wanted to say I'm sorry but now all I want to say is I love you
I'm sorry for what I've done to you
I'm sorry and I'm in love with you
I love you.

Bryan Hardwick, Grade 8
Fertitta Middle School, NV

An Ode to Greg

Your randomness makes the mood in the room brighten
Your strange noises make everyone laugh
Sometimes making class bearable
If you weren't here
School would be an empty shell, no entertainment
No middle of class laughter
No carrots in my hood at lunch
No
School without Greg, wound not be school

Corey Yates, Grade 8
Cedar Ridge Middle School, OR

Gone

I woke up to the morning's sun,
Thinking of what I will do now that you are gone.
Pictures of you churn through my head,
The beautiful times and things you said.
We used to joke around,
Having so much fun, making too much sound.
The trust we held between each other,
Was really awesome, like no other.
Lessons you taught me will be kept forever,
You always said, "never say never."
Following you will be no breeze,
I will work and work, help me please.
Things will never be the same,
Living life will be a game.
Obstacles, twists, and turns,
Got to stay strong, it will take time to learn.

Mason Brozovich, Grade 7
Dunstan Middle School, CO

Roses

Roses are like friends.
Roses come and then go.
Sometimes they have thorns
And sometimes they have petals,
Beautiful and kind.
Friends' hearts grow and grow
And roses mature too!

Lyndsi Mendenhall, Grade 8
Reynolds Middle School, OR

Love

Love is a symbol of honor
A symbol of nature
A symbol for all humans to follow
A symbol for love
Love is a tree that blooms
Love is the blossom on the tree
It is a teaching for all humans
Love is a teaching for all nature
Love is a meaning for darkness
Love is a meaning for light
For whatever the purpose
Love is a part
All Love is a part
Of The world surrounding
Sadness; Happiness
All is for love and joy!

Kristen Lenahan, Grade 7
Oberon Middle School, CO

Another Day

Another shooting,
Another day,
Another life has been taken away.

Another cry,
Another tear,
Another patch of unknown fear.

Another fire,
Another burn,
Another child yet to learn.

Another cry,
Another tear,
Another patch of unknown fear.

Another bomb,
Another shelter,
Another soldier's written letter.

Another cry,
Another tear,
Another patch of unknown fear.

Jessica Drouin, Grade 8
Fertitta Middle School, NV

Sunset

Another day is coming to a close.
The moon rejoices but the sun mourns.
I see the blur of colors like a painting in the distance.
As the sun makes its slow descent of ruling the day,
The moon creeps out of the shadows to be king once again over night.
Never have I seen a sight such as this,
Like a jewel in the dust, a rose among thorns.
The wind sings a lullaby as I am hypnotized by its beauty.
It is a mystery waiting to be told, a story waiting to be read.
The salty sea reaches my nose as I hear the bird's melodic farewell.
It is time for the sun's departure of slumber after a long day of toil.
I've become engaged in the horizon's heavenly glow.
The colors dance before my eyes as they disappear beneath the crashing waves.
A sadness creeps over me knowing that a beauty like this does not last forever.
Yet another masterpiece awaits me, ever more majestic than the last.
For now, a new journey begins, a journey of dreams.

Jasmine Florez, Grade 7
Lighthouse Christian School, WA

Just Because I'm White

Just because I'm white
Doesn't make me different from you
I'm not a nerd or stupid
And I can't do what you can

Just because I'm white
Doesn't mean I have to be picked last on the team
Doesn't mean I have to stick out in crowds
And it doesn't mean you can push me around

Just because I'm white
Doesn't mean I can't be your friend
Doesn't mean you can hate me without knowing me
And it doesn't mean you have to speak a different language around me

Hunter Cooper, Grade 7
Sevilla West School, AZ

Memories

I remember cooking in the kitchen with Grandma Sue.
I remember falling asleep after school with my cat Samy.
I remember getting my 2 new kittens.
I remember my dog when he got surgery on his 2 front legs.
I remember eating my favorite candy before I got braces.
I remember the day I graduated kindergarten.
I remember the day I moved to Colorado.
I remember passing notes in math class but never getting caught.
I remember getting lost in Hamilton with Brandon and Barry at night.
I remember getting my new puppy.
I remember learning the alphabet in French.
I remember the first day I went to Book Club.
I remember when I came to tour Sagewood Middle School.
I remember when my family and I were looking for a house in Colorado.

Nicole Laliberte, Grade 7
Sagewood Middle School, CO

You're the Light in My Endless Tunnel

I'm in my endless tunnel
running to the light…
Once you go I'm all alone
in my own dark and endless
tunnel of loneliness…
So please don't go.

Marcos Villegas, Grade 9
Arizona Agribusiness & Equine Center, AZ

If…

If all of us are different
Is there such a thing as normal?
And if there's no such thing as normal
Do we have the right to say abnormal?
If we say abnormal
Does that make us abnormal too?
And if every culture has norms
Is there such a thing as weird?
If all the norms are different can you be weird everywhere?
But then humans created these norms
So are the norms themselves weird?
And if the norms are weird
How do we base people off of them?
If you have followed this speech
Without getting lost you have officially
Succeeded in becoming abnormal by societies standards
But then is there such a thing as abnormal?

Morgan Murphy, Grade 7
Sky Vista Middle School, CO

Friendship Love

Friendship is like a movie,
What's going to happen?
Someone's going to get hurt.
Don't go in there!
Boring. Slow.
Here comes the end — here comes the tears.

Other times friendship is like a rollercoaster,
Up and down,
All around.
Once you leave, you want to go back.

Sometimes friendship is like a light bulb,
A brand new one shines bright.
But — if you over work it,
It will burn out.

Most of all, friendship is like love.
You hug each other, you cry together.
You laugh together and yell at each other.
When you are apart, you want to be together.
Friendship has all the ups and downs of love,
Friendship is love.

Brittany Agate, Grade 7
Mears Middle School, AK

Ten Little Wolf Pups

Ten little wolf pups wandered through a pine
One ran after a bird and then there were nine.
Nine little wolf pups went home and ate
One got too full and then there were eight.

Eight little wolf pups pounced on a raven
One got bitten and then there were seven.
Seven little wolf pups tugged on some sticks
One got bored and then there were six.

Six little wolf pups were very much alive
One got sick and then there were five.
Five little wolf pups found a bear with a snore
One get too scared and then there were four.

Four little wolf pups played with a bee
One got stung and then there were three.
Three little wolf pups looked at a sky so blue
One saw a lane and then there were two.

Two little wolf pups raced on a long run
One fell off a cliff and then there was one.
One little wolf pup just wanted some fun
She went back home and then there were none.

Jacque Composanto, Grade 7
Beacon Country Day School, CO

Kitchen Bash

Swivel twist with a flick of the wrist
Elbows inching in boiling hot crisp
Bombarding booms that knock over brooms
Vanilla pie, lathered white whip that makes tongues drip
Glossy china soil and soak
Just like old country folk
Deep inside the bumbling foamy sink
Taps of feet in a blink
Boom, click, bang, wham!
Nothing's the same when you try the lamb
Exhilarating whiffs of crisp mouth watering food
Letting your nostrils slip in the mood
Sizzling patties on the grill
Smoking smothering for the thrill
High above plates tall and askew
The main dish — waiting till' tim buck two
Climbing and scuttling to the top
The saucers slant from side to side
Till finally — pop!
There goes the cake round and flat
Just like that in a splat!

Alyssa Saxton, Grade 9
Mountain Ridge Jr High School, UT

Numbers
A thousand nations,
Present and past.
Sworn to protect,
Sworn to last.

Win the great wars,
Live in the peace,
Enjoy the facts,
Of life's new lease.

We live together,
Happiness and splendor,
A happy life for all,
A happy death it will render.
Thomas Hill, Grade 9
Lakewood High School, CO

Super Mario
You Super Mario
You are Italiano
Just because you are a plumber
Your brother is always dumber
You may be a hero
But some people think you are a weirdo!
Isaiah Avila, Grade 8
Place Middle School, CO

Games
Games are played in many ways,
Some played over many days.
I play ping-pong,
Sometimes all day long.
We play the Wii,
Both you and me.
We race the horses,
Over many courses.
When my chores are done,
I finally have some fun.
Christian Stephens, Grade 7
La Center Middle School, WA

Perfection
Of all the people in the hall,
I see his grace above all,
His perfect smile,
His perfect face,
Has got me in a daze,
He speaks nothing,
But says so much,
With a heart that's out of touch,
I wish he'd see,
The love he shares is all I need.
Lucia Cervantes, Grade 9
Selah Jr High School, WA

Quiet Now: It's Snowing
I watch as the quiet snow
falls all around me.
Quiet and cold,
turning my world white.

No force on Earth can stop
the gorgeous, lovely snow
from falling…
Hush, now; silence now;
not a murmur, not a sound,
except the beating of my heart.
Eloisa Rodriguez, Grade 7
Phoenix Preparatory Academy, AZ

Love
Love is a treasure,
There is no pressure,
It's something real,
That you can feel,

Love is not rough,
It may be tough,
But never rough,

You should not cry,
There is no reason why,
Love is a bright light,
Let it light your life.
Leticia Aranda, Grade 7
Somerton Middle School, AZ

Peaceful Bliss
I love you with all my heart,
I can't stand being apart.
Just to see you smile,
I would walk ten-thousand miles.
Our love grows every day,
I never run out of things to say.
My love for you is burning red,
You keep going through my head.
I fall into a peaceful bliss,
Every single time we kiss.
I want you to just hold me tight,
And hug me with all your might.
Just being with you,
Is all that I want to do.
When I am with you I get a rush,
And it always makes me blush.
I can't wait for what morning brings,
Because my heart always sings.
I love you with all my heart,
I can't stand being apart.
Brianna Johnson, Grade 9
Shelley Sr High School, ID

My Mom Only…
My mom only swears,
When I mess up her hair.
My mom only curses,
When I steal from her purses.
My mom only screams,
When I don't make the team.
My mom thinks I'm joking,
When I tell her I'm smoking.
My mom only smolders,
When I tell her I can't wait till I'm older.
Munro C. Kipp, Grade 7
Luther School, MT

Puppy
Sprinting along
Across the open field
Wagging his tail
As happy as can be
Chasing the grasshoppers
Then I call him in
Because it's getting dark
He is so happy
He is sparkling like
A firecracker
Kaitlin Stampfly, Grade 8
Round Valley Middle School, AZ

The Land of Cotate
The land of Cotate
Was a very happy place
But then some things happened
It is now a disgrace

It used to have oceans
It used to have trees
It used to have many things
That delight you and please

But why? One may ask
Why did all these thing happen?
Why did something so wonderful
Become so misshapen

The answer is simple
And you should so know it
They corrupted the environment
And all things that grow it

So listen to the warning
Of the land of Cotate
Save the environment
Before it is too late
Anthony Faraco-Hadlock, Grade 9
Lakewood High School, CO

Creamy Cheesecake

I *love* cheesecake
I never had it until my dad made one
I was a little hesitant about trying it
The cheesecake was amazing

It was smooth and sweet
I could have savored that bite forever
It looked perfect
No splits in the top
I pressed it in my mouth with my tongue
It was as fluffy as a cloud

The shell is soft and has a quiet *crunch*
The flavor is fantastic
I slowly savor each bite
The slight *click* as the fork slides through and hits the plate
I could eat it forever

And *chocolate* cheesecake...
I am speechless
Two wonderful things combine in one
I can taste the cool crunchy creamy cheesecake now

Corey Bruggeman, Grade 7
Mandalay Middle School, CO

Ricky the Raccoon

Ricky is my stuffed animal raccoon
But I'm pretty sure he will fall apart soon
On my second birthday my big brother bought him for me
He is my favorite stuffed animal and always will be
His nose has been bitten off by my friend's dog
He has gotten dirty from sitting with me on a log
He has been stained countless times
Left in many places but I've never heard him whine
He's there for me when I am sick
He keeps me warm for his fur is so thick
I take him everywhere I go
But if he can't make it he's in my heart I know
He is now 11 years old
And to me he is my pot of gold

Hannah Shelpuk, Grade 8
Colorado Connections Academy, CO

X-Games

The day before X-Games all tickets were sold out.
The kids who loved boarding were all very bummed out.
Sheckler, Hawk, and Margera were ready to skate
when they saw all the kids locked out at the gates.
Burnquist and Lasek jumped down from the big half pipe.
They unlocked the gates because they knew it was right.
The kids were happy, they got to see tricks.
The skaters did great, the problem was fixed.

Wyatt Bonertz, Grade 7
Mandalay Middle School, CO

Seasons

Flowers awaken with morning dew
Branches fill with sap to fuel leaves anew
Blades of grass cut through the Earth
Sounds of young blessings cry out their birth
It's spring

Temperatures rise with the closeness of the sun
Beaches come to life with kids old and young
Fire threatens wildlife with every lightning strike
Oceans and meadows alive with brightness alike
It's summer

Crimson and gold extend across the canvas
Life sheds its leaves in the cycle mysterious
Fog blankets the morning with moisture for the day
Stars multiply in the heavens reminding of far away
It's fall

Icicles decorate the scene with streams of delight
Animals seek solace from the chill of the night
Holidays fill the calendars with days of family love
Color all but vanished as directed from above
It's winter

SaLena Elledge, Grade 7
Mandalay Middle School, CO

Pebble

A pebble lays in the dirt
Thinking "Why am I here"
Never assuming life was near

Through the dirt and cracks
Came a drop of H_2O
Landed on the pebble and soon it will grow

Over a couple of days passed
And the pebble started to sprout
Roots and stems created a spout

Three years passed
And the pebble is a tree and happy
About its new look and beauty

But the sun starts to cool off
And the seasons start to change
Tree is not happy
Because the tree has exchanged

Its gorgeous leaves
For gloomy branches
The tree wonders if it will ever see leaves again

Jordan Shouse, Grade 7
Ingleside Middle School, AZ

The Intenseness of Call of Duty 4

I pull the left trigger,
and raise up my sights.
This single shot,
will start a great fight.

I pull the right trigger,
the "tango" is dead.
A fierce piercing bullet,
right through his head.

With the enemy neutralized,
we get in the building.
We got the package,
and home we are heading.

I shut off the Xbox,
hungry for more.
All I want to do is play,
Call of Duty 4.

Austin Poulson, Grade 9
Duchesne High School, UT

Mice

Mice everywhere, ah, mice
under the bed
Under the chair —
everywhere —
mice, mice.
Scary, creepy, crawling, hairy beasts
under my dresser drawer.
Mice, ah, mice, they're everywhere.

Open the pantry door to find holes —
holes in everything.
Creepy, crawling, icky mice.
Mice, ah, mice, everywhere,
even in my underwear.

Holes, holes in all you see —
in my socks,
in my pants,
even in my swiss cheese.

Ahhhhhh!
Mice, ewe, mice, everywhere —
call the exterminator!

Liam Stokes, Grade 7
St Pauls Catholic School, ID

Jack Bauer

Jack Bauer guns smart —
Fighting, running, shooting,
Always on the move —
Last man standing.

Kaden Shumway, Grade 7
Elk Ridge Middle School, UT

Writing

Call the author an artist, delicately perfecting their work.
Call the words a river, flowing from the pen.
Call imagination a guide, helping you find your way.
Call time the enemy, passing by too fast to see.
Call the book the home stretch, hey look! You're almost there!
Call the mind a whirlpool, ideas swirling 'round and 'round.

Kristen Ratcliffe, Grade 7
Mears Middle School, AK

Weeping Willow

The long limbs stretch like arms in the steadily blowing wind.
It bows its head as if it were crying.
The soft cry of the wind through the branches haunts me
Its arms protect me from all that is not wanted.

Then the snow begins,
The snow is like little angels dancing as the wind blew it.
The willow tightens its grip around me,
And does not let anything in.

Its soft leaves move slightly,
The only sign that there is something,
Something beyond the small sanctuary.
It cries a low cry that I can barely hear.

Then it begins to sing a haunting tune,
How sad I thought,
Something so sweet could be filled with so much sorrow.
When the wind and snow settled it seemed to say that it was safe,
And that it was okay to go outside.

Melissa McDermott, Grade 8
La Plata Middle School, NM

My Friends

Seven years ago, I was caught in darkness
No people would call me friend
No one who I could rely on
Then I began going to school

During school I met someone, a candle with light
Someone who called me friend
Then three more lights appeared in the darkness
Then there was no more darkness, but illumination
However, it did not last for long

As we progressed through school, one by one, the lights died out
Until one remained still glowing bright and strong
But eventually that last candle died out and I was alone trapped in darkness yet again

But almost immediately as the last candle died out, four appeared
More lights to help me find my way in the darkness
People who were even brighter than the other lights
People who would call me friend

Marc Gutierrez, Grade 7
St Elizabeth Ann Seton Catholic School, AZ

The Man in the Moon

How can he just stay in the sky?
He sits up there oh so high.
Just waiting for night to come being extremely glum.
Watching all the stars shoot by.
He does not care if you see him cry.
Oh, the man in the moon.
He is in his forever tomb.
Always watching what we do.
He does not care if we do kung fu.
He circles earth day and night,
Watching over the earth with fright.
Oh, the man in the moon.

Zoah Gordon, Grade 7
21st Century Public Academy, NM

Breaking Through

The times you thought
You had no fear
Were the times you knew
You would cry no more tears.
You believed in the truth
And you believed in me
And look at us now
Both wild and free.
You feel in your heart
That you are too strong to fall apart
But so many things have proved you wrong
You won't give up
You will stand up tall
It soon will be time to put down your wall
To let someone in
To walk through the dark hall
Find the truth
And call out the name
Time to break through the
Childish frame.

Kasey Casias, Grade 9
Estancia High School, NM

Sarcasm

Sarcasm gets me mad after too much,
I begin to complain from the anger.
My heart begins to pump and pound at such,
My head is sweating and getting hotter.
Minutes go by before I start to calm,
My body cools and my heart rate slows down.
I feel less dampness on both of my palms.
The frustration of it becomes unfound,
I burst with adrenaline and quiver.
The world slows and I leave to escape,
I then forget it all, and feel languor.
As I go on, I start to irritate,
With sarcasm which makes me smile wide,
From the ironic terms, from which I hide.

Barada Moncravie, Grade 9
Clark High School, NV

Ode to the Run

My heart pounds,
Adrenaline takes over.
The starter's gun blazes,
I fly from the line.

I am focused,
Seeing nothing but the course before me.
I am one with the track,
My heart screams with pure joy.

Pain sets in,
I welcome it, embrace it,
And let it go.
I break through the wall and reach a new level,
I float toward the finish.

I sprint, focusing on the end,
I cross the line.
I am calm,
At one with the track,
At one with myself.

Jaime Miguel McCarthy, Grade 8
La Plata Middle School, NM

Let's Just Say I'm Working on It

Like most people, I can't talk when nervous.
The words come out all strange.
My tongue gets all twisted (although not on purpose)
And my ideas come out deranged.

But when I write it down, it's a wonder!
My voice is beyond compare.
The vivid descriptions cause one to ponder
My writing is more than just fair.

My characters have highs and lows,
The setting is as great as my wit,
The conventions are great, but as how it flows,
Let's just say I'm working on it.

The sentences may be a little choppy,
My wording may be stuck in a groove,
Maybe the events seem a little too "hoppy"
Or the characters don't really move.

The plot line may be too thin,
Or the conflict not worked out
Maybe the ideas are too maxim,
But writing makes me want to shout!

Kennerley Roper, Grade 8
Fertitta Middle School, NV

The Walking Plant*

'Twas gleaming and the brightly girl did run and migrate in the day.
All clumsy were the newborn squirrels and the new bays away.

"Beware the Walking Plant my girl the thorns that scratch, the leaves that clasp.
Beware the Talking Stone and curl the odd-looking Snitcher Slap."

She took her daisy wreath on head, long time the wicked plant she looked.
So rested by the Pumcum tree, and sat awhile and cooked.

And as she stood and thought, "I can't." The Walking Plant with vines to shun,
came grumbling through the other plants yelling as it swung.

Hop, skip! Hop, skip and run and run the daisy wreath went whosh, way, whoo.
She left it dry and with a leaf, she ran home as the wind blew.

"And have you dried the Walking Plant? Come hug me dear, oh, brilliant girl!"
"Oh, wonderful day, hip, hip, hooray," she yodeled in her pride.

'Twas gleaming and the brightly girl did run and migrate in the day.
All clumsy were the newborn squirrels and the new bays away.

Cassie Sharp, Grade 7
Bear Lake Middle School, ID
*Patterned after Lewis Carroll's "Jabberwocky"

I'm From

I'm from the streets of Burque to the streets of El Cerro mission,
I'm from a beautiful two story house to a broken down trailer,
I'm from blue eyes and white skin to brown eyes and brown skin,
I'm from home cooked meals to beans and rice day and night,
I'm from Hollister, Hot Topic, and Anchorblue to Dickies, Locs and yard sales.
I'm from paved roads and big houses to dirt roads and trailers,
I'm from safety and feeling secure to drive bys and fights,
I'm from jobs and ambitions to saving cans and selling drugs,
I'm from a mom who's always here and judgmental to a dad who's never sober and always locked up.
I'm from hitting and problems to cruising day and night.
I'm from Republicans and Christians to Democrats and Catholics,
I'm from tears and smoking to laughing and drinking,
I'm from friends and family one day to death and funerals the next,
I'm from going to school all day and sleeping all night to sleeping all day and partying all night,
I'm from a mom who's already achieved to a dad who's trying,
I'm from peace and tranquility to sirens, gunshots, and basses,
I'm from stuck up and self centered to sweet and kind,
I'm from two different homes, but I'm from both.

Patricia Ocanas, Grade 9
Cibola High School, NM

Something About Him

There is something about him that makes me happy. I don't know if it's his smile or his laugh, but it's something about him. When he hugs me and kisses me with his little lips and hands he makes me feel special. Even though he is only one year old he is still the cutest thing I have ever seen. Besides that he is my baby brother I call him my baby bear.

Claire Elizarraras, Grade 7
Somerton Middle School, AZ

Sister

If you can keep control and have fun at the same time
If you can play games together and be kind
If you can deny peer pressure and do what's right
And be positive
Without getting into a fight

If you can talk and not be hurt
If you can understand
If you can lend a shirt and lend a hand
If you can show compassion but not be shy
And help her with her fashion as time does fly

If you can follow the right path and hold your courage
And do it all with a laugh
And make your friendship a bridge
If you can be kind hearted, always share
And be warm hearted, love her like a teddy bear

If you can be enemies never and be compassionate
If you can be clever
If you can be considerate
If you can be together and never keep your love far
You'll be friends forever
Then your sister will love you for the sister you are

Alyssa Kirsch, Grade 7
Sky Vista Middle School, CO

Love

I hold your hand, you hold mine.
I'm always there till the end of time.
You love me, I love you.
That's all it takes is just us two.
The good and the bad times we share.
They are always there, they're hard to bare.
You are the only one I need.
To be happy for all eternity.
The bad times made you sad.
But I was there to make you glad
The horrid times made me depressed.
You were there to prevent me from eternal rest.
Times haven't changed.
And neither will our love.
I won't separate from you, until I go up above.
I will never fall for another.
You're all I need, no other.
I hold your hand, you hold mine.
Those times really made me shine.
You love me, I love you.
I will die for you, and that will always stay true.

Christopher Vessey, Grade 8
Grand Canyon Middle School, AZ

Beautiful Inside and Out

The touch of her smooth skin
Felt so good it should have been a sin.
The sight of her big brown eyes
Sparkled as bright as fireflies.
The sound of her sweet soft voice —
Not loving her was never a choice.
Her short black hair was silky,
Which smelled like the flowers of Eden.
If her heart wasn't brittle like pure gold,
She would have lived to be 100 years old.
With an innocent and sincere smile,
She could brighten up anyone's day.
Her personality sang such a beautiful song
'Till her last breath she held so strong.
So many stories she had left to tell,
So many memories —
Such a loving family was at her bedside
'Till the very moment she died.

Mark Mazzucco, Grade 9
Stapley Jr High School, AZ

Mike and Michael Atchley

Mike the one with a different side,
Michael, the one whose funny.
Mike the addicted one.
Michael the bright.
Mike the faint.
Michael the muffled —
the Michael who hides.
Mike who tells me he loves me.
Mike who lies.
Michael who tells me he loves me and tells no lies.
Michael who used to be in my life.
Mike who's always present but his mind is always gone.
Michael the amazing.
Mike the rewind.
Mike never going forward, always back.
Mike my father.
Michael my daddy.

Amber Atchley, Grade 9
Independence High School, UT

Behind the Mask

Behind the mask there are tears,
Behind the mask I hide my fears,
Behind the mask I feel the pain,
Behind the mask where it always rains,
Behind the mask where silence is unbroken,
Behind the mask it is given a token,
Behind the mask I ask myself why,
Behind the mask is where I hide,
Behind the mask where I'm safe to cry.
The things that hurt me are cracking this mask,
Now they will all see what I've been holding back.

Katie Bonstein, Grade 8
Rosemary Clarke Middle School, NV

Why?
There has been a
family accident.

I felt scared,
my heart
pounding,
throat throbbing.

As I sit on the couch with my
family,
they tell me the news.

Why him?
He was
too young,
too active,
and too
alive.

I didn't think I would say
goodbye
this
soon.
Amanda R. Hultz, Grade 7
Valley View Middle School, WA

Spring Break
A week off from school in Florida
Get to do whatever we want.
With the pool and the ocean
Comes long awaited rest.
Nothing bothers me
Lay on the beach
Close my eyes
Sit back
Relax.
Brianna Cattelino, Grade 8
Beacon Country Day School, CO

Praying for Safety
Looking up to God and praying
For safety.
Holding on tight
Afraid to look
Down.
Looking across to
The horizon
The sun
Gets
In my eyes
I slip and hold on tight
So I don't fall down,
Gripping, pulling myself up
God was with me.
Amelia Kelkenberg, Grade 8
Skyview Middle School, CO

Dusk in Larken Meadow
On my back, in the meadow,
I gaze at the clouds as they amble on by
A soft breeze plays across my cheek
The clouds move in time with the wind
As the sun buries itself beneath the tundra, west
Notice the layers of painted color, just above its master
The sky darkens and lightning bugs are out
They flash as if to say they're here to guide you along your way
Still on my back, frogs sing,
In a melody like no other, harmony
The sweet aroma of honeysuckles reach my nose
I inhale deeply, relaxing my body
A fawn and doe approach my locale
The fawn bows deeply as an ostrich with grace
I stay perfectly still, awaiting their departure
Before long the spotted animals leave in peace
All is quiet,
All is still
I inhale deeply, one last time
Gathering my thoughts,
I come to my feet, and stride back to the land of haze and disruption.
Jessica Notestine, Grade 9
A G West Black Hills High School, WA

Faith
Faith is blind love,
The binding hope that your belief exists and cares just as much for you.

Faith is leaping from the tall pedestal down into the dark,
murky depths of mysterious, uncharted ground.

Faith is occasional doubt,
A wondering if your efforts to believe are in vain.

Faith is taking your loved one's hand.
In the darkest of times, your loyalty ties strong.

Faith is a pinnacle of confidence.
Trust the unknown, stand next to your belief while leaping into the air,
unsure whether you'll reach the bottom.
Sarah Thompson, Grade 7
Les Bois Jr High School, ID

I Am
I am from Detroit where the wrong colors speak cautious.
I am from Detroit also called Motown, AKA motor city.
I am from a place where people struggle for money and live on the streets.
I am from the community which is trying to build for the future.
I am from a city where the auto industry controls the area's economy.
I am from Detroit, which is also called Hockey Town due to the Red wings.
I am from Detroit, called the Murder Capital of the USA.
I am alive, I have survived Detroit.
Christian Weidle, Grade 8
Our Lady of Lourdes Catholic School, UT

High Merit Poems – Grades 7, 8, and 9

This Is a Sad Love Story

This is a very sad love story
This love showed no glory
He liked her and she liked him
But in the end the light was dim
She told him that it was over
What happened to his four leaf clover
She told him that her love was free
But I don't think I can handle thee
She heard his voice
But she had no choice
She told him that night
That there was just no light
She liked it better just as friends
But our relationship had come to its ends
People talk and people stare
But they know it's no longer there
As you can see this will probably be
One of those really sad love stories

Jessica Robertson, Grade 7
Shadow Ridge Middle School, CO

Lead the Way

Walking down the narrow pathway,
With the sun gleaming in my eyes.
My feet slowly moving along,
And the black top steaming underneath.
Feeling like I am going on and on forever,
My thoughts are wandering.
Where was I going?
I had no idea.
So I closed my eyes,
Letting my feet take the lead.

Emma Keefe, Grade 8
Academy Charter School, AK

Pondering Love

As I sit here and ponder what to do,
My mind begins to wonder between me and you,
I still sit and ponder what will I do,
Am I sane? For I still ponder of you.

Adam Felsheim, Grade 9
Coquille High School, OR

A Cold Dark Night*

Lying on the cold hard floor.
Darkness falls, shadows surround me.
I become lost in the cries of others,
my head filled with thoughts and fears.
I try to block out all the emotions,
but I still hear all the cries and prayers of others.
Dark figures walk by.
emotionless faces look down at me.
As I can only wait until it's my turn to be sent off.

Brittany Jorgensen, Grade 7
Eureka Middle School, MT
*Inspired by the Holocaust

Take My Hand

Take my hand lift me up
Take me away from reality
Take me somewhere, where there is no stress,
No bullies, or people who put you down.
Take me away.

CHORUS
Take me away today up to the clouds
Take me away out of the world
Take me away from this reality.
Take me away

Take my hand lead me away from this place I called home
No more fighting for me I am done with it
(Repeat Chorus)

Take my hand and fly away
Take my hand, take my heart and we'll never be apart
Take my hand and love me.
No one could ever take your place
No one could ever see the world the way you do
No one could ever touch the sky the way you do
(Repeat Chorus)

No one could ever touch my heart the way you do.

Hailey Pelroy, Grade 9
Lowell High School, OR

The Sphere and Cube

I see one thing,
He sees the other.
One leaves you solid,
One does another.
The Sphere runs down,
The Cube stays still.
The Sphere never stays,
The Cube lays on a hill.
The Sphere can be fun,
But it is good to stay in place one.
The Sphere is rugged and clean not.
The cube is free of ink blots.
The Sphere is incapable to stop and enjoy,
The Cube stops to find nature's joy.
The Sphere is one,
The Cube is the other.
They represent the traveling one,
And the traveling none.
The Sphere is the traveler,
The Cube is the enjoyer.

Sydney Tipton, Grade 7
Sequoia Village School, AZ

Each Apple Is Unique

Each apple is unique,
With the round solid touch
Divided among detailed slices
Some shiny, speckled, or grimy
Some as golden as the sun,
But each complete,
Each with the juicy sweet taste
All are part of the same family,
Nutritious and pure,
Crunchy and bruised,
Each apple is unique
Carolyn Hofmeister, Grade 9
Xavier College Preparatory School, AZ

Winter

Wind is blowing,
Leaves are flowing,
Winter's almost here,
Winter's really near.

Christmas coming,
Fire humming,
With Santa Claus
And deck the halls.

Kids are sleeping,
Mice are peeping,
Santa Claus is on the way,
Oh, what a lovely day.
Shannon Rowley, Grade 7
Duchesne High School, UT

Mother's Day

A Mother's love determines
How we love ourselves and others.
There is no sky we'll ever see
Not lit by that first love.

Stripped of love, the universe
Would drive us mad with pain;
But we are born into a world
That greets our cries with joy.

How much I owe you for the kiss
That told me who I was!
The greatest gift is a love of life
Laughing in your eyes.

Because of you my world still has
The soft grace of your smile;
And every wind of fortune bears
The scent of your loveliness there.
Kiersten M. Gurule, Grade 9
Intermountain Adventist Academy, CO

America

America the bravest of all
Has never tripped or faulted
The eagle soaring proudly in the sky
Roaring planes ready to fly
Soldiers ready to fight not die
Everyone waiting for America to come
People laugh and play
World peace every day
Friends helping in every way
That's America!!!
Adrian Bogart, Grade 7
Timberview Middle School, CO

War

The war is so bad,
It makes people sad.
Many innocent die,
Making their families sad.
Bullets fly all day,
Killing whatever is in their way.
Some may never be back,
Families lose them without a track.
I hope the war will end soon,
God bless the troops.
Alejandro Andazola, Grade 9
Hinkley High School, CO

Walk with Me, Mommy

Walk alongside with me, mommy
And hold my little hand
I have so many things to learn
That I don't yet understand
Teach me things to keep me safe,
From danger everyday
Show me how to do my best
At home, at school, at play
Every child needs a gentle hand,
To guide them as they grow.
So walk alongside me, mommy,
We have a long way to go.
Melissa Wollman, Grade 7
King Colony School, MT

Melting Snow

Snow-covered field lies forlorn
Leaves and grass poke sword-like
Through the ice and snow.
A weasel emerges dashing across
Ripples of snow.
An icicle, still in the form of water
Flowing down
Is bound to a solitary tree.
Mark Pfeiffer, Grade 7
Reid School, UT

Reign Over Me

Rain down on me
Satisfy my thirst
Rain down your mysterious miracles
Intrigue my mind with wonders
Rain down your roaring fire
Burning in me a deep passion
Rain down your incredible challenges
Force me to reach higher
Rain down your fierce boldness
Teach me to be intrepid and steadfast
Rain down your keen willing spirit
So that I may work hard for others
Rain down your joy
Let it be contagious
Rain down your abundant hope
Let me never be in doubt
Rain down your unconditional love
Always
Reign over my soul
Keep me in your indelible refuge
Jordan Nylander, Grade 8
Komachin Middle School, WA

Believe

When something is in front of you,
But nothing you can see,
You have to put your doubt behind you,
And continuously believe.

People might insult you,
When they don't see what is there.
But don't let temptation come 'bout you,
And doubt the thing that is there.

People might say you're crazy,
People might say you're insane.
But don't let these insults take thee,
For it is a truth that naught be contain'.
Christopher Keihl, Grade 7
Albuquerque Christian School, NM

Monochromatic Winter

Covering Earth
Like an icy net
Ready to capture prey
Without a sound
White has conquered
Vanquishing green once more
Monochromatic
Spring, summer, fall
Forgotten
Frost's frigid touch overwhelms all.
Abby Hawes, Grade 9
Reid School, UT

Windstorm and the Red Hat

Ripping through the tall trees,
I can feel the breeze,
As I walk through the debris,
I will tell you what I see,
The leaves dance in the air,
They move without a care,
Branches sway, this way and that,
And out of nothing I see a red hat,
Gliding so gracefully in the fog,
Then landing on the nearest log,
With a start it again left the ground
Out of nowhere I heard a strange sound,
Like the howl of a wolf,
And the stamp of a horse hoof,
A tree cracked and came a crashing,
It went through smashing,
The red hat below the falling mess,
Well you know the rest,
Flat as a piece of cloth,
As quiet as a moth, the storm and hat are gone.
Gone.

Kylee Woodman, Grade 7
North Bend Jr High School, OR

Moved from Mexico

Moved from the land of rolling hills, desserts, and oceans.
To the land of concrete, street lights, and motion.

Our skin tan, our hair dark, our eyes brown.
Here everyone looks different which makes me feel down.

Life is hard up north.
When you're trying to move on forth.
Where I recite.
Most aren't white.

Moved from the land where my family lives.
To a land where nobody gives.

I had some happy times.
Now here, it's just crimes.

Life is hard up north
When you're trying to move on forth.
Where I recite.
Most aren't white.

That's where I will stay.
I'm never going away.

Ayme Bejarano, Grade 7
Lincoln Jr High School, CO

Game Time

I put on my shirt, my shorts and socks
My mind starts to race
Game time is coming, not a minute to waste
Tic Toc, Tic Toc, seconds pass
Within each second my heart races faster
It's finally time to jog to my spot
My hands start to shake, they start to get clammy
There are girls from my team
There are girls from the other team
The whistle blows, girls begin to run around
The ball moves from foot to foot
It flies in the air, it comes towards me
I start to dribble up the field, I pass it off to a team mate
My nerves are on fire
They start to burn as the game goes on
It's still zero to zero
It's seconds before the final whistle is blown
The ball gets closer and closer to the opponents' goal
Someone takes a shot, swish the ball hits the back of the net
Right after the kick off the whistle is blown
The game is finally over and my nerves go away

Alison Gonzales, Grade 8
Fertitta Middle School, NV

Knight Arthur

The dragon emits fire
Knight Arthur fought brave
But in the end
I was digging his grave

A.J. Salinas, Grade 8
St Anthony of Padua Catholic School, AZ

Kerby Jack

Those big brown eyes and
soft velvety muzzle,
big and bony
but way bigger than a pony,
powerful legs,
and a mane that ripples gaily in the wind.
Kerby Jack is my one and only horse,
half Clydesdale and half Quarter horse.
Why I love him? I don't know,
the first time I saw him is when we just clicked,
he follows me around like a puppy dog.
He is nosy for treats
and has a big temper,
he is the stallion of the herd
or so I wish.
He listens to my problems
and gives his advice
by nudging my shoulder with his head.
Kerby Jack is the best horse
in the whole world,
so you better live with it!

Natalia Robson, Grade 7
21st Century Public Academy, NM

Hidden

Alone, MY soul sits.
My HEART cracks in bits.
I hear loud BEATS of music from below.
I stay quiet FOR you, you know.
I wait forever, to be saved by YOU, and only you.

MY eyes dry.
My HEART can't cry.
I dance to the BEATS of music,
FOR walls of powder blue.
Life is meant for YOU.

MY life is full of waiting.
The HEART ice skating.
Love BEATS alone and scared.
FOR eyes become visually impaired.
I wonder, do YOU sit alone too?

MY eyes are dry.
I see again my mended HEART.
Happiness BEATS in a fresh start.
AGAIN, I see what lies at heart.

Chelsi Lopez, Grade 7
Shadow Ridge Middle School, CO

Love

Love is a giant wave that will swallow you up
Feelings you once could control
Love will set free
A key that will unlock every emotion
Love is a flame that will burn inside
Melting away the ice of your heart
A cure to all hatred
A ray of sunshine in the darkness

Aspin Mecham, Grade 7
Les Bois Jr High School, ID

Skateboarder vs Snowboarder

I am a skateboarder.

I am a snowboarder,

I ride on pavement.

I ride on snow.

It hurts when we fall.
I go to the skate park.

It hurts when we fall.

I go to resorts.

We both go places.
I can kick flip.

We both go places.

I can tail grab.

We can both grind.
I ride in summer.

We can both grind.

I ride in winter.

We both ride.

We both ride.

Roman Beck, Grade 7
Elk Ridge Middle School, UT

Doves

Doves
Always truthful to your partner
Your friendship — the sun
The light never goes out
The flames continue to burn
Always there the next day

The peace between you is a
Waterfall
Always comes down
Never runs out
The most precious sound
Your melody

Your love is roses
Beautiful and relaxing
This rose lasts forever
Petals never fall
The loyalty you have for each other
Is a dog
The anger between you is a dormant volcano
No ashes, no lava, no smoke
Doves

Kiana York, Grade 7
Sky Vista Middle School, CO

Last Race

Everything depends on this last race.
Nothing could mean more,
You could see it on her face.
Plenty of times wasted,
She had walked out the door.

One year has passed,
Yet the race still thrives on inside her head.
The trophies won are still hung,
Even though nothing is said,
For the melody has been sung.

Soon the memories come back,
For the once forgotten that tainted,
Now develops to stay.
She had once painted,
Herself and "it" that wonderful day.

The last race forgotten,
With the end of a winning streak.
She sat upon her bed,
Wishing "it" didn't peak.
Remembering how the last words were said
Because now, the race is dead.

Stephanie Grier, Grade 9
Lake Havasu High School, AZ

Clouds

The clouds are burning in the skies.
They float and fly in front of my eyes.
What do you hide clouds,
surrounding the mountains.
Above you I am in wonder.
A clean white on a sea of blue.
A cloud, like a mountain in the sky.
I see your wispy fingers stretching out to fly.
The clouds sleeping high in the sky.
Do you see it when the clouds sweep low?
A soft white that looks like snow.

Chase Dimsha, Grade 7
Lone Rock School, MT

I Believe

I believe in honesty
The respect of not lying
The courage of telling the truth
The dirtiness of lying
Respect, strength, caring
But I don't believe in swearing
I believe in good sayings
I believe in thoughts
I believe in the responsibility of saying honest things
Courage, strength, honesty
And I believe in the fact that you shouldn't lie to get
Yourself out of something you have done wrong.

Anna Fredrickson, Grade 7
Terry 7-8 School, MT

My Childhood

Childhood is the most carefree time
Fighting my brother for a toy that's mine
Watching Jurassic Park for the one-hundredth time
Memorizing the movie line for line
Eating my Cinnabon at the kitchen table
Under my covers reading a fable

Running around the house and acting crazy
Sleeping in late because I'm lazy
Molding Play-Doh with my brother
Being chased in the grass by my mother

Riding my bike outside on a rainy day
Disobeying what my dad would say
Me and my brother running around
Climbing on trees that we found

Listening to my brother whine
Going to Duke's where we would dine
Riding horses at the stable
Watching Saturday cartoons on cable
Playing at Discovery Zone as much as I was able
My childhood was truly like a remarkable fable

Ashton Durbin, Grade 9
Tempe Preparatory Academy, AZ

Love

Love is great and awesome
It comes from your heart,
Not who you love
No matter ugly or cute
It's all about your feelings
Angry or happy you wish
That love can never end.

Every moment of life depends on love
What is love?
It's a funny question for you
But when you think about what it is
Love is happiness
And joy until you get hurt.

Then when love passes away
Hate moves in
What made you hate was terrible
Hate, betrayal, untrustworthy
Was the main key.

Hate or love is always there
Re-trust and forgiveness
Now everything is loved and hate is once gone.

Karen Nguyen, Grade 7
Shadow Ridge Middle School, CO

Soccer

Soccer is my favorite sport
It is fun
To play with friends and teammates
Under the hot, hot sun
The ball is a pinball being passed back and forth
A beautiful shot
And the amazing sound of the swish
When the ball hits the back of the net
The fields is as green as a John Deere
The ball black and white like a Dalmatian
I love to hear the scream of the crowds
That is as loud as a booming firecracker
The gifted, talented players
Work very hard
Trying to win
Hoping they don't foul or get a card
The whistling of the wind
And the beating of the rain
Make it hard to play
But when it is nice weather
Soccer is very fun

Matt De Groot, Grade 8
Sunnyside Christian Elementary School, WA

Who Do You Think I Am
am I the kid who sits behind you,
or the one who sits in front
am I the kid who is short,
or do I seem tall to you
am I the kid with long straight hair,
or is my hair wavy like yours
am I the kid who wears stylish clothes,
or do you hate my style
am I the kid that is fit and toned,
or do I weigh much more than you
am I the kid who is beautiful and all the kids like,
or do my looks make you cringe your toes
when I say I do not care what you see
you will begin to wonder why
it is all because I am more than you can see with eyes

Katelin Bartles, Grade 8
Lewis and Clark Middle School, ID

That Boy
Yes, he's a little weird,
But he's got me wrapped around his finger.
When he's around,
I just seem to linger.

He says he loves me,
But he's hard to believe.
When I look into his eyes,
He makes my heart unweave.

My heart desires him,
But my mind says no.
There's something about that boy,
That makes my heart glow.

Why he plays games,
It will never be explained.
Hopefully one of these days,
My heart will be tamed.

Shelby Marra, Grade 8
La Plata Middle School, NM

Forgiveness
When I thought everything is doing good,
another one comes and ruins it all;
One little thing can change every small mood,
we both get mad then our feelings just fall.
One tires to forgive the other for this,
while he cries and begs for her forgiveness;
"How can I not see, how can I miss?"
tried to act cool about it until he confesses;
Getting hurt every time I hear all these,
what's done is done, but this is just a mess.
Come to think of it, it's also my fault,
for not giving him all his needs and rights;
Us calming down is better than assault,
understanding is needed before fights.

Anne Sanchez, Grade 9
Clark High School, NV

Weather
Icy raindrops, brush my skin,
it wakes me up, I drink it in
I stand up strong, as downpour falls
a top this dreary mountain,
and as I draw close, to the ledge,
the winds mutter answers in my ear,
but quickly thunder does appear,
and scolds me for my stupid questions,
and the lightning does suggest,
that ignorance may be the best,
Antidote for my rebellion,

but I stand strong upon my ridge
Oblivious to the dangers that surround me
I let my winds rage all around me

And in my safe tempest I plot and plan
these silent hopes that have never bloomed before,
and in my heart I must admit, that I shall never ever quit
fighting for the dreams I've dreamt before.

Kelsey Bryant, Grade 9
Cedar Ridge Academy, UT

The Nightmare
Deep in the night,
Comes a dark blight.
It calls you, it calls you,
And fills you with fright.
Into the dream.
Without hope it may seem.
It grabs you, it grabs you.
Terrified, you scream.
Down in the dark,
Fear leaves its mark.
It holds you, it holds you.
With hands cold and stark.
It wants you to die;
You let out a cry.
It swallows you, it swallows you.
All goes black, by and by.
Suddenly, you've woken,
Just as dawn has broken.
It warms you, it warms you.
The nightmare? Revoken.

Miriam Johnson, Grade 7
Heritage Middle School, ID

Index

Aalbers, Remington 373
Abuliel, Ahdriana 184
Acevedo, Victoria 219
Ackling, Taylor 258
Acosta, Jonathon 355
Adams, Emily 210
Adams, Holly 263
Adams, Jakob 296
Adent, Kelsey 80
Afoa, Sierra 377
Agate, Brittany 387
Aggarwal, Rohit 93
Agron, Kimberly 317
Aguero, Korinne 260
Aguilar, Jose Luis 374
Aguilar, Viviana 365
Aguirre, Ilse 344
Aguirre, Marissa 197
Akers, Lucy 35
Akre, Kelsie 133
Alam, Taosif 129
Alden, Jonathan 165
Alder, Kristin 112
Aldous, Jed 111
Allan, Kimmy 311
Allen, Dominic 221
Allen, Hayley 159
Allen, Michelle 303
Alley, Liz .45
Allred, Anne 123
Allred, Tiffani 113
Almanzor, Mara 285
Altaha, Tewana 369
Altmiller, Justin 301
Alvarez, Vivian 350
Ambrose, Shelby 298
Ammons-McCarron, Brinna 293
Amodemo, Amanda 156
Andazola, Alejandro 396
Anderle, Emylee 227
Anderson, Amber 55
Anderson, Ariel 52
Anderson, Cassie 249
Anderson, Emma 286
Anderson, Grace 320
Anderson, Jacob 316
Anderson, Jalisa 93
Anderson, Kayla 60
Anderson, Lauren 122
Anderson, Sara 295
Anderson, Wyatt 157

Andrade, Daniel 163
Andreasen, Jordan 163
Andrew, Alicia 162
Andrews, Michael 44
Angarola, Christina 227
Angulo, Ivonne 22
Anhold, Alisa 343
Anthony, Paige 146
Apodaca, Destyni 352
Aranda, Jon-Mikal 170
Aranda, Leticia 388
Arbuckle, Alyssa 301
Archer-Hostetler, Lisa 380
Archibeque, Michael 353
Archuleta, Anisa Ann 291
Archuleta, Greg 335
Arguello, Karina 174
Arkulari, Amanda 113
Arnold, Jayce 264
Arredondo, Christian 227
Artale, Josh 35
Artman, Kayla 225
Ashbaugh, Camille 378
Ashby, Cheyanne 148
Ashby, Paul 338
Ashcroft, Dallen 352
Askey, Brooke Ellyn 47
Asztalos, Zoe 279
Atchley, Amber 393
Atkinson, Kai Olivia 106
Atwood, Tara 276
Austin, Don'Jhanae 254
Avila, Anthony 195
Avila, Brittnie 321
Avila, Clarissa 322
Avila, Isaiah 388
Avila, Megan 150
B., Carli .69
B., Erika 297
Babcock, Shannon 202
Babilonia, Silas 304
Baca, Missy 95
Bacon, Jessica 336
Badiola, Lorenzo 264
Bagha, Shanti D. 382
Bailey, Lauren 363
Bailey, Lauren 377
Bain, Madeline 117
Bakel, Kaleb 255
Baker, Chelsea 311
Baker, Donald 79

Baker, Kandice 329
Baker, Katrina 296
Baker, Matthew 127
Baker, Maureen 347
Baker, Rachel L. 380
Baker, Sierra 29
Bakken, Danny 241
Balchunas, Emily 30
Baldwin, Hannah 266
Ballard, Mandy 269
Ballard, Sadee 259
Banda-Torres, Jenifer 196
Banuelos, Mayra 121
Bañuelos, Samantha 213
Barber, Aquaila 302
Barfuss, Chris 109
Barik, Alisha 178
Barker, James 368
Barkis, Ray 329
Barksdale, Kelsey 384
Barlow, Andrew 356
Barnes, Samantha 316
Barnett, Rose 102
Barney, Brevin 268
Barney, Jackie 94
Barney, Jackson 299
Barringer, Spencer 196
Barrio, Joseph 164
Barry, Hannah 348
Bartholomew, Brianna 256
Bartles, Katelin 400
Barton, Hannah 185
Barzee, Chelsea 250
Basey, Nola 196
Basha, Scott 85
Bates, Kylee 372
Baudek, Natasha 75
Bauer, Erin 331
Bautista, Janice 247
Baxter, Catherine 352
Bayhan, Lizzi 89
Beagles, Amy 164
Beard, Breanna 55
Beck, Ashley 87
Beck, Brady 68
beck, cade 327
Beck, Roman 398
Beckner, Berit 262
Beckstead, Stacee 119
Beckwith, Sydney 151
Beene, Kayla 295

Beeten, Brandie 149	Bonham, Heidi 382	Burdi, Josh 166
Begay, Ashleigh 44	Bonstein, Katie 393	Burge, Heather 128
Begaye, Daisha 173	Boonstra, Jayme 380	Burk, Nathan 326
Bejarano, Ayme 397	Booth, Josiah 172	Burkett, Samantha 240
Bellamy, Alyssa 176	Booton, Eric 97	Burns, Wade 62
Bemis, Christa 91	Borneman, Abigail Joy 213	Busby, Alexa 253
Benavente, Ryan 284	Borré, Brittany 239	Busse, Michael 193
Bencomo, Ashley 156	Boshes, Lindsey 253	Bustamante, Kurissa 336
Bencomo, Nestor 154	Bosman, Chantl 78	Butler, Coltan 253
Benedetti-Peters, Mailee 223	Bottlemy, Parker 270	Butler, Corey 120
Bennett, Danielle 219	Botts, Micheala 194	Buttram, Derek 287
Bennett, Max 173	Boucher, Ryan 214	Byers, Jules 336
Bennetts, Natasha 103	Bower, Lauren 44	Bylbie, Tyler 221
Benningfield, Ashley 22	Bowker, Shara 48	Byrum, Brittany 226
Benton, Emily 329	Bowles, Garrett 58	C. J., Chie 92
Benton, Leon 77	Boyce, Jackie 274	Caballero, Rosie 278
Berglund, Jamee 58	Boyer, Melissa 341	Cain, Alesha 227
Berglund, Samantha 69	Boyett, Wesley 283	Calhoun, Dar-Ci 130
Bermudez, Carlos 302	Bradford, Ashley 212	Callahan, Meghan 86
Bernal, Mark 161	Brand, Anelle 369	Callaway, James 252
Bernards, Tyler 316	Brandner, Chelsea 88	Callsen, Amanda 53
Berndsen, Jessie 346	Brantley, Jordan 84	Calvelli, Alexander 179
Beronilla, Nadija 74	Brantner, Aryssa 324	Calvi, Chase 130
Berry, Caitlyn 217	Brazil, Daniel 267	Calzavara, Casie 114
Berry, Mitch 226	Breedlove, Hope 50	Campbell, Shannon 127
Best, Leah 355	Brehon, Mary 165	Campbell, Vincent 201
Bettinson, Heather 120	Breisblatt, Faith 78	Campos, Emily 309
Betts, Stephen 276	Brichacek, Harlan 218	Campos, Katherine 56
Beul, Jasmine 303	Bridge, EJ 316	Cannon, Jamie 218
Bevilacqua, Melissa 321	Brito, Ricky 296	Cano, Lluvia 186
Beville, Samantha 94	Broberg, Kristy 79	Cardona, Alexis 276
Bigler, Lauren 316	Brocco, Katrina 39	Carlile, Scott 27
Bilodeau, Vanessa 328	Brodie, Adam 232	Carlson, Sierra 165
Binetti, Cynthia 246	Broersma, Brandon 339	Carmen, Maitreya 346
Bingham, Randy Lynn 65	Broersma, Marisa 150	Carnahan, Pat 38
Bingham, Tiffany 38	Brouwer, Alex 160	Carpenter, Ashley 170
Birch, Wesley 205	Browitt, Devon 290	Carpenter, Matt 69
Bird, Kailey 215	Brown, Jeremy 24	Carrero, Charlene 279
Bisch, Shanta 54	Brown, Kelsey 122	Carrier, Tatiana 245
Bishop, Dillon 125	Brown, Libby 32	Carsten, Kayla 70
Black, Everett 71	Brown, Sarah 84	Cartwright, Juli 257
Blackburn, Shelby 205	Brozovich, Mason 385	Casados, Aaron 298
Blaine, Heather 342	Bruce, Jasmine 89	Casap, Elaine Mahoney 203
Blanchard, Chelsea 158	Bruckner, Megan 12	Casias, Kasey 391
Bland, Kimberly 55	Bruggeman, Corey 389	Casimier, Kristen Jean 114
Blasdel, Lytaunie 105	Bruni, Jennifer 160	Castillo, Emmanuel 323
Bliek, Ashlee 53	Brunner, Becca 336	Castor, Rose 119
Block, Lindsay 327	Brunsdale, Sarah 269	Cattaneo, Deryn 239
Bloom, Elisabeth 136	Bryant, Kelsey 400	Cattelino, Brianna 394
Bloomingdale, Kristin 268	Bryant, Trey 263	Caylor, Ryan 345
Blundell, Kyle 195	Bryant, Zack 88	Cecil, Kylie 294
Bobak, Skyler 376	Bublitz, Jakob 307	Celis, Javier 282
Bobo, Lauren 249	Buck, Jacob 258	Cervantes, Ignacio 105
Boehm-Reifenkugel, Gem 286	Bull, Amanda 243	Cervantes, Lucia 388
Bogart, Adrian 396	Bullock, Samantha 333	Chaffee, Sarah 115
Bolton, Gabe 231	Bunts, Tori 194	Chai, Shung 247
Bonertz, Wyatt 389	Burch, Ashly 28	Chambers, Samantha 371

Index

Chan, Doris 312
Chapnick, Amanda 152
Charlie, Calandra 265
Chatterton, Joseph Demar 92
Chaudoin, Alexandrea Rae 34
Chavez, Daniel 186
Chavez, Demi 329
Chavez, Gracie 169
Chavez, Mikaila 207
Chavez, Rebekah 223
Chavez, Satarra S. 359
Chavira-Nieto, Pablo 156
Chidester, Michael 294
Christensen, Alexandra 154
Christensen, Brenna 148
Christensen, Cayla 186
Christensen, Jamie 295
Christensen, Jessica Dawn 29
Christensen, Joshua 58
Christensen, Mackenzi 373
Christensen, Miranda 187
Christensen, Rachel 328
Christenson, Mikayla 325
Christiansen, Julie 255
Christianson, Jamie Kay 68
Chu, Tiffanie 321
Chung, Billy 337
Chung-Hoon, Lauren 28
Church, Austin 82
Church, Katie 336
Cibicki, Alina 182
Cirila, Maricruz 328
Clappisi, Lauren 303
Claric, Rachel 97
Clark, Chyanne 31
Clark, Corinne 53
Clark, James 62
Clayton, Austin 126
Cleary, Charlotte 52
Clement, Brennan 340
Cline, Shelby 93
Coca, Amber 321
Cocchiola, Emily 175
Coffman, Alex 385
Cohen, Allison 370
Coil, Britany 306
Cole, Brianna 308
Collings, Kira 344
Collins, Doug 37
Collinson, Kaylee 113
Composanto, Jacque 387
Compton, Briana 362
Conklin, Abigail 379
Connell, Jordan 185
Conner, Barbara 353
Conover, Hailie 328
Constable, Jennifer 358

Cook, Brody 180
Cook, Trevor 274
Cooper, Hunter 386
Cooper, Ryan 356
Cooper, Sydney 212
Copeland, Nicole 364
Corder, Brittany 25
Cordero, Noemi 222
Cordier, Madeline 206
Corral, Jasmin 177
Correa, Miranda 218
Correll, Kourtney 232
Corson, Robert 31
Cortes, Alex 109
Cortez, Alexis 362
Cotter, Megan 189
Cottrell, Cody 237
Counce, Josh 27
Courkamp, Hannah 304
Court, Preston 244
Covington, Mary 319
Cox, Kim 100
Cox, Makala 285
Cox, Tanner 174
Cozzie, Jonathan H. 114
Craig, Kaitlyn 118
Craig, Kelsie 119
Cramer, Maddie 151
Crawford, Ellis 13
Croissant, Sallie 250
Cruz, Taralyn 157
Cruz, Tina 63
Cuellar, Isis 272
Cueto, Jose 212
Culmer, Jessica 356
Culp, Andrew 281
Culwell, Dylan 191
Cunningham, Kahner 291
Curson, Danielle 102
Curtis, Coleton 277
Curtis, Victoria 217
Cuthbertson, Ashlie 146
D., Katie 155
Dahl, Laura 385
Dahlhauser, Hayley 289
Dahms, Jesse 377
Dain, Aundraya 199
Dalley, Stacy 275
Dalrymple, Rita 187
Dameron, Lauren 85
Damge, Olivia 283
Daniel, Diego 378
Daniels, Emily 119
Dao, Taylor 215
Darst, Sarah 221
Daugherty, Brian 258
Davick, Ashley 50

Davis, Cerina 38
Davis, Temperance 111
Davis, Tori 44
Dawlatzai, Safiya 146
Day, Celina 239
De Groot, Danika 191
De Groot, Matt 399
De La Cruz, Evelyn 336
De Money Gross, Brychan 204
Deaver, Megan 346
DeBarge, Katherine Mae 146
DeBolt, Sophie 330
Debowski, Devin A. 166
DeCent, Sadie 157
deDecker, Tanys 297
Deleon, Ezekiel 230
Deleon, Molly 80
DeLeon, Ralph 193
DeLude, Alexis 370
Demaniow, Quianna 280
DeMaster, Nicole 44
Den Hoed, Kara L. 265
Dennis, Paulina 237
Derks, Alysa 153
Derrera, Marcus 309
Dervin, Emily 64
Despain, Jack 165
Despain, Peter 358
Devati, Architha 372
Diamond, Brad 73
Dietrich, Joshua R. 67
Diltz, Michael P. 223
Dimsha, Chase 399
Dinsmoor, Chelsea 27
Diraviam Kannan, Sarmishta 262
Dixon, Savannah 225
Dodsworth, Treavor 74
Doiron, Andrew 238
Domingo, Jovena 371
Dominguez, Tessie 257
Donnelly, Shannon 159
Doroteo, Laura 285
Douglas, Savannah 269
Douglass, Jackson 207
Downs, Kyle 206
Dozsak, Chelsea 254
Driesen, Ricky 327
Driggers, Katelyn 173
Drott, Angel 37
Drouin, Jessica 386
Drumright, Breanna 334
Dufowe, Irene Allen 313
Duggan, Katelyn 220
Duncan, Torri 240
Dunham, Kaitlin 315
Dunn, Allyssa 200
Dunn, Ashley 214

Dunn, JaLene 100	Fenton, Kylie 83	Fructueux-Bocco, Charmaine 169
Dunnavan, Jacqueline 312	Ferguson, Bailley 211	Fry, Alan 338
Duong, Tung 102	Fernandez-Fisher, Jordan 174	Fuchs, Kyrie 271
Dupree, Tatyana 326	Ferran, DJ 210	Fuentes, Jacqueline 277
Duran, Marina 163	Ferree, August R. 334	Fulford, Michelle 351
Durbin, Ashton 399	Fetzer, Jecelle 331	Fuller, Ashley 156
Duresky, Nikki 260	Fields, Casey 37	Fuller, Chet 54
Dust, Lilly 311	Fierro, Graciela 158	Fumagalli, David 367
Dye, Jake 45	Figueroa, Cecilia 281	Furgeson, Braeden 115
Dykema, Arbor 204	Figurniak, Agata 368	G., Arnetia 22
Dykes, Donovan 213	Fimbres, Alyssa 365	G., Erica 75
Earle, Alisha 361	Finkbeiner, Jen 357	G., Nicole 25
Earley, Sean 236	Finn, Joseph 316	Gaba, Priyanka 256
Eayrs, Paul 165	Fiori, Ellen 204	Gaffney, Trevor 170
Ebert, Ryan 205	Fischer, Allie 266	Gage, Jesse 245
Edmund, Cassandra 174	Fischer, Matthew 361	Gailey, Anna 57
Edwards, Brandon 85	Fisher, Jordan 34	Gallegos, Angela 215
Edwards, Phillip 330	Fite, Ashley 95	Gallegos, Jacob 81
Edwards, Reid 235	Fjerstad, Ben 77	Gallegos, Paul 346
Egging, Rachel 250	Flagg, Erin 245	Gallegos, Sandra 234
Eiffert, Jessica 106	Fletcher, Chelsea 290	Galloway, Kayla 366
Eimers, Megan 61	Fletcher, Nathan 226	Galvez, Efrain 309
Eklund, Hans 296	Flood, Nicole 68	Gaona, Stephanie 194
Elias, Erica 273	Florence, Audrey 314	Garcia, Brett 130
Elizarraras, Claire 392	Florence, Kiera 364	Garcia, Bryce 260
Elledge, SaLena 389	Flores, Christina 197	Garcia, Demi 214
Ellis, John "Miles" 334	Flores, Ingraid 25	Garcia, Gabby 212
Ellison, Tanner 203	Florez, Jasmine 386	Garcia, Kayla 206
Emery, Keenan 165	Florio, Shannon 226	Garcia, Michael 363
England, Chris 222	Floyd, Jacqueline 31	Gardea, Troy 311
Engle, Kelsey 175	Floyd, Kara 133	Garner, Brianna 244
Engstrom, Terani 349	Fobia, Haley 339	Garrett, Tracy 341
Erhart, Christy 94	Fontaine, Jessica 237	Garrison, Adam 232
Esparza, Chris 30	Fontanez, Kathryn 40	Gearhart, John 209
Estadilla, Shaina 22	Forcella, Tyler 252	Gee, Heather 33
Estevan, Felecia 332	Fornelli, Bryan 356	Gee, Levia 312
Estrada, Julie 33	Foster, Emily S. 39	Gemberling, Tess 22
Estrellado, Alayshia 147	Foster, Mitchell 123	Gerdes, Caleb 284
Evangelista, Arjayne 126	Fournier, Kyle 117	German, Alexis 363
Evans, Becca 83	Fowler, Jenaya 241	Gettman, Lydia 126
Evans, Corrie 345	Fowler, Michelle 229	Gianniny, Cori 302
Evans, Kapri 281	Fox, Marissa June 384	Gibbins, Sammi Jo 199
Evans, Kellie 42	Foxlee, Cullyn 128	Gibbons, Cody 294
Eyre, Daniel 34	Fraley, Tara 49	Giesbrecht, Gabrielle 190
Faber, Stephanie 126	Francis, Tori 30	Gil, Julie 54
Falgout, Zack 37	Francisco, Sarah 241	Gilbreath, Rachel 333
Falk, Emily 231	Franck, Kelly 231	Gill, Justina 282
Fanelli-Poole, Nicco 372	Franke, Cheyanne 195	Gillard, Dustin 236
Faraco-Hadlock, Anthony 388	Fredrickson, Anna 399	Gima, Rachel 344
Farmer, Tessa 84	Free, Rachel 381	Giorgi, Kara 201
Farquhar, Nick 183	Freeman, Ray 70	Givens, Shayla 276
Fasel, Christopher J. 112	Frei, Megan 314	Gleason, Mollee 306
Feather, Ashleigh 267	Frerichs, Phoebe 322	Glocker, Sabine 304
Fedchun, Nadia 213	Frisby, Chelsea 313	Goin, Timothy 52
Feller, Janelle 332	Fritz, Hannah 93	Gomez, Andria 309
Felsheim, Adam 395	Fritz, Kyle 361	Gonder, Abigail 202
Fenstermaker, Jessica 320	Frost, Kelsey 377	Gongora, Jennifer 338

Index

Gonzales, Alison 397
Gonzales, Austin 172
Gonzales, Bryan 277
Gonzales, Josh 352
Gonzalez, Cintia 265
Gonzalez, Diana 158
Gonzalez, Jairo 215
Goodenow, Zachary 291
Goodman, Dallin 369
Goodman, Dani 380
Goodro, Pyper 291
Goodrum, Emily 297
Goodson, Mekenzie 304
Goodwin, Jamie 230
Goodwin, Kachine 151
Goody, Madisson 217
Gordon, Zoah 391
Gorkovchenko, Angelina 220
Gottfredson, Jason 273
Goughnour, Daniel 226
Gould, Ryan 345
Grabow, Vance 202
Graham, Haley 375
Graham, Maggie 217
Graham Feldman, Christian 266
Grant, Kristen Amy 183
Gray, Lindsay 343
Green, Brandon 176
Green, Tyonna 224
Greenhalgh, Erin 14
Greenwaldt, Lindsey 339
Greer, Riley 298
Greulich, Johnny 188
Greybull, Mallory 279
Grier, Stephanie 398
Griffith, Brian 354
Griffor, Larkin 297
Griggs, Chelsea 62
Grill, Chanel 123
Grim, Hannah 355
Grimm, Taylor 200
Groninger, Alli 359
Gross, Alan 304
Grubb, Brian 330
Gubka, Steven 110
Gulliksen, Steve 272
Gurule, Kiersten M. 396
Gustin, Gentry 51
Guthrie, Connor 149
Gutierrez, Alicia 306
Gutierrez, Britney 338
Gutierrez, Marc 390
Gutierrez, Rhett 327
Gutkosky, Kelby 171
Guyton, Shantell 221
Guzman, Cindy 225
H., Amber 60
H., Rhonda 59
Haas, Bree 303
Haasl, Heather 234
Hackworth, Samantha 180
Hadd, Emily 315
Hadley, Sara 116
Hager, Carrie 71
Hahn, Kaylie 148
Hahn, Rachelle 203
Hale, Jessica 287
Hale, Shianne 272
Hall, Christopher T. 56
Hall, Eva 243
Hall, Magin 359
Hall, Nathan 287
Hallada, Liam 267
Ham, Aubrey 148
Hamblin, Emily Blake 196
Hamblin, Rex 242
Hamilton, Cassie 252
Hamilton, Simone 122
Hance, Caleb 153
Hancock, Callie 82
Handy, Stephanie 232
Haner, Annatje M. 242
Hanke, Amanda 72
Hankins, Natalia 238
Hanley, Amber 172
Hanover, Andrew 366
Hansen, Andrew 157
Hansen, Jade 378
Hansen, Michelle 105
Hansing, Erica 302
Hanslovan, Jordan 324
Hanson, Chase 108
Hanson, Dillon 380
Hanytskyy, Denys 355
Harbert, Jessica 314
Harding, Alisha 374
Hardison, Titus 149
Hardwick, Bryan 385
Hardy, McKenzie 310
Hardy-Gonzales, Tiffany 331
Harju, Christie 155
Harlan, Michael 346
Harlow, Casey 261
Harmon, Ashley 169
Haros, Dulce 189
Harper, Joshua David 113
Harris, Amanda 353
Harris, Kaelina 344
Harris, Reyna 183
Harrison, Adrianna 279
Hart, Heather 80
Harvey, Devon 250
Hatch, Riley 155
Hatch, Sarah 207
Hawes, Abby 396
Hawkins, Jenna 99
Hawkins, Jessica 383
Hawkinson, Lane 189
Hawley, Alaina 234
Hayes, Kristine 333
Hays, Jacob 296
Hays, Mariah 179
Hayward, Michael 185
Haywood, Sami 35
He, Jing 255
Head, Makenzie 251
Heath, Patrick 131
Heber, Cali 247
Heitman, Andrew 356
Helgesen, Becky 326
Hemphill, Josh 23
Henley, Maggie 79
Henrich, Angela 199
Henry, Andy 254
Henry, Brittany 270
Henry, Lacy 211
Henry-Brown, Ali 103
Henson, Danni 210
Hepworth, Ricky 129
Her, Kaxee 210
Herbert, Amber 281
Hermida, Arianne 381
Hernandez, Alejandra 223
Hernandez, Bethany 188
Hernández, Jazmine 277
Hernandez, Laura 383
Hernandez, Manuel 104
Hernandez, Martin 32
Hernandez, Scarlett 344
Herrera, Andrea 162
Herrera, Anna 129
Herring, Tyler 181
Hesler, Roshell 344
Heupel, Heather 360
Heyrend, Sydney 292
Hibbert, Jessica 173
Hickey, Ronald 257
Hicks, Althea 379
Hicks, Donavan 108
Higbee, Alexa 221
Hill, Crissy 228
Hill, Lisa 101
Hill, Shania 238
Hill, Thomas 388
Hills, Emily 77
Hilton, Davis 179
Hindeyeh, Saphiya 103
Hines, Andrew 299
Hines, Ashley 86
Hoang, Tony 252
Hobbs, Koltyn Robert 45

Hodge, Maggie 335	Ikeda, Greg 80	Jones, Julian 36
Hoefft, Kourtenay 187	Illingworth, Luis 97	Jones, Larisa 188
Hofer, Lori 336	Inscoe, Alex 290	Jones, Melissa 96
Hoffman, Ashlyn 249	Irons, Davion 212	Jones, Natalie 137
Hofmeister, Carolyn 396	Ivey, Austin 210	Jones, Scott 74
Hokanson, Bethanie 196	Jackoski, Matthew 353	Jones, Shannon 242
Holbert, Connor 244	Jackson, Gillian 162	Jones, Shyla 372
Holbrook, Jadan 59	Jackson, Nathan 276	Jones, Sinjin 92
Holik, Cody 305	Jacobs, Kyle 39	Jones, Tiffany 260
Holland, Kyrsten 83	Jacobsen, Brittany 276	Jorgensen, Brittany 395
Holland, Laura 68	Jacoby, Hannah 311	Joslin, Shaylee A. 15
Hollingsworth, Clyressa 274	Jaeamillo, Janae 255	Judd, Cynthia 275
Hollingsworth, Emily 130	Jaehning, Meijiao 112	Judkins, Chelcee 101
Holloway, Mason 220	Jahanpour-Burke, Julia 202	Jueschke, J. 88
Holm, Kayloni 199	Jaime, Dulce 304	Julious, Kimani 161
Holstein, Nicole 29	Jaimes, Perla 384	Kaliszewski, Kyle 86
Homann, Elsa 286	James, Emma 182	Kamas, Katherine 169
Honeycutt, Samuel 261	Jamison, Lorrin 171	Kampfe, Brian 197
Hook, Ashley 350	Janke, Marisa 153	Karas, Hanna 229
Hook, Jennifer 94	Jankowski, Nick 24	Karcher, Tyler 352
Hook, Tyler 172	Janus, Caricia 125	Karr, Dylan 164
Hoops, Nicole 47	Jaramillo, Ashley 80	Karratti, Keenan 116
Hoppe, Wil 190	Jargalsaikhan, Namuun 148	Kasch, Ryan 208
Horne, Ashley 224	Jarvis, Jordan 156	Kassem, Rehab 26
Horton, Adam 381	Jay, Rachel 23	Katz, Alex 224
Horton, Larissa 126	Jayne, Seth 332	Kau, Linsey 75
Hoshiko, Trenton 191	Jednat, Angela 321	Kauffman, Kaylee 232
Hosler, Cody 105	Jenkins, Makelle 211	Kecherson, Kelsey 39
Houghtaling, Kyle 100	Jensen, Annie 216	Kee, Matthew 203
Housley, Billy 309	Jensen, Clarissa 67	Keefe, Emma 395
Howard, Celicia 160	Jensen, Cynthia 105	Keihl, Christopher 396
Howard, Landon 353	Jensen, Elspeth 290	Keiki, Crystal 67
Hruby, Kate 310	Jensen, Lisa 171	Keith, JT .85
Huang, Kaixi 152	Jerome, Amelia 238	Kelkenberg, Amelia 394
Hubbert, DJ 313	Jerome, Caitlin 96	Keller, Natalie 362
Hubert, Alexa 153	Jimenez, Cristian 172	Kelley, Joshua 32
Huckabay, Cody 196	Johnson, Alexis 187	Kelton, Dallas 248
Huey, Stephen 120	Johnson, Ben 28	Kennedy, Tyler 82
Hughes, Shelby 239	Johnson, Brianna 161	Kenney, Patrick 177
Hugill, Kaeleigh 221	Johnson, Brianna 388	Kerschner, Laura 26
Hull, Celie 268	Johnson, Cody 372	Kessler, Anna Monika 73
Hulse, Aerica 98	Johnson, Cory 274	Kettles, Elizabeth Jane 323
Hulsey, Elise 222	Johnson, Heather Elise 121	Keyshae, Madison 301
Hultz, Amanda R. 394	Johnson, Julie 73	Kibel, Jesse 193
Humphreys, Breanne 186	Johnson, KC 244	Kiel, Macy 333
Hunkele, Katie 107	Johnson, Kole 49	Kielbasa, Kylie 202
Hunsaker, Zachary 37	Johnson, Miriam 400	Kieler, Ciera 343
Hunt, Izy 319	Johnson, Olajuwan 156	Kieling, Chris 112
Huntsman, Adam 272	Johnson, Peyton 357	Kight, Haley 159
Huntsman, Hayley 259	Johnson, Sydnee 175	Kilkenny, Shantel 216
Huntsman, Keegan 24	Jones, Abbigail 185	Kim, Yuri 181
Hurd, Mike 33	Jones, Amy 273	King, Ashley 237
Hurlburt, Aurora 325	Jones, Ashlee 74	King, Ben 261
Hutchinson, Nicholas 224	Jones, Breann 56	King, Harley 312
Huynh, Jenni 32	Jones, Courtney 342	King, Parker 172
Ige, Jayson 167	Jones, Hannah 109	King, Sarah 204
Iglinski, Arissa 351	Jones, Jordan 328	King, Stephanie 23

Index

Kingeekuk, Darcie 26
Kinsey, Emily 157
Kipp, Munro C. 388
Kirkpatrick, Natalie 376
Kirn, Jessica 172
Kirsch, Alyssa 393
Kirscher, Maggie 138
Kitchens, Kaitlin Marie 163
Klager, Hannah 382
Klas, Mikayla 308
Kleinman, Andri 217
Klukkert, Wesley 72
Knights, Kayla 350
Knoshaug, Bethany 66
Knowles, Gregory 229
Knowles, Perry 212
Knowlton, Jodie 177
Knox, Kelsey 293
Knudsen, Tayler 241
Koerth, Kim 373
Kohagen, Victoria 317
Kokojan, Sapphire 118
Konig, Kayla 61
Koontz, Mariah 106
Kortan, Emily 251
Kosydar, Lauren 185
Kovac, Danielle 194
Kraus, Jessa 325
Kroeger, Ashley 167
Kroeger, Rachael 259
Krollpfeiffer, Cody 268
Krueger, Matthew 310
Kumferman, Elise 49
Kuntz, Morgan 180
Kuo, Anita 193
Kurns, Brandon 316
LaBonde, Sarah 273
LaBonville, Tracy 124
Labra, Eric 241
Lackey, Grace 375
Laliberte, Nicole 386
Lallatin, Audrey 40
Lam, Dam 93
Lam, Mathia 232
Lam, Stephanie 374
Laman, Lanette 372
Lamb, Eryn 222
LaMont, Maddi 98
Landin, Roxanne 184
Landis, Zach 127
Lane, Frankie 293
Lane, Will 287
Lang, André 243
Lang, Maia 229
Langham, Michelle 23
Lanier, Renee 64
Laning, Courtney 299
Laos, Olivia 334
Lara, Jessica 350
Larios, Paulina 39
LaRose, Timothy 80
Larsen, Alysa 103
Larsen, Crystal 348
Larsen, Shay Christine 261
Larson, Nikki 117
Larson, Summer 109
Lash, Eric 232
Latta, Anton 264
Laveway, Katherine 201
Lawlor, Samantha 237
Lawrence, Mackenzie 164
Lawrenz, Bryon 49
Laywell, Kayla 295
Leaf, Rebecca 344
Ledall, Aimee 172
Ledezma, Christy 87
LeDuff, Alina 199
Lee, Grace 226
Lee, Kierra 75
Lee, Marilyn 76
Lee, Miranda 383
Lee, Timmy 342
Leeuwenburgh, Maitreya 188
Leiba, Shelby 296
Leising, Shelby 45
Leithead, Teresa 304
LeLusche, Andrew 48
Leman, Ryan 349
Lemley, Garrick 234
LeMon, Zachary 362
Lenahan, Kristen 386
Lenz, David 177
Lenz, Jasmine 382
Leonard, Erin 122
Leonhardt, Taylor 268
Lepkoske, Zachary 229
Leung, Ming 23
Levitan, Kristopher 60
Lewis, Ariela 146
Lewis, Crystal 347
Lewis, Dakota 320
Lewis, Danielle 233
Lewis, Dezmond 288
Lewis, Jordan 292
Lewis, Maria 74
Lewis, Tanner 338
Li, Fran .156
Li, Yolanda 289
Liljenquist, Ryan 233
Lin, Jeanne 228
Lindow, Josiah 375
Linton, Aimee 359
Lippitt, Savannah 370
Little, Danielle 286
Lloyd, Sara 335
Lobato, Marcus 146
Lockhart, Henry 339
Lofley, Rebecca 70
Logan, Olivia 55
Loghry, Natasha 380
Lohmeyer, Dustin 65
London, Sara 293
Long, Anna 379
Long, Nigel 372
Long, Rebecca 175
Long, Robert 158
Long, Tynesha 367
Longenecker, Julie 88
Longmore, Lydia 59
Lopez, Abdi 303
Lopez, Amy 221
Lopez, Chelsi 398
Lopez, Esmeralda 272
Lopez, Eva 180
Lopez, Heather 355
Lor, Dolly 295
Loretto, Conztancia 280
Losee, Chance 260
Loveless, Dallin 235
Lovern, Emily 239
Low, Nick 288
Lowe, Jordan 167
Lowe, Kesha 320
Lowery-Rowley, Rachael 306
Lowrey, Shannon 300
Lucero, Samantha 300
Ludeman, Shannon 159
Luft, Alli 270
Lund, Haylee 106
Lund, Kendra 300
Lunt, Abrie 320
Luu, Sandra 248
Luvio, Sharon 96
Lyle, Savannah 296
M., Lauren 69
M., Melissa 108
Mabry, Cortney 152
Macedone, Jordan 115
Machado, Ofelia 147
Macias, John 295
Madrid, Cullen 257
Madrid, Kalla 151
Madueno, Ariana 198
Magana, Francisco 42
Magaziner, Samuel 265
Mahrt, Megan 196
Mairose, Carly 178
Majkowycz, Andrea 366
Makaron, Chris 286
Malakhov, Ludmila 235
Malone, Carolyn 319

Malowney, Taylor 362	McInnis, Caroline 367	Milstead, Nicole 222
Malta, Wendy 234	McIntyre, Michael 185	Minster, Andrea 283
Mangold, Chelsea 103	McKenzie, Meghan 17	Mints, Brittany 212
Mangum, Jayce 367	McKern, Gabriel 102	Minyard, Lauren 50
Mann, Devon 182	McKernan, Christie 251	Mitchell, Nick 204
Manning, Bailey 54	McKune, Daniel 244	Mitchell, Stephanie 166
Manning, Joshua 235	McMinn, Sarah 340	Mitu, Alexander 149
Manuelito, Joseph 365	McNair, Emily 188	Moczary, Selyna 357
Mapother, Geoffrey Ray 77	McNair, Zach 100	Moedl, Simeon Thomas 63
Marchant, Elise 32	McNeace, Wendy 303	Moffat, Forrest 266
Marcle, Kellie 275	McNeal, Joshua 361	Moglia-MacEvoy, Bryce 73
Marett, Grant 305	McPhail, Grace 294	Mojardin, Rebecca 154
Marin, Ivan .63	McPherson, Scottie 26	Moncravie, Barada 391
Marin, Karina 333	McRae, Fallon 63	Monks, Andria 290
Marinetti, Ariel 323	McVey, Kylie 150	Monson, Dominic 204
Marion, Donovan 33	McWain, Heather 220	Montes, Janae 117
Marquart, Pat 29	Meade, Jared 255	Montgomery, Aliyah 204
Marra, Shelby 400	Mecham, Aspin 398	Montoya, Faith 188
Marrama, Cora 242	Mecham, Natalie 253	Montoya, Melissa 354
Martin, Candace 364	Mecham, Rylee 304	Montoya, Sabrina 147
Martin, Gabriel 214	Mecozzi, Renatte 159	Moon, Kat .354
Martin, Gilana 228	Medina, Adriana 276	Mooney, Ashley 346
Martinez, Aimee 96	Medina, Kamron 326	Moore, Amber M. 261
Martinez, Isaiha 211	Medina, Lucia 42	Moore, Meagan 297
Martinez, Matt 34	Medina, Madison 267	Morales, Luis 117
Martinez, Paulena 249	Medran, Nicole 370	Morales, Tanisha 310
Martz, Katlin 56	Meeker, Chryssa 113	Moran, Marcus 312
Marugg, Michael 242	Mehr, Chloe 200	Moreno, Paula 338
Masters, Erica 164	Meikle, Karlee 112	Moreno, Spencer 326
Mathieson, Danielle 337	Meisinger, Alie 161	Morgan, Chase 187
Matsumoto, Sara 167	Melonas, Nikko 90	Morgan, Deisha 308
Mauer, Tessa 16	Melusky, Daniel 264	Morrell, Haley 228
Mauthe, Aaron 316	Mendenhall, Lyndsi 386	Morris, Aubrey 95
Maya, Connie 79	Mendez, Emiliano 184	Morris, Ruthie 86
Mayer, Elizabeth Grace 367	Mendez, Jacob 178	Morris, Tanner 180
Mayfield, Brittney 92	Mendoza, Georgina 235	Morrison, Brandon 306
Mazzucco, Mark 393	Mendoza, Omar 275	Morrison, Calder 110
McArthur, John Michael 206	Mendoza, Sandra 246	Morrow, Nicola 225
McBride, Patrick 204	Menefee, Jasmine 357	Morse, Samantha 56
McCabe, Meagan 33	Merino, Alma 254	Mortensen, Cade 183
McCafferty, Max 191	Merkley, Chris 130	Mosier, Claire 67
McCaleb, Morgan 278	Merrill, Heather 214	Moskowitz, Jared 371
McCarter, Ariel 64	Merriman, Devon 296	Moss, Summer 276
McCarthy, Jaime Miguel 391	Mesa, Priscilla 307	Mosso, Ivette 178
McCaw, Mitchell 305	Metcalf, Duncan 343	Mott, Kiah 260
McCloud, Madeline 52	Metzentine, Chelsie 352	Moyer, William 186
McComas, Sierra 263	Miers, Jessica 304	Moyle, Roman 266
McCrary, Ricardo 285	Mikhaylyuk, Lyuda 23	Moynihan, Maeve 374
McCrory, Patrick 41	Milford, Augusta 219	Much, Austin 252
McCulloch, Alexandria 90	Miller, Aaron 174	Muldoon, Lawrence 351
McDermott, Melissa 390	Miller, Alesha 104	Mulhern, Amy 380
McDonald, Juliana 276	Miller, Amber 52	Mulica, Brooke 98
McEntire, Shayna 371	Miller, Bethany 315	Muljadi, Patrick 382
McFadden, Damon 53	Miller, Daniel 317	Muncy, Monica 252
McGrady, Shelby 40	Miller, Natalie 335	Muniz, Brice 209
McGuire, Jenna 55	Mills, Cassidy 372	Munns, Joshua 84
McGuire, Morgan 30	Milner-Souders, Kelly 60	Munsen, Nick 374

Index

Murphy, Cara 132
Murphy, Mikayla 258
Murphy, Morgan 387
Murphy, Peter 42
Murphy, Zac 335
Murri, Sam 97
Myers, Bailey C. 347
Myers, Kathy 176
Myers, Nina 150
Nagle-Heim, Lizzy 270
Nair, Pooja 240
Nan, Rebecca 276
Napp, Clayton 312
Nash, Christi 18
Natwick, Hannah 281
Navarrette, Kendra 347
Navolynski, Amanda 328
Nay, Sharisa 40
Neely, Brandon 238
Neils, Betty 158
Neiman, Alex 89
Neitzke, Taylor 91
Neubig, Brooklyn 294
Nevarez, Alexandra 212
Nevarez, Clarisa 331
Neves, Summer 92
Newland, Sheena 151
Nez, Raudell 299
Ngirachedeng, Isaac 352
Nguyen, Chau 133
Nguyen, Karen 399
Nguyen, Thao 25
Nichols, Haley 292
Nicoll, Brandon 230
Nies, Shelby 318
Nieto, Malorie 359
Nikkel, Madison 252
Nish, James 127
Nite, Kayla 26
Noble, Richard 123
Nolan, Scott 272
Nolte, Amber 198
Norris, Adrian 150
Norris, Rachel 43
Norsworthy, Erin 166
Northup, Andrea 170
Norton, Autumn 98
Norton, Stephanie 282
Notestine, Jessica 394
Nowak, Carolyn 260
Nufer, Holly 382
Null, Hunter 252
Nunez, Santiago 46
Nye, Michelle 96
Nylander, Jordan 396
O'Brien, Jared 19
O'Brien, Lila 70
O'Dowd, Jason 378
O'Grady, Katie 66
O'Harra, Taylor 198
O'Leary, Alexis 325
O'Leary, Julianne 87
Oaxaca, Fred 182
Ocanas, Patricia 392
Odegard, Elisha 99
Oestman, Kaci 99
Ogle, Samantha 118
Ojeda, Kendra 218
Oldeschulte, Christopher D. 244
Olguin, Alexandria 201
Oliva, Erika 127
Olivas, Jaime 370
Oliver, Jessica 273
Ollerton, Byron 288
Olsen, Diana 306
Olsen, Laura 271
Olson, David 169
Olson, Kayla 346
Oppenheim, Brandon 28
Oramas, Mateo 223
Ornelas-Lopez, Ivan 65
Ortega, Alec 259
Ortega, Brianna 267
Ortega, Mireya 343
Ortega, Shante 271
Ortiz, Joshua 58
Ortiz, Priscila 321
Ortiz, Raul 198
Ortolani, Alexa 41
Osborne, Jon 374
Osborne, McKenna 307
Oswald, Chris 260
Otamendi, Vanessa 157
Owens, Quinton 236
Owens, Sierra 117
P., Genny 174
Page, Cassie 296
Paget, Tanner 42
Pagni, Amber 331
Pahissa, Kathleen 268
Pahl, Emily Michel 332
Palacios, Juan 290
Palafox, Angie-Marie 168
Palizzi, Sean 362
Palmer, Cara 30
Palmer, Hannah 243
Palmer, Myles 181
Pan, Monica 267
Papenfuss, Dillon 298
Pappageorge, Jovanna 63
Paquet, Tiffany 132
Pardos, Jessica 364
Paredes, Nic 178
Parker, Logan 342
Parks, Sarah 181
Parry, Anna 162
Parson, Ashley 98
Pastier, Danielle 261
Pathak, Krisha 373
Patten, Josh 58
Pattison, Jenny 220
Patton, Emily 306
Patula, Shawndel 108
Pavlova, Ulianna 262
Payne, Mathew 83
Peaker, Chana 369
Pearson, Claire 296
Peatross, Rebecca 244
Peck, Emily 344
Pederson, Justin 95
Peery, Kenzie 278
Pehrson, Sarah 124
Pelaez, Melissa 124
Pelroy, Hailey 395
Pena, Destri 246
Peplinski, Brandi 139
Peppers, Shelby 383
Perez, Alina 263
Perez, Andrew Ramon 118
Perez, Joseph 206
Perkins, Celeste 203
Perkins, Ian 73
Perona, Emily 378
Peters, Lorrin 173
Petersen, Michelle 47
Peterson, Austin 205
Peterson, Autumn 245
Peterson, Elizabeth 57
Peterson, Hillary 285
Peterson, Jessica 65
Peterson, Mary 232
Petreman, Johnathan 262
Petrie, Ben 212
Pettingill, Jessica 166
Pezoldt, Randi 88
Pfeiffer, Mark 396
Phan, Shawna 357
Pharo, Ashley 382
Phelan, Andrew 366
Phelan, Merval 207
Phelps, Hailey 109
Pickett, Tim 128
Piehl, Bethany 249
Pielemeier, Jasmine 376
Piersol, Britnee 108
Pierson, Nikki 272
Pitchios, Kira 381
Pizano, Andrea 233
Polanco, Keenan 147
Poling, Beth 164
Polyakov, Greg 49

Name	Page	Name	Page	Name	Page
Ponath, Rachel	352	Reece, Lacey	164	Rogers, Megan	257
Ponce, Jaime	28	Reed, Kalinda	280	Rogers, Rebecca	154
Poon, Hing	314	Reese, Rayven	203	Rohr, Koby	277
Pope, Lauren	341	Regan, John	62	Rojo, Amanda	171
Poppleton, Erik	192	Regnier, Christopher	211	Rollins, Amber	270
Porras, Taylor	168	Rehr, Serena	43	Romano, Katherine	315
Porter, Leah	170	Reid, Kelly	72	Romano, Kristen	344
Porter, Michael	168	Reilly, Kaela	67	Romero, Chantel	240
Poulson, Austin	390	Reimer, Zachary	27	Romero, Michael	179
Powell, Chase	354	Reinert, Jessica	240	Romero, Patrick	84
Powell, Laci	105	Reinhardt, Savannah	337	Romick, Lyndsey	104
Powelson, Megan	337	Remirez, Julian	177	Roper, Kennerley	391
Preece, Margaret	99	Restivo, Carli	230	Ropp, Cody	342
Prell, Glen	70	Reyes, Paulette	263	Rose, Taylor	279
Pretty Weasel, Haylee Jo	192	Reynolds, Jennifer	238	Rose, Thomas	341
Price, Damon	35	Rhinehart, Forrest	198	Ross, Kaylene	191
Price, Naomi	231	Rhodes, Kristen	220	Rossiter, Illaura	27
Prichard, Austin	251	Rice, Cory	278	Rotvold, Megan	124
Proctor, Owen	269	Richard, Hollie	358	Rouane, Stephanie	34
Promes, Kayla	166	Richardson, Dallin	358	Rounds, Cameron Lee	112
Pruett, Summer	220	Richardson, Makeri	234	Routon, Silicia Leanne	77
Pruneda, Rosemely	125	Richison, Brandon	75	Rowley, Shannon	396
Puente, Samantha	211	Ricks-Scanlon, Harlie	352	Rowsell, Justin	167
Pullara, Andrew	288	Rider, Cheyane	256	Roy, Christopher D.	54
Purdy, McKenzie	328	Riggin, Breana	149	Rozich, Travis	363
Putnam, Alyssa	180	Riley, Jordan	85	Ruehl, Erik	299
Pyne, Mikelle	190	Riley Jr., Antonio	337	Rumsey, Amanda	126
Q. Anderson, Elizabeth	385	Ringen, Erica	115	Rusden, Isabelle	147
Qin, Zhiyin	361	Riscen, Sarah	337	Rushing, Shelby	218
Quan, Anna	33	Rivas, Darcys	380	Russell, Brittney	381
Quent, Kimberly	305	Rivera, Anthony	237	Russell, Erica	193
Quezada, Cameron	27	Rivera, Kirsten	110	Russell, Kimberly	179
Quigley, Erin	375	Robbins, Jennifer	61	Russell-LaFave, Kimberlie	319
Quinn, Tristin	68	Robbins, Maranda	302	Rust, Amelia	272
Quintana, Joseph	268	Roberts, Ashley	299	S., Courtney	57
Quirk, Rowan	197	Roberts, Audrey	378	S., Crystal	29
Quiroz, Maritza	189	Roberts, Felicia	358	Sabin, Anna	342
Quiroz, Monique	57	Roberts, Jacob	283	Sadler, Destiny	102
R., Ramsey	255	Roberts, Jennifer	25	Sagers, Christian	279
Radcliffe, Eric	345	Roberts, Vickie	168	Sahagun, Ahmed S.	40
Rader, Claire	289	Robertson, Jessica	395	Salazar, Josh	278
Raffaghello, Katie	93	Robertson, Madi	128	Salinas, A.J.	397
Ragels, Brianna	219	Robertson, Will	347	Salinas, Ashley	119
Ramirez, Jazmine	275	Robinson, Crysta	238	Salinas, Jazmine	336
Ramirez, Jessica	153	Robles, Ismael	155	Samhouri, Mai	364
Ramirez, Melisa	245	Robson, Natalia	397	Sammons, Zoie	354
Ramirez, Nicole	140	Rockey, Erin	236	Sample, Preston	293
Ramos, Joaquin	314	Rodal, Kristen	147	Sampson, Isaac	253
Ramp, Heidi	124	Rodgers, Kevin	125	Sanchez, Adrianna	380
Randall, Neal	64	Rodrigue, Vanessa	125	Sanchez, Alexandra	47
Raney, Katelynn	366	Rodriguez, Deybin	213	Sanchez, Anne	400
Rastrelli, Paul	304	Rodriguez, Eloisa	388	Sanchez, Derek	227
Ratcliffe, Kristen	390	Rodriguez, Erik	79	Sanchez, Gladys	38
Rathbone, David	36	Rodriguez, Vianka	215	Sanchez, Lauren	379
Ray, Cheyenne	120	Roeber, Chelsea	65	Sanchez, Michael	172
Razinkov, Alena	190	Roetting, Alycia	266	Sanchez, Sunday	192
Reagan, Patricia	379	Rogala, Jacob	177	Sanchez, Vitalia	43

Index

Sanchez, Yesenia 239
Sander, Madelyn 288
Sanders, Aj 186
Sandford, Áine 383
Sandlin, Elizabeth 20
Sandoval, Melissa 173
Sandy, Taylor 188
Sanford, Rachel 109
Sanger, Collin 282
Santerre, Stephanie 43
Santos, Amarelis 89
Sarobhas, Narisara 42
Sato, Tori .310
Satterthwaite, Randy 204
Saunders, Jennifer 100
Saville, Brook 370
Saxton, Alyssa 387
Schafer, Ryan 63
Scheer, Brittany 364
Schermerhorn, James 260
Schlageter, Miwako 187
Schmidt, Alyssa 294
Schmidt, Carley 324
Schneider, Jessica 270
Schnurr, Teal 334
Schott, Nick 204
Schouten, Tyran 60
Schrag-Toso, Aaron 110
Schrand, Melissa 199
Schreiner, Joshua G. 45
Schroeder, Emily 219
Schroeder, Kyle 377
Schubel, Chandlar 262
Schwartz, Andrea 128
Schwartz, Kate 175
Schwarz, Joel 151
Schweizer, Charles 274
Schwoch, Kayla 66
Scothorn, Madeleine Joy 141
Scott, Christian 341
Scott, Joshua 326
Scribner, Ellen 296
Scully, Madie 307
Sealock, Hannah 230
Seamons, Melissa 107
Searle, Kylee 107
Seawalt, Tristan 220
Sechrest, Erica 51
Secretan, Kevin 46
Seely, Jacob 251
Seiber, Jaimie 95
Sellers, Emily 87
Sells, P.J. .37
Selshi, Beth 209
Semon, Mary 247
Senogles, Sean 233
Sessions, Brandon 318
Sether, Kyle 316
Setser, Kendall 256
Settle, Kayla 223
Sewell, Nick 323
Shackett, Jayde 29
Shannon, Christina 58
Shannon, Elizabeth 54
Sharp, Cassie 392
Shaw, Nikayla 201
Shearer, Annie 356
Sheehan, John 207
Shelpuk, Hannah 389
Sheng, Julietta 323
Shepard, Jessica 348
Shephard, Hannah 114
Shepherd, Molly 100
Shepherd, Sky 119
Sheridan, Michael 26
Shoemaker, Morgen 162
Shotts, Haleigh 225
Shouse, Jordan 389
Shrum, Audie 301
Shulsen, Heather 247
Shumway, Kaden 390
Shumway, Katrina 289
Sickler, Kaylee 59
Sidenstick, Jordon 329
Siegrist, Kelly 38
Sierra, Sonny 368
Siguenza, Stephanie 179
Siliga, Kasey 123
Silva, Ashlene M. 364
Silveira, Elizabeth 123
Simmons, Victoria E. 229
Simonson, Emily Virginia 142
Simovic, Kathryn 62
Sinclair, Ryan 291
Singleton-Reich, Jade 206
Sisneros, Jordan Juan 339
Sisson, Devan 88
Skinner, Riley 149
Skompinski, Jessica 46
Slade, Whitney 246
Sleight, Jessica 82
Slinkard, Ashley 81
Smaciarz, Olivia 235
Smedley, Emily 288
Smith, Aric 55
Smith, Devyn 317
Smith, Emily 213
Smith, Jacob 220
Smith, Jennica 309
Smith, Justine 183
Smith, Kaylin Marie 59
Smith, Kelly 327
Smith, Laryssa 129
Smith, Lisha 194
Smith, MacCoy 162
Smith, Mariah 297
Smith, Melyzjah 288
Smith, Nick 66
Smith, Rachel 50
Smith, Rashaad 46
Smolenski, Alex 197
Snyder, Ciara 242
Snyder, Courtney 171
Snyder, Lindsie 283
So, Lilian 333
Sobe, Kelly 189
Soiza, Nataly 360
Sok, James 90
Solis, Bianca 25
Solomon, Brooke 328
Sorensen, Kelsey 258
Sorensen, Natalee 22
Spangle, Michele 293
Spencer, Jesse 47
Spencer, Jonathan 110
Spencer, Tedra Kay 282
Spillane, Clayton 116
Spillman, Trenton 289
Spinnie, Kassi 247
Spruit, Brittany 178
Spurlock, Callie 71
St. Pierre, Tyler 227
Stafford, Amy Jeane 363
Stampfly, Kaitlin 388
Stan, Cristina 35
Starbuck, Melissa 181
Stark, Clara 97
Statley, Brittney 66
Stavile, Sara 365
Steagall, Ashlee 372
Steel, Mary 87
Steeves, Samantha 272
Stefanich, Celine 196
Stegman, Hayden 334
Stein, Derek 372
Stein, Jacob 243
Stephens, Christian 388
Stephenson, Ashley 313
Stephenson, Erin 268
Sterba, Amereece 106
Stevens, Amanda 191
Stevens, Kylie 38
Stewart, Ashley 76
Stewart, Kelsey 76
Stickel, Emily 107
Stickel, Lindsay 163
Stock, Alyssa 188
Stocks, Jordan 204
Stockton, Hailey 277
Stoker, Tayler 329
Stokes, Liam 390

Stonehocker, Van 59	Thompson, Myles 280	Vaughn, Helen 170
Story, Sara 198	Thompson, Sarah 394	Velasquez, Damaris 94
Strand, Jennifer 129	Thompson, Zachary 375	Venaglia, Hallie 319
Stratton, Karalie 116	Tillotson, Sarah 313	Vernon, Liza 195
Straub, Amanda 50	Timm, Tasha 186	Versey, Rachael 210
Streeter, Amy 69	Tipton, Sydney 395	Vessey, Christopher 393
Strong, Austin 318	To, Angel 169	Vice, Rachel 161
Stryker, Jake 131	To, Wilson 202	Vider, Julia 116
Stueve, David 57	Tokash, Zakk 317	Vierthaler, William (Blaine) 189
Stuhr, Sandra 36	Tomlinson, Aaron 301	Villamor, Marissa 350
Styer, Zach 268	Toms, Brittney 244	Villarreal, Gabe 48
Sudan, Travis 62	Toolie, Dinah 154	Villegas, Francisco 288
Suen, Wilson 231	Torgerson, Devin 380	Villegas, Marcos 387
Sullivan, Patrick 349	Toscano, Juan Ignacio 24	Vining, Michaela 291
Summarell, Ty 322	Towner, Christian 318	Virgo, Amber 127
Sundt, Steven 43	Tracht, Rebekah 84	Vizcaino, Aracely 193
Swank, Rowee-Jane 365	Tracy, Austin 373	Vogels, Rachel 89
Swatzell, Willard Michael Howard . .91	Tracy, Taylor 180	Vosgerau, Mercedes 259
Swearingen, Justin 219	Trepanier, Michael 164	Vu, Tammy 107
Swenson, Kylie 330	Trevino, Xanadu 182	Waggoner, Amelia 118
Swindler, Jen 325	Trevizo, Alexis 188	Wagner, Ellery 286
Swinehart, Sarah 298	Trimble, Stephanie 57	Wagner, KriSjaan 43
Symons, Chelsea 228	Trinklein, Izzy 315	Wahlert, Ross 156
Sysak, Ashlee 330	Troussel, Myriah 271	Waliezer, Kierston 166
Szalwinski, Dylan 208	True, Leah 143	Walker, Kristi 103
Tafoya, AJ 196	Trujillo, Cheyenne 205	Walker, Melanee 125
Taft, Joshua 209	Trujillo, Kayla 155	Walker, Nalani 259
Tago, Luisa 233	Trusler, Jonathan 49	Walker, Stephanie 288
Tai, Breanna 289	Tsang, Serena 70	Walker Jr., Ronald W. Lee 208
Talaro, Stacey 246	Tseng, Kenneth 345	Wallace, Allie 115
Talmadge, Sho 252	Turner, Chris 228	Waller, Danielle 250
Taylor, Alison 122	Turner, Diana 21	Walling, Anna 205
Taylor, Katie 164	Turner, Gabie 262	Ward, Alexis 144
Taylor, Mackinzi 245	Turner, James 201	Ward, Katelyn 181
Taylor, Morgan 159	Turner, Keaton 273	Ward, MacKenzie 153
Taylor, Zachary 322	Turpin, Mary 39	Ward, Paige 269
Teadtke, Anna 276	Tutt, Megan 111	Warner, Kristin 260
Teglas, Chris 243	Tuttle, Austin 60	Warren, Amanda 354
Tegtmeyer, Alyssa 254	Uddin, Durin 257	Warren, Megan 307
Tello-Gonzalez, Bella 340	Ung, Angel Antonio 271	Watson, Kodi 156
Terrell, Kayla 207	Uriarte, Elodia 129	Watson, Tabitha 145
Thacker, Jessica 360	Uribe, Norma 190	Waugh, Sofia 90
Theriault, Hayley 225	Urquidi, Isana 287	Webb, Clyde 92
Thevenin, Melinda 86	Vail, Bonnie 72	Webber, Colten S. 115
Thomas, Caroline 64	Valdez, Cameron 208	Webster, Samantha 148
Thomas, Cody 214	Valentine, Katie 180	Weeks, Estes 244
Thomas, Derek 53	Valentine, Peter 350	Weidle, Christian 394
Thomas, Edwin 281	Valentine, Suzanne 122	Weisiger, Emily 36
Thomas, Liz 170	Valenzuela, Gabriela 194	Welch, Cate 154
Thomas, Loren 248	Van Deren, Stella 30	Welch, Lise 232
Thompson, Alyssa 209	Van Loan, Emily 287	Welter, Allison 133
Thompson, Brianne 233	Van Valkenburg, Ingrid 78	Wenzel, Mariah 369
Thompson, Danny 47	Vance, Dallin 241	Werner, Anna 209
Thompson, Darlene 322	Vande Brake, Melanie 249	Werner, Ryan 318
Thompson, Emily 253	VanderHoogt, Brooke 113	Wert, Gene 133
Thompson, Kiera 317	Vangrove, Carla 82	Westfall, Euripides 188
Thompson, Matthew 285	Varela, Gabriela 195	Westmoreland, Hayley 78

Index

Wettstein, Jamie 45
Wheeler, Kyle 107
Whitaker, Dylan 254
White, Alexa 216
White, Amber 197
White, Elishia 72
White, Gabe 108
White, Kelsi 311
White, Shayne 24
Whitfield, Miranda 163
Whitfield, Tress 364
Whyte, Alei 44
Wibel, David 175
Widmark, JayLynn 50
Wierleski, Brandon 60
Wilbur, Alison 24
Wild, Erin 278
Wiles, Colton 282
Wiley, Kelli 66
Wilfong, Michelle 196
Wilkerson, Johnny 275
Wilkinson, Miquela (Kella) 148
Wilkison, Kevin 195
Wille, Anna 314
Williams, Anna 46
Williams, Hailee 340
Williams, Jamie 96
Williams, Jamison 156
Williams, Josh 310
Williams, Karl 120
Williams, Laurel 161
Williams, Sara 156
Williams, Taggart 46
Willmann, Johannes 74
Wilson, Branden 265
Wilson, Breanna 34
Wilson, Ciera 298
Wilson, Derek 217
Wilson, Kelsie S. 172
Wilson, Leticia S. 246
Wilson, Sarah 131
Wilson, Tyson 305
Wiltbank, Kaeli 351
Wiltz, Samantha 265
Wimett, Matthew 99
Winter, Kyle 53
Winters, Samantha 158
Winters, Shavenor S. 83
Woelber, Amy 90
Wojtowitz, Christopher 240
Wollman, Melissa 396
Wonder, Jacob 231
Wong, Dickson 118
Wood-Jenkins, Jasmine 194
Woodbury, Merrisa 350
Woodland, Stephanie 331
Woodman, Kylee 397
Woodrum, Chelsea 251
Woods, Marion 182
Woolstenhulme, Kyrsten 328
Woolston, Catherine 284
Wooten, Kurtis 212
Worthington, Kayla 215
Wright, Ian 336
Wright, Morgan 148
Wright, Rossa 352
Wright, Tia 101
Wrobel, Jacqueline 250
Wynn, Elizabeth 72
Wyss, Blain 106
Xanthos, Sarah 78
Xian, Jennifer 176
Yamada, K'lah 148
Yanez, Luis 218
Yates, Corey 385
Yepez, Yesenia 351
Yokel, Robin Bonneau 35
Yoo, Alexandria 283
Yordy, Brooke 214
York, Kiana 398
Yoshida, Tori 183
Youkhana, Cecilia 216
Young, Tae 171
Zachary, Samantha 349
Zaeske, Amanda 371
Zamba, Jacob 150
Zamora, Stephen 180
Zeigler, Andrew 320
Zeigler, Kate 356
Zelenka, Lyndee 190
Zeuch, Jonathan 114
Zhou, Vivian 263
Zikmund, Sierra 230
Zintzun, Jessica 68
Zugschwert, Ashley 349
Zuniga, Junior 280
Zwolinski, Anna 155

Author Autograph Page

Author Autograph Page

Author Autograph Page

Author Autograph Page

Author Autograph Page

Author Autograph Page

Author Autograph Page

Author Autograph Page

Author Autograph Page

Author Autograph Page